Keep this book. You will need it and use it throughout your career.

About the American Hotel & Lodging Association (AH&LA)

Founded in 1910, AH&LA is the trade association representing the lodging industry in the United States. AH&LA is a federation of state lodging associations throughout the United States with 11,000 lodging properties worldwide as members. The association offers its members assistance with governmental affairs representation, communications, marketing, hospitality operations, training and education, technology issues, and more. For information, call 202-289-3100.

LODGING, the management magazine of AH&LA, is a "living textbook" for hospitality students that provides timely features, industry news, and vital lodging information.

About the Educational Institute of AH&LA (EI)

An affiliate of AH&LA, the Educational Institute is the world's largest source of quality training and educational materials for the lodging industry. EI develops textbooks and courses that are used in more than 1,200 colleges and universities worldwide, and also offers courses to individuals through its Distance Learning program. Hotels worldwide rely on EI for training resources that focus on every aspect of lodging operations. Industry-tested videos, CD-ROMs, seminars, and skills guides prepare employees at every skill level. EI also offers professional certification for the industry's top performers. For information about EI's products and services, call 800-349-0299 or 407-999-8100.

About the American Hotel & Lodging Educational Foundation (AH&LEF)

An affiliate of AH&LA, the American Hotel & Lodging Educational Foundation provides financial support that enhances the stability, prosperity, and growth of the lodging industry through educational and research programs. AH&LEF has awarded hundreds of thousands of dollars in scholarship funds for students pursuing higher education in hospitality management. AH&LEF has also funded research projects on topics important to the industry, including occupational safety and health, turnover and diversity, and best practices in the U.S. lodging industry. For information, call 202-289-3180.

Educational Institute Books

HOSPITALITY FACILITIES MANAGEMENT and DESIGN

Second Edition

David M. Stipanuk

EDUCATIONAL INSTITUTE
American Hotel & Lodging Association

Disclaimer

This publication is designed to provide accurate and authoritative information in regard to the subject matter covered. It is sold with the understanding that the publisher is not engaged in rendering legal, accounting, or other professional service. If legal advice or other expert assistance is required, the services of a competent professional person should be sought.

—*From the Declaration of Principles jointly adopted by the American Bar Association and a Committee of Publishers and Associations*

The author, David M. Stipanuk, is solely responsible for the contents of this publication. All views expressed herein are solely those of the author and do not necessarily reflect the views of the Educational Institute of the American Hotel & Lodging Association (the Institute) or the American Hotel & Lodging Association (AH&LA).

Nothing contained in this publication shall constitute a standard, an endorsement, or a recommendation of the Institute or AH&LA. The Institute and AH&LA disclaim any liability with respect to the use of any information, procedure, or product, or reliance thereon by any member of the hospitality industry.

Editors: Donald Peterson
         Timothy J. Eaton
         Jim Purvis

Contents

Preface

Hᴏsᴘɪᴛᴀʟɪᴛʏ ꜰᴀᴄɪʟɪᴛɪᴇs regularly call for managerial attention. Modifications are needed due to (among other things) various levels of facility obsolescence, the Americans with Disabilities Act, and the growth of governmental and corporate requirements for additional safety and security. Remodeling to meet these needs and stay competitive in today's increasingly competitive markets requires managers who understand the basic elements of facility management, design, and renovation. And, of course, new facilities will continue to spring up as entrepreneurs seek to develop new concepts and chains seek to expand.

Hospitality facilities are complex and unique in many ways. Creating and managing them requires special knowledge, skills, and dedication. In *Hospitality Facilities Management and Design*, Second Edition, we provide an introduction to the key issues involved in the management and design of hospitality facilities, illustrated with examples drawn from the industry itself. Owners and operators of hospitality facilities should benefit from the coverage of key areas of interest and concern to them. After reading this book, managers and management students should be much better prepared to deal with facilities-related questions and problems as they arise (and they will arise!).

The text is divided into four parts and two appendixes. Part I presents a look at the nature of hospitality facilities and an overview of the issues involved in managing maintenance needs. The discussion of emerging issues in waste management and environmental legislation highlights the changing responsibilities involved in facilities management.

Part II continues with chapters devoted to each of the primary facility systems—safety and security, water and wastewater, electrical, HVAC, lighting, laundry, telecommunications, and food service. In this era when cost control and extending equipment and building life through better maintenance are more important than ever, these chapters provide much-needed information.

Part III examines important aspects of the building itself and its grounds and parking areas. Roofs, exterior walls, foundations, drainage systems, parking lots and garages, and landscaping are among the topics discussed.

Part IV presents the basics of lodging and food service design and renovation, preparing the reader for the challenges involved in creating new facilities or renovating existing ones. The design chapters introduce key terms, criteria, and methods employed in the design of lodging and food service facilities. Readers with a design orientation should find these discussions especially stimulating. Those more interested in operations will see how the design process unfolds and should be able to more effectively influence this process to help create a product that "works."

The text concludes with two appendixes not directly referenced in the chapters. Although this text is designed for current and future hospitality managers rather than engineers, we have included Appendix 1 on engineering principles for those readers who want a better basic understanding of the more technical elements of the engineering and maintenance world. Also, recognizing that managers should be aware of those elements that influence the air quality and temperature conditioning they provide their guests and employees, we have included a discussion in Appendix 2 on the factors that can work toward increasing a building's air quality and therefore guest and staff comfort.

Acknowledgments

This second edition of *Hospitality Facilities Management and Design* has provided an opportunity to introduce a number of changes. A new facilities overview chapter summarizes the types of building systems found in hospitality facilities and some of the key characteristics of them. Integration of environmental issues (energy management, solid waste management, and more) into a single chapter (Chapter 4) provides a framework that is more in keeping with the global approach to these topics. To provide a more international approach, data, exhibits, and terminology have been selected that better portray facilities in a global context. We hope the many purchasers of this text worldwide will find it easier to use. The adoption of the first edition by hospitality programs in so many countries around the world was heartening.

One feature that has been added at the end of every chapter is a listing of Internet sites pertinent to the chapter. The lists have been kept short intentionally, with the knowledge that the sites listed will often have their own lists of recommended or relevant sites. Readers are encouraged to find these and refer to them.

Input for revisions to this text was solicited from a wide array of sources. Members of the Engineering and Environment Committee of the American Hotel & Lodging Association should be recognized for their individual contributions as well as for the general support provided by the committee. Those making particularly substantial contributions include: Val Lehr of Lehr Associates, August Crannen of Manhattan East Suites Hotels, Chad Callahan of Marriott International, April Berkol of Starwood Hotels & Resorts, Jerry LaChapelle of Harrah's, and John Salmen of Universal Design. Ed Golden of Outrigger Hotels & Resorts took the excellent telecommunications chapter contributed to the first edition by Byrne Blumenstein of MCI and updated it. In addition, those providing products and services to the industry who have helped with this edition should be thanked as well. Fred Hoth of Phillips Lighting, Susan Kary of Kary Project Management (formerly with Marriott), along with others have assisted in a variety of ways.

I'm also deeply appreciative of the chapter contributions by Richard Penner and Jan deRoos, School of Hotel Administration at Cornell, and Carolyn Lambert, Pennsylvania State University. Their chapters make valuable enhancements to the text and broaden its content. Comments and suggestions from my colleagues Stephani Robson and Mike Redlin are also acknowledged. The general support provided by the resources and environment of the School of Hotel Administration at Cornell University has also been a major help in this revision. I must also recognize my former student and now co-instructor in Cornell's Professional Development Program, Richard Manzolina of Hilton Hotels—he is keeping his former hotel professor a bit more aware of what is happening in the real world of hospitality facilities. Conversations with other industry professionals such as Claire Kevill of Marriott Corporation and educators such as Nancy Scanlon of New York University have also been useful in preparing the text. Guest lecturers from Marriott and Hyatt who have addressed students at Cornell over the years have left their mark on the book's content, providing many useful ideas and observations during their visits.

The contributions to this text by the late Harold Roffmann are acknowledged as well. His insights, incorporated in the chapter dealing with "the outer envelope," are of great value for hospitality managers, not least because the building's structure and its exterior facilities have a great influence on the first impressions formed by guests.

In closing, we must acknowledge the contributions of the industry advisory and review committee for this text. The committee set us on our course and we hope we have not strayed too far from it. Special thanks go to Craig Flickinger, Regional Director of Engineering, Radisson Plaza Hotel, Southfield, Michigan. The editors at the Educational Institute have served the readers well with their quest for clarity and quality. Their development of the key terms for each chapter, the preparation of review questions, and their thoroughness in general are much appreciated.

Finally, our students (past and present) are acknowledged. They have contributed to the book's development in several ways and their comments and input are valued. We hope *Hospitality Facilities Management and Design,* Second Edition, will help them in their academic pursuits and assist them in their careers.

David M. Stipanuk
Ithaca, New York

About the Author

David M. Stipanuk, a registered Professional Engineer, has been a member of the Property Asset Management faculty of the School of Hotel Administration at Cornell University since 1983. His teaching responsibilities include courses in sustainable development, facilities management, hospitality risk management, and hotel development and construction. He is also an active participant in the school's Executive Education Program, offering coursework in Property Operations and Maintenance in the program each year.

Professor Stipanuk's service to the university community includes membership on transportation services committees and on the faculty senate. He has also served for many years as the de facto department chair for Property Asset Management and for three years as the faculty coordinator of Cornell's General Manager and Advanced Management programs.

Professor Stipanuk is the author or co-author of three textbooks published by the Educational Institute of the American Hotel & Lodging Association: *Managing Hospitality Engineering Systems* (with Michael H. Redlin), *Hospitality Facilities Management and Design*, Second Edition, and *Security and Loss Prevention Management*, Second Edition (with Raymond C. Ellis, Jr.). Professor Stipanuk provides training to lodging corporations on engineering certification programs offered by the Educational Institute. He has also published articles on environmental issues for the lodging industry and on workplace-safety benchmarking for travel and tourism. Most recently, he helped to prepare AH&LA's *Energy Management and Conservation Guide*.

He is a member of the American Society of Heating, Refrigerating and Air-Conditioning Engineers (ASHRAE) and the Executive Engineers and Environmental Officers Committee of AH&LA. He has also been involved with the Environmental Concerns Task Force of the White House Conference on Travel and Tourism, the Pan American Health Organization, and the Caribbean Hotel Association in developing environmental audit criteria for hotels.

Part I

Introduction

Chapter 1 Outline

The Role of Facilities in the Hospitality
    Industry
Costs Associated with Hospitality Facilities
    The Costs of Development and
        Construction
    The Costs of Operation
    The Costs of Renovation and
        Modernization
The Impact of Facility Design on Facility
    Management
    Components and Layout
    Materials, Methods, and Types of
        Construction
    Equipment
    Systems
Management's Responsibilities
    Management Contracts and Franchise
        Agreements
Responsibilities of the Facilities Department
Facilities Managers in Lodging Operations

Competencies

1. Identify a number of important roles played by hospitality facilities. (pp. 4–6)

2. Explain why construction costs vary by facility type and why proper construction practices provide long-term benefits. (pp. 6–7)

3. Identify the two primary categories of facility operating costs, the components of each category, and various factors that affect those costs. (pp. 7–12)

4. Explain the purpose and limitations of the reserve for replacement.(pp. 12, 21)

5. Describe how facility components, layout, materials, methods and types of construction, and systems affect facility management. (pp. 12–17)

6. Identify several equipment concerns that affect maintenance needs. (pp. 14–17)

7. State management's responsibilities with regard to facility management. (pp. 18–19)

8. Outline typical maintenance requirements found in management contracts and franchise agreements. (pp. 19–21)

9. Summarize the basic responsibilities of the facilities department and the facilities manager. (pp. 22–26)

1

The Role, Cost, and Management of Hospitality Facilities

In 1877, a San Francisco reporter, evidently weary of the endless hoopla over the city's new Palace Hotel, described the hotel's remote signaling device. Twenty-five thousand numbered bellboys, he wrote, one for each guestroom, wait in a basement for lodgers to ring. "Down goes the clerk's foot on a corresponding pedal and up shoots the bellboy...he is put in a box, shut up in a pneumatic tube and whisked right into the room designated by the bell-dial. A door in the wall opens to receive him, an automatic clamp catches him by the coat-collar, and he is quietly dropped to the floor." This whimsy satirized a very real tradition of technological innovation in the hotel industry. In fact, the idea of luxury in a hotel had already come to be defined as much by plumbing, heating, and machinery as by rich fabrics, furniture, and architecture.[1]

FROM THE EXOTIC AND LUXURIOUS ENVIRONMENT of the fantasy resort to the gleaming stainless steel and specialty equipment of the commercial kitchen, the hospitality industry of today relies on well-designed and well-maintained facilities as a key element of its business. Guests desire a safe and comfortable environment in which to conduct business, entertain, relax, dine, and sleep. The hotel, motel, or restaurant is their home away from home, and they usually want it to be better than home.

Hospitality managers' involvement with facilities takes several forms. All departments use the facilities, relying on efficient design and proper equipment and systems to perform their duties. Department heads may be consulted for ideas concerning the design of new facilities. They are also often involved in either planning for or coping with renovations. Meetings of the executive committee at most hotels place department heads in formal contact with the engineering manager. Managers also have day-to-day involvement with the maintenance/engineering/facilities department as they use its services. (For our purposes, the terms maintenance, engineering, and facilities will generally be used interchangeably.)

The Role of Facilities in the Hospitality Industry ————

Facilities play critical and varied roles in the hospitality industry. They can provide an appealing visual environment that contributes to the overall ambiance, experience, and comfort of the guest. These elements, created by the artistic efforts of architects, interior designers, and craftspeople, are sustained by the diligence of the maintenance and housekeeping staff. For some components of the industry, such as destination resorts, theme restaurants, casinos, theme parks, and water attractions, the facilities themselves are the attraction that engages and entertains guests. Other elements also contribute to ambiance, experience, and comfort but in more subtle ways. Often, unseen facilities components create comfortable thermal environments by controlling indoor air conditions while others provide needed supplies of clean water at the proper temperature for bathing, swimming, and relaxing in spas. The environment for the guest is also enhanced by the control or elimination of unwanted sounds that could disturb the guest's experience and, in the most basic terms, by protection from the elements—whether inside the building or under sheltered areas near pools. Safety is another important factor related to facilities. Guests expect to be safe. They expect to be provided an environment in which they are protected from injury and from loss of their possessions. For many of these roles, the skills of the engineer and technician are required, although the guest (who *expects* comfort) may not directly notice their contributions.

Besides contributing to the pleasurable experience of the guest, facilities play a role as "manufacturing plant" in the creation and delivery of services and products. Facilities house and interconnect the equipment and systems that allow the operation to function, whether it be the power and communication cabling connecting point-of-sale devices; the elevators that move guests; or the collection of utilities, equipment, and controls that make up a modern kitchen or laundry facility. In their manufacturing plant role, the facilities are also the workplace for the employees. This means that back-of-house spaces need to be efficient, comfortable, and safe. Specialized consultants in fields such as food service, laundry, and other technical areas are called upon to design these spaces.

Facilities help to define the industry and provide identity in the marketplace. Characteristic roof shapes, signage, colors, and other trademark elements create an image for various products and serve to draw customers. Travelers quickly develop the ability to identify various hospitality businesses by the characteristic appearance of their facilities. Children who can't yet read have no trouble identifying their favorite quick-service restaurant at 300 yards from a speeding auto.

It must also be recognized that industry growth largely comes as a result of additions to the number or size of facilities. In an era of e-commerce, when many services are accessed or delivered electronically via cyberspace, the hospitality industry remains a service that requires a unique "space" (facility) to produce and deliver its service. And while some growth is achievable by higher prices and more customers served (better occupancy), a significant portion of the growth of many hospitality enterprises comes through the addition of facilities. This is also true of restaurant operations, where most sales growth for chain operators is due largely to additional stores rather than increased sales at existing stores.

Hospitality companies such as ARAMARK and Sodexho have further recognized the potential for facilities management to be a contributor to corporate growth in another way. These companies have entered into the **facilities management** business, providing services such as housekeeping, grounds, and physical plant management to hospitality companies, schools, universities, and various industries. Recognizing the opportunities and challenges involved in the operation of facilities provides another role for facilities management within the hospitality industry—that of business opportunity.

Hospitality (and particularly lodging) facilities provide owners with a return on investment in two basic ways. First, they are the location where the business generates operating profit. Second, hospitality firms enjoy a portion of their "return" in the change in market value of their property. In this regard, the return considerations resemble those of real estate, an industry where facilities certainly play a major role.

Finally, facilities play a key role in the amount of revenue generated at the property. On one level, this is obvious: the presence of guestrooms, meeting spaces, dining opportunities, and even recreation spaces provides the appeal guests recognize in choosing your property. The proper design and mix of these facilities is important to meet the customers' needs. However, the existing facility has little latitude to make extensive changes with what it has in terms of facilities except through the infusion of massive amounts of new capital. What the existing facility *can* do is maintain the facilities it has.

A recently published study illustrates the value of facilities maintenance.[2] The study, conducted in early 2001, investigated the relationship between the defects identified in quality-assurance reports and the revenue per available room (**RevPAR)** of the properties. Properties with one or more "failed" items related to facilities on the quality-assurance reports showed significantly different RevPAR values than those that had no failed items. For example, "hotels with at least one defect in the exterior had a RevPAR of $3.12 less than hotels with no defects in the exterior. Hotels with at least one defect in the guest bath had a RevPAR of $1.32 less than hotels with no defects in the guest bath." These are very significant findings. The study estimates that the effect of facilities deficiencies for the chain studied amounted to lost revenue of $20 million over the three-year period studied (February 1990 through January 1993). The study concludes by stating:

> This study demonstrates a direct relationship between product quality and operation's financial performance, when product quality is gauged by the level of facility defects... the defective hotels in my sample recorded a RevPAR of approximately $2.80 less than hotels that did not have defects. This difference was consistent over time and represents an annual revenue shortfall of approximately $200,000 per deficient hotel. The study also indicates where hotels might best invest their capital-improvement and maintenance funds. What seems to count is the exterior, the guest rooms and the guest bath.

This text strives to provide the reader with the tools needed to effectively manage energy, environmental, maintenance, and capital projects. Successful managers recognize that these expenditures are not only "costs" but also contributors to guest satisfaction, employee productivity, revenues, and profits. Delivery of effective, well-managed facilities services plays a key role in the successful operation of a hospitality business.

Costs Associated with Hospitality Facilities

Hospitality facilities generate several types of cost. First, the facilities must be designed, developed, and constructed. Once occupied, they must be operated. And eventually, they must be renovated and modernized. Each of these phases incurs unique expenses.

The Costs of Development and Construction

The facilities of the modern hospitality industry vary greatly. Budget and economy lodging operations have relatively small and simple physical plants, while convention, resort, and luxury properties may resemble small cities. And the facilities of food and beverage (F&B) outlets can range from an airport kiosk to a large themed restaurant. Such differences in complexity and in the overall luxury level of finishes and furniture contribute significantly to the differences in the construction costs of various types of facilities.

Exhibit 1 contains a historical overview of new hotel development costs subdivided into various levels of service. Even a 100-room economy property represents an investment of several million dollars, and a large luxury property could cost several hundred million dollars. The maintenance, operation, and renovation of these multimillion-dollar facilities are ultimately entrusted to the engineering staff.

Exhibit 2 further delineates the cost categories of new hotels. Besides the significant (60 to 65 percent) costs associated with construction, relatively large outlays are made for furniture, fixtures, and equipment (FF&E), development, and financing. Hotels also incur pre-opening and shortfall reserve costs—categories not commonly found at this level of cost for other types of facilities. The cost of land is not incorporated into these percentages, since it varies widely.

The development and construction of a hospitality facility represents a commitment of capital by an owner who naturally expects a return on this investment. As mentioned earlier, this expected return is driven by two elements: operating profit (from the sale of rooms, food and beverages, and meeting services) and real estate appreciation. To provide both types of return, the facility must be operated and maintained in a manner that maximizes operating profit potential and real property appreciation.

A facility constructed with appropriate quality and good budget control should have predictable costs for maintenance, renovation, and operation. Conversely, one that was poorly designed or built with cost overruns and cost-cutting due to poor budget planning, poor project management, or poor construction practices may well face major problems within the first few years of operation. This often means larger than expected infusions of cash and a nightmare for maintenance and other property staff.

Exhibit 1   Hotel Development Costs: Dollars per Room

	Improvements	Furniture Equipment	Pre-Opening	Operating Capital	Total
1990					
Luxury	67,000– 28,000	15,400– 33,000	3,500– 5,700	2,500– 3,500	88,400–170,200
Standard	42,000– 65,000	10,800– 18,500	2,200– 4,000	1,600– 2,800	56,600– 90,300
Economy	22,500– 41,000	5,600– 10,000	1,200– 1,800	1,200– 1,600	30,500– 54,400
1992					
Luxury	64,000–120,000	14,200– 30,900	3,800– 6,100	2,700– 3,700	84,700–160,700
Standard	39,000– 62,000	9,800– 17,400	2,300– 4,400	1,800– 3,000	52,900– 86,800
Economy	21,000– 38,000	4,900– 9,300	1,400– 2,100	1,300– 1,800	28,600– 51,200
1994					
Luxury	64,000–121,000	14,300– 31,100	3,900– 6,200	2,800– 3,800	85,000–162,100
Standard	40,000– 63,000	10,000– 17,600	2,400– 4,600	1,800– 3,000	54,200– 88,200
Economy	22,000– 40,000	5,100– 9,500	1,500– 2,200	1,300– 1,800	29,900– 53,500
1996					
Luxury	66,000–126,000	15,000– 34,200	4,300– 6,500	2,900– 4,100	88,200–170,800
Standard	42,000– 67,000	10,500– 18,500	2,500– 4,900	1,900– 3,100	56,900– 93,500
Economy	23,000– 43,000	5,600– 9,900	1,600– 2,300	1,300– 1,800	31,500– 57,000
1997					
Luxury	68,000–131,500	15,000– 36,000	4,500– 6,800	3,000– 4,300	90,500–178,600
Standard	43,000– 69,500	10,500– 19,000	2,800– 5,000	2,000– 3,100	58,300– 96,600
Economy	24,000– 47,000	5,600– 10,000	1,750– 2,500	1,500– 2,000	32,850– 61,500
1998					
Luxury	70,000–139,400	15,300– 37,800	4,600– 7,100	3,100– 4,400	93,000–188,700
Standard	43,900– 71,200	10,600– 19,600	2,900– 5,100	2,000– 3,200	59,400– 99,100
Economy	24,500– 48,600	5,700– 10,100	1,800– 2,600	1,500– 2,000	33,500– 63,300
1999					
Luxury	73,900–149,200	15,800– 39,700	4,700– 7,500	3,200– 4,500	97,600–200,900
Standard	45,700– 75,500	10,800– 20,600	2,900– 5,100	2,000– 3,200	61,400–104,400
Economy	25,200– 50,500	5,900– 10,600	1,900– 2,700	1,500– 2,000	34,500– 65,800

Source: *2000 Hotel Development Cost Survey,* HVS International.

As Exhibit 3 illustrates, restaurants are particularly costly to build. This is because of the food and bar equipment required and extensive mechanical equipment needed for efficient operation. Though restaurants in hotels would not normally have parking and land costs assigned to them, their base building costs would be higher.

The Costs of Operation

Following the construction of the facility, there will be ongoing costs of operation. The two principal cost entries on the operating (or income) statement pertaining to facilities operation are the *property operation and maintenance* (or **POM**) and the *utilities* accounts. In the United States, lodging properties expend more than $7 billion annually for POM and utilities.

Exhibit 4 is a summary of typical utility and POM expenditures for U.S. hotels. Most hotels pay at least 10 percent of revenue for these two items, with

Exhibit 2   Hotel Development Costs: A Percentage Breakdown*

Cost Category	Percent of Total
Construction	60–65
Base building, utilities, site work, recreation facilities, contingency	
Furniture, Fixtures, and Equipment	15–18
Interior design, food service equipment expendables, back-of-house equipment, miscellaneous systems, contingency	
Development	10–12
Fees (architectural, engineering, consultant, legal, accounting, project management, development, franchise) Payments (feasibility studies, insurance, soils tests, surveys) Contingency	
Financing	8–10
Pre-opening	3–4
Salaries, training, advertising, promotion, office expenses	
Working Capital	1–2
Reserve for Operating Shortfall	3–5

Note: A good starting point for cost information on franchises is the Uniform Franchise Offering Circular (UFOC) available from the franchisor. Many franchisors provide fairly detailed cost estimates for their various products, providing break-downs of costs for not only the building but a number of the systems required by the UFOC.

*Excluding land, which can be 10 to 20 percent of the final total. Exhibit is based on data prepared for Cornell University courses by Richard A. Penner.

POM usually the larger of the two. The POM account includes all labor and fringe benefit costs in the maintenance department, maintenance supplies and expend-ables, and all contract maintenance costs. Labor and fringe benefit costs are usually about one half of the POM expenditure.

The utilities account includes electricity, fuel, steam, and water. The major ele-ment of the utilities expenditure is electricity. Fuel includes such items as natural gas, oil, and propane. A steam cost is generally incurred by hotels (and a few resorts) that derive their heating energy from steam purchased from a local district heating system or from a central heating plant for those in mixed-use complexes. Water costs include potable (drinkable) water purchases and sewage charges.

Exhibit 3   North American Restaurant Capital Costs ($ per Square Foot)

Cost Category	Quick/ Limited Service	Cafeteria	Restaurant
Base Building	47	40	37
Construction and FF&E	254	220	217
Smallwares and Pre-opening	30	31	32
Parking	32	32	32
Land	75	75	75
Approximate Gross Square Feet Per Seat	22	25	30

Sources: Cornell University course materials prepared by Professor Jan deRoos; data from Cini-Little International; Means Construction Cost Estimates (1999).

Exhibit 4   U.S. Hotel POM and Utilities Costs: 1998 Median Values

	Percentage of Revenue		Cost per Available Room ($)	
	POM	Utilities	POM	Utilities
Full-Service Hotels	4.8	3.6	2053	1519
Limited-Service Hotels	5.8	4.9	864	729
Resort Hotels	5.6	3.3	3870	2235
All-suite Hotels	4.3	3.7	1321	1146
Convention Hotels	4.6	2.9	3000	1852

Source: *Trends in the Hotel Industry—USA Edition* (San Francisco: PFK Consulting, 1999).

The high absolute cost of POM for various types of properties will generally correlate with initial construction costs. That is, the more you spend to build the property, the more you spend to maintain it. Utilities expenditures also vary by type of property, but not as greatly as the POM expenditure.

A U.S. full-service hotel has an average expenditure of 8.4 percent of revenues for POM and utilities, while a limited-service hotel averages 10.7 percent of revenues for these services. The manager who effectively controls utilities and maintenance expenses can contribute both significant dollar amounts to the bottom line (especially at larger properties) and a potentially significant percentage to property profits (possibly even turning a losing operation into a profit center).

While we will deal primarily with lodging facilities, information about restaurants provides an interesting contrast with that of hotels, as shown in Exhibit 5. The repair and maintenance (R&M) costs for restaurants do not include labor, since these are included in the overall operation labor account; for hotels, the R&M (POM) account includes labor. This is one reason for the restaurant facilities maintenance value being as low as it is. And restaurants are actually more energy

Exhibit 5   U.S. Restaurant POM and Utilities Costs: 1998 Median Values

	Percentage of Revenue		Cost per Seat ($)	
	POM	Utilities	POM	Utilities
Full-Service Restaurants				
Check under $10	1.5	3.2	84	178
Check over $10	1.6	2.6	94	171
Limited Sevice				
Restaurants	1.8	3.4	139	255

Source: *1999 Operations Report,* National Restaurant Association, Washington, D.C., and Deloitte & Touche, Los Angeles, Calif., 1999.

(utilities) intensive than hotels, consuming more energy per unit of floor area than almost any form of commercial building. However, they also generate more revenue per unit area than almost any kind of commercial building. This is why the percentage of revenue expended for utilities (and R&M) is as low as it is.

Factors to Consider. An often-debated question concerning hotel utilities and POM expenditures is the degree to which these costs vary with hotel occupancy. Any discussion of this issue should consider a couple of points. First, utilities costs *are* influenced by occupancy, but the building is heated or cooled (at least somewhat) and much of the equipment is operated whether the building is occupied or not. Weather plays a much larger role in determining energy costs. Sometimes occupancy and energy needs are correlated, and sometimes they are not. A resort in the southwest United States may see occupancy peak in the winter, a time of lower outside temperatures and therefore lower cooling needs than in the summer. A ski resort located in Colorado may see peak heating requirements and occupancy exactly coincide. It is possible that as much as 80 percent of a facility's utilities costs can be fixed, that is, unaffected by occupancy.

Second, while the usage of the building and systems during periods of high occupancy clearly creates increasing *needs* for maintenance, the high occupancy itself may make it difficult to *perform* the maintenance. Management may choose to delay maintenance (and therefore expenditure) until periods of lower occupancy. While this tactic may frustrate managers hoping to cut costs when occupancy is low, it is hard to find the time to perform needed maintenance when occupancy is high. During such periods, rooms are occupied, equipment is heavily used, and the maintenance staff lacks the access it needs. Periods of low occupancy are a good time for maintenance staff to deal with backlogged work, shut off systems, and get "behind the walls." Management needs to be aware of this and to plan accordingly, especially in budget preparation. Estimates of the percentage of fixed POM costs range from 50 to 75 percent.

Exhibit 6 shows the percentage of revenue and expenditures (in equivalent U.S. dollars) for POM and utilities for various locations around the world. The highest expenditures for POM are in Africa, the Middle East, and Asia. The highest

Exhibit 6 International Hotel POM and Utilities Costs: 1998 Median Values

Region	Percentage of Revenue		Cost per Available Room ($)	
	POM	Utilities	POM	Utilities
Asia	5.7	5.6	2035	2010
Africa and Middle East	5.4	3.3	2168	1324
Australia and New Zealand	3.6	2.0	1691	968
South America	5.9	4.6	1680	1325
North America	5.1	3.6	1944	1401
Europe	4.3	2.7	1763	1108
World	4.7	3.4	1846	1315

Source: 1999 Worldwide Hotel Industry Study, Horwath International, New York.

expenditures for utilities are in Asia. As a percentage of revenue, South America has the highest POM expenditures, with Asia a close second. Asia clearly has the highest utilities cost as a percentage of revenue. Australia and New Zealand have the lowest expenditures in each category.

Each of these regions has specific locations where costs are substantially greater than these median values. For example, Malaysia reports expenditures of 13 percent of revenues for utilities and the Dominican Republic 9 percent. Other countries reporting POM values substantially in excess of their regional values include Malaysia (8.2 percent), Colombia (7.7 percent), Dominican Republic (7.5 percent), Argentina (7.2 percent), and Mexico (7.0 percent). Therefore, it is quite likely that some locations around the world can expect POM and utilities to consume as much as 15 percent of revenues.

The POM and utility figures cited here are snapshots of where the industry was in the late 1990s. Where the industry will stand in the future regarding these costs is unknown, but it is likely costs will escalate at rates higher than the relatively low rates of the 1990s.

In Exhibits 4 through 6, data about hotel and restaurant properties are presented either on a per-room basis (for hotels) or on a per-seat basis (for restaurants). While this approach produces interesting comparisons, it can create problems when comparing two properties. First, despite the fact that much energy usage is fixed, some of the utilities and POM expense will be related to occupancy or cover levels. Comparing properties without controlling for occupancy or cover differences may lead to incorrect conclusions.

Another problem arises when large differences exist in the business mixes of the two properties. If a hotel has a large banquet business and all the related facilities, its expenditures, when expressed per available room, will look high compared to a facility with the same number of rooms but without the banquet business.

The commercial building sector expresses its costs for utilities and POM on a cost-per-square-foot basis. This is probably a better way in that much of these costs are more related to building area. Most hotel energy management programs use this measure, although it is somewhat rare for measuring POM expenses.

Other factors to consider when comparing two facilities are the ages of the facilities, types of building systems, local utility rates, local labor rates, and identifiable differences in construction (such as single- versus double-glazed windows).

The Costs of Renovation and Modernization

One large expenditure category that is clearly facilities-related is that of capital expenditures, or **CapEx**. CapEx includes not simply "the replacement of worn-out furniture, finishes, and soft goods… CapEx must also cover wear and tear, obsolescence, regulatory requirements such as the Americans with Disabilities Act (**ADA**) and life safety, franchise product demands, changing technology, market demand for product change, and replacement and renovations of building components and heavy equipment."[3] Recognition of the unique and expensive nature of CapEx, planning for its needs, and managing its implementation represent a significant portion of the facilities manager's duties, especially as buildings age.

Historically, management contracts for lodging facilities provided for three to four percent of revenue in what was often called a *reserve for replacement* account. This percentage was sometimes lower during the first couple of years after opening, because these years were often not profitable. The low percentage level of the reserve conveyed confusing signals to ownership about the actual costs and timing of CapEx over the life of the facility. CapEx can range from near zero to as much as 30 percent of revenue in a given year, something not conveyed by a small fixed percentage number. Some industry consultants believe the "poor planning for CapEx was a major reason for the operating losses and bankruptcies the industry experienced in the early 1990s."[4] Estimates of CapEx needs for well maintained properties (where capital expenditures do not also have to compensate for neglected ongoing maintenance) indicate that, over a full-service hotel's first 30 years of life, CapEx will approximately equal and may exceed seven percent of total gross revenues. Exhibit 7 illustrates the wide variation in this expenditure over the first 30 years of product life. Facilities managers can assist owners and operators in becoming aware of these needs and planning accordingly.

The Impact of Facility Design on Facility Management ——

"Good design can clearly increase a hotel's top-line performance, as evidenced by the ability to command higher room rates and increased revenue. Good design also helps build a better bottom line by reducing staffing costs, energy costs, and operations and maintenance expenses… Poor design can accelerate a hotel's physical and functional obsolescence, thereby decreasing it value. When valuing hotels, we look closely at operating costs that are out of line with the norm. If the hotel is under-performing, the problem may be inherent in the building's design."[5]

Our primary focus is on *managing* rather than *designing* facilities. Nonetheless, a facility's design will clearly dictate the scope of the facility management function. The role of facility design, then, can be understood by focusing on such factors as:

Exhibit 7   Capital Expenditures as a Percentage of Revenue by Year

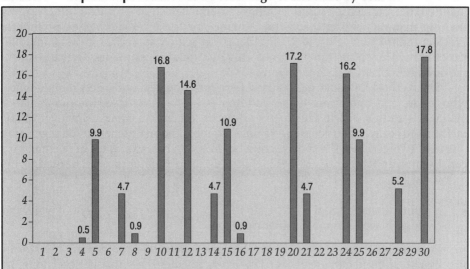

Source: Gregory A. Denton, "Managing Capital Expenditures," *Cornell Hotel and Restaurant Administration Quarterly,* April 1998, pp. 30–37.

- Facility components
- Facility layout
- Materials
- Methods and types of construction
- Equipment
- Systems

Components and Layout

The facility components dictate the needs for facility maintenance, renovation, and operation. The presence of recreational facilities, kitchens, food and beverage outlets, convention space, meeting rooms, and extensive landscaped grounds will all create maintenance needs.

Layout also affects maintenance needs. A high-rise structure generally has more complex building systems and concerns. In addition, high-rise facilities bring needs and costs for such items as elevator maintenance and window cleaning. Low-rise facilities that spread over multiple acres, such as those found at some resorts, create maintenance needs for transportation equipment and long travel times around the facility.

Materials, Methods, and Types of Construction

The materials used in a building will affect not only the maintenance needs, but also renovation needs and such operating costs as energy and insurance. Most seasoned hospitality personnel (and a number of homeowners) have experienced maintenance problems caused by poor material selection—for example, slippery flooring material, siding that is not suitable for the local climate, or premature product failure due to a defect. Problems caused by materials increase maintenance costs. They often can be solved only by capital investments. They also affect the operation of several departments.

The methods of construction used for a building also will affect maintenance, renovation, and operation. If the building is well constructed, the maintenance manager's duties will in fact focus primarily on maintenance. However, if the methods used in construction were substandard, the maintenance manager may quickly be forced into the construction business. Actual examples of substandard construction and its consequences include, but unfortunately are not limited to, the following:

- A poorly installed roof soon began to leak, requiring replacement of walls and ceilings as well as more cosmetic changes.

- Poor construction of the exterior skin of a hotel subject to driving rainstorms in a hot, humid climate allowed moisture to enter the skin and flow along the dividing walls between guestrooms. This led to mold, mildew, and deterioration of the walls.

- Not too many years ago, hotels in the southeast United States failed to properly insulate water pipes. This resulted in massive failure due to freezing.

- In a Midwestern hotel, unapproved changes made to the building's design during construction resulted in the collapse of a walkway and the deaths of scores of people.

- A new urban hotel was built with knockdown (multi-piece) doorframes rather than one-piece doorframes. The frames sagged, aligned poorly, and caused operating problems with locks. Panicked guests often found themselves unable to leave their rooms.

Besides the problems that can result from substandard design and construction, the type of construction itself can affect the costs of the physical plant. A wood frame structure will have higher insurance rates than a masonry one. An exterior surface that requires painting will have higher maintenance costs than one that does not. A facility with plaster walls will cost more to repair than one with drywall. The retrofit of sprinkler systems in older buildings will be easier if a drop ceiling is in place in the guestroom corridor rather than just a finished slab. Facilities with poorly insulated exterior walls and roofs and inefficient windows will all have higher-than-average utility costs.

Equipment

The equipment installed at the facility will have an impact on the need for maintenance. An island resort operating its own electrical generators, desalination plant for fresh water, sewage treatment facility, and large refrigerated storages will

Exhibit 8   Equipment Service Life

Equipment Item	Median Years	Equipment Item	Median Years	Equipment Item	Median Years
Air conditioners		Hot water or steam	25	Cooling towers	
Window unit	10	Air terminals		Galvanized metal	20
Residential single or		Diffusers, grilles, and		Wood	20
split package	15	registers	27	Ceramic	34
Commercial through-		Induction and fan-coil		Air-cooled condensers ..	20
the-wall	15	units	20	Evaporative condensers .	20
Water-cooled package .	15	VAV and double-duct		Insulation	
Heat pumps		boxes	20	Molded	20
Residential air-to-air ...	15	Air washers	17	Blanket	24
Commercial air-to-air ..	15	Duct work	30	Pumps	
Commercial water-		Dampers	20	Base-mounted	20
to-air	19	Fans		Pipe-mounted	10
Roof-top air conditioners		Centrifugal	25	Sump and well	10
Single-zone	15	Axial	20	Condensate	15
Multizone	15	Propeller	15	Reciprocating engines ...	20
Boilers, hot water (steam)		Ventilating roof-		Steam turbines	30
Steel water-tube ..	24 (30)	mounted	20	Electric motors	18
Steel fire-tube	25 (25)	Coils		Motor starters	17
Cast iron	35 (30)	DX, water, or steam ...	20	Electric transformers	30
Electric	15	Electric	15	Controls	
Burners	21	Heat exchangers		Pneumatic	20
Furnaces		Shell-and-tube	24	Electric	16
Gas- or oil-fired	18	Reciprocating		Electronic	15
Unit heaters		compressors	20	Valve actuators	
Gas or electric	13	Package chillers		Hydraulic	15
Hot water or steam	20	Reciprocating	20	Pneumatic	20
Radiant heaters		Centrifugal	23	Self-contained	10
Electric	10	Absorption	23		

Source: *1991 ASHRAE Handbook—HVAC Applications* (Atlanta, Ga.: ASHRAE, 1991), p. 33.3.

clearly have greater and more complex maintenance needs than will a suburban 100-room economy motel. Equipment concerns that will affect maintenance and operating needs involve such issues as equipment *durability, lifetime, repairability, efficiency,* and *accessibility.*

Durability and Lifetime. Some equipment is clearly designed with a throwaway mindset—a light bulb, for example. Other equipment may be suitable for residential use, but not durable enough to last under constant usage. The nature of the hospitality environment mandates the use of commercial-duty equipment for such items as vacuum cleaners. Information about equipment lifetime and maintenance cost can be helpful in understanding maintenance needs and in planning equipment purchases.

Lifetime data for building equipment are presented in Exhibit 8. The figures shown are median values. This means that, in a large sample of the products, one-half of the sample would have failed in the period listed. These data illustrate the variations in the life of equipment commonly found in commercial buildings. The data also point out the potentially large number of expensive items that will need to be replaced 10 to 20 years after they are installed. This has major implications for property capital and maintenance expenditures.

The information in Exhibit 8 does not mean that the equipment cannot continue operating beyond the times given. With a good maintenance program, the life of the equipment can be prolonged somewhat. However, as the equipment reaches and exceeds this expected service life, management should anticipate more frequent failures and a need to invest additional labor and materials to keep the equipment operational.

Repairability. The repairability of equipment involves several issues. Property staff can repair some equipment, while other equipment clearly requires the services of specially trained mechanics. This is one of the reasons 50 percent or more of the POM account is expended on items other than payroll. The decision to repair or replace an item involves several factors. Equipment near its expected life is probably not worth repairing unless the repair will result in a large extension of its life. In addition, the repair of equipment sometimes reduces the efficiency of the equipment. An electric motor, for example, is generally less efficient when it is rewound.

Repairability also depends on the availability of parts and the ability to remove equipment from service while it is repaired. Some operators have purchased imported equipment and discovered that service and parts were virtually impossible to get domestically. Though operators of off-shore facilities often face such problems, this distressing and costly experience has happened even regionally within the United States. This is one good reason to check on service and parts availability and quality *before* you sign the purchase agreement.

The repair of equipment (and facilities) must never jeopardize safety. Equipment (and facilities) should not be repaired in a way that bypasses, disables, or compromises safety features. A repaired electric cord with the grounding plug removed, a repaired lawnmower without a discharge guard, or a repaired fan with its belt guard removed may function properly, but each is a potential safety hazard to both employees and guests. One hotel "repaired" a leaking roof by installing a false guestroom ceiling below. Eventually, the true ceiling collapsed and killed a guest sleeping in the bed below. The lesson is clear. Safety *first*.

Efficiency. Selecting equipment with efficiency in mind involves being aware of the life-cycle implications of equipment decisions. Some pieces of equipment have operating costs per year that are two to four times their purchase price—for example, a water heater for the laundry. Others, like incandescent light bulbs, will cost 30 to 50 times more to operate than their initial cost. Therefore, choosing a more efficient piece of equipment at a higher initial cost could provide some real payback.

Management sometimes finds itself with inefficient equipment that was purchased to keep the initial cost of the building on budget. While there may be no immediate remedy to this problem, the worst decision management can make is to choose the same inefficient equipment when a replacement is required.

Understanding the factors that contribute to the efficiency of various types of equipment can help you make wise purchase decisions.

Accessibility. Accessibility to equipment is essential to ensuring proper maintenance. A few years ago, one of the major auto manufacturers built a car that required partial removal of the engine to change spark plugs! In another case, a water heater was boxed in behind a paneled wall in a private residence. Though defying common sense, these things can and do happen. And building design and equipment location are not exempt. While it is tempting to squeeze mechanical space to reduce building costs, the result can be a near disaster for future maintenance. Maintenance staff may forget equipment located in remote areas with difficult access, either accidentally or deliberately.

Systems

The types of systems found in a building will clearly affect facility management needs. Older buildings with steam heating systems need experts who specialize in this type of equipment maintenance. Local codes may even require such buildings to have on-site boiler operators. Newer facilities often use hot water for heat distribution, reducing the need for maintenance in general and eliminating the need for boiler operators altogether.

To provide guests the option of regulating heating and cooling of their guestrooms and to avoid using through-the-wall packaged room units, many hotels choose centralized (fan-coil) heating, ventilation, and air conditioning (**HVAC**) units for guestrooms. In contrast with packaged units, centralized units have a large amount of additional equipment besides what is in the guestroom, but, from a cost-to-operate perspective, are much more efficient. Constituting these units are boilers, chillers, cooling towers, pumps, and a variety of control devices. All of these components will need specialized maintenance and will incur costs consistent with that level of maintenance expertise.

Systems installed in modern buildings can be quite complex. Computers often must interpret input from a number of sensors in order to control the operation of various pieces of equipment. In addition, the systems are themselves integrated, with the operation of one having an influence on the other. For example, a building fire control system and a building HVAC system may both want to control the operation of certain pieces of equipment, while the building energy management system may want to turn this equipment off.

Introduction of new systems, such as cable or satellite TV and computers, and the addition of increasingly sophisticated entertainment venues to casino hotels and other facilities have increased facilities-related needs. This trend is certain to continue. Today the installation of international standard data network (ISDN) lines for Internet access and of increasingly sophisticated locking and control technology for guestroom security is broadening the sphere of maintenance knowledge and activity. Landscaping features using precision-controlled (computerized) fountains and lights are increasingly being used. What the future may see in terms of new systems in buildings and the maintenance implications of these new systems could truly redefine the skills set of today's facilities engineer. (Imagine the building and other systems necessary to launch the much-discussed era of Space Tourism!)

Management's Responsibilities ────────────────────

The management of facilities is not the responsibility of just the building engineer. While this person has budgetary responsibility for utility, POM, and often CapEx funds, these funds are really spent to provide services for the guests and for the other departments in the operation. And the actions and expectations of other departments relative to facilities need to be the same as those in the facilities area if the customers—paying and internal—are to have their needs met. Since all managers and departments are involved with facilities to some degree, understanding the responsibilities and priorities of facilities management is a shared need.

We can think of the responsibility of facilities management as involving four major areas:

- Safety and security

- Legal and regulatory compliance

- Service

- Cost control

"Safety is always the first concern; legality is tied for second with customer service."[6] The responsibilities of facilities managers as to safety and security are numerous. Facilities staff are often responsible for the proper operation of building systems installed specifically to provide a safe and secure environment. These include fire protection systems, water purification and treatment systems, and locking and security systems. In addition, the proper repair and operation of a variety of building equipment and systems are required to ensure safety. Examples here include such items as ensuring furniture is in good repair and that no electrical shorts exist in lamps and around pool areas. Safety and security also involve the standards, methods, and procedures used to maintain and care for the facility. Facilities employees need to safely conduct their work following procedures that do not endanger themselves or others. And, with ongoing renovation at many properties, the safety of the facility and its guests as part of the renovation "construction zone" is also an important consideration.

Legal compliance includes attention to local building codes, health department regulations, emissions and environmental requirements (including such items as mandatory recycling), and such issues as ADA mandates. The need for legal and regulatory compliance is driven not only out of a need to comply with laws at a variety of levels but also by contracts entered into by the property. To remain valid, equipment warranties may mandate certain maintenance requirements. Management contracts and franchise agreements may also require specific levels of maintenance and refurbishment. And agreements with tour providers may stipulate certain levels of maintenance, environmental performance, and availability of amenities and services.

By design and in practice, the facilities department is a service operation. Facilities staff provide services to the guests, to other departments, and—directly and indirectly—to the owner of the building. The level of maintenance and care of the facility should contribute positively to the guests' experience. There are numerous ways in which a well-maintained facility can contribute in a positive manner and possibly more ways in which a poorly maintained facility can create a negative experience. More often than not, guests make their comments about the facility to employees of another department. The impact of the facilities department is felt throughout the operation and can boost or impair productivity and quality in other departments. Properly operating equipment allows staff in departments such as housekeeping, food service, and laundry to perform their tasks quickly and efficiently.

Finally, the efforts of the facilities staff in caring for the overall physical plant provide an important asset management and protection service to the building owner. Facilities professionals represent the long-term interests of the owner by preserving his or her investment and contributing to the monetary appreciation of the building.

Cost control has high priority in the activities of the facilities department; at times, it is top priority. Costs over which the facilities manager can exercise some control are utilities (fuel, electricity, water, and related items), maintenance and operations (including labor, materials, and contracts), and capital expenditures (including furniture, fixtures, and equipment [FF&E] and major building equipment and systems replacement). Controlling the costs of each major category requires attention to differing issues and can, at times, be in conflict with each other. For example, if an operation focuses too intensely on the control of capital expenses, there may be a rise in maintenance operations expenses and energy deriving from repairing rather than replacing aging equipment and systems.

Finally, the management contracts and franchise agreements that characterize so much of today's lodging and food service environment often make management responsible for providing levels of facility maintenance. Let's look at these in more detail.

Management Contracts and Franchise Agreements

Management contracts may require management to fund reserves for future maintenance and repair needs, to solicit the owner's approval before making building-related expenditures, and to report to the owner regarding how funds are used. A requirement that the operator fund reserves for replacement of FF&E is a common provision of management contracts. Less common are reserves established for non–FF&E repairs. Exhibit 9 presents two sample clauses.

In the 1990s, management contracts underwent some significant changes, as owners were able to garner more control. These changes, as described in the sidebar by James J. Eyster, a leading expert on these contracts, bring **replacement reserves** more in line with actual expenditures and require operators to analyze and document proposed expenditures.

Under terms of most management contracts, the operator generally needs the owner's approval to spend the reserves. Getting this approval can be a difficult point of negotiation when the operator and the owner disagree over whether a certain expenditure should come from the POM budget, the reserve account, or the owner's capital. If the expenditure is categorized as a POM item, it will decrease income before fixed charges (or another profit line) and may therefore decrease the

Exhibit 9   Sample Management Contract Clauses

---

1. Reserve for Replacement of Furniture, Fixtures, and Equipment

Owner shall establish and maintain a separate account to be known as "Reserves for Capital Improvements and Replacements of and Additions to Furniture, Fixtures, and Equipment," for use solely for capital improvements and replacement of, and additions to, furniture and equipment so as to maintain the Hotel in a first-class condition.

2. Reserve for Structural Repairs

Operator shall establish, in respect of each Fiscal Year during the term of this Agreement, a reserve cash amount from which shall be drawn funds for structural or extraordinary equipment repairs, replacement, or maintenance at the discretion of Owner. During each Fiscal Year of the Agreement, funds shall be transferred into the Structural Component Reserve in accordance with the following percentages: (a) None (0%) for all Fiscal Years through and including the Fiscal Year in which the Renovation Program is completed; and (b) One half of one percent (0.5%) in each full Fiscal Year thereafter.

Source: Stephen Rushmore, *Hotel Investments—A Guide for Lenders and Owners* (Boston: Warren Gorman & Lamont, 1990), pp. A3–10, A3–12.

management fee (if it is based on financial performance rather than a flat fee). On the other hand, if the expenditure is categorized as a capital or reserve item, income before fixed charges is not affected and the management fee will be higher. This is a financial basis for debate and potential conflict between owners and management.

Similar disagreement can occur regarding contract services, which are also covered in management contracts. Issuing contracts for "emergency" services may become a point of friction when operators and owners have different definitions of what constitutes an emergency. For example, the owner and operator may disagree over whether a given amount of flooding in the building should be handled by current staff or treated as an emergency calling for contract service.

The management contract will generally contain provisions specifically assigning responsibility for the operator to perform needed repairs, replacements, and improvements. These clauses may contain limitations based on dollar amounts or a percentage of revenue, may contain provisions for owner approval of expenditures, and may allow the owner the option of performing the work using outside contractors. The contract may also specify guidelines for determining whether the expenditure will be considered a POM, reserve, or capital item.

Negotiating and interpreting these clauses is a challenging task. As operating margins tighten, owners become more reluctant to authorize capital expenditures and may even question repair and maintenance expenditures. Conflict results, especially when the pressure on economic performance is caused by the entry of new or renovated facilities into the marketplace. These problems can have major effects on the condition of the physical plant and on the options available to meet perceived needs.[7]

The Funding of Reserves

The basis for funding replacement reserves for furniture, fixtures, and equipment has generally increased in recent years to better match actual expenditures. Most contracts base the initial calculation of annual reserve amounts on at least three percent of gross revenues. The base is stepped up to five percent after the first several years of operation. The issue of whether the owner funds all or a partial amount of the reserve remains a topic of strenuous negotiation. Owners want the reserve funds to be on call, while operators want all or a significant portion of the funds to be placed in escrow. Often a management-discretion slush fund is established for minor expenditures for operators to use without obtaining owner approval.

Owners frequently require approval of competitive bids on all reserve-for-replacement requests and cost-benefit analyses on major expenditures over a negotiated amount. Since significant owner-operator differences can exist in classifying expenditures as repairs and maintenance on one hand or as capital expenditures on the other, recently negotiated contracts often contain appendices describing in detail what types of expenditures are to be classified in each of the two categories—with the arbitrator making the decision for items contested or not included.

Owners and operators both are negotiating for additional capital expenditure budgets separate from the reserve-for-replacement. The funding base for such capital-expenditure budgets is usually one to two percent of gross revenues. Operators seeking to spend those budgets are required to submit cost-benefit analyses for owners' approval or disapproval. Operators have the right to expend funds without owners' approval in emergencies and for situations involving health, safety, licensure, law, or brand compliance.

Many owners require that operators submit three-to five-year plans for replacement and capital improvement with the annual budgets. These plans permit the owner and the operator to focus on the upcoming year's priorities, which often compete and change during the year. The two parties agree in general terms to the expenditures at the beginning of the year, but before the expenditure is made the operator submits actual bids with supporting documentation for the owner's approval.

Source: James J. Eyster, "Hotel Management Contracts in the U.S.," *Cornell Hotel and Restaurant Administration Quarterly,* June 1997, p. 30.

Franchise agreements also establish important requirements for property operation and maintenance. Most franchisors require that facilities be developed and operated in accordance with the franchisors' operating manuals. These manuals establish minimum standards and requirements for constructing, equipping, furnishing, supplying, operating, maintaining, and marketing the establishment. Exhibit 10 presents sample phrasing that might be used.

Responsibilities of the Facilities Department

A complete discussion of the responsibilities of the facilities department in hotels can be quite involved. The following discussion briefly illustrates the potential scope of duties and responsibilities of the facilities staff. Not all operations require all of these, and in some instances, the responsibility may be given to another department.

Exhibit 10   Sample Franchise Agreement Clause

Licensee's Duties

Operate, furnish, maintain, and equip the hotel and related facilities in a first-class manner in accordance with the provisions of this Agreement and the Operating Manual, in conformity to the high service, moral, and ethical standards of the System, and in compliance with all local, state, and federal laws, customs, and regulations, including, without limiting the generality of the foregoing, maintaining and conducting its business in accordance with sound business and financial practice.

Systems and Building Design. It is highly beneficial to have the facilities manager for a new facility provide input regarding building systems and building design from a facilities perspective. This will help to ensure that the facility has been designed with maintenance and operating costs in mind and that the facilities manager is as knowledgeable as possible about the systems and components of the building.

Systems and Building Commissioning. When the actual construction work on the building or system is complete, a commissioning and startup process should be implemented. Commissioning is the "quality assurance facet of systems installation. It is a process for achieving, verifying, and documenting the performance of each system to meet the operational needs of the building, within the capability of the documented design and specified equipment capacities, according to the owner's functional criteria. It is a process that ensures the quality of the installation."[8] Typical of the elements of commissioning HVAC and water systems is what is referred to as TAB—testing, adjusting, and balancing.

Building and System Operations. Building and system operations are the day-to-day activities that ensure the building and its systems continue to operate as intended and provide needed services. To the operators of the facility, this means attention to details, such as proper operation of doors and locks, resetting circuit breakers when appropriate, making sure meeting room schedules are entered into the building management computer system, and a host of other seemingly small but meaningful activities. In the best circumstances, these activities are transparent—everything is working when it should and it becomes invisible to those receiving the resulting service.

Building Maintenance. The building structure and components are a significant investment and serve as the first line of protection for the building's occupants and contents. Facilities staff need to pay attention to the building structures' needs. Elements such as roofing, exterior surfaces, windows, driveways and parking areas, and steps all require regular inspection, maintenance, and other care. Your building's exterior is the first image guests are exposed to; its appearance has a strong influence on their impression of your operation.

Guestroom, Furnishings, and Fixtures Maintenance. The importance of the guestroom, its physical condition, and the proper operation of the equipment serving it cannot be overstated. Regular guestroom preventive maintenance three to four times a year is a signature responsibility of maintenance that helps make the guest experience a positive one.

Equipment Maintenance and Repair. Property facilities contain a vast and varied amount of equipment whose proper operation requires maintenance and repair by facilities staff or by suppliers contracted by facilities staff. Also, facilities staff are often responsible for maintenance and repair of equipment used in or by other departments, such as housekeeping, laundry, and food and beverage.

Equipment Selection and Installation. The equipment operated in hospitality operations changes over time. As new food service, laundry, and other equipment is acquired, it is important that facilities staff be involved in its selection and installation. Facilities staff involvement helps ensure that the equipment is suitable, that its installation can be accomplished cost-effectively, and that its ongoing maintenance can be performed efficiently and in a cost-effective manner.

Contract Management. A host of facilities services are provided by outside contractors. Managing the contracts and contractors for these services is important if costs are to be controlled and the necessary services provided. Facilities managers are central to providing contractor oversight and coordinating and negotiating contract responsibilities.

Utilities Management. The task of utilities management is one of growing complexity and opportunity. Facilities professionals are increasingly finding they have a broader field of utility service vendors from which to choose. Evaluating the cost, dependability, and service levels of each calls for even more managerial decisions than before. Moreover, decisions need to be made about how to control costs of services once they are purchased. And, for water in particular, some utilities managers may find they have potential curtailment or shortage issues to contend with, which may also involve regulatory restrictions with significant cost penalties for over-consumption. Finally, with utilities management now a key component of the growing environmental consciousness arena, compliance, conservation, and communication become priority issues for facilities staff and management.

Waste Management. The facilities department usually is charged with the task of managing waste; its cost is usually in the facilities budget, facilities staff possess the knowledge of the regulatory environment, and facilities professionals have traditionally taken on this task, sometimes even viewing it as a way to reduce the operation's environmental impact.

Budgeting and Cost Control. Facilities professionals must be able to plan and budget for their financial needs (utilities, POM, and CapEx), properly explain and justify these needs, and control the expenditures in all areas under their purview. With 15 to 20 percent of property revenue budgeted for these categories, proper management skills are clearly needed.

Security and Safety. Contributions involving security and safety are twofold. First, the facilities department must be sure its own staff are working in a safe manner. Second, facilities staff must do all that is appropriate to ensure a safe and secure environment for other employees and for the guests. These responsibilities can range from attention to the building and grounds to the proper operation of security and locking systems.

Contractual and Regulatory Compliance. Many elements of facilities operations come under regulatory oversight. Examples include fire codes, building codes, sanitary codes, and environmental regulations. In addition, franchise agreements and management contracts—along with contracts with customers—have elements requiring actions involving the facility.

Parts Inventory and Control. The potentially large number of specialized parts and equipment needed for facilities operations requires that inventory be adequately controlled. Because much of this inventory is also usable outside the building, control of inventory is needed to prevent theft as well as to ensure that parts and materials are available when needed.

Renovations, Additions, and Restorations. Almost immediately upon opening a property, there begins an unending process of renovation, addition, and modification. These can range from a minor installation of a bookshelf to the addition of a new guestroom tower. Involvement and coordination with the facilities department of all these needs are critical. Since adequate service to guests and other departments cannot be jeopardized, maintaining high safety levels and controlling costs during these activities are a major concern of the facilities staff.

Special Projects. Special projects include "unexpected" tasks that fall to facilities staff and those tasks that meet unique guest demands and needs. Building custom facilities for performances and special events, configuring lighting and sound systems, creating special effects, and a host of other unique demands provide not only the opportunity to be resourceful and creative, but generate new streams of revenue for the property.

Staff Training. The continued education and training of departmental staff is essential to orient new employees and learn emerging and changing technologies. Local technical institutions and vendors may offer training services that help facilities staff to update their skills consistent with advances in technology. Another important source for upgrading skills is internal training, in which property-specific and general awareness issues—such as OSHA requirements—can be addressed.

Emergency Planning and Response. Because of their knowledge of the facility and its systems, facilities staff play leadership roles in the property-level emergency planning and response effort. Facilities staff are often key members of emergency response teams as well. If a catastrophe results in damage to the facility, the staff must be prepared to secure the facility from further damage and know the steps to take to restore the facility to operation.

Corporate Reporting. Documenting the activities of the facilities department is important to the success of the operation, as it provides a living history of facilities-related events. The facilities staff will have requirements for corporate reporting and measurement via benchmarking, based on their efforts to keep the facility operating regardless of systems, environmental, or natural problems.

Staff will also be called upon to gather and report specific additional information on facility maintenance, repair, and restoration and on compliance with internal and governmental requirements. These reports serve as the basis not only for recording system and facility breakdowns and slowdowns, but as repair and restoration guides for future reference in similar circumstances.

Facilities Managers in Lodging Operations

Individuals in charge of the lodging facility may have one of a variety of titles such as Director of Engineering, Chief Engineer, Director of Property Operations, or Director of Facilities. Their responsibilities vary as well. Small economy lodging operations have Directors of Engineering (DOE) who do much of the work themselves and require more technical than managerial skills. At larger properties and those with more elegant interiors, the DOE is much more of a manager, controlling a large budget and staff and working to accommodate more complicated demands.

Facilities managers in lodging generally do not oversee housekeeping activities. They are also unlikely to oversee security, except at smaller properties. However, in the world of commercial buildings, housekeeping and security often report to the facility manager. The separation of these activities in lodging is not universal; some operations have initiated a management structure that has engineering and housekeeping reporting to a Director of Facilities staff person, though this is unusual.

Lodging facilities managers are likely have some technical background generated in military service, contracting firms, or trade and technical schools. Managerial skill development is largely on-the-job or derived from in-house managerial seminars. Most property level managers do not hold four-year engineering or technical degrees, having gained much of their knowledge through experience. Exhibit 11 summarizes the skills typically expected from a facilities director.

The salaries of lodging facilities managers (chief engineers) are on the lower end compared with other members of the executive committee of the property, ranking 9 out of 11 nationwide, as shown in Exhibit 12. A significant trend seen in this exhibit is that the relative salary of chief engineers improves with the property's average daily rate (ADR). Mid-rate property chief engineer salaries rank 9 out of 11, first-class 7 of 11, and luxury 6 of 11. This is perhaps reflective of the more significant role that facilities departments play and the care they take at higher end operations. Hourly employees in facilities are among the better-paid staff at the properties.

Facilities staffing varies with the age of the property, services offered, types of systems, commitment to in-house versus contract services, and a host of other factors. Staffing levels of 2.5 to 4 facilities staff per 100 rooms covers the likely range.

Exhibit 11   Summary of a Facilities Director's Position and Required Skills

Scope of Position

Manages and coordinates the work of skilled engineering staff, placing particular emphasis on guest satisfaction and maintaining the property in good working condition.

Position is responsible for supervising, managing, and overseeing the following departments:

- Maintenance
- Engineering
- Security

Position Requirements

Technical

Current on all safety and sanitation policies and procedures that affect the property.

Familiar with chillers, cooling towers, chemical treatments, pneumatics, control systems, water systems, boilers, refrigeration, compressors, etc.

Strong energy management background.

Strong technical skills in HVAC, electrical, mechanical, plumbing, carpentry, etc.

Managerial

Participative management style.

Instill a 'can do' attitude in employees.

Use a 'hands-on' approach to management.

Demonstrate ability to lead by example.

Ability to sell concepts and ideas to management, peers, and employees.

Instill a guest service attitude in all employees.

Clear, concise written and oral communication skills.

However, luxury and first-class operations with large rooms and suites and extensive grounds can have significantly more.

Conclusion

One goal of this chapter has been to drive home the importance of facilities in the hospitality industry. Some of the material about facilities is a bit technical, but then, the industry is increasingly so—just look behind the front desk at most hotels! The manager who wants to control costs, create value for owners and stockholders, and have high departmental efficiency and productivity, happy guests, and a safe and secure operation should find this material helpful. The manager who lacks these concerns should probably look for another line of work. The services provided by a properly funded and well-run maintenance department are of significant value to the property. When it comes to facilities maintenance, you can pay now or pay more later.

Exhibit 12   Lodging Facilities Manager Salary Comparison

	Average Base Compensation (1998)			
Position	Nationwide	Mid-Rate	First-Class	Luxury
Chief Engineer	$43,624	$37,836	$ 50,408	$ 63,163
Controller	$55,938	$48,185	$ 56,559	$ 70,516
Director of Food and Beverage	$61,671	$56,884	$ 62,476	$ 69,946
Director of Human Resources	$50,576	$45,545	$ 47,399	$ 47,383
Director of Rooms	$56,149	$53,739	$ 56,266	$ 55,032
Director of Sales and Marketing	$62,749	$52,285	$ 66,430	$ 86,382
Director of Security	$40,438	$33,109	$ 41,384	$ 47,383
Director of Management Information Systems	$48,559	$45,955	$ 45,624	$ 50,132
Executive Housekeeper	$34,105	$30,698	$ 40,174	$ 48,164
General Manager	$77,950	$66,486	$106,605	$129,356
Resident Manager	$67,512	$53,460	$ 77,311	$ 82,517

Source: *1998 Lodging Property Annual Report*, Hospitality Compensaton Exchange, Mineola, New York.

Endnotes

1. Molly W. Berger, "The Old High-Tech Hotel," *Invention & Technology,* Fall 1995, p. 46.

2. Cheryl E. Kimes, "How Product Quality Drives Profitability—The Experience at Holiday Inn," *Cornell Hotel and Restaurant Administration Quarterly,* June 2001, pp. 25–28.

3 Peggy Berg and Mark Skinner, "CapEx: Do You Spend Enough?" *Lodging Hospitality,* April 1995, p. 48.

4. Peggy Berg and Tom French, "CapEx in the '90s," *Lodging,* April 1995, p. 103.

5. Russell Kett, Managing Director of HVS International (London), quoted in Howard J. Wolfe, "Maximizing the Top and Bottom Line by Design," *Hotels Investment Outlook,* September 1999, p. 68.

6. David G. Cotts, *The Facility Management Handbook,* 2d Ed. (New York: AMACON, 1998), p. 10.

7. Further information on management contracts may be found in James J. Eyster, *The Negotiation and Administration of Hotel and Restaurant Management Contracts,* 3d ed., (Ithaca, N.Y.: Cornell University, 1988).

8. ASHRAE, 1999 *ASHRAE Applications Handbook,* 1999, Chap. 41.

Key Terms

ADA—Americans with Disabilities Act. U.S federal legislation enacted in the early 1990s mandating that owners and operators of public facilities provide certain accommodations for individuals with disabilities as specified in the legislation.

CapEx—Capital expenditure. A major expenditure category in the hospitality industry covering replacement of worn-out furniture, finishes, and soft goods; and wear and tear, obsolescence, regulatory requirements such as ADA and life safety, franchise product demands, changing technology, market demand for product change, and replacement and renovations of building components and heavy equipment.

facilities management companies—Companies with the expertise to provide services such as housekeeping, grounds, and physical plant management to hospitality companies, schools, universities, and various industries.

FF&E—Furniture, fixtures, and equipment, a major portion of CapEx.

franchise agreement—An agreement under which one entity that has developed a particular pattern or format for doing business—the franchisor—grants to another entity—the franchisee—the right to conduct such a business provided it follows the established pattern.

HVAC—Heating, ventilation, and air conditioning. The general term applied to a property's temperature management system. It includes heat and refrigerated air systems and attendant ductwork, airflow machinery, and control devices.

management contract—An agreement between the owner/developer of a property and a professional hotel management company. The owner/developer usually retains the financial and legal responsibility for the property, and the management company receives an agreed-upon fee for operating the facility.

POM—Property operation and maintenance. One of two principal cost entries (with utilities) in the hospitality industry detailing ongoing costs of operation following construction of the facility.

R&M—Repair and maintenance. Generally applied to costing procedures, R&M comprise the maintenance expenses incurred in the regular and unanticipated repair and maintenance of a property's physical assets.

replacement reserves—Cash reserves (the amount usually based on a percentage of gross revenues) set aside largely for maintenance and repair needs. Management contracts commonly require that operators fund replacement reserves for FF&E.

TAB—Testing, adjusting, and balancing. In the building commissioning process, TAB is one of the verification elements that ensures the quality of the installation of systems in the facility (for example, the HVAC and water systems).

Review Questions

1. How do facilities contribute to a hospitality business's profitability?

2. What effect does occupancy have on POM and utility costs? Why might POM costs be higher during periods of low occupancy?

3. What are some advantages of gathering utility and POM data on a per-room basis? What are some disadvantages?

4. How might knowledge of equipment lifetimes affect maintenance decisions?

5. What are management's general responsibilities with regard to the maintenance function? Why is knowledge of the facility important for all managers?

6. Why is there sometimes a question over whether to allocate an expense to the POM, reserve for replacement, or capital account? When are such questions likely to arise?

Internet Sites

For more information, visit the following Internet sites. Remember that Internet addresses can change without notice. If the site is no longer there, you can use a search engine to look for additional sites.

Association of Higher Education
Facilities Officers
www.appa.com

Building Owners and Managers
Association
www.boma.com

Chartered Institute of Building Services
Engineers—UK
www.cibse.org

Energy Decisions
www.facilitiesnet.com/energy
decisions

Energy User News
www.energyusernews.com

Facilities Net
www.facilitiesnet.com/fm

FM Data
www.fmdata.com

FMLINK
www.fmlink.com

Institute of Real Estate Management
www.irem.org

International Facilities Management
Association
www.ifma.com

Today's Facility Manager
http://www.facilitycity.com/tfm/

Chapter 2 Outline

Facilities Maintenance and Repair
Maintenance Management Systems
    Outsourcing
Computerized and Internet-Based Facilities
    Management
Budgeting for POM and Utilities
Contract Services, Responsibility
    Accounting, and Facilities Costs
Capital Expenditure (CapEx) Management
Facilities Benchmarking
Personnel Management in Maintenance
Training and Certification

Competencies

1. Describe several types of maintenance. (pp. 32–34)

2. State the goals of maintenance management systems. (p. 34)

3. Identify and explain the function of several important forms and documents typically used in a maintenance management system. (pp. 34–41)

4. Describe the role played by maintenance schedules and detailed instructions in a preventive maintenance program. (pp. 41–48)

5. Outline the various types of plans and specifications that may be needed for equipment repair and building renovation. (p. 48)

6. List several tactics that could help during maintenance emergencies. (p. 48)

7. Describe elements to consider when hiring contract maintenance services. (pp. 49–52)

8. Describe computerized and Internet-based facilities management. (pp. 52–53)

9. Explain basic elements of budgeting for POM and utility costs. (pp. 53–58)

10. Describe the role of the maintenance department in capital projects and renovations, and explain facilities benchmarking. (pp. 59–64)

11. Outline several considerations involved in managing personnel issues in the maintenance department. (pp. 64–66)

2

Hospitality Facilities Management Tools, Techniques, and Trends

The ideal [engineer] is he who sees further than the mere production of power—who also follows it to the logical conclusion: satisfactory service to the guest at the lowest possible costs to the management. The engineer to succeed must be able to work with department heads and employees in departments that consume the products he manufactures. They must be impressed with the necessity for the engineer and his associates.

Next to the manager I believe the engineer can serve as the most valuable man in the organization of a hotel that has a complete modern plant. The engineer in such an organization should be responsible for the physical upkeep of the house. Under his direction should be the electricians, plumbers, carpenters, decorators, masons, machinists, telephone men, laundry superintendent, silversmiths, and all engine room employees. He should be responsible for the inspection and maintenance of every piece of mechanical equipment in the house.

And it should be possible for him to requisition for whatever he needs in his department. His department should operate on a carefully prepared budget. He should at all times receive reports from the accounting department so that he will know where he stands.

One of the greatest weaknesses in the American hotel system is the manager's failure to work more closely with the man who is responsible for the "Heart of the House." In order to do so it is not necessary that he know all there is to know about different types of heating systems, refrigerating units, and ventilators. But he can learn the highlights about these in a few hours of study.

An engineer does not expect a manager to know as much about engineering as he does, but he appreciates a sympathetic interest in his problems—which after all are the manager's problems as well.

—*Gaston Lauryssen, 1929*[1]

WHETHER it is 1929 or today, "satisfactory service to the guest at the lowest possible cost" and being "able to work with department heads and employees in departments that consume the products he manufactures" remain the facility manager's goals. Achieving them requires the use of the correct managerial and physical tools and techniques, as well as continued attention to relevant trends and opportunities. In this chapter, we discuss the management of the facilities function, focusing on types of maintenance, maintenance management systems, budgeting, and personnel management. Our goal is that you, as a person applying "a few hours of study," will develop an understanding and appreciation of management of operations within the "Heart of the House."

Facilities Maintenance and Repair

A significant portion of the property operation and maintenance (POM) budget is consumed by maintenance and repair demands. Maintenance activities are those done to keep something in an existing state or to preserve something from failure or decline. Repair activities are those that restore something by replacing a part or putting together what is torn or broken. There is intrinsic value in functioning in a maintenance mode rather than in a repair mode. Using an appropriate mix of maintenance methods and capital expenditures is a sound approach to keeping repair to a minimum. But when repair is needed, the skills, parts, and even time should be available to allow the repair to be done in the most efficient manner, on time and within budget.

The types of maintenance at any property can be grouped under a variety of labels. One possible grouping classifies maintenance types as routine, preventive, guestroom, scheduled, emergency/breakdown, and contract.

Routine Maintenance. **Routine maintenance** is that which pertains to the general upkeep of the property, recurs on a regular basis, and requires relatively minimal skill or training to perform. Activities such as grass cutting, leaf raking, and snow shoveling are in this category, as are such housekeeping activities as carpet and floor cleaning.

Preventive Maintenance. While some confusion seems to exist concerning **preventive maintenance** (often abbreviated PM), most practitioners agree that it has several common elements: inspections, lubrication, minor repairs or adjustments, and work order initiation. Preventive maintenance on equipment is generally performed using manufacturers' information concerning maintenance needs as a guideline, coupled with a healthy dose of good mechanical knowledge and common sense. Preventive maintenance may also result from test and inspection activities that indicate action is needed.

Guestroom Maintenance. A unique category found in the maintenance manuals of most hospitality firms, **guestroom maintenance** is actually a form of preventive maintenance. It involves the inspection of a number of items in the guestroom, filter changes in air conditioning units, minor lubrication of doors and other equipment, repair of obvious small problems, and, when needed, the initiation of a work order for more substantial problems or needs.

Scheduled Maintenance. Certain forms of maintenance clearly require advance planning, a rather significant amount of time to perform, specialized tools and equipment, and high levels of coordination between departments. **Scheduled maintenance** includes preparing equipment for changes in the seasons (such as draining cooling towers or winterizing pools) and other activities that are periodically required to keep equipment operating at an efficient level (such as descaling boilers and water heaters). It may also involve more substantial activities, such as replacing major equipment or equipment components or major elements of the building itself (such as a window).

Scheduled maintenance activities usually involve more than inspection, simple cleaning, and lubrication as their primary activities, making them somewhat different from many preventive maintenance actions. Scheduled maintenance may require that major pieces of equipment be removed from service for several hours or longer. In addition, the needed repair may be costly and may be performed by contract service personnel—for example, the repair of a leaking piece of refrigerant piping in a rooftop air conditioning unit. Scheduled maintenance activities may result from PM inspections when the maintenance worker notices a need for repair beyond the scope of PM.

Another action that could be considered a form of scheduled maintenance is the replacement of equipment. Replacement sometimes requires only a minor amount of scheduling. For example, if a through-the-wall guestroom HVAC unit needs replacing, the maintenance staff probably needs access to the room only for about half an hour to remove the old unit and install the new one. On the other hand, if the item to be replaced happens to be all the windows at the property or the roof-mounted HVAC unit for all the public space at the property, the time and scheduling issues may be critically important.

Emergency and Breakdown Maintenance. For the lodging property, **emergency** and **breakdown maintenance** (referred to as corrective maintenance by some) have some important connotations. The emergency or breakdown forms of maintenance are those that either have an immediate revenue effect (the room is out of service and cannot be rented until the problem is solved) or are likely to have a revenue effect if allowed to continue (the leaking pipe threatens the potential rentability of guestrooms if not repaired, or the poorly operating food service refrigeration system will not properly chill food). These forms of maintenance are particularly costly for the operation because:

- They are usually solved only with the application of premium pay (overtime).

- They often bypass the traditional parts or supplies purchasing system, leading to premium parts cost.

- They often have other costs associated with their solution (for example, a leaking pipe may also damage walls and ceilings).

Contract Maintenance. At all properties, the maintenance effort is a mix of in-house and contract activities. **Contract maintenance** activities are undertaken for a variety of reasons, including (but not limited to):

- A desire to minimize the commitment of staff on the payroll to handle these needs.

- A recognition that special tools or licenses are required to perform the work effectively.

- A temporary staffing shortage.

- A need to deal with emergencies.

- A recognition that the complexity of the task is beyond the skills of the existing maintenance staff.

Elevator maintenance, trash haulage, window cleaning, kitchen duct cleaning, yard work, herbicide and pesticide application, water treatment, and HVAC control calibration are common contract maintenance services.

Maintenance Management Systems

To effectively manage the types of maintenance outlined above, the hospitality business uses a variety of maintenance management systems. The goals of these systems are:

- To handle the maintenance needs of the property effectively.

- To record essential information concerning the equipment and systems at the property.

- To establish standards for the performance of the maintenance workers.

- To provide the feedback necessary for management to assess the performance of the maintenance department and the status of work in this department.

This discussion of maintenance management systems uses a paper systems model. While it is relatively easy to visualize these systems, maintenance management is increasingly being computerized. Computer systems are also discussed in this chapter.

The **work** or **repair order** is one of the most commonly used maintenance management forms. Used to initiate requests for maintenance services, this very simple document (usually a sequentially numbered form) provides basic information concerning the needed repair (room, nature of the problem, initiator of the request), a place for the name of the individual assigned to the task, and some area for this individual to respond when the task is completed. This response sometimes includes an estimate of time spent, material used, and other information that might be used for recordkeeping. Exhibit 1 is a sample work order.

At smaller properties, the work orders may be issued from the front desk or from the housekeeping department. Front desk work orders are generally the result of comments or complaints received from guests. Housekeepers may generate work orders in response both to guest comments and to problems that come to their attention in the course of their duties. Some small properties consolidate all work orders in a log at the front desk, while others maintain separate logs in several areas of the hotel. If logs are maintained, they can identify the overall activity in maintenance, the promptness of response, and the size of any backlog.

Many maintenance manuals contain written instructions and flow charts that describe the steps to be taken when a need for maintenance arises. Exhibit 2 illustrates various potential "initiators" of a maintenance need. In this instance, guests, housekeeping, quality assurance (QA) checks, preventive maintenance (PM) checks, and insurance or manager inspections may all identify the need to initiate a

Exhibit 1   Sample Maintenance Work Order

DELTA FORMS - MILWAUKEE USA

(414) 461-0086

HYATT HOTELS®

MAINTENANCE REQUEST

1345239

TIME _____

BY _____ DATE _____

LOCATION _____

PROBLEM _____

_____

_____

_____

_____

ASSIGNED TO _____

DATE COMPL. _____ TIME SPENT _____

COMPLETED BY _____

REMARKS _____

_____

_____

_____

_____

_____

RPHK-04

HYATT HOTELS MAINTENANCE CHECK LIST

Check (☒) Indicates Unsatisfactory Condition
Explain Check In Remarks Section

BEDROOM - FOYER - CLOSET

☐ WALLS   ☐ WOODWORK   ☐ DOORS
☐ CEILING   ☐ TELEVISION ☐ LIGHTS
☐ FLOORS   ☐ A.C. UNIT ☐ BLINDS
☐ WINDOWS   ☐ DRAPES

REMARKS : _____

_____

_____

BATHROOM

☐ TRIM   ☐ SHOWER
☐ DRAINS   ☐ LIGHTS
☐ WALL PAPER   ☐ PAINT
☐ TILE OR GLASS ☐ DOOR
☐ ACCESSORIES   ☐ WINDOW

REMARKS : _____

_____

_____

_____

Courtesy of Hyatt Corporation

maintenance work order. Most of the steps result in some sort of log entry regarding repair.

A property contains many pieces of equipment. Since the continuity of information from manager to manager or employee to employee cannot be expected, several types of written records are maintained concerning the building and equipment. **Equipment data cards** are used for all major pieces of equipment to record facts and information of importance for maintenance purposes. Exhibit 3 is a sample of one such card. When a property is opened or a piece of equipment is purchased, the equipment data card is completed using information from the equipment specifications, nameplates, and other sources. The equipment data card provides the maintenance staff with a summary of key facts and specifications that will assist them in making repairs and in determining correct operation of the equipment.

Cards are also used to record maintenance performed on the equipment, as shown in Exhibit 4. Information contained on these maintenance log cards can be very helpful in determining if equipment is nearing (or has exceeded) its useful or design life. This information is especially helpful when making repair or replace decisions for a piece of equipment.

Exhibit 2   Maintenance Work Order Flow Chart

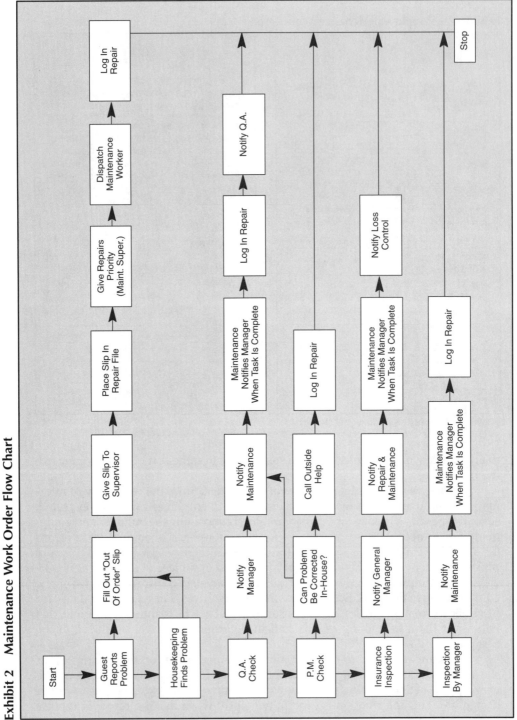

Courtesy of Days Inns of America

Exhibit 3   Sample Equipment Data Card

EQUIPMENT DATA

PROPERTY NO	EQUIP. ID NO	EQUIP. LOCATION
EQUIP. DESCRIPTION	MANUFACTURER	
PURCHASE FROM		
DATE INSTALLED	P O NO.	COST
WARRANTY/REPAIR AGENCY		

MECHANICAL DATA		AIR COND/REFRIGERATION DATA	
ITEM:		ITEM:	
MFG	CFM	MFG	FILTERS
TYPE/MODEL	PULLEY	TYPE/MODEL	BLOWER
SER. NO.	BELTS	SER. NO.	CONTROL
SIZE	BEARING	BTU	REFRIGERANT
GPM	SHAFT SIZE	GPM	PRESSURE
RPM	BLOWERS	RPM	CAPACITY
TYPE OIL		TEMP. RANGE	
CAPACITY		COIL: HEATING	COIL COOLING

ELECTRICAL DATA

MANUFACTURER			SER. NO.		PURCHASE DATE	
VOLTS	PHASE	CYCLE	RPM	PF	HP	AMPS

MOTOR:		MOTOR:		THERMOSTAT/CONTROL	
TYPE	SHAFT SIZE	TYPE	SHAFT SIZE	MFG	
FRAME	PULLEY	FRAME	PULLEY	ITEM	
FLA	LRA	FLA	LRA	MODEL	
WATTS	STARTER	WATTS	STARTER	TYPE	
CAPACITOR	HEATER NO.	CAPACITOR	HEATER NO.	VOLTS	AMPS

MAINTENANCE REQUIREMENTS

Courtesy of Days Inns of America

Exhibit 4   Sample Maintenance Log Card

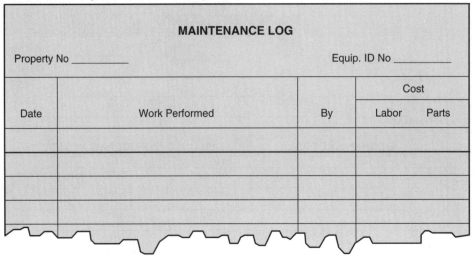

Courtesy of Days Inns of America

Since a key element of the guest experience in hotels is the guestroom itself, some companies maintain information specifically concerning the guestrooms. Exhibit 5 is a sample **room data card** used to record information concerning an individual guestroom. This card contains information about the basic physical characteristics of the guestroom and data on all major elements of the room, whether fixed or movable. The merit of such information usually is not apparent until the need arises to replace some element of a guestroom. Also note that there is space for scheduling and verifying the preventive maintenance dates for the room.

Besides the items contained on the first page of the room data card (usually referred to as FF&E, or furniture, fixtures, and equipment), the second page of the card contains information about the major HVAC and electrical services in the room. The equipment portion of the room card contains an area for entry of warranty information (as does the equipment data card). For the newer property or for newly acquired equipment, this can be very useful and potentially valuable if maintenance problems arise during the warranty period.

Another important recordkeeping system is the **inventory record** kept by maintenance. A large number of items go into the physical plant of a hospitality facility, many of which are listed on the equipment and room data cards. The choice of *what* to put into the maintenance inventory and *how much* of the item to stock affects the responsiveness of maintenance, the storage space needed for maintenance supplies, and the overall investment in the inventory.

The need to maintain an inventory of supplies must not be overlooked when facilities are designed. Failure to consider this need results in a space shortage. It also leads to difficulty in locating inventory, because the supplies that do exist often must be stored in various nooks and crannies. This also contributes to inventory loss or excess inventory. Establishing a formal inventory list for maintenance,

Exhibit 5   Sample Room Data Card

ROOM DATA

NAME OF UNIT						UNIT NO:	
LOCATION						ROOM NO:	

AREA	LENGTH	WIDTH	HEIGHT	SQ. FEET	SQ. YARDS	P.M. DATES	
	✕	✕	=	=			
CARPET	YARDS	COLOR	MAKER	COST	DATE INSTALLED	JAN	JULY
DRAPES							
VINYL							
WINDOWS	SIZE		WINDOWS	SIZE			
DOORS	SIZE		DOORS	SIZE		FEB	AUG
LOCKS	MAKE	TYPE	LOCKS	MAKE	TYPE		
BEDS			HEAD BOARDS				
DRESSER			CHEST DRAWER				
NIGHT STANDS			LAMPS			MAR	SEP
TABLES			LAMPS				
CLOSETS			LAMPS				
MIRRORS			DESK				
SOFA			CHAIRS				
BATHROOM	LENGTH	WIDTH	HEIGHT	SQ. FEET		APR	OCT
	✕	✕	=				
ITEM	TYPE	MAKE	ITEM	TYPE	MAKE		
TUB/ SHOWER			PLUMBING				
TOILET			FLUSH VALVE				
TOILET SEAT			TOILET TANK				
VANITY LAMP			BASIN			MAY	NOV
HEAT LAMP			FLOOR TILE				
JACUZZI			WALL TILE				
STEAM BATH							
ACCESSORIES						JUNE	DEC
ITEM	MAKE	MODEL	ITEM	MAKE	MODEL		
REFRI- GERATOR			COFFEE TABLE				
BAR			END TABLE				
TV/RADIO			EASY CHAIR				
SMOKE DETECTOR			RECLINER				
SPRINKLER			OTTOMAN				
MESSAGE CENTER			STOOL				
ARMOIRE			DR TABLE & CHAIRS				
SAFE			PICTURES				
TELEPHONE			PICTURES				

HEATING & AIR CONDITIONING ON REVERSE SIDE

(continued)

Exhibit 5 *(continued)*

ADDITIONAL COMPONENT DATA

PROPERTY CONTROL NO.	MANUFACTURER	
PURCHASED FROM		
DATE INSTALLED	P.O. NUMBER	COST
WARRANTY/REPAIR AGENCY		

AIR CONDITIONING DATA

	ELECTRICAL HEATING	COILS	
		COOLING	HEATING
MFG	MFG	CAPACITY	CAPACITY
TYPE	VOLTAGE	PRESSURE	PRESSURE
SERIAL NO.	KW	MEDIUM	MEDIUM
BEARINGS	AMPS	MFG	MFG
R.P.M.		REMARKS	REMARKS
SIZE			
BELT & NO.			
FILTER SIZE		NO. FILTERS	MFG. FILTERS
MODEL NO.		SERIAL NO.	THERMOSTAT
TYPE		COOLANT	MFG.
R.P.M.		CAPACITY	MODEL
G.P.M.		REFRIGERANT	TYPE
TEMP. RANGE	PRESSURE	DRIVE	VOLTAGE

ELECTRICAL DATA			MAINTENANCE CODES
MANUFACTURER			
SERIAL NO.		PURCHASE DATE	
H.P.		R.P.M.	
VOLTS	PHASE	CYCLE	PF
MOTOR		MOTOR	
TYPE	FRAME	TYPE	FRAME
FLA	LRA	FILA	LRA
BEARINGS	WATTS	BEARINGS	WATTS
PULLEY/SHEAVE	CAPACITOR	PULLEY/SHEAVE	CAPACITOR
SHAFT SIZE	CAPACITOR	SHAFT SIZE	CAPACITOR
STARTER	HEATER	STARTER	HEATER
PANEL	CIR #	PANEL	CIR #

Courtesy of Days Inns of America

stocking target levels for these items, and conducting periodic inventories of maintenance supplies helps ensure that what is needed is in stock and that excess supplies are not acquired. Some chain establishments with relatively uniform physical plants develop inventory lists for their properties. Still, all properties need to develop their own lists to address the unique items needed at their facilities.

Preventive maintenance schedules and instructions are certainly the backbone of the PM system. Exhibit 6 is a PM schedule for one lodging chain. This listing illustrates several features typical of PM schedules—for example:

- Not every element of the building and physical plant is on the list to receive preventive maintenance. Elements of the building that are critical to guest satisfaction, overall property image and marketing, safety and security, and the performance of other departments' duties are often included in a PM program.

- PM frequency varies with type of equipment. Some elements of the building require PM on a weekly basis. This is likely to consist largely of an inspection or the performance of some repetitive task. Other equipment requires attention monthly, quarterly, or even less frequently. But, when attention is required, the work often involves more than just a simple inspection.

- The scheduling of PM activity is done to attempt to smooth the workload. Activities are not "bunched" into the first week of the month or in some other way accumulated, but rather are staggered throughout the months to allow for productive use of labor.

- The schedule is only a schedule. Information about what is to be done to each system, piece of equipment, or area is not found on the schedule. This information is contained in specific preventive maintenance instructions, which vary for each item on the PM list.

Preventive maintenance instructions are derived from several sources. Equipment suppliers often suggest maintenance activities and frequencies in their equipment manuals. PM instructions for FF&E, building features, and building grounds are generated through a combination of experience, input from vendors and suppliers, and information from various professional and technical organizations. PM instructions may also contain a listing of specialized parts or equipment required to perform the PM task.

Exhibits 7–9 are sample PM procedures for an HVAC wall unit, a convection oven, and a clothes dryer. They are provided for illustrative purposes and are not suggested as the only recommended procedures for such equipment. Nonetheless, they verify that much of the PM activity involves basic inspection, cleaning, and lubrication. PM is not a troubleshooting activity directed at diagnosing and solving a problem. The instructions for PM generally do not state how to repair a piece of equipment. Obviously, to perform PM, the maintenance person must have access to specific tools and supplies.

Like PM activities, many guestroom maintenance activities involve inspection, lubrication, and cleaning. Most hospitality firms have some form of **rooms checklist**, which is used for guestroom maintenance. Exhibit 10 is a sample of one

Exhibit 6   Sample Preventive Maintenance Schedule

Weeks	1	2	3	4	5	6	7	8	9	10	11	12	13	14	15	16	17	18	19	20	21	22	23	24	25	26	27	28	29	30	31	32	33	34	35	36	37	38	39	40	41	42	43	44	45	46	47	48	49	50	51	52
1 Air conditioners—1st floor																																																				
2 Air conditioners—2nd floor																																																				
3 Air conditioners—3rd floor																																																				
4 Air conditioners—roof																																																				
5 Air conditioners—service areas																																																				
6 Bathroom vent filters																																																				
7 Boiler room																																																				
8 Building exterior																																																				
9 Carpets																																																				
10 Caulking/weatherstripping																																																				
11 Circulating pumps																																																				
12 Clean hot water systems																																																				
13 Clean ice machines																																																				
14 Cribs/rollaways																																																				
15 Door closers																																																				
16 Dryers																																																				
17 Elevators																																																				
18 Emergency lighting																																																				
19 Exterior lighting																																																				
20 Fire alarm systems																																																				
21 Fire extinguishers																																																				
22 First aid kits																																																				
23 Flush hot water system																																																				
24 Gutters																																																				
25 Keys/vingcard																																																				
26 Key machine																																																				
27 Landscaping																																																				
28 Laundry/washers																																																				
29 Lawn mower																																																				
30 Lobby floor																																																				
31 Locks																																																				
32 Maintenance shop																																																				
33 Mattress rotation—1st floor																																																				
34 Mattress rotation—2nd floor																																																				
35 Mattress rotation—3rd/4th floor									To have all mattresses rotated by the 15th of the first month in the current quarter.																																											
36 Mechanical room																																																				
37 Meeting room																																																				
38 Mini computer																																																				
39 OSHA 200 log																																																				
40 Parking lot																																																				
41 Pool area																																																				
42 Pool Filter																																																				
43 Pruning/fertilizing																																																				
44 Quik fix-it carts																																																				
45 Roof																																																				
46 Room attendants cart																																																				
47 Signage																																																				
48 Smoke detectors																																																				
49 Stairways, entrance & exits																																																				
50 Storage areas																																																				
51 Telephone room																																																				
52 Vacuum cleaners																																																				
53 Van (*check oil daily)																																																				
54 Walk off mats																																																				
55 Water softener																																																				
56 Water temperature																																																				

Courtesy of La Quinta Motor Inns, Inc.

Exhibit 7   Sample PM Procedures: HVAC Wall Units

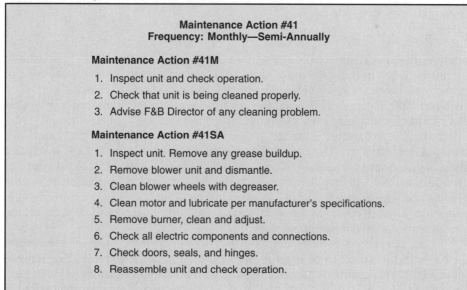

Maintenance Action #7
Frequency: Bi-Monthly—Annually

Maintenance Action #7BM

1. Check unit for proper operation.
2. Clean or replace filter.
3. Ensure coils are clean.

Maintenance Action #7A

1. Remove unit from room and blow out whole unit.
2. Clean coils with coil cleaner and steam or pressure wash.
3. Clean blower wheels thoroughly.
4. Clean condensate pan and paint with bituminous paint.
5. Lubricate fan motors to manufacturer's specifications.
6. Check all electrical components and connections.
7. Run unit and check full operation.
8. Record amp draw against manufacturer's specifications.
9. Clean and repaint any deteriorated surfaces.
10. On units in coastal locations—after full service, recoat unit with tectyl corrosion treatment.

Courtesy of Days Inns of America

Exhibit 8   Sample PM Procedures: Convection Oven

Maintenance Action #41
Frequency: Monthly—Semi-Annually

Maintenance Action #41M

1. Inspect unit and check operation.
2. Check that unit is being cleaned properly.
3. Advise F&B Director of any cleaning problem.

Maintenance Action #41SA

1. Inspect unit. Remove any grease buildup.
2. Remove blower unit and dismantle.
3. Clean blower wheels with degreaser.
4. Clean motor and lubricate per manufacturer's specifications.
5. Remove burner, clean and adjust.
6. Check all electric components and connections.
7. Check doors, seals, and hinges.
8. Reassemble unit and check operation.

Courtesy of Days Inns of America

Exhibit 9   Sample PM Procedures: Clothes Dryer

Maintenance Action #49
Frequency: Daily—Monthly—Semi-Annually

Maintenance Action #49D

1. Inspect machine and check operation.
2. Clean lint trap.

Maintenance Action #49M

1. Check and tighten base hold-down bolts.
2. Blow out dust and lint from top compartment and burner assembly.
3. Blow out dust and lint from lower electrical compartment.
4. Check for loose wires and connections. Tighten as required.
5. Check belt for wear and tension.
6. Lubricate chain per manufacturer's specifications.

Maintenance Action #49SA

1. Carry out Maintenance Action #49M.
2. Lubricate bearings per manufacturer's specifications.
3. Open front loading door. Check rotating basket for clearance. Use adjustment bolts in rear if required.
4. Thoroughly clean dryer.
5. Check pulley alignment. Adjust as required.

Courtesy of Days Inns of America

of these. The checklists used for guestroom (preventive) maintenance will usually list all the items in the guestroom and provide a brief explanation of the type of inspection, lubrication, or cleaning activity to be performed. Since the goal of guestroom maintenance is to keep the guestroom in proper operating order, completing the checklist also involves some repair and replacement activities.

To be able to handle the guestroom maintenance activities efficiently and with minimal downtime for the room, the guestroom maintenance person is usually given a guestroom maintenance cart. This cart contains basic tools and supplies necessary to deal with problems or needs typically encountered. Exhibit 11 is a list of tools and supplies included in a guestroom maintenance cart for a typical motel operation. The selection for any particular hospitality facility will depend on the design and contents of the guestroom.

Many operations provide detailed instructions to the employee concerning the tools and methods to be used to perform maintenance. Exhibit 12 contains a sample of this type of instruction for the touch up and repair of damaged furniture. Note that the quality of the finished product is stressed. Note also that safety is addressed in the use of the paint remover. The **material safety data sheets** (MSDS)

Exhibit 10   Sample Rooms Check List

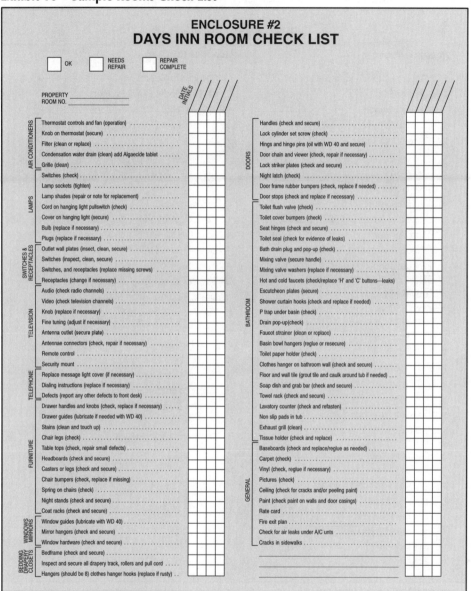

Courtesy of Days Inns of America

that are referenced serve to inform employees about potentially hazardous materials used in the workplace, how to work safely with these chemicals, and what to do in case of an accident. In the United States, OSHA requires vendors and suppliers of hazardous materials to provide an MSDS for each product. The hospitality operation must then maintain these forms and make them available to employees.

Exhibit 11   Guestroom Maintenance Cart Tools and Supplies

QUICK FIX-IT PROGRAM

Required Tools:

- 1 3/8 Electric Drill—variable speed
- 1 Set Drill Bits
- 1 8″ Pipe Wrench
- 1 10″ Pipe Wrench
- 1 6″ Vice Grip Pliers
- 1 8″ Pliers
- 1 Linesman Pliers
- 1 Claw Hammer
- 1 Ball Peen Hammer
- 1 Electricity Tester 0–250 V. AC/DC
- 1 Hand Sander
- 1 7 Piece Punch and Chisel Set
- 1 6 Piece Combination Wrench Set ($^7/_{16}$, $^1/_2$, $^9/_{12}$, $^5/_8$, $^{11}/_{16}$, $^3/_4$)
- 1 Putty Knife
- 1 6″ x 10″ Clear Plastic Tray for assorted bolts, nuts, screws
- 1 3″ Paint Brush
- 1 2″ Paint Brush
- 1 6″ Three Cornered File
- 1 6″ Tailed File
- 1 6″ Flat File
- 1 Set Allen Wrenches
- 3 Phillips Screwdrivers (small, medium, large)
- 3 Regular Screwdrivers (small, medium, large)
- 1 Package Assorted Sandpaper
- 1 Large Sponge
- 1 Plumber's Friend
- 1 Plumber's Snake
- 1 Wire stripper
- 1 Utility Knife

Supplies for Cart:

- 1 Commode Seat
- 2 #1 Wax Toilet Bowl Gasket
- 6 Hinges, Pins, Nuts for Commode Seats
- 1 Can Rossite Drain Opener
- 1 Can Tile Grout
- 1 Elmers Contact Cement #1602
- 1 Can Elmers Carpenter Wood Filler
- 3 Lamp Sockets
- 2 Showerheads
- 2 #782 Double Hooks for Bathroom Doors
- 4 Rate Cards and Holders
- 4 Liability Law Cards
- 4 Aerators
- 2 Shower Cartridge Assembly
- 3 Drain Release Assembly
- 2 Tub Drain Stoppers
- 2 Tank Balls
- 4 Plug Bottoms
- 4 Faucet Handle Caps
- 3 Toilet Water Control Repair Kits
- 3 Ballcock Repair Kits #41071
- 1 Smoke Detector
- 1 Carpet Repair Kit
- 1 Furniture Touch-up Kit

Courtesy of La Quinta Motor Inns, Inc.

Detailed instructions help maintain a standard of work. This is especially useful when personnel turnover occurs and when employees have different perceptions of how to do a task.

The best PM program will not eliminate all breakdowns and emergencies, but it will help extend the time between these events. The familiarity that the employees develop with the equipment while doing PM should prove useful

Exhibit 12   Sample Task Breakdown: Refinishing Wood Furniture

TASK BREAKDOWN		
WHAT TO DO:	**HOW TO DO IT:**	**ADDITIONAL INFORMATION**
Refinish wood furniture.	Refinish wood furniture when scratches cannot be covered.	Formby's paint remover is recommended.
	a. Brush paint remover on the damaged part of the furniture. See MSDS #25.	Use caution while working with paint remover. Read and follow the container instructions carefully.
	Allow the paint remover to set for at least 20 minutes.	Be careful to keep the putty knife parallel to the surface to avoid damaging the wood.
	When the finish begins to bubble and blister, use a putty knife to scrape the finish off the furniture.	
	Wipe off the remaining finish with a clean rag.	
	b. When sanding upholstered furniture, insert a broad knife between the wood surface and the upholstery to protect the upholstery.	
	Use a vibrating sander with #180 fine grade sandpaper to sand heavily damaged areas.	
	If nicks are still present after sanding,	
	Place a damp, heavy cloth on the area.	The moist heat will cause the wood to swell and the nick to pop out.
	Place a hot, flat iron on the damp cloth for about 5 seconds.	
	c. Apply a stain that matches the furniture.	The longer the stain is allowed to set before wiping, the darker it will become.
	Wipe along the wood grain.	
	Allow the stain to set.	
	Wipe off excess with a dry rag.	
	d. Spray the repaired area with the clear lacquer. See MSDS #86.	A stained piece can be immediately sprayed with a polyurethane spray that will give a gloss finish and dry faster, approximately $1\frac{1}{2}$ to 2 hours. Minwax is recommended.
	Let the lacquer dry completely to avoid smudges, fingerprints, etc.	

Courtesy of La Quinta Motor Inns, Inc.

when the need to repair equipment occurs. In order to have at hand the information necessary to perform equipment repairs, it is useful to maintain files of equipment specifications and manuals supplied by the manufacturer with the equipment. These are the same items that often contain the PM recommendations, another good reason to retain them. These specifications and manuals often contain troubleshooting lists that can help greatly in diagnosing the problem and deciding upon a solution. Another useful item is a **control schematic,** which shows the relays, timers, fuses, switches, and basic wiring of controls within electrical equipment.

When maintenance staff must deal with renovations, the building itself, and equipment installed as part of the building, the plans and specifications for the building are key. *Structural plans* allow the maintenance staff to determine locations of key building structural elements, a most important piece of information for certain proposed modifications. *Mechanical plans* identify flow patterns for air and water, control schemes, equipment and system interconnections, and basic operating parameters. *Electrical plans* provide information about circuit capacities, wire sizes, circuit connections and routing, and emergency power circuits. Plans for specialty services such as laundry, telecommunications, lighting, and sound systems assist the maintenance staff or outside contractors in repairing or updating these systems.

How you store plans is very important. Plans should always be accessible to the technician needing them when he or she needs them and stored such that they remain in good condition over time. Purchasing a suitable plans storage unit can be well worth the investment. It is also very helpful to update the plans as changes and modifications are made to the building and systems. When the time arrives to renovate, the lack of updated, current plans often leads contractors either to overbid or to request numerous change orders in the project. Both can result in excess cost and delays.

As mentioned, emergency and breakdown maintenance are costly. The use of the maintenance management systems outlined so far in this chapter will help to greatly reduce the need for emergency and breakdown maintenance. Still, it will be impossible to eliminate this need entirely. Because of the inevitability of emergencies, a property should be prepared. The following are some tactics that can help make a difference during maintenance emergencies:

- Keep a current listing of all telephone numbers for maintenance staff. This list should be available to the maintenance manager and the general manager.

- Train the appropriate night staff concerning procedures to be followed in the event of the more common emergencies. In the context of maintenance emergencies, this would include knowing the location of key water valves and electrical shutoffs.

- Maintain some ongoing relationship with contract maintenance and cleaning firms. Know their telephone numbers (day and night). Adequate manpower and equipment during a maintenance emergency (such as a windstorm which damages a roof) can make a major difference in the extent of damage that might follow and the cost of repairs.

- Consider appropriate backup systems for use during emergencies. This could include using multiple pieces of equipment for key system components (for example, two pumps on the building's chilled or hot water circulation systems, so that a backup exists) or stocking replacement items for key system components (for example, one pump on the system and a spare in stock).

Contract maintenance services are commonly used to supply various services for hospitality properties. Managing these services begins *before* the contract is put out for bid. The following were identified by two authors as some key provisions in drafting a maintenance contract.

- *Insurance:* The contract should require that the contractor have adequate insurance coverage and specify both the type and limits of coverage. The property owner and management company should be a named insured on the contractor's insurance policy.

- *Term:* The contract should be for a specific term with no automatic renewal provision.

- *Cancellation:* The property manager should have the right to cancel the agreement on short notice for lack of performance, and either party should be able to cancel the contract in 30 days for no cause. Penalties for nonperformance may also be included.

- *Contractor not an employee:* The agreement should state that the contractor is not an employee or agent of the property owner or management company.

- *No assignment of contract:* The contractor should be prohibited from assigning the contract.

- *Specifications:* The contract should include very detailed specifications of the work to be performed and the frequency of each task. The specifications should be attached as an addendum to the agreement.

- *Contract fee:* The contract should be specific on the fees for the services named and address fees for extra services. A retention fee would be advisable if the contract is for a one-time maintenance job. A 10-percent retention fee payable after the work has been inspected and approved is appropriate.

  All non-technical maintenance, such as janitorial service, snow removal, parking lot sweeping, and most landscaping maintenance, can be negotiated on a property's standard maintenance contract. Have all contract forms reviewed by an attorney before use. However, technical maintenance, such as elevator or HVAC, requires a maintenance agreement designed specifically for that service.

  Most [hospitality] companies do not have specific technical maintenance agreements and must use the contractor's agreement. When this is the case, the property manager must thoroughly review the contract and negotiate provisions out of the agreement that might be detrimental to the property or its owner.[2]

In addition, it is suggested that you use a relatively short contract term, especially in the early stages of a relationship with a contractor, and take great care with the form of the insurance and indemnification wording found in the contract. A current certificate of insurance should be required and kept on file for all contractors.

Once a contract is signed, it is the responsibility of the maintenance manager or other responsible individual at the property to ensure that the work that has been contracted and billed for has been performed. One property had contracted and been billed for boiler water treatment from one firm for several years. When failures in the heating system began to occur, an inspection of the system revealed major corrosion and a need to replace the boiler and several elements of the piping system. The contractor had never performed the specified work and no one at the hotel had ever followed up to ensure that it was performed.

Outsourcing

A growing trend in commercial real estate is **outsourcing**, a process by which facilities services are provided not by in-house staff but by contract service firms. This is an extension of a common practice in real estate and the lodging industry of what is sometimes referred to as out-tasking, purchasing specific facilities services (such as window washing and elevator maintenance) from outside contractors. Hospitality industry firms such as ARAMARK, Sodexho, and ServiceMaster are active in providing facilities outsourcing.

The U.S. lodging industry has not embraced facilities outsourcing to any significant degree, though there are indications that activity is on the rise. Outside of the U.S., lodging facilities are outsourcing at a somewhat greater level. U.S. outsourcing is primarily associated with large building complexes, either individual large hotels or hotels that are part of larger complexes, in which case outsourcing is not yet at full facilities level. The sidebar on the next page depicts a property where many of the facilities services are outsourced. Lesser outsourcing of energy services occurs when steam or chilled water is purchased from a local utility or from a centralized plant serving a building complex of which the hotel is a part. Of course, the use of contract services for a variety of needs is commonplace in the lodging industry.

Facilities outsourcing can go in both directions. A lodging property could decide that it will, in effect, go into the facilities management business for other properties. This generally involves offices, retail space, or apartments, rather than other hotels, because of proprietary and competitive issues. It is certainly reasonable that hotels occupying portions of buildings (for example, with retail on the ground floor and apartments either above or below the hotel) could provide facilities services to these other spaces. This could turn the typical facilities cost center into a revenue center.

Operators may choose to develop their own maintenance management records and systems or they may choose to purchase sets of cards and recordkeeping systems from various vendors. The key is *using* the systems and maintaining the appropriate controls and records that enable the maintenance operation to be kept productive and under control. Some operations (especially larger ones) use computerized systems to perform maintenance record keeping and to generate the reports and maintenance instructions needed by employees. These computerized systems vary from ones that are operated at the property on either personal

Gaming Industry Bets on Outsourcing

In one example of energy infrastructure outsourcing—or integrated energy management services (IEMS)—Sempra Energy Solutions (formerly known as Energy Pacific), an affiliate of Southern California Gas Co., and Atlantic Thermal Systems, Inc. (ATS) in Atlantic City, N.J., through a new joint venture called Atlantic-Pacific Las Vegas LLC, will own and operate a $70 million, state-of-the-art energy system for The Venetian, a Las Vegas hotel, casino, and convention center.

The system will provide a complete "lighted, conditioned and powered environment" for the hotel and casino and the related convention center and shopping mall complex being developed by Las Vegas Sands Inc. (LVSI).

The joint venture will develop a "turn-key," high-efficiency energy operation for The Venetian, providing a package of energy services that includes energy infrastructure development, equipment financing, operations and maintenance services, and energy procurement.

In addition to saving the $70 million cost of building the energy infrastructure, The Venetian will reduce energy system operating costs in the resort by as much as 20 percent, according to Sempra officials.

Atlantic-Pacific will actually provide the bundled services to three separate affiliates of LVSI. The three customers are The Venetian Resorts Hotel Casino, which will own the hotel and casino; Interface Group, which owns the Expo and Convention Center; and Grand Canal Shoppes Mall, which will own the shopping mall complex.

The IEMS Package Provides For:

- Energy infrastructure ownership. Atlantic-Pacific will finance and own $70 million of energy production and distribution assets, including the central plant, thermal energy distribution system, HVAC delivery systems, fire protection, control systems, and backup power.

- Central plant operating services. Atlantic-Pacific will handle all central plant operations and provide labor and materials for scheduled preventive maintenance and daily operating functions.

- Facility operations and maintenance services. Atlantic-Pacific will be responsible for operation and maintenance of facility systems and controls, including all equipment owned by the joint venture and other systems owned by the customers.

- Energy procurement services. The joint venture will manage energy procurement services for The Venetian, including natural gas and electricity. Customer choice in Nevada's electric industry is expected by the end of 1999.

At the completion of the first two phases, The Venetian will include two hotel towers totaling over 6,000 luxury suites, two casino floors totaling over 200,000 square feet of casino space, The Grand Canal Shoppes, an indoor mall featuring 150 executive shops and boutiques, and 1.6 million square feet of convention and meeting space in the adjoining Sands Expo Center.

Source: *Energy User News,* January 1999.

computers or the property management system to those that are provided by outside service firms.

Computerized and Internet-Based Facilities Management

During the 1990s, a number of lodging companies adopted various computerized and Internet-based facilities management systems. In most instances, these are systems operating separately from the existing "property management" systems, a term that in commercial real estate often includes a facilities management element. Lodging's use of this term does not generally include facilities management, a subtle but important difference.

Computerized facilities/maintenance management systems (CFMS/CMMS) in lodging are used for a variety of functions. Larger operations often control primary building systems (HVAC, for example) by computer. The capability of these systems varies, with the most sophisticated not only controlling equipment operation and building comfort but also fire protection interfaces, security, and electric power management. Even freestanding restaurants have versions of these systems, with varying degrees of "smart" electronics for operating the building's HVAC system and often other equipment.

The management of the "paperwork and dispatch" of maintenance and repair is also increasingly being handled by computerized systems. Preventive, scheduled, and guestroom maintenance and work orders can all be established on computerized systems. These systems can also direct this work to the appropriate staff, account for the time and materials used on the task, and establish a record of the work. In some cases, this feature is a part of a package that provides building systems operations—a CFMS module—and management. More commonly today, however, it is a standalone system (a CMMS module). While a computer does central coordination and recordkeeping, a variety of other technologies and tools can be used. Work orders can be printed, faxed, or dispatched via pager or personal digital assistant (PDA). Communication can be via phone, pager, or PDA as well. Data can be input by way of keyboard, electronic transfer, or barcode reader.

CFMS/CMMS have provided a way to help bridge the gap that sometimes exists between the housekeeping department and facilities. Maintenance management packages can provide multilingual precoded information for housekeeping that allows housekeepers to have information in their native language via prerecorded messages and other information. Housekeeping responds to a given problem with an appropriate telephone signal (a code 555, to mean "light bulb needs replacing," for example, and depending on the system, also the room number). When the computer system receives the signal, it generates a work order to the appropriate employee and sends it via pager. The employee completes the task and enters the work order number (if not already displayed) to indicate the task is done. Inventory is relieved of one light bulb. All the interim steps of the former manual system (housekeeping reports bulb outage to floor supervisor, supervisor writes work order, supervisor sends work order to dispatcher, dispatcher logs and dispatches work order, employee picks up work order, the employee completes the work, employee makes a record of completed work, employee makes manual entry to relieve inventory) are done automatically in a fraction of the time.

CFMS/CMMS not only improve productivity and provide for more complete records, they also provide the basis for more knowledgeable and well-advised decisions up and down the chain of operation. These systems generate information in ways that former systems could not. A ready overview of maintenance backlogs, average time to respond, employee productivity, types of repairs, location of repairs, and a host of other databases can be created. Managers now can actually use maintenance data to help influence decision-making—a much talked-about wish in the era of manual systems, but one often difficult to achieve.

CFMS/CMMS systems are being used both at the unit level and the regional and corporate level. It is possible for access to be set up to these systems in a remote mode. In this manner, a regional or corporate manager can oversee unit level facilities activity. Or a manager in charge of multiple operations can access the data for these without having to be physically at each location. Under the best of all scenarios, this could mean that an engineering manager is able to connect with the CFMS/CMMS and "solve" an operational problem with a piece of equipment without having to drive an hour each way in an ice storm.

An additional feature of some CFMS/CMMS packages, though one not widely used in lodging, is the integration of building plans and specifications with the facilities management software. Managers of office buildings, universities, corporate headquarters, and even manufacturing plants are finding this a particularly helpful tool to effectively and efficiently manage, plan, and allocate the space they occupy. Lodging properties have not seen a particular need for this type of usage, but the application potential is apparent and such a feature may become a common tool for hoteliers in the future.

It is almost assured that in the future many CFMS/CMMS implementers will not load their systems into individual computers at the property level, but will use an Internet connection. Some interesting activities already are emerging and taking place in building monitoring and energy management that use the Internet. By using CFMS/CMMS in Internet mode, facilities professionals and outside vendors alike have access to historical and (at times) real-time information about the building and its systems.

Budgeting for POM and Utilities

The maintenance department's expenditures for property operation and maintenance (**POM**) and utilities equal 10 percent of a U.S. property's revenue. Here we discuss the components of these two elements of the budget, some considerations for budget development, and some of the factors that may result in variations from the budget. The discussion uses the "standard" form of the POM and utility accounts as found in the *Uniform System of Accounts for the Lodging Industry (USALI)* and an actual listing of these accounts for a sample property.

The POM and utility accounts as defined by *USALI* are shown in Exhibits 13 and 14. For most operations, salaries, wages, and employee benefits constitute approximately 40–50 percent of the POM expenditure. Note that contract expenditures may be found in several areas of the POM account. Contract maintenance

Exhibit 13   POM Schedule

Property Operation and Maintenance

	Current Period
PAYROLL AND RELATED EXPENSES	
Salaries and Wages	$ _____
Employee Benefits	_____
Total Payroll and Related Expenses	_____
OTHER EXPENSES	
Building Supplies	
Contract Services	
Curtains and Draperies	
Electrical and Mechanical Equipment	
Elevators	
Engineering Supplies	
Floor Covering	
Furniture	
Grounds and Landscaping	
Heating, Ventilating, and Air Conditioning Equipment	
Kitchen Equipment	
Laundry Equipment	
Life/Safety	
Light Bulbs	
Locks and Keys	
Operating Supplies	
Painting and Decorating	
Removal of Waste Matter	
Swimming Pool	
Telecommunications	
Training	
Uniforms	
Vehicle Maintenance	
Other	_____
Total Other Expenses	_____
TOTAL PROPERTY OPERATION AND MAINTENANCE EXPENSES	$ _____

Source: *Uniform System of Accounts for the Lodging Industry,* 9th Rev. Ed. (Lansing, Mich.: Educational Institute of the American Hotel & Lodging Association, 1996), p. 118.

costs can constitute 25 percent or more of the non-labor element of the POM budget; rubbish removal is a quickly growing cost for many operations. Utility costs include not only what is typically considered to be energy (fuels and electricity), but also water (and sewage) charges. While the fuel and electricity portions of this account have been relatively stable in most areas in recent years, the water and sewage component has substantially increased due to water shortages and/or increased costs of sewage disposal. The utility costs schedule also recognizes the potential for cost recovery due to sales (of office space in a nearby building, for example) or charge backs to departments (such as the laundry).

Exhibit 15 presents annual budget information for the POM and utility budgets for a 485-room suburban full-service hotel. The POM expenditures total approximately $2,860 per room or six percent of revenues. Payroll and Benefits

Exhibit 14   Utility Cost Schedule

	Current Period
Utility Costs	
Electricity	$
Gas	
Oil	
Steam	
Water	
Other Fuels	_____
Total Utility Costs	
Recoveries	
Recoveries from other entities	
Charges to other departments	_____
Total Recoveries	_____
Net Utility Costs	$_____

(Table heading: Utility Costs)

Source: *Uniform System of Accounts for the Lodging Industry,* 9th Rev. Ed. (Lansing, Mich.: Educational Institute of the American Hotel & Lodging Association, 1996), p. 122.

represent just over half this amount. The overall POM expenditure is often divided approximately equally between the Labor and Other POM categories. In this instance, only about 30 percent of the Other POM category is contracts. This figure can be as much as 50 percent of the Other POM expenses.

The utilities expenditures total approximately $1,830 per room or 3.9 percent of revenue in Exhibit 15. As is usually the case, electricity represents the largest component of utilities, here costing $1,240 per room.

The budget in Exhibit 15 is an actual for this hotel, illustrating realistically the impact of various factors on facility needs. The hotel recently changed franchise affiliations and management, at least in part because maintenance needs were neglected by the previous management. This neglect is one of the reasons for the relatively large portion of revenue allocated to POM. In addition, the property is largely responsible for grounds maintenance, which not only creates a large POM cost, but also contributes to the high water/sewer costs. The electric utility serving this property has comparatively low rates so these costs are somewhat low. (These low rates, coupled with a moderate climate, prompted the hotel to select electricity for space heating.)

The process of preparing the POM and utility budgets should use data from several sources. For POM, the labor portion should be approached as it would be for any department, using expected staffing levels, projected hourly wages, and estimated benefit costs. The non-labor portion of the POM account requires a somewhat different treatment. While many operations budget this portion by adding a percentage to the previous year's amount, this approach can create problems. In particular, when either the base year or the year being budgeted involves extraordinary expenditures, this method may produce unreliable figures. For

Exhibit 15   Sample Facilities Department Budget

485-Room Full-Service Suburban Property

Management Salaries	$ 124,623	
Hourly Wages	373,625	
Overtime Wages	31,242	
Annual Bonus	15,600	
Total Payroll Cost	545,090	(2.4% of Revenue)
Employee Benefits	183,443	
Total Payroll and Benefits	728,533	(3.2% of Revenue)
Other POM Expenses		
General POM	9,600	
Refrigeration POM	27,000	
Pool	6,200	
General Electrical	24,000	
Exterminating/Pest Control	9,600	
Automotive	18,700	
Heating & Plumbing	24,000	
Kitchen Equipment	21,000	
Laundry Equipment	21,000	
Elevator Supplies	6,000	
Fire Safety Equipment	600	
Paint—Interior	26,400	
Curtains/Drapes	300	
Floor Covering Supplies	12,000	
Furniture Supply	3,000	
Paint—Exterior	300	
POM Supplies	30,000	
Building Supplies	66,000	
Bulbs	12,000	
Common Grounds	143,600	
Permits & Licenses	2,400	
Waste Removal	34,400	
Elevator Maintenance	96,000	
Hood Cleaning	5,700	
Generator Maintenance	1,200	
Fire Pump Maintenance	1,800	
Chiller Maintenance	4,400	
Soda System	1,000	
Energy Management	12,600	
Life Safety	9,000	
Guestroom Security	3,000	
TV	4,900	

Exhibit 15   *(continued)*

Marble Maintenance	12,000
Water Treatment	7,800
Total Other POM	**$ 657,500**
Total POM	**$ 1,386,033** (6.0% of Revenue)
Utilities	
Electricity	$ 602,000
Gas	112,500
Water	174,000
Total Utilities	**$ 888,500** (3.9% of Revenue)
Total POM & Utilities	**$ 2,274,533** (9.9% of Revenue)

example, a renovation, whether it is upcoming or just finished, will probably reduce the need to expend resources on basic repairs.

Budgeting the utility portion is best handled by dealing with the actual units of energy purchased (kwh, gallons, liters, or whatever is appropriate) and attempting to secure price estimates for these fuels for the coming year from suppliers. During the 1970s and early 1980s, budgeting energy was a major challenge because of double-digit annual escalation rates. The situation in the 1990s was somewhat more stable. The new millennium seems to be headed a bit more toward uncertainty with oil prices fluctuating and electricity showing potential for lower or higher costs due to deregulation.

Contract Services, Responsibility Accounting, and Facilities Costs

There have been instances when the costs for contract services for specific departments in the property, such as computer or copier repair and food service equipment cleaning, have been included in the POM budget, rather than in the individual department's budget. The *Uniform System of Accounts for the Lodging Industry* recognized a change was needed in this practice. In the 1996 edition, *USALI* made a change to include "any contracted service expense within the department that is responsible for the contract. For example, contracted service related to the property management system is charged to the rooms department, while a contract to service point-of-sale devices is charged to the food or beverage department. To facilitate recording these expenses, a new expense item—Contract Services—has been created for each department or cost center."[3]

While properties are not required to follow the *USALI*, the change noted above is potentially significant, especially when combined with another provision and comments found in the 1996 *USALI* related to responsibility accounting and facilities costs.

The department income of the revenue department (for example, rooms, food, and beverage) is computed by charging against revenues only a limited number of expenses that are traceable to the department. For instance, undistributed operating expenses, such as marketing and property operation and maintenance, and expenses that are charged against gross operating profit such as rent, insurance, depreciation, and property taxes are not charged against revenue departments. This measurement approach to departmental income is chosen to help ensure account uniformity. Uniformity is important for the comparability of operating units.

Because of this approach to departmental income measurement, departmental expenses omit a number of significant costs that may be incurred by a revenue department. It may be necessary to ascribe many of the undistributed operating expenses and deductions from gross operating profit to the revenue departments to have a complete and legitimate measure of department performance. There may be times when managers wish to know the overall cost of operating a department. This information is useful for assessing the profitability of a department, for determining prices for services and goods, and for determining whether outsourcing for the services is practicable. Identifying the costs incurred by a department is also useful for making managers responsible for the consumption of resources that drive costs. Managers who are charged for resources may consume them more judiciously than those who do not feel responsible for certain costs. Charging costs to revenue departments may also provide departmental managers with more incentive to monitor the costs of service departments, since these costs will be assigned to their departments.[4]

It is certainly possible to submeter utilities within hotels and track specific information on the usage of utilities by various areas. This is most readily done when the property is constructed, since the installation of the meters at that point is easiest. There are also other methods to allocate utilities costs based on area or other factors. With the growth of food and beverage (F&B) outsourcing in hotels, there may be a growth in interest of both hoteliers and the F&B operators in getting metered information about utility usage.

Arguably, the easiest facilities expense to charge to areas using the service is that of POM. Computerized maintenance management systems can readily account for the POM activity of the major revenue areas of the property as well as other areas (such as the laundry).

Finally, although not addressed in the *USALI*, an additional opportunity is to allocate the capital expenditure costs to departments. This large expenditure could shed some most interesting (and possibly unwelcome) light on the actual costs and profitability of various activities in the hotel.

Charging costs to "tenants" in a building is not a new idea. Many lodging companies already do this within their timeshare/condominium divisions and, when the hotel is part of a mixed-use complex, a central plant with submetering often supplies utility services. There is increasing interest in this activity for all utility services since it is generally acknowledged that submetered customers paying directly for their own usage are more frugal than those who are not metered. There is little reason to believe that the same would not be true for departments in the hotel.

Capital Expenditure (CapEx) Management

The management of capital expenditures is a significant task. At the unit level, the magnitude of responsibility will vary with the size of the property and the corporate organizational structure. At small properties, the owner or general manager may be extensively involved in the planning decision and implementation of capital expenditures. This responsibility at large properties may again be in the hands of the owner or general manager, or the facilities manager may play a more significant role. In any event, two major managerial functions related to capital expenditures must be addressed: (1) planning and budgeting and (2) execution.

Planning and budgeting for CapEx requires knowledge of the expected lifetime of various elements of the facility and the cost of their replacement. Lifetime is defined as a function of the item itself (kitchen equipment lasts longer than office equipment), the durability of the item (commercial grade lasts longer than residential), the care of the item (periodic and proper cleaning of carpeting extends its lifetime), the degree of use (a space with 90 percent usage will wear faster than one with 50 percent), the degree of abuse (items cannot withstand high levels of guest or employee abuse), and the overall level of appearance expected by management and guests (a "worn and tired" piece of FF&E unacceptable at a five-star property could be quite acceptable at a two-star hotel).

Property-specific data tailored to the unique issues facing the property itself is the most pertinent to CapEx planning. Exhibit 16 provides one company's view of equipment life expectancy and replacement cost (expressed in 1997 dollars) for a 200-room full-service hotel constructed in 1997. The exact life and cost of these items will vary from property to property. An item worthy of note is that CapEx activity becomes heightened beginning approximately in year five. A property should have a plan for CapEx to address at a minimum the near-term needs (two to five years) and at least be aware of the needs in the longer term (5 to 25) years. A study conducted by the International Society of Hospitality Consultants serves both as a model and a benchmark for CapEx needs. The most recent version of this study is titled *CapEx 2000—A Study of Capital Expenditures in the U.S. Hotel Industry.*[5] Updates are planned at five-year intervals.

Exhibit 17 is the capital budget for the 485-room property featured in Exhibit 15. This property was recently acquired so the capital budget also reflects the deferment and neglect associated with its previous management. The capital budget of nearly $10.7 million dwarfs the annual combined POM and utilities budget of almost $2.3 million. Almost 50 percent of revenue earned in this year will be spent on capital expenditures. The facility manager is charged with managing contracts for all these items.

The execution of CapEx plans is in many ways similar to the process of facilities construction. Detailed plans and specifications may need to be prepared. These are placed out to bid and vendors and contractors must be selected. Contracts must be negotiated and signed. Timelines and plans must be coordinated with hotel operations. When the process begins, conformance to budget and timetable must be monitored, along with the quality of the work and materials supplied. Often, the oversight of the process is tasked to the facilities manager. Depending on the

Exhibit 16   Estimated Replacement Cost and Life Expectancy of Hotel Equipment

200-Room Hotel (1997)	Life Expectancy (years)	Cost	Subtotal
Guestrooms			
Drapes, sheers, carpet	5	$255,000	
Vinyl wall covering, upholstery, TV	7	240,000	
Light fixtures, artwork	10	75,000	
Beds, case goods, in-room HVAC	12	630,000	
Electronic locking system	15	70,000	
			$1,270,000
Bathrooms			
Vinyl, towel racks	5	$70,000	
Tile, lighting	10	100,000	
Mirrors, vanity, liners	12	125,000	
Fixtures	12	100,000	
			$395,000
Corridors			
Carpeting, vinyl	5	$114,000	
Doors, lighting, ceilings, artwork, mirror	10	40,000	
Ice machines	10	21,000	
			$175,000
Lobby, Front desk, Public areas			
Carpeting, vinyl	5	$27,500	
Upholstered items	7	8,000	
Front desk, ceilings, tile, case goods	10	35,000	
Restroom vanities, tile, fixtures	10	15,000	
			$85,500
Administrative offices			
Faxes, copiers, computer equipment	4	$10,000	
Carpet, vinyl	5	2,000	
Employee dining room furniture, tile	7	2,500	
Case goods, furniture	10	5,000	
Central reservations equipment	10	24,000	
			$43,500
Restaurant and lounge			
Carpet, vinyl, upholstery	5	$75,000	
Lighting, displays, tile flooring	7	25,000	
Case goods, artwork	10	45,000	
Kitchen equipment	24	75,000	
			$220,000
Meeting rooms			
Carpet, vinyl, drapes	5	$20,000	
Equipment	7	2,500	
Lighting, fixtures, partitions, furnishings	12	42,500	
			$65,000

Exhibit 16 *(continued)*

Exterior and back of house		
Parking lot (seal and stripe)	4	$20,000
Pool deck, furniture, landscaping	5	40,000
Paint	5	50,000
Laundry equipment	12	39,000
		$149,000
Building systems		
Exercise room	7	$34,000
Property management system	8	30,000
Elevators (interior finishes)	8	15,000
Phone switch, front-office systems	10	100,000
Water heaters, softeners	12	24,000
Roof	20	125,000
Central HVAC	24	50,000
Elevators (cable)	24	30,000
		$408,000
Total		$2,811,000

Source: Gregory A. Denton, "Managing Capital Expenditures Using Value Engineering," *Cornell Hotel & Restaurant Administration Quarterly*, April 1998.

size of the staff/task, skills of the staff, and the preferences of the owner-operator, the actual execution of the CapEx activity may be by in-house staff, outside contractors, or a combination of the two.

In some cases, the planning and even the execution of CapEx at hotels is under the oversight of an **asset manager**, an official of the property who serves as a combination of owner representative, investment manager, financial and marketing consultant, and project manager. The asset manager evolved during the late 1980s and early 1990s, as owners of lodging properties recognized that their interests might not have been adequately served in CapEx projects.[6]

Facilities Benchmarking

The concept of **facilities benchmarking** —developing numerical (and other) standards that allow comparison of a given facility to itself and to other facilities—is not new. Facilities costs and utilities usage have long lent themselves to this concept. And, with the right tools in place, it is also possible to benchmark facilities service itself, providing insights into effective areas and those needing improvement. The desired result is improved cost control and better service.

Given the accounting system used by the industry, it is not unusual to attempt to benchmark utilities based on cost per room as a percent of revenue. As was indicated previously, facilities-related costs and other measurements are best compared on a per-square-foot or -square-meter basis. This is how benchmarks are developed for other types of commercial real estate. An example of a benchmark is shown in Exhibit 18 that represents fuel usage benchmarks (in this instance, average consumption) for various types of commercial buildings.

Exhibit 17   Sample Facilities Department Budget

485-Room Fullservice Suburban Property	
Project Description	**Budget**
Guestroom Renovation—Main Tower	$ 3,358,200
Plaza Club Lounge	120,000
Elevator Interiors	60,000
Ice Machines	75,000
Retreat Building	1,425,000
Tower Meeting Space and Ballroom	1,950,000
Public Restrooms	150,000
Lobby	600,000
F&B Outlets	200,000
Public Areas	50,000
Administrative Offices	200,000
Back of the House	250,000
Banquet Chairs and Tables	100,000
Signage	175,000
Landscape	175,000
ADA Compliance	425,000
Aluminum Oxidation	100,000
Exterior Sealing	250,000
Chiller Conversion	50,000
Bathroom Exhaust Motors	50,000
New Roof	50,000
Public Area Ceiling Cracks	100,000
Parking Structure/Lot	60,000
Y2K Mechanical/Energy Management	100,000
LAN	325,000
Telephone	200,000
Front Desk/Point of Sale	75,000
CCTV	42,000
Total	**$ 10,690,200**

The most readily used benchmarking data source is the property itself. Comparing performance with similar periods in previous years or monitoring long-term trends in performance is readily done. Internal benchmarking gets around the challenge of comparing like with like that exists when outside comparisons are made. However, looking only internally for benchmarks and best practices can result in a complacent attitude and a potential failure to strive for significant improvements in performance.

The creation of benchmarks for the POM budget can be expressed in total expenditures per room or as a percent of revenue. Facilities labor per room could also be compared (as either staff per 100 rooms or rooms per staff member). As with utilities, a per-room benchmark can make comparisons between properties

Exhibit 18   Energy Consumption Benchmarks

Principal Building Activity	Energy Consumption Benchmarks BTU/Ft² Year
Educational	79,300
Food Sales	213,500
Food Service	245,500
Health Care	240,400
Lodging	127,300
Mercantile and Service	76,400
Office	97,200
Public Assembly	113,700

Source: United States Department of Energy, 1995.

Exhibit 19   Sample Benchmarks for Commercial Hotels

Benchmark	Range
Rooms per Person	21–47
Sq. Ft. per Person	12,700–39,000
POM% of Revenue	3.7–7.1
POM Cost per Room	$1,820–$6,500
POM Cost per Sq. Ft.	$2.10–$6.00
Energy % of Revenue	1.9%–5.3%
Energy Cost per Sq. Ft.	$1.14–$3.36

misleading. Commercial real estate firms might use a value such as facilities staff full-time equivalents (FTE) per unit area.

Exhibit 19 contains benchmarking data from one major lodging corporation. As the data show, significant variation exists in the actual benchmark values for the properties in this company. Age of the property, extent of services, local costs of utilities, labor and material, and a variety of other factors contribute to these variations.

The introduction of computerized maintenance management systems has significantly increased the ability of managers to use other benchmarks. Benchmarks readily available in these systems are:

- Work orders completed per unit time—total by trade, location, piece/type of equipment, and employee
- Work order backlog—total by trade, location, age, and employee
- Work order response time—total by trade, location, age, and employee
- Work orders created—total by location, employee, department, and time of day

Benchmarking can be a useful tool to the hotelier, and there are indications that its use will be more widespread, especially as environmental issues develop. However, caution must be used when applying this tool. The needs and even abilities of properties vary significantly due to climate, facilities, systems, and age. A good first step to initiating benchmarking as a management tool is to use a property's own parameters. After this, comparison with other facilities is appropriate when done with care. The result should help create a measurable path for improved service and reduced costs.

Personnel Management in Maintenance

Key concerns in the management of maintenance department personnel include job qualifications, on-the-job supervision, and employee productivity. Depending on the size of the property and the complexity of the equipment, the way in which the departmental organization is structured will vary, as will the needs for management.

Management personnel for the engineering department will need to have some level of mechanical and electrical skill. The smaller the property, the more the engineering manager will have a "hands-on" role with regard to maintenance. As staff size grows and departmental responsibilities increase, the engineering manager becomes much more a manager and much less a line worker.

Line staff for engineering need very broad skills in maintenance at the small property level, where they perform a varied list of tasks. Usually, these staff members need an education in the electrical, mechanical, and plumbing trades beyond that available in high school. Ideally, they would have several years of experience in these fields. As a screening technique, many operations develop a set of technical questions about maintaining the types of equipment they own. Applicants then must try to answer these questions. In addition, since maintenance staff are sometimes required to lift heavy objects, they should be in good health and physical condition. You should consider using a physical examination as part of the hiring process. If you do use physical examinations, in the United States you must by law require them for everyone applying for a given job; requiring physical examinations selectively violates the Americans with Disabilities Act.

Since engineering staff work all over the property, often under minimal direct supervision, individuals need to be reliable and capable of working on their own. In addition, they need to be aware of what constitutes good workmanship and proper safety procedures and of what complies with local codes. While their trade training should provide much of this, the property still needs to establish and communicate its own standards regarding, for example, appearance and how to address guests and fellow employees.

Training and Certification

Providing the necessary training for engineering staff and management is not difficult, but it does require commitment, time, and money. With low turnover common, little is invested over time in recruitment and job familiarization training of staff. A "fair share" approach suggests that money and time be budgeted to

Exhibit 20   Certified Engineering Operations Executive (CEOE) Program

As a Certified Engineering Operations Executive, you are recognized worldwide as having achieved a distinctive level of excellence in the lodging industry. Created and administered by the Educational Institute of the American Hotel & Lodging Association, the certification program requires a mix of education, experience, and examination. The five steps to certification are:

1. Select from one of three plan types:

    a. Education emphasis, in which you must possess at least a two-year hospitality degree from an accredited institution or successful completion of the Educational Institute's five-course certificate of specialization program.

    b. Experience emphasis, requiring a minimum of three years' full-time experience in the qualifying (facilities manager, for example) position.

    c. Early entry, in which the candidate must hold a qualifying position before taking the examination. Upon successful completion of the examination, the candidate is required to complete specific courses, workshops and seminars to earn points toward the designation. This plan has no educational requirement, but a degree reduces the length of time required in the qualifying position.

2. Submit an application to the Educational Institute Professional Certification Customer Support Center, 800 Magnolia Ave., Suite 1800, Orlando, FL 32803.

3. Verification, in which the candidate's general manager or corporate representative recommends the candidate and verifies employment.

4. Preparation and examination, in which, upon acceptance, candidates have six months to complete all program requirements, including the examination. Study guides and review classes are available.

5. Recertification and maintenance, in which candidates are recognized for their continuing efforts to grow in their hospitality career.

The Certified Engineering Operations Executive designation links the profession to the hospitality industry and establishes a level of expectation and recognition within one's company and the lodging industry.

allow these long-term staff to continue to upgrade their skills. This is especially important for staff holding positions and performing tasks that require licensing and certification.

Engineering line staff can benefit from programs offered by local technical schools and a host of trade associations. Groups such as the International Facilities Management Association (IFMA) and Building Owners and Managers Association (BOMA) offer course and certification sequences geared toward developing the skills and knowledge of the technical staff.[7] Also, most equipment suppliers offer a variety of technical training that may be a requirement of new equipment acquisition. Such training is either included in the purchase price of the equipment or offered for a fee. [8]

Training for engineering management staff is also widely available. Not only can management staff benefit from the programs for line staff, they can take advantage of certification programs offered for facilities managers. Both IFMA and BOMA have certification sequences of various types oriented toward corporate and speculative office building managers and not-for-profit building managers. The American Hotel & Lodging Association (AH&LA), through its Educational Institute, offers the Certified Engineering Operations Executive (CEOE) program that recognizes individuals possessing a specified combination of experience and knowledge in the field. See Exhibit 20 for more information about this certification.

Endnotes

1. Gaston Lauryssen, "Proved Plans that Have Reduced Engineering Costs," *Mid-West Hotel Reporter*, 1929, reprinted in *Hotel Engineering* 1 (1941).

2. Richard F. Muhlebach and Frank E. Ryan, "Developing the Maintenance Agreement," *Journal of Property Management*, March/April 1988, p. 40.

3. *Uniform System of Accounts for the Lodging Industry*, 9th Rev. Ed. (Lansing Mich.: Educational Institute of American Hotel & Lodging Association 1996), p. ix.

4. *Uniform System of Accounts for the Lodging Industry*, p. 183.

5. *CapEx 2000* is published by the International Society of Hospitality Consultants, 515 King, Street, Suite 420, Alexandria, VA 22314, *www.ishc.com*.

6. Further information about asset management can be found in Deborah S. Feldman, "Asset Management: Here to Stay," *Cornell Hotel and Restaurant Administration Quarterly*, Oct. 1995, pp. 36–51.

7. For further information, visit and *www.ifma.org* and *www.boma.org*.

8. A company offering extensive technical training courses is Johnson Controls. For more detailed information visit www.johnsoncontrols.com.

Key Terms

asset manager—an official of the property who serves as a combination of owner representative, investment manager, financial and marketing consultant, and project engineer.

CapEx—capital expenditure; expenditures for capital items such as FF&E and building systems.

computerized facilities/maintenance management system CFMS/CMMS—Computerized maintenance scheduling, recordkeeping, and archiving systems that streamline the "paperwork and dispatch" of maintenance and repair.

contract maintenance—maintenance performed by contract service companies.

control schematic—a document showing the relays, timers, fuses, switches, and basic wiring of controls within equipment.

emergency/breakdown maintenance—maintenance required for problems that either create an immediate negative revenue effect or are likely to created a negative revenue effect if allowed to continue.

equipment data card—a card used for all major pieces of equipment to record facts and information of importance for maintenance purposes.

facilities benchmarking—a continuous-improvement initiative of developing numerical and other standards to allow comparison of a given facility to itself and to other properties or facilities.

guestroom maintenance—a form of preventive maintenance involving the inspection of a number of items in the guestroom, minor lubrication of doors and other equipment, repair of obvious small problems and, when needed, the initiation of work orders for more substantial problems or needs.

inventory record—a maintenance recordkeeping system that keeps track of the equipment and other items in physical inventory.

material safety data sheets (MSDS)—OSHA-mandated forms that inform employees about potentially hazardous materials used in the workplace, how to work safely with these materials, and what to do in case of an accident. Vendors and suppliers of hazardous materials must provide and MSDS for each product. These forms must be available to employees.

outsourcing—a practice in which facilities services are provided by contract service firms rather than by in-house staff.

preventive maintenance—maintenance stressing inspections, lubrication, minor repairs or adjustments, and work order initiation. Generally performed using manufacturers' information as a guideline.

preventive maintenance instructions—maintenance instructions derived from experience, input from vendors and suppliers, and information from various professional and technical organizations. May contain a listing of parts or equipment required to perform each task.

preventive maintenance schedule—a schedule for maintaining elements of the building that are critical to guest satisfaction, overall property image and marketing, safety and security, and the performance of other departments' duties.

POM—Property Operation and Maintenance. One of two principal cost entries (with utilities) in the hospitality industry detailing ongoing costs of operation following construction of the facility.

repair order—a document used to initiate requests for maintenance services. Also called a work order.

room data card—a card used to record information concerning the basic characteristics and major elements of an individual guestroom.

rooms checklist—a checklist used for guestroom (preventive) maintenance, usually listing all the items in the guestroom and providing a brief indications of the type of inspection, lubrication, or cleaning activity to be performed.

routine maintenance—maintenance that pertains to the general upkeep of the property, recurs on a regular basis, and requires relatively minimal skill or training to perform (for example, grass mowing, leaf raking, snow shoveling, carpet and floor cleaning).

scheduled maintenance—significant maintenance requiring advance planning, a significant amount of time to perform, specialized tools and equipment, and high levels of coordination among departments.

work order—see *repair order.*

Review Questions

p32 1. What are the basic activities associated with preventive maintenance?

p 33 2. Under what circumstances might it be appropriate for hospitality managers to use contract maintenance services?

p 38 3. How are equipment data cards similar to and different from room data cards?

4. Why is it important to consider inventory needs when designing a facility? What problems can arise if these needs are ignored at this stage?

5. How does preventive maintenance contribute to the productive use of labor?

p 48 6. What are the possible consequences of failing to update building plans as changes are made?

p55-56 7. What is the best way to determine the energy budget? the labor portion of the POM budget?

8. How does property size affect the maintenance function's role in capital projects and renovations?

9. What factors affect the size of the maintenance staff?

p 61-64 10. What are some possible measures of maintenance department productivity? What are the pros and cons of using these measures? What steps can be taken to improve maintenance productivity?

p63-64 11. What are the principal benefits of CFMS/CMMS?

12. What is facilities benchmarking?

13. How can benchmarking aid the facilities engineer?

14. What is submetering? How does it help in managing costs?

15. What is CapEx management?

16. Where does the asset manager fit into the CapEx management?

p66 17. What are the tasks of the asset manager?

Internet Sites

For more information, visit the following Internet sites. Remember that Internet addresses can change without notice. If the site is no longer there, you can use a search engine to look for additional sites.

American School and Hospital Maintenance magazine
http://www.facilities management.com/

Buildings magazine
http://www.buildings.com

Building Operating Management magazine
http://www.tradepress.com/ publicat/bom

Energy Decisions
http://www.facilitiesnet.com/ energydecisions

Energy User News
http://www.energyusernews.com

Facilities Net
http://www.facilitiesnet.com/fn

Institute of Real Estate Management, *Journal of Property Management*
http://www.buildings.com

International Society of Hospitality Consultants
http://www.ishc.com

Maintenance Solutions magazine
http://www.tradepress.com/ publicat/ms/index

United States Department of Energy, Energy Information Agency, Commercial Buildings Energy Consumption Survey
http://www.eia.doe.gov/emeu/cbecs

Chapter 3 Outline

Competencies

1. Identify the basic facilities-related concerns associated with guestrooms and corridors. (pp. 72–77)

2. Outline the basic facilities-related concerns associated with public space and recreation and exterior areas. (pp. 77–80)

3. Summarize the basic facilities-related concerns associated with back-of-the-house areas. (pp. 80–85)

4. Identify the basic facilities-related concerns associated with a building's structure and exterior. (pp. 85–86)

5. Outline in general terms the steps of the building system design process. (pp. 86–87)

3

Hospitality Facilities— An Overview

Hotels and restaurants are unique (and expensive) facilities designed to make a profit and provide a reasonable return to the owners by serving the needs of customers and employees. Creating and operating the facility so that the product, service, or experience is provided at levels at least meeting, but preferably exceeding, those expected best serve customer and employee needs. Facilities offering a comfortable and safe environment also engender enhanced customer and employee satisfaction. The result is a pleasant experience for the customer, a productive work site for the employee, and a reasonable return on investment for the owner.

W ITH INVESTMENTS OF $50,000 to sometimes more than $300,000 per hotel guestroom or $500,000 to $2.5 million for a freestanding restaurant, it's clear that a huge initial commitment is necessary just to construct a hospitality facility. But cash outlays do not stop there. Ongoing maintenance, utility costs, and capital expenditures needed to operate the facility can be as much as 15 to 20 percent of annual revenue. Obviously, with a commitment of this magnitude, owners and operators want to receive the highest return on the investment they are making and the risk they are taking. For you to help make that happen, you need a comprehensive understanding of the various components of the facility, the options available to you when you design or replace them, operational guidelines and items of concern for the facility, and—importantly—ways to control costs. In this chapter, we address these issues by providing an overview of hospitality facilities, with particular focus on their functions and the issues and concerns affecting them.

We take a look at the principal areas of hospitality facilities and discuss comfort and service issues as well as these areas' links with building systems and components. The intent is to provide a general explanation of these issues without going into deep technical detail. Local building codes, corporate standards, and the individual needs and desires of owners and operating companies understandably will cause variations in design and operation from facility to facility. What we discuss here represents common practices, not universal standards. More detailed study and the counsel of specific professionals would be the next step in more fully understanding, designing, and managing a hospitality facility.[1]

Guestrooms and Corridors

Full-service hotels devote as much as 70 to 80 percent of their space to guestrooms and corridors; limited-service properties use an even higher percentage. These areas are highly visible to guests, and guestrooms are obviously the predominant source of revenue. Providing a comfortable environment in these locations requires attention to visual, acoustical, and thermal comfort issues as well as those of fire and personal safety and security. To deliver this high level of comfort and the expected level of safety, planners and architects incorporate a number of complex and sophisticated systems in their building designs.

Interior corridors are usually provided with artificial lighting 24 hours a day, except in locations where sunlight can be used as the daytime lighting source. Individual wall sconces located at each guestroom or pair of guestrooms can provide artificial lighting. Most modern energy-efficient hotels use long-lived compact fluorescent lamps instead of less efficient, short-lived incandescent lamps. Lamps in exterior corridors should use compact fluorescent lamps rated for operation in the expected outdoor temperatures and conditions of the geographical area. Light for interior corridors can also be provided by overhead lighting located at the entry to each guestroom or along the corridor itself. Lighting in this form is usually provided by four-foot fluorescent lamps.

The air in interior corridors generally requires conditioning to maintain proper temperatures and remove odors. This conditioned air is usually provided via diffusers that direct conditioned air to the corridors either from the end of the corridor or into the elevator vestibule area. In most hotels, the conditioned air moves down the corridors and enters the guestrooms under the door. Envisioned for the future are systems that provide a separate source of fresh air for the guestrooms to address concerns about adequate air quality and fire protection.

Depending on the size and requirements of the building, corridor floors may be of concrete or wood (plywood or a composite material) with a flooring material overlaid on this. In concrete construction, the concrete can also serve as the ceiling of the floor below. Wood floor decking is generally found in smaller one- to three-story properties. Interior corridors are generally carpeted for aesthetic reasons and to reduce noise. The walls and sometimes the ceilings of the corridor are built with fire-resistant gypsum wallboard (drywall) that provides a durable and repairable surface that can be painted or wallpapered. Some economy lodging properties use concrete block for interior walls.

Corridors provide the primary means of exit and as such require protection from fire. The wallboard and concrete are inherently fire resistive and the carpet and wall coverings are designed to meet fire protection standards. Sprinkler systems are usually installed in interior corridors, especially when structures are higher than three stories. Corridors will also have horns and strobe lights to alert guests to fire. Smoke detectors are also generally installed in corridors. Finally, pull stations that activate a building fire alarm are located in corridors near exit doors.

The door providing entry to guestrooms should be fire resistive, self-closing, have a view port, feature automatically latching and locking door hardware, and have a dead bolt. Doors usually have a safety device on the inside that allows the guest to partially open the door while not offering complete access to the room. Guestroom doors have often been undercut to allow air to enter the guestroom (this also provides a way to slip messages and newspapers under the door). Of course, if the opening is too large, there can be noise migration into the guestroom from the corridor.

Electronic locks are increasingly used in new hotels and for retrofits, since they can greatly reduce the potential problems of lost keys and unauthorized entry. However, because electronic intervention with these systems is possible, certain guidelines should be followed in their use. Guestroom cards should be programmed to expire the day the guest checks out of the hotel. Cards should be issued only to registered guests upon the presentation and verification of ID. Room numbers should not be written on guestroom cards. Staff should not admit guests to guestrooms when guests claim to have lost their key or left it in the room. Staff should refer guests to the front desk or in some other way provide assistance and verification that the guest belongs in the room.

The guestroom itself is provided with conditioned air by a variety of means. One approach popular with many guests is simply an operable window allowing fresh air to enter the guestroom directly. If this option is considered, safety and security concerns exist. The window should not open wide enough for room furnishings to pass through. Nor should the window opening be of a size that would allow occupants to get through, especially small children. Other means of providing fresh air include ducting of the air into the guestrooms from a supply plenum or by introduction through the exterior of the building via a wall room HVAC unit.

Accommodations that use **through-the-wall conditioning units** (also known as a PTAC or PTHP—packaged terminal air conditioner or heat pump) generally position the unit below the window. These units use electricity as their energy source and, though their initial cost is moderate compared to other options, they can be noisy and expensive to operate. The units are readily replaced, however, so repair of units can be done offsite with little disruption to use of the guestroom. Air entering the units is filtered to some degree and the units have a provision to allow introduction of fresh air as well. Cleaning of their interior and exterior on a regular basis is required, as is replacement of the filters. These units will typically have cooling and heating capacities of 7,000 to 12, 000 Btu/hr. Integral heat pump units provide lower cost heating operation.

A variation of the through-the-wall unit is what is referred to as a **split system**, in which the compressor and condenser of the air conditioning unit—the principal noise-producing components—are located remotely from the evaporator, where the space cooling occurs. The split of these components into different locations allows the evaporator and its fan to be located almost anywhere in the room—installation on an outside wall is not required. The result is a quieter and less visual HVAC (heating, ventilating, and air conditioning) system, much of which can be repaired without entering the guestroom.

Many hotels (especially larger facilities) use fan coil units to condition guestrooms. These units circulate hot or chilled water through the coils and circulate air from the room past the coils to provide heating or cooling. They also contain filters that remove dust and other contaminants from the air. Fan coils are quieter than

In this guestroom, a vertical fan coil unit is installed along the outside wall. Air distribution louvers are visible directly above the floor lamp. (Courtesy of Hyatt Hotels Corporation and Lisa Masson Photography. © Lisa Masson Photography. Used by permission.)

through-the-wall units and can be installed in a variety of locations in the room. Most common installations are along the outside wall and in recessed ceiling areas in the room's vestibule. Boilers and chillers located elsewhere in the building supply hot or chilled water. Operational costs of fan coil units may be less than those of through-the-wall units, especially for space heating applications. They are also less prone to mechanical problems, but do require the operation of other components in the HVAC system (pumps, boilers, chillers, etc.) to function.

Some hotels have chosen to use a two-pipe fan coil arrangement instead of a four-pipe arrangement. The **two-pipe system** has a single supply line and a single return line, while the **four-pipe system** has two of each. This means the two-pipe system can operate in either a heating mode or a cooling mode, but all units must operate in the same mode—heating of one room and cooling of another at the same time is not possible. The exception to this is a two-pipe system with electric resistance heat. A two-pipe system can be frustrating to both hotel guests and hotel operators. During spring and fall, needs for heating and cooling may alternate from evening to morning on the same day, and from the north or east side of the building to the south or west side during the day. A two-pipe system does not have the flexibility to operate in these alternating modes. Guests are not able to achieve desired comfort, and the hotel operating staff become besieged by unhappy customers. A partial solution is the installation of electric heating coils when fan coils are replaced. It may also be possible to install water source heat pumps in place of the fan coils, although the weight, electrical needs, and noise of these units needs to be evaluated.

Historically, hotel guestrooms have relied upon the airflow from the corridor to replace the air extracted by the bathroom exhaust fan. This has contributed to several problems. First, undercutting the guestroom door to allow air migration compromises the ability of the door to stop the spread of smoke into the guestroom. Second, if the corridor is not supplied with conditioned air at a high enough pressure, the replacement air may enter the guestroom from another source, which could be the outside wall, resulting in the introduction of outside air into the walls of the guestroom or elsewhere—wherever a leak of air is possible. In the walls, moisture can condense and create mold and mildew.[2] Finally, the introduction of replacement or makeup air via the guestroom door does not ensure that this air actually enters and mixes with the air in the guestroom. It may just move from the door to the bathroom vent, failing to freshen the room or remove its odors. Building codes in some locations are now calling for ductwork to introduce fresh air into the guestroom, no longer allowing the practice of makeup air being introduced under the guestroom door.

Control of the temperature in guestrooms traditionally has been done by a simple thermostat activating heating or cooling based on the temperature chosen by the guest. In packaged units, this thermostat may be located on the unit itself. Thermostats may also be wall-mounted (common for fan coil installations). The fan in the fan coil may be operated by the thermostat or may be controlled by a separate control. This basic method of temperature control can result in high operating costs.

Hotel operators should investigate more sophisticated control devices whenever constructing or retrofitting guestroom facilities. One such system is guestroom occupancy control. Sensors in the systems detect whether the room is occupied and automatically adjust the temperature accordingly. Using infrared or ultrasonic sensors to determine occupancy, the units have pre-set temperature limits for unoccupied modes, while still allowing the guest to control the room temperature during occupied times. Some systems also connect with the property management system or front desk and allow unsold rooms to be held at temperatures that further reduce energy use. Energy savings in room heating and cooling of 15 to 30 percent are possible with guestroom occupancy controls. These devices can also interface with room security hardware and other features in the guestroom to provide further value to guests and operators.

Guestroom lighting has undergone at least one notable change in recent years: the replacement of incandescent lamps with compact fluorescent lamps. Improved color characteristics of the compact fluorescent lamp, along with other design changes, have resulted in these energy-efficient lamps becoming the lighting source of choice for hotels. Table or floor lamps generally supply guestroom lighting, with some hotels using wall-mounted lamps by the bed.

Guest bathrooms are provided with a source of cold and hot water, as well as a drain system for sinks, tubs, showers, and toilets. Cold and hot water are supplied via pressurized lines that may require boosting in buildings higher than five stories. Drain systems operate by gravity, so proper pipe pitch is required for water removal, as is a vent line to allow air to escape. Hot water should not be supplied at temperatures in excess of 115° F (46° C) at the point of use. Unless mixing valves are used, maintaining water temperature at no more than 120° F (49° C) at the water heater itself provides heated water well within safe parameters. Water may be need to be treated to control mineral content, odor, and staining.

Attempts to limit water usage have resulted in the installation of faucet aerators, use of low-flow showerheads (some as low as 1.5 gallons [5.7 L] per minute), and low-flow toilets. While faucet aerators have caused few problems, low-flow showerheads have not met with universal guest acceptance because of their poor performance, especially when accompanied by low water pressure. Low-flow toilets have also been problematic, failing to totally clear material from the bowl and being more prone to clogging than high-flow models. With further redesign and incorporation of various flush enhancing features (including pressure assist), the low-flow models are likely to operate satisfactorily.[3]

Bathrooms in hotels are an area where incandescent lamps are still preferred: their color rendering characteristics and decorative possibilities make them the lamp of choice. One problem with bathroom lighting is that guests often leave them burning to function as night-lights. A number of hotel chains are installing night-lights of various types in the guest bath (some in the light switch for the bath and others as part of the hair dryer) to provide for guests' night-light needs without incurring the higher energy costs of operating the bathroom lights all evening.

Guestrooms are equipped with smoke detectors that most municipal codes require be connected to a central building system. In most installations, these trigger the building fire alarm, although in some areas codes allow for an alarm only at the fire panel, with a delay for fire department notification. Sprinkler systems are also widely used in guestrooms, providing a high degree of safety for occupants and the structure. Building codes may not require sprinklers for low-rise structures, but some lodging companies require them as part of their design standards.

Electrical service to U.S. guestrooms is generally supplied at 120 volts, 60 hertz, and single-phase, the same type of service found in a typical U.S. home.[4] Guest bath areas have at least one outlet with a ground fault circuit interrupter (GFCI) to provide protection for the guest against electrical shorts in this potentially wet environment. With the increased use of personal computers, the layout of electrical service in guestrooms needs to take into account access to power outlets for computers as well as the access for housekeeping equipment. Guestroom HVAC units may be served at higher voltages (208/230/480) and may be three-phase rather than single-phase.

Managers quickly become aware of a common and sometimes awkward design feature of hotels: **utility grouping**. Potable water supply, wastewater removal, electrical, centralized HVAC, and other systems are generally grouped vertically in hotels. Guestrooms are located back-to-back, with two rooms sharing a riser that contains piping and electrical service. What this means in terms of servicing is that to repair a system component in a 03 room (say, room 303) service to all 03 and 05 rooms in the hotel (from the first floor of guestrooms to the top floor of rooms) will have to be shut down. This is not only awkward under normal operations, but when renovations are made, those involving building systems are performed, vertically, while others are floor by floor.

The ceiling of the Scandinavian Ballroom in the Radisson Plaza Hotel Minneapolis contains the distribution system for the HVAC systems, various lighting fixtures, and the largely disguised location of sprinkler heads as well. (Courtesy of Radisson Plaza Hotel Minneapolis)

For today's market, various convenience systems are provided in guestrooms: telephone, free and pay television, in-room entertainment, and, increasingly, Internet connection. Some hotels also use more elaborate electronic systems for locking and in-room temperature control. Some of these systems interface with the front desk or other consoles in the building and provide information about room status as well.

Public Space

Besides the corridor areas already discussed, a property's **public space** houses meeting rooms, ballrooms, retail spaces, food and beverage outlets, recreation facilities, and parking. Obviously, these call for vastly differing considerations; we only briefly discuss some of their key issues here.

For high-rise hotels in particular, a critical engineering system that services both guestroom and public spaces is that of **vertical transportation**. Elevators are the primary means of traveling up and down in hotels, although escalators are used for access from lobby levels to other public spaces. Most hotels place elevator and escalator maintenance under contract to outside providers so the major responsibility of the property is to ensure that this maintenance is done properly and per contract. While elevators are needed to provide transportation during normal operations, they should not be used during a fire except under the direction of the fire department. Most operations find that elevators return to the lobby when an alarm sounds and go offline until activated by the fire department.

Meeting rooms may be heated and cooled by either a centralized HVAC system (with conditioned air provided via overhead air ducts and diffusers) or by fan coil or package units located along exterior walls, similar to those used in guestrooms. Centralized meeting room HVAC may be supplied by what is called a **variable air volume system** that adjusts the amount of air to the space depending on the amount of heating or cooling needed, but supplying a minimum amount at all times. Use of variable speed motors with these systems results in the most efficient operation.

HVAC for some meeting rooms and for food and beverage spaces may be supplied from rooftop-mounted package units. This is a common way to heat and cool freestanding restaurants as well. Rooftop units provide heat either by burning a fuel in the unit or using hot water from the building boiler. Cooling is provided by a typical vapor compression refrigeration system. The advantage of these systems is that all equipment is removed from the building and therefore does not take up valuable space. The disadvantage is that they fall victim to an "out-of-sight, out-of-mind" syndrome that results in maintenance neglect. Such neglect results, in turn, in poor environmental conditions in the areas being served and potentially higher operating costs.[5]

Some hotels have created small meeting rooms from guestrooms by removing the dividing wall between guestrooms or have created hospitality suites on guestroom floors in the same manner. This can create problems with providing proper temperature control if guestroom-type HVAC units are used. These units are sometimes not large enough to handle the additional people and equipment loads, resulting in insufficient cooling. Also, buildings with two-pipe systems often find the bulk of the building in need of space heating, while the converted space needs cooling.

Meeting rooms often need lighting that can be dimmed for presentations. In the past, this meant that only incandescent lamps could be used. However, with the availability of electronic ballasts, it is now possible to provide a dimming capability for fluorescent lamps. Another new development worth considering is the occupancy sensor to control lighting so that the lights do not operate when the space is not used. Occupancy sensors also work well in recreation spaces such as fitness centers.

Recreation and Exterior Areas

Resort hotels and properties not located in the center of a city or at airports often have extensive recreation facilities as well as landscaped and parking areas. These contribute significantly to the maintenance function. Swimming pools, tennis courts, golf courses, beaches, and other recreation facilities require continued care to ensure they meet guest expectations. Moreover, care in the maintenance of exterior areas of hotels is a major selling factor not only to those looking for luxurious resort holidays but also to customers drawn to more modest highway lodging facilities.

The Hyatt Regency Scottsdale Resort at Gainey Ranch has 10 swimming pools in its 2.5-acre "water playground" as well as 27 holes of golf and extensive landscaping. All of these facilities create extensive and unique requirements for the facilities management department. (Courtesy of Hyatt Regency Scottsdale Resort at Gainey Ranch)

Indoor pool areas pose special challenges for property maintenance. They require dedicated HVAC systems, owing to the conditions of the air itself (damp and containing chlorine). Pools also require special care to maintain their safety, appeal, and comfort levels. Pool heaters must be supplied with adequate amounts of combustion air to operate properly and safely. Chemicals used to maintain the cleanliness of the water can be hazardous and need to be stored and used properly. Particular care must also be exercised in the use of electricity in and around pool areas.

Sidewalks, driveways, and parking areas have simple but important maintenance needs. First, they must be kept adequately lighted to allow pedestrians and drivers to see where they are going and who or what is around them—proper lighting contributes to safety and security. Cleanliness is also important—debris poses a slip or trip hazard to those using the areas. In locations where snow and ice are present, its prompt removal is important. Finally, these surfaces are subject to deterioration over time, which can result in tripping hazards for pedestrians and, possibly, damage to vehicles. Inspection, repair, and replacement of these surfaces will not only reduce the possibility of injury and damage but also prolong the life of the surfaces themselves.

The amount of work required to care for landscaping varies widely from property to property. Operation of the equipment can be dangerous, requiring the use of special gear for ear, eye, and respiratory protection. Prudent watering and attention to how the water is applied (on the grass, not the driveway) can cut water costs substantially. Certain chemicals used to control landscape pests require a licensed individual to apply them. For this reason and because other equipment and knowledge is needed for proper care of landscaping and lawns, managers often outsource this function.

Back of House

There are a number of important building systems that are not primarily thought of as front-of-the-house equipment, but nonetheless provide vital services to the front of the house. Among these are central plant HVAC equipment, building electrical transformers and control equipment, emergency generators, potable and waste water systems, solid waste handling and removal facilities, and telephone and cable television. Most of these systems are under the managerial oversight and budgetary responsibility of the facilities or engineering department. These "heart of the house" components are critical to the operation of the property, but are often out of sight and sometimes out of mind. Managers operating in destination resorts and in settings where reliance upon local utilities (private and public) is not an option are well aware of the critical importance of these systems and the real challenge of operating them.

Central plant HVAC equipment consists largely of boilers, chillers, cooling towers, circulating pumps, central station air handlers and control systems, and ancillary equipment needed to deliver conditioned air. Care in the selection and operation of this equipment is key to energy-efficient operation. It is particularly important to match the size of the equipment to the load needed. Pay special attention to the steps required for safe operation, since the fuels and electricity used by this equipment—along with its size and power—make it potentially dangerous.

Fossil fuel-fired boilers and water heaters may be fueled by natural gas, fuel oil, or liquefied petroleum gas (LP). Oil and LP require onsite storage tanks that create a potential for leakage. Oil leakage is a potential environmental hazard, while LP leakage is a major safety hazard. Your system must be designed so that combustion of fuels occurs in the most efficient manner possible within the parameters of stringent safety precautions. Supplying adequate combustion air is critical to proper combustion so that the production of carbon monoxide is minimized. Water used in the boilers must be treated to avoid buildup of scale-mineral deposits on waterside surfaces of the boilers. These deposits decrease boiler capacity and efficiency and shorten the functional life of the boiler.

Chillers and cooling towers are commonly found at midsize and larger properties, as well as many commercial buildings. These can be large and expensive pieces of equipment, and their operation needs to be monitored to ensure efficient and safe operation. Efficient operation starts with the selection of equipment designed for efficiency, followed by a disciplined, ongoing maintenance program. Many operations rely on a service contract for chiller maintenance, which includes normal lubrication and refrigerant inspections as well as the cleaning of the waterside of coils to reduce fouling. Critical to efficient and safe cooling tower operation is the careful matching of the tower operation to the cooling load and to the water chemistry of the tower. The first part involves your continual oversight; the second is usually a combination of an installed monitoring system and contract services.

Most operations purchase electricity from an electrical supplier, with the property's responsibility for electrical usage starting at the meter. Hotels and many restaurants are billed for both their electrical energy usage and their electrical demand—the peak rate at which they use electrical energy. From 20 to 50 percent of a property's electricity cost can be demand-related, depending on the tariff of the local utility. Understanding the local utility tariff and its implications for the cost of energy and the value of energy-conserving options is important. There is generally a significant difference between the average price of electrical energy (calculated by taking the entire bill and dividing by the amount of electricity used) and the marginal price (the price of the next additional unit of usage or conservation). Make sure that you audit your electrical bills for correctness and investigate to be sure the tariff is the most economically beneficial that your property qualifies for.

For engineering departments to effectively manage the usage of electricity and other utilities, it is important that they be provided with the appropriate kind and amount of information. This means, at minimum, a copy of the utility bill, which engineering staff should see and approve before it is paid. To truly understand the usage of utilities, it is quite helpful to have **submeters** for utilities on the property. Submeters permit you to monitor utility consumption by specific area (rooms, food and beverage, laundry, landscaping, etc.). This information can help you measure the effectiveness of conservation efforts. Submeters also allow for the charge back of utilities to operating departments and areas, something that could be of more interest as hotels outsource operations such as food and beverage outlets.

In many areas, destination resorts produce their own electricity. Even in areas with access to public utility electricity, some resorts choose to produce their own for reasons of cost and reliability. Whatever the source, the distribution of electricity within the property becomes the responsibility of the property itself. Electrical switchgear and panels provide the means of control and of partitioning the electrical service to various areas of the facility. Fuses and circuit breakers serve to limit excess flows of electricity. Transformers are used to change the voltage of the electricity to match various loads. Transformers need to be kept well ventilated to avoid overheating, and the rooms in which they are located should be adequately secured and not used for storage. Most hospitality buildings are supplied with electricity at 480 volts. Small restaurants and lodges might be supplied at 208/230/120, and very large establishments could be supplied at thousands of volts. All will have alternating current and voltage: 60 cycles per second (hz) in North America and 50 cycles per cycles elsewhere.

Power quality issues are becoming more important as more building controls and property systems incorporate microprocessors to provide automated operation. While some protection for electronic equipment is provided by surge suppressors with multi-strips, the operation looking to provide protection against a variety of electrical problems should consider an uninterruptible power supply unit or other methods of circuit design and equipment that provide protection from power interruption.

An emergency supply of electricity is often required by municipal code, but even if it is not, it makes good business sense to have it. Exit signs and hallways/ stairwells require a backup lighting supply, powered by either battery or emergency generator. Various fire protection systems (for example, detectors, alarms, fire pumps) need to operate even when main building power is disconnected, as do elements of the elevator systems and some portions of the HVAC system. For these reasons, a property often has an emergency generator. Regular testing of the generators (not only starting them but also putting them under load) is important to ensure operation when needed.

For many operations, potable water is provided from a municipal source. Property responsibilities then consist of maintaining this potability by avoiding cross connections with contaminated sources and improving the suitability of the water for human and equipment needs. Municipal water supplies may still need treatment to reduce mineral content, odor, or color problems. If you produce your own potable water (from a well, lake, or desalination plant, for example), the responsibility for water potability is yours.

Wastewater disposal is most easily handled by a municipal sewer system. In this instance, the property faces the responsibilities (and costs) of meeting the discharge requirements of the system. These could involve requirements for grease removal, control of levels and types of chemicals added in laundry operations, and sometimes restrictions on the temperatures of discharge. Operations running their own wastewater treatment plants have greater responsibility (and quite likely costs) in the operation of these plants, in the allowable characteristics of their liquid discharges, and in the disposal of sewage sludge that results. They also have greater options, since the treated wastewater can be used for irrigating landscaped areas and golf courses.

Another responsibility of the facilities department is the disposal of **solid waste**. In the past, this task consisted solely of managing a contract for a dumpster to haul the waste away. This still exists today, at least in part, with today's managers keeping a closer eye on the way they are billed for waste (pull fee, price per lb/kilo, or price per cubic yard/meter) and using devices such as pressure sensors on compactor rams to automatically signal when the compactor needs to be pulled. However, environmental sensitivity, legislation, and the costs of waste disposal have also moved responsibility for solid waste management into such areas as waste reduction, reuse, and recycling. Operations are requiring vendors to take shipping materials (such as pallets) back and encouraging them to use reusable materials in other ways. Many operations have programs to recycle metals, glass, plastic, paper, and cardboard as well. And those with large amounts of landscaped area are composting yard waste along with their food waste.

Laundry

Laundry operations vary widely in size, from relatively small and simple washers and dryers to quite complex tunnel washing systems, many computer-controlled.

Commercial kitchens have a large number of facilities-related concerns. They typically have many pieces of equipment that must operate smoothly together. Kitchens also use a lot of energy and present various potential safety hazards.

Washers require an adequate supply of properly conditioned water; dryers require adequate supplies of makeup air and fuel. Washers and dryers add heat and moisture to the space in which they are operating, requiring proper ventilation and sometimes cooling to maintain a comfortable working environment. Important to the entire operation is that appropriate fire suppression systems be installed and that needed maintenance be performed, especially that which reduces the risk of fire. Of particular concern in the operation of dryers are the removal of lint from lint traps to reduce the fire risk and the cleaning of laundry chutes. Given the cost of water and water heating, operating washers as close to full capacity as possible can help in controlling costs.

Food Service

Kitchens are among the most costly areas in the facility to equip and maintain. While individual pieces of food service equipment are typically not complex, a well-equipped kitchen has dozens of different elements that must all work together smoothly while integrating with building-wide engineering systems.

Electrical power needs in the kitchen are substantial, as many pieces of equipment require 208-volt service and may draw several kilowatts. Most cooking equipment uses natural gas (or propane in some locations), or may require steam, which can be generated either in the kitchen or drawn from a building source.

Venting cooking equipment requires a dedicated exhaust hood and ductwork, along with provisions for replacing the air that is vented. Fire suppression systems are also needed in the exhaust hood and ductwork and these must be integrated with the building fire protection system. Because wastewater from the dishwasher and other equipment contains greasy residues, in-floor grease traps are necessary to help prevent hotel plumbing from clogging and corroding. Backflow protectors are needed on equipment such as dishwashers so that they do not allow contaminated water to be pumped into potable water lines. Finally, refrigeration equipment works most effectively when it is cooled by the building's chilled water loop or uses condensers mounted outside the normally hot kitchen.

Lighting in both kitchens and dining rooms should to have good to excellent color rendition. Food needs to have the same appearance when plated as when consumed. To impart a particular mood or experience in the dining areas, you may wish to have variable control over lighting by time of day as well as take advantage of natural light when available.

Proper air balance for HVAC operation is important in food service; without it, uncontrolled air will enter dining areas, ventilation equipment will not function properly, cooking odors will migrate into dining areas, and other problems can occur. An HVAC system separate from the kitchen's is needed for the dining area since desired temperatures differ in each area.

Food service equipment lasts longer, performs better, and may even save energy if it is cleaned daily and maintained on a regular basis. Strategies to recover waste heat from refrigeration, reduce water use by recirculating dishwasher rinse water, and minimize space conditioning costs by drawing in supply air through the exhaust hood all contribute to reduced operating expenses.

Offices

Lodging and restaurant operations require office space for planning, record-keeping, and day-to-day management functions. While many offices can be located in the back of the house, offices needed for sales and some executive functions must be accessible from guest areas and designed in a way that will enhance the facility's image.

Managers who oversee goods receiving and purchasing typically have offices that overlook or adjoin the loading dock to facilitate prompt processing of incoming supplies. Likewise, in a larger hotel, a security office may be located at the loading dock or other employee entrance. Offices for front office and reservations functions are typically located behind the front desk, while accounting and general administration offices are best located nearby to support the frequent interactions these functions may have. Most other offices (engineering, housekeeping, human resources, chefs, and food and beverage managers) can be located near their functional areas.

Office space in a hotel is rarely luxurious, except perhaps at the executive and sales offices. As long as they are provided with adequate space, lighting, ventilation, and storage, most offices can function effectively with simple office equipment, phone lines, and computers.

Where computers are heavily used, indirect fluorescent lighting is suggested for reducing eyestrain. Office equipment design for ergonomic computer operation is also needed with monitors at the correct height and alignment with the operator, keyboards adjustable, mouse at the same level as the keyboard, and a chair with adjustable height. In areas where computer applications are critical, the computer should be installed with uninterruptible power supplies, ideally supplied by the emergency power system.

Building Structure and Exterior

The building structure provides the needed horizontal stiffness and load carrying capability to allow the building to resist wind loads, the loads of the building itself and its contents, and the potential loads imposed by seismic actions. The structure can be made of wood or steel studs (for restaurants and low-rise lodging), masonry blocks, poured in place or prefabricated steel reinforced concrete, or structural steel (generally with a concrete deck providing floor/ceiling). Elements that are load bearing (that contribute to the stiffness and load-carrying capability of the structure) are unchangeable elements of the building—they generally cannot be removed or altered and therefore any building modifications must deal with these as "untouchable."

The building exterior (or cladding) can be constructed of a variety of materials. Masonry block may be used for one- to approximately three-story building exteriors (and for structure as well). Often a brick face, or veneer, covers the masonry block. Some properties use a wooden, aluminum, or vinyl siding similar to that used on homes. What is referred to as a "curtain wall" may also be used. This is an assembly of glazing (window) and other materials that rest on the building structure and provide the exterior of the building. Precast and cut masonry products are also used as cladding. Most cladding materials are backed by insulation and vapor barriers to inhibit the movement of moisture. Exterior finish insulation materials combine a tough exterior surface with board insulation, integrating the cladding itself and the insulation.

Glazing serves several purposes. Besides admitting light into the building, it also controls heat loss or gain and reduces the transmission of noise. Heat loss and gain are controlled by installing double- or triple-paned glazing and using tints or surface treatments to reduce solar transmission and heat loss. Multiple glazing helps reduce noise transmission.

Roof areas of hotels and restaurants are often flat, although some building designs do have sloped surfaces. Those with sloped surfaces may have enough of a slope to accommodate shingles of some kind. Shingles are commonly made of fiberglass or asphalt, although wood, tile, and stone can also be used. Sloped surfaces also accommodate metal roofing available in a wide assortment of colors. Insulation for these roofs is usually installed in the area above the ceiling, but can be applied to the sloped roof itself. Flat roofs use built-up materials consisting of an insulation material, various covering materials to provide a weather/waterproof surface, and sometimes a material (referred to as ballast) to provide weight for protection against wind and deterioration from sunlight. Membrane roofs are quite common, with seams welded so that the roof surface consists of a continuous piece of material. To reduce the heat load the roof can place on the building during summer months, application of white or reflective coatings is highly recommended.

The multitude of penetrations through hotel and restaurant roofs (to accommodate air handling equipment, exhaust ducts, refrigeration condensers, etc) underscores the importance of proper installation of the roofing system to prevent leaks. Moreover, the nature of discharges from kitchen equipment also creates the potential for contaminants on the roofs that can damage certain roofing materials. Another potential hazard to roofs is pedestrian traffic. To prevent damage during service and inspection, care must be taken when walking on roofs. Where feasible, roofs should be protected by walkways or other non-intrusive means.

A Comment on the Design of Building Systems

Building systems design involves several steps. Corporate design standards for the systems are a starting point, coupled with applicable local code requirements. Design standards involve the conditions under which the system is to operate and the expected performance of the system. For example, a water heating system for a building may be expected to take 40° F (5.5° C) water in the winter and heat this to 120° F (50° C) with the necessary capacity to supply heated water for the needs of 200 guestrooms. Next is selection of the systems from the options available. In the water-heating example, this could include tradeoffs between water heater capacity (gallons or liters per hour) and storage tank size. The designer also needs to consider the possible fuel sources for heating water (e.g., oil, natural gas, electricity) and the cost of heating water using these various sources.

Having determined the size of the equipment and the equipment and system options, there should be an evaluation of the life-cycle cost of various options (for example, water heater, tank, fuel source, maintenance, etc.). Careful consideration should be given to the potential equipment interconnections and interactions. Electric water heating will probably require the building's electrical supply to be increased, while using oil may mean that the oil storage tank needs to be larger and that a flue will be needed to remove combustion gas from the structure. These considerations could cause a revision to the life-cycle cost analysis. With these factors evaluated, it is now possible to proceed to final design. Of course, the system's design should also account for such issues as reliability, noise, maintainability, flexibility, and appearance.

The final designs of all systems are generally specified for the peak load of operation (for a water heater, this could be an assumption of two persons per room and full occupancy) plus some excess to protect the designer legally. The result can be rather large systems and high initial costs. While both may be warranted in some new construction, given the uncertainties of the design information (what if the hotel ends up with three persons in the room when it is full?), the systems purchased may never operate at anywhere near rated capacity. This becomes important when the property reaches the point of needing to replace equipment.

If a property has implemented any water or energy conservation actions over its lifetime and has oversized equipment, it is probably not a wise investment to replace existing equipment with equipment of the same size without at least taking a careful look at the actual needed capacity. This will not only save in the cost of the equipment replacement but also provide further efficiencies as the equipment operates in more of a full-load (i.e., peak-efficiency) mode.

Guiding the design and equipment selection process are the applicable building and other codes and standards. Codes may not allow certain types of systems or equipment to be used (for example, refrigeration systems using ammonia in commercial buildings) and the standards of parent (hotel and restaurant) companies may require certain levels of reliability or commonality in types of design.

Conclusion

Since a building—its equipment, systems, and finishes—defines not only the maintenance needs but also the level of guest and employee comfort and services, it is important to have a working knowledge of the various building components, the cost, comfort, and service options, and the managerial issues associated with facilities operations. In addition, because building owners make substantial investments in the buildings, they value managers who are able to protect and enhance this investment through proper management and sound decision-making. The intent of this chapter is to help hospitality managers better understand their facilities and help these managers better communicate with the professionals they hire to manage the facilities side of the business, whether they be on-site staff, consultants, or contractors.

Endnotes

1. Further information about this topic can be found in "Hotels, Motels, and Dormitories," *ASHRAE Applications Handbook,* American Society of Heating, Ventilating, and Air-Conditioning Engineers, Chapter 5; and Valentine A. Lehr, "Current Trends in Hotel HVAC Design," *Heating/Piping/Airconditioning Engineering,* February 1995, pp. 38–42, 45, 46, 78.

2. More information on mold and mildew problems and how to solve them is found in *Preventing Moisture and Mildew Problems in Hospitality Industry Buildings: Problem Avoidance Guidelines,* published by the American Hotel & Lodging Association.

3. Detailed information on management of waste in lodging establishments is found in "Water Resources for Lodging Operations" published by the Educational Institute of AH&LA.

4. Non-U.S. readers of this text recognize that voltages supplied in their homelands are probably higher than 208 or 240 and that the frequency of the electrical supply is 50 hertz (cycles per second). American travelers frequently outfit their appliances (especially hair dryers) with adapter plugs and then find that they burn out when used in circuits overseas.

5. The causes of failure and malfunction of rooftop units and potential ways to reduce them are discussed in "Smart Maintenance for Rooftop Units" by Breuker, Rossi, and Braun, *ASHRAE Journal,* November 2000, pp. 41–47.

🔑 Key Terms

four-pipe system—A fan-coil unit for temperature conditioning that incorporates two supply lines and two return lines. This arrangement permits simultaneous heating and cooling of different rooms.

HVAC system—The heating ventilating, and air conditioning system. Containing various individual units, this system provides temperature control and fresh conditioned air to an area.

public space—Common areas in a hotel available to all guests, such as meeting rooms, ballrooms, retail spaces, food and beverage outlets, recreation facilities, parking, etc.

solid waste—Materials such as metals, glass, plastic, paper, cardboard, yard waste, and kitchen scraps that require handling and disposal.

split system—A type of through-the-wall conditioning system in which the compressor and condenser of the air conditioning unit (the noise-producing elements) are located remotely from the evaporator (the cooling unit).

submeters—Devices that permit the monitoring of utility consumption by specific areas for purposes of measuring effectiveness of conservation efforts.

through-the-wall conditioning units—Electrical powered air conditioning units generally positioned under guestroom windows and protruding through the wall of the building.

two-pipe system—A fan-coil temperature conditioning unit that incorporates one supply line and one return line. This system can operate in either a heating mode or cooling mode, but all units must operate in the same mode; heating of one room and cooling of another at the same time is not possible.

utility grouping—An arrangement in which potable water supply, wastewater removal, electrical, centralized HVAC, and other systems are generally grouped vertically in hotels, requiring that, for repair of one of the components in one guestroom, service to all guestrooms in the hotel sharing that vertical grouping would have to be shut down.

variable air volume system—A temperature control system that adjusts the amount of air to the space depending on the amount of heating or cooling needed, but supplying a minimum amount at all times.

vertical transportation—Any device that provides travel up to and down from various floors of the hotel, such as elevators and escalators.

wastewater—Any water discharged by the hotel that is not suitable for drinking.

❓ Review Questions

1. What means do hotels use to provide fresh air in guestrooms? Chilled air? Heated air?

2. What is a "split" temperature control system?

3. What is the primary limitation in a two-pipe fan-coil system?

4. What are the principal problems inherent in supplying fresh air to guestrooms via airflow under the room door?

5. What benefits does a guestroom occupancy control thermostat provide?

6. What are some of the unique challenges facing the property maintenance manager at resort properties offering extensive recreational facilities?

7. What are the two principal sources of electrical power for hotels? What are the benefits and drawbacks of each?

8. Why are kitchens among the most costly areas in a hotel?

9. What is glazing? What are its advantages?

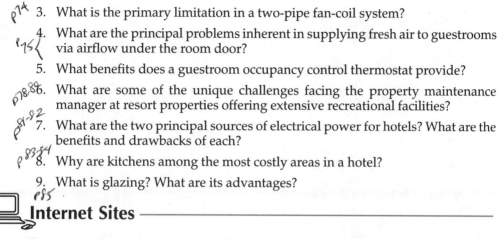

Internet Sites

For more information, visit the following Internet sites. Remember that Internet addresses can change without notice. If the site is no longer there, you can use a search engine to look for additional sites.

American Hotel & Lodging
Association
www.ahla.com

American Society of Heating,
Refrigerating and Air-Conditioning
Engineers
www.ashrae.com

Burnham Boilers
www.burnham.com

The Trane Company
www.trane.com

Chapter 4 Outline

Motivations for Environmental Concern
    Economic Considerations
    Regulatory Issues
    Market Factors
    The Social Responsibility Dimension
Waste Minimization and Management
Energy Conservation and Management
Management of Fresh Water Resources
Wastewater Management
Hazardous Substances
Transport
Land-Use Planning and Management
Involving Staff, Customers, and
    Communities
Design for Sustainability
    Partnerships for Sustainable
        Development
Conclusion

Competencies

1. Describe sustainability and its role in the overall business strategy of a hospitality operation. (pp. 91–92)

2. Explain the impetus of environmental issues in the context of global commerce and the economic, regulatory, market, and social responsibility forces at play in the world business arena. (pp. 92–95)

3. State some of the principal measures facilities managers can take to minimize and manage waste. (pp. 95–100)

4. Describe the liabilities of poor energy management in terms of its effect on both the hotel's bottom line and the local/world community. (pp. 100–105)

5. Outline the issues involved with proper water and wastewater management. (pp. 105–107)

6. Describe the dangers inherent in the commonly recognized hazardous substances and ways to safeguard against them. (pp. 107–109)

7. Explain the negative aspects of operating a diverse fleet of vehicles on and to and from a property and what measures the facilities engineer can take to reduce or eliminate them. (pp. 109–110)

8. Explain the economic and social nuances of appropriate land-use planning and management. (pp. 110–112)

9. Describe the benefits of involving staff, customers, communities, and partnerships in a hospitality company's environmental and sustainabilty concerns. (pp. 112–117)

4

Environmental and Sustainability Management

Hotel environmental programs come in many shades of green, but most sprout the same way. Someone gets an idea and plants it with the "why don't we ...?" ... At Canadian Pacific Hotels, the "why don't we ...?" came from Ann Layton, vice president of Pubic Affairs and Communications for Fairmont Hotels & Resorts. "I think I was in the right place at the right time," Layton says. "I care about the environment in my private life. I recycle at home. Why shouldn't a hotel? We have the same issues. Why not try to take the things people do at home and do them here?" ...

She hired a professional environmental consultant and asked for suggestions from staff—"people who have worked here for 20 years know what goes on." Layton distilled those recommendations into 16 ambitious goals. CP would reduce waste sent to landfill by 50 percent, launch an extensive recycling program (including blue boxes for collecting recyclables in guestrooms), redesign purchasing policies to ensure waste reduction at source, and use nature-friendly hotel supplies. "I knew from the get-go the program would be in all hotels, and it worked better this way," Layton says. "Now it seems basic, but it wasn't at the time." ...

[Layton] believes CP Hotels did two things right. First was polling employees before the program started, and second was to develop a chain-wide incentive program as part of Phase Two. The green Incentive Program sets up teams at each property to create and achieve eco-initiatives across the board. Environmental progress and new programs then earn "CP Tree" stickers for the employees of that property.... At year's end, teams with the most 'trees' win trips to places like Jamaica or Acapulco. "Employees want to earn these trees," says Layton. "No one wants to be last, and so many hotels have submitted incredible ideas we have now incorporated into the program."[1]

CONCERN CONTINUES TO GROW about the impact of hospitality operations on the natural environment. While this impact may not be as significant as that of other industries, the size and growth of the hospitality industry, especially at major tourism destinations, means its overall impact on the environment can be substantial. Recognizing a need for attention to the environment, the American Hotel & Lodging Association (AH&LA) in the early 1970s formed a standing Committee for a

Quality Environment. The committee's charter is to study the potential effects of industry operations on their surroundings and devise methods and procedures to address them. Within AH&LA today, there is an Engineering and Environment Committee addressing these issues. In addition, the Educational Institute of AH&LA has produced a video for hotel owners and managers that focuses on the unique environmental issues in hospitality (see the sidebar on the next page).

During the 1990s, the Travel Industry Association of America, The White House Conference on Travel and Tourism, and the United Nations added travel and tourism environmental concerns to their agendas. A large number of corporations from all sectors of hospitality have also launched initiatives to evaluate and reduce the environmental impacts of their operations.[2]

Internationally, leadership at both the association and corporate levels has emerged to evaluate and reduce environmental impacts. The International Hotel and Restaurant Association, World Travel and Tourism Council, and International Hotels Environment Initiative have introduced a host of initiatives to heighten awareness in both identifying and reducing environmental impacts. Local and regional travel and tourism associations have also been active, providing training materials, technical assistance, and awards programs for best practices. Inter-Continental, Scandic, and Canadian Pacific Hotels were also early innovators in this effort.

Environmental issues often are limited to only the natural environment and tend to focus on issues of global climate change (especially CO_2 emissions and CFCs), pollution (air, water, noise, visual, and other forms), habitat/ecosystem degradation, and resource consumption (including issues of solid waste). Closely related but broader in context is **sustainability.** Sustainability embraces not only typical environmental concerns but also dimensions such as the three E's—economics, environment, and equity.

The hospitality industry has addressed environmental sustainability concerns in a variety of ways. Economic sustainability is a major concern and a major challenge of all hospitality businesses. Correcting environmental problems can prevent hospitality firms from "killing the golden goose,"[3] a concern of operators whose appeal is the natural environment. Equity aspects are potentially more challenging. The distribution of the income and profits from hospitality operations, the impacts of these operations on local communities and cultures, and the potential for the operations to not only minimize damage but also make positive contributions to the environment are just a few of many equity issues.

Sustainability is a major theme pervading the global (business) community. Its importance to the success of the hospitality industry is indisputable. More detailed discussions of this topic are available in references in the end notes of this chapter.

Motivations for Environmental Concern

Corporations and individual operations have various motivations for environmental concerns and actions. Among these motivations are economic considerations, regulatory issues, market factors, and social responsibility.

Shaping Change and Changing Minds

This video from the Educational Institute of AH&LA highlights the environmental efforts of four very different hospitality operations in the United States. The operations range from small to large, center city to resort, and new to old. Featured is a wide range of activities, not only within the property, but also reaching out into the local community.

Space Shuttle Inn—Florida

In this segment, the owner of the property describes the contributions made to the bottom line by environmental actions, as well as how actions have improved the property's surroundings and guest perceptions. The use of energy-efficient lighting and water conservation measures reduced operating costs and increased profits. The restoration of adjacent wetlands creates a natural environment on the property doorstep that enhances the guest's experience.

Westin Hotel—Oregon

On the West Coast, an urban property identifies and addresses energy conservation opportunities. Engineering staff devise creative ways to recover waste heat and in other ways reduce the energy usage and costs for the property. The environmental contributions of the energy reduction are explained and summarized for the property and the Westin Hotel company as a whole.

Walt Disney World—Florida

Featured in this segment are the Wilderness Lodge and the Walt Disney World (WDW) solid waste management efforts, as well as initiatives that contribute to the community. Wilderness Lodge illustrates a property designed with a view toward the environment. The solid waste management efforts include large-scale recycling and compost efforts for the entire WDW complex. Also highlighted are efforts at integrated pest management for the landscaping and wastewater treatment. The sharing of excess food products with the local community is a unique element of the program at WDW.

Saunders Hotels—Massachusetts

The Saunders Hotels segment features the multi-faceted and award-winning efforts of this company to address environmentality at older urban properties. Included are a number of innovative staff initiatives, including heat and water recovery for laundry operations and linen recycling and reuse. The segment also describes this company's efforts to incorporate environmental standards into purchasing decisions.

Economic Considerations

The economic dimensions of environmental actions are often both compelling and significant. Many environmental initiatives have significant economic benefits: converting incandescent lamps to compact fluorescent lamps, for example, results in a reduction of energy use and, by extension, reductions in emissions from power plants that now produce less electricity. Paybacks from such a conversion can come within a few months (reduced maintenance costs due to fewer replacements resulting from longer lamp life). Another example is solid waste management. The cost of waste disposal can be reduced by implementing a recycling program. Recycling is both environmentally and economically beneficial. Keeping a location clean makes good economic sense: hospitality businesses in many locations clearly rely on the beauty and visual appeal of the natural environment as a key feature in attracting customers (and their money).

Regulatory Issues

Legislation requiring recycling, restrictions on water use due to shortages, emissions and discharge regulations, and other environmental limitations mean that concern for environmental issues is not only good business, it is the law. Environmental impact must be addressed from the feasibility stage of new product development through operations and into renovations—all within the context of regulations. Failure to do so can jeopardize new developments and result in fines and penalties.

Market Factors

The role of market factors in motivating concern about environmental issues has several dimensions. First, there are market segments that put a high value on "environmentality" and seek this in their purchases. The **ecotourism** market that emerged in the 1990s is certainly a prime example of this. Second, there are dimensions of environmental concern such as air and water quality and food safety that are pertinent to global tour operators. Tour operators have begun to require that businesses with which they deal comply with standards promulgated by the tour industry. Operators who find that economics (cost savings) and regulations provide little incentive to be concerned about the environment may become motivated when major tour operators refuse to do business with them. Third, the increasing requirements by the global business community for supplier/vendor environmental certification through the **ISO 14000 standards** series (Environmental Management Systems) means customers will be looking for ISO certification and hospitality companies will be looking for this certification from their vendors.[4] It's quite possible that in the near future, certification of (high) environmental performance will be a requirement of doing business, just as adequate credit and insurance coverage is today.

Additional market factors continue to emerge. For example, in 2001, the Coalition for Environmentally Responsible Economies (**CERES**) developed its Green Hotel Initiative. What CERES is trying to do with this initiative is to get its corporate members to include environmental considerations when making lodging purchasing decisions. At this writing, it is too early to tell what effect the Green Hotel Initiative will have. But with Ford Motor Company, General Motors, and Bank of America as endorsing CERES members, the potential purchasing clout is formidable.

During the latter part of the twentieth century, a clearly global economy emerged. Nations recognized they were affected by the political, social, and economic issues not only within their borders but by those of other countries as well.

Corporations came to understand this well. Environmental issues also were present at national and global levels. Recognition of global citizenship came with recognition of global impact. The individual actions of hospitality businesses were recognized as potentially significant to the environment, particularly given the large and growing size of the industry. And the actions of non-hospitality businesses had a significant potential for affecting the business of hospitality firms: consider the impact on tourism to Indonesia in the late 1990s when widespread fires created clouds of smoke that drove visitor numbers down and air travel problems up. A broader social responsibility of firms was one byproduct of globalization.

The Social Responsibility Dimension

Many firms both within and outside the hospitality industry recognize the interaction of environmental policy with corporate social responsibility. Six Continents Hotels incorporates its environmental activities in its corporate social responsibility actions on its web site.[5] Marriott International recognizes its responsibility to protect the environment for its associates, guests, and communities, stating its policy in the opening of its environmental operations manual.[6] Fairmont Hotels & Resorts, which now includes former Canadian Pacific properties, has embraced the excellent environmental program of Canadian Pacific.[7] Accor is yet another hospitality firm taking a highly proactive approach to environmental issues.[8] The actions of these companies exemplify the attention given within the lodging industry to the environment and social responsibility.

In the food service sector, too, companies have become environmentally conscious. Starbucks has recognized and responded to issues of environmental and social concern.[9] Their Green Bean Awards recognize outstanding environmental efforts by their units, and their corporate social responsibility is evidenced by their involvement with CARE and international development activities. McDonald's has implemented an extensive effort, including waste management innovations as a result of its partnership with the Environmental Defense Fund and rainforest preservation efforts through its partnership with Conservation International. McDonald's social responsibility has been clearly visible through its Ronald McDonald House support as well.[10]

The items considered to be part of an environmental program can and will vary depending on the company, location, and a host of other issues. For guidance regarding the content of environmental programs, look to efforts such as the International Hotels Environment Initiative and Agenda 21 for the Global Hospitality Industry. Exhibit 1 contains summary information about Agenda 21 for the travel and tourism industry, on which the following discussion is based.

Waste Minimization and Management

Waste minimization and management involves reduction, reuse, recycling, and waste transformation, as well as cost structure and management of waste haulage contracts. These efforts combine to minimize the amount of waste disposed and

Exhibit 1   Agenda 21 for the Travel and Tourism Industry

Priority area 1: waste minimization
Objective: to minimize resource inputs, maximize product quality, and minimize waste outputs.

Priority area 2: energy conservation and management
Objective: to reduce energy use and reduce potentially damaging atmospheric emissions.

Priority area 3: management of fresh water resources
Objective: to protect the quality of water resources and to use existing resources efficiently and equitably.

Priority area 4: wastewater management
Objective: to minimize wastewater outputs in order to protect the aquatic environment, to safeguard flora and fauna, and to conserve and protect the quality of fresh water resources.

Priority area 5: hazardous substances
Objective: to replace products containing potentially hazardous substances with more environmentally benign products.

Priority area 6: transport
Objective: to reduce or control harmful emissions into the atmosphere and other environmental effects of transport.

Priority area 7: land–use planning and management
Objective: to deal with the multiple demands on land in an equitable manner, ensuring that development is not visually intrusive and contributes to conserving environment and culture while generating income.

Priority area 8: involving staff, customers, and communities in environmental issues
Objectives: to protect and incorporate the interests of communities in developments and to ensure that the environmental lessons learned by staff, customers, and communities are put into practice at home.

Priority area 9: design for sustainability
Objective: to ensure that new technologies and products are designed to be less polluting, more efficient, socially and culturally appropriate, and available worldwide.

Priority area 10: partnerships for sustainable development
Objective: to form partnerships to bring about long–term sustainability.

Source: Agenda 21 for the Travel & Tourism Industry—Towards Environmentally Sustainable Development. WTTC, WTO, The Earth Council. 1997.

the cost of its disposal, and help ensure that final disposal is done in an approved and environmentally suitable manner.

The waste stream obviously varies with the type of services provided and the scope of the facilities. Economy lodging operations without food service, having a small and minimally landscaped site, and lacking conference facilities will have a relatively small amount of waste per room. Full service resort/conference facilities with extensive food service, large areas of highly landscaped grounds, and catering to customers making purchases of a variety of types during their more extended stays can produce more waste per room. Quick-service restaurants have a waste stream consisting largely of disposable final product packaging (cups, plates, napkins, and similar materials) with food production waste minimized by pre-processing activities. Full-service restaurants dispose of smaller amounts of final product packaging but have more food production waste.

The potential economic benefits of waste minimization and management are significant. Waste haulage contracts can be a large part of the Property Operations and Maintenance budget of hotels, with costs in excess of $100 per room per year not uncommon. Supervision and inspection of dumpster contents can also reduce unnecessary losses, such as tableware or other materials that should not have been discarded. Management of waste haulage contracts can minimize the cost of disposal by ensuring that:

- Only full waste containers are removed (haulage contracts often pay for the "pull" of the dumpster as well as for the weight of the contents).

- Weight tickets are submitted with bills to verify waste quantities (where costs are based on weight rather than volume).

- Competitive bidding determines the contractor.

Minimizing waste generation begins with the purchasing function. Purchasing products in bulk, using products manufactured from recycled materials, controlling the usage of products to avoid waste, and working with suppliers to minimize product packaging are all proven ways to minimize waste generation. And don't forget that selecting products with greater durability (and hence a longer lifetime) and employing proper maintenance and housekeeping procedures reduce product deterioration and extends their functional life. An electronic locking system, for example, might be powered by six AA batteries per lock or a singe nine-volt battery, depending on the system selected. The AA batteries could last for two years on average, while the nine-volt battery lasts for four years. Every four years you would have to replace 1200 AA batteries for every 100 locks, at a cost of $600. With the nine-volt system, for every 100 locks you would replace 300 batteries every four years at a cost of $90, a significant reduction in cost and battery disposal.

Reuse as a means of waste reduction has been practiced in the hospitality industry for many years; beverage containers such as those holding syrup concentrate and beer kegs are typical. In some parts of the world, soda and beer are still sold in refillable bottles. And operators have long returned shipping trays and pallets to suppliers for reuse. Reuse does not have to happen on the property itself— used linens can be donated to shelters or other charitable organizations for reuse. Furniture and equipment from renovations is often sold to liquidators or in other ways reused and given an extended lifetime.

Recycling as a means of conservation can be turned into a revenue stream. The price paid for recycled materials varies geographically and over time. Geographic variations are due to proximity to potential processors and the users of recycled

Exhibit 2   Recycling Cost and Savings, Hyatt Regency Chicago

Savings	1997	1998
Hauling cost saving	$200,787	$176,720
Recovered items, equipment	28,459	33,500
Revenue	8,842	6,000
Total Savings	**$238,088**	**$216,220**
Costs		
Labor costs	$73,508	$74,000
Supervisor costs	65,000	55,400
Supplies	8,250	9,740
Total Costs	**$146,758**	**$139,140**
Net Savings	**$91,330**	**$77,080**

Source: Hyatt Regency Chicago annual recycling reports as reported in C. A. Enz and J.A. Siguaw, "Best Hotel Environmental Practices," *Cornell Hotel and Restaurant Administration Quarterly*, October 1999.

materials as well as the degree of development of recycling in the area. Variations over time occur due to market forces that are not only related to the supply of materials but also the demand for recycled products. The real economic value to a property of a recycling program is usually in the savings in waste haulage rather than in the money received for the recycled products. This is illustrated in Exhibit 2.

A recycling effort will generally focus on the following materials:

- Glass

- Metals

- Plastics

- Paper

- Cardboard

- Yard waste

Purchasing records are a rich source for identifying the potential volumes of recyclable materials. Knowing the quantity of various products purchased and the packaging used allows for a quick estimate of the potential volume to be recycled.

With glass recycling, it may be necessary for you to separate the containers by color to receive the best prices. To reduce the volume of the glass, a glass crusher may be a worthwhile investment (depending on the volume of glass waste you generate). A clean product without lids also receives better prices. Some glass recycling occurs when reusable bottles are used for beverages. A significant incentive to recycle glass also comes when beverage bottles can be returned for a deposit refund.

Metals recycled in the hospitality industry are usually from beverage containers (generally aluminum) and food cans (containing steel and tin). Aluminum has

Exhibit 3   Symbols Identifying Various Common Plastics

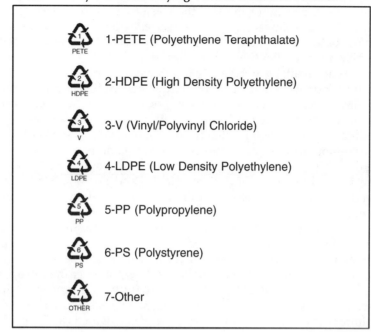

1-PETE (Polyethylene Teraphthalate)

2-HDPE (High Density Polyethylene)

3-V (Vinyl/Polyvinyl Chloride)

4-LDPE (Low Density Polyethylene)

5-PP (Polypropylene)

6-PS (Polystyrene)

7-Other

the higher value, making separation important. In certain areas, beverage containers have a deposit, providing a significant incentive for their return. Food cans need to be clean and in some instances without their paper labels. Can crushing can help to reduce volume and the space required for storage.

Plastic recycling can be more challenging—particularly in developing countries—since not all locations have the capability. As with other materials for recycling, cleanliness of the product and separation of various types of plastic are key to receiving a good market price for the plastics. Exhibit 3 contains information about common symbols used to identify different plastics and the products commonly using these plastics.

Paper recycling is an option available to many operations. Separation of various types of paper—newsprint, office copy paper, and other paper—is sometimes appropriate if large enough amounts exist, since the prices for mixed paper are significantly lower than those of separated papers. Operations have also tried to add paper to composting operations; few have been successful.

Cardboard has long been recycled. There is generally a stable market for this material and, because of its characteristics, it lends itself to on-site collection, compression, and baling. If large quantities of cardboard are collected, a baler may be warranted. Besides the day-to-day accumulation of scrap cardboard from receiving department activities, a potentially large amount can also be generated when renovations or replacements are undertaken. Working with vendors at these times can help ensure that cardboard is recycled.

Yard waste and seaweed from beach cleanups is non-existent at some operations, but can be 40 percent or more of the waste stream for others. If space and time permit, on-site composting of these wastes, along with non-meat kitchen waste, can not only reduce the cost of waste disposal but also provide a valuable soil and fertilizer source. For those operations that elect not to compost this waste on-site, haulers are available to take it to locations for composting.[11]

Waste transformation is an opportunity that may be worth considering under certain circumstances. Incineration of wastes was once common and is still used today in some locations. This can be at the unit level or in a large waste-to-energy facility. Unit-level incineration is often the option of choice where landfill disposal is not feasible—for example, at locations in or near national parks where animals would be drawn to landfills. If heat recovery is combined with incineration, the process is highly efficient and, if recyclables and potentially toxic materials are removed from the waste before burning, viewed as minimally harmful to the environment.

Pulping is another method of transforming waste, in which a pulping machine mixes food waste with water, grinds it up (much like a garbage disposal), presses and as a result extracts water from the tank in which the waste is ground. It then expels the pulp into a holding bin. Waste does not enter the sewage system. The pulper recycles the water it used during the grinding process. Pulpers can handle typical food service waste such as plastic utensils and containers, paper napkins, aluminum foil, straws, milk cartons, and corrugated cardboard. Garbage volume is reduced by 75 to 80 percent, which dramatically lowers waste disposal costs. It is also possible to transform food service wastes with a pulper and make them easier to handle for eventual composting.

Exhibit 4 provides a summary of the information discussed in this chapter on solid waste disposal and other suggested actions. Selecting and implementing waste minimization practices appropriate to your property will help to address economic and environmental issues.

Energy Conservation and Management

Energy conservation and management has long been a concern to the industry, especially to facilities managers. Energy (sometimes referred to as utilities) typically represents four to six percent of hotel revenues. In the U.S. lodging industry, this translates into an annual expenditure for energy of more than $3.7 billion.[12]

Energy includes usage of electricity, fossil fuels, water and sewer (according to the *Uniform System of Accounts for the Lodging Industry*), certain vehicle fuel, and in some instances, purchased steam, hot water, and chilled water. A byproduct of energy usage is carbon monoxide and the emission of other products of combustion such as nitrous and sulphur oxides and particulate matter. Efforts directed at energy conservation and management attempt to reduce energy usage with resultant cost savings and reduction in environmental pollutants.

Good facilities management practices involve actions that will control energy usage. Examples of the kinds of management actions that help control energy usage are:

Exhibit 4   Agenda 21 Waste Minimization

Priority area 1: waste minimization

- Reduce the waste burden by selecting products that have minimal waste implications.

- Select suppliers who agree to minimize the waste implications of their products or insist that manufacturers minimize or reuse non–essential packaging.

- Reuse products wherever possible.

- Recycle where reduction and reuse is not possible or where more environmentally sound waste disposal routes (e.g., biomass) are not appropriate.

- Dispose of unavoidable wastes responsibly.

- Encourage staff to employ the principles of waste minimization at home.

- Work with governments and other authorities to establish labeling schemes that provide realistic environmental information about products and disposal.

- Open recycling or disposal facilities to employees and local communities to improve overall destination quality.

- Records of energy usage and energy costs
- Proper maintenance of equipment
- Proper operating methods and records

To monitor the usage of energy, it is necessary to keep adequate records of energy used and the amounts paid for the energy. Unfortunately, the process used by some operations does not provide the facilities manager with the needed information. If bills for utility services are not provided to the facilities manager for review, not only does the operation lose a needed check on charges being incurred, but the facilities manager also is denied the opportunity to maintain a record of the quantity and cost of the energy. On the other hand, some operations have developed sophisticated methods to know how much energy is being used at a facility. In the 1990s, Inter-Continental Hotels developed an extensive database of energy consumption information and used this to benchmark its hotels' performance.

Using computerized controls at the building, the facilities manager is able to not only obtain records of energy usage over time but also monitor instantaneous usage. Some multi-unit operators have contracted with providers who monitor their buildings and provide them with utility usage reports, either in paper or on-line.

Another helpful option is to actually submeter energy usage (including water) within the building. This allows for usage to be accurately matched to specific operations (the laundry, for example) and, if the property wishes, charged to those operations. This can help offset the problem of the way information is recorded in the hotel industry. Costs and consumption are often viewed on a per-room basis. This conveys the impression that the actual usage of energy occurs in

Exhibit 5   Total Cost Breakdown—Energy and Water Audit

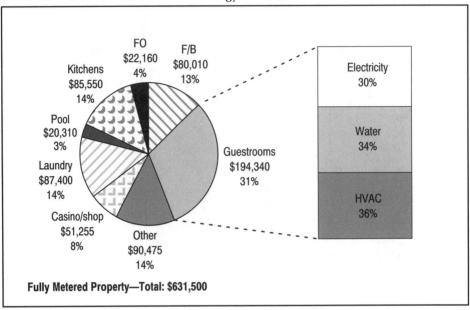

Fully Metered Property—Total: $631,500

the guestroom. For many operations, this is not the case. Energy is used by a host of systems and energy management needs to focus on those systems and the areas they serve. **Submetering** is relatively inexpensive during new construction. As operations conduct more outsourcing of operations such as food and beverage, they may find submetering to be more common. Exhibit 5 illustrates the information that can be obtained from submetering.

Proper maintenance of equipment is key to achieving its rated performance. Cleaning can affect efficiency, as is illustrated by the decreased efficiency of boilers and chillers when they are not cleaned regularly and properly. And failure to provide proper water treatment for boilers and chillers can increase the rate at which fouling of this equipment occurs. Lubrication and alignment of equipment reduces friction and resulting losses. Making certain that valves are not sticking open will ensure that equipment does not simultaneously try to heat and cool or that water is discharged only when it should be, rather than all the time.

Proper operation of equipment and systems by facilities department staff and other employees is also an important component of energy management. Facilities staff need to know—and use on a daily basis—the factors that affect equipment performance and operations. This involves issues such as what equipment to operate during periods of low usage or demand to maximize efficiency. It also involves controlling the operation of equipment so that unnecessary operation does not occur—for example, there is no need to provide full air conditioning to unoccupied meeting rooms. Other staff need to understand the impact of their actions on energy usage and costs. Using hot water to melt ice from buffets, not fully loading washing machines, failing to turn off lights in unoccupied meeting rooms, and a host of similar practices can, in total, waste a significant amount of energy.

Options for energy conservation include:

- Improving efficiency
- Reducing operating hours
- Reducing the load being supplied
- Recovering and reusing waste energy
- Using the least costly energy source

The amount of energy used by any equipment is significantly influenced by the efficiency of the equipment. A vivid (and visual) example is lighting. An incandescent lamp has a typical efficiency of 20 lumens per watt. A fluorescent lamp may have an efficiency of 60 lumens per watt. This means three times the energy is required to produce the same amount of light from an incandescent versus a fluorescent lamp. Knowing the way in which efficiency is expressed for various pieces of equipment, the cost of energy, and the amount of energy used by the equipment, you can conduct an economic analysis to assess the feasibility of purchasing more efficient equipment. Or a manager may simply decide that the combination of economics and environmental benefits from more efficient equipment are enough of a justification.

Another way to reduce energy usage is reducing operating hours, that is, turn the equipment off. Operating storage area lighting 24 hours a day, leaving computers/copies/printers running at all times, operating parking lot lighting on time clocks rather than on photocells, and a host of other all-too-common practices result in excessive and unnecessary energy usage.

Reducing energy loads is an often-overlooked option. Window films can reduce solar heat gain. Low volume showerheads and toilets reduce the amount of water required. Providing additional roof insulation cuts down on heating and cooling loads. The opportunities are extensive.

Hospitality operations have a number of opportunities to recover and reuse waste energy. One option for all commercial buildings is recovery of heat or cold from exhaust air. Pre-heating or cooling the building's incoming air via the exhaust air is a way to recover and reuse waste energy. The laundry provides further opportunities for recovery of heat, from both exhaust air and from discharged water. For the resourceful, the opportunities are almost limitless. Imagine using water to cool refrigeration equipment, then using this water in the laundry operation. Not only is water recovered that might have been discharged, but so is heat. And for some operations, the path to recovery and reuse of waste energy may mean producing power on-site by either an engine-driven generator or, not so far in the future, a fuel cell. Creative facilities professionals and managers who want to encourage creativity have the opportunity to accomplish some amazing things.

Using the least costly fuel source can require careful recordkeeping and research. Consulting historic consumption records and information about prices provides the information necessary to consider fuel cost options. This can involve such decisions as the electric utility tariff under which electricity is purchased, the

Exhibit 6   Agenda 21 Energy Conservation and Management

Priority area 2: energy conservation and management

- Implement programs to reduce energy wastage; simple measures such as switching off equipment when not in use can bring substantial financial and environmental benefits as the first step in an energy management program.
- Research alternative, environmentally benign methods of energy generation, such as solar, wind, or biomass power.
- Develop, use, and disseminate energy-saving technology.
- Integrate energy efficiency considerations into all new developments.
- Train staff about the environmental benefits of initiatives to save energy.
- For trans-national corporations, employ energy-efficient technologies in all facilities in developed and developing countries.

electricity supplier, and consideration of direct purchase of natural gas. It could also involve evaluation of a dual-fueled boiler (operators installing such a system become eligible for what are known as interruptible gas rates), and the evaluation of the cost-effectiveness of purchasing steam from a local distribution system rather than running a boiler at the property. Researching the available options can be daunting, but the results can be highly rewarding. Some firms have found it worthwhile to contract with companies to audit utility bills for errors or for the correct tariff. The fact that such companies provide this service for a portion of the savings they find suggests this may be an area of substantial opportunity.

A number of resources are available to assist facilities managers and owners in reducing and managing energy usage. Many U.S. lodging corporations are members of the U.S. Environmental Protection Agency's Energy Star Buildings programs.[13] These programs provide a wealth of information about energy management and facilities management in general. Groups such as the Association of Energy Engineers, American Society of Heating Refrigerating and Air-Conditioning Engineers, and various facilities organizations such as IFMA (the International Facilities Management Association) and BOMA (the Building Owners and Managers Association) are also valuable resources.[14] Finally, trade publications commonly read by facilities professionals, such as *Buildings and Building Operating Management* and specialty publications such as *Energy Decisions* and *Energy User News*, can help you stay abreast of the latest technology, challenges, and opportunities in the energy domain.[15]

Exhibit 6 lists environmentally benign methods of energy generation such as solar, wind, or biomass along with the use of other energy-saving and energy-efficient technologies. U.S. hospitality operators have not adopted environmentally benign methods of energy generation in large numbers. In urban areas, there are some real challenges to doing this. For others, the economics of these options have either not been favorable or have not been objectively investigated. For many operations, conservation and waste energy recovery provide attractive options; as the costs and reliability of these technologies improve, more hospitality firms may well adopt them. Another option would be to contract only with electricity suppliers that produce their power from "green" sources. Placing the production of the energy in the hands of those with specific skills and expertise in environmentally benign methods and purchasing from them is a worthy consideration for the environmentally concerned operator.

Management of Fresh Water Resources

Because global supplies of fresh water are limited—they represent less than one percent of the total water on the earth—hospitality firms need to be good stewards of this valuable resource by using as little as possible and helping to protect the quality of what remains. As with other environmental initiatives, a reduction of fresh water use brings potential cost savings. With hotels using 100 to 200 gallons (380 to 760 liters) of water per room per day (36,500 to 73,000 gallons [138,000 to 276,000 liters] per room per year) and fresh water costing $2.00 to $4.00 per 1000 gallons ($0.50 to $1.00 per 1000 liters) (and sometimes that much again for wastewater disposal), efforts to reduce water usage may potentially affect the bottom line significantly and positively.

Hospitality operations may find themselves subject to regulations limiting water usage because of supply shortages caused by dry weather, high consumption, or water system breakdowns. Regulations can also prohibit certain uses of water or the time of its use; for example, lawn watering may be prohibited or limited to the evening hours. Regulations may also set maximum usage levels, with fines imposed for exceeding them.

Resort operations are the most likely to pay particular attention to social responsibility as it relates to fresh water. Resorts proposing to build in any area need to be conscious that their large demands for fresh water will affect water supplies in the local community. These demands may also create needs for costly increases in water infrastructure that could raise the price of water for local people. And during their construction and in ongoing operations, the resort needs to pay attention to sustaining the quality of fresh water supplies by not allowing site runoff or hazardous wastes to be discharged into water supplies.

Though not all-inclusive, Exhibit 7 contains a list of some of the possible considerations—and opportunities—that exist for effective management of fresh water resources. Rainwater capture is widely used in locations with limited water supplies. Directing refrigeration condenser cooling water through laundry cycles is another option. Staff creativity at the unit level plays a huge role in identifying other opportunities.

Wastewater Management

Most of the fresh water used by hospitality operations ends up leaving the operation as **wastewater,** the notable exceptions being water used in cooling towers and for landscape irrigation. Operators pay for wastewater disposal as a component of their "water" bill, as a separate charge, or in the form of their own wastewater treatment plant (where no wastewater treatment facility exists). Costs can range from $75 to $200 per room per year for wastewater treatment.

Exhibit 7   Agenda 21 Fresh Water Management Actions

Priority area 3: management of fresh water resources

- Take all possible measures to protect the quality of fresh water reserves and establish appropriate emergency procedures should reserves be under threat.

- Provide fresh water facilities for use by local communities in communal areas or pay for water infrastructure to be installed to serve the needs of both tourists and local communities.

- Minimize wastage of water by undertaking regular maintenance checks.

- Work with customers to reduce water demand; placing notices explaining to guests the importance of conserving water is just one example of a commonly used and effective initiative.

- Use water-saving devices to reduce water consumption while maintaining service quality.

- Plant drought-resistant species in landscaped areas.

- Develop appropriate environmental impact and design criteria to ensure that water conservation is a key element of new projects and, if water is scarce and construction may result in local shortages, be prepared to make the decision *not* to build.

- For trans-national corporations, disseminate water-saving technologies and techniques to facilities in developing countries.

- Reuse and recycle water wherever possible.

- Encourage staff and customers to incorporate components of the water management program into daily procedures at home.

Most commonly, local regulations govern the quality levels of water discharged from wastewater treatment plants. Moreover, there may be regulations governing the content of wastewater discharged to the wastewater system.[16] These regulations were the impetus for creating the grease traps in kitchen areas. In many locales, regulations also require that receiving dock drainage be routed to sanitary rather than storm sewers and prohibit the discharge of site runoff and general storm runoff to the sanitary sewer system.

Market factors can clearly be influential in wastewater management. Coastal locations with poor waste water management have contaminated beaches, resulting in at best an unpleasant environment and at worst illness of guests and local people. From a business perspective, this is disastrous. Circumstances such as these have prompted tour operators to refuse to bring groups to these destinations until assurances were given that the problems had been corrected. And even when guests do not directly react to the problem, the local flora and fauna do. Reef areas severely damaged by sewage discharges lose their attractiveness, which severely reduces the appeal of the operation and the local economy that depends on it for their livelihood.

Exhibit 8   Agenda 21 Wastewater Management

Priority area 4: wastewater management

- Use wastewater treatment facilities in all outlets around the world to ensure that all effluent is treated to match WHO standards as a minimum and reused for secondary purposes where appropriate.

- Where wastewater facilities do not exist, work with other companies and governments to establish appropriate facilities and procedures.

- Establish appropriate catchment ponds to ensure that potentially damaging chemicals do not enter the waste system through runoff.

- Establish programs with staff, tourists, and communities to clean up degraded aquatic environments.

- Establish emergency procedures to ensure that the aquatic environment is protected from disasters within the facility.

- Wherever possible, avoid products containing potentially hazardous substances which may eventually find their way into the water system.

- Dispose of wastewater responsibly.

Discharge of untreated wastewater to the environment is socially irresponsible. While customers may be exposed to this wastewater during the short stay of their visit, it is the local population that is most exposed both to the water itself and to possible diseases the water may carry. Owners and managers need to ensure that wastewater treatment plants in their area are operating properly—not only their own on-site plants, but also those of other businesses in the area. Owners and managers also should take responsibility to ensure that waste processing by municipal agencies is not harming the environment. Failure in doing this could mean that the clean environment so essential to business survival will be irreparably damaged.

Exhibit 8 is a summary of several of the items discussed here regarding wastewater management, as well as some topics for additional involvement and concern. Those operations exhibiting proper responsibility regarding wastewater will help to ensure the ongoing environmental health of their destination for guests, employees, and local people.

Hazardous Substances

Hospitality businesses do not create or generally use large quantities of **hazardous substances.**[17] However, there are operations and activities in the industry that *do* use hazardous substances. By definition, hazardous materials include those that are:

- *Toxic*—substances that cause damage to health, physical or mental impairment, or death when inhaled, ingested, or absorbed; for example, pesticides and herbicides

- *Flammable*—substances that can be easily ignited by sparks or flames and cause fires. Of particular concern are those liquids with low flash points; for example, solvents and fuels

- *Explosive*—substances capable, by chemical reaction within themselves, of producing such a temperature, pressure, and speed to cause damage to the surroundings

- *Corrosive*—materials that destroy other materials by chemical reaction. When in contact with human tissues these substances may cause burns and destroy tissue. At greatest risk are skin, eyes, the lungs, and stomach. Oven and toilet cleaners are usually corrosive

- *Infectious*—substances that contain viable microorganisms and their toxins, capable of causing disease. Examples of infectious items are medical waste or contaminated food (botulism, salmonella, and legionella)

An action plan related to hazardous materials is needed and should include the following objectives:

- Minimizing the use of hazardous materials

- Using more environmentally acceptable alternatives

- Limiting the use of hazardous materials to trained personnel

- Ensuring that hazardous materials are stored, labeled, used, handled and disposed of in accordance with local and international standards and regulations

Recommended steps to include in the action plan are:

- Identify and record where hazardous materials are being used, what they are being used for, and the reasons for their use.

- Assess the hazards associated with their use.

- Identify, where possible, environmentally preferable alternatives.

- Review handling, storage, labeling, and disposal procedures.

- Compile a hazardous materials manual.

On-site storage of the fuels needed for vehicles and possibly to fire boilers is common in the industry. Fuel leaks and discharges can be highly damaging to the environment. Proper procedures and regular inspection of tanks and supply pipes are critical to maintaining the integrity of these storage systems. Fuel storage tanks should be located above ground to help minimize undetectable leaks and to contain fluids that do leak.

During the 1980s and 1990s, particular attention was given to two hazardous substances: PCBs and asbestos. PCBs (polychlorinated biphenols) were in transformers and certain other electrical devices. Ensuring that PCBs do not leak from these devices and that PCB-contaminated products are disposed of in an approved manner continues to be a concern, especially in developing countries.

Asbestos problems center primarily on the potential for this material to become airborne and then inhaled by building occupants. Proper procedures to identify and manage asbestos are well developed and need to be followed.[18]

Exhibit 9   Agenda 21 Hazardous Substance

Priority area 5: hazardous substances

- Examine the necessity for use of products containing potentially hazardous substances and, where possible, use more environmentally benign products.

- Assess the full environmental as well as financial implications of new products prior to purchase.

- Where environmentally benign alternatives do not exist, form partnerships with governments and manufacturers to develop them.

- Reduce use of products containing hazardous substances to the lowest possible quantity and recycle or reuse any residue that can be captured.

- Dispose of any unavoidable wastes responsibly.

- Set up inventories and storage procedures to guard against theft/accidents.

- Ensure that all appropriate staff are trained in handling of hazardous substances and in emergency procedures.

- Start routine emissions of toxic substances to the environment as part of a "right-to-know" program for employees and host communities.

- Transfer benign technologies and know-how to developing countries.

Exhibit 9 provides a set of actions that can help reduce problems of hazardous substances. Following the guidelines in this chapter and those in Exhibit 9 will significantly reduce the usage and release of hazardous substances.

Transport

The hospitality industry obviously would not exist without means of transport for customers, employees, and supplies. The combustion of fuel by autos, buses, trucks, trains, planes, and ships clearly contributes to emissions and air pollution. Building the infrastructure to meet transportation needs, such as roads, airports, and terminals, requires alterations to the landscape and contributes to environmental concerns. Congestion resulting from transportation "gridlock" further contributes to a less-than-pleasurable experience for guests and employees.

To help curb the emissions at the unit level, lodging operators can purchase fuel-efficient vehicles, consider powering these with clean fuels such as natural gas, and encourage car-pooling and public transportation by employees. Coordinating the ordering of supplies to help ensure a minimum number of deliveries and looking to purchase supplies produced locally can also help to reduce the environmental impact of transportation.

Finally, with environmental programs focusing not only on the natural (non-human) environment, but on the human environment as well, an active program to encourage safe transportation is important. Encouraging use of seat belts, safe operation of vehicles, and minimizing overcrowding of bus and other vehicular transport is needed. Transportation-related injuries and deaths are all too prevalent and clearly represent a place where improvements are needed.

Exhibit 10   Agenda 21 Transport Actions

Priority area 6: transport

- Use well-maintained and modern transport technology, thus minimizing emissions into the environment; this is particularly important for airlines, which should seek to operate the most efficient fleet possible.

- Help developing countries to acquire relevant technological skills or equipment.

- Develop and manage car share, cycle, or walk-to-work schemes for employees and provide incentives to ensure success.

- Provide information to customers to help them use public transport, cycle ways, or footpaths.

- Work with planning authorities to ensure that coach stops and other drop off points are well located.

- Work with suppliers to ensure that purchases are not delivered at peak times (congestion contributes to emissions) and that deliveries are fully loaded.

- Work with local farmers and other local businesses to purchase supplies locally whenever possible.

- Work with governments to implement measures to reduce congestion and hence pollution; this is particularly relevant to the air transport sector and to city environments.

- Work with governments to integrate transport modes and thus reduce reliance on the private car.

- Consider transport as a part of development plans.

- Operate demand management to reduce the need for polluting modes of transport in favor of less polluting modes and activities.

Exhibit 10 offers additional ideas for transportation-related measures. Many of these involve activities that encourage the use of mass transit and consider the potential environmental impacts of transportation when purchasing decisions are made.

Land-Use Planning and Management

Probably tens of thousands of hospitality facilities are developed each year if one includes restaurant, lodging, and amusement facilities. Facilities development is a time of a unique opportunity to examine the environmental, cultural, social, and economic impacts of the business. The potential benefits of such an examination can be substantial.

Economically, appropriate **land-use planning** and management can result in reduced or, at the very least, more controlled costs for development and operation. Reuse of existing buildings (either existing hotels and restaurants or converting other structures to these uses) is just one example of appropriate land-use planning and management that reduces initial costs. Reusing existing structures also helps to retain a cultural and social fabric for a location that could be more significantly affected by a demolish-and-build approach. Proper site orientation of newly constructed buildings and retention of existing landscaping can result in lower energy costs and reduced costs for landscaping, both initially and in the long term.

From a regulatory perspective, attention to land-use planning and management has become an integral part of the project approval process and is often included in the broader context of the **environmental impact statement (EIS).** The EIS process can be expedited by addressing these issues in the planning stages. Appropriate attention to land-use planning and management can create a product with a greater sense of place and resulting customer appeal.

Customers *do* respond to careful land-use planning and management. A well-designed facility that integrates the setting in which it is located to maximum advantage is a marketing plus. There are subtle issues here as well: selecting landscape materials that are appropriate for a location will have a better chance of thriving in the location, thus avoiding unattractive or difficult-to-care-for landscaping. Working with and around site terrain conditions has its payoffs as well. By not altering the landscape in ways that create erosion or flooding problems, you help ensure the protection of the property and your guests. Attention to areas outside the property boundaries is also important. An environmental eyesore (especially one created by or contributed to by the property development) en route to the property does not reflect well on the quality of management decision-making.

Social responsibility means that land-use planning and management considerations should not stop at the property boundaries. The development of a new property can create additional demands for land and services to accommodate transportation needs, staff housing, and the general needs for community services (particularly schools and medical care). Supporting initiatives in the local community to meet environmental good practice should be given due consideration. The quality of service to guests is a reflection of the quality of the employees rendering the services: employees should have access to good health services and proper sanitary conditions, reside in good quality housing, and in general live in an environment that is somewhat comparable to the environment they are in while at work.

Describing the practices of operations exhibiting social responsibility helps to define the concept. The Victoria Falls Safari Lodge (Zimbabwe) and Turtle Island (Fiji) are environmental award winners that exhibit social responsibility in both their design and operations (see the sidebars in the following pages). From the outset, they were concerned about their impact in the community and on the environment and took strides to benefit local people by their presence. Another socially responsible operation is the Punta Cana Beach Resort in the Dominican Republic.[19] The Resort helps provide schooling for the children of employees, medical care for employees and families, and has established the Punta Cana Ecological Foundation, which protects 2,500 acres (1,000 hectares) of land and provides a location for environmental research.

Exhibit 11 lists some typical land-use planning and management measures as suggested in Agenda 21. Applying these and other creative ideas to local situations is the responsibility of not only the hotel ownership and operations, but also of design professionals involved in the creation and modification of the facility.

Exhibit 11   Agenda 21 Land-Use Planning and Management

Priority area 7: land-use planning and management

- Assess the potential environmental, cultural, social, and economic impacts of new developments.

- Take measures to avoid negative impacts or minimize unavoidable impacts.

- Monitor the impacts of all new processes and procedures.

- Use local materials (from substantially managed sources) and labor when constructing new facilities.

- Employ technologies and materials appropriate to local conditions in new developments and refurbishments.

- Work with regional and national authorities to ensure that adequate infrastructure is in place for new developments and refurbishments; this may include making provision for wastewater treatment facilities or electricity supply within the development or ensuring support for local craft industries.

- Involve the local community in major development decisions (see priority area 8).

- Consider overall carrying capacity and resource restraints when developing new products, especially on small islands.

- Work with other sectors to ensure balanced and complementary development patterns.

Willingness to constrain development can often help create a location that is more desirable to all concerned, resulting in sustainable economics as well as environmental and equity benefits.

Involving Staff, Customers, and Communities

The development and operation of a hospitality business can benefit from the involvement of staff, customers, and the community in environmental issues. A staff empowered and involved with a property-level environmental program can be a positive contributor to the program itself and take the ideas and concepts developed outside the property into their homes and communities. Saunders Hotel Corporation in Boston, Massachusetts, was an early innovator in getting its staff involved in its environmental program. The Saunders' SHINE program (Saunders Hotels Initiative for the Environment) involved and rewarded employees for their environmental initiatives and involvement. The Saunders program is featured in a video, *Shaping Change and Changing Minds*, dealing environmental issues and the hotel industry.[20]

Some hospitality managers believe that certain environmental actions may result in a negative customer reaction. In this case, market testing of environmental initiatives is needed just as it is with any guest service. Providing some guest

---

Victoria Falls Safari Lodge, Zimbabwe

Victoria Falls Safari Lodge is a privately owned lodge set in 160 acres of natural bush veld with a natural game waterhole on site. The lodge has 61 standard rooms, including one for disabled access, five deluxe rooms and six split level suites.

The Lodge has been built with no expense or effort spared to ensure that the site remains as undisturbed as possible, using thatch, local hard woods and commercially grown Eucalyptus poles. Its intricate split levels and indigenous trees, some even growing through the roof structure, give the impression of a vast, open-plan tree house.

Prior to commencement of any work on the Lodge, an environmental impact assessment was carried out which included identifying mature trees, natural features and rock formations. An ongoing policy is that no tree may be cut down without the express permission of the Chief Executive.

In an excellent example of sustainable development partnerships, the Lodge has a sister project over the border in Zambia known as Songwe Point Village. Working with people and Chief of the local Mukuni village, a traditional village was created as authentically as practicably possible. This operates as a tourist experience incorporating accommodation, culture, archaeology, history, music and traditions of the Mukuni people. Funds received also benefit the Mukuni community at large via health, education and social services.

All the stakeholders in the Lodge, including employees, suppliers and the local community are committed to following ethical business practice in respect to the environment including projects that benefit the local community, through education of employees, guests and local residents, and working with local and central government to protect the environment.

Source: Green Globe 21, www.greenglobe.org.

education to go along with the testing is also appropriate. The responses of customers to the Saunders initiative were generally positive and even resulted in new business, as customers with an interest in environmental issues selected Saunders.

The Colony Hotel, a seasonal resort in Kennebunkport, Maine, earned an award for "Best Hotel Environmental Practices." It was said of the resort:

> "Customers are actively using the guest-friendly environmental practices of the Colony Hotel, and the guest-comment cards indicate a high level of satisfaction. In addition, the resort's corporate business has increased in part because of its environmental programs. Property managers believe that they gain marketing leverage from the numerous awards the hotel's programs have won. All of the champions report their environmental practices have a positive impact on employee morale and enhance staff members' pride in the hotel."[21]

Exhibit 12 provides additional ideas on stimulating employee involvement. By being involved with and sensitive to the concerns of all sectors of the local community, you can better integrate and cooperate with these very important stakeholders.

Exhibit 12   Agenda 21 Staff, Customer, and Community Involvement

---

Priority area 8: involving staff, customers, and communities in environmental issues

- Take into account the opinions of all sectors of the community in the management of tourism developments; this can be facilitated by a local tourism forum or by formal meetings between staff and community members.
- Provide economic outlets for local tradespeople.
- Discuss development plans and opportunities with local communities.
- Open company recycling, water, or waste disposal facilities to the local community.
- Tell communities about the risks and environmental benefits of the business.
- Ensure that all members of the community, including women, indigenous people, the young, and the old, have access to employment and promotional opportunities within the company.
- Improve the local environment by staff sponsored clean-ups, etc.

To realize Travel & Tourism's potential for educating communities, customers, and staff and raising public awareness, companies should:

- Train all staff, from top management to temporary employees, in environmental issues.
- Provide specialist training to staff in key positions.
- Tell customers about company environmental initiatives, both to inspire product loyalty and to ensure that the environmental messages learned on holiday are put into practice at home.
- Work with local schools and colleges to integrate environmental issues into primary and vocational education.
- Encourage or sponsor training for community members to enable them to participate in the environment and development process.
- Involve employees' families in environmental activities and events.
- Offer training opportunities to other businesses in the area.

Design for Sustainability

Significant potential exists for improving the design of hospitality facilities to incorporate more sustainable elements. This potential resides at all levels of the industry and applies not only during new construction but also during renovation planning and when making other capital decisions. To help realize this potential, research is needed to develop new products that have minimal environmental impact. Research results then need to be communicated within the industry and the educational community and corporations need to incorporate these concepts into their policies and mission statements.

Leadership in sustainability within the hospitality industry has come in many forms. Companies such as Scandic Hotels, a company with more than 100 hotels

---

Turtle Island, Fiji

Turtle Island is a remote destination in the South Pacific, part of the Yasawa Group of volcanic islands in the Republic of Fiji. The Resort, situated in the warm clear waters of Fiji, is host to only 14 couples at a time. It provides an individual thatched, hand–built bure (accommodation) for every couple—cool and quiet cottages with windows opening onto the Blue Lagoon.

In order to preserve the environment of the Island, the owner, Richard Evanson, strove to become self-sufficient—including setting up a full workshop and a busy furniture factory turning out handmade pieces from local timber. There has also been a vigorous tree–planting scheme which has added more than 300,000 trees to the island during the past decade. The island has been placed under the control of an irrevocable trust which prohibits the sale of the island, limits the number of guests to 14 couples, and protects wildlife. In recent years Evanson has funded twice-yearly eye clinics providing free services and surgeries for neighbouring island villagers.

Turtle Island commissioned a "cultural audit" in 1998, which aimed to examine the organization within the context of its vision statement, and the economic, social and cultural impact of Turtle Island on the groups and individuals who make up the social fabric of the tikina and its surrounding areas. The audit is the first of its kind in the world, and has established new paradigms for operators with concerns about their social impacts.

Source: Green Globe 21, www.greenglobe.org.

throughout Scandinavia, illustrate ways in which corporations are responding to the challenge of sustainability. Scandic has received a number of awards for its environmental programs and has pioneered what they refer to as the 97-percent recyclable room, in which "choice of materials is guided by optimum consideration for the environment and our care for our guests. This means wooden floors, furniture made from Nordic tree species, pure wool or cotton textiles, and a minimum of chrome and other metal parts." Scandic's corporate business mission includes striving for "A future in which resource conservation and concern for the environment will bean integral part of our daily lives and in which we take our share of responsibility for the development of society."

LaQuinta Inns, a mid-market lodging firm with more than 300 properties primarily in the United States, was recognized as the Environmental Protection Agency's Energy Star Buildings Hospitality Partner of the Year for 2000. This award was given for changes LaQuinta made to building systems, including energy efficient lighting, conversion of all guestroom heating and cooling units to heat pumps, and its general commitment to energy efficiency. La Quinta is also involved in an evaluation of guestroom digital controllers that create energy savings when rooms are unoccupied.

Exhibit 13 offers a number of additional suggestions on achieving sustainability. Understanding the issues in designing for sustainability requires adoption of creative ideas from other industries, which in turn requires knowledge of effects and ways to address them in design decisions.

Exhibit 13   Agenda 21 Design Actions for Sustainability

Priority area 9: design for sustainability

- Establish company-wide policies on sustainable development.

- Increase research and development activities.

- Examine the potential environmental, social, cultural, and economic impacts of new products.

- Seek solutions to environmental problems in developed and developing countries.

- Within the transport sector, strengthen efforts to collect, analyze, and exchange information on the relation between transport and the environment.

- Provide information and support to schools and colleges about environmental issues to help build up institutional, scientific, planning, and management capacities.

- Make adequate preparations for natural disasters, including designing and building new tourism facilities to withstand such disasters.

- Exchange information on solutions to environmental problems through resource centers such as the World Tourism Organization and the World Travel & Tourism Environment Research Centre.

- When developing facilities in other countries, ensure than environmental standards are as high as those in the country of origin.

Partnerships for Sustainable Development

Creating coalitions to encourage sustainable development is integral to the concept of sustainability. Input and cooperation of all stakeholders is needed to achieve the economic, environmental, and equity concerns inherent in sustainability. Though individual operations have scored significant sustainability gains, guidance has been provided through the leadership of various industry organizations.

The Green Globe 21 organization, founded in 1994 to promote environmental awareness, provides a location for coordinating information and conducting dialogue related to sustainability issues throughout the globe. Green Globe was founded to:

- Encourage companies and communities of all sizes to join Green Globe 21 to show their commitment to sound environmental practice.

- Promote the truth that adopting good environmental practice makes good long-term business sense.

- Collect, explain, and distribute examples of industry best practice to businesses and governments.

- Sustain the quality of our vacations for our children—and our children's children.

In addition to publications, studies, conferences, and other activities, Green Globe 21 provides certification for operations run in an environmentally sound manner, as well as annual awards for members exhibiting particularly outstanding efforts relative to Agenda 21.

ECoNETT, the European Community Network for Environmental Travel & Tourism, is an organization dedicated "to increasing overall awareness of sustainable Travel & Tourism" and in turn stimulating changes in management practices, in destinations, and in corporations to achieve sustainable travel and tourism development. A great deal of additional information is available at the ECoNETT web site maintained by Green Globe 21.[22]

Another partnership focusing on sustainability issues has emerged in the Caribbean: The Caribbean Alliance for Sustainable Tourism (CAST) has as its goals to:

- Expand awareness of the region's hotel and tourism operators by providing high quality education and training related to sustainable tourism.

- Promote the industry's efforts and success to the traveling public and other stakeholders.

- Serve as a vital link to all stakeholders with sustainable tourism interest in the Caribbean region.

Formed as a subsidiary company of the Caribbean Hotel Association, CAST has an advisory board consisting of industry and public sector members. CAST is illustrative of a regional grassroots effort to improve the overall environment for tourism as well as the environmental impact of tourism. Further information on CAST can be found at its web site.[23]

Still another organization that integrates environmental and sustainability issues is Business Enterprises for Sustainable Tourism (BEST)[24] formed under the leadership of Conference Board.[25] Representing an extension of the Board's efforts in environment, health, and safety, BEST has drawn together industry, environmental, and other sectors to promote sustainable practices in travel and tourism.

Exhibit 14 provides suggestions for individual operations and others interested in sustainability partnerships. Those establishing partnerships can significantly enhance the environmental and equity aspects of their operations, and in the process they may well find they have also made a positive economic contribution to their bottom line.

Conclusion

A large number of properties, companies, and organizations around the world are working to improve the sustainability of travel and tourism. Those mentioned here highlight these efforts. Space does not permit a full discussion of even a small fraction of the many commendable approaches being made. That so much is happening is heartening. However, there remain industry scofflaws and laggards whose lack of concern and action reflects negatively on the industry as a whole.

Recognition of the economic, regulatory, market, and social responsibility aspects of environmental/sustainability issues should be sufficient to motivate

Exhibit 14   Agenda 21 Partnerships for Sustainability

Priority area 10: partnerships for sustainable development

- Contribute to the economic development and improve the well being of the local community.

- Use representative sectoral bodies to host jointly funded initiatives to test the constructs of sustainable development.

- Foster dialogue between industries, based on formulating solutions to joint problems.

- Work with small and medium–sized enterprises to exchange management skills, market development, and technological know-how, especially as regards the application of cleaner technology.

- Work with governments to establish an enabling framework for the achievement of sustainable development.

- Promote interaction between tourists and host communities and so enhance the industry's potential to contribute to increased understanding of other cultures.

- Promote and support access to markets for the wide range of interests involved in the Travel & Tourism industry.

- Incorporate the concerns of communities—especially indigenous communities—in the planning process so that they effectively participate in sustainable development.

most hospitality managers to take some action. As the items discussed here illustrate, there exist a wide variety of approaches to a wide variety of issues. Sustainability is more about a process than an ultimate destination. Some things are more sustainable than others, and some practices are more environmentally sound than others. Almost all have impacts. The challenge is to minimize the impacts on the environment, achieve equity in the distribution of costs and benefits, and operate in a manner that provides an acceptable economic return.

Endnotes

1. Lou Cook, "Shades of Green," *Lodging,* October 1999, pp. 66–70.

2. For further discussion of the history of environmental programs in the U.S. lodging industry, see David M. Stipanuk, "The U.S. Lodging Industry and the Environment—An Historical View," *Cornell Hotel and Restaurant Administration Quarterly* , October 1996.

3. See also E.W. Manning and T.D. Dougherty, "Sustainable Tourism: Preserving the Golden Goose," *Cornell Hotel and Restaurant Administration Quarterly,* April 1995.

4. ISO standards are developed by the International Organization for Standardization. Another ISO series with which the hospitality industry has experience is the ISO 9000 series dealing with quality.

5. www.pressoffice.sixcontinentshotels.com/social.cfm.

6. *An Environmental Guide for Marriott International—Environmentally Conscious Hospitality Operations (ECHO)*, Marriott International, July 1998.

7. *The Green Partnership Guide—A Practical Guide to Green Your Hotel*, 2nd ed, Fairmont Hotels & Resorts, 2001.

8. www.accor.com/sa/groupe/env.htm.

9. Further discussion on Starbucks environmental efforts can be found on their Web site at www.starbucks.com.

10. Information on environmental measures at McDonald's can be found on their Web site at www.mcdonalds.com/countries/usa/community/environ/news/index.html.

11. Information on composting can be accessed at www.cfe.cornell.edu/compost.

12. Based on data from Alex Brown, "Energy the Revolution by Deutsche Bank, *Hospitality B2B*, May 2000, p. 27.

13. See www.energystar.gov.

14. See www.aeecenter.org; www.ashrae.org; www.ifma.org; www.boma.org.

15. See www.buildingsmag.com; www.facilitiesnet.com; www.energyusernews.com.

16. Standards from organizations such as the World Bank and World Health Organization may be used as references when local regulations are lacking.

17. This discussion is based on *Environmental Management for Hotels: The Industry Guide to Best Practice* (Oxford: Butterworth-Heinmann, 1993), Chapter 12.

18. For an example of asbestos management policies and procedures, see *Environmental Management for Hotels*, Chapter 13.

19. See www.puntacana.com.

20. This video is available from the Educational Institute of the American Hotel & Lodging Association. The Institute is accessible via www.ei-ahla.org.

21. C.A. Enz and J.A. Siguaw, "Best Hotel Environmental Practices," *Cornell Hotel and Restaurant Administration Quarterly*, October 1999.

22. www.greenglobe.org/econett.

23. www.cha-cast.com.

24. www.sustainabletravel.org.

25. www.conference-board.org.

🔑 Key Terms

CERES—Coalition for Environmentally Responsible Economies, an environmentally conscious group who, among other things, is urging its corporate members to include environmental considerations when making lodging purchasing decisions.

corrosive—Any materials that destroy other materials by chemical reaction. When in contact with human tissues, these substances may cause burns and destroy tissue.

ecotourism—A segment of the tourism market that places high value on the "environmentality" of a destination.

environmental impact statement (EIS)—A document stating the effect a planned construction project will have on the surrounding community.

explosive—Any substance capable, by chemical reaction within itself, of producing such a temperature, pressure, and speed to cause damage to the surroundings.

flammable—Any substance that can be easily ignited by sparks or flames and cause fires.

hazardous substances—Any substances that have the potential to damage health or property.

infectious—Any substance that contains viable microorganisms and their toxins, capable of causing disease.

ISO 14000 standards—A set of environmental guidelines established by the International Organization for Standardization that are recognized as the global standard for environmental management. Certification by the ISO to the ISO 14000 standards is acknowledged in the industry as benchmark achievement.

land-use planning—A facilities development function in which careful and appropriate planning and management is applied to existing real property, structures, and natural resources to preserve the cultural and social fabric of surrounding community.

pulping—A method of transforming waste (such as that generated in kitchens) from solid form into a type of slurry by adding water and processing it through a pulping machine. The pulping machine acts much like a household garbage disposer, grinding the waste, pressing out the water, and expelling it into a holding bin.

recycling—Separating certain items of refuse for eventual shredding or melting to their basic materials to be used to make new products.

reuse—The practice of using items more than once, thereby substantially reducing trash and throwaways. Beverage containers, beer kegs, shipping trays, and pallets are typical reuse items.

submetering—A method of tracking and recoding energy usage by department or function such that usage can be accurately matched to specific operations (such as the laundry) and charged to those operations (if desired).

sustainability—A broad approach to environmental consciousness in which environmental issues are addressed within the context of economics, ecology, and ethics.

social responsibility—The recognition by hospitality owners and managers of an obligation to protect the environment for their associates, guests, and communities.

toxic—Any substance that causes damage to health, physical or mental impairment, or death when inhaled, ingested, or absorbed.

waste minimization—An approach to environmental good practice involving reduction, reuse, recycling, and waste transformation to minimize the amount of waste disposed and the cost of its disposal. Its ultimate goal is to ensure that disposal is done in an approved and environmentally suitable manner.

waste transformation—The practice of converting waste products into another usable form, such as incinerating burnable items and capturing the heat energy thus created to generate power.

wastewater—The majority of water leaving a hospitality operation (exceptions being cooling tower water lost to evaporation and irrigation water for the grounds).

Review Questions

1. Why do hospitality companies initiate environmental awareness programs?

2. Why is waste management important to hotel operators?

3. What are examples of re-use? Recycling? Waste transformation?

4. What is pulping? What are its benefits to the hotelier?

5. What does good energy management contribute to environmental good practice? To the bottom line?

6. What is submetering? Why is it a good management practice?

7. What are some examples of energy load reduction?

8. Why is fresh water resource management a critical issue to hoteliers, especially those managing resort operations?

9. How does the nature of wastewater management affect the market appeal of a given hotel/resort operation?

10. What are the five commonly recognized hazardous substances? What danger potential does each present?

11. What are some of the business-related benefits of appropriate land-use management?

12. Why is employee involvement important to the success of an environmental program?

13. What is sustainability and what impact does it have on the success of a property?

Internet Sites

For more information, visit the following Internet sites. Remember that Internet addresses can change without notice. If the site is no longer there, you can use a search engine to look for additional sites.

American Solar Energy Society
http://www.ases.org

Association of Energy Engineers
http://www.aeecenter.org

Blue Flag
http://www.blueflag.org

Business Enterprises for Sustainable
Travel
http://www.sustainabletravel.org

Caribbean Action for Sustainable
Tourism
http://www.cha.cast.com

Coalition for Environmentally
Responsible Economies
http://www.ceres.org

ECoNETT
http://www.greenglobe.org/econett

Energy User News
http://www.energyusernews.com

Environmental Data for hotels
http://www.benchmarkhotel.com

Environmental Good Practice for
Hotels
http://www.ih-ra.com

Environmental Management for Hotels
http://www.bse.polyu.edu.hk/BEP/
hotels14000/ems.html

Florida Energy Extension Service.
http://www.agen.ufl.edu/~fees
programs/hotels.htm

GEMI—Global Environmental
Management Initiative
http://www.gemi.org

Green Globe 21
http://www.greenglobe21.com

Green Seal
http://www.greenseal.org

International Hotels Environment
Initiative
http://www.oneworld.org/pwblf/
ihei/index.htm

ISO 14000
http://www.iso.ch

Links related to sustainability and
tourism
http://www.yorku.ca/research/
dkproj/string/rohr/index.htm

National Renewable Energy Laboratory
http://www.nrel.gov

Project Planet
http://www.projectplanet

Recycling in the Hotel/Motel Industry
http://ndep.state.nv.us/recycle/
reshot.htm

The United Nations Commission on
Sustainable Development
http://www.un.org/esa/sustdev/
csd1999.htm

U.S. DOE—Energy Information
Agency
http://www.eia.doe.gov

U.S. EPA-Energy Star for Buildings
http://yosemite1.epa.gov/star/
business.nsf/webmenus/Business

U.S. Green Building Council
http://www.usbgc.org

Part II

Facility Systems

Chapter 5 Outline

Safety and the Hospitality Industry
Building Design, Maintenance, and Safety
Safety in the Guest Bath
Fire Safety
    Fire Prevention
    Fire Detection
    Fire Notification
    Fire Suppression
    Fire Control
Evacuation Plans
Security
    Key Control
    Electronic Locks

Competencies

1. Describe how to reduce occupational injury rates in the hospitality industry. (pp. 126–130)

2. Outline how building design and maintenance affect safety. (pp. 130–132)

3. Identify several safety concerns with regard to the guest bathroom. (pp. 132–133)

4. Cite evidence that concern over fire safety is growing. (pp. 134–135)

5. Identify critical elements of fire prevention, fire detection, and fire notification. (pp. 135–142)

6. Identify components of fire suppression and fire control devices and systems. (pp. 142–150)

7. Outline several elements that should be addressed in evacuation plans. (pp. 148, 151)

8. Describe various ways in which facilities design and management can enhance a property's security efforts. (pp. 151–152)

9. Identify the elements of key control and guestroom locking systems. (pp. 152–159)

5

Safety and Security Systems

When you lay your head on a pillow at night, you're statistically safer from fatal fire when that pillow is in a hotel or motel than virtually any other place—safer than in a single-family house, a duplex, a manufactured home, an apartment, a townhouse, rooming house, boarding house, or lodging house.

The current situation (re: hotel fires) is a result of an industry transforming itself. While the number of people the lodging industry serves continues to grow, fires have been cut by more than half in the past 15 years, and fire deaths by more than three-fourths, because the industry responded to major disasters with determination and sustained efforts to make their properties safe.[1]

THE HOSPITALITY INDUSTRY has long been expected to provide guests with a reasonably safe and secure environment. This safe environment has changed from the stout walls and barred doors of the travelers inns of years ago to the electronic locks, fire sprinklers, smoke detectors, and closed-circuit television of many modern lodging properties. Today's hospitality manager must understand safety and security needs as they affect the well-being of both guests and employees and how they influence the financial success of the business.

Managers can be motivated to address safety and security issues by several factors, including:

- A sense of moral and ethical responsibility for the welfare of guests and employees.

- Concern over the cost of losses associated with safety and security problems.

- Concern over potential legal liability for failure to exercise "reasonable care."[2]

- Corporate policies and procedures that establish standards.

- Contractual responsibilities related to union contracts.

- Governmental regulations.

- Concern for employee welfare, productivity, and retention.

- Market issues related to safety and security standards expected by guests.

125

Exhibit 1   Occupational Injury and Illness Incidence Rate per 100 Full-Time Workers, 1989 vs.1999

	Total Cases		Lost Workday Cases		Nonfatal Cases w/o Lost Workdays		Cases Involving Days Away From Work		Cases Involving Restricted Work Activity	
	1999	1989	1999	1989	1999	1989	1999	1989	1999	1989
Eating and Drinking Places	5.6	8.5	1.8	3.2	3.8	5.3	1.4	3.0	0.4	0.2
All Retail Trade	6.1	8.1	2.5	3.4	3.6	4.6	1.7	3.1	0.8	0.3
Hotel and Other Lodging Places	7.8	10.8	3.7	4.7	4.1	6.1	2.1	4.2	1.6	0.5
All Services	4.9	5.5	2.2	2.7	2.6	2.8	1.5	2.4	0.8	0.2

Source: U.S. Department of Labor, Bureau of Labor Statistics, Washington, D.C., Selective Access Statistics (www.bls.gov).

Safety and the Hospitality Industry

Safety involves avoiding those causes of injury and damage that we might call accidental—slips and falls, cuts, burns, and other personal injuries, as well as related property damages. Safety issues are important for their impact not only on guests and employees but on profitability as well.

Lodging and food service industries have demonstrated significant improvements in the safety of their workplaces over the past decade, as evidenced by the statistics in Exhibit 1. Substantial reductions have been achieved in not only the total number of injuries and illnesses (down 34 percent for eating and drinking places and 28 percent for hotels and other lodging places) but also in the more serious injuries and illnesses—those resulting in days away from work. Eating and drinking places have reduced the incidence rate of cases involving days away from work by 53 percent (from 3.0 to 1.4) and hotels and other lodging places have reduced these by 50 percent (from 4.2 to 2.1). These reductions result from a combination of improved safety within the workplace and the increased return to work of employees with restricted duties. Eating and drinking places increased their use of restricted workers by 100 percent over this time (from 0.2 to 0.4) and hotels and other lodging places increased theirs 220 percent (from 0.5 to 1.6).

The good news of Exhibit 1 should certainly be celebrated. At the same time, however, certain concerns and opportunities remain. Hotels and other lodging places continue to have relatively high overall injury rates compared to other service industries. And with the large employment in eating and drinking places and hotels, each of these categories continues to make the "top ten" list of industries in terms of total injuries and illnesses. In 1999, approximately 300,000 injuries and illnesses were reported in eating and drinking establishments and 108,000 in hotels and other lodging facilities.[3] These figures put both of these hospitality sectors once again in the "top ten." In eating and drinking establishments, the sheer numbers of people employed will almost guarantee their position on this list. However, hotels and other lodging facilities could drop off the list if they could achieve a little more than a 10 percent reduction in their overall injury and illness rates.

Some U.S. lodging companies have achieved injury and illness rates that are substantially lower than the national averages. They have achieved this by implementing programs of loss prevention as part of their overall corporate risk management efforts. Risk management and loss prevention programs are designed to pinpoint major potential risk areas and identify options to reduce either their frequency or the severity of their losses. Implementation of restricted duty programs, as evidenced by the data in Exhibit 1, is an effort to reduce the severity of losses. Exhibit 2 lists 14 elements that the U.S. National Safety Council suggests are necessary for a successful safety and health program. The emphasis a property places on individual elements is dependent on the type of business or unit.

Establishment of a safety committee is key to encouraging a safe work place. Involving employees in the development of safety policies, reviewing details of accidents, recommending corrective action, and participating in safety inspections and other safety functions helps ensure interest and buy-in. It is quite helpful to draft a policy statement setting the organization, responsibility, recommendations, and procedures for a property-level committee. Numerous resources exist to assist in this endeavor, ranging from those of the corporation itself, to the Educational Institute of AH&LA,[4] to the National Safety Council.[5]

Occupational injuries and lost workdays affect the capability of operating departments to function properly. This degraded functionality in turn affects the operation's profit picture. In addition, injuries affect employees and their families. A property with a good safety program should be able to reduce both the rate at which injuries occur and the severity of the injuries that do occur.

Some hospitality operations have reduced their injury rates below the industry average by implementing safety programs. Such programs are often part of an overall program of **risk management,** an integrated effort to reduce the causes and effects of safety- and security-related incidents of all types. One of the most important factors in risk management programs is having the support and involvement of top management. One researcher has noted:

> The effectiveness of a risk management program depends greatly on the support of top management, both at the property and corporate level...The most effective programs held property managers accountable for losses, either through charge backs for losses or incentives for safety. Moreover, properties that have implemented ongoing training programs as part of their culture have better risk management programs. In these litigious times, a solid risk management program is a sound investment.[6]

It is also very important to place either an individual or a safety committee in charge of safety. This person or committee should have the authority to enforce compliance with safety rules. The membership and leadership of a safety

Exhibit 2   The 14 Elements of A Sucessful Safety and Health Program

The 14 Elements

The U.S. National Safety Council established the following 14 Elements as the standard for a successful safety and health program. All effective programs contain these elements, but the emphasis on each will vary according to individual company needs. For example, a service organization might place less emphasis on some activities that receive top priority in a heavily regulated manufacturing company.

Element 1: Hazard Recognition, Evaluation, and Control

Establishing and maintaining safe and healthful conditions require identifying hazards, evaluating their potential effects, developing ways to eliminate or control them, and planning action priorities. This process is the essence of successful safety and health management.

Element 2: Workplace Design and Engineering

Safety and health issues are most easily and economically addressed when facilities, processes, and equipment are being designed. Organizations must incorporate safety into workplace design, production processes, and equipment selection. They also need to evaluate and modify or replace existing processes, equipment, and facilities to make them safer.

Element 3: Safety Performance Management

As in all areas of operations, standards must be set for safety performance. They should reflect applicable regulatory requirements, additional voluntary guidelines, and best business practices.

Element 4: Regulatory Compliance Management

The Occupational Safety and Health Administration (OSHA), the Mine Safety and Health Administration (MSHA), and state safety and health agencies establish and enforce safety and health regulations. Other agencies, such as the Environmental Protection Agency, also issue and enforce regulations relating to safety and health in the United States.

Element 5: Occupational Health

Occupational health programs range from the simple to the complex. At a minimum, such programs address the immediate needs of injured or ill employees by providing first aid and response to emergencies. More elaborate medical services may include medical surveillance programs and provision for an in-house medical capability. In addition, some companies are beginning to focus on off-the-job safety and health through employee wellness and similar programs.

Element 6: Information Collection

Safety and health activities, including inspections, record keeping, industrial hygiene surveys and other occupational health assessments, injury/illness/incident investigations, and performance reviews, produce a large quantity of data. Safety and health professionals must collect and analyze this data. Small incidents often provide early warning of more serious safety or health problems. Complete and accurate records can be used to identify hazards, measure safety performance and improvement, and, through analyses, help identify patterns. The recording, analysis, and

Exhibit 2 *(continued)*

communication of safety and health data are greatly simplified through the use of computers and commercially available software.

Element 7: Employee Involvement

Design and engineering controls are limited in their ability to reduce hazards. Companies now understand that their real assets are people, not machinery, and they also realize that employees must recognize their stake in a safe and healthful workplace. As employees become more involved in planning, implementation, and improvement, they see the need for safer work practices. Solutions to safety and health problems often come from affected employees.

Element 8: Motivation, Behavior, and Attitudes

Motivation aims at changing behavior and attitudes to create a safer, healthier workplace.

Element 9: Training and Orientation

New and transferred employees must become familiar with company policies and procedures and learn how to perform their jobs safely and efficiently. The use of on-the-job, classroom, and specialty training can contribute to a successful safety and health program. A complete program includes hazard recognition, regulatory compliance, and prevention. The training is reinforced through regular follow-up with both new and veteran employees.

Element 10: Organizational Communications

Effective communication within the organization keeps employees informed about policies, procedures, goals, and progress. Effective two-way communications among employees and managers is critical, as is publicizing safety and health information in the community.

Element 11: Management and Control of External Exposures

Today's safety and health programs must address risks beyond the organization's walls. Contingency plans and "what if" worst-case scenarios are part of planning for disasters, contractor activities, and product and other liability exposures.

Element 12: Environmental Management

Environmental management often requires a complete program of its own. Many companies, however, address environmental issues along with safety and health as part of their comprehensive programs.

Element 13: Workplace Planning and Staffing

Safety and health considerations are important when planning for and staffing the company's work force. Issues include work safety rules, employee assistance programs, and requirements resulting from the Americans with Disabilities Act.

Element 14: Assessments, Audits, and Evaluations

Every organization needs tools to measure conditions, monitor compliances, and assess progress. A variety of evaluative tools can be used to meet the needs of the organization, including self-assessments, third-party assessments, and voluntary regulatory assessments.

committee should be rotated among management employees and perhaps key line employees as well. One study indicated, "The most effective committees included the general manager, certain department heads, and some line employees." This study found the seemingly least effective technique to be that reported by one manager:

> We meet every month, review the accident records, and make recommendations. The minutes are sent to the GM, but nothing ever really changes unless corporate [management] calls screaming that we've got to lower our accident rate. Then the GM has us start contests and do more training. This lasts for about two or three months, and then it's back to business as usual. [7]

A note of caution is needed. *Responsibility* for safety and security cannot be delegated to a committee or to a department. Safety and security must be viewed as a responsibility of all employees—line and management.

Some key elements of safety programs that have helped reduce employee injuries include:[8]

- Composing and communicating to all employees a written policy relating the organization's commitment to safety and what it expects of its employees.

- Soliciting and using the input of line employees on safety matters

- Conducting regular safety inspections of the property

- Setting realistic goals for accident reduction, closely monitoring progress, and rewarding reductions

- Requiring accountability for accident reduction

- Offering a modified- or transitional-duty program to return injured employees to work sooner

- Creating a heightened sense of safety awareness through signs, contests, rewards, and health fairs

- Training, retraining, and more training

- Establishing specific safety-oriented behaviors as a performance consideration

Building Design, Maintenance, and Safety

The proper design and maintenance of the physical plant are important contributors to employee and guest safety. Properly maintained and adequately illuminated walkways, stairs, and parking lots reduce the likelihood of falls and related injuries. Using slip-resistant flooring materials and finishes helps protect employees and guests from injury due to slippery surfaces. Another important design consideration is the Americans with Disabilities Act of 1990, which spells out accommodations to be made for people with disabilties.

The glass installed in sliding doors to balconies, other patio doors, and exit/entrance doors is another potential source of safety problems. Tempered glass should always be installed in such locations. Tempered glass is harder to break

Safety and Security Systems and the ADA

Guests with disabilities may often be at greater risk in emergency situations due either to a diminished ability to hear warning signals or an inability to exit a building quickly. Guests with hearing or other cognitive disabilities may be unable to perceive some types of emergency warnings, while guests with some types of mobility impairments may be unable to independently evacuate floors that are above or below grade if the elevators are out of service. Although such potential situations have been recognized for many years, possible solutions have only recently been addressed by accessibility standards.

To alert guests who cannot readily hear audible alarms, the Title III ADA Standards for Accessible Design require the installation of visual fire alarms (strobe lights) in various areas, especially where an individual might be isolated, such as in restrooms, meeting rooms, and guestrooms. The strobe lights are required to meet certain minimum requirements such as spacing, installation heights, flash rates, intensity, and synchronization.

All wheelchair accessible guestrooms plus a percentage of other guestrooms are required to have audible/visual alarms that are triggered by a local smoke detector and the building's general fire alarm. Accessible guestrooms are required to be configued and distributed to provide choices of room types and amenities comparable to those offered to the general public, including room types, levels of service, smoking/non-smoking rooms, views, etc.

The ADA Standards for Accessible Design require that new hotels be fully sprinklered or that each floor have either direct at-grade egress or an area of rescue assistance. Areas of rescue assistance are designated protected spaces that connect directly to a means of egress (usually a fire stair), are large enough to accommodate two wheelchairs out of the path of normal egress, and have a two-way audible and visual communications system that connects to a fire command location. In these protected areas, guests who are unable to use stairs are expected to wait to be evacuated. Unfortunately, areas of rescue assistance can cause collateral security problems in hotels/motels. Spaces with immediate access to an exit, where persons are out of sight of security personnel, can potentially cause a threat to other hotel guests. Also, if storage space is at a premium, it typically becomes an ongoing management challenge to assure that areas of rescue assistance are kept clear *at all times.*

It is important that hoteliers establish backup operational procedures to ensure the safety of guests with disabilities. The simple task of flagging the folio of each guest with a hearing or mobility impairment at the time of check-in can provide an effective means of identifying rooms that staff should notify in case of an emergency or that fire professionals should check to ensure that guests have been safely evacuated.

and, when shattered, breaks into rounded pieces, reducing the chance of injury. Take care when replacing glass that the correct type is used. In addition, when glass doors may be mistaken for open doorways, the glass should have decals affixed or bars of some type placed across them to alert people to its presence.

Besides the physical plant, the furniture, fixtures, and equipment also need attention as part of a safety program. When these items are cleaned, they also should be inspected for loose connections and worn or frayed parts. This is yet another example of the need for a close working relationship between maintenance and housekeeping. If any problems are noted, the item should be either repaired immediately or removed from service until it is repaired.

Attention should also be paid to product recall and defect notices. In recent years, defective sprinkler heads and high-chairs were among a host of product recalls.

Safety in the Guest Bath

An area of particular concern in guest safety is the guest bathroom.[9] Some of the safety concerns are:

- Hot water temperatures
- Slip resistance of bathtubs, showers, and bathroom floor coverings
- Electrical shock
- Proper bathroom construction

The scalding of guests in lodging bathrooms has resulted in injury and death. This problem occurs primarily in older establishments due to system design and operation. The resulting lawsuits can bankrupt smaller operations and significantly affect the bottom line of larger ones. To prevent scalding, it is suggested that operators:

- Set guest-use water temperatures no higher than 120° F (49° C) at the source and 110° F (43° C) at the tap.
- Separate hotel water systems supplying commercial facilities, guestrooms, and locker rooms from those supplying kitchens and laundries.
- Install bath and shower valves that provide pressure and temperature compensation. These valves maintain a preset mix of hot and cold water and automatically adjust to system changes.

The slip resistance of bathtubs is also a concern, since slippery bathtubs can cause injuries. The American Society for Testing and Materials (ASTM) has defined indices of "slipperiness." When purchasing new bathtubs and showers, ask for a nonslip surface per ASTM F462.

The slip resistance rating of a bathroom tub and shower can decrease over time due to wear and the effects of cleaning chemicals. Tub and shower suppliers can recommend cleaning materials and methods. When resurfacing these fixtures, be sure to specify the required slip resistance as part of the contract; require the contractor to submit test results per ASTM F462 on samples of the finished product.

The location and installation of grab bars is also important in bath safety. Suggested guidelines for positioning and mounting grab bars appear in Exhibit 3. All wall-mounted items need to be installed with adequate blocking to ensure secure anchoring.

Exhibit 3 The Position and Mounting of Grab Bars

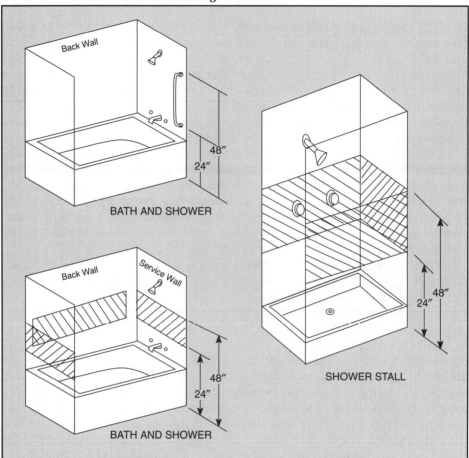

Source: Robert L. Kohr, "The Safety Factor in Bathroom Design," *Lodging,* May 1989, p. 28.

Any glass used in shower stalls and mirrors should be safety glazed. Shower stall doors should be of tempered glass to reduce the possibility of cuts should the door break.

Bathroom flooring should also have proper slip resistance. When specifying floor surfaces, require the manufacturer to submit certified copies of slip resistance test results from independent laboratories. The test results should represent conditions appropriate to the expected use of the flooring material. The manufacturer can also recommend cleaning materials that maintain the floor's slip resistance. These steps will help minimize slips and falls.

To reduce the hazard in the guest baths due to electrical shocks, furnish ground fault protection on selected electrical outlets. If your property provides hair dryers, the fan and coil should be mounted on the wall with a built-in GFCI capability.

Fire Safety ⎯⎯⎯⎯⎯⎯⎯⎯⎯⎯⎯⎯⎯⎯⎯⎯⎯⎯⎯⎯⎯⎯⎯⎯

The U.S. lodging industry has had great success in improving the fire safety of hotels and in reducing the number and severity of hotel fires. In the late 1970s, an average of 11,500 hotel/motel fires were occurring yearly. By the early 1990s, this figure had dropped to about 6,000,[10] and the number of deaths in hotel/motel fires had dropped from more than 100 per year to an average of about 35. This occurred amid a substantial increase in the number of hotel/motel rooms. The National Fire Protection Association remarked that it was in fact a milestone in the dramatic and remarkable progress of fire safety in the lodging industry.

How did the industry manage to achieve this? A major factor was attention to fire prevention—identifying possible causes of fires and striving to reduce or eliminate them. Hotels have also greatly improved the ways in which they detect the presence of a fire and the policies and methods they use to notify and evacuate building occupants. Finally, there is technology. Vastly improved fire suppression systems are installed today and systems to control the spread of fire and smoke effectively control even those fires that do flare up.

With all these improvements, the reader may ask why we continue to discuss these topics. The admirable fire safety record of U.S. lodging establishments can be lost through complacency, a false sense of security, and a lack of managerial attention to fire issues. A classic case in point is a hotel fire in Cambridge, Massachusetts, in 1990. Banquet staff brought a 20-pound propane tank into a function room to operate a buffet warming grill. The grill created smoke and set off the room's smoke detector. To dissipate the smoke, the staff set up fans. Later, when the staff disconnected the propane tank, they failed to notice that the fuel line was still open. The escaping propane was circulated around the room by the fans, encountered an ignition source, and a fireball surged across the room. Amazingly, only one person died and 10 others were hospitalized. In a news story reporting the fire, the writer stated, "Fire safety know-how may or may not trickle down to the people who need it most—the banquet staff."[11] This incident is a reminder that management not only needs to know what to do, it needs to convey this information to the staff and ensure that policies and procedures are followed.

Continued attention to fire safety is mandated also by rapidly advancing fire detection and suppression technology. New technology, systems, and devices require continued maintenance and testing and, unfortunately, may be subject to operational problems. The greatly reduced numbers of lodging fires, coupled with the presence of increasingly sophisticated fire technology, can give managers a false sense of security. Smoke detectors and sprinkler heads do require maintenance; they cannot be installed and then forgotten. Moreover, various components of systems need checking and, possibly, replacement.

Market factors also favor operations with the proper technology and systems related to fire safety. For example, the federal government continues to follow the Hotel and Motel Fire Safety Act, which stipulates minimum fire protection standards for the lodging establishments at which federal employees stay. Federal employees will not be reimbursed for stays at properties not complying with federal fire safety requirements. Since the federal government is the largest employer in the United States, it represents a huge market for the lodging industry.

Though major strides have been made in hotel fire safety, major gaps in hotel fire protection still exist. Some of these are within the U.S., but during the 1990s, the major loss of life due to fires in lodging was offshore. The last major loss of life in a hotel fire in the United States or its territories was in 1986 at the Dupont Plaza Hotel in Puerto Rico. The 1990s also saw major loss-of-life fires in hotels and various social and dance clubs outside the United States. Exhibit 4 presents a summary of a hotel fire that claimed 91 lives and seriously injured another 51.

A fire safety program involves fire prevention, detection, notification, control, suppression, and evacuation. No fire safety program will ever eliminate the possibility of a fire. However, a well-conceived and well-managed fire protection program can reduce the frequency and severity of fires. Lodging industry efforts over the past decade have significantly reduced deaths in lodging fires. In addition, the number of lodging fires has dropped substantially over the same period.

Major hotel companies have improved their fire safety records through design of new facilities, retrofitting fire protection features into older facilities, and developing and implementing various fire safety procedures. The use of property-level checklists to identify and remedy hazardous situations is one feature of these procedures. Exhibit 5 is a checklist from the National Fire Protection Association that identifies a number of key concerns in fire safety at the property level. Checklists such as these should be prepared and used to help maintain a fire-safe facility.

One key provision is that all fire protection equipment must be able to operate during a power outage. Therefore, checking the connection and operation of fire protection equipment under conditions of a simulated power outage is very important.

Fire Prevention

Fire prevention is *everyone's* job. It is clearly linked with maintenance, but fire safety itself pervades all departments and tasks of a property. An "It's not my job" attitude toward fire safety just isn't acceptable.

Many links exist between maintenance activities and fire prevention. Establishments with on-site laundry facilities need to clean dryer ductwork regularly and remove lint from filters frequently to minimize the risk of fire. If a linen chute is used, it should also be cleaned periodically as needed. In addition, all linen chutes should be kept locked and provided with automatic fire sprinklers. Regularly scheduled inspections of the building's electrical systems (and especially thermal scanning of electrical wiring) also help prevent fires. Critically important, especially in the lodging industry, is a well-informed staff. Managers should make fire prevention and response training a priority in their operation. Materials are available from a host of sources, including fire prevention agencies, local fire departments, government, and trade associations. The Educational Institute of AH&LA, for example, has produced a fire prevention training video in conjunction with the National Fire Protection Association that addresses the fire safety issues unique to the lodging industry.[12]

Exhibit 4 Hotel Fire in Thailand

At approximately 10:20 a.m. on July 11, 1997, a fire began in a ground-floor coffee shop at the Royal Jomtien Resort at Jomtien Beach in Thailand, approximately 200 kilometers (124 miles) southeast of Bangkok. The fire killed 91 hotel guests and staff and seriously injured 51....

The fire was first reported by a crew from the local beach rescue foundation, which was patrolling nearby....

The nearest fire station crew, monitoring the radio traffic, overheard the first call and responded immediately, arriving on the scene in 7 to 10 minutes. At the hotel, they saw a well-advanced fire with flames emanating from the third-floor [of the 17-story structure] roof of the discotheque. Smoke was also visible from the top of the hotel towers, and fire was visible on the third floor.

The first-arriving crews also noticed that 14 people had climbed out a second-floor window onto a canopy above the hotel foyer and that they were exposed to the fire....

During the early stages of their operations, firefighters concentrated on rescuing and protecting those exposed to the fire. Once the first on-scene apparatus had exhausted its water, firefighters had to leave the scene to replenish its supply....

An aerial apparatus with a turntable ladder that arrived with the second wave of responders positioned itself near the hotel entrance, and its crew rescued the 14 people from the canopy above the foyer....

Once inside the hotel, firefighters tried to mount an attack using the standpipe, but they found it dry. The post-fire investigation revealed that no standpipe connections existed to permit the fire brigade to boost the standpipe system, and that an electric fire pump would have been needed to do so....

The only external city water source at the resort was in the southwest section of the complex near the hotel's swimming pool, where it was used to maintain the pool's water level. It was impossible to position a piece of apparatus close to the valve outlet, and when firefighters tried to connect [a] hose to it, they discovered that the connection wasn't compatible with that of their hoses.

The firefighters' only alternative water supply on the property was the swimming pool, which contained approximately 336,000 liters (88,763 gallons) of water. They suctioned the water from the pool using a floating pump and five portable pumps. Tankers were refilled at water sources outside the property....

Fire cause and origin

Before the fire started, approximately eight staff members smelled what they thought was gas emanating from the buffet area of the coffee shop. Investigating its source, a male staff member noticed that gas was leaking from the valve assembly of a 9-kilogram (20-pound) liquid propane gas cylinder. The cylinder was connected at the valve assembly to a Y-shaped breaching piece connected by [a] flexible rubber hose to two wok-type burner jets. The jets were regularly used to cook breakfast for the hotel guests.

Noting the leak, the man tried to shut down the cylinder's main control valve. However, he inadvertently turned the valve the wrong way and, instead of shutting off the flow of gas, actually increased it. The vapor, expanding as it was released, quickly ignited. . . The fire, which grew rapidly as it consumed combustibles near the cylinder, soon became too big to contain with a portable extinguisher.

Exhibit 4 *(continued)*

> According to the local police officers responsible for the initial investigation, the sister of one of the hotel's senior managers had fled the area of the fire before she realized that no one had begun to evacuate the resort's guests. When she re-entered the complex to do so, she was overcome by the fire....
>
> Combustible interiors, the westerly breeze, and the lack of fire separation, compartmentation, and active suppression systems allowed the fire to spread rapidly through the lower levels of the complex. As the fire grew, the lack of pressurization in the stairwell, the lack of self-closers on many of the upper-level doors, and the lack of firestopping in the service shafts allowed smoke to penetrate the upper levels, causing the hotel to fill with smoke....
>
> According to NFPA Chief Fire Investigator Ed Comeau, the lessons learned from this disaster are those that have been repeated time and time again, both in the United States and throughout the world.
>
> "While significant progress has been made through code adoption and fire safety education, there's still much work to be done," says Comeau.

Source: *NFPA Journal*, March/April 1998. Written by Garry J. Martin, inspector for the Fire Investigative and Analysis Department of the Metropolitan Fire and Emergency Services Board of Melbourne, Australia.

Kitchen areas pose great risks for fire. Attention to proper housekeeping practices in the kitchen and regular cleaning of ductwork can help prevent fires and reduce their severity if they do occur. Quick attention to problems with poorly operating kitchen equipment will help to prevent the outbreak of fire.

Particularly important from both a fire safety and sanitation perspective is the kitchen ventilation or hood system.[13] This system must be properly designed and maintained. Cleaning a hood system is a major maintenance task, the extent and nature of which depends on the type of hood system and the filtering method used. Some old hood systems are difficult to clean, yet require frequent cleaning. New designs incorporate automatic wash cycles, minimize potential pockets and crevices where grease can accumulate, and incorporate grease extractors rather than mesh or baffle filters. Periodic cleaning of ductwork and fans is also required to reduce the risk of fire and avoid a "grease dump" on the roof or wall area near the fan outlet. This cleaning is often done by a contract service.[14]

Trash storage and disposal should also be viewed with the possibility of fire in mind. Storing combustible trash near the building (on the loading dock, for example) provides an arsonist with a supply of fuel for which only a match is needed. Failure to secure trash rooms and other storage areas in the building may also provide an arsonist with a relatively isolated location loaded with fuel.

Fire prevention is also a key issue during renovation. Renovation may involve nothing more than replacing interior finishes, or it may consist of substantial changes to the building. When replacing interior finishes, be sure to consider the relative flammability and smoke development potential of the materials. Local fire codes and corporate standards usually establish minimum requirements for these finishes. If such standards do not exist, refer to publications of the National Fire Protection Association (NFPA), such as *NFPA 10—The Life Safety Code*. Also, be

Exhibit 5   NFPA Hotel Fire Safety Checklist

To be completed by Chief Engineer, Director of Safety or Equivalent:

1. Is there a fire alarm system to alert the attendees of a fire? What does it sound like?

    a. Bell   b. Horn   c. Slow whoop   d. Other:

2. Are exit doors and routes to them indicated by illuminated EXIT signs?

3. Is there emergency lighting for the exit ways and exit stairs?

4. Are there any obstructions in corridors, exit doorways, exit stairs, and other routes that constitute exit ways for occupants?

5. Do exit doors from meeting, food service, or casino areas swing out?

6. Are exit doors locked or secured in any way that would prevent ready use of the door?

7. Are doors which could be mistaken for an exit marked properly? At least, DO NOT EXIT.

8. Do doors to exit stairs close and latch automatically after use and remain properly closed?

9. Are you able to access the guestroom floor from the exit stairs?

10. Are instructions prominently displayed in each attendee's room giving details of the fire alarm signal and indicating locations of the nearest exits?

11. Are attendee's room doors self-closing and free of transoms or louvers that might permit penetration of smoke into the room?

12. Is there a sign clearly visible in each elevator lobby station that states "Elevators are not to be used during a fire"?

13. Are there signs posted at the principal entrance to meeting and facility rooms, specifying maximum number of occupants?

14. Are the provided exits remote from each other so that occupants are able to use alternatives if one exit becomes unusable in an emergency?

15. Are folding partitions or air walls arranged so as not to obstruct access to required exits?

16. Are there mirrored surfaces near exits that might create confusion for evacuees?

17. Do meeting rooms have sufficient exits to allow the number of occupants to leave readily, based on the following rate?

More than 1,000	4 exits (minimum)
300–1,000	3 exits
50–300	2 exits

18. Are all corridors, stairways, and aisles free of temporary or permanent storage, including laundry, chairs, tables, room service trays, and trash?

19. Is there a designated senior staff person responsible for on-site firesafety inspections?

    Name:_____   Title:_____

Exhibit 5 *(continued)*

20. Are you subject to a fire code? If so, which one?
21. Are any violations related to fire safety inspections outstanding or uncorrected? If so, please list.
22. Does your facility have an established operating emergency procedure in case of fire? Please include a copy with this completed checklist.
23. Is your facility fully sprinklered? If no, indicate where sprinklers are located.

    a. Meeting Rooms   b. Corridors   c. Public Lobbies   d. Guestrooms
    e. Public Washrooms   f. Other

24. Are smoke detectors located in all areas of the facility? If no, indicate smoke detector locations.

    a. Meeting Rooms   b. Corridors   c. Public Lobbies   d. Guestrooms
    e. Other

25. Are all smoke detectors hard-wired into a central signaling system or directly to the fire department? If no, which are not?

careful about where new furniture, carpeting, and other combustible items are stored. Don't create an opportunity for either an arsonist or a carelessly thrown cigarette to create a fire. Some major hotel fires have started this way.

More extensive renovations sometimes create additional risks. To demolish and remove portions of the building, contractors often bring equipment on-site that may create a fire risk (cutting torches and fuel tanks, for example). Stress fire safety with your contractors, specify designated smoking areas and storage locations for hazardous materials, inspect their work for unsafe practices, and be sure that both you and they have the necessary insurance coverage. It is also important that you know if any elements of the fire detection, notification, or suppression systems have been disabled during the renovation. A system for scheduling notification and a fire watch must be determined prior to any shutdown.

Fire Detection

Fires are often first detected by human observation. Nonetheless, methods of fire detection that operate independently of human presence are needed. These methods include heat detectors, smoke detectors, and sprinkler activation detectors.

Heat detectors react to the absolute temperature in a location (fixed temperature detectors), to a change in the temperature of a space (rate-of-rise detectors), or to a combination of the two (rate-compensation detectors). They are likely to be used where the use of smoke detectors would be problematic, such as in dusty locations.

Smoke detectors are of two types. Photoelectric detectors are triggered when smoke particles either scatter or obscure light. Ionization detectors contain a small amount of radioactive material that establishes a flow of ionized air between charged electrodes in the conductor. The presence of smoke changes this flow of ionized air and triggers the detector.

Dust buildup on smoke detectors can result in "nuisance" alarms. Therefore, periodic cleaning of detectors is required. In addition, detector sensitivity changes over time. Too large a change can either compromise system operation or result in nuisance alarms. Because of this drift in detector sensitivity, it is necessary to calibrate detectors from time to time. Some detection systems monitor detector sensitivity, adjust this sensitivity automatically, and signal operators when detectors exceed allowable changes so that maintenance can be performed. For other systems, periodic calibration is necessary. Consult manufacturers' information for testing methods and frequencies.

Many lodging establishments now contain sprinkler systems. Besides their contribution to suppression, these systems also detect fires and trigger an alarm. The alarm is triggered by flow in the sprinkler piping, which is sensed by piping flow sensors connected to the building alarm. The alarm also identifies the particular flow sensor involved, making it possible to identify the approximate location of the fire.

Fire Notification

Notification involves all means used to inform guests and employees not only about an existing fire, but also about the correct procedures to follow in case of a fire. Notification is accomplished in several ways, each of which requires some maintenance attention and consideration. Elements of the notification system are:

- Emergency instructions and floor plans

- Building horns and alarms

- Voice alarms, visual alarms, and communication systems

- Single-station smoke detectors

- Exit lights

Local fire codes will dictate minimum standards with regard to all aspects of building fire protection. Most fire codes will address the items listed above.

Emergency instructions are typically posted on the guestroom door. They tell guests what to do in case of a fire or other emergency. Floor plans should be part of these instructions and should show the locations of the nearest exits. If elevators are present, guests should be instructed not to use them during a fire. Guests are also instructed to keep their room keys with them (to allow them to get back into their rooms either after an all-clear signal is given or if the fire has them trapped). If stairwell doors are self-locking, guests should be warned of this. Other property-specific emergency instructions should be included as well. With the growing number of international travelers, management should include graphic instructions and instructions in languages commonly spoken by the hotel's guests.

Some hotels have created videotapes that provide safety and security information. These tapes are shown on an information channel on the guestroom television. The set may tune to this channel automatically when it is turned on. At some locations, there are several such channels, each in the language of a major guest group.

Building alarms should be checked regularly, in accordance not only with local codes but also corporate standards. Special testing and inspection is also warranted whenever work is performed on or near these circuits. Alarms must be clearly audible inside guestrooms; codes usually specify some noise level that the alarm must produce inside the guestroom. Adjustments may be necessary to meet these standards.

Some alarms have test switches or reset keys that are used during testing. Other alarms are activated only when the user breaks a glass panel. When these alarms are tested, the glass should be removed; afterward, the glass should be replaced. The maintenance staff should have the replacement links needed to restore the system following activation.

To provide better information to guests, lodging properties have been installing more voice and visual alarms and communication systems. **Voice alarm systems** usually integrate a warning alarm with a pre-recorded message providing guests with information about proper procedures in case of a fire. The systems normally allow property staff or the fire department to override the recorded message so that additional instructions can be given. Keep in mind that speakers of foreign languages may not understand these spoken instructions. Just as multilingual written information about emergency procedures may be needed in the guestrooms, multilingual spoken instructions may be needed when appropriate. Voice alarms and other communication systems should be tested periodically for proper operation.

To notify hearing-impaired guests of fires, visual signaling devices are now regularly used. Strobe lights are installed on alarm speakers in hotel guestrooms and hallways and on the exit signs in hallways. These visual devices may go off in all rooms or only in rooms identified as having hearing-impaired guests, depending on local codes.

As already discussed, smoke detectors are a key feature of fire detection systems. Some detectors also serve as local notification devices—that is, they do not sound a building alarm. Called **single-station smoke detectors,** these devices are similar to those used in residences in that they contain both a smoke detector and an integral alarm. They differ from most residential types in that they are powered by a dedicated electrical circuit, not by batteries.

Since guests at most hospitality facilities are only slightly familiar with the physical layout of the building, the role of exit signs and lighting in a fire is very important. In addition, exit signs are almost always included in a fire department inspection. Management has the clear responsibility to keep exit signs illuminated and clear of obstruction. Emergency lighting should be installed and operational. Inspecting and maintaining emergency lighting often involves using emergency test switches and checking battery fluid levels (for battery lighting systems). Systems powered by emergency generators should always be checked with the generator under load. Doors and hallways that are dead ends should be clearly marked "NOT AN EXIT." Changes in exit patterns as a result of ongoing renovations must also be noted.

It is appropriate to comment on the dangers of overriding the protection devices of fire doors and exit passages. Far too often when a hotel is opened, wooden wedges are placed to hold open every fire door in the hotel. This compromises the fire protection designed into the building. Fire and smoke control doors should *not* be held open by anything other than an approved device that will release the door in the case of a fire. Similarly, exit passages should *not* be used to store equipment and furnishings (or anything else, for that matter). Doing so not only reduces their ability to serve as exit passages, but also may provide a fuel source for a fire.

Fire Suppression

Despite the successful initiatives by designers and operators to reduce the number of fires, outbreaks of fires in hospitality establishments still occur. It is therefore necessary to have adequate fire suppression and control equipment, to know how to use this equipment, and to keep it in proper operating condition.

Fire suppression equipment includes such items as sprinklers, standpipes and hose systems, portable extinguishers, and all related equipment (such as fire pumps, emergency generators, and hoses).

Sprinkler systems are becoming much more prevalent in hospitality applications as their effectiveness becomes better known and as fire codes are modified to require them. Wet-pipe sprinklers are commonly found in hospitality applications. These systems consist of pipes filled with water, individual temperature-activated sprinkler heads, and a water source with sufficient pressure. For low-rise buildings, the water source is generally the local water supply, which provides adequate pressure without a supplemental pump. For high-rise buildings (usually those higher than five to seven stories), a fire pump is generally installed to provide the necessary water pressure and quantity.

A 1998 AH&LA survey revealed that installation of sprinkler systems, while widespread, is still not universal in lodging establishments. Exhibit 6 depicts the results of this survey. Many smaller establishments are not required by code to install sprinklers, particularly if the guestrooms open directly to the outside. What is surprising in the survey is that of the various classifications of properties, only the casinos category had sprinkler systems installed in more than 80 percent of their hotel properties. In contrast, smoke detectors were installed in more than 99 percent of the properties surveyed.

Properties should stock a supply of sprinkler heads to replace those damaged or needing replacement after a small fire. If these are not on hand, occupants may be denied re-entry to the building after a small fire. This causes at best an inconvenience for guests and employees and at worst a significant revenue loss.

Portable fire extinguishers are useful for extinguishing fires in their early stages. To be effective, however, an extinguisher must be the correct type and must be operated properly. Exhibit 7 summarizes the types of extinguishers suitable for use on various types of fires. The extinguishers in a given area should be appropriate for the type of fire likely to be encountered in that area (that is, a water extinguisher should not be located in an electrical room). Some extinguishers are labeled for multiple applications (the ABC extinguisher, for example), while others are labeled for a specific type of fire.

Exhibit 6   Percentage of Hotels with Sprinklers in Room

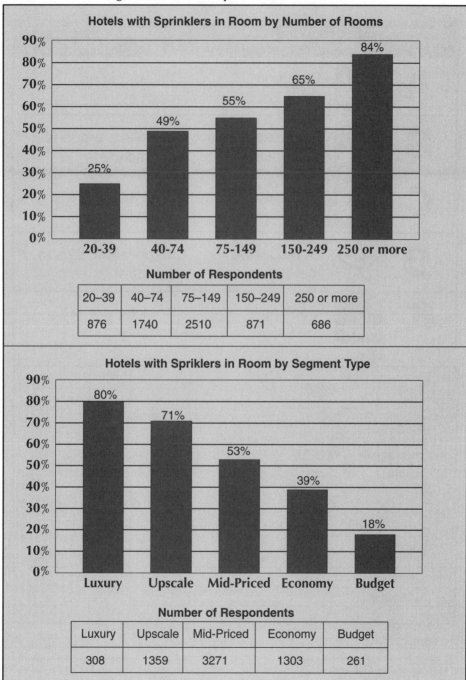

Hotels with Sprinklers in Room by Number of Rooms

Bar chart values:
- 20-39: 25%
- 40-74: 49%
- 75-149: 55%
- 150-249: 65%
- 250 or more: 84%

Number of Respondents

20–39	40–74	75–149	150–249	250 or more
876	1740	2510	871	686

Hotels with Spriklers in Room by Segment Type

Bar chart values:
- Luxury: 80%
- Upscale: 71%
- Mid-Priced: 53%
- Economy: 39%
- Budget: 18%

Number of Respondents

Luxury	Upscale	Mid-Priced	Economy	Budget
308	1359	3271	1303	261

Source: AH&LA 1998 Lodging Survey.

Exhibit 7   Types of Fires and Extinguishers

CLASS	SYMBOL	TYPE OF FIRE	EXAMPLES
A		Common Combustibles	Wood, paper, cloth etc.
B		Flammable liquids and gases	Gasoline, propane and solvents
C		Live electrical equipment	Computers, fax machines
D		Combustible metals	Magnesium, lithium, titanium
K		Cooking media	Cooking oils and fats

TYPE	A	B	C	D	K
Foam	✓	✓			
Water (Pump Tank) (Cartridge) (Pressurized)	✓			Not Normally Found in Hotels	
Loaded Stream	✓	✓			
Dry Chemical		✓	✓		
Dry Chemical (A,B,C-Triplex)	✓	✓	✓		
Dry Chemical (Foam Compatible)		✓	✓		
Wet Chemical					✓
Carbon Dioxide		✓	✓		
Halon	✓	✓	✓		

Note: Halon is banned for refills under the Montreal Protocol and should gradually be replaced under that protocol and its time limits. Halon is being replaced in many establishments by traditional water sprinkler systems or water fogging or misting systems. (Courtesy of Sheraton Corporation and Badger Fire Protection)

Two recent developments regarding portable fire extinguishers should be noted. First, a new type and classification of extinguisher has been added, the class K. This new extinguisher was created to cope with fires in large fryers and other appliances using large quantities of vegetable or animal fats. The new extinguisher reduces the potential for fire flashback. Before development of the class K, auto-ignition was a problem because, though other extinguishers smothered the fire initially, heat retained in the fat could re-ignite the fire. Class K units are designed to effectively prevent re-ignition. Class K extinguishers are used in addition to and following activation of the installed fire protection system.

The other new development is an expansion of the extinguisher ratings. A numerical value has been added to the previously used letter value. The number now appearing before the "A" letter classification denotes the amount of fire suppression material contained in the extinguisher. An extinguisher rated 2A has approximately 2.5 gallons (9.5 liters) of extinguishing agent. The number before the "B" letter classification denotes the total square feet of a class "B" fire that the extinguisher is rated to cover. A unit rated 20B is suited for suppression of approximately 20 square feet (1.9 square meters) of a surface with a class "B" (flammable liquid) fire. No numbers are assigned to the "C" and "K" letters.

All portable extinguishers should be included in the operation's preventive maintenance program. Maintenance staff should regularly inspect hoses, fittings, gauges, pressure levels, and the weight and condition of the extinguishing media. You should also ensure that the correct type of extinguisher is readily available. If you hire outside contractors to service portable extinguishers, make sure that someone at the property monitors their work.

For many years, the standard fire suppression system in kitchens used dry chemicals discharged through a set of nozzles located over key equipment and sometimes in ductwork. Dry chemical hood systems are particularly sensitive to pipe runs, so any change in piping should be done only after an engineering study. Check chemical levels in the systems periodically and inspect all plumbing for propellant leaks. These systems are activated manually or by a fusible link (which melts to activate the system) in the hood or ductwork. In several restaurant fires, the fire protection equipment has not operated properly because of problems with its installation, the installation of food service equipment, or maintenance-related failings.

Because of the need to suppress and control vegetable oil and animal fat fires, and in recognition of the large cleanup task associated with dry chemical systems, some food service operations have begun using wet agents in their kitchen hoods. One version of the wet agent system uses a mixture of potassium salts and water spray. These extinguishing agents are used on Class K fires (those involving large quantities of cooking oils in appliances such as fryers). These wet chemical extinguishing systems create a foam layer on the surface of the hot or burning grease, thereby smothering the fire and preventing reflash. In addition, the liquid spray provides a cooling effect. The cooling effect is important to reduce the potential for re-ignition of the fire due to auto-ignition. Advantages of the wet agent system include its easy cleanup and low corrosiveness. Dry agents use sodium bicarbonate, which is not only quite messy, but also somewhat corrosive if left in contact with kitchen equipment. Wet agents result in more localized application of the agent and can be cleaned up with sponges and towels. Agents used in these systems must pass UL 300 tests.[15]

A variety of kitchen hood systems exists, several of which are designed to reduce energy usage. Some of these energy-saving designs fail to provide adequate kitchen ventilation. Maintenance and food service managers considering energy-saving ventilation systems should make sure the systems provide ventilation adequate to meet all applicable code requirements.

Maintenance staff should check that (1) the hood system is properly connected, (2) the nozzle caps are in place to protect nozzles from grease, (3) the nozzles are aimed correctly, and (4) the fusible links are not covered with grease and dirt. Fusible links may need to be replaced on a regular (usually annual) basis per manufacturer's instructions. Spare fusible links should be in continuing inventory. Cable connections for manual activation should also be inspected.

When the kitchen fire suppression system is activated, it should also interrupt the supply of fuel to equipment. Care should be taken when installing new equipment or modifying equipment installations so that the interrupt capability of the fire protection system is not affected. One operation connected a new range to two gas lines but installed a shutoff on only one, resulting in a problem when a fire occurred. This can easily happen when maintenance staff replace equipment or modify installations to reflect changing needs. Periodically inspecting the fire suppression system can help to ensure its operation when needed.

On the other hand, not all equipment needs to be shut off automatically. Do not connect such equipment to automatic shutoffs, because this may interrupt some equipment unnecessarily—for example, a kitchen alarm that shuts off all gas in the building. Either provide a separate gas line for the kitchen or use another fuel (such as electricity) as the primary or backup energy source for the rest of the building.

Studies of restaurant fires indicate that sometimes the plumbing connecting the dry chemical tanks, piping, and spray nozzles either was never completed or was disconnected for maintenance and not reconnected. In other instances, the fusible links were replaced with wires, bolts, and other inappropriate items. The result was suppression systems that failed when needed. You need to be aware of these problems. You should not compromise the operation of the system. Work done by outside contractors on the restaurant fire suppression system should always be inspected.

Maintenance staff are often part of the emergency response team—particularly at smaller properties—and should be instructed in the proper operation of extinguishers and other equipment. Exhibit 8 contains information concerning the discharge time and distance of several common types of portable extinguishers. Familiarity with such data is important for any operator of extinguishing systems.

Kitchen staff should also be trained to use portable extinguishers. Particular emphasis should be placed on instructing the staff on how to use them on grease fires. An improperly handled CO_2 extinguisher can spread a grease fire rather than smother it. Also, employees should practice removing extinguishers from wall mountings. Ensure that extinguishers are not located in places that are too high

Exhibit 8   Portable Fire Extinguishers: Typical Discharge Times and Distances

Type and Capacity	Discharge Time	Discharge Distance	UL Classification
Water 2.5 gal. (9.4L)	60 seconds	30–40 feet (9–12m)	2–A
Dry Chemical, 2.75 to 5 lb (1.2 to 2.3 kg)	8–25 seconds	5–20 feet (1.5–6.1 m)	5 to 20–B:C
Wet Chemical, 2.5 gal. (9.4L)	45–85 seconds	8–12 feet (2.4–3.7m)	1–B;C or 2–A:1–B:C
Carbon Dioxide 2.5 to 5 lb (1.1 to 2.3 kg)	8–30 seconds	3–8 feet (0.9–2.4m)	1– to 5–B:C
Halon, 2 to 3 lb (0.9 to 1.4 kg)	8–10 seconds	6–10 feet (1.8–3m)	5–B:C

or that otherwise make access difficult. Employees should become familiar with handling extinguishers *before* there is a fire. Further training in extinguisher operation can be obtained from most local fire departments, corporate training resources, or the NFPA.[16]

Fire Control

Fire and smoke control equipment includes such items as fire and smoke dampers in air handling systems, smoke sensors in HVAC ductwork, stairwell pressurization systems, automatic guestroom door closers, and alarm-initiated fire and smoke control door closers. Fire control also involves elements of building construction and operation that control the spread of fire and smoke. Understanding the role of these elements is important when conducting building maintenance and renovations.

Fire dampers are installed in ductwork where the duct penetrates walls and floors. The dampers, which limit the spread of fire, are activated by the melting of a link that holds them in their normally open position. Maintenance workers have been known to wire these dampers open when links break or are lost. This seriously compromises the fire control built into the building by the designers. Investigation of one of the major hotel fires of the 1980s showed dampers held open with wires and steel straps so they could not close. Whether done by in-house personnel or outside contractors, such changes to the building fire control design clearly increase the risk of damage, injury, and death due to a fire. Maintenance staff need to be attentive to the design intent of these features and not compromise this intent.

Smoke dampers are installed to inhibit the movement of smoke through ductwork. **Smoke sensors** control smoke dampers. Smoke sensors may also control smoke by shutting down the air handling system when smoke is detected.

Stairwell pressurization systems increase the air pressure in stairwells, thereby keeping the stairwells relatively smoke-free.

The automatic door closers on guestroom doors should be inspected as part of guestroom preventive maintenance. One major deadly hotel fire would probably have been a minor incident if a self-closing door had been able to operate properly. Fire and smoke control doors should never be blocked or have their complete closure inhibited.

Some doors are connected to automatic release devices. These doors are normally held open by the release devices, but are designed to close automatically when a fire alarm is sounded. Unfortunately, they will also close if a power outage occurs. Since these doors are installed for fire and smoke control, they must meet certain minimum construction standards—for example, any glass used in these doors must be fire tested (which usually means it must be wired glass).

The walls that surround any means of egress (such as the guestroom corridor or the fire stairs) must meet a minimum fire resistance rating. Renovation must be done with this in mind. Any replacement of walls, doors, or windows that involves spaces along a means of egress will need to have the proper fire resistance rating. In addition, smoke and fire stops (means of sealing gaps that result from construction work) should be installed in plumbing chases and other penetrations of walls and floors. Maintenance clearly has a role in keeping these features operational.

The importance of replacing smoke and fire stops when performing maintenance and the need to close fire doors are illustrated by another hotel fire from the early 1980s. A fire on the second floor of a Toronto hotel resulted in deaths on the sixth, twelfth, and twenty-third floors of the building. Smoke and fire were able to spread throughout the building because a fire door was held open by a doorstop, and fire stops were not replaced in pipe chases when maintenance work was performed. These factors facilitated the vertical movement of fire and smoke in the building.

This discussion of fire safety deals with only some key issues in hotel fire safety. Most hotel corporations have standards for building design that incorporate fire safety concerns. Many have developed other corporate training materials to assist in keeping staff informed of fire safety issues and systems on their properties. Exhibit 9 is an excerpt from a sample maintenance schedule for fire protection. Such a schedule should be developed for each facility on the basis of the equipment installed at the facility. The schedule should use information from the building designer and equipment suppliers. Another source of maintenance information is the NFPA, which includes maintenance suggestions as a component of its standards for various pieces of fire protection equipment.

Evacuation Plans

The probability of facility evacuation is real and must be planned for accordingly. The process of evacuation and re-entry should occur as easily as possible. Though detailed discussion of all aspects of these plans is not possible here, plans should include:

Exhibit 9   Periodic Test Requirements: Fire Protection Systems

Device	Frequency	Comments	NFPA Code
Private Hydrants	Annually	Flow water minimum of 1 minute, until water has cleared. Close and observe for proper drainage.	25 4–2.2.4 4–2.2.5 4–3.2
Control Values	Annually	Physically verify open position quarterly, annually operate valve through full range—shut and re-open.	25 9–3.3.1 9–3.4.1 9–3.4.3
Main (2') Drain	Annually		25 9–2.6 9–3.4.2
Back Flow Prevention Devices	Annually	Per code requirements, must measure flow and calculate friction loss.	25 9.6
Dry Pipe Valves	Annually	Annual trip tests, full flooding every 3rd year. Test quick opening devices.	25 9–4.4.2.2.1 9–4.4.2.2
Fire Pump	Weekly	Churn (no flow) test of motor driven pump— 10 minutes minimum. Engine driven— 30 minutes minimum.	25 5–3.2.1 5–3.2.2
Fire Pump	Annually	Full flow test.	25 5–3.3.1
Fire Pump Alarms		Verify pump running alarm in conjunction with weekly test run. Other alarms to be verified in conjunction with annual pump test.	
Water Flow Alarm	Quarterly		25 9–2.7
Standpipe		Hydrostatic test and water supply test—5 years. Pressure reducing valves (hose connection)—5 years.	25 3–2.3 9–5.2.2
Valve Supervisory Switch	Semi-Annually	Verify alarm signal after two turns of the valve or after it has been moved one-fifth of the distance from it's normal position.	25 9–3.4.3

(continued)

Exhibit 9   *(continued)*

Device	Frequency	Comments	NFPA Code
Smoke Detectors	Annually	Distance from its normal position.	
Heat Detectors	Annually	For nonrestorable type, test electrically. For restorable type, use listed aerosol acceptable to the manufacturer.	72 Table 7–3.2
Fire Alarm Pull Stations	Annually		72 Table 7–3.2
Alarm Notification —Audible & Visual	Annually		72 Table 7–3.2
Elevator Capture/Return		Falls under ASME/ANSI A17.1. Required monthly operation and written records on premises.	101 7–4.8
Electromechanical Door Releases	Annually	In conjunction with Pull Station Tests.	
Stairwell Pressurization	Semi-Annually	All operating parts must be tested by semi–annually "approved" personnel—recorded results.	101 31–1.1.10 5–23.13
Restaurant Hood Extinguishing System	Semi-Annually		96 10–6.5 8–2
Engine-Driven Generator	Weekly	Inspect/exercise weekly. Exercise monthly under load.	110 6–4.1

NFPA 25   The Standard for Inspection. Testing and Maintenance of Water Based Fire Protection Systems, 1999 edition.

NFPA 72   The National Fire Alarm Code, 1999 edition

NFPA 96   The Standard of Ventilation Control and Fire Protection of Commercial Cooking Operations, 1999 edition.

NFPA 101 The Code for Safety to Life From Fire in Buildings and Structures (Life Safety Code), 1997 edition.

NFPA 110 The Standard of Emergency and Standby Power Systems, 1999 edition.

- Designation of staff members to supervise the movement of guests down exit stairwells, out exit stairs, and to pre-arranged locations of assembly.

- Designation of locations of assembly for hotel staff outside the building.

- Preparation of lists of registered guests and their room numbers, as well as one duty staff in case there is a need to account for all building occupants.

- Designation of staff members to ensure that special needs guests, such as those with physical handicaps, receive information and special care as needed.

- Designation of individuals to meet fire department personnel and provide whatever assistance and information they require.

- Instruction for the securing of cash and other valuables.

Security

As mentioned, market issues stand as one of the motivating factors of managerial concern for safety and security. Guests care about security!

A hotel that maintains a high level of security does so through a mix of facility design and managerial practices. Physical facilities designed with security in mind help restrict hotel access to guests only. They are designed to inhibit forced entry, to allow supervision of entrances and exits, and to provide adequate lighting. Managerial practices that increase security range from instituting procedures to ensure guest privacy, to keeping adequate records to support security-related decisions, to training employees to recognize and deal effectively with security-related needs, and to adhering to procedures that enhance the security of the property.

To reduce the potential for security problems at hotels, several design and operational features should be considered. These include:

- Providing guests with information about property security and safe behaviors for guests. Use of AH&LA's "Traveler Safety Tips" or equivalent material is one way to do this. Exhibit 10 lists the Traveler Safety Tips.

- Equipping guestrooms with phones to enable guests to make emergency calls.

- Installing guestroom doors that self-close and lock automatically. They should be provided with deadbolt locks, viewports or the equivalent, and security chains or bars that allow the door to be partially opened and yet secure.

- Installing deadbolt locks on both sides of the connecting doors.

- Ensuring that operable guestroom windows and sliding glass doors have a means of being locked. Windows should not open wide enough to allow a person or object to pass through. For sliding glass doors at ground level (and others where access may be possible via the balcony) consideration should be given to the installation of secondary access-restricting devices as well (hinged bars, metal or wood placed in the door channel, or additional locks).

Hotel guests may have valuables that they wish to secure during their visit. Historically, this was done via a safe deposit box near and often under the purview

Exhibit 10   Traveler Safety Tips

1. Don't answer the door in a hotel or motel room without verifying who it is. If a person claims to be an employee, call the front desk and ask if someone from their staff is supposed to have access to your room and for what purpose.

2. When returning to your hotel or motel late in the evening, use the main entrance of the hotel. Be observant and look around before entering parking lots.

3. Close the door securely whenever you are in your room and use all of the locking doors provided.

4. Don't needlessly display guestroom keys in public or carelessly leave them on restroom tables, at the swimming pool, or other places where they can be easily stolen.

5. Do not draw attention to yourself by displaying large amounts of cash or expensive jewelry.

6. Don't invite strangers to your room.

7. Place all valuables in the hotel or motel's safe deposit box.

8. Do not leave valuables in your vehicle.

9. Check to see that any sliding glass doors or windows and any connecting room doors are locked.

10. If you see any suspicious activity, please report your observations to the management.

of the front desk. A variety of procedures and regulations cover the use of safe deposit boxes, with the responsibilities of the facilities department often limited to drilling out the locks when guests lose their keys.[17] Recently, properties have installed in-room safes to secure quest property. Several factors are involved in this trend. First, today's customers are often interested in a secure place to store personal computers. Many existing safe deposit box systems do not have the space to store these. Second, guests prefer the convenience of an in-room storage location for computers (and other items) to a front desk location. Finally, hotels have been able to realize some revenue from the in-room safes. It is likely that the in-room safe will become a more common amenity in the future. Exhibit 11 shows in-room safe availability by hotel size and segment type.

All employees should keep security in mind with each decision they make. Training employees to recognize and report suspicious individuals and unsafe conditions is also strongly recommended. AH&LA's Educational Institute has produced a security videotape series that is an excellent source for the needed training.[18] It should be supplemented with property-specific information.

Key Control

Central to security for hotels is **key control.** Key control for locking systems is critical to establishing and maintaining security at the facility. Whether mechanical or electronic locks are used, the need for key control is essentially the same.

Exhibit 11   Percentage of Hotels with In-Room Safes

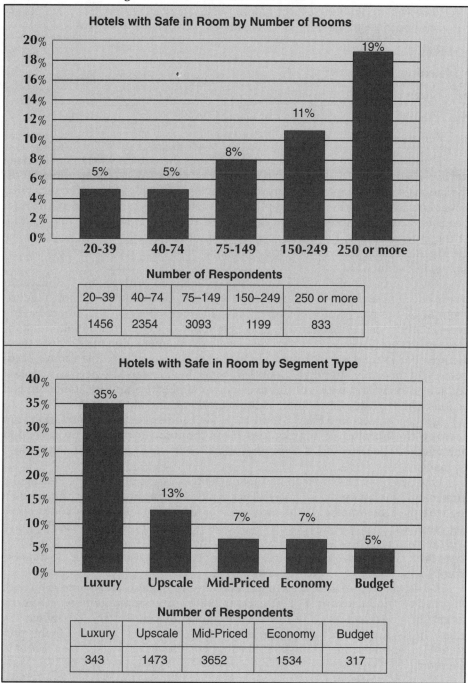

Hotels with Safe in Room by Number of Rooms

20–39	40–74	75–149	150–249	250 or more
5%	5%	8%	11%	19%

Number of Respondents

20–39	40–74	75–149	150–249	250 or more
1456	2354	3093	1199	833

Hotels with Safe in Room by Segment Type

Luxury	Upscale	Mid-Priced	Economy	Budget
35%	13%	7%	7%	5%

Number of Respondents

Luxury	Upscale	Mid-Priced	Economy	Budget
343	1473	3652	1534	317

Source: AH&LA 1998 Lodging Survey.

Mechanical systems rely more on continuous management involvement, while electronic systems embody a large amount of key control within the system itself.

One approach to the topic is to remember "the five R's of key control":

- Rationale

- Records

- Retrieval

- Rotation

- Replacement

The *rationale* of a key control system includes the criteria used to develop the keying schedule and to identify who will have what level of access. In other words, the rationale determines how many keying levels there will be and who gets what keys. Considerations include the physical layout of the building, departmental needs for access, the interaction of these needs with the productivity and staffing of these departments, the needs of guests, and the overall security needs of the facility. A rationale lets you develop a coherent hotel keying schedule such as that shown in Exhibit 12.

Key control *records* involve a number of elements. With regard to the guestroom, effective key control calls for keeping information about the status of guestroom keys, the names of room occupants, and the names of any others having access to the room. With regard to keys issued to employees, records should indicate which employees have which keys. Policy implementation may rely on these records. For example, a room key should be given out only to the room's occupants, and then only after their identities are verified. Hotels also need to maintain records of problems with guestroom locks (maintenance and incidents) and of actions taken to enhance security, including rotation and replacement.

The mechanical key blanks need to be kept under control. Information concerning the number of blanks and their disposition should be recorded and checked. Records of the lock cores installed in each guestroom should also be made.

One practice of recordkeeping (not currently recommended) is recording the guestroom number on the key itself. This practice—or a similar one of attaching a tag with the room number to the key— has far too much potential for compromising guest security. If your property still uses guestroom keys, provide the guest with room numbers separate from the keys themselves—on a printed key envelope, note paper, etc—similar to the manner commonly used at hotels with electronic locks.

Retrieval involves all actions to retrieve keys from guests and employees when they leave the building. For guests, these involve management attempts to get the guest to leave the key for the room. Asking for the key when the guest checks out and providing drop boxes for keys at exit points assist in this process. Also, housekeeping staff should be told what to do with guest keys found in the room.

It is also important to retrieve keys from employees. Employees should take no keys off the premises. Keys needed for the work shift should be signed out at

Exhibit 12   Sample Hotel Keying Schedule

Master Key	Submaster Key	Privacy Key
Administration	Executive offices Sales and catering offices Accounting offices Personnel	Cashier's office (safe) Accounting files Safe deposit area
Rooms division	Front office Entrances Guestrooms (by floor)	Retail shops
Food and beverage	Kitchens Food outlets Beverage outlets Food and beverage storage Food and beverage offices, purchasing Receiving area	Wine and liquor storage Refrigerators and freezers China and silver storage Entertainers' dressing rooms
Function areas	Function rooms Function storage	Audiovisual equipment storage
Housekeeping	Guestrooms (by floor or other maid unit) Linen/housekeeping Lockers and employee dining	Lost and found
Laundry	Laundry Linen storage	
Engineering	Engineering offices Engineering shops Mechanical areas Electrical areas	Electric transformer room
Recreation	Health club and pool Remote facilities (tennis club, golf club, pool)	

Source: Walter A. Rutes and Richard H. Penner, *Hotel Planning and Design* (New York: Whitney School of Design, 1985), p. 220.

the start of the shift and returned at the end. They should be placed in a secure location, whether in use or not. Housekeepers should keep keys on their person, not on their carts. Keys are all too often not retrieved from terminating employees, as they should be. Annual surveys of hospitality students continue to find that they have keys to hotels or restaurants at which they previously worked.

Pay particular attention to keys given to outside contractors for access to a portion of the building. Avoid this practice if at all possible.

Rotation involves moving locks from room to room to maintain security—a sort of preventive security action. Some properties rotate locks on a regular basis (every six months or every year), while others rotate when a given number of guestroom keys have been lost. Rotation is also a good practice when it appears guestroom security has been compromised. A system should be implemented to avoid creating guest dissatisfaction due to rotation. For example, when locks are rotated for occupied rooms, use a "lock change" notice card on the guest-room door.

Despite efforts to deal with proper key control, the *replacement* of part or all of the locking system will eventually be necessary. Locks for food and beverage storage areas and other back-of-the-house locations should be replaced if it is believed that security has been compromised. The loss of master keys may trigger the replacement of all locks at the hotel. Replacement of locks also should be considered when the property is sold, especially when there is a major change in staff.

The replacement process for those operations currently using mechanical/ hard key locks will likely involve the installation of electronic locks. For many operations currently using electronic locks, the next 10 years will probably see them replacing these systems. Exhibit 13 shows that as of the 1998 survey date, there were still a substantial number of smaller properties without electronic locks. Until these operations convert their systems, the five Rs of key control certainly will apply.

Electronic Locks

Electronic locks inherently perform many of the elements of key control described already. The process of purchasing and installing the system includes developing a rationale for key issue and the master/submaster hierarchy. The central computer for the locking system maintains records of keys issued. The need to retrieve keys is greatly reduced, since the combinations of the rooms are changed when a new guest enters the room. In essence, locks are "rotated" automatically for each new room occupant. If a master key is lost, the costly replacement of all locks is not necessary, since the central computer and individual units can be reprogrammed. In addition, the cost of most keys used in electronic lock systems is much less than that of mechanical locks.

Some individual locks maintain records of the keys used to gain entry to the room. The ability to "interrogate" these locks when security problems are encountered is a clear benefit. It has not only assisted in the investigation of thefts, but also served a significant preventive role. Employee theft from guestrooms has been greatly reduced at properties installing these systems. Since every entry is recorded and every key used for entry is identified, employees know that they can neither enter a room without leaving recorded evidence nor blame some nonexistent unseen intruder.

Electronic locks have greatly improved guestroom security. Although these systems add some unique maintenance responsibilities (for example, battery changes), these added duties are more than offset by the systems' overall savings and convenience.

Electronic lock technology continues to change. Some locking systems now automatically engage the dead bolt when the door is closed, reducing the potential for forced-entry room thefts. Some electronic locks now incorporate **"smart card" technology** that allows guestroom key cards to be used throughout a hotel to

Exhibit 13   Percentage of Hotels with Electronic Locks

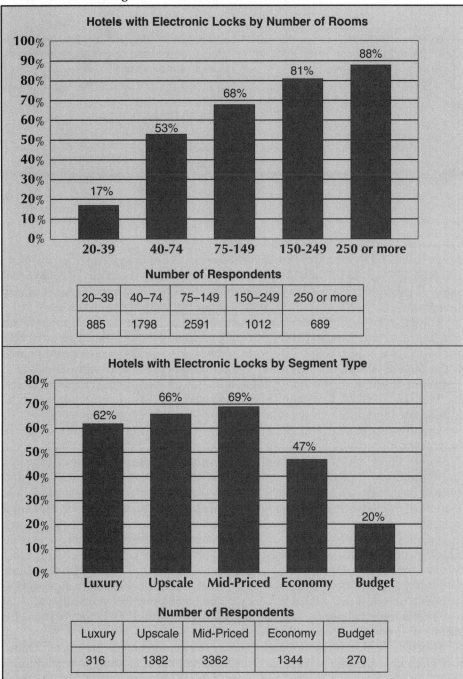

Hotels with Electronic Locks by Number of Rooms

20–39	40–74	75–149	150–249	250 or more
17%	53%	68%	81%	88%

Number of Respondents

20–39	40–74	75–149	150–249	250 or more
885	1798	2591	1012	689

Hotels with Electronic Locks by Segment Type

Luxury	Upscale	Mid-Priced	Economy	Budget
62%	66%	69%	47%	20%

Number of Respondents

Luxury	Upscale	Mid-Priced	Economy	Budget
316	1382	3362	1344	270

Source: AH&LA 1998 Lodging Survey.

Exhibit 14   Safety and Security Reference Sources

Loss Prevention Management Bulletin Loss Prevention Management Institute Conrad N. Hilton College University of Houston Houston, Texas	*Hotel Security Report (*formerly *Hotel/* *Motel Security and Safety Management)* Rusting Publications Port Washington, New York
Security and Loss Prevention *Management, 2nd Edition* Raymond C. Ellis, Jr. and David M. Stipanuk Educational Institute of AH&LA	*Guide to Occupational Safety and* *Health Compliance for the Lodging* *Industry* Raymond C. Ellis, Jr. Educational Institute of AH&LA

charge to the room account. Moreover, there are locking systems that integrate with other systems in the hotel to provide information on the status of room occupancy. These systems interact with the guestroom HVAC control system, notify housekeepers of room occupancy, and communicate with the front desk.

The general overview we have presented in this chapter can be supplemented using the resources listed in Exhibit 14. The previous edition of this text described a visit by an American traveler to Europe in the late 1980s. The traveler commented on the lack of smoke detectors, emergency instructions, and sprinklers in the guestroom. In addition, the independent four-star property lacked a viewport and deadbolt was well. Unfortunately, problems such as these continue in both the United States and international marketplaces.

During recent visits to the Caribbean, this author encountered newly constructed high-rise hotels whose single exit stairwell (centrally located on the guestroom floor) had no fire doors or any other means of separation from the guestroom floors. This meant fire and smoke could readily enter the stairwell and render it essentially useless. There was also no safety chain on the guestroom door. At another property, there was no viewport or safety chain on the door, making it impossible for a guest to see the person at the door without opening it. Finally, at a property at which a major regional tourism meeting was held, the hotel doors were of highly combustible wooden construction and were not self-closing. Guestroom keys had the room number on the key tag, and there was no deadbolt on the doors. In addition, the door providing outside egress from one fire exit was locked during the night, the exit stairwell doors were propped open, one exit stairwell was used to store furniture and debris, and the unused upper level of the property (used for additional storage) was open to the exit stairwell.

Problems such as these are not limited to locations outside the United States. In 2000, an investigative news program visited a motel operation in the south-east United States where attacks and guestroom robberies had occurred. Despite these incidents, the motel did not rotate or replace door locks even when it was obvious the assailants had keys to gain access. In another instance, the same news program videotaped motel security guards sleeping in their vehicles in parking lots—this at a motel having a history of security problems. Another security shortfall uncovered by this investigative effort was that, in spite of having electronic locks and locked exterior doors, motels were failing to code expiration dates on the keycards, leaving cards valid long after guests had checked out.

Endnotes

1. "Top to Bottom Hotel Fire Safety," *NFPA Journal*, March/April 2001, pp. 72–76.

2. In the United States, hotel operators are generally responsible for providing "reasonable care"—a legal concept—for guests at their establishments. However, the legal dimensions, implications, and limitations of this responsibility are not the subject of this chapter. For more information on this aspect of hospitality safety and security, see Raymond C. Ellis, Jr., and David M. Stipanuk, *Security and Loss Prevention Management*, 2d ed (Lansing, Mich.: Educational Institute of the American Hotel & Lodging Association, 1999), and Jack P. Jefferies and Banks Brown, *Understanding Hospitality Law*, 4th ed. (Lansing, Mich.: Educational Institute of the American Hotel & Lodging Association, 2001), Chapter 10.

3. http://www.bls.gov.news.release/osh.t04.htm.

4. See *Security and Loss Prevention Management*, published by the Educational Institute of AH&LA at www.ei-ahla.org or call 1-800-752-4567.

5. Of particular interest is the National Safety Council publication, *Accident Prevention Manual for Business*, a three-volume set dealing with several aspects of workplace environmental health and safety.

6. Jamelia Saied, "Approaches to Risk Management," *Cornell Hotel and Restaurant Administration Quarterly*, August 1990, pp. 45–55.

7. Saied, pp. 54–55.

8. Saied, pp. 45–55.

9. Robert L. Kohr, "The Safety Factor in Bathroom Design," *Lodging*, May 1989, pp. 27–30.

10. John R. Hall, "A Tale of Fire Safety Programs that Work—Two Decades of Hotel/Motel Fires," *NFPA Journal*, July/August 1996.

11. Nichole Bernier, "Hotel Cited in Blaze," *Meeting News*, July 1990, pp. 21–23.

12. For the video "Fire Prevention and Response for the Lodging Industry," contact the Educational Institute of AH&LA, 800 N. Magnolia Ave., Suite 1800, Orlando, Florida 32803, 1-800 752-4567.

13. Safety aspects of kitchen ventilation equipment are addressed in *NFPA 96—Removal of Smoke and Grease-Laden Vapors from Commercial Cooking Equipment*. Contact the National Fire Protection Association, 1 Batterymarch Park, Quincy, Massachusetts.

14. Further information on kitchen ventilation system cleaning and maintenance is available from the International Exhaust Cleaning Association (IKECA), www.ikeca.org.

15. See National Fire Protection Association 17A, "Standard for Wet Chemical Extinguishing Systems."

16. The National Fire Protection Association videos *Fighting Fires with Portable Extinguishers, Fire Extinguishers: Fight or Flight,* and *Fire Brigade Training Program* are all useful for this purpose.

17. Ellis and Stipanuk, Chapter 3.

18. The titles in the series are *Employee Awareness and Problem Prevention, Key Control and Guest Privacy, Protecting Your Property and Guests,* and *Handling Disturbances.* For more information, contact the Educational Institute, P.O. Box 1240, East Lansing, Michigan 48826, or call (517) 372–8800. The Internet address is www.ei-ahla.org.

Key Terms

fire damper—A device installed in ductwork that limits the spread of fire, usually activated by the melting of a link that holds it in its normally open position.

heat detector—A device that reacts to the absolute temperature in a location (fixed temperature detectors), to a change in the temperature of a space (rate-of-rise detectors), or to a combination of the two (rate-compensation detectors). Likely to be used where smoke detectors function poorly, such as in dusty locations.

key control—The coordinated effort to establish and maintain the security of a property's locking systems.

risk management—An integrated effort to reduce the causes and effects of safety- and security-related incidents of all types.

single-station smoke detector—A smoke detector containing an integral alarm powered by a dedicated electrical circuit.

smoke damper—A device installed in ductwork that inhibits the movement of smoke.

smoke detector—A photoelectric or ionization device that reacts to the presence of smoke.

smoke sensor—A device that controls smoke by operating smoke dampers and by shutting down the air handling system when smoke is detected.

stairwell pressurization system—A system that increases the air pressure in stair-wells, thereby keeping the stairwells relatively smoke-free during a fire.

voice alarm system—A system integrating some sort of warning alarm with a pre-recorded or live message providing guests with information about proper proce-dures in case of a fire.

Review Questions

1. What are some factors that may contribute to the high employee injury rates in hotels? In food service?

2. What actions might help reduce employee injuries? How might some of these actions cause other problems at the operation?

3. What steps can be taken to reduce the chance that guests and employees will injure themselves in the guest bathroom?

4. What are some of the challenges facing lodging and food service operators with regard to fire safety? How can an operator deal with these challenges?

5. What are the five basic elements of a fire safety program? How do these elements fit together into a coherent whole? What happens when one or more of the elements are missing?

6. What are the purposes of a fire notification system? How might this system differ from property to property? What elements of the system will depend on the types of guests that typically visit the operation?

7. Why is it critical that in-house and contract maintenance personnel understand the design intent of the fire control system? What sorts of maintenance actions all too often compromise this design intent?

8. How do physical facilities and managerial practices combine to create a high level of security? How can facility design help to prevent crime?

9. What are the "five R's of key control"? What role does key control play in a hotel's security efforts? What problems can arise when key control is lax?

10. What are the advantages of using electronic locks? Are there any disadvantages?

Internet Sites

For more information, visit the following Internet sites. Remember that Internet addresses can change without notice. If the site is no longer there, you can use a search engine to look for additional sites.

Federal Emergency Management Administration
http://www.fema.gov

Loss Prevention Management Institute
http://www.hrm.uh.edu

National Fire Protection Association
http://www.nfpa.org

U.S. Department of Labor—Bureau of Labor Statistics—Safety and Health Statistics
http://www.bls.gov/oshhome.htm?H6

U.S. Department of Labor— Occupational Safety and Health Administration
http://www.osha.gov

Chapter 6 Outline

Competencies

1. Outline water usage levels and patterns in the lodging industry, and describe the basic structure of water and wastewater systems. (pp. 163–168)

2. Identify various potential water quality problems, outline major water heating concerns and options, and identify various water system maintenance concerns. (pp. 168–176)

3. Explain how lodging properties can use water for entertainment and recreational purposes, describe issues associated with swimming pool water systems, and summarize water conservation issues pertinent to the lodging industry. (pp. 176–181)

6

Water and Wastewater Systems

Outside of a few private homes, hotels were the bastions of luxury and comfort—and indoor plumbing. In 1829, the brilliant young architect, 26-year-old Isaiah Rogers, sent ripples of awe throughout the country with his innovative Tremont Hotel in Boston. It was the first hotel to have indoor plumbing and became the prototype of a modern, first-class American hotel.

The four-story structure boasted eight water closets on the ground floor, located at the rear of the central court. The court was connected by glazed corridors to the bedroom wings, dining room and rotunda.

The bathrooms in the basement were fitted with cold running water which also went to the kitchen and laundry. The bathtubs were copper or tin and probably had a little side-arm, gas furnace attached at one end. Perhaps shaped like a shoe as the French and English models, the water in the tub would flow and circulate backwards until the entire bath was heated to satisfaction.

In the Tremont, water was drawn from a metal storage tank set on top of the roof, the recently invented steam pump raising the water on high. A simple water carriage system removed the excretal water to the sewerage system. As with other individual buildings of the time, each had its own source of water and removal.

Five years later in New York City, Rogers surpassed his achievements of the Tremont Hotel. He built the Astor House with six stories, featuring 17 rooms on the upper floors with water closets and bathrooms to serve 300 guest rooms. The Astor and the Tremont were the first modern buildings built with extensive plumbing. (In contrast, the Statler Hotel in Buffalo caused a sensation in 1908 by offering "A room with a bath for a dollar and a half.")

— The History of Plumbing[1]

WATER IS USED at lodging establishments for bathing and sanitary purposes in guestrooms, for drinking, and for cleaning activities in and about the facility. In addition, water is used for sanitizing purposes and cooking in restaurants, for cleaning in laundry operations, for recreational or landscaping purposes (such as in swimming pools or decorative ponds), for fire safety systems, and as a cooling

Exhibit 1   Water Consumption in the Lodging Industry

By Size	Gallons per Available Room per Day Median Usage
<75 rooms	101
75–149 rooms	124
150–299 rooms	153
300–499 rooms	184
500+ rooms	208
By Group	
Resort/Casino/Conference Center (N=56)	254
Convention/Midmarket (N=170)	153
Limited Service/Economy (N=72)	94
Deluxe (N=14)	232
Luxury/First Class (N=185)	174
All Suite: Economy & Upscale (N=11)	139

Source: Michael Redlin and Jan deRoos, *Water Consumption in the Lodging Industry* (Washington, D.C.: Research Foundation of the American Hotel & Lodging Association, 1990).

medium for various pieces of equipment. Most of the water "used" at a property is disposed of through the property's sewer system. Exceptions to this are the makeup water used in cooling towers and swimming pools and the water used on lawns and shrubs.

An important subcategory of water usage is hot water usage, which costs the property not only for the water but also for the energy used to heat the water. Depending on the fuel sources used for water heating, the cost of the heat can range from 4 to 20 times the cost of the water.

The hospitality industry is clearly concerned about water and wastewater issues. Many resort operations rely on access to pristine bodies of water as major guest attractions. The expansion of hospitality facilities is limited in some areas by the availability of adequate water supplies or the capacity of wastewater treatment systems. In other locations, water shortages have led to water rationing. Even where water sources are adequate, water treatment costs sometimes skyrocket or water quality deteriorates significantly as more marginal supplies must be used. For resorts and other facilities that rely on wells or non-municipal water supplies, the quality of these sources is a major concern.

Water Usage in the Lodging Industry

Annual water usage by the U.S. lodging industry is in the hundreds of billions of gallons and costs millions of dollars. Levels of actual usage and cost for individual hotels vary significantly by type of hotel, location, facilities, and managerial attention to water usage. Exhibit 1 shows median water consumption data for lodging properties of different sizes and types or markets. These data show that:

- Larger properties generally use more water per room than do smaller properties.

- As the level of services and amenities increases, so does the amount of water consumption.

Further analysis of water consumption data indicates that the presence of on-site laundry, kitchens, extensive irrigation, and cooling towers can significantly affect total water consumption. For example, hotels with on-site laundry operations for which study data are available showed laundry water consumption ranging from 5 to 29 percent of total water usage. Similar ranges existed for the percentage of total consumption represented by kitchens and cooling towers. For some properties, landscaping represented 20 percent or more of total water usage. The type of services, facilities (interior and exterior), and equipment affect not only total consumption, but also the distribution of this consumption in use categories.

The property manager will probably be most concerned about water costs. These costs are composed of two components, purchase and disposal (or potable water and sewer). The average cost for water (purchase and disposal combined) in lodging properties is $4.60 per 1,000 gallons. On the average, purchase costs account for about 50 percent of water costs; disposal costs account for the remaining 50 percent.

Utilities often assume that the amount of water disposed of in the sewer system matches the amount of water purchased. However, not all water used at hospitality facilities enters the sewer system—for example, that used for cooling towers and irrigation. In consideration of this fact, many water utilities do not charge for the disposal of water that can be shown not to have entered the sewer system. The high cost of disposal highlights the potential benefit of using a **deduct meter** on the water supply to cooling towers, irrigation, and (to a lesser extent) the swimming pool, which together can constitute 50 percent or more of a facility's total water usage (although about 20 percent is more typical). The deduct meter submeters water used for these purposes so that it can be deducted from the disposal bill. The data indicate that this would reduce the cost of water used for these purposes by about 50 percent—a significant potential savings.

The study showed that 60 percent of those facilities with cooling towers and 40 percent of those with irrigation use deduct meters. Since 75 percent of the water utilities studied allow for deduct metering, these percentages indicate that many properties that would benefit from deduct metering do not use it.

Given the relatively low water usage attributable to swimming pools in the study, the benefit of using deduct meters on pools is much more limited than on cooling towers or irrigation. This is probably one of the reasons only 22 percent of properties with pools use deduct meters.

Water Systems

Water may be supplied from a variety of sources, including rivers, lakes, wells, rainwater collection, and the ocean (via desalination). Operations may purchase water from a water utility or get it from a facility they operate.

Exhibit 2   Building Water Systems and Uses

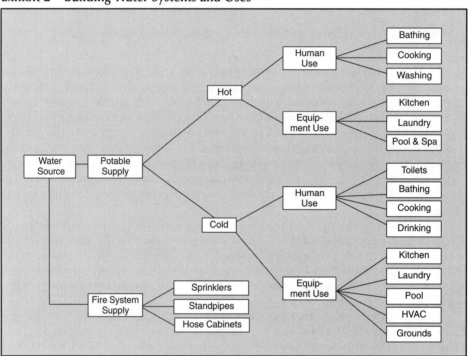

Building water and wastewater systems actually consist of a number of sub-systems with appropriate isolation devices between the subsystems. Exhibit 2 illustrates the more common of these various subsystems. Each subsystem may have special equipment installed to create water conditions appropriate for the use being served. For example, in providing hot water for use in the laundry, the property will often put the water through a softener and then a water heater dedicated to the laundry application.

The subsystems shown in Exhibit 2 often have their own subsystems. The chilled and heated water circulated in the building cooling and heating systems is *not* part of what is typically considered the building water system. The water in such systems is *not* potable (drinkable).

In the building water system, pipes made of galvanized iron, steel, copper, or plastic (PVC or CPVC) contain water under pressure. The pressure is supplied by the water utility, pumps at the property, or a combination of these. The pipes contain valves that may be used to isolate various elements of the system, shutting off the supply of water to these elements or to the entire system. Other valves, called **backflow preventers,** are used to prevent water from flowing from one subsystem to another—for example, a backflow preventer or an outside hose connection can prevent water standing in the hose from re-entering the building water system.

Building wastewater systems and their subsystems are shown in Exhibit 3. The **storm sewer system** is involved in the disposal of rainwater. It flows directly

Exhibit 3 Primary Subdivisions of Property Wastewater Systems

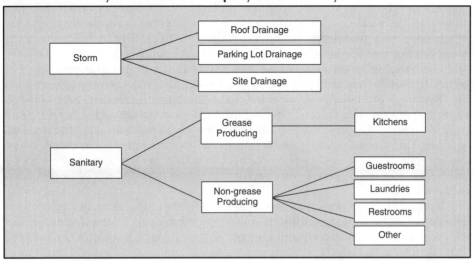

to some discharge location where the rainwater enters a river, lake, or other drainage system. In contrast, the **sanitary sewer system** is involved in the removal of waste products from the facility. This system carries waste products to a sewage treatment facility.

Building wastewater systems are generally designed to use a gravity flow system. Pumps are used only when necessary. This is the reason the bathroom ceilings in lodging facilities are often lower than the ceilings in other parts of the guestrooms—the facilities in the rooms above need space to run waste lines which rely on a gravity flow. Piping systems for wastewater use cast iron or plastic piping (usually PVC) and are designed to withstand lower pressures than water systems. Valves are rarely found in wastewater systems at the property level. Anything that slows or constricts flow in gravity flow systems should be avoided.

The grease-producing wastewater systems will flow through a **grease separator** (also known as a grease trap). Most municipal sewage treatment systems require the removal of grease because of its negative effect on waste treatment system operation. Grease separators are mounted either in the floor area or attached to a piece of equipment. Wastewater enters the top of the unit, slows its flow in a holding tank (which encourages separation of grease), and then moves toward the outlet, where it is filtered before discharge to the sanitary sewer. Grease separators should be periodically cleaned or pumped to remove the grease buildup; this task is often performed by a contract service. If additional filters are present in the separator, these should be checked, cleaned, and replaced as needed.

A few properties operate their own sewage treatment facilities. While some small operators function with a septic tank under these circumstances, most others operate packaged wastewater treatment plants. Proper operation of these facilities is extremely important because of the potentially adverse environmental consequences that can result from malfunctions. However, this extremely specialized operating and maintenance need is beyond our scope. Operators with on-site sewage treatment facilities are encouraged to contact their state office of environmental protection, their state health department, or the equipment supplier for operating suggestions and guidelines. One good source for operating instructions is the Water Environment Federation, 601 Wythe Street, Alexandria, Virginia 22314-1994.

The building water systems are usually designed to group rooms together vertically, particularly in high-rise designs. In addition, whether high-rise or low-rise, buildings are usually designed to have the guest bathrooms back-to-back. These two design features result in a grouping of rooms in sets of two by floor and vertically within the guestroom blocks for the supply of potable water and removal of waste. This grouping into plumbing **risers,** as they are known, has maintenance implications. It will sometimes be necessary to shut down groups of rooms above and below a location with a water system problem in order to perform needed maintenance.

Water supply systems may use a small recirculation loop on hot water lines to keep hot water flowing within the pipes of the building. Doing this minimizes the chance that a guestroom will end up at the end of a long pipe full of cold "hot" water.

Because wastewater systems rely on gravity flow and are open to atmospheric pressure on the user's end, they are vented to the atmosphere and have **traps.** Traps are water-filled sections of pipe that keep sewer gases and odors from entering the building.

Both water and wastewater systems may utilize insulated pipes. Water system pipes are insulated to prevent heat loss from hot water piping and to prevent condensation on cold water piping. Roof drain piping is also often insulated to prevent condensation that can lead to wet walls and ceilings. When maintenance or renovation involving water systems is performed, replacement of this insulation is very important.

Water systems for fire protection include sprinklers and fire standpipes. Standpipes are used for hose systems installed at the property and for supplying hoses brought by the fire department. These fairly simple systems require little actual maintenance, relying on water supplied from the water main or the hydrant and pump of the fire truck.

It is much easier to meet maintenance and emergency needs related to water systems if the elements of each subsystem are clearly identified. Each pipe, valve, and pump should indicate the subsystem it belongs to and the flow direction within the piping. Since pipes are also used to circulate water for HVAC applications, a code is sometimes developed to identify piping. Often, the code is alphabetic (CWR for chilled water return, for example); sometimes, a color code system is used. Maintenance staff and key management personnel should know the location of water system shutoffs in order to reduce potential damage during emergencies.

Water Quality

Water quality involves a number of elements that differ in importance, depending on how the water is used. The most important concern is clearly related to

potability—that is, suitability for drinking. Potability is of specific concern to guests and employees. It involves examining a variety of criteria, including the presence in the water of bacteria, nitrates, trace metals, and organic chemicals. Other water quality concerns not directly related to potability include color, odor, taste, clearness, mineral content, and acidity/alkalinity.

Any property relying on wells, lakes, streams, or water supplied by small water utilities should regularly test the quality of its water source. The Environmental Protection Agency estimates as many as 20 percent of the public water systems in the United States do not meet minimum water quality standards. The number of private systems failing to meet these standards is probably higher.

Potability concerns were at one time largely limited to concerns about coliform bacteria (which indicate the presence of human or animal feces in the water supply). Such contamination can occur when a well is used and the well becomes contaminated by a nearby septic system. Treatment via chlorination is the common solution, although iodinization or ultraviolet radiation is applied in some instances.

More recent potability concerns have extended to fertilizers, pesticides, herbicides, gasoline and other hydrocarbons, and a variety of heavy metals. These contaminants may have little effect on guests (because their stays are short). However, if present in sufficient quantities, they may well affect employees. Removing most of these contaminants is possible with the installation of rather expensive treatment systems, such as reverse osmosis. Because some water quality tests offered by local health departments and by vendors selling water treatment equipment are not comprehensive, specific testing for these contaminants should be requested. See Exhibit 4 for a list of maximum permissible levels for several contaminants.

Water quality concerns also involve a number of issues not directly related to potability. These problems may be largely aesthetic (odor and turbidity, for example), or they may be relevant for water-using equipment (such as hardness—that is, the presence of dissolved minerals). These problems are generally solved through the use of firms specializing in water treatment. Specialists are particularly required when the problems involve microbial growths in locations such as cooling towers (a topic we will return to later).

A common treatment method is the **softening** of water to reduce high levels of calcium, magnesium, and low levels of manganese and iron in the water supply. Calcium and magnesium will create scale (a buildup of the minerals) in boilers and water heaters and on heating elements. In addition, hard water makes it difficult to generate a lather with soap, creates an irksome soap scum, and leaves mineral spots when it evaporates—which can reduce linen quality and life. Iron and manganese stain plumbing fixtures and linens. A water quality expert should determine the level of softening required, because over-softening can create problems with pipe and equipment corrosion. Since softening involves the replacement of the hardness-causing minerals with sodium, softened water should not be used for potable purposes except under special circumstances.

Water softening systems are generally low maintenance. Refilling the brine tank with salt and checking the backwash circuit timing may be all that is required. Periodically, the zeolite (that is, the material in the softener that actually removes

Exhibit 4   Water Quality Standards: Maximum Contaminant Levels of Selected Contaminants

Contaminant	Maximum Contaminant Level
Distribution System Turbidity	5.0 NTU (MCL)
Coliform Bacteria	5% positive (MCL)
Free Chlorine	0.05 mg/l (minimum level)
Arsenic	0.05 mg/l
Chromium	0.05 mg/l
Fluoride	2.2 mg/l
Lead	0.015 mg/l
Copper	1.3 mg/l
Iron	0.30 mg/l
Manganese	0.30 mg/l
Sulfate	250.0 mg/l
VOCs	0.005 mg/l

MCL = Maximum contaminant level—the maximum concentration of a contaminant that, by law, may be present in potable water

Mg/l = milligrams per liter

NTU = Nephelometric Turbidity Unit—a measurement of the amount of suspended solid (Turbidity) in water

VOCs = Volatile organic chemicals

iron and so forth from the water) will need replacing. This decision requires input from the supplier.

Discharge/Sewage Water

There was a time when hotels and restaurants did not pay much attention to the amount of water or the condition of the water they discharged into the sewer system. Managers only had to make sure that storm water was not entering the system and that grease traps were functioning. But times have changed.

Because of the high cost of waste treatment and the costs of enlarging water treatment plants, local governments are taking a closer look at the wastewater of hotels and restaurants. Of particular concern can be the water's discharge temperature and the BOD, FOG, and TSS values of the discharge. "BOD" stands for Biochemical or Biological Oxygen Demand—the quantity of oxygen used in the biochemical oxidation of organic matter under standard laboratory procedures for five days. "FOG" stands for Fats, Oils, and Grease—the amount of free-flowing and/or emulsified vegetable-, animal-, or petroleum-based fat, oil, and/or grease detected in standard laboratory test procedures. Total Suspended Solids—TSS—is the total suspended matter that floats on or is suspended in water and is removable by laboratory filtering. In addition, discharges of ammoniacal nitrogen and

Escherichia coli (E-coli) can be of concern. Allowable levels of these elements are established by the local sewage treatment authority.

Water conservation at hotels and restaurants can result in a more concentrated waste, with higher BOD levels. Poorly performing grease traps can increase the amount of FOG being discharged. Use of garbage disposals and pulpers can increase TSS values. Restaurants can find their annual sewer charges significantly affected by high BOD, FOG, and TSS levels in their wastewater. Data on 134 food service outlets in one region of the United States showed surcharges as high as $50,000 per year for quick-service restaurants; the average surcharge for the region's restaurants was $4,500 per year. Well-designed wastewater systems, properly maintained, along with chemical and biological treatments all can help to control wastewater costs.[2]

Legionnaires' Disease

Another important aspect of water treatment for operations with cooling towers involves Legionnaires' Disease (formally called *legionella pneumophila).* First diagnosed in 1976 at the Bellevue–Stratford Hotel in Philadelphia, this potentially deadly disease has since been encountered at a number of other buildings, including, but not limited to, hotels. The bacteria involved in this disease are widespread in the environment. A cooling tower, with its warm, wet, algae-containing environment, is a good place for bacterial growth. The cooling tower plume provides a means to place the bacteria into the air, where people may inhale them. A professionally designed and implemented cooling tower treatment program is among the best preventive tactics available for this disease.

Some hotels that have faced major lawsuits dealing with Legionnaires' Disease have been shown to have had essentially no cooling tower treatment program. Locating the cooling tower discharge near an air intake for the building has also been a contributing factor to outbreaks of the disease. While most major outbreaks in the U.S. lodging industry have been linked to cooling towers, the potential exists for transmission via showers, humidifiers, and spas as well. In fact, many non-U.S. outbreaks involved facilities other than cooling towers.

In addition to its harmful effects on guests and employees, an outbreak also causes long-lasting, extremely negative publicity. The Bellevue–Stratford, site of the first U.S. outbreak, was forced into bankruptcy as a result of guest cancellations and abandonment. Clearly, it is very important that management be aware of, and take action regarding, the Legionnaires' Disease problem.[3]

Water Heating

Hotels require large amounts of hot water for uses ranging from guest showers to laundry. The cost to heat water almost invariably exceeds the cost of the water that is heated. Hot water needs for guestrooms, laundry, and kitchen applications are probably the largest at the facility. Employee locker rooms and health club facilities can also be significant users. All of these needs are potentially different and should be approached separately.

Guestroom hot water needs exist at all hotels. These needs may be rather concentrated at some properties, occurring primarily during the early morning wakeup time. Properties generally try to meet these needs by using a combination of hot water storage and production equipment. In order to meet these concentrated needs, some hotels have resorted to increasing the supply temperatures of the hot water. This is a potentially risky method, since water temperatures above 115°F (46°C) at fixtures can scald users.

Mixing valves are commonly installed to control hot water temperatures. These valves are connected to hot and cold water lines and modulate the flow of these two water sources to deliver water at a constant temperature. These devices are often an integral part of a guestroom water system or a system component, such as a shower control valve. If installed properly, they serve to protect the user from high water temperatures and the resulting burns and scalds.

Hotels have faced major lawsuits as a result of high temperature water supplies. A burn case in Texas led to an award to the burn victim of over $3.5 million! In this case, a high water temperature and an improperly installed mixing valve combined to severely burn a guest who had taken care to test the water temperature before entering a shower. The operation of the hot water system was so erratic that, even with this level of care, the guest was seriously injured.

The lessons from this example are at least two. The first is that hotels need to keep safety in mind when establishing operating conditions for equipment and building systems. The second is that the installation of safety equipment must be done properly if this equipment is to function properly. The failure to do this at the Texas hotel not only created great pain and suffering for a guest, but also cost the hotel a large amount of money. There is no substitute for proper design, installation, and operation of building systems.

Since kitchens require water at 180°F (82°C), most system designers include a separate water heater or booster heater for kitchen needs. This sometimes involves a booster heater in a dishwasher. Laundry operations have such large needs for hot water over relatively short periods of time that they generally have a dedicated water heating system. The kitchen and laundry are sometimes provided with hot water from the same hot water system. This water is usually softened to help achieve proper equipment operation.

Water Heating Options

Choosing from among the various available water heating options involves making decisions about equipment and fuel sources. Exhibit 5 illustrates the equipment options and the fuel source options for each of these. **Directly fired water heaters** are probably the most common. These are the typical water heaters found in many homes, restaurants, and lodging establishments. A fuel is burned and heat is transferred to the water. For all fuel sources but electricity, a source of combustion air is required; the combustion gases are sent up a flue. Directly fired units may have integral or separate storage tanks.

Indirectly fired water heaters are more likely to be found at facilities with steam. The steam enters a coil or heat exchanger which transfers heat from the steam to the water. The steam is generally kept separate from the water in these

Exhibit 5   Water Heating Equipment and Fuel Options

Water Heating Equipment	Fuel Source(s)
Directly Fired	Natural Gas, Oil, LPG (liquefied petroleum gas), Electricity
Indirectly Fired	Natural Gas, Oil, LPG, Electricity
Heat Pump	Electricity
Waste Heat Recovery	Waste Heat (from refrigeration equipment or other waste heat source)
Solar	Sun

devices. Since a flue is required only where the steam is produced (rather than at the water heater), indirectly fired units can be placed in basements without access to outside air or at similar locations.

Heat pump water heaters (HPWH) extract heat from the air within a space, the outside air, or a water source. The HPWH uses a refrigeration cycle to remove heat from the air (or water) and transfer it to the water being heated. Since the refrigeration system operates on electricity, there is no combustion or need for a flue. HPWHs can produce relatively cheap hot water because the refrigeration cycle uses less energy than electric resistance heating. Also, the refrigeration cycle *transfers* heat with greater efficiency than electric resistance and gas-fired water heaters *create* heat. HPWHs can pay for themselves very quickly, sometimes in less than one year.

With regard to operating costs, waste heat recovery and solar energy are probably the least expensive types of water heating equipment. However, the capital investments associated with each can be rather substantial. Waste heat recovery water heating is most commonly done from the condenser of a refrigeration system, where as much as 15,000 Btu of energy are rejected for each ton (or 12,000 Btu per hour) of cooling capacity.[4] Consider installing waste heat recovery devices on equipment with long operating hours per year, such as large food service refrigeration systems. Waste heat recovery water heating is also done at operations that have on-site electric power production.

Solar energy has seen limited use for water heating, primarily in sunny locations. While the fuel cost to provide hot water in this manner is low, the equipment itself can be somewhat costly. Solar water heating requires an expanse of sun-facing area, usually on a roof, and provision for hot water storage (since hot water is needed when the sun is down). At this time, solar water heating is not the option of choice for most operations, although island resorts and some warm climate locations use it rather extensively.

All water heating systems will have their costs of operation dictated by the efficiency of the water heating appliance, the cost of the fuel, the amount of hot

Exhibit 6   Water Heating Costs per 1,000 Gallons for Various Fuel Sources

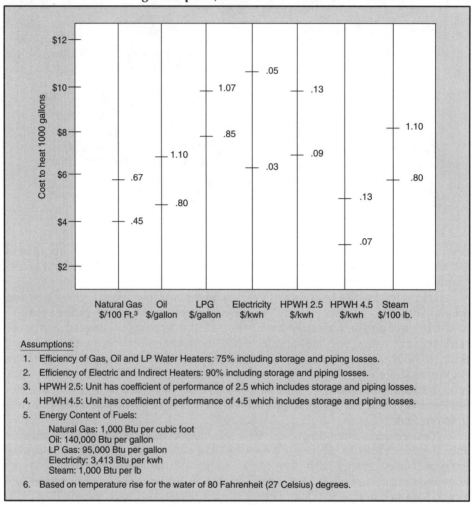

Assumptions:
1. Efficiency of Gas, Oil and LP Water Heaters: 75% including storage and piping losses.
2. Efficiency of Electric and Indirect Heaters: 90% including storage and piping losses.
3. HPWH 2.5: Unit has coefficient of performance of 2.5 which includes storage and piping losses.
4. HPWH 4.5: Unit has coefficient of performance of 4.5 which includes storage and piping losses.
5. Energy Content of Fuels:
   Natural Gas: 1,000 Btu per cubic foot
   Oil: 140,000 Btu per gallon
   LP Gas: 95,000 Btu per gallon
   Electricity: 3,413 Btu per kwh
   Steam: 1,000 Btu per lb
6. Based on temperature rise for the water of 80 Fahrenheit (27 Celsius) degrees.

water used, and the overall temperature rise of the water. Exhibit 6 illustrates the cost of water heating for various fuel sources as a function of the cost of the fuel source. Electric resistance water heating is generally the most expensive option. Heat pump water heating systems (which use electricity) can be competitive from an operating standpoint with oil or gas water heating systems.

Not shown in Exhibit 6 is the cost of water heating for waste heat recovery units. These units incur little or no energy cost for their operation, but they do have a capital cost greater than that of conventional water heating units. They are often used with a conventional water heating system as a backup, either because they are a retrofit item or because the backup is needed to ensure adequate supplies of hot water when the waste heat source is unavailable or hot water demands are very high.

Water System Maintenance Concerns

Although water systems require periodic maintenance, they are generally not a major consumer of maintenance time or cost unless they deteriorate to the point of needing major work or replacement. The preventive maintenance activities involved with water systems include such tasks as:

- Treating water to make it appropriate to the application or need
- Replacing sacrificial anodes (which decrease pipe corrosion) in water heaters
- Cleaning filters and strainers
- Lubricating pumps
- Checking hot water temperature settings
- Checking pressure relief valves on water heaters for proper operation

In addition, guestroom maintenance consists of the repair of leaking valves and general caulking and sealing around fixtures.

A facility manager (and owner) should be aware of the potential for corrosion and erosion of water piping systems. Corrosion is the destruction of a metal or alloy by chemical or electrochemical reaction with its environment; erosion is a literal wearing of a pipe's inner surface due to friction.

There are many types of corrosion possible; leading causes include:

- The pH of the water
- The amount of oxygen in the water
- The chemical makeup of the water
- The amount of galvanic corrosion from the use of dissimilar metals within (or in contact with) the piping system
- The temperature of the water

Facility managers can test the water's pH to determine whether the supply is overly acidic (or, in rare cases, overly alkaline) and requires treatment. Highly oxygenated water (say, in recirculating fountains) may also have a higher tendency to create corrosion. The chemical makeup of water can be quite involved, with a number of different chemicals contributing to the water's corrosive potential. Salts are corrosive; managers and others involved with maintaining swimming pools recognize the corrosive potential of the chlorinated water used in pools. Galvanic corrosion occurs when different metals come in contact with each other. Finally, any corrosion will occur at a faster rate as the temperature of the water increases. Corrosion is also possible on the exterior of pipes, particularly those that are buried underground. In these instances, there may be a reaction between the pipe and the soil/fill around the pipe, or there may be a leakage of groundwater into the soil/fill around the pipe (especially troublesome is the salt-laden runoff from streets and parking areas that have been salted to clear them of snow and ice).

Erosion of the piping system is another concern. Turbulence in water systems (resulting from water flowing at high velocity, pipe turns, and obstacles) causes a wearing of pipe surfaces and of protective oxides produced on the inside of copper piping. Water velocities in excess of four feet (1.22 meters) per second should be avoided. A factor that can accelerate pipe erosion is the presence of particulates (sand, metal filings, and so on) in the water itself. Adequate filtering of the water should help to keep these at a minimum.

The flame of fossil-fueled water heating appliances should be inspected periodically to ensure that proper combustion is taking place. The flue should also be checked for blockage. All water heating units should be inspected regularly for water-side mineral buildup and periodically cleaned and drained to reduce this buildup. If this is not done, the unit's efficiency and lifetime will be reduced.

Wastewater systems may require periodic clearing to reduce the chances of blockages and resulting backups. Traps may require periodic filling with water at some locations (such as floor drains in generally dry areas). Gutters, roof drains, and site drainage, all of which enter the storm sewer system, should be inspected and cleaned of debris. This can be particularly important before times of the year when heavy rains occur and when debris, such as leaves, is likely to have built up.

Guestroom maintenance generally involves the repair of leaking faucets and valves and the cleaning of clogged filters in aerating faucets (that is, faucets that spray water through a screen that spreads the flow). When problems occur, clogged drains need to be cleared either chemically or mechanically. When maintenance staff work on plumbing in guestrooms, they should also inspect the tile and caulk around plumbing fixtures and perform any necessary repairs.

Emergency and breakdown maintenance of water systems requires knowledge of the key water shutoff valves, the piping layout for both potable and waste water, and the appropriate cleanup equipment. Such equipment includes, at a minimum, a wet/dry vacuum and usually a pump as well.

Water for Entertainment and Recreation

Water is more than just a utility; at some hotels, it is a key element of the entertainment and recreational facilities of the property. Water is commonly used in exterior landscaping treatments—ponds, flowing streams, fountains, and more. Sometimes these elements are brought indoors. For example, at the Wilderness Lodge at Walt Disney World, a stream emerges in the lodge's lobby and flows to the outside. This is only the beginning. Outside, the stream becomes a waterfall; a geyser erupts as well. Disney also makes extensive use of water features in its theme parks

Many hotels and casinos in Las Vegas use water for entertainment purposes. The Treasure Island resort features a mock naval battle in a large "sea" where an eighteenth-century battleship sinks—every hour! The Bellagio resort created the "Fountains of Bellagio."[5] Completed in 1998 and taking up most of a small lake, the fountains employ 1,200 water jets (many of them motorized and synchronized) and more than 5,400 individually programmed underwater lights, choreographed to the music of Luciano Pavarotti, Aaron Copland, Frank Sinatra, and others. Designers, musicians, and performance artists helped mesh the movement of the water with the music. For many observers, the fountains seem to be alive, with a heart, soul, and emotions of their own. The fountains were designed to express the romantic spirit of the Bellagio.

The Fountains of Bellagio are a spectacular water attraction. (Courtesy of Bellagio, Las Vegas, Nevada)

Water features on the scale of those at Walt Disney World and Bellagio are certainly impressive and unusual. More common is the usage of water for recreational facilities such as water parks, slides, and surf pools. These features are becoming more and more elaborate and more and more common. Eight resorts in the vicinity of Phoenix, Arizona, have invested millions in water features such as falls, rivers and grottos, and slides. The resorts have seen 4- to 5-point increases in occupancy and 5- to 10-percent increases in average rates during the summer as a result of these water features.[6]

For those operations taking advantage of natural water features such as oceans and lakes, the water quality of these bodies of water is obviously very important. Blue Flag is an organization formed in Europe to improve and maintain the quality of beaches, marinas, and other marine environments. It concentrates on the following areas:

- Water quality
- Environmental education and information
- Environmental management
- Safety and services

Blue Flag works with local communities as well as the operators of beaches and marinas; it recognizes that businesses and communities must work together to

Exhibit 7   Typical Swimming Pool Piping, Filtering, and Heating Schematic

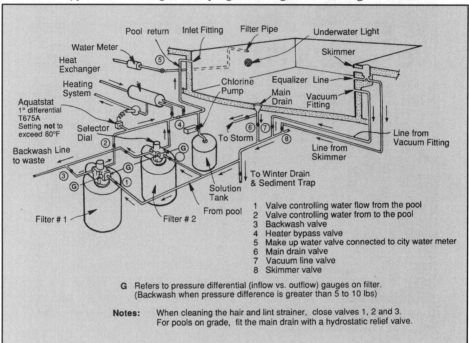

1   Valve controlling water flow from the pool
2   Valve controlling water from to the pool
3   Backwash valve
4   Heater bypass valve
5   Make up water valve connected to city water meter
6   Main drain valve
7   Vacuum line valve
8   Skimmer valve

G   Refers to pressure differential (inflow vs. outflow) gauges on filter.
   (Backwash when pressure difference is greater than 5 to 10 lbs)

Notes: When cleaning the hair and lint strainer, close valves 1, 2 and 3.
   For pools on grade, fit the main drain with a hydrostatic relief valve.

Source: Mel A. Shear, *Handbook of Building Maintenance Management* (Reston, Va.: Reston Publishing, 1983), p. 318.

improve and sustain their marine environments. Blue Flag is currently expanding globally.

Swimming Pool Water Systems

Many lodging facilities have swimming pools. Maintaining a safe and comfortable pool environment is an ongoing challenge requiring a significant amount of time and labor. The failure to do so can result in major problems.

Exhibit 7, which presents a schematic of a typical swimming pool piping, filtering, and heating system, helps to illustrate the areas of concern in pool maintenance and operation. Pool maintenance involves cleaning the pool, the equipment, and the water.

Pool cleaning involves skimming to remove floating debris and vacuuming to remove debris on the bottom. Walls, steps, and other areas by the pool should be brushed to remove dirt. Tile at and near the water level of the pool should be cleaned periodically (using an appropriate tile cleaner and equipment) to remove lime buildup.

Pool equipment is specially designed for the pool environment. Pumps are usually factory-lubricated and require little maintenance other than cleaning of the strainer and skimmer basket, which should be done daily. When the strainer is cleaned, various valves must be closed to avoid either draining the pool (if the strainer is located below pool level) or draining the pump suction line of the strainer (if the pump is located above pool level). The filter requires regular cleaning or backwashing (depending on the type of filter) in order to keep the water clean and to ensure sufficient flow in the piping system.

The cleanliness of pool water involves maintaining a proper balance of water temperature and acidity/alkalinity. Since the number of bathers, the intensity of the sunlight, and wind and rain (for outdoor pools) can all affect pool chemistry and conditions, the maintenance of proper pool conditions can be challenging. Failure to maintain proper conditions can result in disease or discomfort for swimmers, corrosion of metal pool parts, and leaching of plaster pools.

The balance between acidity and alkalinity is established by measuring the pH of the pool with a test kit. The pH should be between 7.2 and 7.6 (slightly alkaline). Pools naturally tend to become more alkaline than is desired. The pH can be controlled by treatment with muriatic acid or sodium bisulfate. Testing of pH levels should occur before chlorine is added, since residual chlorine levels can affect pH readings.

Another problem with pool water quality involves algae. Algae will clog filters and impart a disagreeable odor or taste to the water. In addition, algae interfere with disinfectants and can create slippery floors and steps. While normal chlorine levels are generally effective in controlling algae growth, they do not completely kill the algae. Killing of algae requires use of an algaecide on a regular basis.

Pool water treatment is also possible using ozone, ionization, or with chemicals other than chlorine. These methods may be used to supplement or replace chlorine or bromine. All pool chemical usage should be done in a safe manner, complying with the recommendations of suppliers and with local laws and ordinances.

Pool heating is necessary in many locations and is usually provided for all indoor pools. A temperature range of 70–80°F (21–27°C) for pool water and air conditions of 75–80°F (24–27°C) and 50–60 percent relative humidity are comfortable to most people. Pool water may be heated by a directly or indirectly fired dedicated pool heater or by a type of heat pump designed specifically for pool applications. Directly fired heaters for indoor pools have been implicated in incidents of carbon monoxide poisoning. This is caused by inadequate provision of combustion air and/or inadequate venting of exhaust gases. Managers need to check pool heaters for these conditions and rectify any problems they may find.

Heat pumps have seen increasing use as a means to control the interior environment around indoor pools, conserve pool water and chemicals, and reduce energy costs. Some units are installed in the pool exhaust airstream where they extract water (which is returned to the pool) and heat (which is used to keep the pool air comfortable). Others are located within the pool area and dehumidify and heat the air in this area. However installed, their overall effect is to reduce the humidity around the pool. This helps reduce corrosion, odor, and other problematic effects of humid, chlorine-laden pool air.

Pools and similar water-based recreational facilities pose some unique safety risks. One suggested checklist for pool safety is given in Exhibit 8.

Exhibit 8   Swimming Pool Safety Checklist

- *Review applicable state, county, and municipal regulations.* These provide the minimum standards you must comply with under the law.

- *Hire a certified, trained lifeguard.* If you choose not to have a lifeguard present, post a sign warning guests to swim at their own risk. Have an employee trained in emergency first aid present during pool hours.

- *Post a diagrammatic illustration of artificial respiration procedures.* Provide clear instructions to indicate when resuscitation should begin and advise that it should continue until professional aid arrives.

- *Make safety equipment, such as a life pole, immediately available.*

- *Make breaks between shallow water and deep water obvious.* Use ropes, floats, or a different color on the floor of the pool.

- *Enclose the pool with a fence.* This will control access and may prevent child-drowning incidents.

- *Clean, inspect, and repair the pool regularly.* Make sure all ladders are secure.

- *Install slip-resistant surfaces around the pool.*

- *Provide an emergency telephone.* Have emergency phone numbers posted.

- *Clearly mark water depth.* If your property attracts many foreign visitors, consider marking the pool in meters as well as feet.

- *Post a sign prohibiting diving.*

- *Post a sign prohibiting swimming solo.*

- *Post a sign with the pool's hours.* Make sure pool hours are strictly enforced.

- *Prohibit intoxicated guests from swimming.* Consider a ban on alcoholic beverages near the pool. If this is unrealistic, keep a close eye on intoxicated guests and restrict them from swimming.

- *Prohibit rough-housing at the pool.*

- *Keep a log.* Document the times you stop unacceptable behavior in and around the pool.

Source: Adapted from *Hospitality Law,* July 1999.

Water Conservation

With rising water costs, decreasing water availability, and governmental restrictions on water usage, hospitality businesses have several reasons to reduce water usage. The chapter appendix illustrates some possible water conservation methods as suggested by one governmental agency. In addition to these suggestions, proper maintenance and operation of valves on dishwashers and washing machines can help keep water usage at acceptable levels by reducing leaks.

The lodging industry has already done some things to reduce water usage. Some actions, such as installing low-flow shower heads, are common, due in part to the fact that they also save energy used to heat water. However, actions to reuse water (known as *gray water*) are less common (but growing). With increased pressure to reduce water usage, we may see further use of water recycling. But the need to have local officials approve such actions (in some instances) and to modify existing plumbing connections (calling for capital expenditure) are two major obstacles to water recycling.

Initiating water conservation practices that may affect guests should be done cautiously. One operation that installed low-volume shower heads received so many guest complaints that it chose to reinstall the previous shower heads. Another operation discovered—*after* it had installed new low-volume shower heads—that the poor condition of its piping did not allow it to raise water pressure high enough to operate the shower heads properly! Managers who are contemplating using water conservation devices should try a few as a test, monitor results, and evaluate the test before installing the devices throughout the property.

Water usage can often be reduced with little effort. Controlling landscape irrigation, installing foot-operated faucets in kitchens, and doing basic maintenance on water systems can be very effective conservation measures.

Endnotes

1. "The History of Plumbing—Part Two—Plumbing in America," *Plumbing and Mechanical Engineer,* July 1996.

2. Data provided by Foodservice Wastewater Consultants Inc., to the multi-unit architects, engineers, and construction officers' group of the National Restaurant Association, May 2000.

3. Further information on this topic is available in *Minimizing the Risk of Legionnaires' Disease*, available from the Chartered Institution of Building Services Engineers, Delta House, 222 Balham High Road, London SW12 9BS.

4. A Btu, or British thermal unit, is a measure of heat defined as the amount of heat required to raise one pound of water by one Fahrenheit degree. To convert Btu to kilocalories, multiply Btu by 0.252.

5. Information in this paragraph was pulled from J. Koski, "Going Where No Fountain Has Gone Before," *Plumbing and Mechanical Engineer,* July 1999.

6. Emergy H. Trowbridge, "The Marketing of Water Parks, Slides and Surf Pools at Resorts and Hotels in Arizona: A Case Study," *Journal of Vacation Marketing,* 1998, vol. 5., No. 1, pp. 82–93.

Key Terms

backflow preventer—A valve used to prevent water from flowing from one subsystem to another—for example, to prevent water standing in a hose from re-entering the building water system.

deduct meter—A device that submeters water that is used by a property but does not flow into the sewer system (for example, water used in cooling towers, irrigation systems, and swimming pools) so that it can be deducted from the sewage disposal bill.

directly fired water heater—The most commonly found type of water heater, in which a fuel is burned and heat is transferred to the water. For all fuel sources but electricity, a source of combustion air is required; the combustion gases are sent up a flue. May have integral or separate storage tanks.

grease separator—A device used to capture grease in wastewater before it enters the sewer system. Also called a grease trap.

heat pump water heater (HPWH)—A water heater that extracts heat from the air within a space, the outside air, or a water source and, using a refrigeration cycle, transfers it to the water being heated.

indirectly fired water heater—A water heater in which steam enters a coil or heat exchanger that transfers heat from the steam to the water.

potability—Suitability for drinking.

riser—A grouping of rooms in sets of two by floor and vertically within the guest-room blocks that share piping for the supply of potable water and removal of waste.

sanitary sewer system—A system that removes waste products from a facility and carries them to a sewage treatment facility.

storm sewer system—A system for the disposal of rainwater that flows directly to some discharge location where the rainwater enters a river, lake, or other drainage system.

trap—A water-filled section of pipe that keeps sewer gases and odors from entering the building.

water softening—The removal of calcium, manganese, and iron from the water supply.

 Review Questions

1. What factors could cause large variations in water usage for hotels of similar size?

2. When is using a deduct meter a good idea? What should you know before installing a deduct meter?

3. What is the difference between the storm sewer system and the sanitary sewer system? Which water subsystems flow into each?

4. How does the organization of plumbing risers affect maintenance needs?

5. What is the most important water quality concern? What are several secondary quality concerns?

6. What is Legionnaires' Disease? What steps should be taken to help avoid an outbreak of this disease?

7. When selecting a water heating fuel source for a new property, what factors besides price might be involved?

8. What safety concerns must be addressed when directly fired water heaters are used to heat indoor swimming pools? What advantages might heat pump water heaters have in such a setting?

9. What water conservation measures are widely applicable to, and used by, hospitality properties?

Internet Sites

For more information, visit the following Internet sites. Remember that Internet addresses can change without notice. If the site is no longer there, you can use a search engine to look for additional sites.

American Water Works Association
www.waterwiser.org

Plumbing and Mechanical Magazine
www.pmmag.com

Consulting-Specifying Engineer
www.csemag.com

PM Engineer
www.pmengineer.com

HPAC Engineering Interactive
www.hpac.com

Water Online
www.wateronline.com

National Spa and Pool Association
www.nspi.org

Water Web
www.waterweb.org

Chapter Appendix

Water Conservation Checklist

General Suggestions

Increase employee awareness of water conservation.

Seek employee suggestions on water conservation; locate suggestion boxes in prominent areas.

Conduct contests for employees (e.g., posters, slogans, or conservation ideas).

Install signs encouraging water conservation in employee and customer restrooms.

When cleaning with water is necessary, use budgeted amounts.

Read water meter weekly to monitor success of water conservation efforts.

Assign an employee to monitor water use and waste.

Determine the quantity and purpose of water being used.

Determine other methods of water conservation.

Building Maintenance

Check water supply system for leaks and turn off any unnecessary flows.

Repair dripping faucets and showers and continuously-running or leaking toilets.

Install flow reducers and faucet aerators in all plumbing fixtures whenever possible.

Reduce the water used in toilet flushing by either adjusting the vacuum flush mechanism or installing toilet tank displacement devices (dams, bottles, or bags).

As appliances or fixtures wear out, replace them with water-saving models.

Shut off water supply to equipment rooms not in use.

Minimize the water used in cooling equipment, such as air compressors, in accordance with the manufacturer recommendations.

Reduce the load on air conditioning units by shutting air conditioning off when and where it is not needed.

Keep hot water pipes insulated.

Avoid excessive boiler and air conditioner blow down. (Monitor total dissolved solids levels and blow down only when needed.)

Instruct clean-up crews to use less water for mopping.

Switch from wet or steam carpet cleaning methods to dry powder methods.

Change window cleaning schedule from periodic to an on-call/as-required basis.

Pools

Channel splashed-out pool water onto landscaping.

Lower pool water level to reduce amount of water splashed out.

Use a pool cover to reduce evaporation when pool is not being used.

Reduce the amount of water used to clean pool filters.

Kitchen Area

Turn off the continuous flow used to clean drain trays of the coffee/milk/soda beverage island; clean the trays only as needed.

Turn dishwasher off when not in use. Wash full loads only. Replace spray heads to reduce water flow. If necessary, use ponded water.

Use water from steam tables to wash down cooking area.

Do not use running water to melt ice or frozen foods.

Use water-conserving ice makers.

Recycle water where feasible, consistent with state and county requirements.

Recycle rinse water from the dishwater or recirculate it to the garbage disposer.

Presoak utensils and dishes in ponded water instead of using a running water rinse.

Wash vegetables in ponded water; do not let water run in preparation sink.

Use water from steam tables in place of fresh water to wash down the cooking area.

Bar

Do not use running water to melt ice in the sink strainers.

Laundry

Reprogram machines to eliminate a rinse or suds cycle, if possible, and if not restricted by health regulations.

Reduce water levels, where possible, to minimize water required per load of washing.

Wash full loads only.

Evaluate wash formula and machine cycles for water use efficiency.

Exterior Areas

Convert from high-water using lawns, trees, and shrubs to xeriscape—landscape design incorporating plants providing beautiful color and requiring less water. In the future, design landscapes requiring less water.

Inventory outdoor water use for landscaped areas.

Do not water landscape every day; two to three times a week is usually sufficient.

Stop hosing down sidewalks, driveways, and parking lots.

Wash autos, buses, and trucks less often.

Avoid plant fertilizing and pruning that would stimulate excessive growth.

Remove weeds and unhealthy plants so remaining plants can benefit from the water saved.

In many cases, older, established plants require only infrequent irrigation. Look for indications of water need, such as wilt, change of color, or dry soils.

Install soil moisture overrides or timers on sprinkler systems.

Time watering, when possible, to occur in the early morning or evening when evaporation is lowest.

Make sure irrigation equipment applies water uniformly.

Investigate the advantages of installing drip irrigation systems.

Mulch around plants to reduce evaporation and discourage weeds.

Remove thatch and aerate turf to encourage the movement of water to the root zone.

Avoid runoff and make sure sprinklers cover just the lawn or garden, not sidewalks, driveways, or gutters.

Water in winter only during prolonged hot and dry periods. (During spring and fall, most plants need approximately half the amount needed during the summer.)

This checklist provides water conservation tips successfully implemented by industrial and commercial users. This list has been revised from the original copy first published and distributed by the Los Angeles Department of Water and Power. The ideas presented are not intended as an endorsement by the California Department of Water Resouces of any method, process or specific product but are merely suggestions.

Source: California Department of Water Resources, "A Checklist of Water Conservation Ideas for Hotels and Motels."

Chapter 7 Outline

Competencies

1. Describe briefly various aspects and components of electrical systems, and cite important considerations regarding system design and operating standards. (pp. 188–192)

2. Identify elements of an effective electrical system and equipment maintenance program. (pp. 192–197)

3. Describe electrical system components: fuses and circuit breakers; distribution panels and wiring; electric motors, controls, and drive elements; electronic equipment; emergency power systems; and electrical maintenance equipment. (pp. 197–207)

4. Explain the billing methods of electric utilities, describe how to read electrical utility meters, state why electric bills should be checked for errors, summarize issues involved in deciding on a tariff (rate) for electric service, and discuss electric utility deregulation. (pp. 207–214)

7

Electrical Systems

If the electric current is to be generated on the premises, it should be, by all means, direct current. There is no possible point in using an alternate current generating plan for this character of building, unless it be to conform to the characteristics of an outside service. The cost of generating and distributing direct and alternating current for the building is approximately the same, but direct current is somewhat better for motors which require speed variation, and very much better for elevator work.

With current from an outside source, it is a case of take what you can get; but if this happens to be 25-cycle, alternating current, something has to be done about it. This low frequency gives a constant flicker in the lights which is noticeable, and in fact objectionable, to anyone who has not been educated down to it. If the frequency is 60-cycle, the character of the illumination and the wiring for lighting are the same as with direct current, and the lighting of the building can be thrown at pleasure from a direct current plant to an alternating service. In this case the converter equipment need be only large enough for the direct current motors, while with a 25-cycle service it will be called on to convert the total load of power and light.[1]

OBVIOUSLY, THE WORLD OF ELECTRICITY has changed since this excerpt, taken from a 1923 magazine article, was written. Today, alternating current and 60-cycle power are the rule in the United States rather than the exception, and most operations purchase their electric power rather than produce their own. The world of hotels has changed as well. Much more so than did hotels in the 1920s, modern hotels rely quite extensively upon electricity to provide for the needs of their guests and their employees.

Electricity is the most costly and widely used energy source within the hospitality industry. A high-quality, reliable source of electrical energy is required for the operation of equipment ranging from lights to computers to kitchen equipment to the air conditioning system. With the electric bill accounting for potentially as much as 90 percent of a property's utility costs, it is clear that controlling utility costs involves controlling electricity consumption in particular. Correct design, proper operation, and attention to the maintenance of electrical systems all contribute to a safe and comfortable environment for both guests and employees. And, as hoteliers in California were forcibly reminded during California's energy crunch in 2000 and 2001, reliable electrical supplies are crucial to daily operations.

Exhibit 1 Conceptual Diagram of Electrical Systems

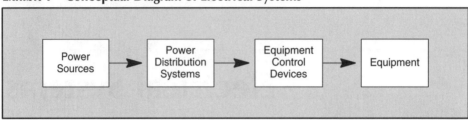

A Brief Introduction to Electrical Systems ————————

As illustrated in Exhibit 1 , electrical systems consist of a source, a distribution system, and control devices connected to various pieces of equipment. A proper understanding of these components will help a building operator to have a safe and efficient electrical supply system.

Although most lodging properties have the capability of producing power only to meet emergency needs, a few produce some or all of their own electricity. Lodging facilities may choose to produce their own power when the local utility's rates are high or the utility service is unreliable. Lodging facilities in remote locations (such as island resorts) are likely to have onsite electrical production capabilities.

Most hospitality operations, however, have their electricity delivered by a local utility. For some facilities located within larger complexes, the electricity may be provided by the building owner (who in turn generally gets it from the local utility). The utility is responsible for providing power at a correct voltage and frequency. The utility provides power through an electric meter that measures the rate and amount of power consumed. These data are used to generate the electric bill.

The utility services the building with electricity at a specified voltage and number of phases with the capacity to deliver a rated amount of current at a given frequency. The **voltage** of the system is a measure of the electrical potential provided by the utility (often compared with water pressure in a water system). **Frequency** refers to the rate at which an alternating current (AC) power supply alternates the direction of the current flow. This frequency is 60 hertz, or cycles per second, for North American electric utilities, but is different elsewhere in the world; many countries use a 50-hertz system. The number of **phases** (which is almost always either one or three) refers to the number of energized or "hot" wires in the electrical supply. The ampere capability of the service refers to the maximum current flow (measured in **amperes**) for the system. It is essentially defined by the wire size feeding the building. When facilities are expanded or significant amounts of electrical equipment are added, it may be necessary to increase the size of the electrical wires, thus increasing the ability of the service to deliver more amperes. Rewiring is a common need during renovations of older buildings.

In practice, a small U.S. restaurant might have a 120/208 volt, 500-ampere, three-phase electrical service at a frequency of 60 hertz. Larger hotels, motels, or

Onsite Power Production

While most hospitality businesses choose to rely on an electric utility for their power, there are instances where hospitality businesses produce their own power. Internationally, the term "combined heat and power" (CHP) is used to describe one mode of onsite power production; in the United States, the term "cogeneration" is used. Both of these terms refer to a situation where both a usable thermal output and electrical power are produced. This is mostly done with an engine generator, where the heat from the engine is used to heat water as a heat source for a heat-driven (absorption) refrigeration system. Some operations that are either supplied with steam from a steam utility or produce steam onsite may use the steam to drive a turbine to produce electricity and then use the "waste" steam that results. A few of these operations bypass the electrical production process and use the turbine to power equipment directly.

The Opryland Hotel in Nashville, Tennessee, has nearly 3,000 guestrooms, 600,000 square feet (55,800 square meters) of meeting space, and numerous restaurants, shops, and ballrooms. It also has a 5-megawatt, gas-driven turbine generator in a hybrid plant that includes 1,000 tons of absorption cooling. Thermal heat from the turbine is fed into a heat-recovery steam generator. This generator is capable of producing the 13,000 pounds (5,850 kilograms) of steam per hour that is used to drive the absorption chiller. The absorption chiller carries the hotel's air-conditioning baseload and runs all year long. The hotel enjoys huge savings through its efficient plant operation. In fact, operational savings provided a 5-year payback on installation costs.

Of increasing interest are smaller options for onsite power production. Chain restaurants and some hotels are investigating the use of microturbines (25 to 75 kilowatt) to provide some of their power needs, both to save on utility costs and ensure access to a reliable power source. This technology clearly has advantages for hotel and restaurant chains considering expansion into parts of the world that do not have reliable power systems. Several of these units can be used together, so this technology can be used for large facilities as well. Also being considered is heat recovery for domestic hot water and absorption cooling.

Finally, any discussion of onsite power production should include the use of emergency generators. It is possible for a hotel to configure its emergency generator to operate during peak electrical demand periods and thus reduce the peak power demand of the hotel. This can result in a substantial reduction in the hotel's demand charge (this charge is discussed later in the chapter). In some areas where the power grid is heavily loaded, electric utilities have requested that hotels and other commercial businesses use their emergency generators for this purpose, and have offered a reduced electricity rate for those businesses that comply.

In the future, we may see more and more hospitality properties using onsite power produced by photovoltaic (solar) cells integrated into the building's structure, fuel cells operating off natural gas or even hydrogen, and wind turbines (for properties in locations where this option would be feasible).

---

restaurants would be served with a 277/480 volt, three-phase, 60-hertz system with a current capability of up to several thousand amperes.

After the electricity is metered, it enters the distribution and control system at the property. Exhibit 2 illustrates the layout of a building's electrical system. This

Exhibit 2   Diagram of a Building Electrical System

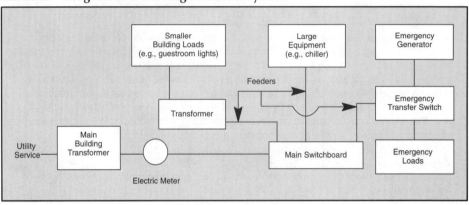

system splits the electrical supply into what are called **feeders.** Feeders deliver electricity to various portions of the building and to major equipment.

If the voltage supplied by the utility is not appropriate for all uses, the system will include **transformers,** which are devices that change (technically, *step up* or *step down*) the voltage of the electrical supply. In most larger hospitality facilities, the major equipment is operated at 208/277 or 480 volts. When guestroom applications require (for example) 120 volts, a transformer is used to step down the voltage. The main service transformer for a building may be owned by either the utility or the operation. Utility ownership saves the operation the cost of the transformer and the energy it consumes and relieves the operation of the responsibility for its maintenance. On the other hand, the business owning its own main service transformer usually pays a lower utility rate. A hospitality business may also own and operate other transformers to meet its electrical needs.

As we will discuss later in the chapter, certain loads are considered to be emergency loads. These are supplied from the utility service under normal circumstances and from an emergency generator or battery backup in other circumstances. The emergency transfer switch in Exhibit 2 serves to detect the interruption of utility power. When utility power is interrupted, the switch activates the emergency power source and transfers the emergency loads to this source.

U.S. hotels should be aware that electrical equipment brought in by guests from other countries may not work at all, may work erratically, or may even be damaged when connected to a typical domestic electrical system. For example, equipment that requires a 240-volt power supply sometimes can be connected to a 120-volt system, but with a large decrease in performance. In addition, since most such equipment is expecting a 50-hertz signal, the use of the equipment at 60 hertz may create other problems. Any device using the 50-hertz signal for speed or time control will run faster on a 60-hertz signal, even when a transformer has changed the voltage to 240. There are also problems with the reverse situation—U.S. travelers staying in hotels abroad. A U.S. traveler who puts a plug adapter on something like a hair dryer (manufactured for the U.S. market) and tries to use it abroad may

Exhibit 3   Plug Configurations Used in Overseas Locations

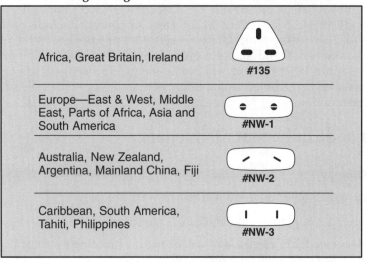

Africa, Great Britain, Ireland	#135
Europe—East & West, Middle East, Parts of Africa, Asia and South America	#NW-1
Australia, New Zealand, Argentina, Mainland China, Fiji	#NW-2
Caribbean, South America, Tahiti, Philippines	#NW-3

be greeted by sparks and a destroyed unit; this may even trip a circuit breaker in the hotel.

Plug configurations throughout the world are varied on purpose in an attempt to avoid the problems that can occur when equipment designed for one electrical system is plugged into another. Exhibit 3 shows plug configurations for electrical equipment in various countries.

System Design and Operating Standards

The electrical distribution system at the property should be designed and maintained according to all relevant codes and standards. These codes and standards are established to provide safe and reliable sources of electrical power. Failure to follow the codes and standards can result in problems ranging from equipment failure to a major fire.

In the United States, the codes for the electrical system are established by local governments. Generally, these codes are patterned after the *National Electrical Code (NEC)* developed by the National Fire Protection Association. The *NEC* and other codes are primarily concerned with safety. Their provisions should be viewed as minimum standards. The *NEC* and similar local codes cover such topics as proper wire size and type (depending on the load and location), methods to determine circuit loading and capacity, proper wiring conventions, and so forth. The codes change over time as new information is discovered and new materials are developed.[2] An older facility making major renovations may need to extensively upgrade its electrical system—both to meet current electrical needs and to meet the current code. Safety issues for employees operating or maintaining electrical systems are covered in the National Fire Protection Association's "NFPA 70E—Electrical Safety Requirements for Employee Workplaces."

Further legal requirements for electrical systems and safety are contained in the Occupational Safety and Health Act (OSHA). OSHA contains a large number of provisions for electrical safety. Major areas of concern include design safety standards for electrical systems, safety-related work practices, safety-related maintenance requirements, and safety requirements for special equipment. OSHA standards should be consulted when maintenance procedures are developed. They should also be included as minimum standards for electrical safety during maintenance.

System and Equipment Maintenance

Keeping electrical equipment from breaking down is particularly important, since this equipment is so important to the ability to occupy the building. For an effective electrical maintenance program, the following are needed:

- A current set of plans for the building's electrical system

- Good knowledge of electrical practices and the building's electrical system by maintenance personnel (and others when appropriate)

- Good housekeeping practices in areas containing electrical equipment

- Knowledge of and adherence to proper safety procedures

- Incorporation of electrical maintenance procedures into the facility's preventive maintenance program

Electrical Plans

A number of building electrical systems have terminals in the guestroom of a lodging facility. Therefore, the electrical plan of a guestroom provides a good reference for viewing a number of elements of the system. The electrical plan and the interior design plan must be closely coordinated to ensure that electrical services are provided at key locations.

Exhibit 4 is a copy of the electrical plan for a king standard suite. It also provides an introduction to some of the symbols used on electrical plans. This plan shows not only the electrical power systems, but also the location of the telephone, fire alarm speaker, smoke detector, TV antenna, and air conditioner control. The wires are generally not shown on the plan, since they would clutter the representation.

A building's electrical plans will be quite extensive. A major challenge with regard to these plans is to keep them current as modifications are made to the building. While updating plans is sometimes not thought of as a maintenance activity, it should be. Operations that do not update plans are essentially relying on the memories of their maintenance personnel. Such operations invariably find that, as the years pass, their maintenance employees leave or retire, taking important information about the building with them. A good set of plans on file can greatly speed the solution of a problem and may save a lot of money during renovations or other modifications to the building.

Exhibit 4   Sample Electrical Plan for a King Standard Suite

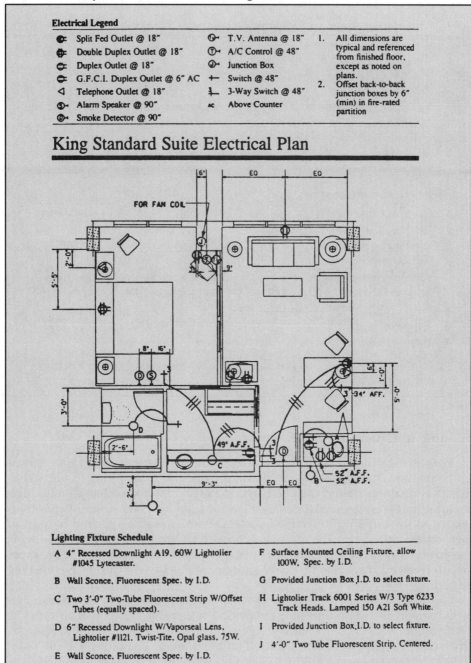

Electrical Legend

c: Split Fed Outlet @ 18"	**⊕** T.V. Antenna @ 18"	**1.** All dimensions are typical and referenced from finished floor, except as noted on plans.
⊕: Double Duplex Outlet @ 18"	**⊤** A/C Control @ 48"	
c: Duplex Outlet @ 18"	**⊕** Junction Box	
c: G.F.C.I. Duplex Outlet @ 6" AC	**+** Switch @ 48"	**2.** Offset back-to-back junction boxes by 6" (min) in fire-rated partition
◁ Telephone Outlet @ 18"	**ᒪ** 3-Way Switch @ 48"	
Ⓢ Alarm Speaker @ 90"	**ᴬᶜ** Above Counter	
Ⓓ Smoke Detector @ 90"		

King Standard Suite Electrical Plan

Lighting Fixture Schedule

A 4" Recessed Downlight A19, 60W Lightolier #1045 Lytecaster.

B Wall Sconce, Fluorescent Spec. by I.D.

C Two 3'-0" Two-Tube Fluorescent Strip W/Offset Tubes (equally spaced).

D 6" Recessed Downlight W/Vaporseal Lens, Lightolier #1121, Twist-Tite, Opal glass, 75W.

E Wall Sconce, Fluorescent Spec. by I.D.

F Surface Mounted Ceiling Fixture, allow 100W, Spec. by I.D.

G Provided Junction Box I.D. to select fixture.

H Lightolier Track 6001 Series W/3 Type 6233 Track Heads, Lamped 150 A21 Soft White.

I Provided Junction Box, I.D. to select fixture.

J 4'-0" Two Tube Fluorescent Strip, Centered.

Courtesy of Sheraton Corp.

Exhibit 5   Screening Questions for Electrical Maintenance Applicants

1. What color of wire is used for an equipment ground?
2. What color of wire is used for your power source?
3. What causes a hermetic motor compressor burnout?
4. How do you check a compressor to see if its windings are grounded to the compressor case?
5. If a three-phase motor is running backwards, what should you do to correct the problem?
6. How much voltage drop does it take to cause problems to a motor?
7. How many terminals does a domestic hermetic motor usually have? Name them.

Answers to Above Questions*

1. Green or bare.
2. Any color but green, white, or bare.
3. Moisture, high head pressure, single phasing on a three-phase unit, start winding not dropping out.
4. With an ohmmeter, you check for grounding between the case of the compressor to the start, run, and common windings and between the start and the run.
5. Switch any two legs of power to the motor.
6. Ten percent.
7. Three—(1) Start, (2) Run, (3) Common (Neutral)

*Note: Although these answers are correct for many countries, they may not be correct in every country.

Courtesy of Hampton Inns, Inc.

Training in Operating and Safety Procedures

Maintenance staff and other key personnel should receive training in those aspects of the building's electrical system that are pertinent to their jobs. Their performance evaluations should then be based in part on their knowledge and understanding of the system. Maintenance staff should be given a set of questions related to the building's electrical system. These questions should be part of their training program. The questions can also be used to test employees being considered for retention and/or promotion. It may also be advisable for the property to receive a magazine that covers electrical practices for use by engineering personnel.[3]

Basic questions about electrical system practices could also be included as part of an employment questionnaire for prospective maintenance staff in order to verify an applicant's competence with electrical systems (see Exhibit 5). Competence can be further verified by asking an applicant to demonstrate basic skills, such as wiring a circuit or testing a circuit for problems.

While most staff do not need specific training in electrical fundamentals, certain staff clearly need to have some understanding of the building's electrical system. Staff on duty at the front desk, especially in the evening hours, should know the location of circuit breakers and controls for various electrical systems, especially if an engineer is not always on duty. Staff should also know the location of the electrical disconnect switch for the building and the emergency generator. Staff responsiveness to guest and staff needs can be enhanced by clear labeling of breakers and controls.

Staff should also have a familiarity with the characteristics of the hotel's electrical system (voltage, frequency) and be able to answer guest inquiries as to the basic compatibility of foreign electrical equipment such as shavers, hair dryers, computers, and so on. Staff should also know where guests can find adapter plugs, either in the hotel or in nearby stores.

All staff should be made aware of the importance of reporting needed electrical repairs and of not operating equipment that has become unsafe due to electrical (or other) problems. Staff-caused electrical maintenance needs can be reduced if the staff observe good operating practices, which include the following:

- Keep equipment that uses electricity clean.

- Avoid storage of this equipment in damp or wet locations.

- Use a firm grip on the plug when unplugging equipment rather than pulling on the electrical cord.

- Match the equipment to the task. Overloading equipment may result in motor failure or other problems.

- Promptly report malfunctioning electrical equipment so that needed repairs can be performed.

- Do not perform do-it-yourself repairs or modifications to electrical systems and equipment.

- Do not use electrical rooms for the storage of items that block access to electrical panels, reduce air circulation to transformer rooms, or otherwise create potential safety problems or contribute to premature equipment failure.

When electrical maintenance is performed, safety concerns are very important. Lockout/tagout procedures should *always* be followed when work is performed on electrical equipment. (In the United States, OSHA mandates their use.) This involves locking out of service those circuits to be worked on so that another individual cannot accidentally energize the circuits while someone is working on them. Exhibit 6 presents excerpts from the procedures and forms used at one hospitality firm.

Electrical safety can often be an issue even in non-electrical maintenance. Because electrical service is needed for so many uses, electrical wiring can be found almost everywhere. Care must be taken when performing other maintenance tasks to avoid accidental contact with electrical lines. The following are some key safety tips:

- When performing onsite excavations, refer to a site map for the location of any buried electrical cables (or other utility services). This is one more reason to keep a good set of as-built and modified drawings. If any questions exist, use

Exhibit 6 Sample Safety Lockout Procedures

SAFETY LOCKOUT SHUTDOWN PROCEDURES

Depending on the type of equipment that is shut down for service or repair, the employee responsible for the shutdown must do one of the following:

Lockout the electrical disconnect and apply the appropriate lockout tag,

or

Throw the breaker at the electrical panel and attach the appropriate lockout tag.

or

Shut off the valve or equipment at the service location and apply the appropriate lockout tag.

If any piece of equipment is removed from service for a period of eight (8) hours or more, the reason for the lockout MUST be recorded in the Engineer's Log Book.

Failure to comply with the safety lockout procedures will result in the issuance of a written warning or possible employee termination.

THE ONLY PERSON AUTHORIZED TO REMOVE A WARNING TAG OR SAFETY LOCK IS THE EMPLOYEE WHO LOCKED OUT THE EQUIPMENT OR THE MAINTENANCE ENGINEER/AGM FACILITIES.

ELECTRICIAN'S BLOCKING TAG

FRONT   BACK

Courtesy of Hampton Inns, Inc.

a cable locator to determine the exact location. Anyone using onsite cranes, hoists, and front end loaders should always watch for overhead electrical lines. It is often easy to overlook these while concentrating on the load or the ground.

- Avoid electrical service locations when painting eaves and drain troughs or doing other work on the roof or sides of buildings.

- Avoid downed electric wires. Keep people away from these and call the electric company immediately.

- Avoid any tree or limb touching electrical wires. If a tree or limb falls over the wires, don't attempt to remove it. Call the electric company.

- Wear safety glasses and rubber-soled and -heeled safety shoes when working.

One other concern warrants attention. Older electrical transformers that contain oil as an insulating/cooling medium may contain PCBs (polychlorinated biphenyls). If an electrical fire occurs involving these transformers, dangerous chemicals can be produced. The U.S. government (through the Environmental Protection Agency) has issued numerous rules and regulations that establish conditions for the continued use of these transformers in commercial buildings. These rules and regulations cover such topics as registration with the local fire department, limitations on their location within the building, procedures for their removal and disposal, and a variety of other conditions. A failure to comply may result in significant fines and other penalties. Management should know and comply with these regulations. Contact the EPA for a complete set of regulations if you believe that PCB-containing transformers are present at your property.

System Components

We have already looked briefly at transformers and feeders. Other components of the electrical system are fuses, circuit breakers, motor controls, relays, and emergency power supplies and circuits.

Fuses and Circuit Breakers

Some elements of the electrical system are quite literally designed to "break down." These are fuses, circuit breakers, and light bulbs or lamps. Fuses and circuit breakers serve to interrupt the electrical supply when a current flow in excess of safe levels is detected. Safe levels are determined by the carrying capacity of the wires and local code requirements.

Fuses, more common in old properties, are designed and sized to fail when the current in the circuit in which they are installed is too great for the circuit capacity. The fuse failure indicates either an existing safety problem due to a short circuit or a potential safety problem due to wire overloading. Some fuses have a replaceable element and reusable fuse body, while others are completely disposable. Fuses may be screw-in plugs or cylindrical cartridges with either cylindrical ends or (knife) blade ends.

When fuses are used, care should be taken to replace them with units of the correct amperage and type. When installed on circuits with electric motors, fuses are often of a time-delay type. Such fuses allow a brief flow of higher current without burning out; this is necessary because a higher current is needed to start the motor than to keep it running. If regular fuses are used in place of time-delay fuses, they may fail whenever a motor starts.

Circuit breakers serve a similar function, but differ from fuses in that the circuit breaker may simply be reset, while the fuse or fuse element must be replaced. Normally, a tripped circuit breaker merely must be turned off and then back on. The ease of resetting these devices and their inherent safety make them the device of choice for many applications today.

One type of circuit breaker is the **ground fault circuit interrupter (GFCI).** This device, which provides a much higher level of protection than a standard circuit breaker, is largely designed to protect people. GFCIs are installed in such areas as bathrooms, outside receptacles, swimming pools, spas, and other areas where required by code, usually where electricity and water may both be found. A GFCI may be part of the wall receptacle or it may be a separate breaker in the breaker box. A built-in testing device is included. GFCIs should be tested as part of the regular preventive maintenance activity.

Fuses or circuit breakers should never be replaced with items of a larger capacity (amperage) unless an analysis of the circuit reveals that the wiring and other elements are capable of handling the larger load.

The burning out of fuses or tripping of circuit breakers—especially if it is frequent—is a sign of a potential problem with the electrical system that should not be ignored. Maintenance personnel should inspect fuse and breaker boxes. They should look for discoloration, a burnt odor, and other evidence of overheating or short circuits, debris and dirt, and moisture.

To avoid potential problems with vandalism and with electrical system tampering, fuse and breaker boxes should be kept locked. The key should be in the control of maintenance personnel or otherwise secured. Of course, it should always be readily available when needed.

Distribution Panels and Wiring

Next to the fuse and breaker boxes are the panels and wiring that distribute electricity to the building and its equipment. While these elements generally do not require much maintenance, there are preventive maintenance activities that may be undertaken with panels and wiring. Loose connections or overloaded wires can create safety hazards—for example, overheating can cause a fire. In addition, overheating and overloading can cause equipment to operate at conditions of voltage and current that lead to inefficient operation and even damage or failure.

Diagnosing problems in distribution panels and wiring is made easier when the following preventive maintenance actions are carried out:

- Check the tightness of all wiring connections to ensure adequate electrical contact.

- Measure the current flow in electrical circuits to be sure it is within acceptable limits.

- Measure supply voltages to electrical equipment to be sure proper voltage levels exist. This should be done under load (operating) conditions.

- Check the operating temperatures of wires, motors, and other elements of the electrical system. These should be within the rated limits of the equipment.

- Check the temperature rise in wires, terminal blocks, and motors. Values of 15 to 25 Fahrenheit degrees (8 to 14 Celsius degrees) above ambient may indicate potential problems, while those in the range of 45 to 90 Fahrenheit degrees (25 to 50 Celsius degrees) above ambient warrant immediate attention.

- Check the flow of electricity in three-phase circuits and supplies to ensure that the load on the three phases is approximately balanced.

Some older hotels may have aluminum electrical cables in lieu of the more common copper wires. Aluminum is a good conductor of electricity and is less expensive than copper. For these reasons, its use enjoyed a period of popularity some years ago. Unfortunately, aluminum suffers from a physical phenomenon called "creep" or cold flow that causes connections, especially those using set screws or crimps, to loosen. Loose connections cause temperature buildups and can be very dangerous. Properties with aluminum wire need to enforce a regular maintenance schedule to ensure tight connections. Later in the chapter the use of thermal imaging will be discussed as a diagnostic tool for overloaded electrical circuits. This is also a very useful tool to identify loose connections in aluminum wiring systems.

Electric Motors, Controls, and Drive Elements

Electric motors are found in many devices in a hospitality operation—for example, air conditioning equipment, vacuum cleaners, dishwashers, and the laundry. In addition, large motors power major pieces of building equipment such as the compressors in the chillers, air handling fans, and chilled water pumps.

Electric motors that are integral parts of other equipment, such as motors in guestroom air conditioning equipment and dishwashers, will be included in the overall preventive maintenance instructions for the equipment. Some equipment with hard-to-access electric motors may have little or no preventive maintenance performed. The level of preventive maintenance performed will vary significantly with motor size and the motor's importance to the operation. Remember, the goal of preventive maintenance is to help keep the *overall* cost of maintenance as low as possible while promoting proper and reliable equipment operation.

The preventive maintenance process will involve regular inspections during which operating conditions (such as voltage, current, and operating temperatures) are measured and noted, general conditions, noise, and vibration are observed, and cleaning and lubrication are performed. Operating conditions may indicate a need to change the frequency of maintenance. For example, a particularly dirty environment may warrant more frequent cleaning and inspection.

Exhibit 7   **Sample Preventive Maintenance for Electric Motors**

P.M. PROCEDURES: Electric Motors
MAINTENANCE ACTION #21
FREQUENCY: Quarterly – Annually

Maintenance Action #21Q

1. Inspect motor and check for unusual noise.
2. Clean motor.
3. Blow out dirt and dust.
4. Lubricate per manufacturer's specs.

Maintenance Action #21A

1. Carry out Maintenance Action 21Q.
2. Check bearings.
3. Check electrical connections tight.
4. Check running amps against nameplate.
5. Clean starter and replace contacts.
6. Check running temperature.

Courtesy of Days Inns of America

Exhibit 7 contains a sample preventive maintenance procedure for electric motors from one lodging chain. Quarterly activities involve inspection, cleaning, and lubrication. Annual actions include those normally performed quarterly, plus additional inspections, the measurement of key operating parameters, and some parts replacement. Because of the variety of electric motors and their applications, it is very important to write preventive maintenance procedures for each motor based on its type, its usage (especially its operating hours), and the manufacturer's recommendations for maintenance. Equipment warranties can often be voided if the purchaser does not follow the manufacturers' established maintenance procedures.

When electric motors are used to power larger devices, they do so via some sort of a drive mechanism. This may be a belt and pulley, a drive chain, or some sort of drive coupling. Preventive maintenance inspections of this equipment will involve not only the motor but also the drive mechanism.

In addition, the motor controls will need periodic attention. Motor controls are devices that provide an interface between an electric motor and the electrical system. They control the motor's operation, generally by turning it on and off, but sometimes by changing its operating speed. Relays also serve a control function; they open and close circuits in response to signals from control equipment.

When motors wear out or malfunction and cease operation, managers face a "repair or replace" decision. Some guidelines for this decision are as follows:

• When buying new motors (or equipment with motors), specify EPAct-efficiency motors. "EPAct" refers to the U.S. Energy Policy Act of 1992. This

---

Electric Motor Replacement Issues

Hospitality operations use numerous electric motors, some contained in equipment and others connected to equipment such as fans and pumps. When purchasing equipment, the efficiency of the electric motor used in the equipment is a contributing factor to the equipment's overall efficiency. However, it is often the case that there are few or no motor options to choose from when purchasing equipment; a piece of equipment tends to come with a standard motor, and no choice is given. It is when electric motors are up for repair or replacement that the operation has the opportunity to make a decision about motor efficiency.

In the United States, new government regulations have established minimum efficiency levels for electric motors. The motors sold today are therefore more efficient than those sold 10 or 15 years ago. It is possible to purchase motors that exceed these minimum efficiencies. This especially makes sense when the hotel is in a location with high electricity rates or when it is purchasing motors that are expected to have a large number of operating hours.

When purchasing a replacement for an electric motor, it is a very good idea to inquire as to whether the motor being replaced was correctly sized to begin with. Unfortunately, motors are often significantly oversized, and conservation efforts can make this situation worse by reducing the load served by the motor. If investigation reveals an oversized motor (that is, a motor that always operates at a current draw of approximately 85 percent or less of its full load amperage), managers should consider replacing it with a smaller motor. The property will not only save money on the motor, but also on the operating cost of the motor.

---

act specified minimum efficiency levels for equipment manufacturers to follow; motors produced after October 24, 1997, are stamped with their EPAct efficiency rating.

- If a repair will cost more than 60 percent of a new EPAct motor, buy the new motor.

Another thing to keep in mind when evaluating whether to repair or replace a motor is the effect repairs will have on the motor's efficiency. Efficiency losses of from three to five percent are possible when repairing standard motors; a loss of one percent efficiency is possible when repairing energy-efficient motors.

Another way to reduce the operating costs of electric motors is to install variable-speed drives on the motors. Variable-speed drives match the speed of the motor to the needs of the connected load, making the motor run more efficiently. The result is reduced energy usage, increased life of the connected equipment, and a better matching of motor output to the application.

Finally, when considering electric motors and their operation, attention to the motors' power factors is appropriate. "Power factor" is another measure of motor efficiency, having to do with the motor's use of alternating current and voltage. The goal should be to operate equipment with power factors in excess of 90 percent. When motors are operated below about 65 percent of rated capacity, their power factor suffers. Making the right decision on motor size helps to keep the power factor as high as possible. The result can be reduced electric bills.

Electronic Equipment

Although electric motors have long been subject to various power supply problems, the proliferation of electronic equipment in the modern hospitality industry has heightened the need for a high quality electrical supply system. Electronic equipment is especially sensitive to such power quality problems as voltage transients, momentary voltage sags and surges, momentary power loss, electrical noise, and harmonic distortion. (To a somewhat lesser degree, these power quality problems can also harm electric motors.)

Transients involve high voltage, short, fast electrical pulses that can destroy electronic equipment instantly or over a period of time. Sags and surges involve lower or higher than normal voltages. Sags may cause motor heating and disk drive problems, while surges may cause incandescent lights and computer circuits to burn out. Momentary power losses can disrupt data processing, electronic memory, and program functioning. Electrical noise and harmonic distortion are electrical signals injected into the electrical system by faulty equipment or certain types of electric equipment. They give wrong "signals" to sensitive electrical equipment, resulting in erratic operation and possible equipment damage.

The sources of these problems include natural phenomena (for example, lightning), normal utility operations (for example, equipment maintenance), neighboring utility customers (for example, a faulty electrical system in the business next door), and a business's own internal electrical problems. There are various possible solutions to electrical quality problems.[4] These include:

- Wiring-intensive solutions such as wiring upgrades, grounding/bonding upgrades, and isolation of equipment loads

- Equipment-intensive solutions such as surge suppression equipment, voltage regulators, isolation transformers, and battery backup units

Wiring upgrades involve the installation of large wires capable of handling the larger starting and operating loads of equipment. Such upgrades should help to eliminate voltage sags. Upgrading of grounding/bonding involves establishing good connections within the building to the electrical ground system and of the ground to the earth. This will help reduce stray voltages that can create noise problems. Load isolation places sensitive loads on separate circuits where the possibility of their being influenced by noise, sags, and other problems caused by other pieces of equipment is minimized. Exhibit 8 shows suggested equipment isolation where the "victim" is the electronic equipment and the "culprit" is another type of electrical equipment. Operations should also not operate portable equipment such as vacuum cleaners and other cleaning equipment on circuits that supply electronic equipment.

The equipment-intensive solutions will generally be the more expensive option, although extensive rewiring can also be costly. Surge suppression equipment limits the magnitude of voltage transients in order to avoid damage to sensitive electronic equipment. Installation of surge suppressors may be necessary at

Exhibit 8   Equipment Isolation Chart

Do not connect equipment shown in the victim column of this chart into the same circuit as devices in the corresponding culprit column.		
PROBLEM	**VICTIM**	**CULPRIT**
SAGS and SURGES	Check/Credit Approval System Main/Personal Computer Order Entry Terminal	Air Conditioning Unit Conventional Oven HVAC Equipment Industrial Mixer Refrigeration Equipment Water Cooler
TRANSIENTS	Bar Code Scanner Check/Credit Approval System Digital Scale Fax Machine Fire/Security System Main/Personal Computer Order Entry Terminal Phone System Point-of-Sale Terminal Video Product Display	Conventional Oven HVAC Equipment Industrial Mixer Lighting Control Refrigeration Equipment
NOISE	Audio System Energy Management System Fax Machine Fire/Security System Phone System	Copy Machine HVAC Equipment Industrial Mixer Refrigeration Equipment

Source: Edison Electric Institute, *Quality Power in Your Restaurant*, p.13.

the electrical service entrance itself, at the electrical panel where the circuit feeding the electronic equipment is located, or at the electronic equipment itself. Data lines feeding the equipment and such items as antenna leads are also candidates for this type of protection. Equipment purchased for this purpose should be UL (Underwriters Laboratories) listed as a transient voltage surge suppressor. It should have indicators that reveal whether it is functioning.

Voltage regulators address both sag and surge problems by providing automatic voltage adjustment. Response times of 1.5 cycles or less and operating efficiencies of 90 percent or better are recommended. Isolation transformers help remove noise from the system, but provide no protection against sags or surges. The device's ability to reduce noise is expressed in a dB (decibel) rating. A rating of 80 dB or higher should be chosen for adequate noise reduction.

Battery backup units help to supply power during utility power outages. They are discussed later under emergency power systems.

Exhibit 9 is a summary of the more common symptoms associated with electrical system disturbances, the problems that may cause them, the solutions, and a

Exhibit 9 Power Problem Ready-Reference

SYMPTOM	PROBLEM	SOLUTION	COST
Scanner Lockup Scanner Damage Inventory Data Lost Frequent Service Calls Digital Scale Damage	Transients (Spikes)	Transient Suppression	$1,000 to $7,000
Computer Reboots Early Compressor Failure Dim or Flickering Lights Early Lamp Failure	Sags and Surges	Upgrade Wiring Rearrange Loads Line Conditioner	$500 to $20,000
Order Files Lost Scanners and Computer Must be Restarted	Power Loss (Blackout)	Battery Backup System Reduce Exposure	$500 to $30,000
Unexplainable Order Errors Noise on PA System Random Data Error	Noise	Line Conditioner Battery Backup System Relocate Equipment Isolation Transformer	$500 to $20,000
Compressor Heating	Harmonic Distortion	Harmonic Filtering	$500 to $5,000

Source: Edison Electric Institute, *Quality Power in Your Restaurant*, p. 15.

range of costs. The cost effectiveness of any particular solution is clearly dependent on how likely the problem is to occur and the cost of the symptom. Many operations find that some form of protective equipment is warranted due to the large losses of time and money that can result from problems with electronic equipment.

Emergency Power Systems

Emergency power systems are present to provide power during temporary interruptions in the electrical supply to the building. Emergency power supplies and equipment include such items as generators and batteries to provide lighting and uninterruptible power supplies for computer systems. Although these devices are (one hopes) seldom used, they are greatly needed when called upon; therefore, their proper operation is very important.

The *National Electrical Code* provides for specific types of businesses in which emergency power is required and the types of loads that shall be connected to this power. Local code authorities may adopt this code or may modify it. Emergency systems are generally required in all types of hospitality businesses with the possible exception of very small food service establishments. Among the items generally required to be connected to this system are artificial illumination, fire detection and alarm systems, fire pumps, and public safety communications systems.

Battery backup units may be either standby power supply (SPS) units or uninterruptible power supply (UPS) units. The SPS units switch from utility power to battery backup when the utility power is interrupted. There is therefore a momentary power outage. One selection criterion for such equipment is the transfer time, which should be no more than 15 milliseconds. Another criterion involves voltage regulation, which should be within eight percent of the rated equipment operating voltage.

In contrast, the UPS is always on line. Power from the utility feeds the UPS, which stores this power in batteries and supplies the equipment with a "clean" power source using the batteries and electronics that create AC power. For UPS selection, efficiencies of 70 percent or more should be specified. For both UPS and SPS systems, the quoted prices of the systems should include the necessary batteries.

Emergency power may be provided by batteries alone in smaller buildings. Batteries will generally power lights in corridors, stairwells, and certain interior spaces such as meeting and conference rooms. If more than this level of power is needed, the operation will generally install an onsite emergency generator powered by an engine.

Onsite engine generators may be installed to operate only essential or code-required loads (such as emergency lighting and fire protection systems) or may be installed to provide power to additional loads. Among these additional loads could be the uninterruptible power supply for the computer systems, food service refrigeration, and key building heating systems (especially in colder climates). Engine generators are usually diesel-fired and require onsite fuel storage. Various provisions should be made to prevent the unit from transmitting noise and vibration to the building. Emergency loads are connected to the emergency generator by an automatic transfer switch (as was seen in Exhibit 2). This device supplies these loads from the utility service when it is present and switches to the emergency source when utility service fails.

Because code requirements usually call for a fuel supply capable of providing only two hours of full-load operation, the generator is of limited usefulness during long outages unless provision is made for extended operation. Battery-powered lighting systems provide light for even shorter periods of time.

Maintenance of emergency power systems is often a weekly task which involves the following:

- Checking fluid levels on battery systems. (Note: Batteries may be installed to provide emergency lighting or to provide starting energy for an engine generator.)

- Checking the charge level in batteries.

- Checking proper ventilation of battery rooms.

- Cleaning and lubricating battery terminals to retard corrosion.

- Testing engine generator systems under load. Because of the noise generated, maintenance staff should generally wear ear protection when doing this and should choose a time of day least likely to disturb guests.

- Observing and recording appropriate data regarding each engine generator test. This will include information required by local code authorities and for maintenance records, such as fuel supply, oil and coolant levels, switch settings, oil and water temperatures and pressures, and positions of any key indicator lights or gauges.

- Ensuring that the engine generator is put back on line after any testing or work where the emergency generator must be disconnected.

A properly functioning emergency power system provides insurance in the event of a power failure. The testing and maintenance of the system ensures that this insurance will be available when needed.

While it is not required by code, many operations install an uninterruptible power supply on key pieces of computer equipment. The UPS may be designed to allow either continued operation or an orderly shutdown of equipment. UPS units must be matched with the load being served and the time of operation desired. Computer operation during prolonged outages will be assured only if the UPS is also connected to the emergency power system.

Electrical Maintenance Equipment

The various maintenance activities discussed so far require appropriate equipment. This equipment should include the following somewhat specialized items:

- Multimeter—A device capable of measuring volts, ohms, and current over a wide range. Usable on both major electrical circuits and control and other lower voltage circuits.

- Wall receptacle analyzer—Used to determine the condition of wall outlets (sometimes called convenience outlets). This device plugs into a wall outlet and indicates the circuit condition. Reversal of the neutral and ground wires, the quality of the ground path, and the presence of multiple wiring errors are identified if present. This is a quick diagnostic for these components.

- Fuse pullers for cartridge fuses—These devices allow safe removal of cartridge fuses.

- Rubber boots, gloves, and insulated ladders—Safety equipment designed to reduce the contact with electrical equipment and the resulting flow of current to earth if contact should occur.

- Hydrometer—A device that measures specific gravity and is used to check the charge level in batteries.

Other items of electrical maintenance equipment which may be needed, depending on the complexity of the facility and expected duties of the staff, could include cable fault locators, transformer oil test kits, and vibration analyzers.

Because of the difficulty in accurately measuring temperatures in all elements of electrical systems, it is becoming more common for properties to use a thermal scan of the electrical systems as part of the preventive maintenance program. This scan involves the use of an infrared (IR) video imaging system that represents the object being scanned as an image whose color indicates the temperature of the object. The scan identifies overheating electrical components. Hence, it is possible to inspect the operating electrical system for potential safety or operating problems.

A thermal imaging inspection is generally a contract service. It may be implemented as part of commissioning a new building or as an element of the preventive maintenance program of an existing building. It can be particularly useful for older buildings having extensive wiring modifications that make the connected loads, wire size, and so forth difficult to evaluate. Chains and large hotels may elect to purchase IR scanning guns in order to have them available when needed.

Electric Utility Billing and Building Operations

As was indicated at the start of the chapter, the electric bill represents the bulk of a property's utility costs. Understanding the billing methods of electric utilities and their impact on building operations and operating costs can be very helpful.

First of all, there are literally hundreds of electric utilities in the United States and throughout the world. Virtually every one will have a slightly different way of converting electrical usage into an electric bill. Almost all of these utilities will generate a bill for a commercial establishment such as a hotel, motel, or restaurant in a somewhat different manner from that used for a residence. The major difference lies in the use of both an **energy** (or consumption) **charge** and a **demand** (or capacity) **charge** when commercial bills are determined. Residences typically only have an energy charge.

The energy charge is based on the amount of electricity used by the customer over the billing period. This electricity is measured in *kilowatt-hours* (abbreviated kwh). The kwh may be thought of as the amount of energy used by a 100-watt light bulb burning for 10 hours. As you can guess, the kwh isn't a very large unit of energy. A commercial establishment can use tens or hundreds of thousands of kwh in a 30-day period (the typical billing period used by utilities). The charge is usually in the range of $.06 to $.12 per kwh for business accounts.

The demand charge is something which residential customers generally do not pay (although they pay a higher charge per kwh than business customers to make up for it). The demand charge is based on the business's highest *rate* of energy usage. This rate, measured in *kilowatts* or kw, is usually determined by breaking the billing period up into a series of 15- or 30-minute windows and measuring the energy usage in each window. The bill is then calculated using the highest average rate of energy usage or demand in these windows during the billing period. Demand charges range from $3 per kw per month to as high as $20 per kw per month.

One way to think about the demand and energy charges is to think about the way rental car agencies bill for their product. Among the options is usually one which charges you a fee per day for the auto and a fee per mile. The fee per day is analogous to the demand charge. The larger the auto, the higher the fee. The bigger the demand, the higher the demand charge. The fee per mile is analogous to the energy charge. The more you use the auto, the more you pay because of the increased mileage.

Just as there are variations in rental car rate structures, there are variations in the structures of utility rates. Some utilities have rates that vary according to the time of year or time of day. Others have variations that depend on the relationship between the demand level and the energy used. Yet others will impose a minimum demand charge based on demand during some peak period of the year (rather than just during the current billing period). Under this billing practice, known in utility jargon as a **ratchet clause,** a high demand during one month can result in a high demand charge for the next 11 or 12 months. Often, the peak periods on which ratchet charges are based are months in which utility services are heavily used—summer months in cities and the southern United States and winter months in northern locations.

Because the demand charge is based on peak demand during 15- or 30-minute windows, operating practices can have a major impact on costs. One seasonally operated hotel that was up for sale turned on all the building's systems, lights, and so forth to prove to a prospective buyer that everything worked properly. This action established a high peak demand during a ratchet period and led directly to higher charges for several months. A more common scenario involves the start-up of building equipment following a shutdown or a power outage. Starting everything at once leads to high demand. Starting such equipment up in phases helps avoid an unusually high demand charge. One way to do this is to station an employee at the electric meter. This employee can follow the effect of equipment operations and communicate with other staff by phone or radio. Of course, operators with demand control equipment should be able to use it in this instance, provided the power loss or shutdown does not cause the demand control equipment to need re-setting or re-programming.

The energy and demand charges represent by far the largest portion of the utility bill. The mix between the two varies with the utility and the building. Some utilities have billing methods which weight the energy portion, while others weight the demand. It is not unusual for the demand charge to equal 25 percent or more of the total bill. In rare instances, it might even be more than 50 percent of the bill.

Two other charges are usually found on the utility bill. Most utilities use a fuel clause adjustment to adjust their rates in response to variations in the price of the fuels used to produce electricity. This adjustment takes the form of an additional charge or credit per kwh used in a billing period. The other rather common bill component is sales tax.

If a charge for a poor *power factor* appears on your bill and is a significant dollar amount, call your utility and ask for help to understand the basis of this charge and what to do to lower it.

This discussion of electricity rates is somewhat similar to discussions of how hotels set their guestroom rates. Many hotels today practice revenue management:

that is, they change their guestroom prices depending on their expectations of the demand for guestrooms during a specific time period. Setting electricity rates based on time of use is a form of revenue management originally developed to provide price signals to customers about the cost of their consumption of electricity. This idea was promoted for electric utilities in the early 1970s as a means of trying to control the growth in demand for electrical energy, especially during peak periods. Airlines and later hotels picked up this pricing strategy as a way to enhance their revenue as well as control demand.

Reading Electrical Utility Meters

The utility usually sends a meter reader to record the energy and demand values off the property's meter. A well-run operation will take its own meter readings, usually once per day and sometimes once per shift. This should be part of the shift engineer's daily responsibility. The readings should then be given to the director of engineering or the general manager. The purpose of taking these readings is to diagnose any problems before they become severe—for example, a surge in consumption caused by a theft of electric service. These readings may also prove useful if a dispute arises with the utility over the meter readings used for billing purposes.

Various types of meter dials are shown in this chapter.[5] The actual types or styles of meters used in different properties may vary, but the method of reading the meters will be the same. In general, quantities of energy consumed are determined by subtracting the beginning meter readings from the end-of-period readings. If a multiplier is shown on the dial face, you must multiply the difference between the two readings by the number shown to determine the actual quantity of energy used.

There are two general types of electric meters: the kilowatt-hour meter and the kilowatt-hour meter with kilowatt demand meter.

Kilowatt-Hour Meter. This type of meter is used to determine the number of kilowatt-hours of electricity used. On a kilowatt-hour meter, the meter dials are read in sequence from left to right. The number recorded should be the lower of the two numbers that the hand is between in each dial.

In Exhibit 10, Example A, the first dial is read as 4, the second as 5, the third as 1, and the fourth as 9. Thus, the meter reading is 4519. In Example B, the reading is 4628. To calculate the number of kilowatt-hours used, subtract the first reading (4519) from the second reading (4628). The difference between the two readings is 109. Since the meter face has the words "multiply by 100," you must multiply 109 by 100 to obtain the kilowatt-hours that were actually used (10,900).

Kilowatt-Hour Meter with Kilowatt Demand Meter. In a combination meter, the row of dials on the meter face marked "kilowatt-hours" is read the same way as the dials on a kilowatt-hour meter. There are many types of demand meters and each is read in a different way. When a meter is installed at your property, ask the utility company how to read it. The following section describes three common types of combined meters and provides guidelines for reading each type.

Exhibit 10　Kilowatt-Hour Meter

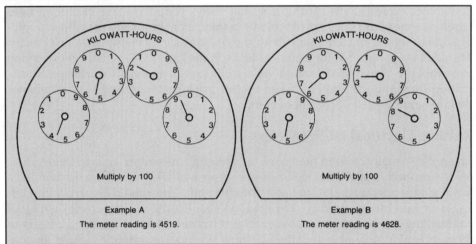

Source: Robert E. Aulbach, *Energy and Water Resource Management*, 2d ed. (East Lansing, Mich.: Educational Institute of the American Hotel & Motel Association, 1988), p. 125.

Exhibit 11　Combination KWH and Demand Meters

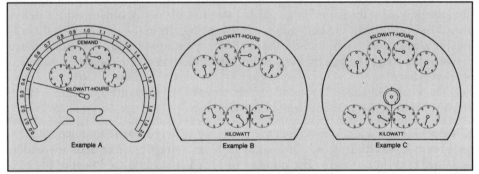

Source: Robert E. Aulbach, *Energy and Water Resource Management*, 2d ed. (East Lansing, Mich.: Educational Institute of the American Hotel & Motel Association, 1988), p. 126.

Maximum demand. The pointer in Example A in Exhibit 11 indicates maximum demand on the outer scale ring. The scale may be read directly or a multiplier may be required. The demand indicated is 0.4 kw. The pointer will be reset to zero by the meter reader. This type of meter only shows maximum demand since the previous reading and billing period.

Demand dials. Example B in Exhibit 11 depicts another type of demand meter that has demand dials below the meter dials. These dials are read from left to right just like those on kilowatt-hour meters. The vertical line between the dials indicates where a decimal point should be placed. If there is a multiplier shown on the dial face, the reading must be multiplied by that number. The demand indicated in

Example B is 96.2 kw. Demand dials of this type are also reset to zero by the meter reader after the reading is taken.

Cumulative demand register. A demand register—like that shown in Example C in Exhibit 11—looks and works somewhat like a kilowatt-hour meter. The dials are again read from left to right. The vertical line again indicates where a decimal point should be placed. The demand in this example is 13.15 kw.

In the cumulative demand register, the meter dials show the sum of the maximum demands up to the time the meter was last read. The meter reader determines the maximum demand for the current period by taking the dial reading, inserting a key in the meter that advances the dials to the new meter indication, and taking the new reading. The maximum demand for the period is the difference between the two readings. The new dial setting then remains fixed until the next meter reading.

The meter reader must use his or her key to advance the meter before the demand for any billing period can be calculated. However, by recording the meter reading just before the meter reader arrives, and by reading the meter after the reader departs, you can have a check on the demand that is used by the utility company during each billing period.

Recording demand meters. With the advent of time-of-day rates, it has become necessary for the utility company to know *when* energy consumption occurs in addition to the number of kilowatt-hours. In its simplest form, this has required the installation of more than one meter to record during certain periods of the day or year. In other instances, especially in larger commercial facilities, recording demand meters are used.

Recording devices also may be required when the rate is based on something other than the maximum demand during the month. For example, the rate schedule might stipulate that the maximum demand will be the average of the two, three, or four highest demands during the month. In another case, recording devices may be used when an individual consumer's load is large in relation to the system load. This enables the utility to determine whether the consumer's intervals of high demand coincide with system peaks.

There are several forms of demand recording devices, including strip charts and circular charts. However, these devices are giving way to those using magnetic tape. The magnetic tape demand recorder records the demand for every 15- or 30-minute time interval during the month on a cassette tape. This tape is removed from the meter each month and fed into the utility company's computer for computation and billing. Some utility companies can access this data through devices that transmit meter information to a computer via telephone lines.

Checking the Bill for Errors

While the electric bill is usually given to the accounting department, it is important for the maintenance department to receive a copy to review. This makes sense because the bill will be paid out of the utility budget, which is the responsibility of maintenance. Next, the maintenance department should record the information on the bill in an energy consumption log. Engineering should review the readings taken by the utility and compare them with their own readings. Sometimes the utility company makes an error. Errors in demand readings are particularly hard to detect when the demand meter is reset to zero after it is read. Finally, the engineering staff are sometimes the only ones who understand how the electric bill is calculated. The bill should *always* be checked for errors.

In fact, billing errors are common enough that some independent contractors offer to monitor and check bills, often simply for a percentage of the savings they find. These firms maintain extensive data files on utility tariffs. They check for errors in both calculation and classification (for example, a company paying residential rather than commercial rates or paying a wrong or less advantageous commercial rate; there may be different commercial rates that apply to the same business and the utility is under no obligation to state which rate is more advantageous). Because billing errors can take many forms, some properties prefer to use the services of these outside contractors. However, with a little care, each property should be able to discover the same errors on its own.

Choosing the Best Rate Schedule

Deciding on a tariff or rate for electric service can be a somewhat confusing decision. There are often a number of options available, and it's up to the utility customer to decide which option is best. The utility provides rate information and leaves the decision up to the customer.

Some hospitality companies hire firms to identify the most advantageous electric rate for them and to audit their utility bills for errors, as just mentioned. Some of these firms provide this service "free"; they are paid by collecting a percentage of the dollars they save the hospitality companies they are working for.

It is appropriate to review the rate a property is paying when any of the following occur:

- Managers are considering replacing the building's electrical transformer.

- Managers are considering making significant additions to the building or making other changes that could increase the amount of electricity being used.

- Energy conservation measures are being implemented.

- The utility company announces changes in its rate structure. (Properties should have a copy of the current electric utility rates on file.)

The chapter appendix provides sample rate sheets from Commonwealth Edison Company, the electric utility serving Chicago. These rate sheets illustrate a number of common features of electric utility bills. For example, the demand charges vary with the time of year, the energy charges with the time of day. Some utilities vary both of these charges according to both the time of year and the time of day. Because these charges vary, the marginal cost of electricity (the cost of one additional unit of electricity used or saved during a given time period) is sometimes substantially different than that of the average cost. Knowledge of the rates will allow managers to calculate potential energy savings using marginal costs rather than average costs.

Knowledge of the rate schedule, coupled with an automated building control system, can help managers create opportunities for significant electricity savings. For example, the Marriott Marquis Hotel in New York participated in a real-time pricing (RTP) experiment with Con Edison, its electricity supplier. Con Edison was investigating the potential response of its customers to electric rates that could vary every day by the hour, with rate information transmitted to customers a day in advance, so they could prepare to adjust their electricity consumption accordingly. The director of engineering at the Marriott saw real-time pricing as a great opportunity for savings.

The Marriott Marquis controlled various building loads (primarily air-handling system fans) and other deferrable non-guestroom loads, allowing these to be shut down or reduced during the hours of high electricity prices. The results were amazing. Key results included the following:

- With automatic control responses to RTP rates, the hotel saved more than $1 million in four years, which represented cost savings of approximately 8.3 percent when compared to conventional time-of-use electric rates.

- Average yearly kilowatt consumption dropped by more than two million kilowatts, from approximately 38 million kilowatts during the baseline period to less than 36 million kilowatts during the monitored period. This represented an energy savings of about 5.2 percent compared to conventional time-of-use rates.

- Peak electric load was reduced by up to 1,400 kilowatts during high-price hours.

- These savings were achieved without compromising guest comfort or service.[6]

Exhibit 12 shows the energy savings that the Marriott Marquis enjoyed during one calendar year of the experiment, and the types of building equipment that contributed to these savings.

Electric Utility Deregulation

The electric utility system in the United States operated for many decades as a regulated monopoly. A single electric utility served a given region, and its prices were largely fixed by filed rates approved by a state utility commission. Choice of utility companies and rates did not exist for customers. However, starting in the mid-1990s, electric utilities began to be deregulated, just as the telephone companies had been.

The result? Deregulation of electric utility companies has presented managers with another decision to make: What company should we choose to provide us with electricity? This can be a hard and potentially risky decision. First, it can be confusing because of the number of companies to choose from; figuring out which companies are reliable and reputable sometimes is not easy. Second, the rates are not fixed in some contracts; the rates are set to vary along with the market price of

Exhibit 12   Kilowatts Saved, by Equipment Type, Using Real-Time Pricing

Month	Air-Handling Systems	Chillers	Exhaust Fans	Lighting	Misc. Loads	RTP kWh Reduction
January	74,386	0	18,498	0	0	92,884
February	174,472	207	38,100	0	0	212,779
March	194,880	1,979	44,115	17,600	11,000	296,574
April	120,140	11,445	4,255	0	0	135,840
May	126,704	28,253	4,485	0	0	159,442
June	132,786	68,652	6,095	0	0	207,533
July	234,648	145,683	40,655	7,200	4,500	432,686
August	145,588	79,152	13,405	3,200	2,000	243,345
September	141,554	49,293	1,035	0	0	191,882
October	150,904	17,222	2,875	0	0	171,001
November	197,254	14,136	28,840	5,280	3,300	248,810
December	173,382	1,589	11,200	800	500	187,471
Totals	**1,866,698**	**417,610**	**213,558**	**34,080**	**21,300**	**2,553,246**

electricity. Experiences with market prices for electricity in the late 1990s have shown that large, short-term jumps in power prices can occur.

Deregulation has introduced another concern for managers. With the electricity market deregulated, the oversight that was provided by regulatory agencies has been reduced, and the more-or-less guaranteed fixed return for utilities is gone. Deregulation has opened the door for larger profits, which has encouraged companies to enter the electric utility industry that are primarily interested in quick, large profits. Other companies, under pressure to increase profits, have reduced maintenance activities and system reserve capacities. This has led to more frequent power outages and power-reliability problems. The late 1990s saw brownouts (voltage reductions) and requests for voluntary power-usage curtailments (power shutdowns) in many regions. Whether these problems will continue and even worsen is yet to be seen.

Hotel and restaurant chains as well as state hospitality associations have responded to the emerging deregulated electricity markets by collecting information and negotiating new electricity purchase agreements. Some hospitality companies have negotiated directly with power companies; others have used the services of firms specializing in purchasing electricity. It is too early to tell what the overall electric-bill savings for the hospitality industry will be, but, if the experience with natural gas purchasing in the 1980s and 1990s is any example, the savings could be substantial. After the natural gas industry was deregulated, some hotels, through efficient purchasing, saw savings of from 10 to 25 percent and even higher. (Of course, natural gas users have an alternative in oil, something that electricity users do not have.)

Endnotes

1. J. F. Musselman, "Power Plant and Refrigeration Equipment," *The Architectural Forum*, November 1923, p. 257.

2. Particularly useful sources of updated information include *Electrical Construction & Maintenance* Magazine, published by Primedia Business, P.O. Box 12914, Overland Park, KS, 66282-2914; and the National Fire Protection Association, 1 Batterymarch Park, P.O. Box 9101, Quincy, MA, 02269-9101.

3. One magazine that can be helpful in this regard is *Electrical Construction & Maintenance.*

4. These solutions are suggested in two publications of the Edison Electric Institute, *Quality Power in Your Restaurant* and *Quality Power in Your Motel,* 701 Pennsylvania Ave. N.W., Washington, D.C., 20004-2696. These publications guide the reader through a process of diagnosing and solving electrical quality problems.

5. This section on meter reading is drawn from Robert E. Aulbach, *Energy and Water Resource Management,* 2d ed. (Lansing, Mich.: Educational Institute of the American Hotel & Lodging Association, 1988), pp. 124–126.

6. S. D. Gabel, L. Carmichael, and G. Shavit, "Automated Control in Response to Real-Time Pricing of Electricity," *ASHRAE Journal*, November 1998, pp. 26–29.

Key Terms

ampere—A measure of the current flow in an electrical system. One ampere represents 6.251×10^{18} electrons per second passing through a cross section of the conductor.

demand charge—That part of a utility bill based on the highest rate of energy use, measured in kilowatts. Also called a capacity charge.

energy charge—That part of a utility bill based on the amount of energy used, measured in kilowatt-hours. Also called a consumption charge.

feeder—Element of a building's electrical system that supplies electricity to various portions of the building and to major equipment.

frequency—With regard to electricity, the rate at which an alternating current (AC) power supply alternates the direction of the current flow. Measured in hertz, or cycles per second.

ground fault circuit interrupter (GFCI)—A particularly sensitive circuit breaker designed to protect people from electrical shocks, usually used in areas where water may be found.

National Electrical Code (NEC)—A publication of the National Fire Protection Association that details recommended safety code standards for electrical systems.

phase—With regard to electrical service, the number of energized wires in the electrical supply. Almost always either single-phase or three-phase.

ratchet clause—A utility billing structure that bases the demand charge on the highest demand over a given period extending beyond the current billing period.

transformer—A device that changes the voltage of the electrical supply.

voltage—A measure of the electrical potential of an electrical system. Electricity flows between two points of different electrical potential. Comparable to pressure in a water system.

Review Questions

1. What factors might lead a hospitality property to choose to produce its own power supply?

2. What are the potential advantages and disadvantages to a hospitality operation of owning its own transformer?

3. What is the purpose of the *National Electrical Code*?

4. Why is it important to update electrical plans as changes are made to a facility?

5. What are lockout/tagout procedures? Why are they critical to electrical safety?

6. Should preventive maintenance be performed on every piece of electrical equipment at a facility? Why or why not?

7. What steps can be taken to reduce the likelihood of electrical problems interfering with electronic equipment?

8. When is the use of battery backup systems most appropriate? What is the difference between a standby power supply and an uninterruptible power supply?

9. What is the difference between a demand charge and an energy charge? Why is it important to know the difference?

10. If a hospitality facility qualifies under more than one rate schedule, how should it select from among the available options?

Internet Sites

For more information, visit the following Internet sites. Remember that Internet addresses can change without notice. If the site is no longer there, you can use a search engine to look for additional sites.

Consulting-Specifying Engineer
www.csemag.com

Electrical Construction & Maintenance Magazine
www.industryclick.com/magazine.
asp?siteid=13&magazineid=31

Edison Electric Institute
www.eei.org

Electric Power Research Institute
www.epri.com

Chapter Appendix

Sample Electric Utility Rate Sheets

RATE 6
GENERAL SERVICE

APPLICABILITY.
Except as provided in Rate 6L, this rate is applicable to any commercial, industrial, or governmental customer with a Maximum Demand of less than 1,000 kilowatts who uses the Company's electric service hereunder for all requirements. Direct current requirements provided under another rate immediately prior to September 2, 1975, will, however, also be provided hereunder.

GENERAL SERVICE – TIME OF DAY.
Time of day charges shall apply to (1) any customer with a Maximum Demand of 500 kilowatts or more, but less than 1,000 kilowatts, in three of the twelve months preceding the billing month, one of which occurs during the three months preceding the billing month, (2) successors to customers served under these charges immediately prior to the date of succession whose estimated Maximum Demands meet the demand requirements in clause (1) above, (3) new customers whose estimated Maximum Demands meet the demand requirements in clause (1) above, and (4) any customer previously billed hereunder pursuant to clauses (1) or (2), except as otherwise provided below.

These charges shall not be applicable to customers or their successors with electric space heating taking service under the Heating with Light provision of Rider 25 prior to November 23, 1977, except upon written application by the customer to the Company.

If a customer at one time was served pursuant to (1) above on General Service – Time of Day and has a Maximum Demand which (A) has not exceeded 400 kilowatts in any month of the 16-month period preceding the billing month, or (B) has not equaled or exceeded 500 kilowatts in any month of the 24-month period preceding the billing month, such customer may elect, in written application to the Company, to be served on General Service – Non-Time of Day. General Service – Time of Day shall not again be applicable until such customer meets the requirements of General Service – Time of Day.

GENERAL SERVICE – NON-TIME OF DAY.
General Service – Non-Time of Day charges shall apply to all other customers qualifying for service under this rate.

CHARGES.
General Service – Time of Day.
Monthly Customer Charge.
The Monthly Customer Charge shall be:... $39.93

Demand Charge.
Charge per kilowatt for all kilowatts of Maximum Demand for the month:
For Summer Months $14.24
For All Other Months $11.13

For the purposes hereof, the Summer Months shall be the customer's first monthly billing period with an ending meter reading date on or after June 15 and the three succeeding monthly billing periods.

Energy Charge.
Charge per kilowatt-hour for kilowatt-hours supplied in the month:
For kilowatt-hours supplied
during Energy Peak Periods.. 5.599¢
during Energy Off-Peak Periods .... 2.341¢

General Service – Non-Time of Day.
Monthly Customer Charge.
The Monthly Customer Charge shall be:... $8.83

Demand Charge.
Charge per kilowatt for all kilowatts of Maximum Demand for the month:
For Summer Months $14.24
For All Other Months $11.13

In accordance with the Application of Demand Charge provisions of this rate, there shall be no demand charge as such for certain small customers, but in lieu thereof, such customers shall pay a charge per kilowatt-hour in addition to the energy charges of this rate.

The in-lieu of demand charge per kilowatt-hour for kilowatt-hours supplied in the month:
For Summer Months .... 6.057¢
For All Other Months .... 4.798¢

RATE 6
GENERAL SERVICE

(Continued from Sheet No. 24)

CHARGES. (CONTINUED)
General Service – Non-Time of Day. (Continued)
Demand Charge (Continued).
For the purposes hereof, the Summer Months shall be the customer's first monthly billing period with an ending meter reading date on or after June 15 and the three succeeding monthly billing periods.

Energy Charge.
Charge per kilowatt-hour for kilowatt-hours supplied in the month:

For the first 30,000 kilowatt-hours... 4.247¢
For the next 470,000 kilowatt-hours .... 3.167¢
For all over 500,000 kilowatt-hours.. 3.118¢

Late Payment Charge.
The late payment charge provided for in the Terms and Conditions of this Schedule of Rates shall be applicable to all charges under this rate.

Minimum Charge.
The minimum monthly charge shall be the Monthly Customer Charge.

Maximum Charge.
For customers with demand meters, the average cost of electricity hereunder in any month, exclusive of the Monthly Customer Charge, shall not exceed the Maximum Charge per kilowatt-hour, provided, however, that such guaranteed charge shall not operate to reduce the customer's bill to an amount less than the Minimum Charge.

The Maximum Charge per kilowatt-hour shall be: .... 20.502¢

MAXIMUM DEMAND.
For General Service – Time of Day customers, the Maximum Demand in any month shall be the highest 30-minute demand established during the Demand Peak Periods in such month.

For General Service – Non-Time of Day customers, the Maximum Demand shall be the highest 30-minute demand established at any time during such month.

APPLICATION OF DEMAND CHARGE.
The Company shall provide a demand meter and the demand charge shall apply when a customer's monthly kilowatt-hour use exceeds 2,000 kilowatt-hours in three of the twelve months preceding the billing month; or if either his Maximum Demand or monthly kilowatt-hour use is estimated to exceed 10 kilowatts or 2,000 kilowatt-hours, respectively, for at least three months of the next 12-month period. Any customer to whom the demand charge would not ordinarily apply under the preceding sentence may, at his request and upon payment of appropriate meter rentals, be provided with a demand meter and be billed the demand charge rather than the charge in lieu thereof. In such case, meter rentals shall be payable for the period during which the customer elects to retain the meter, but not less than twelve months, unless he becomes entitled to a demand meter prior to the end of the 12-month period. A customer who is entitled to a demand meter shall not be required to pay rental or other separate charges for such meter.

Where a demand meter is installed, the demand charge shall apply when the customer's monthly use exceeds 2,000 kilowatt-hours or his demand exceeds 10 kilowatts in three of the twelve months preceding the billing month. The demand charge shall continue to apply until the customer's monthly use has not exceeded 2,000 kilowatt-hours and his Maximum Demand has not exceeded 10 kilowatts in any month of the preceding 16-month period, at which time the in lieu of demand charge shall apply, except for a customer who has requested a demand meter and has elected to be billed the demand charge.

Prior to application of the demand charge, the customer being billed in lieu of demand charges will receive notification on the customer's bill each time the above 2,000 kilowatt-hours or 10 kilowatt requirement has been exceeded and the significance of it.

Chapter 8 Outline

Competencies

1. Describe the basic elements of human comfort and how HVAC systems affect this comfort. (pp. 222–227)

2. Identify heating sources, types of heating equipment, and operating and maintenance concerns for this equipment. (pp. 227–231)

3. Explain how the vapor compression refrigeration cycle operates. (p. 231)

4. Identify cooling system operating and maintenance concerns. (pp. 231–238)

5. Describe several guestroom HVAC systems, including centralized, decentralized, and hybrid systems. (pp. 238–245)

6. Identify the system types and maintenance needs of HVAC systems for other building areas. (pp. 245–247)

7. Outline the nature and maintenance needs of HVAC controls. (pp. 247–249)

8. Identify various maintenance concerns with regard to cooling towers. (pp. 249–250)

8

Heating, Ventilating, and Air Conditioning Systems

Air conditioning is the science of mechanically controlling the (1) temperature, (2) humidity, (3) purity, and (4) movement of the air within buildings and other enclosures, thereby controlling the effects of such air upon the persons and materials exposed to it.

The effects of air upon comfort and health are due to the reactions of the human being to variations in air temperature, humidity, purity and motion. The sense or feeling of warmth is dependent upon the moisture content of the air, rather than upon its mere temperature, and for this reason comfortable and healthful heating requires coincident regulation of humidity. The purity of the air breathed by the human being is, of course, primarily important to his physical well-being. His personal efficiency is materially depressed by air that is contaminated with foreign matter, particularly in congested centers, manufacturing districts, or in proximity to any source of pollution. Drafts, due to improper distribution of air, are dangerous to health, and subversive to comfort. Air conditioning is a sure and sane means of insuring comfort and of eliminating the personal inefficiencies resulting from improper air qualities in spaces enclosing human beings. Just as surely as the first invigorating days of spring bring to you a pulsating sense of new energy, so will conditioned air, duplicating those same conditions perhaps, bringing new energy and comfort to all it reaches. Manufactured weather makes "Every day a good day," so that the increased satisfaction rather than discomfort of the hotel guest and the increased efficiency rather than indifference of the employee yields a day-after-day dividend on the operating cost and investment in air conditioning equipment.[1]

HEATING, VENTILATING, AND AIR CONDITIONING (HVAC) SYSTEMS create and maintain the levels of comfort required by guests and employees. HVAC systems must be properly selected, operated, and maintained if they are to provide an appropriate level of comfort. To maintain comfort, you need to understand the basic elements of comfort. The capabilities, limitations, and operating costs of various types of HVAC systems are important as well, especially as they relate to decisions about equipment selection and overall cost control.

Proper maintenance of HVAC systems not only will create comfortable conditions, but also will help control the operating costs associated with the equipment. Knowledge of fuel and equipment options can help management to make decisions for new and retrofit applications. In addition, certain elements of the HVAC system need special care to avoid potential safety and health problems.

While there are many types of systems, the underlying ways in which they operate are somewhat similar. Knowing how a property creates heating and cooling and provides ventilation will help you to understand the ways in which each of these is used to help produce building comfort.

Factors Influencing Building Thermal Comfort

The concept of comfort involves a number of factors. HVAC systems maintain thermal comfort by modifying and controlling the factors that influence comfort. These systems use equipment such as furnaces and boilers to produce heat, air conditioners and chillers to produce cold, fans and ductwork to move air, and filters and air washers to clean the air.

Factors influencing thermal comfort include:

- Room air temperature

- Room air movement

- Relative humidity of room air or wet bulb temperature

- Activity level in the room

- Clothing worn by room occupants

- Temperature of the room surfaces

Most of these factors will seem quite obvious to you. A room's comfort level can be greatly changed by providing air movement—such as with a fan in the summer. A humid environment can be much less comfortable in summer than a dryer environment at the same temperature. If we are actively exercising, we find cooler conditions more comfortable. An individual wearing a suit or sweater will be warmer than he or she would be in a thin short-sleeved shirt and shorts.

An individual's comfort is the result of balancing the heat produced by his or her body with the surrounding environment. Body heat is lost by **convection, radiation,** and **evaporation.** Convection involves the transfer of heat due to the movement of air over a person's skin and a difference in temperature between the air and the skin. The more rapid the air movement or the colder the air, the more rapid is the transfer of heat. Transfer of heat by radiation occurs when two surfaces are at different temperatures. Energy is transferred in the form of thermal radiation from the warmer to the colder surface. Evaporation transfers heat because, in order to turn water from a liquid to a vapor, heat must be added to the water. With regard to human comfort, this heat is removed from a person's body as perspiration evaporates from his or her skin.

Radiative heat loss is particularly influenced by the temperature of room surfaces. This effect is illustrated when you sit near a window on a cold winter day.

Exhibit 1   ASHRAE Summer and Winter Comfort Zones

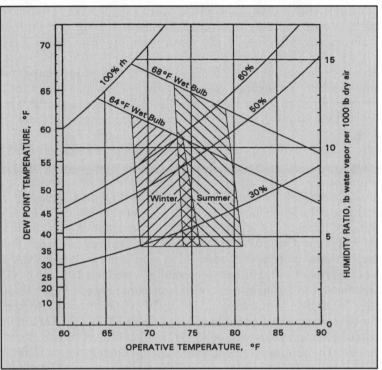

Reprinted by permission from ASHRAE.

The cold glass of the window causes your body to radiate heat in that direction, making the side of your body near the window feel cold. Most building heating systems locate heat discharge points below windows so the heating system can warm the window surface. This reduces the radiative cooling effect the window has on room occupants.

The HVAC industry has provided a simplified way to view thermal comfort by defining a region of temperature and relative humidity known as the **comfort zone.** Through testing of human response to various indoor air conditions, a range of conditions in which 80 percent of the population tested was "comfortable" has been defined. Exhibit 1 illustrates this zone on what engineers call a psychrometric chart. Temperatures and relative humidity levels within the ranges specified represent desired conditions for occupied spaces. The zones numerically express what we intuitively understand. In summer we are comfortable at warmer conditions than in winter. As the air temperature rises, no matter what the season, the range of comfort shifts somewhat to lower levels of humidity.

Interpreting the comfort zone on the chart in Exhibit 1 also provides some background in interpreting the psychrometric chart itself. The lines ascending from left to right and labeled *rh* with a % sign are relative humidity lines. Relative humidity is a measure of the relative amount of moisture the air is holding, with values ranging from 0 percent to 100 percent. These are labeled from 100 to 30 percent in the exhibit, with most of the comfort zones lying between 60 and 30 percent rh—common internal building conditions. The lines ascending from right to left are **wet bulb temperature** lines. If you move vertically from the 64°F (18°C) wet bulb line to the 68°F (20°C) wet bulb line you can see that this also results in the relative humidity increasing. The left (Y) axis is the **dew point temperature**—the temperature at which water condenses. The right axis is a measure of the absolute amount of water in the air, expressed in pounds of water vapor per 1000 pounds of dry air. The bottom (X) axis is the dry bulb temperature, referred to as the operative temperature.

The dry bulb temperature is what we commonly refer to as "the temperature" and measure with a thermometer. The wet bulb temperature is the value that would be measured if the bulb of a thermometer was surrounded by a small swatch of wet cloth. The wet bulb temperature and relative humidity are often used interchangeably. If we have a dry bulb temperature of 85° F (29° C) we can talk of a relative humidity of approximately 30 percent or of a wet bulb temperature of 64° F (18° C). And if we cooled this air to approximately 50° F (10° C) it would reach its dew point and condensation would result. All of these relationships can be illustrated using illustrations similar to Exhibit 1.

The winter comfort zone ranges from approximately 68° F (20° C) at 60 percent relative humidity to in excess of 76° F (25° C) at humidity lower than 30 percent. Summer comfort ranges from a low of about 73° F (23° C) at humidity levels in excess of 60 percent to a high of 81° F (27° C) at humidity significantly lower than 30 percent. The summer comfort zone is approximately the same as the winter zone with 5° F added (i.e., the zone shifted 5° F to the right of the exhibit). This is primarily due to different clothing levels in summer than in winter. The comfort zone in Exhibit 1 is for individuals in sedentary activity and not particularly elderly. It is known that people at age 80 require temperatures three Fahrenheit degrees warmer to be comfortable than those of people in their 20s.

The comfort zone is not an infallible guide. It will not apply universally in all situations because it was developed for specified levels of air movement, activity, and clothing levels. Nonetheless, it is useful for most occupied spaces.

Further needs in the comfort and acceptability of indoor environments concern such elements as noise, odor, and the general quality of the air. Air quality must meet basic requirements for human occupancy, such as the presence of adequate amounts of oxygen and the absence of any toxic gases. Air quality also involves subtler issues, such as the possible impact of mold spores, bacteria, and airborne particles of various types on occupant well-being.[2] A well-designed and properly functioning HVAC system strives to meet all comfort needs.

While striving to meet thermal comfort needs, room and building HVAC systems must meet other comfort needs as well. Acoustical comfort is one of these needs. HVAC systems usually move some fluid—air, water, or both. This movement may make noise, due to either the fluid itself or the pump or fan moving the fluid. Sometimes, a low level of noise is intentionally designed into equipment—for example, an air distribution system—because it can serve to mask other sounds. This is known as the "white noise" approach. Also, air that is discharged at

Exhibit 2   Guestroom HVAC Loads

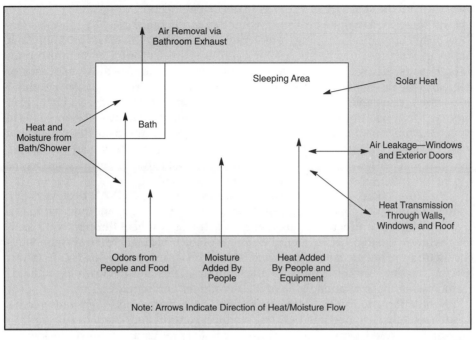

too high a rate can make unwanted noise. Controlling ventilation airflow rates is necessary.

Additional noise and vibration can be generated by the equipment used to move the fluid. A poorly balanced fan, a lack of adequate vibration isolation of fans or pumps, bearing deterioration, and related problems can result in the transmission of vibration to the ductwork, the piping, or the building itself. While these problems should be dealt with in the design of the systems, all of them can occur because of a faulty maintenance program.

Building Loads and Comfort

Exhibit 2 illustrates some of the challenges facing an HVAC system operating in a guestroom. (A similar diagram can be drawn for other spaces.) The exterior wall, windows, and ceiling of the guestroom may add heat to or subtract heat from the space, depending on the season. The windows allow solar energy to enter and add heat to the room. The guest, television, lights, and other equipment add heat to the room. The shower and bath also add heat. Air leakage around the windows (and the door if the guestroom opens to the outside) can add cold or hot air to the room, depending on the season. Moisture is added by the bath and shower and by the breath of, and skin evaporation from, room occupants. The bathroom vent fan removes air that must be replaced. This replacement air eventually enters the building from the outside, which means it must be heated or cooled somewhere.

The HVAC system is ideally able to deal with all of these variable inputs to and outputs from the space (referred to as **loads** by engineers).

Building loads can be broken down into various categories. The simplest are those loads that are sensible and latent. **Sensible loads** involve heat addition (and removal) with resulting increases (or decreases) in dry bulb temperature only. **Latent loads** involve moisture addition or removal with resulting increases or decreases in the relative humidity only. If you move horizontally on Exhibit 1 you'll see the sensible load process. If you move vertically, you'll see a latent load process. Many heating loads involve sensible and latent elements—the air needs to be cooled and moisture removed as well. Sometimes failure to create comfort is a matter of overly addressing one load (usually sensible) without also addressing the other load (usually latent). One contributor to mold and mildew in guestrooms can be too much sensible cooling and not enough latent.

Building loads can also be broken down in other ways. HVAC designers talk about transmission/conduction, ventilation, infiltration, solar, and internal loads. Transmission or conduction loads involve the transfer of heat through walls, ceilings, windows, and other structural elements of the building. Heat transfer always occurs from warmer to colder locations. This means transmission loads can be heat lost (in the winter) or heat gained (in the summer). Transmission loads are reduced by increasing the insulation value of walls, ceilings, and windows.

Ventilation and infiltration loads are similar in many ways. Ventilation loads are deliberately designed into buildings to meet comfort and safety needs. Infiltration loads are not designed into the building but are rather a function of leakage of air either from the outside in or the inside out. If from the outside in, the entering air must be cooled or heated to maintain the space in the comfort zone. If from the inside out, replacement air must be cooled or heated to maintain the space in the comfort zone. One challenge with infiltration loads is that these may occur in locations where the system is not designed to compensate for them—locations such as near a door or a leaking window. Ventilation loads are designed as part of the system. However, in either instance, the load usually requires the use of energy for heating or cooling. Under the right circumstances, the ventilation air can provide cooling if needed and eliminate the need for energy usage to run cooling equipment. A detailed discussion on effective ventilation and infiltration is presented in the appendix to this chapter.

Solar loads are due to sunlight either entering the building through windows or heat generated into a building by surfaces on the exterior of the building (especially roofs). Sunlight entering through windows immediately turns to heat within the space. Sunlight striking building surfaces also immediately turns to heat, but the effect is first to raise the temperatures of these surfaces above the air temperature. Then, the heat produced works its way through the surface to the interior. This process can take several hours. The result is that a solar roof load may not show up in the guestrooms unto 6:00, 8:00, or even 10:00 p.m. Solar loads are one good reason to paint roofs white or some other reflective color in hot climates. To illustrate, consider the difference in the temperature of the hood of a white car versus that of a black car when exposed to bright sunlight. In winter periods, solar loads can reduce the energy needed for space heating.

Internal loads involve anything inside a space that provides heat or moisture. People, a coffee pot, overhead projectors, or computers provide heat or moisture or both. In some unusual circumstances, there can be things that remove heat and moisture—a large urn of iced beverage or an ice sculpture, for example,

To maintain comfort, the HVAC system must remove the loads at the rate they are created. This can be a challenge. Imagine the change in load of an auditorium or convention space at a "comfortable" 77° F (25° C) and 40 percent relative humidity (rh) when a thousand people suddenly enter from outside where the temperature is 95° F (35° C) and 80 percent rh. Not only do the people themselves generate heat (internal loads) but their movement brings with it a large amount of outside air (infiltration). The sensible and latent loads that result are large and sudden. The good news is that the system is usually configured to handle these loads. More of a problem can occur when guestroom HVAC systems, designed for a small number of occupants and minimal internal loads, are called upon to meet the needs of a large number of people and large internal loads. This can be the case when guestrooms are converted to meeting space or to provide concierge or executive lounge areas on guestroom floors. If no changes are made to the HVAC system, it is almost guaranteed that the system will be unable to meet the peak loads created by these conversions. The result will be uncomfortable guests and complaints about the comfort in these spaces. Without HVAC system changes costing many dollars, there is little that can be done.

Heating Sources and Equipment

The major space conditioning need of guestrooms and many other spaces involves cooling. Yet for operations in colder climates, the space heating needs are quite large and the maintenance needs associated with heating equipment are important. Heating equipment usually creates more important safety concerns than does cooling equipment, due to the flame and flue gases that are generally present. In addition, a failure of the heating system can have disastrous effects on the building because of freezing; in contrast, a failure of the cooling system generally has much less important effects on the building itself.

Heat Sources

Options for heating fuel are shown in Exhibit 3. The type of fuel selected for a location will be dictated by factors such as availability, relative cost of the fuel, cost of equipment and systems to use the fuel, environmental constraints, and safety concerns.

While electricity is almost always available and is generally a safe and clean fuel source, its cost is among the highest of the fuel sources. Electricity can be an economical choice when overall needs for heat are low or the cost of equipment needed to use the other fuel sources is high. You might also choose electricity if a reliable supply of an alternative fuel is not available. Electrical space heating equipment most commonly passes electricity through a resistance device that converts electrical energy to heat. Another way to use electricity is to operate a heat pump, a method of heating described later in this chapter.

Exhibit 3   Heating Fuel Options

Fuel Types	Heat Content/Unit Purchased	Comments
Electricity	3413 Btu/kwh	Used in all electric heaters. Requires no flue since there are no products of combustion. Usually the most expensive form of heat.
Natural Gas	1000 Btu/cubic foot (approx.)	Clean burning. Flue required. Complete condensing units very efficient. Delivered to building by underground pipe.
Liquefied Petroleum	95,000 Btu/gallon (approx.)	Relatively clean burning. Requires on-site storage tank located outside of building. Slow vaporization of fuel in winter. Delivered by truck. May also be used for cooking fuel.
Fuel Oil	140,000–150,000 Btu/gallon	More tendency to create dirt and smoke than natural gas. Requires on-site storage tank. Delivered by truck. Various grades of fuel oil with differing energy content and combustion characteristics.
Steam	1000 Btu/lb (approx.)	More common in urban areas where steam is purchased from local steam utility. May also be supplied from central boiler plant in large complexes. Supply line for steam and return line for condensate.

Natural gas, LPG (liquefied petroleum gas—usually liquefied propane), and fuel oil all produce heat as a result of combustion. This combustion requires sufficient supplies of oxygen and produces heat, carbon dioxide, water, and other products. Combustion occurs in a furnace or boiler. A furnace is a device that produces hot air. Furnaces may be found in small restaurants and in individual lodging units such as some timeshares and condominiums. Boilers produce steam or hot water that may be used both for space heating and for other heating needs as well.

During the combustion process, the proper mixing of the fuel and air is required. Generally, the fuel is pressurized and injected into the air. This process both mixes and (in the case of liquid fuels) atomizes the fuel, resulting in the potential for more efficient combustion. Combustion is then initiated by either a pilot flame or a spark.

Furnace and Boiler Operation and Maintenance

The maintenance needs of furnaces and boilers are similar. They include actions that promote efficient and safe operation and that prolong the operating life of the equipment. There is an overlap in actions taken in these three areas. Actions to improve efficiency can also help prolong life and vice versa. Because furnaces and boilers are important in meeting guest and employee needs, their proper and safe operation is critical.

Furnace and boiler efficiency involves two aspects—the efficient combustion of the fuel and the efficient transfer of that combustion heat to the air or water being heated. Efficient fuel combustion requires the correct mix of combustion air and fuel. Too little combustion air will cause the fuel to burn incompletely, which leads to waste. Too much combustion air will reduce the temperature of the combustion gases and, therefore, the amount of heat that can be removed from these gases.

Maintenance staff or outside contractors should check combustion efficiency as part of the semi-annual or annual maintenance of the furnace or boiler. More frequent checks are warranted when on-site personnel are used and when large furnaces or boilers are installed.

Combustion efficiency is checked by measuring the oxygen or carbon dioxide content and temperature of the flue gas. Measuring the oxygen or carbon dioxide content of the flue gas will show whether the unit is receiving the correct amount of oxygen. Most larger commercial units now use a controlled combustion process in which air (oxygen) use is controlled and adjustable. The flue gas temperature may also indicate efficiency problems. A low flue gas temperature may indicate that too much air is being supplied. A high flue gas temperature may indicate that combustion heat is not being transferred efficiently. Both situations call for maintenance attention.

Besides adjusting air and fuel for proper combustion efficiency, regular maintenance should include cleaning of all heat transfer surfaces on both sides. Burner nozzles should be inspected and carefully cleaned of dirt, debris, carbon, and other buildup. Furnaces require the removal of soot and dirt from the combustion side and the cleaning of the air side. Usually a stiff brush and vacuum are required for this cleaning. Boilers require similar combustion-side cleaning and sometimes extensive water-side cleaning.

The degree of water-side cleaning required by boilers will depend on the water quality in the boiler loop water. If water in this loop contains minerals such as calcium or magnesium, there may be a problem with boiler **scale**. Scale is a buildup of calcium or magnesium carbonate on the walls of the boiler. Scale insulates the walls, thereby reducing heat transfer and increasing the operating temperature of these portions of the walls. This can lead to premature failure of these portions of the boiler. The scale problem is addressed by treating and removing calcium and magnesium from (or *softening*) boiler system water and by periodically cleaning the boiler to remove any buildup. The frequency of cleaning should be based on the needs of the individual operation and incorporated into the preventive maintenance (PM) instructions.

Further issues of boiler water quality involve maintaining the proper pH in the boiler to avoid acidic attacks on boiler components and keeping oxygen out of the boiler when adding makeup water. Operations using steam boilers, especially when this steam is also used for laundry operations, may introduce significant amounts of makeup water. Some of this water is required to compensate for blow-down water—water deliberately vented from the boiler to remove mineral buildup and debris.

Some systems provide makeup water automatically in order to avoid dangerous low water conditions in the boiler. You should install a meter on the makeup water line to the boiler system and keep records of the amount of makeup water added. Should a leak occur in a boiler water line or elsewhere, it would be shown by an increased meter reading. In a large property, such leaks could be difficult to identify readily by another means.

Because of the potential for soot buildup and other blockages in the flue, flue inspections and cleaning should be included in the PM program. Failure to remove blockages and buildups may force combustion gases back into the boiler room, leading the boiler to operate with a reduced supply of oxygen. Besides reducing efficiency, this situation can produce carbon monoxide—a potential killer if inhaled for an extended time.

All fossil-fuel-fired heating equipment should be inspected for leakage. Furnaces should receive particular attention in the area of the combustion chamber/heat exchanger, where building air comes closest to the combustion products. All joints and seams should receive particular attention, especially on older units. Flue ductwork should also be inspected for leaks. Any problems with the exhaust of combustion products should be corrected immediately.

You should also pay close attention to the location of flue outlets in relation to building air intakes—especially as buildings are modified over the years. Obviously, flue gas should not enter the building's fresh air intake. There are other concerns as well. One operation located its boiler exhaust quite close to the air inlet for the cooling tower. Since the boiler was used year-round for water heating, the air entering the cooling tower was always abnormally warm. In addition, combustion products were introduced into the cooling tower water. The tower's efficiency was impaired and its life was shortened.

Since the delivery of heat from the boiler or furnace usually requires the operation of various pumps or fans, maintenance considerations for such equipment should be included in boiler or furnace PM instructions. These include basic lubrication, checking of alignment and vibration, and cleaning. Furnaces usually have a filter bank installed on the air inlet side. The filters should be changed regularly; most operations do so monthly. More frequent changes may be necessary under particularly dirty or dusty conditions, such as during building startup or renovation. Filters on water systems should also be included in PM instructions.

For boiler systems to operate properly, all controls and safety devices need to function correctly. The boiler pressure relief valve and low water cut-off switch should be checked. Control systems may use compressed air as a means of operating valves and other devices. If compressed air is used, these controls should also be calibrated. In addition, the air dryer on the compressed air system should be checked and replaced if necessary, pressures checked and adjusted, air intake filters cleaned or changed, and all connections checked for leakage.

If steam above 15 psi (pounds per square inch) is produced, the operation of boilers may require a licensed boiler operator. Most facilities have multiple boilers to provide backup during maintenance outages and to match boiler capacity to the load. Because boiler loads vary and the standby losses that occur when unused or underused boilers are kept on are potentially high, management should shut off unneeded boilers, matching the capacity of units on line to the loads.

There are different methods of rating or expressing boiler capacity. Boilers may be rated in boiler horsepower. A boiler horsepower is equivalent to a heat output rate from the boiler of 33,475 Btu/hr, 9.8 kw, or 34.5 lb of steam per hour at standard pressure.[3]

Cooling Sources and Equipment

Mechanical cooling equipment is used to provide the cooling required in many climates. This equipment extracts heat from either air or water and uses this cooled air or water to absorb heat in the building spaces, thereby cooling the spaces. The equipment may use the **vapor compression** process or the absorption process. Since vapor compression is much more common, the absorption process will not be discussed in this chapter. However, concerns over the impact of vapor compression refrigerants on the environment (discussed later in this chapter) may create a resurgence of absorption systems. Absorption processes are used in some guestroom refrigerators and minibars.

The Refrigeration Cycle

Exhibit 4 shows the basic components of the vapor compression cycle. In this cycle, a circulating refrigerant removes heat from one location and transfers this heat to another location where it is rejected. Heat removal occurs in the **evaporator,** while the heat is rejected in the **condenser.** The **compressor** provides the energy necessary to accomplish this heat transfer. The **expansion valve** controls the flow of refrigerant through the system.

In the vapor compression process, the refrigerant is boiled, or converted from a liquid to a vapor, in the evaporator. The energy used to boil the refrigerant is taken from the air or water being cooled. The refrigerant vapor then leaves the evaporator and enters the compressor, which raises the temperature and pressure of this gas. The compressor is powered by an electric motor; it is the major energy-using component of the cycle.

The high-temperature and high-pressure refrigerant gas then leaves the compressor and enters the condenser. In the condenser, it releases heat to the condenser's cooling medium—either air or water—and reverts to a liquid. The liquid refrigerant then moves to the expansion valve, where its pressure is reduced, which causes its temperature to drop. The cold low-pressure liquid refrigerant then enters the evaporator and the cycle repeats.

Cooling Systems Operation and Maintenance

All refrigeration system components need to function properly. Maintenance activities with regard to these systems include the following:

- Inspect equipment for refrigerant leaks. These can be identified by the presence of oil carried outside the system by the leaking refrigerant. Special devices are also available to test for leaks.

Exhibit 4   Basic Vapor Compression Refrigeration Cycle

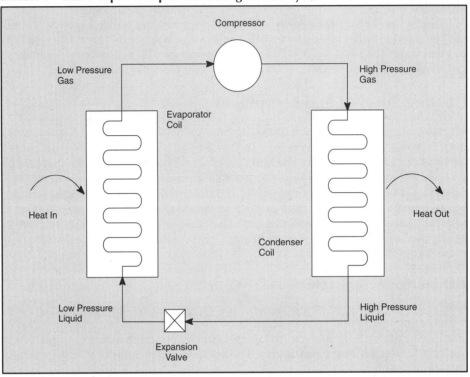

- Check refrigerant dryers for indications of water contamination. (Dryers are devices installed in refrigerant lines that collect and hold moisture.) Replace all dryers showing signs of water and re-inspect these dryers again shortly to be sure the problem has not recurred.

- Clean air-cooled condensers and evaporators.

- Clean condensate drip pans and drain lines from evaporators. Replace algae-cide tablets in drip pans and reapply protective paints.

- Check equipment operating conditions to be sure each unit is operating correctly. Refer to equipment manuals.

- Perform all recommended drive motor maintenance, paying particular attention to operating temperatures and motor starting controls. High operating temperatures and repeated starting and stopping are major factors in refrigeration system motor failure.

Space cooling equipment uses three different types of compressors: reciprocating, centrifugal, and rotary. Each has unique maintenance concerns. Reciprocating compressors use a cylinder moving within a chamber to compress the refrigerant. Maintenance needs resemble those of automotive engines and on-site staff can sometimes handle these needs. Since they may be relatively small and designed to be replaced, units may be exchanged for rebuilt or other replacement units. Operating efficiencies are often already low and poor maintenance can degrade these values to even lower levels.

Centrifugal units are generally larger compressors and require more care in maintenance and shutdown. Particular care is needed to avoid the introduction of air and water, which can cause many components to fail. Because of the complexity of these centrifugal units, maintenance contracts are often used to provide the necessary services.

Rotary compressors are among the smaller compressors found at the property. They are often used in through-the-wall guestroom units and may be used in other similarly sized applications. Because of the small size and applications for these units, they are often replaced with an exchange unit rather than repaired at the property.

Cooling equipment capacities are expressed in several ways. The cooling rate of equipment might be expressed in Btu/hour. A unit installed in a guestroom might have a capacity rating of 7,000 to 14,000 Btu/hr. Cooling rate or capacity is also expressed in *tons*. A ton of cooling is equivalent to a cooling rate of 12,000 Btu/hr. A large hotel could have several chillers rated at several hundred tons each. All equipment ratings use a standard rating point to allow for comparison among equipment. The cost of equipment operation depends on the load on the equipment, the equipment efficiency, and the cost of electricity (the usual source of power for chilling equipment).

An understanding of the factors that define and influence the efficiency of cooling systems can be helpful in achieving optimal performance of these systems, in controlling operating costs, and in evaluating equipment for purchase.

The efficiency of cooling equipment involves measuring the ratio of the amount of cooling achieved (the output) to the amount of energy used to operate the system (the input). This ratio can be expressed in several ways. For smaller equipment, such as packaged terminal units used in guestrooms, the ratio may be expressed as the **energy efficiency ratio** or **EER.** The EER is calculated by dividing the rated cooling output of the unit in Btu/hr by the watts drawn by the unit. The higher the EER, the more efficient the unit.

Exhibit 5 contains information abstracted from manufacturers' specifications for packaged and through-the-wall air conditioners. Units of approximately the same cooling capacity were selected and the capacity chosen is one suitable for many guestroom applications. The operating voltage (230/208) also represents two of the possible operating voltages, with 265 also available (data not shown). The amps value is for operation in the cooling mode. Slightly lower amp requirements exist when in the heat pump mode but substantially higher values exist if operating via resistance heating. Watts divided into the cooling capacity yields the EER value. Unless the cooling season is extremely short, purchase of units with EER values in excess of 10 is warranted.

We could estimate the operating cost of two different units if we knew the cost of electricity and the expected annual hours of operation of the units. The latter can often be supplied by the equipment dealer. If we assume we have a location where

Exhibit 5   Specifications of Various Air Conditioning Units

	Company A	Company A	Company B	Company B
Cooling Capacity	9000/8800	9200/9100	9000/8800	8600/8400
Volts	230/208	230/208	230/208	230/208
Amps	4.5/4.8	3.8/4.0	3.6/ 3.9	3.6/ 3.9
Watts	980/980	815/795	795/780	795/780
EER	9.0/9.0	11.0/11.0	11.3/11.3	10.8/10.8
Moisture Removal (pts/hr)	2.1	2.2	2.7	3.4
Air Circulation	270	310/290	260	230
Heat Pump Rated Capacity	8200/8200	8000	8400/8200	N/A
Heat Pump COP	2.8/2.8	3.2/3.2	3.4/3.5	N/A

there are 2500 full-load-equivalent operating hours, what is the difference in the annual operating cost of a unit with an EER of 9.0 versus 11.3?

The units with the 9.0 EER will require 2450 kilowatt hours of electricity per year. This number is derived by multiplying the unit wattage (980) by the operating hours (2500) and dividing this by 1000 to convert to kilowatt hours. The 11.3 EER unit will require 1988 kwh per year. The calculated savings for the more efficient unit is 462 kwh per year. If electricity costs $.10 per kwh, there would be a savings of $46 per year or about $500 over the life cycle (10+ years) of the equipment. The units themselves cost little more than $500, illustrating the value of buying more efficient equipment.

One of the units from Company B has a substantially higher moisture removal rate. This unit has been designed to produce dryer air in the guestroom. This will help to reduce potential problems due to mold and mildew that can occur when moisture levels are high. A slightly lower cooling capacity and EER also results.

Unit size should be matched to the cooling needs of the space; larger is not better. Larger units typically have a lower efficiency, cost slightly more, and may contribute to more humid conditions in the guestroom. Optimum service to guests and efficient operation is best provided by units matched to the peak needs of the room or slightly less than the peak needs, trading off a little capacity on the warmest days for higher efficiency the rest of the time. Operators who have reduced the heating and cooling needs of their guestrooms via installation of reflective window treatments, energy-efficient windows and doors, insulation, and energy-efficient lighting should not need to replace heating and cooling units with units of the same capacity. Smaller, less expensive units should be satisfactory, resulting in savings in initial costs as well as in energy costs.

Choosing heat pump through-the-wall units rather than resistance heat can be a good choice. Heat pump units can cost 10 to 15 percent more than resistance heat units. However, their annual heating energy usage can be half or a third that of resistance heating units. Paybacks could be as short as one heating season.

One final element of comfort related to PTAC and PTHP units involves noise. Purchasers of units are encouraged to test the noise generation of the units at all fan switch settings and while the compressor is cycling. Determine whether the levels of noise produced are satisfactory. This author's experiences with a unit that had only an ON switch for the fan was that the noise generated was excessive. In another instance, choosing a unit that cycled the fan along with the compressor created a most unpleasant night's "non-sleep" as the unit's cycling was far too noisy. Guest comfort includes acoustic comfort.

Larger cooling equipment, such as a building chiller, may have its efficiency expressed as an EER value or, more commonly, as a value of kilowatts per ton of cooling. The kw per ton value is really an inverse efficiency (input divided by output); that is, efficiency increases as the kw per ton value decreases.

Recent advances in equipment rating methods of larger equipment have improved the way in which efficiencies are defined. Ratings can now consider performance at various load levels. Ratings compiled in this manner are known as **integrated part load values (IPLV).** The information gained using this approach can be significant, since equipment operates for much of the time at partial loads. Selecting equipment with these part load efficiencies in mind can result in lower operating costs.

CFCs, HCFCs, and the Environment

During the 1980s, concern about ozone depletion in the stratosphere and global warming began to grow. Investigation determined that a major contributor to ozone depletion was probably the discharge of chlorofluorocarbons (CFCs) and to a much lesser extent hydrochlorofluorocarbons (HCFCs). CFCs and HCFCs are chemical compounds manufactured for use as solvents and refrigerants.

In past decades, a number of CFCs and HCFCs were commonly used in air conditioning and refrigeration equipment. The CFCs R-11 and R-12 have been used in centrifugal chillers. Reciprocating chillers used R-12. HCFC R-22 has been used in refrigeration equipment as well as some chiller, packaged air conditioning systems, and window units.

Depending on the type of equipment, age, and specific recommendations of suppliers, various options are available to retrofit refrigerants to existing equipment. However, some equipment does not lend itself to retrofitting and new equipment should be purchased using HCFCs with lower ozone depletion or alternative refrigerants such as the hydrofluorocarbons (HFCs) having near zero ozone depletion ratings. Information on the potential substitute refrigerants and other issues of interest regarding refrigerants can be found at the United States Environmental Protection Agency[4] and at the United Nations Environmental Program.[5] Decisions about refrigerant changes should be made only after careful evaluation and consultation with equipment suppliers. Changing refrigerants is not as easy as changing the oil in your car.

New refrigerants may also introduce some safety concerns. There may be a need for refrigerant monitoring devices in mechanical spaces because of potential toxic effects of exposure to refrigerants. Operations may have to purchase breathing apparatus to protect staff in the instance of leakages. These issues should be addressed with the equipment suppliers and the local health and building code authorities.

One possible solution to the potential costs and uncertainty of HCFCs and HFCs is to use an absorption (heat-driven) chiller. Exhibit 6 illustrates one application of an absorption chiller, showing the variety of issues and opportunities that arise when considering this technology.

The Montreal Protocol, signed in 1987 with subsequent modifications over the years, provides a schedule for the phaseout of ozone-depleting refrigerants as well as other rules and regulations including provisions for global taxes on these materials. Many countries are signers of the Protocol and therefore legally obligated to ensure compliance by their citizens. The Protocol represents a major global action to address environmental change caused in this instance by ozone depletion. This depletion is partially caused by refrigerant emissions.

Hospitality firms and individual properties should have monitoring programs in place to ensure they are following applicable local laws related to the Montreal Protocol and should be considering the implications of the HFC and HCFC regulations when performing maintenance and purchasing new equipment. One side benefit of the Protocol has been that new equipment purchased using refrigerants with lowered or zero ozone depletion potential have generally been more efficient than the existing equipment. Responding to an environmental "threat" has in this instance turned out to be good business—providing more reliable equipment with reduced operating costs.

There are increased costs associated with the CFC/HCFC issues. First, the cost of CFCs has risen substantially due to new taxes and restricted availability. The production of CFCs had essentially been eliminated by the year 2000. Production of HCFCs will probably be eliminated by the year 2020 and possibly sooner. Therefore, only recycled forms of these products will likely be available for replacement needs. Scarcity and the cost of recycling will be reflected in a higher price.

A large amount of the refrigerant discharged from equipment in past years was discharged due to either poor equipment maintenance or poor maintenance practices. Refrigerant leaks clearly must be eliminated or reduced to their lowest possible level. In the past, leaks were sometimes tolerated because refrigerants were relatively inexpensive and perceived to be inert and safe. These conditions no longer apply. Maintenance employees will require retraining and certification concerning appropriate practices. Venting of refrigerants as a standard purging method must be eliminated. Proper equipment must be used to remove refrigerants from equipment and either recycle it on-site or store it for eventual reclamation at an off-site reclamation plant.

The decision to repair, modify, or replace existing refrigeration equipment will be more difficult. An operation with an existing chiller may wish to continue to use a CFC refrigerant but take steps to minimize possibilities of refrigerant release. This could mean installing equipment to facilitate the recovery and reuse of refrigerant.

Exhibit 6   Gas-Fired Cooling for Philadelphia Marriott

Over 1400 rooms totaling about one million square feet are air-conditioned mainly by a natural-gas-fired absorption chiller at the Philadelphia Marriott hotel. Philadelphia Gas Works (PGW) developed an economically attractive equipment package, which was selected by the customer based on cost savings and energy efficiency.

The hotel's hybrid cooling system design minimizes operation costs, since the gas chiller provides most of the air-conditioning while an electric unit assists only on hot, humid summer days. The Philadelphia utility benefits from additional gas load year-round and especially during the summer, when sales volumes are lower. PGW's gas cooling load now totals about 250,000 Mcf/season.

Background

The 23-floor Philadelphia Marriott, occupying a city block in the business district, opened in early 1995. The hotel offers 11,000 square feet of meeting space, four ballrooms, four restaurants and lounges, retail space, and many other amenities.

The heating, ventilation, and air-conditioning (HVAC) system was designed by Giovanetti-Shulman Associates (Drexel Hill, PA), which analyzed the economics of various fuels and equipment including city steam, electric chillers, heat pumps, and fan coils. Marriott's choice, based on economics and energy efficiency, was a 1,000-ton Thermachill™ unit manufactured by The Trane Co. The lower gas rate compared to electricity, along with an equipment rebate, were factors in the hotel chain's decision.

Implementation

The Trane Thermachill unit at the Marriott hotel is a direct-fired, double-effect chiller that runs primarily on natural gas. At the height of the cooling season, the gas-fired chiller is assisted by a Carrier Corp. 1,000-ton electric centrifugal chiller. The two units were piped in series to ensure that the absorption equipment takes preference.

For additional operating cost savings, the HVAC system features variable-flow pumping, water- and air-side economizers, and variable-air-flow equipment.

Advantages

As with most gas cooling systems, the biggest advantage of absorption chillers is low operating costs. Commercial electric rates penalize consumption during peak demand periods, mainly hot summer days requiring air conditioning. In hybrid cooling systems, gas-fired chillers give operators more flexibility to minimize costs by selecting the most economical combination of energy sources, gas and electricity.

Demand charges are pegged at $12.72/kw, and electric rates range up to 8.9 cents/kwh in an extremely complex rate structure. Due to a ratchet clause, a high peak demand charge for electricity is enforced year-round. Even during the winter, the customer pays 80% of the worst (highest) 15-minute summer peak demand charge.

PGW offers a very competitive gas cooling rate of $4/Mcf from May through September for interruptible service. Marriott selected a dual-fuel chiller (gas/ #2 fuel oil) to take advantage of this interruptible rate, but during four years of operation, the system has never been interrupted during the cooling season. PGW also offered a rate on the absorption chiller cost, which the utility views as a worthwhile means of increasing summer gas load.

Other advantages of gas absorption technology include quiet operation, low maintenance, and environmentally harmless refrigerants. Brian Mazuk, Marriott's Chief Engineer, says, "We have very few problems. The chiller operates efficiently, even at part-load capacity. We use natural gas as the primary fuel because it is cheaper and cleaner."

Source: "Municipal Case Studies: Philadelphia Gas Works—Absorption Chillers," August 1999.

Exhibit 7   Guestroom HVAC Options

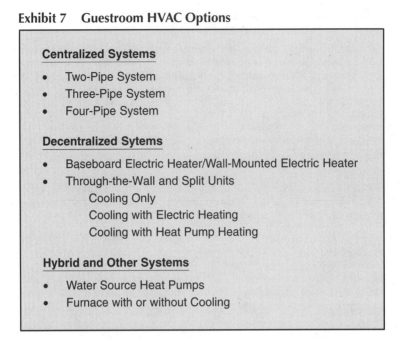

Centralized Systems

- Two-Pipe System
- Three-Pipe System
- Four-Pipe System

Decentralized Sytems

- Baseboard Electric Heater/Wall-Mounted Electric Heater
- Through-the-Wall and Split Units
  Cooling Only
  Cooling with Electric Heating
  Cooling with Heat Pump Heating

Hybrid and Other Systems

- Water Source Heat Pumps
- Furnace with or without Cooling

Another option would be to change refrigerants. Finally, careful analysis may lead you to decide to replace the chiller completely.

Each of these options requires you to evaluate a number of issues. You will need to collect a significant amount of data and to consult knowledgeable individuals. A good source for current information is the American Society of Heating, Refrigerating and Air-conditioning Engineers located in Atlanta, Georgia.

Guestroom HVAC System Types

Exhibit 7 is a summary of the possible options for providing HVAC to guestrooms. The two major types of systems are centralized and decentralized. All modern centralized systems use pipes to distribute hot and chilled water to fan coil units in the guestrooms. The hot and chilled water is produced by large boilers and chillers. Most decentralized units use electrically powered equipment in the guestroom itself to provide heating and cooling. The "other" systems in Exhibit 7 are less frequently found, but they may be used in some applications.

Centralized Systems

Centralized systems use boilers to create hot water and chillers to create cold water. The hot and cold water is circulated to fan coil units in the guestrooms. Air is blown through the fan coils, where heat is transferred either to or from the water, and heating or cooling occurs. Because the only devices operating in the guestroom are small fans, centralized systems are relatively quiet.

Because fan coils require no connection to the outside of the building, they can be placed in a variety of locations in the guestroom. These include under the exterior window, horizontally above the ceiling in entry areas, and vertically on adjoining walls. Vertical units are usually installed back to back; this reduces installation costs by sharing pipe and electrical runs vertically in the building.

The **two-pipe system** allows both heating and cooling, but only one of these at a time. In the two-pipe design, someone must decide whether to provide heating or cooling on a given day. Converting from one option to the other usually takes several hours or even a day or two, so it is important to choose wisely. Since only one mode is possible, the two-pipe system is not capable of dealing with situations requiring both heating and cooling over the course of a day. The operating costs of two-pipe systems are relatively low, since they limit guest HVAC options, allow shutdown of the boiler or chiller during seasons of the year, and provide fuel economies due to the operation of fossil fuel heating and an efficient central chiller.

The guests and management of facilities with two-pipe systems may be frustrated by these systems' lack of flexibility in meeting varying conditions in the building. If a building has cool outside air temperatures but abundant sunshine or widely varying outside temperatures from night to day, it will be very difficult to maintain comfortable conditions in all guestrooms. While little can be done to rectify this in the operating mode, it may be possible to make relatively minor modifications to the building piping layout that will zone the building, allowing portions to be connected to a chiller and others to the boiler. Another option is to install water source heat pumps when guestroom fan coils are replaced, if the existing electrical supply to the fan coils will allow this.

To increase the comfort provided by the two-pipe system, some operations install units that contain small electric resistance heaters. This allows the guest to select heating or cooling. This is often done in locations that have a relatively short heating season, where the expense of a boiler is not warranted. If a boiler is installed as well, the electric heater will have a sensor that disables it when the building heating system is operational.

While modern two-pipe designs use hot water, steam may be used in some older designs. When this is the case, it is not possible to connect the fan coil to a chiller. If needed, space cooling will have to be provided by another means.

The **three-pipe system** is relatively uncommon, especially in recent construction. This system provides both hot and cold water to the fan coil units at all times and mixes the return water from the fan coils. The three-pipe system can provide good guestroom comfort, since heating and cooling can be provided as needed. However, since the boiler and chiller both use this lukewarm return water as input water, their efficiencies are reduced, causing their operating costs to rise. That is, this system must use energy to bring the lukewarm return water back up and down to proper boiler and chiller temperatures.

The **four-pipe system** provides the same level of comfort as the three-pipe system, but keeps the cold and hot water returns separated. This leads to greater boiler and chiller efficiency, since much less energy is needed to reheat and recool the return water. The four-pipe system is the most expensive central system option to install, since it requires more extensive piping and two coils in the fan coil unit.

The control of comfort in the guestroom can involve several different methods, depending on the system. For those systems with a wall-mounted thermostat, the thermostat generally controls one or more valves in the fan coil unit. If a combination heating and cooling thermostat is used, it will activate either the heating or cooling mode of operation (hot or cold water valve setting), depending on the thermostat setpoint (the desired room temperature) and the actual room temperature. Fan operation and speed may be selected by using a switch located with the room thermostat. The thermostat usually controls only the heating or cooling operation. It is rare that the thermostat also controls the fan. Units lacking wall-mounted thermostats have controls on the units themselves which allow selection of heating or cooling, fan speed, and temperature.

Decentralized Systems

Decentralized systems place the heating and cooling sources within the guestroom itself or along the outside wall. An electric baseboard heating system is a decentralized heat source. Electric heaters may also be wall-mounted with a fan, an arrangement found in some bathroom areas. Electric baseboard or fan-forced units generally do not incorporate any method of providing or delivering cooling. For operations in cold climates or those operating seasonally, it may be satisfactory to provide heat only. However, most guestrooms require both heating and cooling, and some require only cooling.

Decentralized systems that provide cooling use a small refrigeration system (compressor, condenser, evaporator, and expansion valve) located within a cabinet that extends through the outside wall of the guestroom. "Split" decentralized systems locate only the evaporator and distribution fan in the guestroom and put the condenser and compressor outside the building on a balcony, roof, or on the ground. The condenser has access to outside air, which it uses for heat rejection. The evaporator is located within the room. Room air is circulated through the evaporator, where it is cooled and dehumidified.

Many decentralized units provide space heating with an electric resistance heater. This may create rather high costs for space heating. One way to reduce the cost of space heating may be to use a **heat pump** unit instead of electric resistance heating.

The heat pump unit uses the refrigeration cycle not only for space cooling, but also for space heating. Reversing the direction of refrigerant flow in a heat pump causes the components functioning as the evaporator and the condenser to switch functions. As a result, heat can be removed from the outside air and added to the inside (and vice versa). The heat pump uses the refrigeration cycle to do this at an efficiency two or more times greater than that of electric resistance heat.

Heat pump efficiency (output divided by input) is defined as heat delivered in Btu/hr (output) divided by the heat equivalent of the electric energy input (with each watt of input the equivalent of 3.413 Btu/hr). This ratio is defined as the **coefficient of performance (COP)**. A unit capable of delivering 8200 Btu/hr (2.4 kw) while drawing 1000 watts has a COP of 2.4.

The COP is less of a constant than the EER because the temperature conditions of operation vary considerably over the heating season. The evaporator will "see" outside conditions ranging from temperatures in the 50s to the 20s Fahrenheit (12 to –7 Celsius), or possibly less. Equipment vendors are able to calculate seasonal performance values for heat pump units and compare these with the performance of electric heat-only units to determine potential savings. Keep in mind your expected operating mode for the units when considering this. If occupancies are low in the winter months and you keep temperatures relatively cool in unoccupied rooms, the vendor's savings figures for replacing an existing unit with a heat pump may be somewhat overstated.

A factor affecting heat pump operation involves the defrost cycle on the evaporator. Since the evaporator extracts heat from the outside air, cold temperatures may result in frost buildup. The unit will go through a defrost cycle to remove this buildup. The controls governing the defrost cycle must operate properly if the heat pump is to function efficiently.

The efficiency of cooling equipment will vary, depending on the conditions at the evaporator and the condenser. The colder the evaporator temperature or the higher the condenser temperature, the less efficiently the equipment operates and, therefore, the less cooling it delivers. While we may think we have little control over evaporator or condenser temperatures, maintenance actions can make a difference. If the evaporator is starved for air as a result of a clogged filter, its temperature will drop and efficiency will suffer. The same is true when the evaporator or condenser is "insulated" by a layer of dirt and dust. Heat transfer is reduced and efficiency suffers.

The operation of virtually any HVAC system in the cooling mode produces condensate on the evaporator. Therefore, a means of condensate removal must be provided. Some older units just drip the condensate outside the building. The current standard involves either using some sort of evaporation or ejection system (which ideally vaporizes the condensate) or draining the condensate from the drip pan to a drain system.

Other Systems

Hybrid systems have characteristics of both centralized and decentralized systems. The water source heat pump system is the most obvious choice for this category. Rather than using outside air as the heat source or location for heat rejection, the water source heat pump is connected to an internal water circulation loop from which it takes, or to which it adds, heat (in the heating or cooling mode, respectively). This allows the heat pump to operate with an evaporator (or condenser) temperature that better maximizes unit efficiency. It also eliminates the need to locate the unit on the outside wall of the building and allows the operator to recover and use waste heat within the building.

In one hotel application, the water source is well water circulated through the pump and then returned to the ground—a "free" source of heat or cooling. In another hotel application, the water pipe connected to the heat pump is also the supply pipe for the sprinkler system, thereby reducing installation costs through dual use of the piping. In addition, this system cools all refrigeration equipment with the same water, providing a heat source for the heat pump throughout the winter months. Supplemental heating is provided by a boiler and the water loop is cooled in summer by the building's cooling tower. The result is a potentially very cost-effective application of heat pump technology.

Still another application emerging in some areas is geothermal heating and cooling. Geothermal has the potential to provide significant cost savings to hoteliers and in most applications to date has proven to be a very reliable technology.

The furnace systems mentioned in the "other" category in Exhibit 7 are sometimes found in condominium or timeshare units. In essence, a residential furnace is located within the unit. The unit may have an air conditioning capability as well. This is a type of decentralized system, but it relies on combustion of a fuel in the furnace and a remote condensing unit for the air conditioner. Therefore, they are rather different in design, appearance, and location from the typical decentralized through-the-wall unit.

Guestroom Ventilation

Providing fresh air to guestrooms can be a problem. Most guestrooms operate at a slight negative pressure due to the bathroom ventilation fan. The air removed by this fan must be replaced from somewhere. Guestrooms with central HVAC systems may rely on airflow under the guestroom door from a corridor to provide makeup air. If air does not enter the room under the door, it must migrate from somewhere and will leak in wherever it can, often along windows and through any opening. Decentralized HVAC units adjust the amount of outside air they admit.

If the outside air admitted to the room is not conditioned and controlled, operational problems can result. During the summer, hot and humid outside air leaking into guestrooms around windows and through the building exterior can result in moisture condensation in, and deterioration of, walls. In the winter, warm, moist interior air can deposit moisture in the walls as it migrates through the walls. Other related problems include mold growth on wall coverings and carpet. Some of these problems can be reduced by sealing and caulking, but the ultimate solution to many problems requires a redesign of building systems and often a resizing and reselection of the guestroom HVAC units as well. Coping with these types of problems can be a real headache for management and staff.

Guestroom HVAC Occupancy Control

While hotels are 24-hour-per-day, 7-day-per-week types of businesses, guestrooms are generally not occupied 24/7. Typical hotel occupancies are often 70 percent or less. This means 30 percent of the days of the year the room does not have even the potential of the guest being in the room. For the 70 percent of the time the room is rented, the guest is only present in the room a fraction of this time. For many operations, the guest may be in the room only 10 or 12 hours out of the day. Conditioning guestrooms 24/7 consumes large amounts of energy whose usage can be reduced. One option for reducing his usage is occupancy control of HVAC equipment.

Occupancy control of guestroom HVAC equipment adjusts the temperature in the room depending on room status (rented or not rented) and on guest (or other person's) presence. In summer, the setpoint for room temperature is raised.

Geothermal Heating and Cooling at the Galt House

Al Schneider is the owner and designer of the Galt House, a complex that now contains over 1.7 million sq ft that includes 100 apartments, 600 hotel rooms, 150,000 sq ft of conference space, and 960,000 sq ft of office space. Mr. Schneider engaged Marion Pinckley, of Pinckley Engineering, Inc., to look into using a GeoExchange system (geothermal) to heat and cool the Galt House East hotel. That 1,700-ton project was completed in 1984. Based on the success of the GeoExchange system in the Galt House East hotel, Mr. Schneider has since completed the Waterfront Office Building in 1993, and the 4,700-ton combined office/hotel/apartment complex Galt House has become the world's largest GHP project.

What made GeoExchange appealing is its economy of installation and operation, ease of maintenance, and environmental benefits. System cost was $1,500/ton. A conventional system (centrifugal chillers, cooling towers, insulated pipes) for such a complex could cost from $2,000 to $3,000/ton. And maintenance is favorable due to heat pump technology, which does not require specialized procedures.

The system is controlled by a combination of thermostats and an energy management system. Each heat pump unit in the public and meeting areas has a normal thermostat with a sensor placed in it reporting to the EMS [energy management system]. The EMS kills the thermostat when it is energized; however, if the EMS fails, the thermostats take over control.

There are four 130-ft deep wells that each can provide up to 700 gpm [2,650 lpm] with 15-hp variable-speed pumps from the aquifer under Louisville. Ground water at 58° F [14.4° C] is pumped into a 150,000-gal reservoir under the mechanical room. Water from the reservoir flows into the Ohio River. Water from the reservoir is circulated through plate and frame heat exchangers which separate the ground water from closed loop circulation systems in the buildings. There is a total of 65,000 gal of water flowing through the entire loop system: 25,000 gal in the hotel loops, and 40,000 gal in the office building loops.

During a typical summer, water is stored at an approximate temperature of 80° F [27° C] while maintaining an average temperature of 55° F [13° C] in the winter. During spring and fall energy can be simply removed from the buildings during the day and put into the loops and 140,000-gal reservoir to be used at night. The Galt House East has a high internal load due to its occupants; therefore, incorporating GHPs with the use of thermal storage has proven to be very efficient. The use of thermal storage allows the controls to shut down the well pumps (sometimes for as long as a week) and use the Btus stored in the reservoir during the day, with a net cooling load, to heat the building during the night if necessary.

The office buildings are conditioned with package heat pumps of 10- to 20-ton capacity for interior areas. The exterior is conditioned by stacked vertical units for each bay. Exterior zones are defined as approximately the outer 12 feet.

The Galt House East hotel energy cost is approximately 53 percent of the adjacent original Galt House, when subjected to the same rented room/meeting room occupancy. The adjacent Galt House has heat pumps in the first three floors, which include meeting and public space. The remainder is served by electric heat from air units and package air-conditioning units with electric heat. An EMS and better insulation in the Galt House East contribute to the total savings, but the all-GeoExchange system contributes the major portion of the savings.

(continued)

(continued)

> Due to water-regulating valves and variable-frequency drives on the Galt House East circulating pumps, the pumps most often operate at 25 to 30 percent of full load. The office buildings are not filled, but similar savings are expected on that system.
>
> Each 4-ft tall [1.2 m], 15-hp, 700-gpm [2,650 L] pump provides the HVAC system with 3.5 MMBtu/hr of heating or cooling, equivalent to a 300-ton chiller/cooling tower combination and a 4-MMBtu/hr input boiler. The well pump and a heat exchanger pump will cost approximately $1.5/hr to operate, versus $15 to $20 for the conventional system.
>
> Maintenance cost and personnel requirements have been very favorable. A heat pump package does not require the skill and experience required by a centrifugal system with four pipe controls, VAV, or other systems common in large complexes.
>
> In addition to saving approximately $25,000/month in energy costs, the GHP has been very reliable because each space has its own system. Such a system also has reduced capital requirements during construction since the major portion of the equipment need not be purchased until required. And, of course, it was not necessary to furnish a 4,000-ton cooling tower, or its space and support. The GHP system saves 25,000 sq ft in space that would have been used for equipment rooms with a conventional system.
>
> All of this adds up to lower initial cost, lower operating cost, and a very friendly system for the owner, occupants, and maintenance personnel.

Source: GeoExchange Heating and Cooling Teleconferences (www.geoexchange.org/cases/ cs0007.htm)

In winter, the setpoint is lowered. Both of these actions reduce the amount of energy used to condition the room.

Some guestroom occupancy controls can also act to turn off the electricity in the guestroom when the guest is not present. Controls of this type have been used for years by four- and five-star hotels in a number of countries around the world. In one of the simpler versions of guest occupancy control, the guest places his or her "key" into a holder upon entering the room. This engages the electrical circuits for television, lighting, and sometimes HVAC (minibar and entry room lighting are on a separate circuit that is always energized). Guests know where their key is and the hotel reduces guestroom energy usage. Such systems will likely be coming to the U.S. in some form. The most recent version of ASHRAE 90.1-1999 (Energy Standard for Buildings Except Low-Rise Residential Buildings) has a provision for a feature similar to this for new hotel construction. How this provision is incorporated into building codes across the U.S. and throughout the world will be seen in the next decade or so.

Occupancy sensors can do more than just assist in energy conservation. This technology can also be integrated with security systems to provide enhanced security of guestrooms. When connected to the front desk, occupancy sensor systems can inform the hotel when guestroom doors are not closed properly or when unrented rooms are entered. Occupancy sensors can also create a signal that will tell housekeepers whether the guest is in the room, thus reducing the instances of those sometimes unpleasant encounters between sleepy, partially clad guests and housekeepers anxious to clean a room.

Guestroom HVAC Maintenance

Guestroom fan coil units are relatively simple devices. Maintenance of these units is generally part of the preventive maintenance (guestroom maintenance) activity. A common PM checklist for these units would include:

- Checking the operation of all valves and control knobs.

- Checking the thermostat for proper operation, appearance, and physical connections.

- Cleaning the filter inlet grill and physical connections.

- Replacing the air filter. (Note: This may be done monthly, while guestroom preventive maintenance may be only quarterly.)

- Cleaning the condensate drain and replacing algaecide tablets.

- Inspecting fans and cleaning and tightening connections.

- Checking the condition and fit of electrical plugs and connections.

- Checking and cleaning the outside air vent.

- Cleaning all coils.

- Lubricating blower motors.

- Painting locations such as condensate pan and any deteriorated surfaces. Reapply corrosion treatment if in coastal areas.

HVAC Systems for Other Building Areas

The fan coil and heat pump systems used in guestrooms may be used elsewhere in the building. Units similar to these are found in office spaces, some corridor and lobby locations, smaller meeting rooms, and similar areas. Other areas may use HVAC systems that differ from those found in the guestroom. Most of these systems operate with an air delivery system.

System Types and Configurations

The HVAC systems for building areas other than the guestroom generally involve some form of all-air system. Some all-air systems use **air handling units,** while other all-air systems use **packaged air conditioning units.** Air handling units (AHUs) consist of coils (through which steam/hot water or chilled water is circulated from central boilers and chillers), filters, fresh air intakes, exhaust air discharges, and sometimes humidification equipment. AHUs are generally located in building mechanical spaces, often somewhat remote from the areas actually being served. They are connected to these areas via duct systems.

Exhibit 8   Air Conditioning System for a Meeting Room or Restaurant

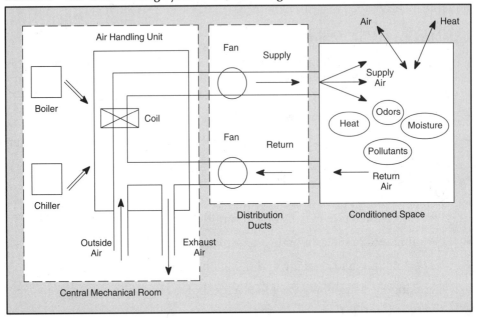

Packaged air conditioning units are generally mounted on the roof. Each packaged air conditioning unit operates separately and is essentially self-contained. A fuel provides heat and a refrigeration system produces cooling. Refrigeration systems of this type are called **direct expansion** (abbreviated DX) units because the evaporator is located directly in the conditioned airstream. Ductwork for these systems is usually less extensive than that for AHUs.

Exhibit 8 shows a very simplified view of an air conditioning system for a space such as a meeting room or restaurant. Within the box representing the space, people, food, and equipment generate heat, moisture, and odors. In addition, heat may be added or lost through the building structure and via air leakage. The air conditioning system in Exhibit 8 removes air from the space, exhausts some of this air, mixes fresh air with the remaining return air, filters this mixed air, and then either heats or cools the air. This "conditioned" air is moved to the space being conditioned, where it either warms or cools the space. It will also pick up moisture and odors as it moves through the space.

Packaged units often supply conditioned air for restaurants and various public areas in low-rise lodging facilities. The self-contained and factory-assembled nature of these units mean they can be installed quickly with relatively little on-site labor. On the other hand, their rooftop location means they may be somewhat neglected and not receive proper maintenance. One corporate director of engineering tells the story of a property in Texas that was unable to cool its ballroom. After numerous attempts to troubleshoot the system by phone failed, the director visited the property. Upon climbing on the roof to view the unit, he discovered that the access doors and ductwork on the unit had come loose. The unit was functioning on 100 percent (hot) Texas outside air.

Maintenance Needs

The maintenance needs of HVAC systems supplying public areas are derived from the maintenance needs of their individual components. These needs include filter changes, fan cleaning and lubrication, cleaning of heat transfer surfaces, cleaning of drain pans, checking of refrigerants for moisture and leakage, belt checking and replacement, and a variety of other maintenance actions. Once again, the equipment supplier should also supply a list of suggested maintenance actions, which should then become part of the units' maintenance program.

Filter replacement (or, in some instances, cleaning) may be done on a regular schedule or on an as-needed basis, with need determined by the degree of pressure drop occurring across the filter. When a manometer (a device that records differential pressure) is installed, it is possible to determine this pressure drop and, with input from fan suppliers or the system engineer, to establish an optimal filter replacement point.

Belt checking and replacement can be a key item. Replacing a worn belt with a new one can reduce the potential for future failure not only of the belt, but also of other fan components whose life may be compromised by worn belts (or by the belt when it breaks). When belts are replaced, the entire set should be replaced because worn belts have stretched and no longer have the tautness and alignment of a new set of belts.

Cleaning fans and heat transfer surfaces will help the system to operate efficiently at rated capacity and will reduce problems with fan imbalance caused by dirt accumulation. For badly neglected systems, it may be necessary to clean ducts as well to remove the buildup caused by neglect.

Other HVAC Components

With the exception of the most basic lodging guestrooms, a large number of components make up the HVAC system. We have discussed chillers, boilers, pumps, fans, and coils. Two other HVAC components warrant discussion. These are the building controls and the cooling tower.

Controls

Various forms of controls allow HVAC systems to operate properly, efficiently, and safely. Early HVAC controls consisted of a manually operated steam valve in a guestroom, an operable window, and a boiler operator who manually adjusted the firing rate of the boiler and kept the steam pressures within acceptable limits. Controls today are often electronic. They may interface with many computers and may be self-correcting and self-adjusting to changing conditions.

The most commonly encountered HVAC control is the thermostat. The thermostat, whether in a guestroom or meeting room, performs several tasks. First, it senses the temperature at the thermostat. It then converts the temperature into a signal (usually on or off) that is sent to the HVAC unit conditioning the space. The signal can be an on/off type or it can be proportional to the measured temperature. An "on" signal tells the HVAC unit to do something—usually to provide either heat or cooling. Some thermostats provide more control, such as time-of-day control, startup and shutdown, and staged heating. Thermostats may also have adjustable "dead bands" that establish a range over which neither heating nor cooling will be required. Units will also have some sort of differential control that establishes the range of likely operation around the setpoint. For example, a room thermostat set at 70° F (21.1° C) that has a two Fahrenheit degree control differential will need to sense room temperatures of 69° F (20.6°C) to initiate heating and 71° F (21.7° C) to stop heating. An appropriate differential will avoid excessively rapid cycling of the unit, while still maintaining the room temperatures within acceptable limits.

Various control devices help operate many other pieces of HVAC equipment. The simpler devices only turn equipment on and off. Others sense not only air temperature, but also relative humidity. The "enthalpy" or "economizer" control found on some HVAC systems determines when the temperature and humidity of outside air make it a potential source of cool air for the building. At such times, the mechanical cooling system can be turned off and cooling accomplished using outside air.

Older control sensors rely upon some sort of mechanical sensing and response to parameters being measured—for example, temperature measured by the degree of thermal expansion of a metal or a liquid. Some more modern systems use sensors that measure changes in electrical properties, relying on an electrical rather than a mechanical connection between the sensor and the controller. Sensors that provide an electrical signal proportional to the value being measured allow the operation of digital control systems. Digital systems use a control algorithm in the processing unit to analyze the signals and control the operation of equipment and systems.

Digital control systems allow the building operator to change the operation of the building from the central control computer. The building operator can also monitor system operation from the computer, determining the operating status and conditions of various pieces of equipment or systems. Digital control also makes variable output operation of equipment more feasible. The widespread use today of **variable air volume (VAV) systems** is largely due to advances in digital control. VAV systems vary the amount of air flowing into a zone based on sensor input of the load in the zone.

Building Automation Systems. Large, modern hotels can have relatively complex HVAC Systems with system components distributed throughout the building. Effective operation of theses systems requires a large amount of information and the coordination of a number of system components. To collect this information and effectively coordinate the operation of the components, hotels are increasingly installing (and updating) various forms of **building automation systems** (BAS).

Building automation systems generally use a digital signal that provides information about the operating status and conditions of a system. Signals could show not only the operating status of a fan but also how much air the fan was moving and the temperature of the air. Information could also be generated on the amount of energy being consumed.

The information collected is then used by the BAS to make decisions as to system operation. For a fan system, the BAS might monitor the outside air temperature, the temperature of the return air from the space, and the amount of air supplied to the space. As the return air temperature rises above a setpoint, the BAS might increase the airflow to the space to provide more conditioned air to keep the space at comfortable conditions. The BAS could monitor the outside air temperature and, if that air is cold enough to provide the cool air needed, shift from mechanically chilling the air to providing it via increased amounts of outside air. Decisions can be made by the BAS itself or an operator can provide control of systems. The operator does not have to be on-site—remote control via the WWW is possible as well. BAS systems attempt to use graphics to represent the system components and their operations.

Maintenance needs for control systems depend on the type of system. Cleaning of sensors may be necessary. Proper calibration of controllers, transmitters, and gauges is important, since incorrect signals will compromise system operation. Calibration may reveal failed sensors that need to be replaced. The sensing device needs to "know" how to correlate a given signal with the condition of a piece of equipment.

Maintaining modern control systems is often beyond the capabilities of property level maintenance staff. Maintenance contracts for these systems are common.

Cooling Towers

When a centralized HVAC system is used, the cooling of the refrigeration system is usually accomplished by circulating water through a **cooling tower.** The cooling tower cascades this water over various forms of tower fill and, at the same time, pulls or pushes air through the tower. As a result, some of the water evaporates, thereby cooling the remaining water. This cooled water is then circulated back to the cooling system to remove more heat from the condenser.

Cooling towers have rather specific operating and maintenance needs. Since not all operations need year-round cooling tower operation, there are also startup and shutdown considerations. Because the cooling tower is often located "out of sight," some operations forget about the startup and shutdown needs until it is too late. One facility was discovered to have a burst makeup water line (the result of a failure to drain the line when the unit was shut down for the winter) and badly corroded fan supports and other tower components. These problems, which were not found until startup began, resulted in an unknown but potentially significant water leak, a "rush" replacement of the tower, and unhappy guests while the building cooling system was out of service.

Since motors are used to power pumps and fans, all necessary motor lubrication needs to be performed. Electrical connections on all motors and controls should be inspected, cleaned, and tightened. Controls for the tower's water supply should be tested for proper operation. If controls fail to operate properly, the tower may consume excess electrical power, have excessive water usage, or fail to provide adequate heat rejection.

Because the tower uses outside air, dirt and other debris will be caught in the tower water. This debris needs to be removed from the tower basin and other locations where it may accumulate. Tower water is a potential breeding ground for various forms of algae and bacteria. Proper chemical treatment is necessary to control the buildup of these contaminants. Treatment is also applied to reduce the buildup of scale—dissolved salts that concentrate in the tower due to the evaporation of the water. Tower water treatment therefore involves using scale and corrosion inhibitors, dispersants to disperse sediments, biocides to kill or prevent multiplication of bacteria, and disinfectants of a variety of types.

Chemical treatment for cooling towers may be provided as a contract service. The manager's job is to ensure that the proper treatment is being provided, whether by in-house personnel or by a contractor. Failure to provide proper treatment can result in a significant decline in tower performance, increased operating problems and energy usage, and premature tower failure. In addition, the potential for Legionnaires' Disease due to bacteria in the tower entering the building ventilation system could pose a real danger to human health.

The metal in cooling towers should be inspected for corrosion. Any corrosion should be treated. Tower components need periodic cleaning and painting with corrosion inhibitors to avoid premature failure.

The startup and shutdown of towers requires attention to special concerns. Exhibit 9 contains suggestions for these special concerns. Some towers must be operated during subfreezing winter conditions because they provide heat rejection for computer rooms or food service equipment. These towers require attention to ensure that ice does not form in the tower. Some of these towers have mechanisms for adding heat to the water to melt ice, while others use tower fan shutdown or fan reversal to accomplish deicing. Large amounts of ice formation can be very damaging to the tower and building structure itself. Management supervision is required to keep these problems from occurring.

HVAC Thermal Storage

Because the cooling of buildings requires a large amount of energy, building operators and designers sometimes chose to use thermal storage as a means of reducing the cost of cooling. Thermal storage involves the storage of cold in the form of ice or chilled water and the use of this stored cold during periods of high energy cost. The ice or chilled water is produced at times of lower energy cost, typically during the late evening and early morning hours. During these times, not only are the costs of electrical energy (kwh) lower but also the costs of electrical demand (kw) can be lower or even non-existent. The additional cost of the chilled water storage systems can sometimes be partially offset by a reduced size of the chillers themselves and of other elements of the chilled water system.

Conclusion

The astute reader can identify in the discussions in this chapter the four major areas of responsibility of facilities management—safety and security, legal and regulatory compliance, service, and cost control. Proper selection, operation, and

Exhibit 9   Shutdown and Startup Considerations for Cooling Towers

Shutdown Considerations

- Disassemble, clean, and reassemble float and ball-cock valves.
- Wash down interior of the cooling tower.
- Clean perforated heat pans and spray nozzles.
- Drain and flush tower pans.
- Drain and flush pipelines.
- Drain and flush pumps.
- Lock closed automatic "fill" valves.
- Remove and clean strainers and screens.
- Inspect tower fans and drives for wear, cracking, and corrosion.
- Cover fan and louver opening subject to airborne dirt.
- Check pump motor bearings and lubricate.
- Paint all metal parts subject to alternate wetting and drying.

Startup Considerations

- Remove all debris from within and around unit, then flush as required.
- Check and clean strainers, bleed, overflow, and drain.
- Lubricate fan and motor bearings per manufacturer's recommendation.
- Change oil in gear reducer assembly per manufacturer's recommendation.
- Check belts, motor pulley, and motor mounts. Replace and adjust as required.
- Inspect electrical connections, contactors, relays, and operating/safety controls.
- Check motor operating conditions.
- Clean float valve assembly and check for proper operation.
- Check operating conditions. Adjust as required.

Source: Johnson Controls, Inc., "Fall Maintenance Checklist" (1985) and "Spring Maintenance Checklist" (1986).

maintenance of HVAC equipment is a major objective in providing a comfortable and safe environment for guests and employees. The operational costs of HVAC equipment can also be substantial, meaning that cost control of operation can make significant bottom-line contributions. Legal and regulatory compliance requires attention to the variety of regulations that cover HVAC equipment and its operation. Maintaining proper indoor conditions also helps to preserve the physical condition of the building and its contents, thus protecting the interests of the owner and operator.

Endnotes

1. Frank H. Randolph, "Air Conditioning," *Hotel Engineering Bulletins*, 1931, Cornell University, Ithaca, N.Y.
2. Further information on mold, mildew, and related problems can be found in the publication *Preventing Moisture and Mildew Problems in Hospitality Industry Buildings: Problem Avoidance Guidelines*, available from AH&LA Publications, 1201 New York Ave. NW, Suite 600, Washington, DC 20005-3931.

3. The heat content of steam as listed in Exhibit 3 is an approximate value, as are the values for natural gas, fuel oil, and LP/LPG. Specifically, the latent heat of vaporization of water is 970 Btu/lb. If you divide 33,475 by 970, you will get 34.5 lb of steam. Use of the 1000 Btu/lb figure is a common "rule of thumb" which is easy to remember and makes for simple math.

4. Visit http://www.epa.gov/ozone/title6/snap. This is the U.S. EPA's Significant New Alternatives Policy site. Substitute refrigerant information can be found at this site. Other information on refrigerants and ozone depletion can also be found on the EPA site.

5. Visit http://www.unep.org.

Key Terms

air handling units—An all-air HVAC system consisting of coils (through which steam/hot water or chilled water is circulated from central boilers and chillers), filters, fresh air intakes, exhaust air discharges, and sometimes humidification equipment.

building automation system (BAS)—A control system that uses a digital signal to provide information about the operating status and conditions of the HVAC system. Information collected by the BAS is used to make decisions as to system operation and automatically adjust for optimum operation.

coefficient of performance (COP)—A measure of heat pump efficiency defined as heat delivered in Btu/hr (output) divided by the heat equivalent of the electric energy input (with each watt of input the equivalent of 3.413 Btu/hr).

comfort zone—A range of conditions in which 80 percent of the population tested is "comfortable."

compressor—The component in a vapor compression refrigeration system that raises the temperature and pressure of the gaseous refrigerant coming out of the evaporator.

condenser—The component in a vapor compression refrigeration system in which a gaseous refrigerant releases heat and reverts to liquid form.

convection—The transfer of heat due to the movement of air over a surface and a difference in temperature between the air and the surface.

cooling tower—In a central HVAC system, the place at which refrigeration occurs. Water is cascading over fill, causing some of the water to evaporate, which cools the remaining water.

dew point temperature—The temperature at which water condenses.

direct expansion (DX) system—A refrigeration system in which the evaporator is located directly in the conditioned airstream.

energy efficiency ratio (EER)—A measure of the efficiency of cooling equipment calculated by dividing the rated cooling output of the unit in Btu/hr by the watts drawn by the unit.

evaporation—With regard to human comfort, a method of heat removal that occurs when a person's perspiration evaporates from his or her skin.

evaporator—The unit in a vapor compression refrigeration process in which the refrigerant is converted from liquid to vapor.

expansion valve—The component in a vapor compression refrigeration system that reduces the pressure and temperature of the liquid refrigerant just before it enters the evaporator.

four-pipe system—An HVAC system that provides both hot and cold water to the fan coil units at all times and keeps the return water lines from the fan coils separate.

heat pump—A device using the vapor compression refrigeration cycle to deliver either heating or cooling, depending on the direction of the refrigerant flow.

integrated part load values (IPLV)—Efficiency ratings that take into account equipment performance at various load levels.

latent loads—Addition or removal of moisture with resulting increases or decreases in the relative humidity only.

loads—In HVAC systems, variable inputs to and outputs from a space (i.e., sources of heat gain or loss and humidity).

occupancy control—A component of certain HVAC systems that adjusts the temperature in the guestroom depending on room status (rented or not rented) and on guest (or other person's) presence.

packaged air conditioning units—Generally roof-mounted, essentially self-contained air conditioning units in which a fuel provides heat and a refrigeration cycle provides cooling.

radiation—The transfer of heat occurring when two surfaces are at different temperatures. Energy is transferred in the form of thermal radiation from the warmer to the colder surface.

scale—A buildup of calcium or magnesium carbonate.

sensible loads—Heat addition and removal with resulting increases or decreases in dry bulb temperature only.

three-pipe system—A relatively uncommon HVAC system that provides both hot and cold water to the fan coil units at all times and mixes the return water from the fan coils.

two-pipe system—An HVAC system that allows both heating and cooling, but only one of these at a time.

vapor compression—A refrigeration cycle in which a circulating refrigerant removes heat from one location and transfers this heat to another location, where it is rejected.

variable air volume (VAV) system—An HVAC system that varies the amount of air flowing into a zone based on sensor input of the load in the zone.

wet bulb temperature—In measuring temperature, the value that would be measured if the bulb of a thermometer was surrounded by a small swatch of wet cloth.

(?)Review Questions

1. What factors affect guest and employee comfort? What is the comfort zone and how is it useful?

2. What are the two elements of furnace and boiler efficiency? How can you determine whether your furnace or boiler is operating efficiently?

3. How is the efficiency of cooling equipment measured? Is using integrated part load values a good way to define the efficiency of large cooling equipment? Why or why not?

4. What types of managerial decisions might be affected by growing concerns with ozone depletion in the earth's atmosphere?

5. What are the operating characteristics, advantages, and disadvantages of two-pipe, three-pipe, and four-pipe centralized HVAC systems? Are guests likely to know the differences between these systems? Why or why not?

6. How can heat pumps be used to provide both heating and cooling in guestrooms? What is the difference between an energy efficiency ratio and a coefficient of performance?

7. Why is makeup air required? What problems may result if the ventilation system provides insufficient makeup air to a guestroom?

8. How are air handling units different from packaged air conditioning units?

9. What sorts of controls are needed on HVAC systems? What is the difference between mechanical and digital controls?

10. Why is chemical treatment of cooling towers needed? What kinds of treatment are needed?

11. What is a building automation system (BAS)? What benefits does it provide the hotelier?

Internet Sites

For more information, visit the following Internet sites. Remember that Internet addresses can change without notice. If the site is no longer there, you can use a search engine to look for additional sites.

American Society of Heating, Refriger-Heating, and Air Conditioning Engineers
http://www.ashrae.org

Air Conditioning and Refrigeration Institute
http://www.ari.org

Consulting, Specifying Engineer
http://www.csemag.com

Cooling Tower Institute
http://www.cti.org

Gas Technology Institute
http://www.gri.org

Heating/Piping/Air Conditioning
(HPAC) Interactive-Engineering Basics
http://www.hpac.com/member/
basics/index.html

U.S. Environmental Protection Agency
—Building Air Quality
http://www.epa.gov/iaq/largebldgs/
baqtoc.html

U.S. Environmental Protection Agency
—Energy Star-Building Upgrades
http://yosemite1.epa.gov/estar/
business.nsf/content.business
resources upgradebuilding.htm

Chapter Appendix

The "Indoor Air Quality Handbook"—reproduced in its entirety on the following pages—is provided through the courtesy of *Options,* Philip Morris USA.

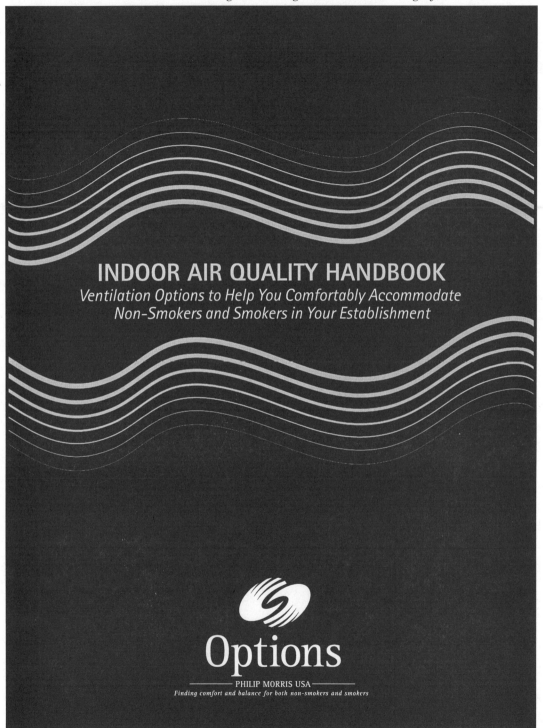

INDOOR AIR QUALITY HANDBOOK

*Ventilation Options to Help You Comfortably Accommodate
Non-Smokers and Smokers in Your Establishment*

Options

PHILIP MORRIS USA

Finding comfort and balance for both non-smokers and smokers

"Providing good ventilation is really no different than providing good food and friendly service. Its just smart business. Continuing to upgrade our ventilation system allows all customers to enjoy time spent at Wizard's Sports Café without complaints of smoke – our business is growing 8 to 12 percent annually."

— Cooper Stewart, Vice President, Wizard's Sports Café, Richardson, Texas

"We have reaped the economic benefits of improved ven tilation. Roughly 20 percent of my customers choose to smoke. We accommodate everyone, and that's a critical issue in our business."

— Bryan McGuire, General Manager, '21' Club, New York, New York

"The ventilation upgrade I chose has been well worth the investment – the indoor air quality is much improved, and my customers are pleased. This has given me a great sense of accomplishment and has allowed my business to stay profitable."

— George Hadler, Owner, The Bowling Palace, Columbus, Ohio

"We wanted an environment that wasn't uncomfortably smoky, but we didn't want to ban smoking – it didn't make financial sense. I believe smoking bans can really hurt business in bars. Improving the ventilation was definitely the route to go, and judging by how popular the bar is these days, the renovation was well worth the investment."

— Bob Harmon, General Manager, The Hitching Post Inn, Cheyenne, Wyoming

INTRODUCTION

Creating a comfortable environment for everyone is important. A smoky and stuffy environment can be annoying and bothersome to customers and employees. Environmental tobacco smoke can be unpleasant and annoying, and many people believe that it presents a health risk. That is why we strongly support options designed to minimize unwanted ETS, while still providing adults with pleasant and comfortable places to smoke. Despite the health issues surrounding ETS[1], recent public opinion research shows that many Americans support the accommodation of both non-smokers and smokers in hospitality establishments.[2]

So, how can you deal with the smoke and create a more comfortable environment for everyone, both non-smokers and smokers alike? One way is through improved ventilation. Ventilation is the method of diluting indoor air with air from outdoors, or with filtered indoor air, which is an important principle of improving indoor air quality, or IAQ. Ventilation helps to freshen the air and reduce the concentration of smoke and odors in the indoor space.

Improved ventilation is one way to make your customers, both non-smokers and smokers, and employees feel welcome and enjoy the time spent in your establishment. Recent public opinion research, conducted by Yankelovich in 2000, shows that the American public supports consumer and business owner choice[3]:

- 80 percent agree that we can find a way to accommodate both non-smokers and smokers in hospitality establishments.

- 86 percent believe that ventilation can have a lot or some impact on addressing smoking issues.

- 91 percent agree that they would be more likely to go to an establishment that had a state-of-the-art ventilation system over one that did not.

This handbook has been designed to demonstrate the potential benefits associated with enhancing your heating, ventilation, and air-conditioning (HVAC) system to improve IAQ in your establishment. By proactively managing IAQ within your establishment you can create a more comfortable environment for all customers and employees, as well as the following:

- Reduce equipment maintenance and housekeeping, thanks to less dust and particles

- Minimize smoke drift from cigarettes and cigars

- Reduce presence of lingering odors from the kitchen, cigarette smoke, and cleaning solvents

- Minimize the introduction of moisture that can lead to mold and mildew

Because the quality of the air in your establishment can make a difference in both comfort and the perception of cleanliness for your customers, ventilation in your establishment is important. By proactively managing the IAQ in your establishment, you can create more comfortable environments for your customers and employees, both non-smokers and smokers alike. Your customers expect you to provide a comfortable environment where everyone feels welcomed, and the success of your business depends on satisfying your customer expectations.

---

1 For more information about ETS and reported health effects in non-smokers, see our website: www.philipmorrisusa.com. *Options*, Philip Morris, USA does not purport to address health effects attributed to environmental tobacco smoke.

2 Omnibus survey conducted by Yankelovich Partners, April 2000, partially funded with a grant from *Options*, Philip Morris, USA.

3 Ibid.

TABLE OF CONTENTS

ONE: DECIDING YOUR ACCOMMODATION POLICY

If you decide to accommodate both non-smokers and smokers in your establishment, you need to consider your current facility layout, your business needs, and any applicable local building codes or smoking ordinances. By selecting an accommodation strategy based on this information, you can make all your customers and employees feel comfortable.

There are several strategies that you can use to accommodate non-smokers and smokers in your establishment:

- Integrated spaces — non-smokers and smokers can move freely throughout the establishment. This is most common in bars or taverns in which there is a variety of activities customers can enjoy.

- Separate designated areas — customers have a choice between a non-smoking area and a smoking area. Areas can be designated using many techniques, include spatial or physical barriers. Separate designated areas are most commonly used in establishments such as restaurants, hotels, and bowling centers which have multiple space usage.

- Separate rooms — areas that are fully enclosed and removed from other areas of an establishment. This is commonly used for private dining rooms, where special events, or banquets may be held. In addition, some larger facilities may choose separate rooms because their establishment may have large rooms that can be designated either smoking or non-smoking.

Let's take a closer look at each of these strategies to help you determine which one will work best for your business.

INTEGRATED SPACES

- Do you have a small space? A centrally located bar? Or a large establishment, in which your customers are frequently moving from space to space to enjoy activities such as billiards or dancing? Do you have a wide mix of customers; some of who smoke and some do not? Then an integrated approach to accommodation might be best suited to your establishment.

With an integrated space, customers can choose to smoke throughout the establishment. There are no designated non-smoking or smoking areas. By following the three principles of IAQ — (1) bringing in enough outdoor air; (2) filtering the outdoor and recirculated air; and (3) managing airflow — you can provide an environment that all customers can enjoy. (See section two for more information on the three principles of IAQ.)

SEPARATE DESIGNATED AREAS

- Do you have a larger facility with an open floor plan? Is your bar area located off to one side? Do you have a fairly steady mix of non-smoking and smoking customers that prefer separate section seating? Using designated non-smoking and smoking areas may be your best option for accommodating all of your customers.

- Does your current space have existing barriers like half-height walls, plants or room dividers? If so, these can be natural points to use as references when designating non-smoking and smoking areas.

Using a strategy to accommodate non-smokers and smokers in separate areas requires planning and thought about where air is supplied to your establishment and where air is removed from your establishment. If your customers' smoking preferences vary from day to day and night to night, you can still have flexibility in your space designation. If you have several areas that are separated by existing barriers, you can vary the designation of the areas based on the needs of your customers for that day or evening.

To avoid smoke and odor from drifting into the non-smoking area from the smoking area, air should be supplied to the non-smoking areas and removed from the smoking areas. (See section two for more information on controlling airflow.)

Designated areas allow you some flexibility in the size of your non-smoking and smoking areas. You can vary the size of the designated areas, based on your expected customer mix. For example, if you have an aisle that runs between your non-smoking and smoking areas, you can shift this aisle by moving tables and changing the number of tables allocated to the non-smoking and smoking areas. Keep in mind, though, that air should be supplied to your non-smoking sections and exhausted or removed from your smoking sections.

SEPARATE ROOMS

• Does your establishment consist of a number of rooms for dining and the bar area? Do you have separate rooms for private groups? If so, you can provide completely separated non-smoking and smoking areas for your customers.

Using a strategy to accommodate non-smokers and smokers in separate rooms requires planning about where air is supplied and where air is removed from your establishment. If a private room is set up to accommodate smoking, you do not want the smoke drifting from the room into a non-smoking area. Air should be supplied to the adjacent non-smoking areas or rooms and removed from the smoking areas or rooms. (See section two for more information on controlling airflow.)

When planning for a separate room, it is a good idea to plan for at least one open doorway or a "transfer grille" to allow for a consistent flow of air between the room and the adjacent space. When a door opens and closes, it causes turbulence in the air. This turbulence creates "puffs" of air that will come out from the room.

Additionally, care needs to be taken if you choose to recirculate air that has been removed from smoking areas so that smoke and odors are not redistributed to other areas of the facility.

ORDINANCES AND CODES

It is important to consider any requirements that your state or locality may have regarding the creation or designation of non-smoking and smoking areas. Some jurisdictions may require a certain percent of your establishment be designated as non-smoking; others may require a certain amount of space between non-smoking and smoking areas or require specific ventilation requirements to accommodate smoking in your establishment.

Call your local contractor or engineer, as they should be familiar with local ventilation codes and ordinances. Another option is to contact your local government's building and zoning department to learn about local codes and ordinances in your area.

> **HVAC Professional Tip:** Ask your HVAC professional if you should use supplemental air cleaning in a closed room in which you allow smoking. Supplemental air cleaner can help further reduce the amount of smoke and odors within the room.

TWO: MAKING VENTILATION WORK FOR YOUR BUSINESS

There are three steps that you can take to improve your IAQ and in turn help create a more comfortable environment for non-smoking and smoking customers and employees. The principles of IAQ involve your HVAC system. Your HVAC system will heat or cool air, deliver either outdoor air or recirculated air to a space, and remove stale air from a space — all for customer and employee comfort.

Three Principles of IAQ

1. Bring in enough outdoor air. Outdoor air must be supplied to a space to help reduce the concentration of particles and odors generated indoors.

2. Filter the outdoor and recirculated air. Filtration removes dust and particles from the air, which can help reduce both housekeeping and equipment maintenance.

3. Control airflow. Air should be supplied to non-smoking areas and removed over smoking areas to help minimize smoke drift.

IAQ PRINCIPLE ONE: BRING IN ENOUGH OUTDOOR AIR

Why is this important?

- Bringing in outdoor air can help reduce your housekeeping and maintenance by diluting odors and particles in the air. This also provides a fresher-smelling establishment for all of your customers and employees.

- State and local building or mechanical codes may require that a certain amount of outdoor air be supplied to buildings

- A complete HVAC system involves equipment to supply and remove air from a space. As shown in Figure 1 and 2, supplying air is just as important as taking it out of a space. The lesson is that air can not just be "pulled," it must also be "pushed."

Think of a lit kitchen match that you want to extinguish. Try to extinguish it by sucking air inward (pulling) — it does not extinguish. Now try blowing air to extinguish the match (pushing) — the match is now extinguished.

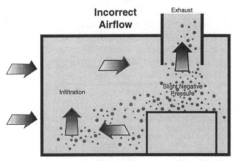

Figure 1: Smoke and odors can spread throughout the space without supply and outdoor air to "push" smoke or odors towards the exhaust.

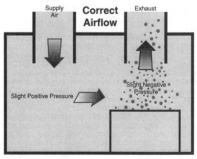

Figure 2: Supply and outdoor air provided to a space can "push" the smoke or odors to the exhaust.

Does increased outdoor air mean a greater out-of-pocket cost?

- Not necessarily. The cost varies on a building-by-building basis and depends on a variety of factors, including the building structure, climate conditions, geographic location, and the ventilation options you select.

- Using high-quality filtration and technologies can result in energy, maintenance, and other cost savings that can help offset the cost of heating or cooling the additional outdoor air.[4] (See section four for more information on HVAC technologies)

- You need to play an active role when working with an HVAC professional to determine what will work best for you based on your business needs and budget.

How to Accomplish Principle One

- Outdoor air can be brought into a building either mechanically or naturally.

  - Mechanical ventilation uses HVAC equipment to heat or cool air, deliver either outdoor air or recirculated air to a space, and remove stale air from a space.

  - Natural ventilation is a means in which air moves in and out of buildings through doorways, windows, and other openings. This type of ventilation is more practical in moderate climates when windows and doorways can be left open year round.

- Check your HVAC equipment. Most equipment has dampers or louvers that can be opened to allow the system to bring in outdoor air. These outdoor air intakes should be set to an "open" position so that outdoor air is being brought in at all times. The amount of outdoor air to bring into your establishment is usually based on the type of establishment and the occupancy. Most of the time existing equipment can be adjusted to bring in more outdoor air levels specified in state and local building or mechanical codes.

- **Renovation or new construction tip:** If you are planning on installing new HVAC equipment, make sure the HVAC unit is capable of bringing in the minimum amount of outdoor air as suggested by your state and local building or mechanical code.

> When you feed your family, one chicken is usually enough. When you have a party, you will need several chickens — the number of chickens you need will depend on the number of guests. It is the same with outdoor air. The more people you have the more outdoor air you need to supply to your establishment.

> **HVAC Professional Tip:** Ask your HVAC professional how much outdoor air your HVAC system is capable of bringing into your establishment and does it meet state and local building or mechanical codes. Your HVAC professional may also be familiar with the American Society of Heating, Refrigerating and Air Conditioning Engineers, Inc. (ASHRAE), which also provides ventilation guidance. ASHRAE Standard 62, *Ventilation for Acceptable Indoor Air Quality*, provides recommendations related to ventilation and indoor air that vary by venue. It is subject to a "continuous maintenance" process that involves ongoing revisions by means of addenda and interpretations. Some of these interpretations may change previous guidance for indoor smoking. You or your HVAC professional may wish to contact ASHRAE to determine the current status of the standard.

---

4 Burroughs, Barney. *Particulate Filtration: A New Look with New Data. Engineering Solutions to Indoor Air Quality Problems,* AWMA, 1995: 513–526.

IAQ PRINCIPLE TWO: FILTER THE OUTDOOR AND RECIRCULATED AIR

Why is this important?

• Upgrading the filtration on your HVAC equipment is usually the easiest and most cost-effective change you can make to improve the air quality in your establishment.

> "A filter is used in HVAC equipment to remove dust and other particles from the air stream before it is delivered to a space."

• Proper filtration can help remove odors and particles from your facility.

  • Most HVAC equipment is equipped with "angel hair" filters that only remove about 20 percent of the particles in the air. It is the smaller particles not removed by these filters that often contribute to odors and smoke haze.

  • Higher-quality filters remove more of the smaller particles from the air which can help improve the air quality, reduce housekeeping costs, and increase operating life and lower maintenance costs of your HVAC equipment

> Particles the size of grains of table salt and smaller pass right through "angel hair" filters. You can test this yourself: take the filter from your HVAC unit, hold it flat, and pour table salt on it. Shake it a little and the salt will fall through the filter. This means that small particles are passing through and in return can contribute to odors and smoke haze. In addition, it can result in your HVAC equipment becoming dirty and inefficient. If the smoke and haze causing particles are not removed by filtration, you may find yourself cleaning the counter tops, bar stools, and windows more often.

How to Accomplish Principle Two

• Read the labels on your HVAC system's filters and check their ratings. If your filters are not rated at least 65 percent dust-spot efficient, consider replacing them with filters that are. Filters rated above 95 percent efficiency, including HEPA filters, can have real economic payback, in addition to improving IAQ.[5]

> **HVAC Professional Tip:** Ask your HVAC professional if your HVAC system is capable of handling upgraded filters and how frequently your filters should be changed.

• Change your HVAC filters on a regular basis — but not too frequently. Filters get better at removing particles as they get dirty. Changing filters too frequently may mean you are not getting the full benefit of their ability to filter out the smaller particles.

> A good rule of thumb is to check your filters monthly, at least at first. Once they begin to develop a "sheen" of black dirt, then it is time to change them. Once you gauge how fast your filters get dirty, you can increase your time between inspections. However, it is always a good idea to check with the filter manufacturer or your HVAC professional on the recommended filter change schedule.

---

5 Ibid.

IAQ PRINCIPLE THREE: CONTROL AIRFLOW

Why is this important?

- By controlling the direction air moves in your establishment, you can minimize the potential for odor and smoke drift into unwanted areas. For example, think about a non-smoking and smoking area in a restaurant. You can control air movement so that smoke stays in the smoking area and does not drift into the non-smoking area.

- Proper management of airflow in you establishment can help provide a more comfortable environment for all your customers and employees. Manage the airflow within your establishment smoking sections so that air is supplied over areas in which your employees frequently are situated, such as the bartender's workspace.

- Controlling airflow allows you to be more flexible in accommodating your mix of customers. You can maintain an open floor plan, as opposed to using walls and partitions to separate non-smoking and smoking areas, which can allow the non-smoking and smoking areas to expand or contract based on seating requests.

> "Did you know that you can actually determine where air will flow in your establishment? All it takes is a little thought about the layout of your establishment and the location of the grilles that supply and remove air from your establishment."

How to Accomplish Principle Three

- Airflow is controlled by either negatively or positively pressurizing an area. Air will always move from a positively pressurized area to a negatively pressurized area. So what does this mean for you? Your non-smoking areas should be positively pressurized and your smoking areas should be negatively pressurized. This will cause the air to move from the non-smoking area to the smoking area.

> **Positive pressure:** More air is supplied to a space than is removed from a space
> **Negative pressure:** More air is removed from a space than is supplied

- Identify where air is supplied to your establishment (air is usually supplied via supply diffusers) and where air is removed from your establishment (air is usually removed via return grilles or an exhaust fan). Are your non-smoking areas located where you have the majority of supply diffusers and are the smoking areas located where you have the majority of return grilles or exhaust fans?

  Think about the lit match again. You cannot suck out (exhaust) the flame, but you can blow it out (supply). It is the same with air in your facility. You use supply air to blow smoke, haze, odors, and particles toward the exhaust. The exhaust alone will not pull the smoke, odors, and particles out of the space.

- Sketching your floor plan with the location of supply diffusers and return grilles or exhaust fans can help you determine how to manage the flow of air throughout your establishment. This type of sketch is called an airflow footprint. See section three for an airflow footprint worksheet, which can help you and your contractor design an airflow footprint based on your establishment.

> **HVAC Professional Tip:** An HVAC professional can help you locate your supply grilles and return diffusers to determine if your floor plan is set up to take advantage of the benefits of moving air from positively pressurized areas to negatively pressurized areas.

> **Renovation or new construction tip:** If you are planning to install a new duct work system, tell your HVAC professional that you would like to locate the majority of supply diffusers over non-smoking areas and the exhaust and return grilles over smoking areas.

- In addition to managing airflow between areas in your establishment, you also need to think about your establishment as a whole. What is your establishment's pressurization relative to the outdoors? Determine the overall pressurization in your establishment by noticing whether air moves in or out of the building. You should supply a little more air to your establishment than you remove from your establishment. This will keep your establishment at a slight positive pressure relative to the outdoors.

Go to the door your customers come in. Does the door open easily? If the door pulls open easily and air flows out, your building is positively pressurized. If the door is resistant and difficult to open and air flows into the space, your building is negatively pressurized.

THREE: DESIGNING AN AIRFLOW FOOTPRINT

An "airflow footprint" illustrates the direction air moves within your establishment and charts the areas of your establishment that are under negative pressure and positive pressure. The airflow footprint includes the floor plan of your establishment, as well as the location of supply diffusers, and the return and exhaust grilles. Creating an airflow footprint can help you determine the ventilation strategy that works best with the layout of your establishment and your accommodation preferences.

You can use this tool to see how air is flowing and make any necessary changes, such as the location of your supply diffusers and return or exhaust grilles. It will also help you understand how to contain odors generated within your facility. Having this diagram will be a helpful tool in communicating with a HVAC professional regarding layout and use of space.

CREATING AN AIRFLOW FOOTPRINT

1. Draw an outline of your establishment with appropriate walls and doorways (the drawing does not need to be to scale); a blank grid is provided on the following page.

2. Label the uses of each area, for example non-smoking dining area, smoking bar area.

3. To determine where the supply diffusers, return grilles, and exhaust fans are located within the facility:

    • Use a single ply of tissue.

    • Hold the tissue up to each supply diffuser, return grille, and exhaust fan.

    • Note the direction that the tissue is moving.

       - If the tissue being blown into the space, then it is a supply diffuser.
       - If the tissue being drawn into the grille, then it is a return grille or exhaust fan.

    • Indicate the location of the supply diffusers, return grilles, and exhaust fans on the drawing by using the correct symbols illustrated in the diagram.

4. To determine directional airflow:

    • While customers are present, pay attention to the direction that smoke moves within your establishment.

    • You or your contractor can use a "smoke pencil", available from safety equipment suppliers. A "smoke pencil" is a devise commonly used by HVAC professionals to determine directional airflow.

    • A match that has been just blown out will also provide the same effect as the smoke pencil.

    • When you notice the direction that the smoke is moving, mark it on the drawing with an arrow.

The following is an example of an airflow footprint with the steps referenced above.

Example of an airflow footprint

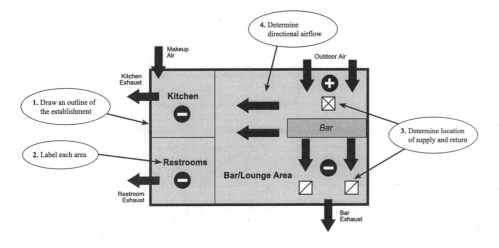

Use the sample airflow footprint chart in the handbook to create a footprint of your establishment. While your establishment space will be different, your airflow footprint should illustrate the space use, location of supply and exhaust vents, and directional airflow. Work with an HVAC professional to determine if you are maximizing the capability of your HVAC system relative to the different space usage in your establishment.

> **HVAC Professional Tip:** Your HVAC professional can test, adjust, and balance (TAB) your supply grilles, return diffusers, and exhaust fans to help ensure that more air is supplied than removed from areas where less smoke and odor is desired, such as designated non-smoking areas or a bartender's work space. This process also helps ensure that air flows in the correct direction according to your airflow footprint

AIRFLOW FOOTPRINT SAMPLE CHART

Date _____
Facility Name and Address
_____
_____
_____
_____

Key

Positive Air Pressure.
Areas where more air is supplied
to a space than is removed from it. Air is
pushed out of a space into other areas.
*Example: The non-smoking area should
be positively pressurized.*

Negative Air Pressure.
Areas where more air is removed from a
space than is supplied to it. Air is drawn in
from other spaces.
*Example: The smoking area should be
negatively pressurized.*

Direction of Airflow.
Indicates the direction air is moving
between spaces.
*Example: The air should be moving from
non-smoking areas into smoking areas.*

Supply.
Air that is being supplied to a space
through a diffuser.
Outdoor air supply should exceed your
total exhaust capacity.

Return or Exhaust.
Air that is removed from a space through
a return grille or from an exhaust fan.
Exhaust fans should be located in
smoking areas, kitchen areas, and
restrooms.

FOUR: VENTILATION TECHNOLOGY OPTIONS

There is no "one-size-fits-all" approach to improve IAQ and comfortably accommodating non-smoking and smoking customers and employees through ventilation. The design and application of ventilation options can vary based on the actual physical space, the accommodation policy you choose (see section one), and the activities in your facility.

Technology options discussed here include air cleaning, energy recovery ventilators (ERV), and demand controlled ventilation (DCV). These technologies support the three IAQ principles you can take to improve your ventilation (see section two). Regardless of the technology you use, the benefits of upgrading your ventilation system can go beyond managing smoke drift and odor. Other common problems such as odor build-up and grease from a cook stove can also be reduced, resulting in housekeeping, maintenance, and potential energy savings. Using one or more ventilation technologies can be a cost-effective, practical investment that can pay for itself over time through higher revenues and lower operating costs.

You should work with your HVAC professional to help determine which technology will work best for your business.

SUPPLEMENTAL AIR CLEANERS

The technologies

There are two common types of supplemental air cleaners:
• Electrostatic precipitators, which remove particles
• Three-phase air cleaners, which remove both particles and odors

"Air cleaners are commonly found ceiling mounted or at your central HVAC system. They supplement the filters used in your HVAC system and can be used to supplement the amount of outdoor air brought into your establishment."

Electrostatic Precipitator

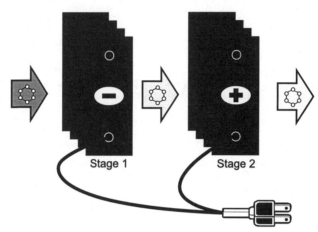

This figure illustrates how electrostatic precipitators use two stages to electronically remove particles from the air.

- The first stage uses a high voltage current that negatively charges the particles in the air.

- In the second stage, the charged particles enter a collector, a series of positively charged plates that attract the particles, much the way magnets attract iron particle

Everybody is familiar with an electrostatic precipitator in the form of a TV set. The screen is always dustier than the cabinet. This is because electricity in the TV tube puts a charge on the glass and that attracts dust particles. Electrostatic precipitators work the same way. They create a charge that attracts the particles.

Three-Phase Air Cleaner

This diagram shows how a three-phase air cleaner removes gas and odors from the air stream.

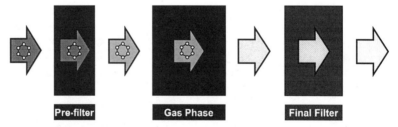

- The pre-filter, or first stage, removes larger particles.

- The gas phase, or second stage, often uses charcoal to absorb gases and odors.

- The fine particulate filter, or third stage, removes very fine particles.

Note: The order in which the stages appear will vary from manufacturer to manufacturer.

The potential benefits

• Reduces housekeeping and maintenance by removing odors and particles from the air.

• Provides a good supplement to the outdoor air that you supply to your establishment.

> HVAC Professional Tip: Some building or mechanical codes will allow the use of air cleaning to supplement the amount of outdoor air that is required by code. Ask your contractor if this option is available to you.

Points to remember

• Air cleaning is not a substitute for outdoor air, it is a supplement.

• Bringing in outdoor air can help reduce your housekeeping and maintenance by diluting odors and particles in the air. This also provides a fresher-smelling establishment for all of your customers and employees.

• In special cases, such as historical buildings, creative engineering alternatives, using a combination of outdoor air and air cleaning, can usually resolve ventilation problems in a cost-effective manner.

• Apply proper care and maintenance of air-cleaning equipment from the start. If air cleaners are not properly maintained they will become less effective at capturing the particles or odors from the air. Follow the manufacturer's recommended filter change or cleaning schedule to ensure the air cleaner is working at optimum levels.

> HVAC Professional Tip: Inquire about a maintenance contract to ensure that your air cleaners are properly cleaned and maintained.

ENERGY RECOVERY VENTILATORS

The technology

• ERVs take energy from the air that is removed from your establishment (exhaust air) and add it to the new outdoor air coming into your establishment. This allows the new outdoor air to be either pre-heated or pre-cooled before it gets to your HVAC equipment. The job of your HVAC equipment is thus reduced, as it will not have to heat or cool the air as much before it enters your establishment.The following diagram shows how the ERV takes temperature from the air removed from the establishment (exhausted air) and adds the temperature to the air entering the establishment (supplied outdoor air). This allows the new outdoor air to be pre-cooled before it gets to the HVAC equipment.

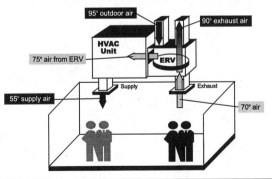

> Note that ERVs can also help pre-heat air when the temperature outside the establishment is colder then inside.

You have a cup of hot coffee and a cup of cold coffee. If you mix them together you have two cups of warm coffee. It is the same with bringing hot outdoor air through a cool ERV wheel or cold outdoor air through a warmer ERV wheel. Because of heat transfer, you end up with warm air and a warm wheel. Now your air-conditioner only has to cool warm air, not hot air; or your furnace only has to heat warm air, not cold air. Your equipment doesn't have to be as big or work as hard which can translate to savings in energy use.

The potential benefits

- Reduces energy costs associated with bringing in and conditioning outdoor air; ERVs can recover up to 80 percent of the energy that would normally be wasted in the exhaust air.[6]

- Can either be bolted onto existing HVAC equipment or used by themselves.

- Can help control humidity.

Points to remember

- Using an ERV can reduce capital costs by reducing the required air tonnage capacity of the HVAC unit.

- ERV technology can provide ongoing energy savings.

- ERV technology can help reduce mold and odors associated with humidity.

HVAC Professional Tip: Check with your HVAC professional to determine if ERV technology will work in your establishment, as facility layout may affect the ability to use ERV effectively if placement of supply diffusers, return grilles, and exhaust fans is restricted. The intake and the exhaust must be adjacent for proper placement of the wheel in both airstreams.

DEMAND CONTROLLED VENTILATION

The technology

- Carbon dioxide (CO_2), a gas exhaled during breathing, is measured and used as an indicator of how many people are occupying a space.

- The CO_2 level is used to control the amount of outdoor air being brought in by the HVAC system. More outdoor air is supplied when there are more people occupying your establishment, and less air is brought in when the occupancy is reduced.

- The amount of people in your establishment varies from hour to hour, day to day. With DCV, your ventilation rate can match that occupancy. Instead of providing air for maximum occupancy all the time, you provide air to match the actual number of people in your establishment.

The potential benefit

- Reduces energy use since outdoor air is provided based on the amount of people in your establishment. If a room has only a few people in it, you need less ventilation air for the room than when it is full.

Demand control ventilation works similar to automatic temperature controls found in some homes. These temperature controls turn on the furnace or air conditioner depending on the actual temperature of the house compared to the programmed temperature. DCV works on a similar principle. As more people enter a room, the ventilation system automatically brings in more outdoor air. Similarly, as more people leave the room, less outdoor air is introduced into the room.

---

6 Caldwell, Rick. *Semco Incorporated Introduces FV–600 Fresh Air Ventilator.*

Points to remember

- DCV can provide the most energy-saving opportunities when there are big fluctuations in the number of people in your establishment, such as in a restaurant when there is a peak for lunch and a peak for dinner.

- DCV works like a thermostat and can be used with most existing HVAC equipment.

THE ECONOMICS OF THE TECHNOLOGIES COVERED

There are many variables that can impact the cost of new HVAC equipment, including the building size and structure. For example, is the establishment in a stand-alone building or is it part of a multi-tenant structure? Other factors include the type and condition of existing equipment, the establishment layout, and your preferences as an owner or manager.

The table below summarizes the technology options presented here to help you see how the different technologies compare with each other with respect to the IAQ benefit, the time it may take to install the equipment, and the potential capital cost and energy savings.

	Air Cleaning Ventilation	Energy Recovery Ventilation	Demand Controlled
IAQ Benefit	Reduced odors and particles	Increased outdoor air	Outdoor air based on occupancy
Installation Time	Hours	Days	Hours
Capital Cost	$$	$$$	$$
Energy Savings	$	$$$	$$

Note:

- Capital costs and savings for technologies vary widely from region to region because of climate conditions and other factors. The $ used here are to be used directionally. Consult with a local HVAC professional for specifications of these and other ventilation technologies.

The payback on ventilation technology can average between two to six years, which can vary widely from region to region because of climate conditions and other factors.

> **HVAC Professional Tip:** Ask your contractor to prepare a cost-benefit analysis to help you determine which options provide the greatest benefits and still fit within your budget.

Note:

- There is not a one-size-fits-all approach to using ventilation to improve IAQ in hospitality establishments. The design, application, and effectiveness of ventilation options vary based on climate conditions, the actual physical space and the activities you allow in the space. Any technology that is selected and used should be reviewed and evaluated with a qualified HVAC professional.

FIVE: FINDING AND WORKING WITH HVAC PROFESSIONALS

Having a basic understanding of how ventilation works and the technology options available is a step in the right direction toward providing a welcoming environment. The next step is finding a reputable HVAC professional to help with your ventilation needs based on your accommodation policy and budget parameters.

The HVAC professional you work with should be able to discuss with you the pros and cons of various ventilation strategies and technology options. In addition to discussing the principles of IAQ — outdoor air, filtration, and directional airflow — your HVAC professional should be able to help you understand how your current HVAC systems operate and what improvements can be made.

A reputable HVAC professional will be knowledgeable about state and local codes and should have appropriate insurance. This professional will also be up-to-date on equipment and technology so that you can choose what will best meet your needs.

When considering finding an HVAC professional who can help you improve the ventilation in your establishment, you will most likely turn to either an HVAC contractor or engineer.

- A *contractor* installs new equipment and maintains and often upgrades existing equipment. Contractors generally sell equipment from manufacturers. They are often trained by those manufacturers in the specifications and applications of the equipment they will be selling. Contractors can install what an engineer has designed. If you need to understand how your current HVAC system is operating or what its capabilities are, you should consult a contractor.

- An *engineer* has schooling and training in a specific area of engineering, such as mechanical engineering. Often licensed or registered by a state authority, such professional engineers, or PEs, have the knowledge to design and specify systems in their area of expertise. If you need a building or HVAC design change or blueprints, you should consult an engineer.

In the case of a new construction or a renovation project, you might be working with an architect. If so, remember to discuss with the architect how you are planning to accommodate your customers and employees, both non-smokers and smokers alike. The architect can then discuss your needs with the contractor or engineer who will be designing the HVAC system for your establishment.

FINDING AN HVAC PROFESSIONAL

There are a variety of ways to find a reputable HVAC professional:

- Get a local referral from the nationwide directory of qualified HVAC professionals available through Options.

- Ask other business owners who they use for HVAC services and if they are satisfied with their service.

- Contact HVAC organizations and request a list of contractors in your area or visit their web site to locate contact information for local chapters of the associations. (See page 22 for a list of HVAC organizations you can call.)

- Check with your trade association to find affiliate members from the HVAC industry.

- Ask questions of the HVAC professional to gauge their experience level with hospitality businesses.

- Ask for references and call these references or visit the establishments to discuss their experiences.

Screening questions to ask HVAC professionals

1. What work have you done in the hospitality industry? Can you tell about or show me some successful examples of working with a hospitality business owner?

2. What technologies have you worked with? Have they been successful?

3. Do you use ventilation, filtration, and directional airflow principles in your work?

4. Who does your installations?

5. To what professional organizations do you belong?

6. Are you licensed? Do you have insurance?

7. What training do you have?

WORKING WITH AN HVAC PROFESSIONAL

- Convey your business needs so the HVAC professional can help identify options that will work for your establishment and within your budget.

- Explain the layout, your smoking policy, and your desire for a welcoming environment.

- Review existing HVAC equipment and options for upgrading to newer technology.

- Request an airflow TAB (test, adjust, and balance) report at the completion of the job to verify that ventilation improvements are working and your objectives were met.

- Walk through your facility during a busy period to see if the improvements have had the desired effect.

- Conduct customer satisfaction surveys before and after the ventilation improvements. (See page 24 for a sample survey template.)

- If you are not satisfied with the results, request that the HVAC professional come back and make the necessary changes.

Questions to ask your HVAC professional

- How much outdoor air is my HVAC system capable of bringing into my establishment, and does it meet local building codes and guidelines?

- Where are my air supply grilles and return diffusers, and are they in the correct position based on my accommodation policy?

- Is my HVAC system capable of handling upgraded filters, and how frequently should the filters be changed?

- What upgrades or improvements can be made to my current HVAC system?

- Is the outdoor air intake damper on my HVAC equipment open, and is the fan is running as designed?

- Do you offer maintenance contracts. If so, what equipment is covered under the contract?

- What HVAC technology will work best in my establishment? Can you provide a cost-benefit analysis to help me determine which option can provide the greatest benefit based on my budget?

MAINTENANCE CONTRACTS

When working with a contractor, you will likely face the question of maintenance contracts. Considering the many duties you have with owning or managing your establishment, having a maintenance contract for your HVAC system and air cleaners may be a wise idea:

- A maintenance contract will ensure that the recommended maintenance program for your HVAC system is being implemented.

- A regular maintenance program by your HVAC professional can free your time while still maintaining the right level of air quality for your establishment.

- Regularly scheduled inspections of your HVAC equipment will provide preventive maintenance opportunities, which can identify small problems before they become more costly.

- Documenting maintenance is part of the contract and can give you a track record of your equipment.

HVAC ORGANIZATIONS

Call for assistance in identifying an HVAC professional in your area

For HVAC Contractors:

- AIR CONDITIONING CONTRACTORS OF AMERICA (ACCA)
  1712 New Hampshire Avenue, N.W.
  Washington, DC 20009
  202/483-9370
  www.acca.org
  Contact: Member Services Department

- MECHANICAL CONTRACTORS ASSOCIATION OF AMERICA, INC. (MCAA)
  1385 Piccard Drive
  Rockville, MD 20508
  301/869-5800
  www.mcaa.org
  Contact: Pat Fink, Director, Affiliate Support Services

- MECHANICAL SERVICE CONTRACTORS OF AMERICA (MSCA)
  1385 Piccard Drive
  Rockville, MD 20508
  301/869-5800
  www.mcaa.org/msca
  Contact: Barbara Dolim, Executive Director

- SHEET METAL AIR CONDITIONING NATIONAL ASSOCIATION (SMACNA)
  1750 New York Avenue, NW
  6th Floor
  Washington, DC 20006
  www.smacna.org

- EXCELLENCE ALLIANCE, INC.
  625 Eden Park Drive, Suite 300
  Cincinnati, OH 45202
  877/324-4822
  www.excellencealliance.net

For Engineers:

- ASSOCIATION OF ENERGY ENGINEERS (AEE)
  4025 Pleasantdale Road, Suite 420
  Atlanta, GA 30340
  404/447-5083
  www.aeecenter.org

SIX: IAQ QUICK REFERENCE AND CHECKLIST

The following is a summary of the sections you just reviewed. Use this checklist as a quick reference guide when evaluating your accommodation policy and ventilation needs.

DIFFERENT ACCOMMODATION STRATEGIES

• Establish an accommodation strategy that will work with your business needs and goals. (See page 5.)

• When developing your establishment's accommodation strategy, always be sure that you are in compliance with all local laws and regulations governing smoking and ventilation in your establishment.

PRINCIPLES OF IAQ

• Check the outdoor air intake dampers on your HVAC equipment to make sure that it is bringing in the maximum amount of outdoor air as required by your state and local building or mechanical codes. (See page 8.)

• Once you have determined that you are using a minimum 65 percent dust-spot efficient filter, change your filter as suggested by your HVAC professional or the manufacturer's instructions. (See page 9.)

• Notice where air is being supplied and removed from your establishment relative to the different areas within your establishment in order to control airflow. (See page 10.)

• Create an airflow footprint of your establishment. (See page 12.)

VENTILATION TECHNOLOGIES

• Think about the IAQ challenges in your establishment:

  • Does your establishment have a stuffy or stale odor?

  • Do you have a lot of humidity odors?

  • Do your filters look old?

  • Do you have accumulation of smoke and odors in specific areas?

If you answered yes to any of these questions, work with an HVAC professional to determine the ventilation technologies that will help you get the most out of your existing equipment while improving customer comfort. (See section four.)

SEVEN: SAMPLE CUSTOMER SATISFACTION SURVEY

Customer satisfaction surveys can be a good way to determine the effectiveness of ventilation improvements made at your establishment as well as other key customer factors, such as customer service. The surveys can be placed on tables and on the bar counter area for customers to rate the key factors of your establishment. To accurately gauge the improvements of your ventilation investment, see the following suggestions:

- Develop a rating scale on the key factors of your establishment.

- Conduct the same survey twice, once before the IAQ improvements have been made, and again after their completion.

- Share the results of the two surveys with the HVAC professional you worked with, and if feedback from the survey indicates customer comfort satisfaction has not improved, have them re-evaluate their original recommendation to address the survey results.

CUSTOMER OPINION SURVEY

Please take a few minutes to complete this survey so that we can better serve you.

1. How would you rate your experience in (fill in establishment name) on (date):

	Very Poor									Excellent
Friendly Service	1	2	3	4	5	6	7	8	9	10
Fast Service	1	2	3	4	5	6	7	8	9	10
Cleanliness	1	2	3	4	5	6	7	8	9	10
Quality of Air	1	2	3	4	5	6	7	8	9	10
Atmosphere and Décor	1	2	3	4	5	6	7	8	9	10
Taste of Beverages	1	2	3	4	5	6	7	8	9	10
Taste of Food	1	2	3	4	5	6	7	8	9	10
Prices	1	2	3	4	5	6	7	8	9	10

2. In your most recent experiences, is the air quality in (establishment name) better, the same or worse than other (your type of establishment)?

Better	
Same	
Worse	

3. Is the air quality in (fill in establishment name) acceptable or unacceptable to you?

Acceptable	
Unacceptable	

4. Given your response to question number three, does the air quality of this establishment affect whether or not you would return in the future?

More likely to return	No impact	Less likely to return

The management of (fill in establishment name) would like to thank you for completing this survey. Making sure we meet your expectations is very important to us.

EIGHT: GLOSSARY OF TERMS

The terminology used when talking about IAQ and ventilation can often seem too technical and complicated. However, increasing your understanding of some common terminology will help you to maximize your conversations with your contractor or engineer. The following are some terms you might discuss.

Air cleaner: Device used to help remove impurities from the air, usually supplemental to the HVAC system.

Air filter: Means of reducing the levels of particles and noticeable odors within a space. Primarily used within the HVAC system, but sometimes used supplemental to the system in advanced cleaners. A minimum 65 percent dust-spot efficient filter is suggested.

Airflow footprint: Diagram that shows how air flows in the space. Airflow footprints are used to map out the various uses in a space, the supply diffusers, and the return and exhaust grilles.

Carbon dioxide (CO2): Odorless, colorless gas that is a by-product of human breathing. In many cases, CO2 measurements can be used as indicators of the number of occupants.

Conditioned air: Air treated to control temperature, relative humidity, purity, pressure, and movement.

Contractor: A person who can install new equipment and maintain and often upgrade existing equipment.

Damper: A louvered covering, controlled either manually or automatically, which usually brings air from the outdoors into an HVAC system to a room or space.

Demand controlled ventilation (DCV): Sensor-driven control system that allows the HVAC system to adjust the ventilation to match occupancy levels. Occupant sensors or other means of detecting occupants are control mechanisms that are typically used.

Dilution: Reducing the concentration of particles and odors in the air

Duct: The means by which air moves from the HVAC system to the supply diffuser, often made of sheet metal.

Electrostatic precipitator: Air-cleaning device used to remove particles from the air by charging and attracting particles to plates.

Energy recovery ventilator (ERV): Unit that is attached to an HVAC system or is used alone and captures energy that would have been lost in the conditioned exhaust stream. ERVs use this recovered energy to pre-condition the outdoor air introduced into the building.

Engineer: A person with schooling and training in a specific area of engineering, such as mechanical engineering. Often licensed or registered by a state authority, such professional engineers, or PEs, have the knowledge to design and specify systems in their area of expertise. Engineers sell services, not equipment.

Exhaust: Air discharged from a space to the outdoors, as differentiated from air transferred from one space to another.

Exhaust grille: Louvered or perforated covering for an opening in an air passage which can be located in a sidewall, ceiling, or floor, through which air is exhausted to the outdoors.

Filtration: Process of helping to remove contaminants from air by passing the air stream through a porous material.

Heating, ventilation and air-conditioning (HVAC) system: A system that provides, either collectively or individually, the processes of comfort heating, ventilation, and/or air conditioning within a space.

Indoor air quality (IAQ): Attributes of the respirable atmosphere (climate) inside a building including gaseous composition, humidity, temperature, and contaminants.

Louvers: An arrangement of overlapping slats with gaps between them so that air is admitted.

Mechanical ventilation: The use of HVAC equipment to heat or cool air, deliver either outdoor air or recirculated air to a space, and remove stale air from a space.

Natural ventilation: The movement of outdoor air into a space through intentionally provided opening, such as windows and doors.

Outdoor air intake: Planned point for outdoor air to enter the HVAC system.

Pressurization: Positive or negative pressurization is one way to refer to the air movement between areas within an establishment, such as the bartender's workspace and the bar counter area, or the building as a whole to the outdoors. When a building or area "pulls" air in through doors or other openings, it is said to be "negatively pressurized" to the outdoors or adjacent areas. With positive pressurization, more air is supplied to the building or area than is exhausted.

Return or recirculated air: Air extracted from a space, then totally or partially returned to an air conditioner, furnace, or other heating or cooling source.

Return grille: Louvered or perforated covering for an opening in an air passage, which can be located in a sidewall, ceiling, or floor through which air is returned to an HVAC system.

Smoke pencil: Used to generate small amounts of smoke that can be used to check direction of air flow between spaces, through doorways and other openings. Also available as smoke tubes, smokes bottles, or smoke matches.

Supply diffuser: A louvered or perforated covering, usually mounted to a ceiling or floor over any air passage, which delivers air from an HVAC system to a room or space.

Test, adjust, and balance (TAB) report: Written report by an HVAC professional documenting the amount of air supplied and exhausted by an HVAC system as well as how it is distributed indoors.

Three-phase air cleaner: Air cleaning device to help in removing particles and odors by using three air cleaning technologies such as filtering coarse particles, absorbing gases and odors, and filtering out fine particles.

Transfer grille: Louvered or perforated covering for an opening which can be located in a wall or doorway which allows air to be supplied from an adjacent space.

Ventilation: Process of supplying or removing air by natural or mechanical means to or from any space. Such air may or may not have been conditioned.

Note:

• Every business owner should seek the advice of ventilation professionals (i.e., contractors or engineers) to develop a plan appropriate to the particular site, use and capacity.

• Business owners should independently assess the level of experience of any HVAC professional being considered to provide design and ventilation guidance.

• Always be sure that you are in compliance with all local laws and regulations governing smoking and ventilation in your establishment.

• *Options*, Philip Morris USA and the INvironment® Hotline do not purport to address health effects attributed to environmental tobacco smoke.

The handbook was prepared by the Chelsea Group, Ltd., for *Options*, Philip Morris USA.

INVIRONMENT® is a registered trademark of Chelsea Group, Ltd., an independent IAQ consultancy.

Educational materials and engineer consulting services are provided courtesy of *Options*, Philip Morris USA.

For more information on environmental tobacco smoke, please visit www.philipmorrisusa.com.

Chapter 9 Outline

Basic Definitions
Light Sources
    Natural Light
    Artificial Light
Lighting System Design
    Design Factors
Lighting System Maintenance
    Cleaning Luminaires and Lamps
    Replacing Lamps
Energy Conservation Opportunities

Competencies

1. Define basic lighting terms, explain how natural light can be used to meet a building's lighting needs, and describe common artificial light sources. (pp. 285–293)

2. Describe the following lighting system design elements: light levels, luminaires, color rendition, safety, and emergency lighting. (pp. 293–299)

3. Describe lighting system maintenance and identify energy conservation opportunities. (pp. 299–305)

9

Lighting Systems

The designer should consider hotel lighting more a design element than a building science. Lobbies, atriums, restaurants, entertainment areas, meeting and banquet rooms, and guestrooms owe their success to comfortable and creative lighting as much as to any other single design element. As in other disciplines, the requirements are often based on common sense. For example, guestroom lighting needs to be adequate for reading in bed, working at the desk or table, and shaving or applying makeup. If the lighting for any of these is poor, the guest registers at least subconscious irritation. Meeting room lighting also must be highly adaptable. It should combine incandescent lighting for ambiance with fluorescent fixtures for meeting use and track lighting for displays or accents. Special decorative restaurant lighting is essential in creating the desired mood in food outlets.[1]

LIGHTING SYSTEMS AFFECT SEVERAL ASPECTS of physical plant management. The character and direction of light influence building colors and textures. Light's optical characteristics affect the appearance of surface finishes and ceilings. Some properties make major use of lighting to attract customers and create an image; casino hotels are obvious examples. The nature and level of illumination affect employee efficiency and customer comfort. A building's lighting system influences HVAC system design and operation (because of the heat given off by the lights), a building's interior design (because of the dimensions of the lighting fixtures), electrical design, and the economics of investment (because the lamps and their controls are part of the initial investment). Finally, lighting plays an important part in safety and security.

Basic Definitions

Before we begin our discussion of light sources and systems, we should briefly introduce some basic terms. **Visible light** is defined most simply as radiated energy that can be seen by the human eye. Light is made up of various wavelengths and frequencies interpreted by the eye as color. At the low end of the spectrum, violet, indigo, blue, and green light are produced by shorter wavelengths, with violet the shortest; at the high end, yellow, orange, and red are produced by longer wavelengths, with red the longest. Sources of visible light contain some or all of these colors.

When light shines on a surface, some of the colors in the light are absorbed and disappear, others are transmitted or reflected. The transmitted or reflected

Exhibit 1   Correlated Color Temperature/Kelvin Ranges

Color Temperature	Warm	Neutral	Cool	Daylight
Kelvin Range	3000K	3500K	4100K	5000K
Associated Effects and Moods	Friendly Intimate Personal Exclusive	Friendly Inviting Non-threatening	Neat Clean Efficient	Bright Alert Exacting coloration
Appropriate Applications	Restaurants Hotel lobbies Boutiques Libraries Office areas Retail stores	Public reception areas Showrooms Bookstores Office areas	Office areas Conference rooms Classrooms Mass merchandisers Hospitals	Galleries Museums Jewelry stores Medical examination areas Printing companies

light is what gives objects their color. For example, a red napkin absorbs almost all light except red; a yellow flower absorbs all light except yellow.

Since an object's color is partially determined by the light that shines on it, a light source's color rendition is important. **Color rendition** refers to a light source's ability to provide a perceived color similar to that which results from sunlight. A lamp's color rendering index (CRI) is a number from 0 to 100 that states how closely a given light source approaches the color rendering capability of daylight or incandescent lighting, both of which have an index of 100.

The color appearance of light can also be referred to as the color temperature or, more specifically, as the Correlated Color Temperature (CCT). CCT is measured in degrees Kelvin or "K" (see Exhibit 1). Lamps with a CCT below 3500K are considered "warm" and give out a yellow or reddish light; lamps above 4000K are considered "cool" and give out a white or bluish light. Color temperature creates the mood or ambiance of the space you are lighting and can influence customer behavior and employee performance. Lamp specifications generally include a CRI value and a CCT value.

Standard light-level units and measurement methods have been developed in order to have some objective means of determining relative light levels. The **lumen** is a commonly used unit of light. Light that strikes a surface is known as **illumination**. Illumination is typically measured in **footcandles;** one footcandle is a light intensity of one lumen per square foot. In countries using the metric system of measurement, light is also measured in lumens, while levels of illumination are measured in lux, a lux being a light intensity of one lumen per square meter.

Light Sources

Light is either natural or artificial. Both sources can be used to meet a building's lighting needs.

The Opryland Hotel makes dramatic use of natural light. (Courtesy of Opryland Hotel, Nashville, Tennessee)

Natural Light

Natural light, or sunlight, is by far the most common and least expensive light source. The use of natural light is currently of great interest to designers of commercial buildings, especially offices and schools where lighting energy is a significant fraction of total energy use. Since clear-sky outdoor illumination levels can approach 1,000 footcandles for over 85 percent of the working day in some locations, natural light's contribution to meeting a building's overall lighting needs is potentially great. It should also be recognized that natural light has drawbacks: it can create substantial solar heat gain, be a source of glare and distraction, and contribute to the fading and physical deterioration of fabrics.

Using natural light for interior hotel and restaurant lighting is generally appreciated by guests and employees. The chance to look through a window, possibly at attractive hotel grounds or some other pleasant scene, is psychologically pleasing and helps employees avoid eye strain because they can occasionally focus their eyes on distant objects. Natural light must be used with care, however. Designers of a building's lighting system have to consider a lot of variables to make natural lighting pleasing—the type of glass used in the windows, whether or to what extent to use window treatments such as drapes or blinds, how reflective the surfaces are in the space being lit, the nature of the view outside, and others.

Artificial Light

Artificial light is light other than sunlight. Artificial light sources can be categorized by many measures, including their efficiency (measured in lumens per watt) and their color-rendering index. The two basic sources of artificial light commonly used today are incandescent lamps and electric discharge lamps (see Exhibit 2).

Incandescent Lamps. An **incandescent lamp** consists of a filament inside a sealed glass bulb. Electric current passing through the filament heats it to incandescence, producing light. The lamp is usually etched or coated to diffuse the light produced by the filament. The electrical connection for the lamp is through the base. The light bulbs commonly used in homes and hotel guestrooms are incandescent lamps.

Incandescent lamps are characterized by relatively short lifetimes (2,000 hours or less) and relatively poor efficiencies (15 to 20 lumens per watt). However, they are capable of instant starting and restarting, are low in cost, and are readily dimmed. The light from these lamps is "warm" (high in reds and yellows) and color rendition is considered good. As a result, they do not "shift" or change the color of fabrics or finishes.

Because of their poor efficiency, incandescent lamps contribute a large amount of heat to a building and have relatively high operating costs. Their short lamp life results in potentially high maintenance costs, since employees must replace them often. **Lamp life** refers to the time it takes half of the lamps in a given sample to fail. If a lamp is rated as having a lamp life of 1,000 hours, for example, 1,000 hours is the expected lifetime for this type of lamp, although a given lamp might burn for more or fewer than 1,000 hours.

The higher the wattage of an incandescent lamp, the more efficiently the lamp operates. Long-life or extended-service lamps (which produce 10 to 20 percent less light per watt of power consumed) are generally less efficient than standard lamps, but have longer lifetimes and should be used where replacement is difficult. Any incandescent lamp will have its efficiency increased (and its life decreased) if it operates at higher than its rated voltage.

Besides the conventional incandescent lamp, other types of incandescent lamps are used for special applications:

- Rough service or vibration incandescent lamps are built to withstand rough handling and vibration.

- Tungsten halogen lamps are incandescent lamps that produce a slightly "whiter" light (higher CCT) and have a longer lamp life (3,000 hours) than standard incandescent lamps. These lamps are used as longer-life replacements for standard incandescent lamps as well as for special applications.

Exhibit 2   Types of Incandescent and Electric Discharge Lamps

	Standard Incandescent	Tungsten-Halogen	Flourescent	Compact Flourescent	Mercury Vapor	Metal Halide	High-Pressure Sodium	Low-Pressure Sodium
Wattage	3–1,500	10–1,500	4–215	4–55	40–1,250	32–2,000	35–1,000	18–180
Average System Efficacy (lm/W)	4–24	8–33	49–89	24–68	19–43	38–86	22–115	50–150
Average Rated Life (hrs)	750–2,000	2,000–4,000	7,500–24,000	7,000–20,000	24,000+	6,000–20,000	16,000–24,000	12,000–18,000
CRI	100	100	49–92	82–86	15–50	65–92	21–85	0
Life Cycle Cost	high	high	low	moderate	moderate	moderate	low	low
Fixture Size	compact	compact	extended	compact	compact	compact	compact	extended
Start to Full Brightness	immediate	immediate	0–5 seconds	0–1 min	3–9 min	3–5 min	3–4 min	7–9 min
Restrike Time	immediate	immediate	immediate	immediate	10–20 min	4–20 min	1 min	immediate
Lumen Maintenance	good/excellent	excellent	fair/excellent	good/excellent	poor/fair	good	good/excellent	excellent

- Reflector lamps (PAR, ER, and R-type bulbs) are incandescent lamps that contain a reflector coating to give the lamps a more directed light output. These lamps are also called spot or flood lamps. They may be installed over food counters with filters to limit the amount of heat in the light beam. They provide interesting options for merchandise and accent lighting but care is needed because of their high operating temperatures.

Electric Discharge Lamps. Electric discharge lamps generate light by passing an electric arc through a space filled with a special mixture of gases. This category of lamps includes fluorescent, mercury vapor, metal halide, and high- and low-pressure sodium.

Electric discharge lamps can't be operated directly from a power supply, as can incandescent lamps. Therefore, all electric discharge lamps require an additional piece of equipment, a **ballast,** that controls their starting and operation and acts as a current-limiting device. The ballast for most tube-type fluorescent lamps (the four-foot or eight-foot lamps commonly used) is a separate item from the tubes. It is usually mounted on top of the light fixture and is replaceable. Some compact fluorescents—small fluorescent lamps developed as energy-efficient alternatives to incandescent lamps—have the ballast and tube as one piece; others have separate ballasts. For many hospitality applications, having a separate ballast is preferable because replacement costs are lower.

Ten to fifteen percent of the energy used by an electric discharge lighting system is consumed in the ballast and given off as heat. Ballasts are rated by their operating temperature, type of overheating protection (those that are thermally protected, self-resetting, and generally specified for commercial uses are denoted as type "P" ballasts), and noise level (rated A through F, with A the quietest). Some recent trends in ballast design have included the development of electronic ballasts that consume up to 25 percent less energy than standard ballasts and can provide a dimming capability.

Ballasts should also be chosen with an eye on how they will affect the building's electrical system. In many applications it is preferable to have ballasts with a high power factor (above .9) to reduce the possibility of electric bill surcharges (for low overall power factor) and to improve electrical system operation. Selecting ballasts with a low total harmonic distortion (under approximately 35 percent) can also help to reduce the potential for electrical equipment problems.

Fluorescent lamps. Fluorescent lamps are the most common type of electric discharge lamp. They are characterized by a long lifetime (7,000 to 20,000 hours) and a higher efficiency (40 to 100 lumens per watt) than those of incandescent lamps. They also put out less heat than incandescent lamps, which means less heat needs to be removed by the HVAC system. Fluorescent lamps come in circular and "U" shapes as well as long tubes.

The development of various types of compact fluorescents throughout the 1980s and 1990s has greatly expanded the potential applications of fluorescent lamps. Compact fluorescent lamps are now commonly used in hotels and restaurants—for corridor lighting, in guestroom lamps, and for downlight applications in dining rooms and elsewhere. Compact lamps with electronic ballasts can be used with dimming systems. When replacing incandescent lamps with compact

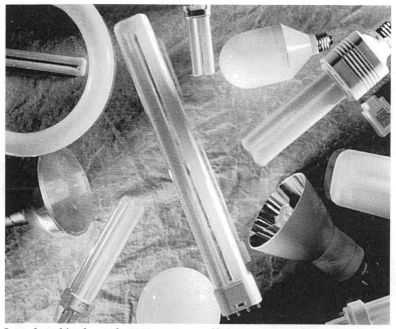

Introduced in the early 1980s, energy-efficient compact fluorescent lamps are small enough to fit into fixtures and spaces that only incandescent lamps fit in before. (Courtesy of the Electric Power Research Institute, Palo Alto, California)

fluorescents, managers must attend to the compact lamps' CRI and CCT values to make sure light quality is approximately the same; otherwise, the space being lighted will not look the same in terms of color and light and the interior designer's intended look for the space will be lost.

Generally, the color rendition of fluorescent lamps is much poorer than that of incandescent lamps, although some fluorescent lamps have been developed to produce a "warmer" light. Fluorescent lamps come in a variety of "whites"—for example, cool white and warm white. A cool white lamp has a color temperature of approximately 4100K; a warm white lamp has a color temperature of 3000K. Improved-color-rendition whites have red added to their light to help them bring out the full range of colors. What type of fluorescent lamp should be used in a hotel or restaurant? It depends on the space, the decor, the activities that go on in the space, the desired atmosphere, and other variables. Generally, fluorescent lamps in the "warm" group blend more successfully with incandescent lighting.

The label on a fluorescent lamp defines several of the lamp's characteristics. A lamp labeled F15T12WW is a fluorescent (F) lamp with 15 watts, a tubular (T) shape, a $^{12}/_8$ inch diameter, and a warm white (WW) color.

Fluorescent lamp life decreases as the average number of burning hours per start decreases. This has led some people to believe that it is cheaper to leave a fluorescent lamp on continuously than to switch it on and off as needed. However, this is not true, especially in areas with high-cost electrical energy. When a room or area is left vacant, fluorescent lights should be turned off. The additional lamp replacement costs associated with the reduced lamp life should easily be repaid by the resulting energy savings.

Operation of fluorescent lamps in locations in and around the building that are warmer or colder than the lamps' recommended operating range can cause problems. The same can be true of ballasts, which also have a recommended operating range. For example, in a cold location, lamps and ballasts that are not rated for operation in cold conditions may either not operate, take a long time to come on, or, once operating, produce light at reduced levels. Hot locations will decrease ballast life, resulting in premature ballast failure. Using a ballast suitable for higher temperatures will result in longer ballast operation and fewer maintenance problems. When fluorescent lamps are installed in cold locations, ballasts that are capable of starting and operating the lamps under cold conditions should be used.

Providing a dimming capability for fluorescent lamps requires an electronic ballast and dimming equipment suitable for the size and type of lighting system.

During much of the late twentieth century, the standard fluorescent lamp in use was the T12 lamp—a lamp 1.5 inches in diameter. At the present time, a more efficient and commonly specified fluorescent lamp in new construction is the T8 lamp—a lamp 1.0 inches in diameter. When coupled with energy-efficient ballasts (and, ideally, with high-efficiency fixtures), the T8 lamp can provide substantial reductions in lighting energy and excellent cost savings.

Lighting technology continues to improve and new products are emerging. An example is the T5 fluorescent lamp. Providing approximately the same lumens as a similar T8 lamp, the T5 does so while consuming 10 percent less energy and doing a better job of maintaining its light output over time. With these advantages, the T5 might become the standard for tubular fluorescent applications in the future.

Other electric discharge lamps. Mercury vapor, metal halide, and high- and low-pressure sodium lamps operate on the same principle as fluorescent lamps and require ballasts for operation. These lamps are sometimes listed in a general category called **high-intensity discharge (HID) lamps.** Each type of HID lamp has possible uses within the hospitality industry.

While incandescent and fluorescent lamps light almost immediately upon being energized, the **strike time** (the time required for a lamp to reach full output from a cold start) for HID lamps can be several minutes. In addition, the time required for a hot HID lamp to restrike is usually longer than the strike time. These longer strike and restrike times can be a problem in certain applications, such as locations that need emergency lighting.

Mercury vapor lamps have long been used for lighting streets and parking lots. They have an efficiency of 15 to 60 lumens per watt and a lifetime of 12,000 to 24,000 hours. Strike times for these lamps are three to five minutes and restrike times, three to eight minutes. White mercury vapor lamps have somewhat better color rendition than clear lamps.

Metal halide (MH) lamps basically are mercury vapor lamps modified by the addition of metallic halides to improve the lamp's color rendition and increase efficiency (80 to 100 lumens per watt). Lamp life is 7,500 to 15,000 hours—less than that of mercury vapor lamps. **Lumen maintenance**—the lamp's ability to maintain its output—is also significantly reduced later in the lamp's life. Newly introduced MH lamps have improved CRI values (80+), improved lumen maintenance, and higher energy efficiency. MH lamps have relatively short strike times, two to three minutes, but can have restrike times of up to 10 minutes.

High-pressure sodium (HPS) lamps are highly efficient light sources (85 to 140 lumens per watt) that have long life (16,000 to 24,000 hours) and a high lumen maintenance over their lifetimes. Strike times are three to four minutes, with a relatively short restrike time of about one minute. Color rendition is poor. HPS lamps are typically used to light parking lots and garages, building exteriors, and entry areas. HPS lamps can be used indoors if color-corrected lamps are selected or the HPS lamps are mixed with other light sources that together produce an appropriate color rendition.

Low-pressure sodium (LPS) lamps are the most efficient light sources, with efficiencies in excess of 150 lumens per watt possible. They have lifetimes of up to 18,000 hours and a high lumen maintenance. Their color-rendering characteristics are generally poor, since they produce a very yellow light. They are primarily used for parking lots and security lighting such as after-hours lighting in restaurants.

Lighting System Design

Lighting system design is an important element of the overall design of any hospitality facility. Interior and exterior lighting are crucial design components that:

- Help attract guests and make them comfortable

- Communicate a concept (your intended position in the market)

- Establish an atmosphere

- Highlight artwork or interior features

- Improve employee productivity

In addition, lighting can substantially affect safety and energy costs, both directly and indirectly.

Design Factors

Factors in designing a lighting system include light levels, luminaires, color rendition, safety, and emergency lighting.

Light Levels. One of the first questions a designer must ask is: How much light should there be in a given space? This question is usually answered by determining what activities or tasks are being or will be performed within the space. Sometimes widely varying levels of light need to be available in a single space. For example, a meeting room may only need five foot candles of light during an audio-visual presentation, but 100 footcandles during a workshop. The meeting room may need several different types of lamps and fixtures with lots of light switches and perhaps dimming capabilities to accommodate the various lighting needs.

Light levels can be measured with portable light meters that indicate the available light in footcandles. These devices are accurate to plus or minus five percent if kept calibrated. Portable light meters will often have multiple scales allowing designers to measure light levels over a fairly wide range.

The Illuminating Engineers Society (IES) lists, for various hotel and restaurant spaces, minimum lighting levels that incorporate a number of task, space, and occupant considerations (see Exhibit 3). These levels are recommended minimum levels, not standards, and designers may want to use more light than these levels.

The design of hotel lighting systems, as with all other building systems, must comply with local and state building codes. Local and state codes often incorporate portions of, or adopt in total, standards developed by engineering and design organizations. In regards to light levels, the standards of the Illuminating Engineering Society of North America (IESNA) and the American Society of Heating, Refrigerating, and Air-Conditioning Engineers (ASHRAE) are of interest for U.S. properties. The IESNA and ASHRAE standards can be found in the ASHRAE/ IESNA publication A90.1—"Energy Efficient Design of New Buildings Except Low-Rise Residential."

Exhibit 4 contains the latest proposed lighting standards for various hospitality building spaces, based on what is referred to as the "building area method." This method provides the maximum amount of power wattage that shall be required by the lighting system in various types of hospitality buildings.

An alternative standard to the building area method is the space-by-space method of calculating lighting power. The standards under this method are shown in Exhibit 5. Which of the methods will apply—or whether both apply—to a particular property depends on the policy of the local code authority. There are also provisions of these standards that allow for adjustments for decorative lighting (chandeliers, for example), retail lighting, and lighting for building exteriors.

Light levels within a given space can also be manipulated through the use of dimming controls. Some systems use photosensors wired directly to dimmable electronic ballasts, so that light levels can be adjusted automatically. Spaces that are exposed to natural light (such as atriums and other interior spaces with extensive glazing) are candidates for this technology; as the sun goes down and the natural light dims, the system can be programmed to adjust artificial light levels upward. Many dimming systems rely on manual switches; light levels are adjusted manually depending on the task at hand or the "mood" that management wants to convey or support through lighting.

Luminaires. Luminaires, also known as fixtures, consist of the following components:

- Lamps
- Lamp sockets
- Ballasts (for luminaires that use electric discharge lamps)
- Reflective material
- Lenses or louvers
- Housing

Exhibit 3 Minimum Footcandles for Hotel and Restaurant Applications, Based on IES Standards

Space	Recommended Minimum Footcandles
HOTELS	
Bathrooms	
General	10
Mirrors	30
Bedrooms	
Reading	30
Subdued environment	15
Lobby	
General	10
Reading and working	30
Power Plant	
Boiler room	10
Equipment room	20
Storerooms	10
Offices	
Accounting	150
Regular office work	
Good copy	70
Fair copy	100
Corridors, elevators, and stairways	20
RESTAURANTS	
Cashier	50
Dining areas	
Intimate restaurant	
Light environment	10
Subdued environment	3
Leisure restaurant	
Light environment	30
Quick-Service restaurant	
Bright surroundings	100
Normal surroundings	50
Food Displays	
Twice the general level but not under	50
Kitchen	
Inspection, checking, and pricing	70
Other areas	30

Source: Adapted from Benjamin Stein, John S. Reynolds, and William J. McGuinness, *Mechanical and Electrical Equipment for Buildings*, 7th ed. (New York: Wiley, 1986).

The main function of a luminaire is to deliver the light produced by the lamp(s) to a space or surface in a way that is visually appealing and comfortable for people. Luminaires are used for direct lighting, indirect lighting, spot or accent lighting, flood lighting, and task lighting.

Exhibit 4   Hospitality Lighting Power Densities, Building Area Method

Space	Lighting Power Density (W/ft2*)
Convention Center	1.4
Dining: Bar Lounge/Leisure	1.5
Dining: Cafeteria/Fast Food	1.8
Dining: Family	1.9
Exercise Center	1.4
Hotel	1.7
Motel	2.0
Office	1.3
Workshop	1.7

*Watts per square foot

Exhibit 5   Hospitality Lighting Power Densities, Space-by-Space Method

Space	Lighting Power Density (W/ft2*)
Office—enclosed	1.5
Office—open plan	1.3
Conference/Meeting/Multipurpose	1.5
Classroom/Lecture/Training	1.6
Lobby	1.8
Atrium—first three floors	1.3
Atrium—each additional floor	0.2
Lounge/Recreation	2.2
Restrooms	1.0
Corridor/Transition	0.7
Stairs—active	0.9
Active storage	1.1
Inactive storage	0.3
Electrical/mechanical	1.3
Guestrooms	2.5

*Watts per square foot

Lamps must be correctly matched to luminaires for optimal and safe operation; a lamp's geometry, heat generation, and size are all issues that must be addressed. Lamp sockets hold the lamps. Ballasts are often mounted above the luminaire. The reflective material is very important to the overall efficiency of the luminaire, because it affects the amount of light that actually exits the luminaire. Another element that affects a luminaire's efficiency is the lens or louver that is used. Lenses are generally made from translucent, ultraviolet-stabilized acrylic plastic; louvers are used when a reduction in the luminaire's glare is desired. The more translucent the lens or the more open the louver design, the more efficient the luminaire in delivering light.

The degree to which the luminaire achieves a glare-free delivery of light is measured by the visual comfort probability (VCP) rating of the luminaire. VCP values range from 0 to 100, with 70 considered to be the lowest acceptable value for a high-performance luminaire. VCP values refer to the percentage of people who would not find the light from a particular luminaire objectionable due to glare.

The overall efficiency of a luminaire is called the **coefficient of utilization (CU).** This value integrates the efficiency of the luminaire's reflective material and reflector design, the efficiency of its lens/louver, and how well the luminaire's lamp interacts with these elements. High CU values can approach or exceed 90 percent.

All luminaires have basic maintenance requirements—they must be cleaned, replacement items (such as decorative globes or safety covers) must be stocked, and repairs must be made. Whenever possible, designers should choose luminaires that are easily cleaned. For most applications, this means that a fixture should have no bottom surface and side surfaces as vertical as possible so dust will not readily collect. Luminaires suspended from the ceiling in relatively dust-free areas should have an opening above the lamp; the opening creates air circulation because the heated air within the luminaire rises through the opening, carrying dust away. Luminaires in areas with a lot of dust or moisture (flour dust in kitchens or moisture in dishwashing areas, for example) should have dust-proof or vapor-tight luminaires—luminaires that completely enclose the lamp.

Color Rendition. Since the color of the light emitted by various types of lamps differs, the types of lamps used by a property have a great impact on the appearance of the surfaces, finishes, and furnishings within the building. For example, restaurants should have lamps in their dining areas that give off a sufficient amount of light in the red and orange frequencies, or foods such as beef and tomatoes that are rich in red and orange colors will appear dull, dark, and unappetizing. As mentioned earlier in the chapter, the color rendering index (CRI) is used to rate the relative performance of artificial light sources (see Exhibit 6). Generally speaking, the higher the CRI value, the truer the colors.

Safety. Designers must keep safety as well as costs and aesthetics in mind when designing a lighting system. Compliance with local safety code requirements is a must. Plastic fixtures should only be used if the plastic materials are slow-burning or self-extinguishing and have low smoke-density ratings and low heat-distortion temperatures. (For aesthetic reasons, long-term durability of plastic fixtures when exposed to ultraviolet light should also be investigated to ensure that yellowing or embrittlement will not occur.) Fixtures should always be installed according to the manufacturer's recommendations, with adequate ventilation and clearance to

Exhibit 6   Typical CRI Values of Various Light Sources

Source	Typical CRI Value
Incandescent/Halogen	100
Fluorescent	
Cool Whie T12	62
Warm White T12	53
High Lumen T12	73–85
T8	75–85
T10	80–85
Compact	80–85
Mercury Vapor (clear/coated)	15/50
Metal Halide (clear/coated)	65/70
High-Pressure Sodium	
Standard	22
Deluxe	65
White HPS	85
Low-Pressure Sodium	0

avoid heat build-up. Luminaires should always be used with lamps with the proper (rated) wattage.

Light sources in locations where the breakage of a lamp could pose a likely health hazard (such as kitchens and pool areas) must have either a luminaire with an acrylic diffuser to retain glass and lamp phosphor materials or (for fluorescent lamps) a tube safety shield around the lamp. This is usually required by a provision of local health codes.

Light itself—or the lack of it—can be the culprit or at least a contributing factor in employee and guest accidents. Insufficient lighting is an obvious hazard, but other light conditions can cause trouble as well—glare from lights that are too bright, blinding reflected glare from polished surfaces, harsh shadows, and so on. Guests who move from a bright hotel lobby into a dark restaurant just off the lobby may stumble or even fall if there is a change in floor level between the areas. This is caused by the delayed eye adaption that individuals experience when they move from bright surroundings into dark ones. For that reason, guests should not be confronted with widely varying light levels between adjacent hotel areas.

Care should be exercised in the maintenance of lighting systems. Failed lamps can have cracked glass or may be subject to breakage while being removed; eye protection and gloves may be in order. Some public-space lighting systems operate at 277 volts; lockout/tagout requirements should be considered when working with these systems.

Emergency Lighting. Emergency lighting requirements for a property will be specified in the local community's building codes. Local codes must be complied with. This discussion will draw on the requirements found in the *Life Safety Code*[2] and the

National Electrical Code (NEC).[3] Local building codes usually follow these two standards.

The *NEC* states that

> emergency illumination shall include all required means of egress lighting, illuminated exit signs, and all other lights specified as necessary to provide required illumination. Emergency lighting systems shall be so designed and installed that the failure of any individual lighting element, such as the burning out of a light bulb, cannot leave in total darkness any space which requires emergency illumination.[4]

Emergency lighting can be provided as (1) an emergency lighting system with its own power, independent of the regular lighting system, or (2) two or more separate and complete regular lighting systems with independent power supplies, each system providing sufficient current for emergency lighting purposes. In the event of a power failure, a delay of no more than ten seconds is permitted in the operation of the emergency lighting system. The system must be capable of providing a minimum of one footcandle for 1.5 hours.

The lighting of exit signs is another emergency lighting concern. Exit signs operate 24 hours a day and must be kept in good repair, with lights functioning properly. That said, exit signs can be excellent opportunities for energy conservation. Exit-sign lighting options include:

- Light-emitting diodes (LEDs)
- Low-wattage incandescent lamps
- Compact fluorescent lamps
- Incandescent lamps
- Electroluminescent fixtures
- Self-luminous signs

Light-emitting diodes are the most energy-efficient option, consuming two to five watts of energy per sign. They have the added advantage of extremely long lifetimes (25+ years). Low-wattage incandescent lamps (8 to 18 watts) in a flexible "light tube" configuration also have long lives (10 years). Compact fluorescent lamps have low power consumption (10 watts or less) but only have a two-year lifetime and are somewhat costly. Incandescent lamps should be avoided, due to their high lifetime operating costs. Electroluminescent sources have relatively high initial costs ($200 per fixture) but have a low wattage (about one watt per fixture) and lifetimes of approximately 10 years. Self-luminous signs require no electricity and have lifetimes of 10 to 20 years but cost in excess of $200 per fixture. Also, since they utilize tritium, they require disposal as a radioactive waste.

Lighting System Maintenance

Operating problems with lighting systems can be caused by several factors. If the voltage supplied to the lamp is above or below the rated voltage for the lamp, the lamp's output and life will be affected. Fluorescent and some HID lamps may not operate properly if placed in an operating-temperature environment for which they are not rated. Choosing ballasts that are not compatible with the lamps can also result in operational problems. Managers should always remember that they are dealing with a lighting *system,* all of whose components and interconnections must be correct if proper operation is to be achieved.

The requirements for lighting system maintenance depend on what types of lamps are used, their locations, and the purpose served by the lighting. The two major activities of lighting system maintenance are cleaning luminaires and lamps and replacing lamps.

Cleaning Luminaires and Lamps

How clean the housekeeping staff keeps a building's luminaires and lamps will affect light output, thereby affecting the ability of the lighting system to deliver its designed light levels. Periodic cleaning of lamps and luminaires will enable the lighting system to deliver a greater fraction of its light output than it does when the light is absorbed by dirt on the lamps and luminaires. Regularly replacing filters in the building's air-handling units can make housekeeping's job easier by removing dust and dirt from the building's air.

How often should luminaires and lamps be cleaned? Semi-annual cleaning is sufficient in many locations; in dustier or dirtier areas, more frequent cleaning may be necessary. Each hotel must establish a cleaning program that works for it.

To prevent them from attracting dirt, plastic luminaires should be de-staticized when they are cleaned. Often, a destaticizer is included in the cleaning solution. Plastic luminaires should be air-dried; wiping them would give them a new static charge. Employees should wear clean gloves when handling the cleaned luminaires; otherwise oil from their hands will leave marks on the plastic and destroy the de-staticization there.

Replacing Lamps

Replacing lamps can be as simple as screwing a light bulb into a guestroom table lamp or as difficult as climbing into a bucket truck to replace a pole-mounted high-pressure sodium lamp and its ballast in the middle of a parking lot. Two factors that help determine how lamps are replaced at a property are lamp characteristics and the property's replacement policy.

Lamp Characteristics. As mentioned earlier, incandescent and electric discharge lamps have different life expectancies. Incandescent lamps need to be replaced much more often. For example, if we assume an incandescent lamp life of 1,000 hours (some may have a life of only 750 hours) and a fluorescent lamp life of 12,000 hours, the incandescent lamp could require as many as 8 or 9 replacements per year if burned continuously. (There are 8,760 hours in a year.) The fluorescent lamp would be replaced about once every 1.5 years under such circumstances. While the use of incandescent lamps in guestrooms may sometimes be appropriate for aesthetic reasons, their use in back-of-the-house spaces where such characteristics are unimportant and daily operating hours are long is certainly unnecessary.

A consideration when replacing fluorescent lamps is maintaining the desired color rendition. Replacing a fluorescent lamp with a lamp that has a markedly different color rendition (warm white with cool white, for instance) results in a mottled lighting effect on the interior design that can be disastrous.

If a property's lighting system maintenance program is designed to maintain the lighting system and its light levels as closely as possible to its initial condition, then the lumen depreciation of the system's lamps is also of concern. **Lumen depreciation** is a measure of a lamp's tendency to decrease its light output over time. With mercury vapor lamps and some other types of fluorescent lamps, light output drops off dramatically as the lamps' operating hours approach the lamps' rated life. Unless the lighting system is greatly overdesigned, it may be desirable to replace lamps before they fail entirely because their light output has fallen so far below what it should be.

Other characteristics of lamps that affect maintenance needs are the average burning time of the lamp and the voltage of the electrical supply to the lamp. Incandescent and fluorescent lamps that are frequently cycled (turned on and off) will have greatly reduced lifetimes, resulting in greater maintenance costs in terms of lamps and labor. Lamps that are supplied electricity at a voltage different from the lamp's rated voltage (even by only a very low percent) will have a reduced life if the voltage is above the lamp's rated voltage, an increased life if the voltage is below the lamp's rated voltage. Electrical system or circuit voltages can change for a variety of reasons, including loads being added or removed, changes in electric utility supply voltages, and malfunctions of electrical equipment.

Replacement Policies. Most discussions of lamp replacement policies include a discussion of group relamping versus replacement upon burnout. Group relamping advocates suggest that wholesale replacement of all of the lamps in the lighting system (or a portion of the system) after some prescribed number of operating hours will result in significantly reduced lamp replacement costs. Cost reductions are possible primarily through a labor cost reduction, although it may be possible to reduce lamp costs as well by purchasing them in bulk. One lamp replacement policy is shown in Exhibit 7.

A group relamping policy does not mean that the visual appearance of the space is compromised by not replacing burned-out lamps, as Exhibit 7 illustrates. Lamps that burn out are replaced as they fail, but rather than doing the relamping on a "failure" basis indefinitely, a group relamping program is proactive with regard to failure—that is, it anticipates failure. When the lamps in a given area reach a portion of their rated life (80 percent in the instance of Exhibit 7), they are all replaced. The result is a space that enjoys a uniform light level, with fewer instances of burned-out or malfunctioning lamps. Group relamping can save the property money as well. Group relamping is particularly appropriate in any area that requires a significant number of labor hours simply to gain access to the lamps or where special equipment is required—for example, convention halls and parking lots.

Labor costs for lamp replacement can vary considerably, depending on the length of time required to replace a lamp and the wages of the individual replacing it. For example, if burned-out lamps in guestrooms can be replaced by

Exhibit 7   Sample Lamp Replacement Procedures

P.M. PROCEDURES: Planned Lamp Replacement
MAINT. ACTION #23
FREQUENCY: Annually

Maint. Action #23A

How to set up this program:

1. List all your lamps by area, such as:

    - Coffee Shop—50 lamps
    - Restaurant—100 lamps
    - Corridors—200 lamps

2. Doing one area at a time, replace all the lamps with new ones. Save 20 percent of the best-looking lamps in a "replacement" box with the area clearly marked on it.

3. Now, let's take the coffee shop with 50 lamps as an example. If you saved 20 percent of the old lamps, you have 10 lamps in a box marked "Coffee Shop."

4. As the lamps in the coffee shop burn out, replace them with the ones you have in their replacement box. When there are no lamps left in the box, you have achieved 80 percent of the coffee shop lamps' life and it is time to re-lamp this area with 50 new lamps, once again saving 20 percent (10) for the replacement box.

<u>EASY, ISN'T IT?</u>

P.S. Don't forget to maintain an inventory of lamps sufficient for complete lamp changes.

Source: Adapted from *Maintenance Operating Manual*, Days Inns of America, Inc., Atlanta, Georgia.

housekeeping employees as part of their normal rounds, the cost of lamp replacement in guestrooms will be low. However, if every time a lamp burns out it's replaced by a member of the engineering staff dispatched via radio, the labor cost to replace a single lamp can approach $5 to $10.

Lamp and Ballast Disposal. Replacing lamps and ballasts brings up waste disposal issues. This is especially true during lighting system upgrades or a group relamping effort; both can result in the accumulation of large numbers of lamps and ballasts that must be disposed of properly. Legal as well as environmental issues must be considered.

Some current and most older fluorescent and HID lamps contain small amounts of mercury. Depending on the lamp type and the quantity involved, the disposal of these lamps may be subject to hazardous waste regulations at the federal or state level. Managers should refer to local environmental agencies and/or the U.S. Environmental Protection Agency to check on whether the lamps they are disposing of fall under hazardous-waste guidelines.

All ballasts manufactured through 1979, and some after this date, contain PCBs. There is legislation in the United States (at both the state and federal level) and in many other countries in the world that specifies proper handling and disposal practices for PCB ballasts. These laws must be followed by the property or the contractor retained by the property. Options for ballast disposal include incineration, recycling, and disposal in a landfill.

Although not available in all locations, recycling of fluorescent lamps and ballasts is certainly something that can contribute to a hotel or restaurant's record of good environmental stewardship. When available, fluorescent lamp recycling typically costs approximately 10 cents per lineal foot of lamp. Or, for another way to look at it, the recycling of fluorescent lamps is approximately 1 percent of the life cycle costs of the lamps. Ballast recycling costs approximately $3.50 per F40 ballast.[5] Freight expenses will add to these costs.

Energy Conservation Opportunities

For lighting systems, the two primary energy conservation opportunities are the use of more efficient lighting sources and the control of operating hours. Secondary benefits may be possible by reducing lighting in overlit spaces, but this must be approached with caution since lighting reductions may affect safety, productivity, or guests' perceptions of the property.

One way to achieve more efficient lighting (fewer watts per lumen) is to replace incandescent lamps with fluorescent lamps in as many locations as possible. Compact or screw-in fluorescent lamps are available that can be substituted for incandescent lamps in downlights, table lamps, and ceiling-mounted lighting fixtures of various designs. The result will be a reduction of up to 75 percent in the electricity consumed by the lamp. In addition, there will be substantial labor savings due to the longer life of the fluorescent lamps. Replacing inefficient exterior lights with more efficient ones usually has a short payback period, since the operating hours of exterior lighting are very long.

Efficiently controlling the operating hours of lights results in fewer operating hours, lower energy usage, and lower costs. The easiest control method is to simply turn off lights that are not needed. This is something everyone employed at a property can do that requires no additional training, investment, or labor hours, and has immediate benefits. Since motivating employees and managers to take this responsibility has sometimes proven difficult, many operations use mechanical methods whenever possible to turn off unneeded lights. Microprocessors can also be used to turn lights on and off on a predetermined schedule. In addition to saving electricity, reduced operating hours also increase the time between lamp replacements.

One area that certainly lends itself to mechanical control is exterior lighting, including parking lot lighting. Photocell control for exterior lighting is highly recommended and, in comparison to either manual or time clock control, should result in substantial energy savings with a minimal initial investment. (Time clock

Since exterior lights operate for long hours, replacing inefficient exterior lights with more efficient ones usually has a short payback period.
(Courtesy of Resorts International Casino Hotel, Atlantic City, New Jersey)

control for this lighting must frequently be reset in order to operate the lighting only when needed.) In locations within the property that benefit from natural light, management may wish to install photocell control as well. In these instances, the photocell control acts to maintain a preset light level in the area and either dims or turns off lamps as the amount of natural light increases, or turns on and brightens them as natural light decreases. This can be quite effective in reducing energy costs.

To control the operation of lights in meeting rooms, storerooms, and other areas where lights do not need to operate continuously, the use of ultrasonic or infrared sensors or twist timers may be appropriate. Sensors turn on lights when they sense movement in the room. Following a preset period of inactivity in the room, the lights are switched off. Twist timers are manually activated by the person wanting to use the space; they automatically turn off after a period of time. The length of time lights stay on is dictated by the type of timer and the degree to which it is turned.

Endnotes

1. Walter A. Rutes, Richard H. Penner, and Lawrence Adams, *Hotel Design, Planning, and Development* (New York: W. W. Norton, 2001), p. 338.

2. NFPA 101—*Life Safety Code* (Quincy, Mass.: National Fire Protection Association, 1985).

3. NFPA 70—*National Electrical Code* (Quincy, Mass.: National Fire Protection Association, 1986).

4. Reprinted with permission from NFPA 70–87—*National Electrical Code*, copyright 1986, National Fire Protection Association, Quincy, Mass., 02269. This reprinted material is not the complete and official position of the NFPA on the referenced subject, which is represented only by the standard in its entirety.

5. U.S. Environmental Protection Agency, *Lighting Waste Disposal*, EPA 430-B-95-004, September 1998.

Key Terms

artificial light—Light other than sunlight.

ballast—A piece of equipment that controls the starting and operation of electric discharge lamps and acts as a small transformer in the lighting circuit.

coefficient of utilization—The efficiency factor that combines the luminaire efficiency (light delivered from the luminaire divided by the light produced by the lamp) with the room characteristics and the light distribution in the room.

color rendition—A light source's ability to provide a perceived color similar to that which results from sunlight.

electric discharge lamp—A lamp that generates light by passing an electric arc through a space filled with a specially formulated mixture of gases. Types of electric discharge lamps include fluorescent, mercury vapor, metal halide, and high- and low-pressure sodium.

footcandle—A measurement of illumination. One footcandle denotes a light intensity of one lumen per square foot.

high-intensity discharge (HID) lamp—A lamp requiring a ballast that generates light by passing an electric arc through a space filled with a specially formulated mixture of gases. HID lamps are types of electric discharge lamps that are characterized by high lumens per watt and long strike and restrike times.

illumination—Light that is incident on a surface.

incandescent lamp—A lamp that consists of a filament inside a sealed glass bulb. Current passing through the filament heats it to incandescence, producing light.

lamp life—The expected operating lifetime of a lamp, defined as the time it takes half of the lamps in a given sample to fail.

lumen—The most commonly used unit of light.

lumen depreciation—A measure of a lamp's tendency to decrease its light output over time.

lumen maintenance—A lamp's ability to maintain its output.

luminaire—A lighting appliance that consists of a lamp, lamp socket, ballast (for luminaires using electric discharge lamps), reflective material, lenses or louvers, and a housing. Also called a fixture.

natural light—Sunlight.

strike time—The time required for an electric discharge lamp to reach full output from a cold start.

visible light—Radiated energy that can be seen by the human eye.

Review Questions

1. What are the advantages of natural light?
2. What are the advantages and disadvantages of incandescent lamps?
3. How do incandescent lamps and electric discharge lamps produce light?
4. What are the various types of electric discharge lamps and their characteristics?
5. Why is a lighting system's design an important element of a building's overall design?
6. What are some safety considerations designers must keep in mind when designing a lighting system?
7. How does the type of lamps used at a property affect lamp replacement?
8. What is group relamping?
9. What are some ways lighting systems can conserve energy?

Internet Sites

For more information, visit the following Internet sites. Remember that Internet addresses can change without notice. If the site is no longer there, you can use a search engine to look for additional sites.

American Lighting Association
www.americanlightingassoc.com

American Society of Heating, Refrigerating, and Air-Conditioning Engineers, Inc.
www.ashrae.org

Consulting-Specifying Engineer
www.csemag.com

Green Lights Program
http://.es.epa.gov/partners/green/
g-lights.html

Illuminating Engineering Society of
North America
www.iesna.org

International Association of Lighting
Designers
www.iald.org

Lighting Research Center
www.lrc.rpi.edu

Philips
www.lighting.philips.com

Sylvania
www.sylvania.com

Chapter 10 Outline

Laundry Equipment
    Laundry Transport Equipment
    Washers
    Extractors
    Dryers
    Flatwork Finishers
    Valet Equipment
Laundry Design
    Design Factors
Laundry Maintenance

Competencies

1. Describe laundry transport equipment. (pp. 310–311)

2. Distinguish a washer–extractor from a tunnel washer. (pp. 311–315)

3. Describe dryers. (pp. 315–318)

4. Describe ironers, folders, and valet equipment. (pp. 318–319)

5. Explain factors in locating a laundry and selecting laundry equipment. (pp. 319–323)

6. Describe laundry layout, utilities, and labor. (pp. 323–326)

7. Outline laundry maintenance. (pp. 326–327)

10

Laundry Systems

The Wyndham Wind Watch Hotel doesn't try to put any marketing spin on its laundry equipment—the staff just knows it works.

Humming behind the scenes at the Long Island hotel is an in-house laundry system which goes unnoticed by guests who just see the soft and clean whites and linens which make their stay comfortable and worry-free. Executive Housekeeper David Jakubowski knows exactly how important that is to a hotel, and to its housekeeping staff.

The hotel uses two 150-pound machines and a single 250-pound machine to accomplish the dirty work, while a custom built automatic folding and ironimg machine puts the finishing touches on hotel whites. That and two industrial-size dryers round out the modest but hardworking equipment at the hotel.

"We haven't had any problems whatsoever with the equipment since I came here," Jakubowski said. "We have an in-house preventive maintenance program which keeps things running smooth."

At a time when many hotel companies are forced to outsource their laundry service, The Wyndham Wind Watch prefers to continue using its in-house system.

"It's definitely cheaper to do laundry in-house," Jakubowski said. "But the real advantage is the convenience to the guests. It's always right there. You don't have to worry about the laundry truck getting stuck in a snowstorm."[1]

DEALING WITH LAUNDRY is a fact of life for hotels. Guestrooms, restaurants, banquets, fitness centers, and employees all have soiled linens, towels, tablecloths, uniforms, and other laundry that must be cleaned. Hotels have several choices in how they handle this chore. They can:

- Use disposable products in some cases (paper rather than linen napkins, for example).

- Rent clean linens from a commercial laundry.

- Buy their own linens and use a commercial laundry to clean them.

- Buy their own linens and use a centralized laundry (either free-standing or in a hotel) run by the hotel chain or some other group of affiliated hotels to clean them.

- Buy their own linens and use an on-premises laundry to clean them.

- Use a combination of these alternatives.[2]

Lodging properties in the United States often operate an on-premises laundry for processing all or most of their laundry. In contrast, lodging properties elsewhere in the world usually have their laundry cleaned and processed by outside contractors. Some U.S. chains operate regional laundry facilities where laundry from several of the chain's hotels are processed, providing an off-site laundry similar to a commercial laundry but retaining corporate control over laundry standards.

There are several advantages to operating an on-premises laundry. Many properties enjoy significant savings because processing their own laundry costs them less than paying a commercial laundry to do it. Properties can get by with smaller linen inventories. The life of laundry items is extended; fewer laundry items are lost or damaged. The quality of finished laundry is higher. And the property has complete control of the operation—there is no dependence on an outside laundry's deliveries.

Laundry Equipment

It takes a lot of equipment to outfit the laundry of a large hotel, especially one that offers in-house valet service to its guests. Laundries of small properties can usually get by with the basics—washers and dryers. In the section that follows, we'll discuss a full range of commercial laundry equipment. Keep in mind that the number and type of equipment a hotel has depends on the hotel's size, level of guest service, and other factors.

Laundry Transport Equipment

Employees have to get soiled linens to the laundry. At small properties, laundry (sometimes called "work" or "goods" by laundry personnel) may be carried by hand. At larger properties, carts or chutes are used to move large amounts of laundry quickly. Some hotels have automated overhead transport systems to carry laundry to the washers once linens, towels, and other soiled laundry items arrive at the laundry room.

Carts. Laundry carts are used to transport linen to the laundry, within the laundry, and to storage areas outside the laundry.[3] There are basic carts, carts with shelves, carts with bars or hangers, and "raising platform" carts—the bottom of the cart rests on springs, so that as workers unload the laundry, the bottom rises and workers don't have to bend over so much. There are open carts, carts with covers, and lockable carts. Other cart options include tow hitches (so a worker can pull more than one cart at a time), drain valves, wheel brakes, special casters, and caster swivel locks.

Laundry carts come in various sizes—common sizes carry 200, 400, or 500 pounds of laundry. There are many color options so that hotels can choose carts that match their decor. One manufacturer offers 15 color choices, including bright lemon, jade green, honey gold, and pink! Carts range from heavy-duty canvas to one-piece plastic types with drain holes for easy washing.

Carts should not have protrusions that can snag or tear. They should move easily, and employees should be able to load and unload laundry without

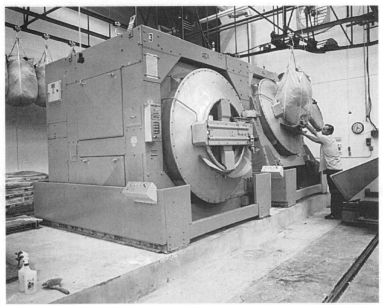

A large laundry with an automated overhead transport system. (Courtesy of the Pellerin Milnor Corporation, Kenner, Louisiana)

excessive bending and stretching. Carts should be cleaned and sanitized on a regular basis. It is a good idea to keep carts for soiled laundry separate from those for clean laundry. The clean-laundry carts can be a different color or made from a different material so that they are not mixed in with the soiled-laundry carts.[4]

Chutes. Laundry chutes are a convenient way to get laundry to the laundry room. They should be cleaned regularly to remove lint and dust. Any fire detection or suppression equipment in the chute should be checked periodically to ensure proper operation in case of fire. Laundry chutes should be locked to reduce the risk that they will be used by a prankster or an arsonist. The locks should be on the engineering department's preventive maintenance schedule to ensure that they are kept in working order.

Automated Overhead Transport Systems. Some large properties have automated overhead transport systems in their laundry rooms. With a typical system, employees sort laundry items and place them in bags that travel on overhead rails to the washers. When a washer is ready for another load, an employee opens the bottom of the bag (or the bag automatically opens) and drops the laundry into the washer. Some machines tilt backward to make this easier. If the transport system is computerized, the computer can keep track of which laundry goes where and make sure it is properly processed.

Washers

There are many types and sizes of commercial washers. Commercial washers not much bigger than the washers found in homes can handle up to 35 pounds of

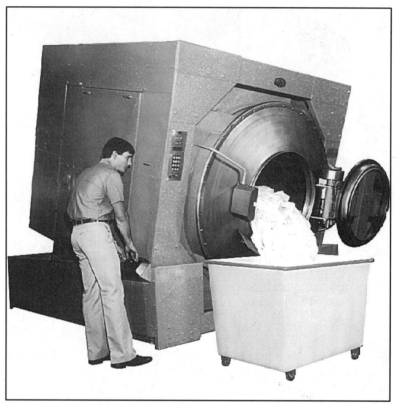

This washer-extractor handles up to 450 pounds of laundry per load. Machines of this size would only be found in large hotels. (Courtesy of the Pellerin Milnor Corporation, Kenner, Louisiana)

laundry per load; at the other extreme are giant washers that can handle as much as 700 pounds. Two common washer types are washer-extractors and tunnel washers.

Washer-Extractors. Washer-extractors, sometimes called conventional washers, are free-standing units made of stainless steel or other heavy-duty materials, used to clean laundry and extract water from it to prepare it for drying. Washer-extractors may be front or side loaders. The type of machine a manager chooses depends on the property's laundry operation. Side loaders, for example, are usually used in laundries that deliver soiled items to the washers by way of an overhead transport system.

Once laundry is loaded into the machine, water must be added that is at the proper temperature. Then the correct mix of chemicals for the laundry being washed are added. Many washers are computerized, so that the correct chemical mixture is added automatically—all an employee has to do is push a button to start the process. The control panel will display such information as the name of the current wash operation ("Rinse," for example), time remaining in the operation, water

Washer-Extractor Capacities

	Double sheets	Pillow-cases	54 x 54 table-cloths	20 x 20 napkins	Bath towels	Shirts	Pants	Uniforms	Mop-heads
35 lb. model	23	116	37	206	61	74	29	38	23
50 lb. model	33	170	54	295	88	106	42	55	33
75 lb. model	50	250	81	442	130	159	63	82	50
95 lb. model	62	315	102	560	165	200	80	105	63
135 lb. model	90	450	145	795	235	286	113	148	89

These sample laundry capacities provide a general idea of how much laundry can be placed in small to mid-size washer-extractors. Of course, the amount of laundry a given size washer-extractor can process will vary from manufacturer to manufacturer (these numbers were provided by the Pellerin Milnor Corporation). How much laundry can be washed per cycle also depends on a number of other factors, including how much the individual laundry items weigh, the type of fabric they are made of, and their degree of soiling.

temperature, and chemicals being injected. Some washers' control panels have two-language capability—messages can be displayed in English or in one of five other languages (French, Dutch, German, Italian, or Spanish).

Some washer-extractors have a **cool-down cycle.** During this cycle, cold water is slowly injected into the wash to prevent blended no-iron fabrics from going into the "thermal shock" that causes wrinkles.

Some of the large washer-extractors tilt forward to help with unloading. Once the machine is tilted, an employee can position a laundry cart under the door and push a button to rotate the cylinder, causing the clean laundry to tumble into the cart. The machine can also unload onto a conveyor that can transport the laundry to a dryer. Some washer-extractors also tilt back to help employees load laundry.

Tunnel Washers. Tunnel washers, also called batch washers or continuous washers, have characteristics that make them different from conventional washer-extractors. As you can see from Exhibit 1, a tunnel washer is, in effect, a series of interconnected washers.[5]

In both conventional washers and tunnel washers, laundry is subjected to successive "baths"—some with chemicals—to loosen, suspend, and rinse away

Exhibit 1   Diagram of a Tunnel Washer

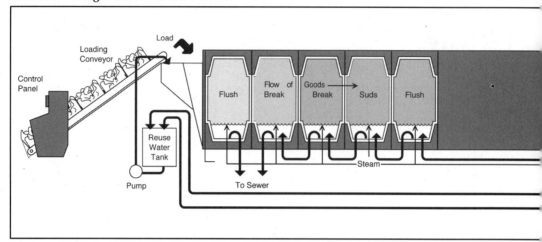

Courtesy of the Pellerin Milnor Corporation, Kenner, Louisiana

soil. These baths are followed by finishing operations (sour, starch, softener, etc.). A conventional washer does this in a single cylinder; baths are changed by draining and refilling the cylinder. A tunnel washer, on the other hand, keeps each bath in a different cylinder and moves the laundry from one cylinder to the next. The laundry is separated into batches, just as with a conventional washer. Computerized tunnel washers can keep track of each batch as it moves through the tunnel and automatically adjust water temperatures and chemical formulas so that each batch receives the treatment it needs for optimum cleaning.

Two basic types of tunnel washers are top-transfer machines and bottom-transfer machines. **Top-transfer machines** lift the laundry out of the water and drain it before transferring it to the next bath; **bottom-transfer machines** transfer both the laundry and the water along the bottom of the washer. Top-transfer machines offer the advantage of draining laundry before moving it along to progressively cleaner baths; this process makes for cleaner laundry. In bottom-transfer machines, dirty water moves forward with the load, so laundry is not as clean.

Tunnel washers are becoming more popular in the United States for a number of reasons. One is that it takes fewer employees to operate them. Tunnel washers are connected to an extractor, and conveyors can automatically move the laundry from the extractor to the dryers, so that instead of a number of employees loading and unloading separate washers, extractors, and dryers and transporting laundry between these machines, only one employee is needed to load the washer and one or two to load the dryers. In addition to labor savings, there can be significant energy and water savings. Where conventional washers can use as much as three gallons of water per pound of laundry, some tunnel washers use just one gallon. By extension, energy is saved because less water needs to be heated.

Tunnel washers have other advantages as well. Laundry is processed faster because there are no delays for filling and draining cylinders. Because water and

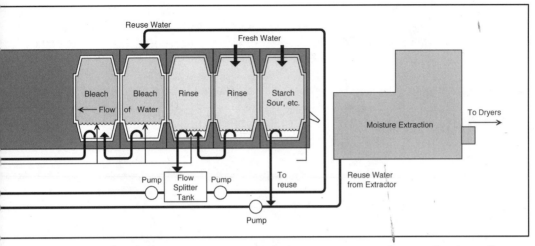

energy demands are constant, support systems—water heaters, water softeners, drains, and so on—do not have to be sized to cover peak demands. Tunnel washing systems are highly adaptable to whatever space is available. If necessary, they can be installed around corners so that the washer, extractor, and dryers are arranged in an L or U shape. Since tunnel washers process laundry steadily in small batches, morning startup time is quicker and throughput is at a steady level. Employees in the finishing sections don't have to wait a long time to get started, only to be buried under hundreds of pounds of laundry all at once.

Extractors

As the name implies, **extractors** extract water from laundered fabrics, usually by the centrifugal force generated when the laundry is spun in a basket, although very large extractors may press the water out. Extractors cut down on drying time and costs. Most extractors have two extraction speeds: fast, for most natural-fiber fabrics, and slow, for easily wrinkled polyester or other no-iron fabrics. Stand-alone extractors are typically used in large laundries or with tunnel washers; as noted earlier, washer-extractors do their own extracting, and many laundries don't need a separate extractor.

Dryers

Dryers are machines that dry laundry by tumbling it in a basket exposed to hot air. There are gas, electric, and steam dryers. Gas is generally the most economical heat source; electric dryers are quiet; steam dryers are best suited for locations where steam power is already available. Dryer capacities range from 15 to 450 pounds.

Today's dryers are more sophisticated than their counterparts of yesteryear because (1) there are more types of fabrics now, some of which have special drying needs, (2) saving energy is of greater concern, and (3) managers are seeking simpler machines that can reduce energy, training, and labor costs.

Two 50-pound washer-extractors. (Courtesy of the Pellerin Milnor Corporation, Kenner, Louisiana)

Many dryers now have microprocessor-driven control systems. All an employee has to do is push the button on the control panel that corresponds to the type of laundry being dried, and the dryer goes through a cycle that has been pre-programmed by the laundry manager or by the dryer's manufacturer (usually with input from the laundry manager). Some dryers dry the load for a set number of minutes recommended for that fabric; others have sensors linked to their micro-processors that can "feel" moisture in the load and turn the dryer off automatically the moment the laundry is dry. Many dryers then go through a cool-down cycle so that wrinkles are not set into no-iron fabrics. Some also have an "anti-wrinkle" feature that automatically tumbles the load without heat at pre-selected intervals—managers may program the dryer to tumble the load for 20 seconds every two minutes for ten minutes, for example. If an employee is busy and can't get to the laundry right after a cycle is completed, the anti-wrinkle feature keeps clothes from sitting at the bottom of the dryer basket and wrinkling.

Energy-saving features on dryers include an ignition system for gas dryers rather than a standing pilot light. Some manufacturers build extra insulation into their "energy-saving" models. One manufacturer offers a "heat reclaimer" pack-age, in which a portion of the hot exhaust air is recirculated into the dryer, saving energy and reducing drying time. Another dryer saves time and energy by using a permanently tilted basket and gravity to position the wettest laundry (which is the heaviest) closest to the hot air inlet.

The Ten Most Common Drying Mistakes

Although these tips were written with large laundries in mind, many of them can also help managers of mid-size and small laundries.

1. **Not loading the dryer to full capacity.** Underloading is the most common and most costly mistake made in institutional laundries. Dryers with microprocessors can eliminate this problem with "small load" dry cycles for each fabric classification.

2. **Allowing laundry to dry too long.** Besides wasting energy and production time, overdrying creates friction, which wears out linen fibers and produces excess lint. Don't pad drying time "just to make sure."

3. **Not running the dryer at constant production rates.** It's a waste of production time to let employees dictate when a dryer is loaded. Often the machine sits idle after a load is dried because employees are engaged in other tasks. There are automatic or semi-automatic dryer loading and unloading possibilities for almost any laundry.

4. **Taking too long to load or unload machines.** Besides wasting time, this allows the dryer's cylinder to cool off between loads, resulting in the dryer having to work harder to bring the temperature back up for the next batch.

5. **Too much heat at the end of the load.** The most effective means of drying is to apply the greatest heat to laundry at the beginning of cycles. It is best to restrict heat toward the end, when goods are most susceptible to damage. Dryers with microprocessors can do this easily.

6. **Not enough cool-down.** If dried laundry is not cooled down enough during the dryer's cool-down cycle, at worst there is a chance that it may smolder—or even catch fire! At best, wrinkles are set into the fabric, which means employees must spend more time in the finishing area trying to get them out. Sometimes the laundry must be rewashed. Ideally, the cool-down cycle should occur when the laundry reaches a certain temperature, not at a pre-selected time. Microprocessors make this possible.

7. **Not keeping filters clean enough to allow the dryer to operate at optimum levels.** Although it should be a given that laundries follow the manufacturers's recommended filter-cleaning schedule, it's amazing how few do.

8. **Not maintaining the dryer's seal.** A dryer's efficiency is directly related to the condition of its seal, since it keeps cold air out and hot air inside the basket so it can flow through the laundry. Most seals wear out quickly since they are subjected to the reverse side of the basket's perforations (a cheese-grater effect). A worn-out seal means the dryer has to work harder and longer to dry goods. You can bypass this problem entirely with new dryers, which have an unusual placement of the seal on a smooth band around the basket.

9. **Not moving laundry to finishing stations quickly.** Optimum use of ironers, for example, relies on a specific amount of moisture in the goods before ironing. Allowing goods to sit too long makes them wrinkle; sometimes rewashing is the only cure. Besides improving scheduling, consider installing a conveyor or some other automated means of transport between dryers and finishing stations.

10. **Not keeping accurate production and cost figures for drying.** To improve anything, you need to know what you're starting with—how much time and fuel are projected for each classification versus actual numbers. New personal computer systems can provide this information in summarized reports.

Source: Mike Diedling, "Avoiding Ten Most Common Errors in Drying Reduces Fuel Costs in Institutional Laundries," *Laundry News.*

Dryers come in various colors to match an operation's decor. Other features include signal lights indicating dryer operation, self-cleaning lint screens, reverse cylinder drives (to help prevent laundry from balling and tangling), "no-snag" baskets with extruded perforations to help protect delicate fabrics, and automatic backdraft dampers (to eliminate downdrafts that chill the dryer). Some dryers with microprocessors have diagnostic boards that allow maintenance employees to locate a problem quickly.

Flatwork Finishers

The two machines commonly used to finish linens, tablecloths, and other laundry items are ironers and folders.

Ironers. **Ironers** give linens a crisp, finished look. Sometimes properties even send "no-iron" blended linens through an ironer to improve their appearance, especially if they have been washed enough times for their no-iron finish to be damaged or worn out.

Ironers can be heated by gas (generally the most economical method), steam, electricity, or thermal fluid, and are available in several sizes. Small units may finish 40 to 100 pounds of laundry per hour; large units can finish up to 1,500 pounds per hour.[6] Ironers are wide enough to take in tablecloths and bed linens. Some ironers also fold and stack linens. Some, called dual-finish ironers, iron linens on both sides. Microprocessors on large units monitor temperatures and production speed. Some ironers can take linens directly from washer-extractors, eliminating the drying step.

Folders. **Folders** can be very simple devices that function like an extra pair of hands to help an employee fold laundry manually. Folders can also be large, rectangular machines that look much like ironers and fold laundry automatically. They take linens fed into them manually or automatically from the ironer and fold them, using blasts of air for the primary folds. There are primary folders and cross-folders. Some machines combine both functions. Some folders have infrared photo sensors that measure the linen as it is fed into the machine; a microprocessor then makes the calculations that determine the fold points and triggers the air blasts. Counters display the number of linens that have been folded. Grading devices signal employees when soiled or torn linens go through the machine. Some folders have attachments that stack folded linens on a conveyor belt; the belt then moves the stacks to the next laundry station.

Valet Equipment

Valet services require many types of equipment.[7] There are body presses, sleeve finishers, collar-yoke-cuff presses, vacuum spotting boards, form finishers, utility presses, mushroom presses, pants toppers, and others. Presses are heated with steam and come in automatic, semi-automatic, or manual models. Presses greatly increase employee productivity. For example, an employee can finish 20 to 35 shirts per hour with a good shirt-finishing press.

Finishing cabinets and tunnels are used to get wrinkles out of no-iron employee uniforms and other garments. Garments are put on hangers and placed in a cabinet or on a conveyor that pulls laundry through a tunnel where wrinkles are steamed out.

Hand irons (electric or steam), water spray guns, and sewing machines are also part of a good valet department.

Laundry Design

Obviously, to run smoothly a laundry needs to be well-designed and have the right equipment, properly installed. What may be less obvious is that such laundries have lower equipment maintenance costs. By having a well-designed facility with correctly installed equipment, equipment modifications and equipment break-down due to overuse and misapplication will be minimized.

Managers at many properties have their laundries designed by outside con-tractors. These contractors should be aware of laundry employees' schedules, guestroom occupancies and quantities of dirty laundry generated, the type and amount of laundry coming from food and beverage operations, and laundry from other sources—for example, a health club facility.

There may be a time in your career when you will be asked to help design or redesign an on-premises laundry. There are several signs that a laundry may need to be redesigned:

- Too many last-minute rush jobs

- Persistent linen shortages

- Too much overtime among laundry workers

- The laundry never seems to catch up

- Work space is tight; often there seem to be too many employees, carts, and equipment for the space[8]

You should ask questions before redesigning a laundry, however:

- Can the laundry's workload be changed to avoid last-minute rush jobs? Would a change in the laundry's operating hours solve the problem?

- Are linen shortages due to inventory depletion because linens have been lost, worn out, or stolen? When was the last time anyone took a physical inventory of sheets, pillowcases, tablecloths, and so on? In hotels operating with 3 par or less, an inventory should be taken at least every 30 days.

- Can the overtime problem be solved in a cost-effective manner by hiring addi-tional part-time or full-time employees? Are there employees from other parts of the operation that can help out in the laundry (for example, room atten-dants who finish their rounds early)?

- If the laundry never catches up, is it because employees are not scheduled cor-rectly? Do you simply need more equipment? Is laundry being washed or dried too long, causing unnecessary delays? Is equipment operating at peak efficiency? Does the laundry lose time because equipment constantly breaks down? If your equipment is more than ten years old, new equipment could dramatically decrease washing and finishing times and eliminate the need to redesign the laundry.

- Even if work space is tight, a redesign of the laundry may not be necessary. Are the laundry carts in the laundry room typically half full? If so, the number of carts in the laundry room can be reduced. Can an area outside the laundry be used as a holding space for soiled laundry? This area would have to be easily accessible with no safety hazards and be secure from theft. As a last resort, perhaps housekeeping personnel can be asked to hold onto soiled goods until they can be accommodated in the laundry.

If these options do not seem to be the answer, then a redesign of the laundry may be in order. You should do a cost analysis first, however. Add total direct and indirect operating costs (salaries, supplies, maintenance, repairs, utilities, depreciation, and so on) for a given period of time, and divide that cost by the number of pounds of laundry processed during that same time period. This will give you a cost per pound of laundry processed. If a redesign of the laundry, including the purchase of new equipment, cannot reduce the cost per pound by 15 percent or more, the redesign is not practical from a cost-savings standpoint.

Design Factors

Basic design factors that need to be thought out when designing or redesigning an on-premises laundry include location, size, equipment, layout, utilities, and labor.

Location. If you are planning to redesign an existing laundry, the location of the laundry has already been decided for you. But since most laundries are expanded when they are redesigned, there is still the question of where to find the additional space. To save labor and utility costs, find the extra space as close as possible to the existing laundry. One hotel moved the valet section of its laundry into an adjacent locker room, freeing up space in the laundry for additional equipment. Another hotel built its new laundry on the floor directly above the old one. The old laundry had washing, drying, and finishing areas in one room. The new laundry housed the washing and drying equipment only, and the old laundry was converted into a finishing area. Clean linens from the new laundry dropped through chutes into waiting carts on the floor below to be separated, folded, and stored.

If you are planning a new on-premises laundry, make sure to locate it far enough from guestrooms so that guests won't be disturbed when laundry equipment is running. Another important consideration: are utilities and drains readily available at the proposed location? If so, installation costs will be lower. Very hot water—160°F to 180°F (71°C to 82°C), cold water, steam, gas, and large sewer drains and water lines are essential plumbing requirements.

Getting carts into and out of the laundry is easier if the laundry is located on the main floor. Remodeling costs can be kept down if the laundry is located in or near the current linen distribution area. And last but certainly not least, ideally a laundry should be located in an area with an outside wall, since dryers and other equipment need to be vented to the outside.

If a hotel has a basement, the laundry is usually located there because (1) laundry equipment can be very heavy, and (2) vibrations from the equipment are better absorbed. There are exceptions to this, however. As noted earlier, one hotel chose to expand its laundry by taking space above the laundry rather than alongside it. The floor of the new laundry was structurally reinforced to bear the added weight, and vibration was not a problem since the new equipment had such anti-vibration features as shock absorbers and self-balancing baskets. In Hawaii, where flooding can be a problem, the Hawaii Prince Hotel in Waikiki located its laundry well above the basement. If an upper floor has not previously supported laundry equipment, it is important for management to consult a structural engineer before moving equipment to that floor.

Wherever the laundry is located, the laundry room's walls should be durable and moisture-resistant, and ceilings should resist moisture and absorb sound. An eight- to ten-foot ceiling is usually sufficient. A cement floor with easily cleanable floor drains and no low spots where water can pool is ideal.

Size. The size for a hotel laundry is dependent on a number of variables: the types and amounts of linen used; the average number of guests per day; the number of restaurants in the hotel; the types and capacities of laundry equipment; whether employees wear uniforms and, if so, whether those uniforms are laundered at the hotel. Laundry equipment manufacturers and laundry design consultants can help you determine the correct size for your hotel's specific needs.

Equipment. Because each lodging operation is unique, it is impossible to give specific advice on equipment selection. However, there are some useful general questions you should ask when selecting a piece of equipment:

- *Is it easy to operate?* Ease of operation is especially important if there is high employee turnover or if employees from other departments help out in the laundry. Many machines have microprocessors to help keep things simple for employees.

- *Is it versatile enough to do the job?* Chances are, a piece of equipment will be called on to handle a variety of tasks. For example, washer-extractors are called on to clean a number of different fabrics with various degrees of soiling, from lightly soiled sheets to heavily soiled floor mats. Therefore, washer-extractors should be able to dispense a variety of chemical formulas and have different cycles to deal with the various laundry items and soiling conditions they will encounter.

- *Will it survive heavy use?* Commercial laundry equipment is designed to stand up under heavy use for many years, but some equipment handles the workload better than others. Also, the laundry's equipment will be operated by a number of different people over the years and, at times, will be abused. Is the equipment well-constructed of strong materials? Does it have life-extending features such as heavy-duty motors and a load-distribution speed?

Of course, another factor to consider when buying equipment is the manufacturer. Does the manufacturer provide good service and parts backup? How long has it been in business? What kind of warranty does it provide? Does it specialize in laundry equipment? Some manufacturers have extensive maintenance manuals, service seminars for maintenance employees, and training videos and workbooks for on-the-job training. Some do not. You may pay dearly for an equipment "bargain" if the manufacturer doesn't stand behind its products or provide good service support.[9]

A question that is sometimes not asked until the last minute is: How are we going to get the equipment into the laundry room? Some washer-extractors and dryers are huge machines, and it is not unknown for a hotel to take off a section of its roof or knock a big hole in a wall to get its laundry equipment into the building. For small hotels buying small-capacity equipment, some manufacturers make machines narrow enough to fit through conventional doorways.

Let's take a closer look at selection considerations for the two most important pieces of equipment every laundry has to have: washer-extractors and dryers.

Washer-extractors. It is usually best to install two small washer-extractors rather than one large one, because:

- It takes less time to accumulate a full load for a smaller machine

- If one machine breaks down, you have a backup

- You can handle small, odd laundry loads more efficiently

- You can wash two different types of laundry at the same time (for example, lightly soiled sheets and heavily soiled cleaning rags)

- Small machines impose less of a peak load on plumbing and electrical systems

However, there may be times when you should buy a single large washer-extractor rather than two smaller ones. The laundry area may not be large enough for two machines. Perhaps the budget won't permit two machines (usually one large model costs less than two small models). And if the choice is between one 35-pound commercial washer-extractor or several home appliance washers, choose the single commercial machine for greater efficiency, durability, and laundry quality.

The size of the washer-extractor's cylinder or basket is a top consideration when choosing a washer-extractor. Commercial washer-extractors use a lifting and tumbling action to wash clothes, as opposed to the agitator action of a home washer. A large cylinder does more lifting and tumbling than a small one. Machines rated at the same capacity may have different-size washing cylinders; those with the smaller cylinders will do a poorer job of washing. Cylinder turning speed is also important. A wash speed that is too fast will plaster the laundry to the cylinder wall, cutting down on the lifting and dropping action.

Because a laundry handles a variety of fabrics, it is best to buy one washer-extractor with a high extraction speed (for thick laundry items and cottons) and one with a low extraction speed (for permanent press sheets, polyester or cotton/polyester employee uniforms, and other polyester or blended fabrics). If only one machine is budgeted, buy one that gives you a choice of high or low extraction speed.[10]

A large, accessible door is important for fast loading and unloading. Door safety locks prevent opening the machine while it is operating.

Finally, ease of operation is important. Choose a washer-extractor that your employees can learn easily and quickly.

Dryers. For faster drying and less wrinkling, a dryer should have a slightly larger capacity than its corresponding washer-extractor. One rule of thumb is approximately 25 percent more.[11]

There are many things to look for in a dryer. Is it the right size for your needs? Is it easy to operate? Is it easy to maintain? Some dryers have diagnostic microprocessors—if there is a problem with the dryer's door, heat sensor, motor, etc., the microprocessor displays information to help maintenance employees locate and solve the problem. Does the dryer have a variety of cycles to handle various types of laundry with differing drying requirements? Does it have an anti-wrinkle cycle? Does it have a no-snag basket? The answers to these and other questions will help you determine the dryer(s) best suited to meet your hotel's needs.

Layout. A laundry layout should position equipment so that laundry flows smoothly with no backtracking from the soiled laundry area to the finished laundry area (see Exhibit 2).

Exhibit 3 shows a laundry layout for a typical small property (150 rooms); Exhibit 4 shows a layout for a property with 500 to 750 rooms. These exhibits illustrate the flow-through nature of laundry design and the need to locate equipment to provide a minimum travel distance between key equipment (such as between washers and dryers). Any modifications to a laundry's layout should always consider work flow and, whenever possible, not interfere with the smooth flow of traffic.

When laying out a laundry room, aim for easy loading and unloading of equipment to reduce turnaround time between loads. Soiled laundry storage and sorting should be done near the washer-extractors. Dryers should be placed close to washer-extractors to save time and employee effort. Hinges on washer-extractor and dryer doors can be placed on the left or right side—the proper choice depends on your laundry's layout. For example, if you have two washer-extractors and two dryers in a row along one wall, it would be best for the washer-extractor hinges to be on the left side and the dryer hinges to be on the right, so that employees won't have to walk around an open washer-extractor door to get to a dryer. The folding area should be located close to or in the direction of the room or area where laundry is stored.

When positioning equipment, you should also pay close attention to the laundry room's entrances, exits, support columns (if any), and drain locations. Check local codes for restrictions or permit requirements before installing equipment.

Have you allowed enough space between adjacent machines? A good general rule is to allow at least 18 inches between washer-extractors. Dryers can usually be placed closer together.[12]

It's also important to allow space around a machine for servicing. One manufacturer suggests you should allow at least two feet between the back of a machine and the wall behind it, although this minimum clearance varies with the machine's design.[13]

Utilities. Many pieces of laundry equipment require an electrical supply, usually three-phase and at least 208/240 volt. Both 115V and 220V grounded electric outlets must also be provided in the laundry area. Machines may use natural gas or

Exhibit 2   Laundry Layouts

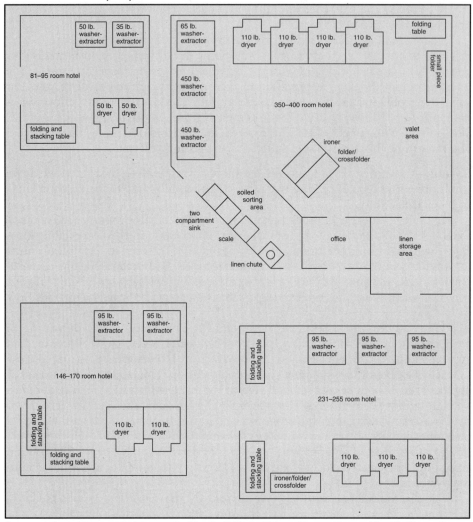

Source: Adapted from materials supplied by the Pellerin Milnor Corporation and Jay D. Chase, "Laundry Service: Consider the Options," *Lodging,* May 1986, p. 34.

(less commonly) steam as their fuel source, requiring a connection to the building's gas or steam system.

A laundry must have an adequate supply of hot and cold water. One to five gallons of water may be required for each pound of laundry processed. If you can operate the laundry during periods of low hot water usage, you may not need to increase hot water capacity, or may only need to add a booster to the existing water heater(s). Otherwise, additional water heaters may be needed. A water softener may also be required. Since both hot and cold water are used in washing, it may be advisable to soften both. Drains must keep up with the rapid rates of discharge

Exhibit 3 Laundry Layout for a Small Property

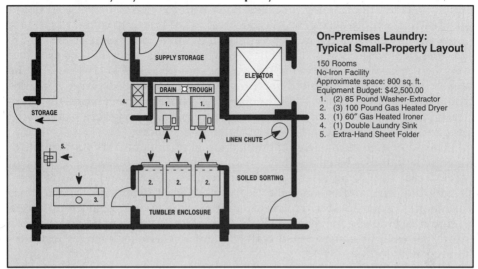

Source: Jay D. Chase, "Laundry Service: Consider the Options," *Lodging,* May 1986, p. 38.

Exhibit 4 Laundry Layout for a Large Property

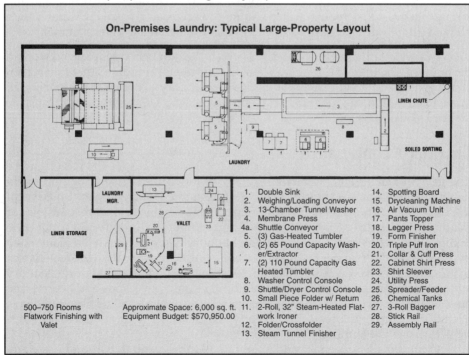

Source: Jay D. Chase, "Laundry Service: Consider the Options," *Lodging,* May 1986, p. 36.

possible from modern laundry equipment. Often a drain trough is used (see Exhibit 3). Other floor drains (installed flush with the floor surface so as not to impede work) remove accidental overflow and normal cleanup water.

Water for the laundry must be supplied at suitable pressure levels. Large laundries have washers with rapid fill rates, which means water must be provided at enough pressure to ensure that the washers are filled quickly. Because of the large quantity of water required and unique temperature needs, large laundries should have their own water-heating equipment. This equipment has all the maintenance needs of any water heating equipment. Only heavy-duty, commercial equipment should be purchased to heat water for a laundry.

The water itself must be free of problem-causing contaminants. As mentioned, water for laundries is usually softened because detergents work better in softened water. It may also be necessary to remove iron, manganese, and sulfur to avoid staining problems and enhance the cleaning action of detergents. Maintenance staff should be sure water treatment equipment is operating at an optimum level and is properly maintained. Periodic water testing may be necessary to ensure the water is being treated correctly and to check for changes in water-supply conditions.

The rapid filling rates of commercial laundry equipment can result in "water hammer," a problem that can also affect other portions of the water system. Water hammer occurs when water flowing rapidly in a pipe is abruptly stopped. In the case of laundry equipment, the solenoid valves used to control water flow can create this problem. Consider installing shock arresters on the water lines, using piping practices that reduce water hammer, or replacing solenoid water valves with adjustable air-operated water valves that can eliminate water hammer.

Labor. One factor that affects laundry design is the number of people who work in the laundry. One rule of thumb for a small institutional laundry is that one person should be able to handle about 80 pounds of laundry per hour.[14] Allow enough space to accommodate the number of employees who will be working during the laundry's busiest times.

Laundry Maintenance

The general manager is indirectly responsible for correctly operating and maintaining the on-premises laundry. Direct responsibility is shared by the housekeeping department and the engineering department. Engineering is responsible for maintaining laundry equipment and keeping the laundry's utility and water costs within limits set by upper management. Laundry equipment may be maintained by engineering personnel or by an outside contractor—usually the dealer from whom the equipment was purchased. Housekeeping employees staff the laundry and are therefore involved in a number of day-to-day decisions and actions that have an impact on how much maintenance a laundry needs. Some properties have a laundry manager; at others, the executive housekeeper or one of his or her assistants manages the laundry.

A laundry's maintenance and operating needs depend in part on its size and equipment. In a hotel that processes laundry for other hotels as well as its own (the

Exhibit 5 Sample Maintenance Actions for Laundry Equipment

CLOTHES WASHER	CLOTHES DRYER
DAILY	**DAILY**
1. Inspect washer and check operation.	1. Inspect machine and check operation.
2. Wipe door gasket to remove soap buildup.	2. Clean lint trap.
MONTHLY	**MONTHLY**
1. Check and tighten base hold-down bolts.	1. Check and tighten base hold-down bolts.
2. Vacuum lint and dust from control housing.	2. Vacuum dust and lint from top compartment and burner assembly.
3. Check for loose wires and connections. Tighten.	3. Blow out dust and lint from lower electrical compartment.
4. Check belt for wear and tension.	4. Check for loose wires and connections.
5. Check drain assembly. Clean out rubbish.	5. Check belt for wear and tension.
6. Lubricate drain solenoid linkage.	6. Lubricate chain per manufacturer's specs and frequency (may be annually rather than monthly.
7. Lubricate bearings per manufacturer's specs and frequently (may be annually rather than monthly).	
8. Clean machine.	
ANNUALLY	**ANNUALLY**
1. Conduct all actions listed under monthly heading.	1. Carry out maintenance actions listed under monthly.
2. Check pulley alignment. Adjust as required.	2. Lubricate bearings per manufacturer's specs and frequency (may be monthly rather than annually).
3. Open front loading door. Check rotating drum for clearance. Adjust from rear as required.	3. Open front loading door. check rotating basket for clearance. Use adjustment bolts in rear if required.
4. Check all safety devices.	4. Thoroughly clean dryer.
	5. Check pulley alignment. Adjust as required.

Source: Adapted from materials supplied by the Pellerin Milnor Corporation and Jay D. Chase, "Laundry Service: Consider the Options," *Lodging*, May 1986, p. 34.

Chicago Hilton and Towers, for example, processes laundry for other Chicago-area Hilton properties), the laundry's size is much larger and it has more equipment than is required just for the hotel itself. The type of equipment in the laundry depends on whether the facility provides all possible laundry services or only the basics. For example, a hotel laundry may do dry cleaning for the hotel or may send it to an outside commercial establishment.

Exhibit 5 contains sample maintenance actions for laundry equipment. Maintenance actions are usually not complex, although troubleshooting and repair of today's computerized equipment can become so. For large laundries, some maintenance employees may be assigned virtually full-time to the laundry, or contract maintenance services may be used. A good preventive maintenance program for laundry equipment is a must, since a breakdown can have immediate effects on many aspects of the hotel.

Equipment is not the only maintenance concern in a laundry. Because of the heat, humidity, and chemicals present in laundries, the only way most laundries can be kept habitable is by using an HVAC system. For this reason, maintenance staff should give any HVAC maintenance request by laundry personnel a priority.[15]

Endnotes

1. Nick Raio, "Wyndham Wind Watch In-House Laundry Custom Fit for Hotel Needs," *Hotel Business,* July 7–20, 1998, pp. 32–33.

2. Adapted from Frank D. Borsenik and Alan T. Stutts, *The Management of Maintenance and Engineering Systems in the Hospitality Industry,* 2d ed. (New York: Wiley, 1987), p. 442.

3. Some of the following information was found in "Poly-trux: Seamless One-Piece Molded Polymer Trucks," a brochure from Meese, Inc., Leonia, New Jersey.

4. "Commissioning Milnor 35 and 50 lb. Machines," a brochure by the Pellerin Milnor Corporation, Kenner, Louisiana, p. 30.

5. Much of the information in this section was found in "Questions People Ask About Tunnel Washing," a brochure by the Pellerin Milnor Corporation, Kenner, Louisiana.

6. From "Chicago's All Star Lineup," a brochure by the Chicago Dryer Company, Chicago, Illinois.

7. Much of the material in this section is drawn from brochures and other materials from the Cissell Manufacturing Company, Louisville, Kentucky.

8. This list and much of the information in this section are based on "How to Spot and Remedy Growing Pains," by Charles A. Emling, Jr., *Laundry News.*

9. "Laundry Equipment Selection Checklist," courtesy of the Pellerin Milnor Corporation, Kenner, Louisiana.

10. "Before Buying a Washer-Extractor…" *Executive Housekeeping Today.*

11. Kenneth A. Penman, "Saving Money with an On-Premise Laundry," *Athletic Purchasing and Facilities.*

12. "A Laundry Planning Checklist," courtesy of the Pellerin Milnor Corporation, Kenner, Louisiana.

13. "A Laundry Planning Checklist," courtesy of the Pellerin Milnor Corporation, Kenner, Louisiana.

14. "A Laundry Planning Checklist," courtesy of the Pellerin Milnor Corporation, Kenner, Louisiana.

15. Two sources for more information about on-premises laundries and laundering are the National Association of Institutional Linen Management and the American Laundry and Linen College, both in Richmond, Kentucky.

Key Terms

bottom-transfer machine—A tunnel washer that moves the laundry and the water along the bottom of the washer.

cool-down cycle—A washer cycle in which cold water is slowly injected into the wash to prevent blended no-iron fabrics from going into the "thermal shock" that causes wrinkles.

dryer—A machine that dries laundry by tumbling it in a basket exposed to hot air.

extractor—A machine that extracts water from laundered fabrics, usually by spinning the laundry in a basket, though very large extractors may press the water out. Extractors cut down on drying time and costs.

folder—A machine that folds laundry. Folders range from simple devices that help employees fold laundry manually to huge rectangular machines that fold laundry automatically, taking linens fed into them manually or directly from the ironer.

ironer—A machine that uses rollers to iron linens, giving them a crisp, finished look. Some ironers also fold and stack linens.

top-transfer machines—A tunnel washing machine that lifts the laundry out of the water and drains it before transferring it to the next bath.

tunnel washer—Also called a batch or continuous washer. Tunnel washers are, in effect, a series of interconnected washers in which each bath, or cycle, is kept in a different cylinder and laundry is moved from one cylinder to the next.

washer-extractors—Sometimes called conventional washers, these free-standing units are used to both clean laundry and then extract water from it in preparation for transfer to drying machines.

Review Questions

1. How can laundry be transported to and within the laundry room?

2. What are the differences between a washer-extractor and a tunnel washer?

3. How do top-transfer and bottom-transfer tunnel washers differ?

4. What are some of the features available on today's sophisticated dryers?

5. What are some signs that a laundry may need to be redesigned?

6. What should you consider when locating a new laundry or finding additional space to expand an old one?

7. What are some general questions you should ask when selecting a piece of equipment?

8. What are some specific selection considerations for washer-extractors and dryers?

9. What should you keep in mind when laying out a laundry room?

10. What are some of the maintenance issues for a laundry?

Internet Sites

For more information, visit the following Internet sites. Remember that Internet addresses can change without notice. If the site is no longer there, you can use a search engine to look for additional sites.

International Fabricare Institute
www.ifi.org

Laundry Today
www.laundrytoday.com

NAILM: American Laundry & Linen College
www.nailm.com

Pellerin Milnor Corporation
www.milnor.com

Textile Care Allied Trades Association
www.tcata.org

Chapter 11 Outline

Competencies

1. Describe changes taking place in hotel telephone service. (pp. 336–338)

2. Describe types of telephone calls. (pp. 338–341)

3. Identify types of hotel telephone equipment, telephone lines, and telephone services. (pp. 342–356)

4. Describe special telephone services offered by hotels. (pp. 356–359)

5. Explain common problems hotels have with their telephone systems. (pp. 359–362)

Telecommunications Systems

This chapter was written and contributed by Edward Golden, Director of Engineering, Outrigger Hotels & Resorts, Honolulu, Hawaii.[1]

In years past, the features and benefits of a guestroom telephone were few. They were designed for simple verbal communication, and were often times linked only to the front desk. Outside access was achieved via the property switchboard, and volume control meant yelling at different levels to the unfortunate listener on the other end. My, how times have changed!

Today's hotel or motel guest places far more demands upon their in-room telephones than were ever considered necessary with the phones of yesteryear. With technological advancements came increased burdens for telephone switches, and indeed for telephones themselves.

The growing needs of the business traveler necessitated that telephones be equipped with data ports, for those all-important Internet and e-mail connections. Laptop computers continue to be more and more the norm of the business traveler, and not the rarity as in years past. With the dramatic increase in Internet usage, the data port has become a required and demanded room convenience, and a telephone feature that is almost expected ....

With the wide variety of demands made by hotel guests, the manufacturing industry has risen to the occasion by offering newer and continually improved models of hospitality telephones. What once was a simple telephone set used for voice communication has now developed into a specialized piece of telecommunications hardware. In making your buying decisions, review all of the features available to you, select those that service the needs of your patrons, and then purchase a model of telephone that best suits those needs.[2]

In a period of less than 20 years, the telephone industry has moved from an analog world of mechanical devices to a sophisticated technology of computer chips and advanced software. In recent years, there has been a technology explosion that is redefining the telecommunications industry. We have truly entered the information age where technology is being driven by the demands for faster and more reliable information. What was previously a closed industry now is rapidly opening its doors to the convergence of voice and data. **Computer-to-telephone interface** (CTI), **open architecture integration** (OAI), voice-over IP, and the ever-present battle for more bandwidth are just some of the examples of the whirlwind changes occurring in this industry. As a result of deregulation, the telecommunications industry worldwide has opened its doors to new architecture, suppliers, and new entrants into the marketplace. The entire effect has created epic changes on an international level. Deregulation has promoted incentives to eliminate monopolies, allowing free enterprise to emerge and challenge existing monolithic government-run phone companies.

With these new challenges facing the hotel industry, corporations and owners alike are focusing on new technology investments as strategic business weapons. Diverse and independent technologies such as voice and data, video, and information networks must now operate together. It is our customers who demand this technology and they will continue to drive the direction of technological development in the future.

When you, as a hotel manager, acquire or manage a telecommunications system for your hotel, you need a solution that will satisfy your guests with the latest in customized convenience. It is therefore incumbent on any hotel manager or aspiring hotel manager to understand the fundamentals of the telecom industry before entering into agreements with system providers or attempting to manage existing telecom installations. The system needs to provide for the hotel's current needs as well as future requirements. A shortsighted decision simply means that your phone system will be changed or upgraded at a higher cost. Today's phone systems should provide voice and data capabilities that can solve the hotel's guest service, accounting, and property management challenges in a cost-effective manner. Exhibit 1 poses questions you as a hotel manager should ask periodically of your telecommunications manager and suppliers. Answers will indicate whether your hotel is providing adequate telephone service to guests.

Telephone service is one of the most common hotel services. However, despite this almost universal offering, most hotel managers know little about the financial and technical nuances of their systems. In fact, telecommunications is perhaps one of the least known and least audited services in the hospitality industry today. Consider that:

- Ninety percent of all hotels overspend on telephone services for either unnecessary equipment or service, or for services that are never received.

- Sixty percent of all telephone bills contain errors.

- Major U.S. hotel companies spend from $500,000 to $3 million and more per year on telephone service, even though many hotel managers do not fully understand what they are buying.

It's amazing how many hotel managers spend little or no time learning what phone service is all about. Many, of course, went through their hospitality education during a period when phone service was a monopoly, and there were few, if any, telephone equipment or service choices to make.

As a hotel manager (or someone perhaps aspiring to be one), you should not assume anything about the communication needs of today's sophisticated travelers. If you fail to offer the level of service a guest is accustomed to, you will risk

Exhibit 1   Questions Every Hotel General Manager Should Ask

> These are questions a hotel's general manager should ask from time to time of the manager in charge of telecommunications or the suppliers of the hotel's telephone equipment and services.
>
> - Is the current telephone system using the latest software updates available from the supplier? If not, what benefits will the upgrade provide the hotel?
> - Has the call accounting system been updated to reflect changes in long-distance rates, new area codes, office codes, and so on?
> - Is the call accounting system using the timeout method for billing guest calls, or has software and/or equipment been installed to accommodate answer supervision?
> - Has the hotel looked at the benefits and feasibility of changing from analog to digital trunk service?
> - Does the hotel comply with state and federal laws (including ADA requirements) regarding telephone services?
> - Does the hotel provide easy access to alternative operator-service providers?
> - How is your hotel currently addressing the needs for Internet access and is it currently meeting the needs of your guests?
> - Does the hotel have a good handle as to the inventory of telephone equipment and trunks on the property?
> - Has the property reviewed its current trunk inventory and is there a more optimum use of trunks that would better serve the property?
> - Does the property have a single point of contact (within the property) where orders are placed for the moves, adds and charges (MACs) of equipment and telephone service?

looking archaic. There are discriminating guests who refuse to return to properties where phone service is poor or inadequate.

Ask yourself, "What do most of my guests do when they first enter the lobby or their guestrooms?" If the answer is that they go to the phone, the impression they form of your telephone service is likely to be the impression they form of your facility overall.

Not only does phone service help create your guests' first impressions of your property, it may create their last impression when paying their bill. Hoteliers have to understand that guests have become savvy travelers. They are aware that there are other methods of placing a telephone call and they also know that most hotels are still charging exorbitant amounts for outgoing calls. If the bill seems high or something is wrong, they will complain and express their displeasure by making their next reservation at your competitor's property.

In this chapter, we discuss recent changes in hotel telephone service, including the types of calls guests make at hotels, various elements of telephone equipment, and the types of trunks over which those calls are made. We examine the selection of guestroom phones and the use of call accounting, voice mail, high-speed Internet access, and the interaction of the hotel's property management system (PMS). We conclude with a look at common problems of hotel telephone systems.

Changes in Hotel Telephone Service

One of the most radical changes for hotel phone service was its shift in the mid-1970s from a cost-based center to a revenue-based center. Before that time, hotels looked on telephone service as an unavoidable expense that had to be kept to a minimum—phone bills were viewed as just another utility bill. In most hotels, the phone bills were rarely reviewed. The bookkeeper routinely paid them each month with the thought that little could be done since the phone rates were government regulated and the phone bills were difficult to interpret.

Earlier phone systems proved to be labor intensive. Front desk employees viewed the phone system as a necessary inconvenience—something that cost the hotel time that could be better spent elsewhere. During these early years, almost all long-distance phone calls were established with the assistance of the local telephone company operator. In some cases, even local calls had to be connected with the assistance of the hotel operator or front desk personnel. Guests could also have the operator bill the calls to their rooms by asking the operator to relay the charges to the front desk agent (often referred to as "time and charges"). In addition, the hotel would often add a service fee (or surcharge) to the operator charges before posting the charges to the guest folio. What resulted was a very expensive call that often infuriated the guest upon checkout. The actual charges for the long-distance calls would show up on the hotel's monthly telephone bill with little or no profit. In effect, hotels often passed the phone charge it collected from guests straight through to the phone company. Hotel phone service generated revenue for the phone company and provided a cumbersome, but effective, service to the guest. Since most long-distance calls were made with operator assistance, this procedure made some sense, but only rarely did it generate any profits for the hotel.

Depending on the desired level of service, most larger hotels still use a dedicated operator to field incoming telephone calls. In a move to reduce the expense of a dedicated staff position for this function, some hotels are moving away from the traditional operator and assigning front desk personnel to answer calls. In addition, to aid in the handling of incoming telephone calls, some hotels are employing an **automated attendant**, which in most cases is an integral part of the hotel's voice mail system. The automated attendant can be programmed to answer all incoming calls immediately or after a pre-defined time length and number of rings. It then provides a recorded announcement to the caller. This announcement could provide the caller with instructions of what number to press to reach certain departments or specific extensions. This system can also connect calls when the hotel operator is busy with another call; guests hear a pre-recorded message and the calls are put on hold momentarily, or are automatically routed to an extension if the caller dialed the extension number.

When long-distance direct-dialing for homes and businesses became available in the mid-1960s, hotels installed phone equipment that allowed guests to dial local and long-distance calls without hotel or operator assistance. Since guests were bypassing the phone company operator, hotels had to purchase equipment that would establish the price for all calls—a service that local phone company operators had done in the past.

Exhibit 2   Telephone Service Cost/Profit Analysis: Before/After Deregulation

	Before Bell Breakup	Today
Long-distance charge to guest (AT&T direct-dial rates)	$ 1.00	$ 1.00
AT&T operator-service surcharge	+ $ .75	+ $ .75
Hotel surcharge (i.e., 25 % markup)	+ $ .44	+ $ .44
Total	**$ 2.19**	**$ 2.19**
Charge to guest	$ 2.19	$ 2.19
Long-distance charge to hotel	– $ 1.75	– $ .80
Gross profit to hotel	**$ .44**	**$ 1.39**

Hoteliers were now faced with the task of pricing calls that would not only cover the expense from the local telephone company, but also include a profit. Through the use of **Call Accounting Systems** (CAS), hotels can base the cost of a **long-distance call** either on the standard AT&T direct-dial or operator-assisted rates. The hotel can also add a flat surcharge and often a percentage increase to these base rates. Unfortunately, when fixed costs such as equipment and monthly trunk (main line) charges were added to the equation, the typical hotel still lost money.

With the advent of deregulation, the U.S. saw the breakup of the Bell telephone system monopoly into AT&T and the seven **Regional Bell Operating Companies** (RBOCs—pronounced "are-box"). In addition to this breakup came the introduction of other long-distance competitors such as MCI, Sprint, and many regional carriers. This deregulation and subsequent competition allowed hotels to find ways to increase their profits without antagonizing their guests. The key was to pay less for calls rather than charge guests more. Competition among the long-distance companies brought down the rates hotels pay for calls, which meant that a hotel could make a greater profit without increasing the price to the guest. Exhibit 2 is a simplified and hypothetical example of how this works for a typical guest call.

As shown in the exhibit, the hotel charged the guest $.95 more for the long-distance call than it paid, and added a hotel surcharge of $.44, for a profit of $1.39. The hotel can now make a greater profit without charging guests more than what they would have previously paid.

The astute hotelier continuously strives to find ways to reduce costs throughout the property, local and long-distance telephone service notwithstanding. Fortunately, competition and the new regulatory environment have helped create such opportunities. You can now shop among MCI, AT&T, Sprint, and other long-distance carriers and **operator-service providers** (OSPs) to find the price structure that makes the best sense for your hotel and your guests. In addition, with the arrival of the digital T-1 and PRI trunk lines (discussed later in the chapter), hoteliers are now able to choose different vendors to handle the local call traffic. The availability of these trunks to specific hotel properties—and the cost savings they may offer—depends on the geographic location of the properties.

Types of Calls

Hotel guests have myriad call choices they can make from a typical property. It is important for hotel management to understand these different types of calls and how they affect the property. Among the types of calls are:

- Local
- Direct-dialed long-distance
- Calling- or credit-card
- Collect
- Third-party
- Person-to-person
- Billed-to-room
- International
- 900 or premium-price

Often, a single call can fit into more than one of these categories. For example, a third-party call can also be a person-to-person long-distance call; a person-to-person call can also be a collect call; and an international call can be person-to-person/credit-card call.

Local

A **local call** can be defined as a call that terminates within a local calling area. Typically, a local call (including those to toll-free 800 numbers) is billed on a per-call basis rather than a per-minute charge. Owing to the popularity of the Internet and the widespread use of computers, some hotels are billing on a per-minute basis for all local and **800-number calls** that exceed a predefined threshold. The purpose of this charge is to help defray the cost to the hotel for purchasing additional trunk lines to accommodate the increased traffic. Local calls are typically handled by the local telephone company, which could be a Bell Operating Company (BOC), General Telephone, or one of many other local phone companies.

As a marketing initiative, some hotels elect to not charge for local and 800-number calls, the thought being that their hotels will be more attractive with this incentive. Hotels need to consider that even though there is no cost for these calls, there is still a fixed monthly charge for each trunk line that comes into a property. In reality, there is a tangible cost for each local and 800-number call made from a hotel. Conversely, revenue that a property can receive for 800-number and local calls can be substantial. A typical 200-room hotel can see revenue of about $4,000 per month just for local calls. This revenue (or the absence thereof) needs to be considered when electing to not charge for this type of call.

Direct-Dialed Long-Distance

Direct-dialed long distance (DDD) calls are the most common placed by guests. A long-distance call by definition is one that terminates outside the local calling area. Once a long-distance number is dialed, it goes out over the hotel's telephone lines to the local phone company office, which routes it to the hotel's long-distance provider. Direct-dialed long-distance calls are also called "1+" calls; guests simply enter a "1" plus the area code and telephone number with no operator involved.

Calling- or Credit-Card

A long-distance company typically bills calling-card calls to a code number on a calling card issued by either the local phone company or by a long-distance company. Many of these codes are in a common computer database that can be accessed by any long-distance or local phone company. Most codes are made up of the caller's area code and telephone number, plus a four-digit personal identification number (PIN). Some codes issued by AT&T are just random numbers with no association with any phone number.

AT&T has issued a limited number of proprietary calling cards that only AT&T operators can verify as valid. When a guest uses a card with one of these codes, calls placed through any other operator-service provider will be denied, since the codes cannot be verified. Most guests will be referred back to the hotel operator for instruction on how to place these calls.

MCI and a few other companies have begun accepting credit cards such as Visa, MasterCard, and American Express for payment of long-distance calls. This offers a significant revenue opportunity to hotels since, although many people still do not have telephone calling cards, virtually every guest has one or more major credit cards. If credit cards can be used to charge calls at your hotel, be sure that information in each guestroom advises guests of this added service feature.

Calls placed with the use of calling cards or credit cards cannot be direct-dialed. They are placed with the help of an OSP. An OSP is a telephone company contracted by the hotel to provide long-distance operator services to guests who want to make calls that cannot be placed without the help of a "live" or automated operator. Hotels can choose among many OSPs, including Sprint, MCI, AT&T and a host of others within different regional areas.

Calling-card and credit-card calls are also referred to as "0+" or "0-" calls. For "0+" calls, the guest dials "0" plus the number he or she is trying to reach. In most cases a live operator is not required. For "0-" calls, a guest dials "0" and the phone number. An OSP operator responds automatically to assist the guest in completing the call. The **"0-"** calls are often used for collect, third-party, and person-to-person calls.

It is important to remember that when calling or credit cards are used, the hotel does not bill the guest; the call is billed to the guest's calling or credit card by the hotel's OSP. For this reason, it is vital that when you select an OSP, you compare the rates and time-of-day discounts offered—not just the commission the OSP will pay your hotel. If guests feel these rates are excessive, their displeasure will be directed toward your hotel, not the OSP.

Collect

With collect calls, the guest dials "0" and informs the OSP operator that it is a collect call. The operator contacts the receiving party and asks if he or she will accept the charges.

The party accepting the call is billed by the hotel's OSP. The hotel pays nothing for the call, and has the option of adding a surcharge if it wishes. Most OSPs pay a commission to the hotel for collect calls.

Third-Party

Third-party calls are similar to collect calls, except that the billed number is a number other than the one called. The guest gives the OSP operator the billing number, whereupon, in most cases, the operator calls the third party for verification that the charges are accepted before putting the guest's call through (verification of acceptance of charges helps prevent fraud). The third party is billed by the hotel's OSP and the amount appears on the third party's phone bill, not in the guest folio. The hotel does not have to pay anything for the call; as with credit-card and collect calls, the hotel has the option of charging guests a small fee for this service.

Person-to-Person

A **person-to-person call** is not connected unless a specific party named by the caller verifies that he or she is on the line. The call costs the guest nothing if the specific person is not reached; however, if the person requested is reached, the call is expensive relative to other types of calls. Unlike credit-card, collect, or third-party calls, once completed, this call is billed to the originating number. If that is a guest's room phone, there is usually no way for the hotel to collect from the guest, since hotel telephone systems are not configured to calculate telephone charges for calls placed and billed by an outside operator. Hotels eliminate this problem in one of two ways: either they instruct their OSP and local phone company to block person-to-person calls altogether or have their local or long-distance company bill such calls directly to the guestrooms. Billing directly to the guestrooms requires that charges be transferred manually to the guest's folio.

With a person-to-person collect call, the receiving party pays for the call, but only if the party named by the caller answers. The hotel is not exposed to a potential loss with this type of call, since the OSP bills the receiving party. To prevent incoming collect calls, hotel trunk lines are class-marked—restricted—so that guests are not able to accept collect calls or make third-party calls that bill the hotel's phone number. **Class marking** provides indication to the OSP that collect calls are not to be placed to the hotel and that third-party calls are referred back to the property with time and charges for the guest initiating the call.

Billed-to-Room

In **billed-to-room calls**, guests ask an operator to place their call, after which the operator advises the hotel of the charges based on a "time and charges" formula, which usually includes a mark-up percentage. This type of call is quite expensive and therefore used very sparingly, mostly in isolated countries and properties where call accounting is not used. Although automated systems are available that electronically post charges to the guest folio, charges are typically entered manually in the folio, broadening the potential for error.

International

International calls are those made to areas outside the North American continent. They can be direct-dialed or placed with the help of an operator. The cost of international calls varies widely depending on the location called. It is important that hotels make certain that their call accounting system includes pricing tables that accurately calculate charges accrued by the guest. When selecting a long-distance provider, pay close attention to the type of international calls made from the property and the rate charged by the long-distance provider. Some providers show lower domestic rates but charge excessively for certain international calls. As is the case with domestic long-distance calls, the hotel bills the guest for direct-dialed international calls and the OSP bills the guest for calling-card or credit-card international calls.

Premium-Price or 900-Number

Calls made to businesses that charge callers a fee for the telephone call (a fee separate from that of the telephone company's) are called **premium-price** or 900-number calls. Typical of the content of these calls are children's stories, astrology readings, adult conversation, sports information, jokes, etc.

Hotels faced a host of serious problems with the advent of 900-number businesses. First, the businesses charge a wide range of rates for their 900-number services. One might charge $1.50 per minute; another may charge $3.50 for the first minute and $2.00 for each additional minute. There are some that charge $99 per call.

Second, the hotel's telephone system is designed to track only the cost involved in placing the call, not the cost imposed by the business providing the 900-number service.

Third, the prefix of a premium-price call does not have to be a recognizable number; some premium-price calls have local telephone numbers that begin with 976 rather than 900.

In the early days of 900-number calls, many hotels found out very soon how financially painful these calls can be. Consider this scenario: a guest checks out and is charged $.50 for what appears on the phone system to be an ordinary local call. Several days (or even weeks) later, the hotel receives its phone bill and discovers that it has been charged $99.50 for the call. It doesn't take very many guests making undetected 900-number calls before the hotel realizes it has a real problem. To prevent such calls, most hotels today have either programmed their systems to block 900-prefix calls or instructed their local telephone companies to do so. Of the two options, the better is to have the local telephone company do the blocking since any errors in programming or changes in the types of calls will be their responsibility, not the hotel's. And in the case of hotel telephone systems lacking the sophistication to block these calls, the only option is to have the local telephone company do it.

Private Branch Exchange

To better manage your telephone system, you as a hotel manager need to have a solid understanding of your telephone system, its related components, and how they integrate to operate as a unit. In this section, we address the **private branch exchange** (PBX) telephone system, call accounting guestroom telephones, voicemail, hotel software, and related interfaces.

The central component of telephone service in a typical hotel is the PBX. The earliest PBX telephone systems required the hotel operator to receive all incoming calls and make all outgoing ones. The operator transferred incoming calls to the appropriate line (extension, room) in the hotel. Guests wishing to make outside calls gave the number to the operator who would make the call, then connect the outside and inside parties.

Today, the modern PBXs are complex computers that perform myriad tasks through a flexible software-based system. The flexibility of the software allows the telephone vendor (and sometimes hotel personnel) to customize the operation of the telephone system for the guest rooms and the diverse requirements of the hotel's administrative functions. It is important that hotel management understand how the PBX works, what its capabilities are, and the system's immediate and future expansion potential. Within the PBX system are printed circuit boards (PCBs) consisting of common control cards and peripheral control cards. Common control cards control the basic functions of the telephone system; peripheral control cards support the PBX's individual lines (extensions) and trunks. Trunks are the main telephone lines that serve the hotel from the local telephone company. For planning and cost-control purposes, it is important for hotel management to be acutely aware of the number of ports available in each type of peripheral card and the number of spare slots in the PBX available for future expansion.

When assessing PBX systems, look for a system that has a strong and proven hospitality software package. Check with other hotels that have the same hardware and software and find out from them what their experience has been with the system. It is not feasible here to mention all the features available in today's PBX, but some of the most popular are wake-up, room status, guest name display, do-not-disturb, house phones, room-to-room blocking, call restriction, automatic route selection (ARS), paging, interface, and a strong property management system (PMS) interface.

PBX Line Cards. Line cards are printed circuit boards that support the different types of lines (extensions) within the PBX telephone system. In most cases, each PBX line equates to a specific telephone in the hotel. To illustrate, imagine there are only two basic types of line cards, each capable of supporting either analog or digital lines. In most cases, a single line card will support from 8 to 32 lines.

- *Analog lines.* Analog lines support all industry standard devices, which means nearly all mainstream communication devices in the hotel: guestroom phones, elevator phones, modem devices, credit card verification machines, facsimile machines, answering machines, and cordless telephones.

- *Digital Lines.* These circuits service all multi-line digital phones provided by the PBX manufacturer. Often referred to as "proprietary phones," these telephones are designed to work only behind the manufacturer's PBX. Multi-line phones that display the guest name and room number are usually proprietary phones that operate off these digital lines.

Trunks and Trunk Cards

A *trunk line* is a main or primary telephone line servicing a hotel. Individual lines or destinations (from your hotel, for example) feed into and rely on the trunk to carry the telephone message from the originator to the receiver. The PBX is the gatekeeper. By analogy, if you view an Interstate highway as a trunk line for automobiles, on-ramps, off-ramps, and surface streets are individual lines carrying you on or off the trunk line. Your hotel may have several trunk lines, depending on the level of service you offer your guests.

The term **trunking** refers to the hotel's mix of telephone lines. If your hotel has too few trunk lines, you will have an unacceptable number of busy signals; conversely, if you have too many trunk lines, you are paying for trunks that are never used. Hotel trunking is generally designed to provide a certain level of service determined at least in part by the property's business plan and vision statement.

A *trunk card* is one of many peripheral cards contained in a PBX. In most cases, there is a different type of trunk card for every type of trunk. Each trunk card supports a varying number of trunk lines, so it is important to know how many trunk lines will be supported for each of the different trunk cards in the PBX. Trunk lines are defined by the technology involved—either analog or digital. Within each category are various types of trunk lines:

Analog Trunks	*Digital Trunks*
Incoming	T-1
Outgoing	Integrated Services Digital Network (ISDN)
	Primary Rate Interface (PRI)
Bothway	ISDN Basic Rate Interface (BRI)
Direct Inward Dial (DID)	
E&M Tie	

Multiple trunks of the same type are often combined and referred to as a **trunk group.** A trunk group is simply a group of trunks with similar characteristics. For example, a bothway trunk group represents the number of trunks available for both incoming and outgoing access. The routing tables in the PBX will determine what trunk group (or route) is used for that particular type of call.

While older analog trunks are the most prevalent, more and more hotels are installing newer digital trunks. Digital trunks provide greater reliability, faster connections, increased flexibility, and lower recurring monthly charges. For example, a digital T-1 trunk will support up to 24 simultaneous conversations on two pairs of copper wire. For the same capability on an analog trunk, you would need to purchase 24 individual trunks, each of which would occupy a single pair of copper wires. In most cases, the monthly cost of 24 individual analog trunks would be greater than the cost of a single T-1 trunk. Hotels should assess their current trunk mix and determine if it is technologically and economically feasible to replace existing analog trunks with newer digital technology.

Exhibit 3 shows the relationship of the various types of lines and trunks and how they connect to other pieces of equipment.

Typical of the types of messages managed by your PBX are local calls, toll calls, WATS calls, and emergency 911 calls.

Local Calls. Local calls are outgoing calls made within the local exchange carrier's (LEC) free calling area. The local phone company processes any calls within the same **local access and transport area** (LATA) with no charges to the hotel. The phone company routes calls going outside the LATA to the long-distance carrier the hotel has selected.

Toll Calls. At some hotels, if a guest dials a toll number the call would automatically be routed over dedicated outgoing toll trunks provided by a hotel's long-distance provider. It was common practice in the past to have dedicated long-distance trunks because the phone companies offered more favorable pricing. Today, however, hotels typically use the same trunk group for both local and toll calls; competition has narrowed the gap between the rates provided by dedicated long-distance trunks and those offered by the regular trunks. Unless the cost differential is substantial, most hotels find that a single trunk group provides greater efficiency than separate trunk groups that handle toll and local traffic.

WATS Trunks. Wide area telephone service (WATS) trunks are available for either incoming or outgoing service. Even though this type of trunk is rarely used for outgoing traffic, most hotels use some form of an 800 WATS trunk for inbound traffic (particularly for reservations). With WATS lines, rates are based on total hourly usage, rather than on a per-call basis. If your hotel offers 800-number service, make certain the service is terminated as a dedicated trunk group. Callers will attempt to dial the 800 number and then request to be transferred to a guestroom, which, in effect, imposes a long-distance telephone charge on the hotel.

Emergency (911) Service. Nine-one-one service provides guests a direct channel for help when faced with an emergency. Most—but not all—modern PBX systems automatically route 911 calls to the emergency operator, even if the guest forgets to dial a "9" first. It is important that you make sure your PBX has this capability, since often an individual thrust into an emergency situation will not know or will forget to enter the access code. The 911 system automatically informs the operator of the name and address of the property whence the call originated, but unless the caller is able to communicate, the operator will not know the actual room number. This has caused serious problems for hotels when it has taken hotel staff hours to locate the victim. Some call accounting systems report an alarm when 911 is dialed, but this usually occurs only after the caller has terminated the call, which will not happen if the guest is suffering from a heart attack and is unable to hang up the phone.

This problem has prompted some states to require that hotels, hospitals, and other extended stay facilities use new technology with an E-911 number. This technology, coupled with special trunk lines, enables the emergency operator to

Exhibit 3 Telecommunications Trunks and Lines

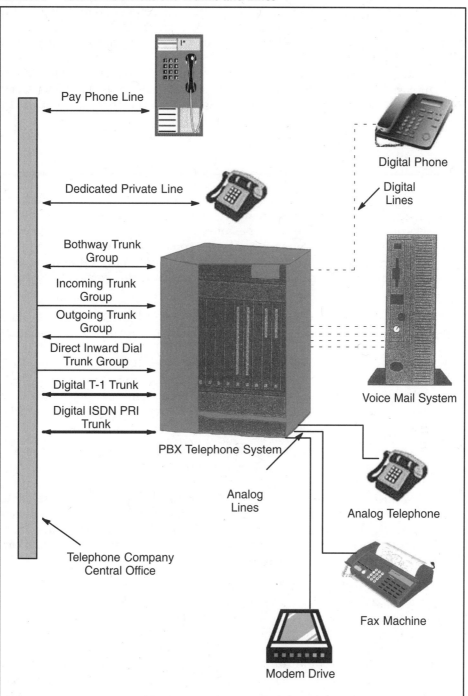

Pay Phone Line

Dedicated Private Line

Digital Phone

Digital Lines

Bothway Trunk Group

Incoming Trunk Group

Outgoing Trunk Group

Direct Inward Dial Trunk Group

Digital T-1 Trunk

Digital ISDN PRI Trunk

Voice Mail System

PBX Telephone System

Analog Lines

Analog Telephone

Telephone Company Central Office

Fax Machine

Modem Drive

stomatically identify the hotel, its address, and the room number of the caller. (E-911 service may require additional hardware and software depending on the age of your telephone system.) In addition, some newer PBX systems are able to alert the PBX operator (or security)—by extension number—the moment a 911 or 9-911 call is placed. You should carefully evaluate your emergency calling capability and incorporate a system that instantly identifies the caller by extension or room number. The specter of potential lawsuits will be dramatically reduced, and should the FCC mandate use of E-911 or similar service in the future, you will be prepared.

Telephone Services

Telephone services provided to hotels fall into various categories: local service, direct-dialed long-distance, and long-distance operator. Deregulation in the communication industry and resultant new entrants in the market have given hotels a wide selection of suppliers of all types of telephone service. This is especially important in the local service market, where formerly there was no competition. Deregulation and the advent of T-1 and ISDN PRI trunks have opened the local service market to a host of sources and spurred the restructuring of the industry as a whole.

Local Service. One of the initiatives of deregulation of the 1980s was the breakup of Bell Telephone into seven Regional Bell Operating Companies (RBOCs) and 22 Bell Operating Companies (BOCs, today called 'Baby Bells'). If a property is using analog trunk lines, a BOC office serving the hotel's area likely provides their local service. However, rapidly moving into these markets are companies offering low-cost local service through digital T-1 or ISDN PRI trunk lines. A hotel with 13 or more analog trunk lines could reduce their monthly telephone costs substantially by upgrading to digital service.

Direct-Dialed Long-Distance Service. Despite the literally hundreds of long-distance carriers in the United States from which users can choose, routing of all calls follows a similar process: the long distance call originates at the hotel and is directed to the local phone company. The local phone company routes the call to the long-distance carrier selected by the hotel, and the long-distance carrier directs the call over trunk lines to the destination. During this process, the call can be handled by any one of three types of long-distance carriers: **nationwide common carriers, regional carriers, or aggregators.**

- *Nationwide Common Carriers.* Nationwide common carriers are telecommunications companies that own their own transmission facilities. The three largest of these are AT&T, MCI Telecommunications, and U.S. Sprint. Each of these companies has the facilities, network, and equipment to transmit long-distance telephone messages without reliance on equipment from other companies. MCI Telecommunications, U.S. Sprint, and other non-AT&T nationwide common carriers are usually referred to as other common carriers (OCCs) to differentiate them for AT&T.

- *Regional Common Carriers*. There are also dozens of regional common carriers, such as Allnet, Williams Telecommunications, and Litel. Most of these service a certain area and purchase the bulk of their calling capacity from one or more to the other carriers. Regional carriers are often referred to as "resellers," though, strictly speaking, a reseller usually owns no transmission facilities.

- *Aggregators*. An aggregator doesn't own a network but resells time purchased from a common carrier. Calling costs are reduced by high-volume discounts made possible by the "aggregation" or adding together of traffic from many smaller customers. Customers are usually billed and serviced not by the aggregator but by the common carrier from which it purchases time. The aggregator promises to resell a large block of time—calculated in call minutes—in exchange for a very low per-minute rate. The aggregator picks the carrier to be used on each business line, and the carrier bills the hotel at the rate for that particular service.

With such a variety of choices, hotel managers cannot be faulted for feeling a bit overwhelmed as they select their long-distance provider. However, there are some basic guidelines that should help the hotelier in selecting a DDD service: the carrier must provide hospitality-oriented service and have a proven track record with other hotels in the area. Importantly, in evaluating any provider, managers should evaluate both service and price equally.

When pricing its service, carriers should offer the standard time-of-day (evening and weekend) discounts. The carrier with the lowest daytime rate may not be the lowest overall when you take into account the unique calling patterns of your particular property. Bear in mind also that national hotel chains and large hotel management companies may have worked out special volume purchase rates with the major carriers. If you represent a smaller hotel, it might be best if you check with your state lodging association, as they often negotiate special discounts on behalf of their members. Local on-site support has to be available, as well as a 24-hour customer service number. Hotel management should have a clear understanding of the vendor's policy on billing disputes and the ease of obtaining credits. The long-distance company you choose should provide a full range of services, including such features as an 800-number line, multi-lingual operators, e-mail, conference call capability, and information services. Limited-service telecommunications in a lodging environment is not consistent with good marketing practice.

Long-Distance Operator Service. Long-distance operator service is a separate issue from direct-dial long-distance service. For example, a hotel using AT&T as its DDD carrier may use a company such as MCI as its operator-services provider.

Operator-service providers carry calls requiring phone company operator assistance such as when a calling card is used or when the use of a card number is required for call connection and billing (0+ and 0- calls). A number of OSPs are available, on both the nationally recognized and regional levels, the majority of which provide very good service. Some OSPs own their networks (telephone lines and equipment), while others supply the operators but lease their networks. Guests are provided the option of making calls through an OSP by way of a credit or calling card or placing their calls with the help of an OSP operator. Each OSP has its own rate structure for calls and its own commission plan, which in the early days of OSP service created a problem: the majority of calls placed by hotel guests were billed to either AT&T or BOC calling cards. The callers, understandably expecting to be billed at AT&T or BOC rates, were not happy when they discovered they were charged at higher rates because the hotel used an OSP whose rates were higher than those of AT&T or BOC.

In answer to guest complaints, most OSP companies lowered rates and improved disclosure procedures. Also, in 1988, a new trade organization—the Operator Service Providers of America—was formed that drafted a code of responsibility emphasizing the consumers' right to know which company is processing their calls. Approximately two-thirds of OSP companies have joined the group and agree to the stipulations of the code. Members are also urged by the organization to price service competitively.

Guest complaints also reached federal levels, which resulted in federal legislation that gives guests the option of selecting a different OSP for their calls. This legislation, it must be noted, applies only to operator-assisted long-distance calls. It does not require hotels to offer guests options on direct-dialed long-distance (1+) calls, since the hotel pays for these calls and bills guests for them, and exercises its right to control costs and potential 1+ fraud or abuse.

When a guest selects an alternate OSP, the hotel does not get a commission for the calls. However, guests have the right to make the choice, and it is critical that each hotel understand how to instruct a guest to bypass the hotel's OSP.

To bypass the hotel's OSP on a pay phone, a guest must dial a six-digit code generally known as a **1010XXX**—or ten-ten-triple-X—code, for the new OSP. Each OSP has its own code. After dialing the 1010XXX code, the guest dials a 0, the area code, and the number. The local phone company then routes the call to the OSP identified by the code rather than the hotel's OSP. The caller is then billed by that OSP at its rates.

It may be necessary to program the hotel's PBX to block 1010XXX dialing from guestrooms to prevent guests from rerouting direct-dialed long-distance (1+0) calls. If such calls are blocked, guests cannot use a 1010XXX code to choose a different OSP when dialing from their room phones; they must call a front desk agent or hotel operator.

The front desk agent or hotel operator can assist the guest in switching to a different OSP by:

- Dialing the 1010XXX code for the OSP the guest wants to use, dialing 0 and the number, and then transferring the call to the guestroom.

- Advising the guest to use the access phone number printed on the back of many calling cards (typically an 800 number or a 950 number now required by government regulation). These calls require no hotel operator involvement in most cases.

Exhibit 4 lists questions you can use in evaluating OSP service. Answers to the questions will help you determine whether you and your guests will be satisfied with a particular OSP. Another consideration in choosing an OSP is whether it has

Exhibit 4   Questions to Ask Candidate Companies When Selecting an OSP

Answers to these questions will help you select an OSP that best meets your hotel's telecommunications demands.

1. Are your rates equal to or better than AT&T rates?
2. What other hotels in the area are using your service?
3. How long has your company been in business and are you well financed?
4. Do you use the standard AT&T time-of-day and day-of-week discounts?
5. Do you offer international calling service? (Some OSPs do not.)
6. Do you provide training for the front desk staff?
7. How many operator centers do you have? (For backup purposes, there should be more than one.)
8. What long-distance carrier do you use?
9. What credit cards do you accept?
10. Are all calling-card numbers validated?
11. Are "billed-to-room" calls allowed? If so, how (and how quickly) are charges transmitted to the hotel?
12. Do you give credit for wrong numbers?
13. Will guests be billed for no answer calls or busy signals?
14. On which calls do you pay commissions? How much are the commissions? When are they paid?
15. Do you operate your own switching and transmission facilities, or do you use someone else's services to complete calls?
16. Are your operator surcharges comparable to those of the local phone company and AT&T?

"branded openings and closings." Required by some states, branded openings and closings are messages by the OSP operator that identify the OSP they represent. Some OSPs go a step further and offer to add another short message. For example, an opening with an additional tag line could be, "Thank you for staying at XYZ hotel. This is the MCI operator, how may I help you?" In many cases, there is a closing message—just before the call is put through—repeating the identification. Branded messaging imparts the idea that the long-distance operator is part of your staff, enhancing your image.

Often overlooked by managers when they evaluate OSPs are the non-English-speaking traveler. Some OSPs have the capability of identifying the language of the caller so they can then transfer him or her to an operator that speaks that language. This is an especially important guest-service feature for hotels whose clientele are predominantly non-English-speaking.

HOBIC Systems. Before hotels began pricing their own calls, the phone company tracked and billed telephone service using a system called **hotel and billing information center** (HOBIC). Guest calls went out over special HOBIC trunk lines. When a guest placed a call, an operator at the local phone company came on the line and arranged for the call to be billed as a collect call, a call to a third-party number, to a phone company calling card, or directly to the caller's hotel room. In the case of the call billed to the guest's hotel room, when the call was completed, the hotel was informed of the duration of the call and its cost (time and charges) and the guest's phone bill was added to his or her folio.

Though HOBIC systems have largely given way to automated call handling and billing systems, their important role in bringing telecommunication into virtually all hotel guestrooms worldwide is undeniable.

Automatic Route Selection. Automatic route selection (ARS) software has been a feature of most PBX telephone systems since about the mid-1980s. When a hotel has more than one type of telephone line, the software will automatically route a call to the type of line that can carry the call at the lowest cost. If that route is busy, it directs the call to the next least expensive route, or transmits a busy signal. Routing parameters are based on the called destination, time of day, and the day of the week. Some PBX manufacturers refer to this feature as least cost routing (LCR). Few differences exist in PBX equipment from the various manufacturers providing ARS and LCR capability.

Guestroom Phones. Keeping pace with other pieces of telephone equipment, guestroom phones are increasing in sophistication and capability. Many hotels are now standardizing on two-line telephones so guests can still receive a call while on another line. Important for hoteliers to know is that to accommodate two-line telephones, the PBX needs to have two analog ports for each room and there needs to be a minimum of two dedicated cable pairs between the telephone room to each of the guestrooms. In most older hotels, cabling is likely not sufficient to accommodate two pairs of cabling to each room; hotel managers will need to consult with vendors to determine how to add cable. In some cases, the hotel can wire a limited number of rooms with two-line telephones based on a determination of how many spare cable pairs are available. Along with two incoming lines, most guestroom phones now come equipped with a data port to provide guests with the capability of connecting to their laptop computer or facsimile machine without unplugging the phone.

Obviously, the best time to cable a hotel is during the construction process. If cabling isn't done correctly from the start, adding cable after the hotel is operating can be cost-prohibitive at best and in some cases not even possible. For best guestroom service, four dedicated cable pairs should be run to each guestroom. This allows two cable pairs for the two-line phone, one for a dedicated fax line, and a fourth as a spare in the event that a cable pair fails or additional resources are needed. The cost differential of running two-pair cable and four-pair cable is insignificant since the labor cost is the same and the difference in the actual cost of the two cable types is minuscule.

Other guestroom phone amenities include multiple speed-dial buttons for voicemail access and other commonly dialed extensions. All phones are equipped with the standard message-waiting light. Fast becoming standard are such guestroom features as speakerphones, bathroom phones, two and sometimes three phones per room, some of them cordless. Still another feature making its entrance into guestroom telecommunication is handset amplification. This has come at the urging of the Federal Communications Commission and the Americans with Disabilities Act to make this feature a requirement for all new telephones. With this feature, guests can increase the volume of the handset to as much as 18 decibels either incrementally or in a one-step jump, depending on the manufacturer. Most telephone manufacturers are incorporating this feature in their new models at no charge, so it is important that you make sure that any new phones you purchase have this feature; if they do not, you have received old technology.

Top-of-the-line guestroom phones today offer a variety of capabilities including conference calling, hold buttons, and call waiting; some guestroom phones can be programmed to dial a number over and over again until the party is reached. Some newer telephones even house such convenience features as controls for the television, lighting fixtures and lamps, AM/FM radio, night-light, alarm clock, and the heating and cooling system.

To accommodate the various individual telephone-using styles of customers, guest-focused hoteliers specify extra-long phone cords to their suppliers and actually use the phrase in their advertising. Business travelers tend to spread their papers and reports around the room. If you make it easier for them to work while they are on the phone, you have accommodated a simple but important need and by so doing have gained an advantage at a very low cost. Just make sure your front desk employees ask guests if they would like a room with a long phone cord. Some guests spend more on their phone bill than on the room itself. It is therefore important that all staff look at room phones as revenue-generating assets, just as guestrooms and restaurants are.

Pay Telephones. Pay telephones are supplied by the local phone company or can be purchased or rented from a private company. Whichever you choose, be sure you know how often the supplier services the phones, as public phones take a lot of abuse. If you buy pay phones from a private company, you are usually responsible for keeping the phones in service. If your pay phones are supplied and maintained by a company other than your local phone company, you may hear them referred to in the industry as "**COCOT**," meaning customer-owned coin-operated telephone.

Some private-company pay phones look or operate differently than what your guests may be expecting. Pay phones that look unusual often have extra features that might increase revenue. Many callers still do not trust—or simply refuse to use—what they see as "non-phone-company" pay phones. Guests who are confused by an unfamiliar or uncooperative pay phone may go elsewhere to complete both their calls and their stays. It is estimated that 70 percent of all public phone calls are made on impulse, so pay phones should be placed wherever traffic flows or congregates—in the lobby, meeting rooms, conference areas, banquet rooms, and restaurants. Be aware, however, that some locations pose security problems, such as secluded parts of the property or in restrooms or foyers. Contact your local phone company or private pay phone provider to relocate phones.

Most pay phones now accept credit cards issued by phone companies specifically for use in pay phone systems. Especially popular with the youth are prepaid calling cards sold in various time denominations. These cards can be used for local, long-distance, domestic, and international calls.

Lines provided by the local telephone company to service the pay phones are not connected to the hotel's PBX system, meaning that, in many cases, the hotel receives no revenue from direct-dialed long-distance calls from a pay phone. However, most OSPs will pay the hotel commissions on operator-assisted long-distance calls made from pay phones; the OSP sets the rates, bills the guest, and sends the hotel an agreed-upon commission.

Call Accounting Systems

A call accounting system (CAS) is a device that takes the information from the PBX and actually prices the call for posting to the guest folio. While these systems are sometimes integrated within the PBX telephone system, more often it is a standalone piece of hardware that receives information from the PBX. For the hotelier, it is important to install two basic types of call accounting systems—one designed specifically for the commercial business market, the other designed for the hospitality industry. Flexibility in pricing methods and the ability to post calls to the property management system define the principal differences between the two systems. Hospitality systems also have different report capabilities as well, such as a profit report and a night audit (or posting) report.

The simplest CAS is a standalone proprietary piece of hardware with rate tables resident within the software. While these systems are less costly than others, they do not usually have the sophistication and report flexibility of a PC-based CAS. A PC-based CAS is a software-based product priced generally on the basis of the number of lines (extensions) the system is able to support. The call accounting software is loaded on an industry standard personal computer supplied in most cases by the hotel.

The CAS receives the real-time data it needs from the PBX. When a call is finished, information about the call such as the date and time the call was begun, the number dialed, the duration of the call, and in most cases the trunk from which the call was made is sent to the PBX. This information is sent to the CAS and, based on the rate tables loaded into the CAS, the price of the call is determined. If the CAS is equipped with a property management system (PMS) interface, the price and essential details of the call are automatically posted to the guest folio. The rate tables loaded in the CAS are either AT&T's direct-dial rates or their operator-assisted rates. The CAS can then add appropriate surcharges, markups, discounts, or tax assessments to the established rate. For those properties that do not have a PMS or the PMS interface, the call charge information can be retrieved from the CAS for manual posting to the guest folio. A graphic flow schematic of the PMS and its integration with the CAS is presented in Exhibit 5

The call accounting system tracks all direct-dialed calls, whether from guestrooms or other non-pay telephones on the property. (Operator-assisted calls are not usually tracked, since they are not normally billed to the hotel.) As in most business environments, employees are not charged for the business-related calls they make, but abuse of the system is certainly possible. The CAS is a tool that can help curb such abuse.

Exhibit 5 CAS/Property Management System Integration

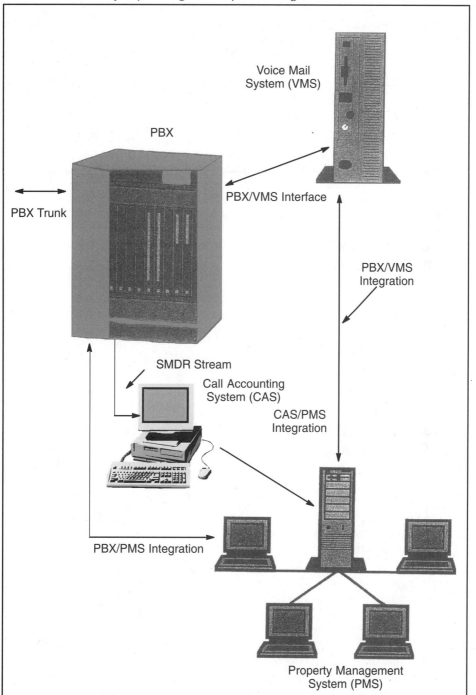

Voice Mail
System (VMS)

PBX

PBX Trunk

PBX/VMS Interface

PBX/VMS
Integration

SMDR Stream

Call Accounting
System (CAS)

CAS/PMS
Integration

PBX/PMS Integration

Property Management
System (PMS)

Key to the effectiveness of the CAS is its software. Software should be updated periodically to reflect new area codes, rate changes, and special services, yet some hoteliers are not even aware that CAS software needs to be updated. Without updating, you may be over- or undercharging guests or not billing guests for calls made to new exchanges or area codes. Or you may be billing long-distance calls as local. Some CAS contracts require the manufacturer to update the software for the first year. Though hotels with this arrangement stay current for a year, if they make no provision to update for subsequent years, they will have problems and likely lose revenue.

Answer Detection/Supervision. A pervasive problem with many hotel PBXs is an inability to detect exactly when a call has been connected. This, of course, has ramifications on billing. Local and long-distance telephone companies receive an indication that a call has been connected when they hear a signal that they call **answer supervision.** This signal lets them know that the call has been connected and they can begin timing and billing the call. Today most PBX systems can detect this signal, but except for very isolated locations, the local telephone company does not pass this signal the hotel's PBX. There are three ways to address this problem:

1. *Timing Method.* This is the oldest and least reliable of the methods of detecting that a call is completed. Under this method, the CAS is programmed to measure various timing thresholds. These timing thresholds may differ according to whether the call is local, interstate, or international. If the minimum timing threshold is not met, the call is not charged to the guest; conversely, if the threshold is reached, the guest is charged for the call. This causes two problems. If the call is actually completed, but is shorter than the minimum threshold, the hotel is charged for the call and the guest is not, hence a loss of revenue for the hotel. On the other hand, if the guest dials and lets the phone ring for a long period of time but the call is never completed, the hotel is faced with a complaint and the need to write off the charge. This has prompted hotels to continually adjust timing thresholds to arrive at the right balance between lost revenue and guest complaints.

2. *Answer Supervision.* In some geographical locations, the telephone company will actually pass the answer supervision signal to the hotel's PBX. If your PBX has the capability to detect this signal, it will send only station message detail reporting (**SMDR**) information to the call accounting system on completed calls. This method is accurate and requires no additional hardware or software and is perhaps the best method of the three, but it is available in only limited locations on analog trunks and through most digital T-1 or ISDN PRI trunks.

3. *Answer Detection.* Answer detection uses equipment and software purchased by the hotel. Depending on its level of sophistication, this method has several ways of determining if a call has been completed. It detects voice cues and the absence of ringing or a combination of both. Once a call is detected as completed, the information is sent to the CAS.

   While this system does increase revenue and reduce guest complaints, it does have drawbacks. First, the equipment will cost the hotel upwards of

$10,000 (2001 dollars) depending on its size. In addition, it is one more piece of equipment and interface that can possibly fail. If it does fail, the CAS will charge for all calls, since the threshold within the CAS is set to zero.

These drawbacks may become non-issues in the future as electronic detection technology improves. Electronics are now capable of 95-percent accuracy in distinguishing between normal ringing sounds, fast busy signals, and a person or fax machine answering the phone with "Hello."

Property Management System Integration

The integration of your PBX, call accounting, and voice mail systems into the hotel's PMS is a critical element in the guest satisfaction/business efficiency equation. The integration of these three elements—discussed here and illustrated in Exhibit 4—with the PMS defines the management, control, and accounting of your hotel's telecommunications system.

Call Accounting System Integration. CAS/PMS integration is a one-way CAS-to-PMS interface with a handshake type of protocol that verifies the accuracy of the information transfer. Once the call charges are received by the PMS, they are automatically posted to the guest folios. If the PMS link fails for any reason, the CAS stores all the call records until the PMS link is re-established.

PBX Integration. The PBX system's interface with the PMS is a two-way communication channel that provides information sharing between the PBX and PMS. This interface, for example, controls the telephone restrictions upon guest check-in and check-out. The interface also updates the occupancy status, room status, guest name, guest directory, do-not-disturb, and message waiting notification. The breadth of information capable of being exchanged between the two pieces of equipment depends largely on the type of PBX and PMS and the degree of sophistication manufacturers designed into their systems. Some interfaces provide VIP notification and guest language preference to the administrative display telephones.

Voice Mail Integration. VMS/PMS integration is also a two-way communication that shares information between the two devices. This interface automatically opens and closes mailboxes upon check-in and check-out. Some of these interfaces automatically alert the voice mail system of the selection of specific foreign language prompts. The VMS alerts front desk staff of any new messages still in the voice mail system prior to guest check-out. When a direct connection between the PMS to the voice mail system is preferred, the hotel must purchase a separate interface. Where the PBX is used as the information transfer device, a third interface is not needed. With this type of configuration the PMS sends a check-in message to the PBX when the guest registers and the PBX then sends a message to the VMS instructing the system to open the voice mail system. Though this type of integration is cost-effective, it may have some performance limitations.

Wireless Communications

As the cost of wireless communications has come down and its capabilities gone up, hotels are now taking a close look at the benefits of this technology. Wireless communications work in conjunction with the hotel's PBX system such that calls can be made and transferred between the wireless system and the PBX as if they were one system. Some systems even display guest names and other information on the wireless display phones.

The devices of wireless communications are a series of handheld telephones and a number of base units installed throughout the hotel property. The base units determine the size of the coverage area and the number of simultaneous users that can operate in that area. A hotel is ideally suited for the application of wireless technology: cordless phones can be used in security, bell services, maintenance, management, engineering, and in other departments in which immediate contact is required or beneficial. Some hotels even supply them to guests so they can receive calls when away from their rooms, eliminating the need for voice or digital pagers.

Pagers

Another of the features a full-service-focused hotel can offer is portable pagers so guests can stay abreast of incoming messages. It is important, however, that hotels weigh the benefit of such an offering with the costs of maintaining control of the individual devices. Another part of the equation is that, like cellular phone service, billing is delayed and hotel profit markups must be done manually. Today, most hotels use pagers only to communicate among staff.

Special Services

Guest telephone services that go beyond basic calling capabilities are called special services. Industry studies and guest comments and surveys suggest that business travelers want and have come to expect the same level of telecommunications service at their hotels that they enjoy in their offices. Fortunately for hotels, this is not a great technological leap.

The special services most requested by business guests are:

- High-speed Internet access
- Toll-free 800 numbers
- Fax connections and machines
- Voice mail
- E-mail
- Telecommunication devices for the deaf (TDDs)

High-Speed Internet Access

One of the most recent dilemmas facing hotels is dealing with the need for high-speed Internet access. Business and resort travelers that arrive with their laptop computers are often faced with very slow data speeds from outside trunks channeled through the hotel's PBX. Moreover, those guests using the hotel's trunks generally dial an 800 number for Internet access, which may tie up the trunks for hours. This has forced hotels to increase the number of trunks to their properties without generating any additional revenue. Some hotel chains are now charging for local and 800 calls on a per-minute basis once the caller exceeds a predefined time threshold. This does not make the hotel popular, but the practice is a growing trend. When guests use an extension from the PBX or the data port on the side of the phone, they are using dial-up Internet access. Though at most hotels this is the prevalent method of accessing the Internet, the maximum speeds available to guests are far from optimal. Understandably, hotels are looking at other methods to provide faster Internet connections (and generate additional revenue). High-speed Internet access can use either existing telephone cable or coaxial cable feeding the pay-per-view movie service. It is totally separate from the PBX telephone system, and since it does not use any of the PBX trunks, some hotels report that their trunk requirements actually go down owing to the alternate choice available to the guest to access the Internet.

Toll-Free 800 Numbers

An 800 number allows guests to call a hotel without charge to make reservations, inquiries, etc. Hotels can have several 800 numbers to service the several guest offerings of the hotel. Since many businesses call to reserve meeting rooms or ask for help with meeting planning, hotels dedicate separate 800 numbers for its sales department. As a special guest "perk," some hotels carry an unpublished 800 number for their frequent guests. This saves time for these guests because they bypass the operator or front desk staff and are connected directly to the reservations agent or the sales office. Another potential application for a separate 800 line is for the restaurant's reservation desk, adding a level of sophistication and convenience to that function. Hotels also have direct 800 numbers for their voice mail and fax lines. Admittedly, these extra lines are a cost item, but in most cases, under the scrutiny of a cost-benefit analysis, the benefit of the revenue they generate outweighs their cost.

Fax Machines

Growing almost exponentially as a result of guest demand is the addition of facsimile service to hotel telephone systems. From a technological perspective, the fax machine is just another analog station on the PBX. The fax machine is usually assigned a **direct inward dial** (DID) extension to allow callers from outside the hotel to dial the fax machine without going through the hotel's operator.

As is true with other telephone services, fax service is a growing revenue opportunity for the hotel. Recognizing this potential, hotels are moving fax machines from their back offices to their lobbies so that guests are more aware of their availability. In some hotels, fax machines are permanent fixtures in suites and other rooms as indicated by demand. Cable patch panels allow hotels to quickly and efficiently assign new extensions to rooms for fax capability.

Voice Mail

Voice mail is an automated message-recording system that allows many guests to receive messages at the same time, thus freeing up the operator for other tasks. Fast becoming a service expected as standard by guests, voice mail is like a private answering machine for each guestroom. An incoming call is automatically connected to the voice mail system after a predetermined number of rings, at which time the caller leaves his or her message. Guests can retrieve their messages remotely or when they return to their rooms. Voice mail is especially valuable for guests whose native language is not English. Depending on the PMS interface and the voice mail system, hotels may be able to change the language selection upon guest check-in, and at check-out the voice mail system automatically reverts back to the default language.

Though voice mail systems are common in virtually all industries, each industry has its unique requirements. A hospitality voice mail system, for example, allows the administrative mailboxes to perform differently from guest mailboxes. A guest mailbox must be simple to operate and will have far fewer options than an administrative mailbox. In addition, for security reasons, guests are not allowed to record their own names and greetings. Pass codes are usually encouraged for administrative mailboxes but are not encouraged for guest mailboxes.

There are two major variables in a voice mail system: the number of storage hours and the number of voice mail access ports. The number of hours determines how many messages and greetings can be stored in the system. The number of ports in a system determines the number of individuals who can place or listen to a message simultaneously.

E-Mail

E-mail is arguably the fastest growing form of telecommunication. Most hotel business guests have it at work and perhaps also at home. An increasing number of mothers and children also have e-mail addresses. Friends, relatives, acquaintances all communicate via e-mail. What this means to the hotelier is another service expected by guests. Though high-speed Internet access is preferable, for limited applications most guests will still be able to use their laptop connected to the data port on the side of the room telephone to dial into the Internet. Also technologically possible is some form of Web-TV product that provides Internet access without the need of a laptop. This technology serves as both an entertainment vehicle for guests and a revenue generator for the hotel.

Telecommunications Devices for the Deaf

The Americans with Disabilities Act (ADA) requires that all hotels make available, upon request, a **telecommunications device for the deaf** (TDD) for use by individuals with impaired hearing or a communications disorder. In addition, a TDD must be available at the front desk to handle in-house calls from hearing or speech-impaired guests.

A TDD (sometimes called a TTY) looks like a small typewriter with a coupler above the keyboard for a telephone receiver. To make a call, the caller places the telephone receiver into the coupler, dials the number, and begins typing when the other party picks up. A small display screen above the keyboard shows what the caller (or the person called) is typing. Commonly accepted TDD abbreviations and a code of etiquette facilitate the call.

The ADA also requires all telephone companies in the United States to provide special relay services that enable persons with hearing and speech impairments to use their TDDs to communicate with anyone having a regular telephone. Callers reach the relay service by calling an 800 number, but they are billed as if they had dialed their calls directly. To illustrate, a relayed call from Las Vegas, Nevada, to Providence, Rhode Island, is billed as a long-distance call even if the office providing the relaying service is within the caller's city. A call across town is billed as a local call, even if it goes through a relay service on the other side of the state. Front desk staff and other employees should be alerted that relayed calls are likely to take more time than other calls because a relay operator will be between the two conversing parties passing messages back and forth. Employees should stay on the line until it is confirmed that all messages have been received and understood. Fortunately, increased use of the Internet has drastically reduced the number of TDD calls. Hearing-impaired individuals find it easier, faster, and less expensive to use the Internet.

Common Problems

Telecommunications in the hotel industry is in a period of rapid change that began in the mid-1980s. New equipment, new suppliers, new telephone companies, and new laws make the telephone environment both exciting and confusing for hotel managers. The days of providing just telephones and service and paying the phone bill have gone the way of the elevator operator.

Staying Abreast of Changing Laws

Not surprisingly, keeping up with new laws that affect hotel service is a common problem facing hotel managers today. The breakup of the old Bell Telephone System and the end of AT&T's monopoly on long-distance calls are relatively recent events, and the federal government and the courts are still creating and ruling on the laws necessary to regulate the new telecommunications environment.

The Hearing Aid Compatibility Act of 1988 made it a requirement that all guestroom phones be compatible with hearing aids (older phones caused electronic feedback between telephone earpieces and hearing aids). The law also includes provisions mandating that hotels have equipment available for the blind. To carry out the 1988 law, the Federal Communications Commission (FCC) ordered that all telephones in hotels be hearing-aid compatible. In addition, laws requiring hotels to provide amplification capability to guestroom phones as well as E-911 service have been enacted. Deregulation of local dial tones has forced hotels to make more choices and decisions.

Since the early 1990s, several new laws have been enacted that affect the level and conduct of hotel telephone service. The Telephone Operator Consumer Services Improvement Act of 1990 is a case in point. One provision of this law requires that hotels display certain long-distance carrier information on or near guestroom telephones. In compliance with the law, hotels must now post the name address, and toll-free number of the OSP the hotel uses; where to call for rate information; and a statement that guests can choose a different OSP to place their operator-assisted calls if they so desire. Other provisions in the law state that guests must be advised that they can file a complaint with the FCC, and that 800 and 950 numbers must be provided for guests to gain access to the alternative OSP of their choice.

In 1997, hotels were required to install software and equipment to allow 10XXX calls. This capability permits guests to choose the operator-service company of their choice for non-direct-dialed long-distance (0+ and 0-) calls by dialing that company's equal access code (10XXX) before making their call. Because of the growing number of **other common carriers** entering the market, this law was refined shortly after its enactment requiring hotels to provide 1010XXX access.

Owing in large part to leap-frog advances in telecommunications technology and the public's increasing reliance on that technology, you as a hotel manager can expect many more laws in the years ahead that will affect your hotel and the telephone service you provide your guests. To stay abreast, you should stay in regular contact with your long-distance provider, who can best keep you apprised of the laws that affect their service to you and, in turn, your service to your guests. Other sources of current information are industry association meetings, industry periodicals, and publications of the American Hotel & Lodging Association's Governmental Affairs Department.

Service on Equipment

Interestingly, one of the major recurring problems hotels have with their phone systems does not involve the local or long-distance telephone companies. The problem is that of service on telephone equipment. Most hotels have at least one story to tell of telephone equipment breakdown during evening peak hours and their inability to get service and repair until the next business day. If the breakdown occurs on a weekend, the problem is compounded.

Because telecommunications is such a critical tool to conducting a lodging business, it is equally critical that you protect your operation from disastrous telephone service interruption. When selecting or upgrading a telephone system, make sure the vendor is experienced in the unique needs of the hospitality business. The telephone needs of hotels are very different from those of non-lodging businesses. Other businesses rarely deal with charging back calls, and are usually open only during traditional business hours. Also, non-lodging businesses normally are not concerned with commissions on operator-assisted calls. Nothing short of a vendor with solid hotel telephone experience who is available 24 hours a day will suffice.

Hotels that have successfully addressed the equipment service problem have found it better to acquire the majority of their equipment—PBX, call accounting system, and voice mail system—from a single vendor. If sole-source procurement is not possible, make sure that there is a clear understanding among all parties involved of the lines of service, maintenance, and warranty responsibility. If you are purchasing equipment from other than the local telephone company, insist that the PBX provider accept all related service calls. As hotel manager, you should not have to be in the position of determining if the problem is with the equipment or with the outside lines serving the equipment. Furthermore, if it is determined by the equipment vendor that the problem lies with the telephone company, your hotel should not incur any charges for the vendor's time. Such a scenario should be covered in the scope of the warranty and maintenance agreements.

Incorrect Trunking

Next to equipment failures, trunking is arguably a hotel's biggest problem. Trunking—the hotel's mix of telephone lines—is usually designed to meet a certain grade of service. The level of service determines an ideal number of trunks needed to meet the hotel's service goals, with a certain allowance for busy signals. For example, a P.01 level of service means that it is acceptable for one out of 100 callers to experience a busy signal. The number of trunks a hotel will need depends largely upon the hotel's peak usage periods. If occupancy bounces from between 70 percent and 95 percent, a hotel will normally size the trunking for a value in between. This creates the interesting balance between cost and service. If a hotel is concerned with the number of their trunks—too many, too few—both the equipment vendor and the local telephone company can conduct traffic studies. But while traffic studies from the equipment vendor can tell the hotel if and when all the trunks were busy, only the local telephone company will be able to tell the hotel the number of people that actually got a busy signal.

Problems also emerge when a trunk is assigned to the wrong carrier and the hotel orders additional trunks to meet needs of a specific function, but neglects to have those assigned to the wrong carrier disconnected.

Another issue is the ever-expanding use of private lines/trunks. Individual hotel departments make decisions to order trunks for their own use, often without clear justification. Over time, additional trunks are ordered for modems, credit card machines, private lines, elevators, alarm systems, and countless other applications. Upon review, hotel management discovers that they have been paying an exorbitant amount of money for trunks that are seldom used.

How does the conscientious hotel manager prevent trunking problems? First and foremost, don't install a phone system and then forget about it. Revisit it and review it regularly. Keep a master list of all trunks coming into your property, and monitor their exact use and frequency of use. If there is indication that lines are underused, overused, out of service, or being billed after they were supposed to have been disconnected, contact your local phone company and request a service billing record. This is the document that shows the phone lines you are paying for. It will help you audit the type and number of lines you have. Also, have a traffic study conducted at least once a year. This analysis calculates your number of trunk hours for the year and is an accurate tool for measuring whether you have enough or too many trunks in your hotel. Your long-distance or telephone system supplier can also help you with this study.

Untrained Staff

Hotel employees usually receive little phone service training, even at hotels where the phone facilities are excellent. What your staff doesn't know can hurt you. Would at least one person at your front desk know what to do if a non-English-speaking person calls, or how to help a guest reach the OSP of their choice (as required by law), or be able to help a guest having trouble placing an international call? Guest phone problems can happen at any hour of the day, any day of the week.

"Free" Calls

As a hotel manager, you must ensure that you are not inadvertently giving away calls to guests. To cite an example: some hotels allow guests to make international calls, but their call accounting systems have no international rate tables. Therefore, the hotel is unable to charge the guests for the calls. The result is that a significant number of calls are falling into a "free" loophole that through vigilance beforehand could have been closed.

Also make sure that your hotel does not accept inbound calls for guests on your toll-free 800 number: you pay for the call, and you have no easy way to charge the guest.

Consider blocking all 900 calls. Some guests try to get a free call by requesting a credit for a "wrong number" that shows up on their guest folio, when in fact they intentionally dialed the number to reach someone they wanted to talk to. To help stop this problem, check to see if the disputed number is the same as the home or office number the guest gave when he or she checked in. Then decide if the request is valid.

Summary

As the information age moves steadily forward and technology continues to advance, hotel managers are increasingly challenged to provide faster access and greater amounts of information to their guests. The telephone system has evolved from a stoic, monopolistic entity to a dynamic, competitive industry.

Hotel managers need to fully understand the capabilities of the telephone system and the associated costs. Hotel telephone systems have evolved from cost centers to revenue centers, but competition from the long-distance industry and the use of wireless technology is making it increasingly difficult for hotels to maintain profits. For hotels to maintain their telecommunications systems as revenue centers, they will have to become more creative and provide competitive choices for their guests. Hotel managers must develop and maintain the discipline to continuously analyze their telephone systems to ensure that they have the most efficient mix of trunks and equipment. The efficiency of a phone system must be reviewed regularly—it is not a one-time exercise. The use of wireless communications, combined with the demand for high-speed Internet access, will continue to play a role in shaping the technology of the future.

Endnotes

1. The views expressed in this chapter are not necessarily those of Outrigger Hotels & Resorts.

    Contributing specific technical material were David Mozdren, Consultant, Hotel Technologies; Byrne Blumenstein, National Account Manager Executive, MCI Telecommunications; and Harry Newton, Author, *Newton's Telecon Directory*, 15th Edition.

2. Jeffrey Powell, "A Variety of Customers, A Variety of Telephones," *AAHOA Buyer's Guide*, Summer 1998, pp. 151–152.

Key Terms

aggregator—A long-distance telephone company that doesn't usually own any network, but purchases calling capacity in bulk on one of the nationwide networks' large customer products, such as AT&T or MCI Vent.

answer supervision—A method of detecting exactly when a call has been connected, so that a call accounting system or other piece of equipment can begin timing and billing the call.

automatic route selection (ARS)—A software-driven system for hotels with more than one type of telephone line that automatically routes calls to the type of line that can carry the call at the lowest cost.

billed-to-room call—An operator-assisted call that allows guests to have an operator place their calls and then advise the hotel of the charges.

branded openings and closings—Messages by an OSP operator that identify the OSP they represent. Some add another short message at the opening and closing personalizing the service to a particular hotel.

call accounting system (CAS)—Telephone equipment that enables hotels to price calls. Usually found in hotels with more than 40 rooms.

calling card—A pre-paid card for making telephone calls, issued by either the local phone company or a long-distance company.

calling-card call—A call typically billed to a code number on a calling card issued by either the local phone company or long-distance carrier, usually with a per-call surcharge.

class-marking—A restriction placed on hotel trunk lines that prevents guests from accepting incoming collect calls or making third-party calls that bill the hotel's phone number.

COCOT—Customer-Owned Coin-Operated Telephone. A pay telephone serviced by or purchased from a company other than one of the local phone companies.

collect call—A call in which the receiving party is asked if he or she wishes to accept the charges for the call; in not, the call is terminated.

computer-to-telephone interface (CTI)—An electronic device, such as a modem, that permits the user to access the Internet and other computer services carried over telephone lines.

direct-dialed long-distance calls—Most commonly used by hotel guests, direct dialing connects the caller with his or her destination number via automatic routing, and without the assistance of an operator.

direct inward dial (DD)—A dedicated extension that allows callers from outside the hotel to dial a fax machine without going through the hotel's operator.

800 number—A telephone number that allows a caller to call a business or individual without charge to the calling party.

e-mail—An electronic system that allows computer users to send and receive messages or documents on their computers by means of a network connection or modem.

HOBIC—Hotel Billing Information Center. With HOBIC, long-distance calls dialed by guests are intercepted by a local operator who records the guest's room number and completes the call. The cost of the call is then transmitted back to the hotel and recorded via a HOBIC teleprinter. The appropriate charges are posted to the guest's folio, and the guest is billed at check-out.

international call—A call made to an area outside North America.

ISDN PRI—Integrated Services Digital Network Primary Rate Interface. An ISDN PRI is a trunk line providing low-cost local service advanced digital technology.

least cost routing (LCR)—Another term for automatic route selection.

local access and transport area (LATA)—The area within which a hotel's local telephone company does not charge per call made.

local call—A call made within a LATA for which long-distance charges are not assessed.

long-distance call—A call made to a destination outside the LATA.

nationwide common carrier—Telecommunications companies that own their own nationwide transmission network. The three largest nationwide common carriers are AT&T, MCI Telecommunications, and U.S. Sprint.

900 or premium-price call—A call for which the business called charges a fee that is separate from the fee the telephone company charges for placing the call.

0- call—Calling- and credit-card calls that are placed with an operator's assistance, and collect and third-party calls.

0+ call—A calling- or credit-card call placed without an operator's assistance.

open architecture integration—Electronic and software protocols that permit device-to-device communication, such as computer-to-computer, computer-to-telephone, and computer-to-Internet via telephone trunk lines.

operator-service provider (OSP)—A telephone company contracted by the hotel to provide long-distance operator services to quests who want to make calls that cannot be placed without the help of a "live" or automated operator.

other common carrier (OCC)—A telecommunications company other than AT&T that owns its own nationwide long-distance network. The two largest OCCs are MCI Telecommunications and U.S. Sprint.

person-to-person call—A call that is not connected unless a specific party named by the caller verifies that he or she is on the line. A person-to-person call is an expensive call, if completed, but has no cost if the party in not able to come to the phone.

private branch exchange (PBX)—The primary piece of equipment controlling phone service at a typical hotel with more than 40 rooms. A PBX, or switchboard, takes inbound calls and delivers them to the PBX operator's console; it also connects in-house hotel telephone extensions directly to outgoing telephone lines.

Regional Bell Operating Companies (RBOCs)—Products of federal deregulation of the telephone industry, these seven companies—formerly parts of the Bell telephone system monopoly—provide telephone service to various regions of the United States.

regional common carrier—A long-distance carrier that owns its own network covering a limited geographic area. Regional common carriers typically use fiber optic digital radio networks.

SMDR—Station Message Detail Reporting. A module that connects to PBX systems that records and stores telephone call activity and provides the data and reports needed for billing, fraud control, and accurate cost-accounting.

telecommunications device for the deaf (TDD)—A device that enables an individual who has impaired hearing or a communication disorder to communicate by telephone with others. A TDD looks like a small typewriter with a coupler above the keyboard for the telephone receiver. It has a small display screen above the typewriter keys that shows each message as it is typed.

1010XXX code—A code that tells the local phone company not to direct a call to the carrier that was pre-selected for the line the call is going out on. Every carrier has a "ten-ten triple X" code.

third-party call—Similar to a collect call, except that the billed number is not the called number. In most cases, operators will require that someone at the third-party number accept the charges before they will put the call through to the dialed number.

trunk line—One of many main or primary telephone lines servicing the hotel from the telephone company. Trunk lines enter the hotel's system through the PBX system, which directs calls or data communication to the intended recipient.

trunking—The hotel's mix of trunk lines. Hotels may have several trunk lines, either dedicated or open, depending on the level of telecommunications service it wishes to provide.

wide area telephone service (WATS)—Long-distance service billed on a total hourly usage basis rather than on individual calls (for example, an 800-number line).

Review Questions

1. Why is providing good telephone service important for hotels?
2. What is the difference between 911 and E911 service?
3. What type of information is transferred between a property management system and the telephone system?

4. What benefits can a hotel derive from providing wireless communications to its guests?

5. What are some of the pertinent questions a hotel manager should ask when evaluating candidate OSPs?

6. What are the differences among collect, third-party, and person-to-person calls?

7. How are guest calls handled under the HOBIC system?

8. What is a call accounting system and what does it do?

9. How are guestroom phones increasing in sophistication?

10. What are the three types of long-distance carriers, and how do they differ from one another?

11. What types of questions should hotel managers ask when choosing an OSP?

12. What is a TDD and how can it be used at hotels?

13. What are some common problems hotels face with their telephone systems?

Internet Sites

For more information, visit the following Internet sites. Remember that Internet addresses can change without notice. If the site is no longer there, you can use a search engine to look for additional sites.

BICSI—A Telecommunications Association
http://www.bisci.org/

Consulting-Specifying Engineer
http://www.csemag.com

Newton's Telecom Dictionary (CMP Books, 2001)
http://www.telecombooks.com/

Chapter 12 Outline

Competencies

12

Food Service Equipment

Has it ever occurred to you that the commercial or institutional kitchen is a factory in every sense of the word? It receives raw materials and, through various manufacturing processes, prepares, combines, machines, finishes, decorates, "packs" and "ships" a finished product.

This processing of raw materials into finished product requires labor and machinery and, as in all factories, the proper organization of all factors into efficient, smooth–running, compact, properly planned operating units.[1]

THERE ARE MANY DIFFERENT TYPES of food service equipment that may be used in commercial kitchens today. This equipment can be powered by gas, electricity, or steam. Almost any type of food service equipment comes in small countertop or large freestanding models. Some can be placed on wheels or on wheeled carts for maximum flexibility. Different types of equipment are often combined in one unit—a range with an oven below it and an overhead broiler above it is a common kitchen appliance.

In this chapter we will talk about preparation, cooking, and sanitation equipment typically used in commercial kitchens. Later sections present information about equipment maintenance and warranties. The chapter concludes with a discussion of the role of equipment consultants and contractors.

Types of Food Service Equipment

Preparation Equipment

In this section we will discuss the major pieces of preparation equipment most commonly found in commercial kitchens: mixers, food processors, and slicers.[2]

Mixers. Mixers combine different types of solid food, solid food and liquid(s), or two or more different liquids. They can knead, whip, emulsify, slice, mix, beat, grind, or chop food, depending on the attachment used.

There are several types of mixers, the most common being the vertical mixer. Vertical mixers range in capacity from 5 to 140 quarts (4.75 to 133 liters).[3] A 20-quart (19 liter) model is generally a countertop or bench model; a 30-quart (28.5 liter) model can be a bench or floor model; and a mixer with a capacity of 40 quarts (38 liters) or more is a floor model. The motor of a vertical mixer is above the bowl, with the attachments hanging from the motor—roughly the same configuration found in small countertop mixers used in homes. When the bowl is filled with

A floor mixer. (Courtesy of Univex)

A vertical cutter/mixer. This model weighs 260 pounds (117 kilograms). (Courtesy of Stephan Machinery Corporation, Columbus, Ohio)

ingredients, it is raised by lever, wheel, or motor to get in position so the attachments can function properly.

Food Processors. For chopping, cutting, grating, pureeing, and combining foods, most commercial kitchens use some form of **food processor.** These units can range from small countertop appliances similar to those used in residential kitchens to large mobile units that discharge food directly into pans. Food processors typically have a number of cutting and blending attachments that slip onto a central shaft as needed for any given task.

Vertical cutters/mixers are older variations on food processors, and typically include a stainless steel bowl with a motor attached to its base, mounted on a stand that puts the bowl at working height. In kitchens where large quantities of vegetables must be roughly chopped, a buffalo chopper might be used. This chopper sits on a counter and has its motor positioned beside, rather than under, the work bowl.

All food processors are electrically powered, and most can be easily moved from place to place in the kitchen as required.

Slicers. A **slicer** has a spinning disk with a sharp edge for cutting food. The food is placed on a tray that slides back and forth, pushing the food against the disk's spinning edge. The tray can be powered manually or by an electric motor; commercial kitchens generally have an electric model.

Slicers are used to slice meats, cheese, tomatoes, and other food for sandwiches and salads. Slicers can be used in so many areas of the kitchen they are sometimes placed on carts and moved wherever they are needed.

Cooking Equipment

Cooking equipment includes ranges, ovens, broilers, tilting braising pans, griddles, deep-fat fryers, steam cookers, and ventilation hoods.[4] Most cooking equipment can be fueled by either natural gas or electricity, although some steam cookers may make use of a building's steam system. In areas where natural gas is not available, propane is often adopted for cooking equipment.

Ranges. Ranges provide flat surfaces for cooking food. There are countertop ranges, but most ranges used in commercial food service are floor models. Ranges usually have a conventional or convection oven beneath them; those that have shelves or storage cabinets beneath them instead are sometimes called skeleton ranges. A range may also have a broiler attachment. Because ranges are great for short-order cooking and are so versatile, they have long been the mainstays of commercial kitchens. But that is slowly changing. Specialized equipment that does the same job—but uses less energy and can be operated by employees with fewer skills—is beginning to take over. In fact, some commercial kitchens are built without ranges now.[5]

The various types of ranges are named after their cooking surfaces. There are solid-top, fry-top, open-top, and induction ranges.

Solid-top. Solid- or hot-top ranges, designed for pots and pans, have solid cast-iron or alloy tops. These ranges can have several different burner arrangements beneath their tops. Some solid-top ranges have uniformly heated tops—that is, no matter where you place a pan on the range, it will receive the same amount of heat. Another type of range, called a radiant hot-top range, has burners underneath its top that look like a series of concentric rings. The range's hottest spot is in the center, and temperatures gradually decrease as you move to the edges of the range. A third type has burners in the front of the range, so the hottest part of the range is in front, and lower temperatures are found at the rear. For fast heating and boiling, the hottest part of the range is used; the cooler parts are used for slower cooking.

Fry-top. A fry- or griddle-top range also has a solid cooking surface, heated from beneath. However, the surface is not for pots and pans. It is a highly polished, smooth surface used as a griddle for frying.

Open-top. An open-top range has grates to hold pots and pans over burners. Open-top ranges are superior to solid-tops for sauté work, because heat is available instantly and individual burners can be turned off when they are no longer needed.

Induction. A newer type of range uses electromagnetic energy to heat foods rather than electrical resistance or burning gas. An induction range consists of a glass plate mounted above a flat inductive coil that, when supplied with electricity, creates an electromagnetic field. This field reacts with any conductive cookware placed on the glass plate to create heat for cooking. The top of the range itself stays cool at all times, making induction ranges a popular choice for cooking on buffet lines and at tableside. However, because only cast iron, steel, or other ferric alloys will generate heat on an induction range, there are some limitations in the choice of cookware that can be used with this type of range.

Double-oven range with an overhead broiler on top. This model weighs 461 pounds (207 kilograms). Note that the left range is an open-top, the right range a fry-top. (Courtesy of The Montague Company, Hayward, California)

Ovens. Ovens are heated cavities in which food is cooked. Ovens can be divided into three basic categories: conventional, convection, and radiation. Within each category there are a great variety of ovens, some of which are known by more than one name, adding to the confusion. In this section we will describe the most commonly used ovens.

Conventional. Conventional ovens are enclosed chambers heated by a heat source from below and in some models by an overhead heat source as well. Food is placed in pans and placed on the oven's deck (the bottom or floor of the oven). Some ovens have a shelf or rack so that more pans of food can be cooked at the same time. In these ovens, the pans usually have to be rotated between deck and shelf halfway through the cooking cycle so the pans of food cook evenly.

Conventional ovens can be used for roasting and, less frequently, baking. A conventional oven's purpose is indicated by the size of its cavity; small cavities are found in baking ovens, larger ones in roasting ovens.[6] Roasting oven cavities are usually about 15 inches (38 centimeters) high, so even large cuts of meat weighing over 100 pounds (45 kilograms) can be roasted. Types of conventional ovens include deck, range, and mechanical.

Deck ovens are ovens in which two or three conventional ovens have been decked or stacked on top of each other. The stacked arrangement saves kitchen floor space.

Inexpensive deck ovens have only one burner and temperature for all the ovens. In more expensive models, each oven has its own heat control so employees can cook food requiring different temperatures at the same time. Deck ovens can cook all types of food. Those with steam-injection equipment are good for baking bread. Sometimes deck ovens are used to reheat frozen heat-and-serve foods as well.

Range ovens are small conventional ovens located beneath ranges. They are used for roasting and baking or as food warmers.

Mechanical ovens, so called because they have moving, mechanical parts within them to assist in cooking, range in size from compact to giant. Three typical mechanical ovens are revolving, conveyor, and rotary ovens.

Revolving ovens (also called reel or revolving tray ovens) move trays vertically within the oven's interior, so that they move within the oven somewhat like the cars on a ferris wheel. Revolving ovens were originally designed for baking. However, kitchen personnel discovered that other types of food could be successfully cooked in them. Advantages to cooking with revolving ovens are that a large number of food items can be cooked at the same time with a minimum of loading and unloading, and roasts and other meats can be cooked more quickly with less shrinkage.

Conveyor ovens are long ovens through which trays of food pass, either on a conveyor belt or on a rack that is pulled through the oven. There can be different temperatures within the various sections of the oven.

Rotary ovens have circular shelves that move trays of food horizontally around a central axis within the heat chamber. There are usually three to five shelves.

Convection. A convection oven is an oven in which heated air within the cooking chamber is circulated rapidly by a fan or blower system. Convection ovens were developed to increase the cooking capacity of conventional ovens.[7] Convection ovens can cook more food by using racks or multiple shelves because the circulated air penetrates food and eliminates the "cold spots" that can occur within a conventional oven. Food does not have to be manually moved from shelf to shelf because the circulating air evenly distributes the heat.

There are many other advantages to convection ovens. Food is cooked faster than in conventional ovens. Meats can be baked or roasted at lower temperatures, saving energy. Foods cooked in convection ovens—particularly meats, fish, and fowl—are more moist and less subject to shrinkage than those cooked in conventional ovens. Types of convection ovens include rack, rethermalization, and combination oven/steamers.

Rack or roll-in ovens are heated enclosures into which employees can roll special racks filled with trays of food. Rack ovens work on the same principle as other convection ovens—the heated air inside the oven is circulated by fans or a system of ducts. There is virtually no time or labor involved in loading and unloading these ovens. Also, because rack ovens have large capacities, they are ideal for cooking large amounts of food in the shortest time possible. Employees can simply roll a rack filled with hundreds of entrées into the oven and roll it back out again when the entrées are ready to be served. The bending, reaching, and lifting associated with conventional ovens are dramatically reduced.

Rethermalization or "retherm" ovens are used to rethermalize chilled or frozen foods. They are specially designed to quickly defrost food without damaging it. Some retherm ovens alternate cycles of heat and refrigeration to reduce dryness on the edges of frozen items while gently thawing the centers.[8] Retherm ovens come in various sizes and have many uses, because most models can also be used as high-speed conventional ovens.

A combination oven/steamer (often called a "combi") is a versatile piece of equipment that can be used as a convection oven, a pressureless convection steamer, and a combination oven/steamer in which food is cooked with hot air from the oven and is kept moist with steam from the steamer. This combination of hot air and steam is great for reheating frozen food or for cooking fish, vegetables, fowl, crusty bread, and delicate specialty items.[9] Combis are space savers, since they can be used in so many different ways. They come in countertop, floor, and roll-in rack models.

Radiation. Radiation ovens cook food by radiating electromagnetic waves. Two types of radiation ovens are microwave and infrared ovens.

Microwave ovens use very short (hence the name "micro") electromagnetic waves to cook food. These microwaves penetrate the food, causing movement within the molecules of the food that creates friction and heats the food internally. Containers made of metal cannot be used in microwave ovens because they may (1) cause sparks, and (2) reflect microwaves back to the oven's microwave tube and destroy it.[10] Glass and other non-metallic materials can be used because microwaves pass through them.

Microwave ovens cook food fast and do not heat the air around them, helping to keep the kitchen cool. Their biggest disadvantages are that they can't cook large quantities of food, and additional cooking with other equipment is usually needed—some meats need to be placed in an oven for browning, for example. For these reasons, in many kitchens microwave ovens are used mainly to reheat foods or to thaw frozen items for cooking on other equipment.

Infrared or quartz ovens use infrared electromagnetic waves to cook food quickly at very high temperatures. Infrared ovens can be used to heat, roast, and brown meats. They can rethermalize frozen foods, or brown foods that have been cooked in a microwave. Some quartz ovens, like those designed to cook pizzas, have conveyors. Like microwave ovens, infrared ovens do not heat the surrounding air.

A rotisserie broiler. This broiler can cook 40 chickens at once. (Courtesy of Hardt Equipment Manufacturing Inc., Lachine, Quebec)

Broilers. Broilers differ from other cooking equipment in that the food is cooked primarily by radiant heat. There are three basic types of "overfire" broilers, so called because the source of the radiant heat is above the surface of the food: one is a broiler with an overhead shelf; another type has an overhead oven instead of a shelf, the oven heated by the burners in the broiling compartment below; the third type is a broiler mounted above a conventional oven. This last type may have an overhead warming oven as well.

Other types of broilers are designed for special needs. These include overhead broilers, rotisserie broilers, and charbroilers.

Overhead broiler. Also called elevated broilers or salamander broilers, overhead broilers are small broilers typically mounted above the top of a hot- or fry-top range. Overhead broilers are useful for melting cheese, browning items quickly, and preparing short orders during slow periods when bigger broiling equipment is shut down.

A tilting braising pan. (Courtesy of Groen, a Dover Industries Company, Elk Grove Village, Illinois)

Rotisserie broiler. A rotisserie broiler holds the food being broiled on a spit that rotates, exposing all sides to the broiler's burners. Rotisserie broilers are often placed where guests can see them and be enticed by the cooking food's appearance and aroma. Chickens and large roasts are commonly prepared in this way.

Charbroiler. A charbroiler has irregularly sized ceramic chunks (simulating the irregularity of a layer of charcoal) forming a bed that radiates the heat produced by burners just below the bed. A grate above the bed holds the food. Juices from the food drip directly onto the hot bed of "coals" and burn. The smoke and flame that result give the food the appearance and flavor of food cooked over a charcoal fire—but without the labor and cleanup problems associated with charcoal fires. This type of broiler is popular in steakhouses.

Tilting Braising Pans. Tilting braising pans—also called tilting pans or tilting skillets—function as oversized skillets. The advantages of a tilting braising pan are that the pan can be tilted for easy loading and unloading, there is a pouring spout, and the pan itself is usually 7 inches (18 centimeters) deep. These pans can be used to produce almost every type of food except deep-fat fried. They can also reheat frozen foods. With some water in the bottom and steamer-pan inserts, they can steam vegetables. They can even be used to hold hot foods or proof bakery items.

Griddles. Griddles are cooking appliances with a one-piece polished steel, chrome-plated, or cast-iron plate. The plate usually has raised edges around the outside (to contain grease) and a grease trough. The plate is heated by burners underneath it; a griddle's smooth, unmarred surface should be evenly heated. Griddles are ideal for short order frying. Most griddles need only six to eight minutes to preheat.[11]

Within the last few years a new type of griddle has been manufactured with grooved surfaces. The tops of these grooves transfer grill marks to food, similar to the way charbroilers mark food. There are some advantages to using a grooved griddle rather than a charbroiler. Grooved griddles use less energy, produce less smoke, and are easier to clean, since grease runs off into collection troughs just as with the more traditional griddles.[12] Food will not have a charbroiled flavor, however.

Deep-Fat Fryers. With **deep-fat fryers**, foods are cooked by immersing them in heated fat. Two deep-fat fryers commonly used in commercial kitchens are open-pot fryers and pressure fryers. Open-pot fryers are the types of fryers used to produce french fries at McDonald's and other quick-service restaurants. They may be equipped with automated basket lifters or computerized timers to streamline production. For pressure frying, food is lowered into the hot fat and the fryer is covered tightly. Steam pressure keeps the cooked food moist and causes the food to roll around in the fat. This produces moist food with a crisp, golden exterior. Food often cooked in pressure fryers includes breaded chicken and fish; onion rings; french fries; breaded mushrooms and zucchini slices; corn on the cob; pork chops; and veal cutlets. Well-designed pressure fryers automatically shut off the heat if temperatures get too high, and have devices to catch the water that condenses on the underside of the fryer's lid (water should not be allowed to get into the cooking fat).

Steam Cookers. Steam cookers are appliances that cook food by converting water to steam. Steam cookers cook food quickly, with a minimum of moisture and nutrient loss. Two types of steam cookers commonly found in commercial kitchens are steam-jacketed kettles and compartment steamers.

Steam-jacketed kettles. In steam-jacketed kettles, steam does not come into direct contact with food. Instead, it is trapped within the kettles' hollow walls. These kettles are usually fully or two-thirds jacketed—that is, their walls are hollow all the way up the sides of the kettle or only two-thirds of the way. Steam-jacketed kettles range in capacity from 10 to 200 gallons (38 to 756 liters); can be mounted on a pedestal, legs, or a wall; and can be stationary or tilting. Although some people mistakenly refer to all steam-jacketed kettles as trunnion kettles or trunnions, only the kettles that tilt are properly referred to as trunnions.

Compartment steamers. Steam comes into direct contact with the food in compartment steamers. The food is cooked in pans placed on shelves or racks. Low-pressure steamers cook food at five psi (pounds per square inch) and are sometimes used in institutions for cooking meats. High-pressure steamers cook food at 15 psi and are good for cooking small amounts of vegetables very quickly.

Ventilation Hoods. Because ranges, broilers, griddles, and other cooking equipment generate heat, steam vapors, and—in some cases—smoke, they should be vented to keep the kitchen safe and relatively comfortable to work in. In most U.S. jurisdictions, any piece of cooking equipment that produces grease-laden vapors must be covered by a **ventilation hood.** (Although many codes do not require it, it is advisable to vent cooking equipment such as ovens and steam cookers even though their cooking vapors are not typically greasy.)

Two steam-jacketed kettles. (Courtesy of Groen, a Dover Industries Company, Elk Grove Village, Illinois)

Ventilation hoods, also called exhaust hoods, consist of a metal box or shelf that hangs roughly 3 1/2 feet (1.07 meters) above the cooking surface, a fan or fans that pull air off the cooking surface, and one or more collars to connect the hood to ductwork that removes air from the kitchen. Ventilation hoods typically include some form of grease-removal mechanism to prevent air ducts from becoming clogged with grease and creating a fire hazard. Grease removal may be via filters or through water-washing or misting devices.

Also included in ventilation hoods is some form of fire suppression equipment. Fire suppression systems may use wet or dry chemicals or a very fine water mist to put out fires that occur at the cooking surface. These systems may also tie into the building's fire protection system, so that fires originating in the kitchen can be immediately identified from a central location.

Other Food Service Equipment

Thus far in the chapter we have discussed the major pieces of food service equipment commonly found in commercial kitchens. There are many other types of food service equipment that do such specialized jobs as making ice or holding food at its proper temperature until it is served. In this section we will mention just a few:

- Holding tables
- Hot and cold beverage equipment

- Refrigerators and freezers

- Ice machines

Holding Tables. Holding tables (also called steam tables) keep food hot until it is served. Cafeterias use holding tables as serving counters that display food and keep it hot for guests who serve themselves. Holding tables can be heated by hot water or by dry heat generated with steam, gas, or electricity.

Hot and Cold Beverage Equipment. Equipment for the preparation and service of beverages can be quite extensive. Beverage equipment includes coffee brewers and urns, juice dispensers, milk dispensers, ice water stations, beer dispensing systems, hot water towers, and soda dispensers. Since almost every food service facility will have some form of equipment for making/dispensing coffee and sodas, we will concentrate on this equipment in this section.

Coffee brewing and dispensing equipment. Coffee may be prepared for service from either a stationary urn or from carafes that can be used by servers or placed on a buffet line. Self-contained coffee brewers are typically electrically heated, and consist of a water tank with a heating element, a thermostat and relay, and a removable basket for holding ground coffee and a filter. Water may either be poured into the unit from the top (as with small brewers), or supplied via a fixed connection to the building's potable (drinkable) water supply. The thermostat controls the temperature of the water used for brewing and, in the case of urns, controls the holding temperature of the brewed coffee. Coffee dispensed into carafes is held at temperature either by a heating element below the carafe or by thermal insulation around the carafe itself.

Stationary urns are typically used in large, institutional settings where substantial quantities of a single type of coffee are needed. Carafe coffee makers are popular because they allow many small batches of different types of coffee to be brewed using the same equipment, and allow the coffee to be served directly to the customer at optimum temperature.

Soda dispensing equipment. While some facilities still rely on single-serve bottles or cans of soda, most food service establishments use a post-mix system to prepare and dispense carbonated drinks. These systems combine a carbon dioxide dispenser with chilled, pressurized water and concentrated soda syrups to provide freshly mixed soda at the point of service, either via a soda fountain or "gun." Post-mix systems require electrical power and a connection to potable water.

When soda must be available in multiple locations, it is common for an operation to install a single post-mix system in an area where it can be easily stocked and monitored, and run lines of chilled, carbonated water and soda syrup to remote soda fountains or guns. There are limits on how far the remote dispensers can be placed from the centralized post-mix system, so managers should consult with the system's manufacturer when installing remote soda equipment.

Refrigerators and Freezers. Refrigerators and **freezers** are used to maintain the quality of stored food. They preserve the color, texture, flavor, and nutritional value of food items by keeping them chilled or frozen. Refrigerators and freezers range from cabinet models and reach-in units to large walk-in units.

Cabinet models are small refrigerators or freezers that are located on or under countertops right at a workstation, to keep food handy for food preparers or servers.

Pass-through and reach-in refrigerators with glass doors are used in some food service operations to store prepared food such as salads or desserts. Employees can then take food items from the refrigerators and serve them as guests order them, or the guests may serve themselves—for example, in cafeterias. To reduce employee trips to the walk-in refrigerator, operations use reach-ins in kitchens to store some food.

Typical upright reach-ins are 78 to 84 inches (198 to 213 centimeters) high and 32 inches (81 centimeters) deep. They commonly come with one, two, or three doors. A one-door unit would be about 28 inches (71 centimeters) wide; a three-door, 84 inches (213 centimeters). Doors are usually self-closing.[13]

Walk-in refrigerators and freezers provide food storage away from the kitchen and allow operators to buy food in large quantities, keeping costly deliveries to a minimum. They should be installed to make the delivery of food and the movement of food from the walk-ins to production areas as convenient as possible. Where possible, walk-ins should be installed so that their floors are flush with the kitchen floor.

Walk-ins are typically built from prefabricated modular panels. Panel sizes vary, and walk-ins can be custom-built. A typical unit may measure 8 feet by 12 feet (2.4 meters by 3.7 meters).[14]

A walk-in can be an integral part of a building, or a prefabricated room installed in sections. Walk-ins can be built outside the building as well. In some cases, outdoor units are installed right next to the main building with a connecting door between them; a door on a different wall is for deliveries. This saves interior space and allows deliveries to be made easily, without disrupting the normal employee traffic flow.

Since the ideal storage temperatures for food items vary, an operation may have more than one walk-in. For example, a large operation may have a walk-in refrigerator for vegetables, one for meats, and one for dairy items, as well as a walk-in freezer for frozen items.

Ice Machines. Ice machines make cubed, crushed, or flaked ice. They can be floor models or mounted on a wall. Capacities range from 20 to 2,400 pounds (9 to 1,080 kilograms) of ice per day.[15] Machines that allow the first ice made to be the first ice dispensed are desirable. So are machines designed to allow employees to run cleaning solutions through them during periodic maintenance.[16]

For large operations, there are machines that make ice in block or bulk form; the ice must then be chipped or crushed. The capacities in these machines run from 40 to 4,000 pounds (18 to 1,800 kilograms) of ice per day.

Sanitation Equipment in Food Service

Two sanitation mainstays within commercial kitchens are dishwashing machines and waste disposals. There are other types of washers besides dishwashers—pot and pan, glass, tray, and silverware washers to name a few. But dishwashers are the most commonly used, and we will focus our discussion on them.

Dishwashing Machines. Because food service operations vary so widely in terms of floor space, number of employees, and amount of dishes to be washed, there are a tremendous variety of **dishwashing machines**. In this section we will briefly cover door-type, conveyor, flight-type, and energy-saving dishwashers.

Door-type. A door-type dishwasher—also called a single-tank or stationary-rack dishwasher—has a tank holding a solution of heated wash water and detergent. This solution is circulated through spray nozzles above and below the dishes. As with most dishwashers, water for washing is at 140°F to 160°F (60°C to 71°C). Rinse water is circulated through the same spray nozzles. To kill bacteria, rinse water is heated to 180°F (82°C) with a booster heater (most tap water only reaches 140°F to 160°F [60°C to 71°C]). Dishes are placed on racks for cleaning; these racks remain stationary throughout the washing process. Doors may be on one or more sides.

Door-type dishwashers are typically 24 inches (61 centimeters) square and about 58 inches (147 centimeters) high. It takes about one minute for a rack of dishes to be washed and rinsed by a typical door-type model. Dishes may have to be presoaked before going into the machine. Typical door-type dishwashers can handle 810 to 1,875 dishes in an hour's time.[17]

Conveyor. With conveyor dishwashers, racks of dishes are placed on a conveyor belt that carries the dishes through the machine. These dishwashers have curtains rather than doors. At one end, an employee loads the soiled dishes into the machine; after going through the cleaning cycle, the dishes are automatically pushed out onto the clean-dish table at the other end, eliminating the need for an employee to open a door and manually remove the racks.

The simplest conveyor dishwasher has one tank of hot wash water. After the dishes are washed, they remain in place for the final rinse. In a two-tank machine, the dishes are washed, then moved down the line to a second tank, where a special rinse takes place before the final rinse. A three-tank machine has a tank for rinsing off food remaining on the dishes before they are moved to the wash tank. Obviously, the more tanks a conveyor dishwasher has, the longer it is.

A single-tank conveyor ranges from 36 to 54 inches (91 to 137 centimeters) in length; a double-tank unit, 64 to 84 inches (163 to 213 centimeters). Conveyor dishwashers can handle 4,500 to 5,650 dishes per hour.[18] A typical single-tank unit can wash 75 racks of dishes, glasses, and silverware in 30 to 40 minutes. It would easily handle the dishwashing needs of a 150-seat restaurant.[19]

Flight-type. In flight-type dishwashers, the conveyor is not a belt upon which dish racks are placed; the conveyor itself acts as one continuous rack because it is made up of pegs on stainless steel bars (see Exhibit 1). Plates, pans, and trays are placed between the pegs. Cups, glasses, and silverware still have to be racked, however.

Flight-type dishwashers are built to handle large dishwashing demands— 6,750 to 24,000 dishes per hour, depending on the dishwasher's size.[20] Typical machines range from 9 to 26 feet (2.7 to 7.9 meters) in length.[21] Most units contain prewash, power wash, power rinse, and final rinse cycles. They are typically used

Exhibit 1   Diagram of a Flight-Type Dishwasher

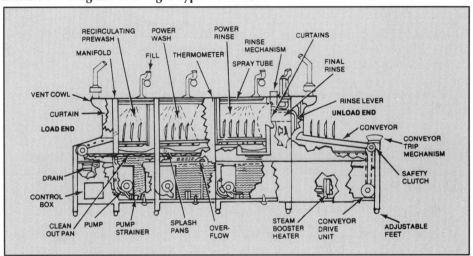

Source: Robert A. Modlin, ed., *Commercial Kitchens*, 7th ed. (Arlington, Virginia: American Gas Association, 1989), p. 259.

in commercial operations or large institutions that serve more than 1,000 people per meal.[22]

Energy-saving. Energy-saving or low-temperature dishwashers come in door-type and single-tank conveyor models. Whereas conventional dishwashers sanitize dishes by heating rinse water to 180°F (82°C), energy-saving dishwashers use water heated to 120°F–140°F (49°C–60°C) and sanitize dishes with a chemical—usually chlorine. These units are useful in settings where energy costs are very high, such as remote resorts.

Waste Disposals. Waste disposals grind or shred food waste and are usually part of a sink. Running water is used to carry food into the disposal where it is cut into smaller and smaller pieces until the water can carry it through drain pipes into the sewer system. Typically, small disposals are installed throughout the kitchen at points where food waste collects. The vegetable preparation area usually has a waste disposal, for example; so does the soiled dish area.

Waste disposals come in a range of horsepower ratings. They are also rated by the pounds or gallons of food waste they can handle per hour. A ³/₄ horsepower disposal can handle 300 pounds (135 kilograms) an hour; a 2 horsepower disposal, 600 pounds (270 kilograms).[23]

A food service operation may generate more waste than can be handled by in-sink waste disposals, or may be located in a jurisdiction that does not permit their use. A pulper/extractor is an alternative piece of equipment for managing kitchen waste that does not put food solids into the building's plumbing system. Like waste disposals, pulper/extractors grind up food waste with water. However, in a pulper/extractor, the ground-up waste is pushed through an extraction screw that squeezes out most of the water, leaving a damp pulp that is ejected into a waste receptacle for disposal. The soiled water is removed via the sanitary sewer.

These units are helpful in food service operations that generate a large amount of food waste.

Maintaining Food Service Equipment

Maintaining food service equipment is an example of how the engineering department contributes to the efficiency of other departments. Well-maintained and properly operating equipment allows food and beverage employees to concentrate on producing quality products for guests. The alternative—working with poorly maintained equipment—can mean frustrated employees who must cope with problems such as inaccurate temperature controls or poorly cleaned dishes.

Maintenance involves keeping equipment operating at or near its peak design capacity. An ice machine whose production rate has declined due to a clogged condenser coil and a buildup of scale can have its production rate improved through a good maintenance program. But maintenance cannot make a machine do more than it was built to do. If an ice machine is purchased that has an ice-making capacity of 50 pounds of ice per day and the operation needs 100 pounds per day, maintenance cannot increase the machine's capacity beyond 50 pounds per day even with the best care in the world.

Maintaining food service equipment is a responsibility of food and beverage department employees as well as maintenance employees. Equipment needs maintenance due to the wear and tear of normal operation, but sometimes, unfortunately, maintenance needs are created when employees abuse equipment. At times abuse occurs because employees do not know how to operate the equipment properly; at other times abuse is the result of poor work habits or lack of attention. Whatever the cause, the abuse must be stopped. Training kitchen employees to take proper care of equipment is an excellent investment. Managers should also continually remind these employees of the importance of equipment care. Chapter Appendix A lists sample maintenance procedures for kitchen employees.

One potential difficulty with food service equipment involves installation. If the food and beverage department purchases equipment without consulting the maintenance and engineering department, installation problems can result. For example, needed utilities are sometimes lacking at the point of installation. When this happens, the maintenance and engineering department must try to provide them on short notice, and often the result is conflict between maintenance employees and food and beverage employees.

Other problems occur if food and beverage personnel choose equipment that needs special maintenance or parts that are not available locally. Maintenance employees also need the control diagrams and maintenance instructions that come with a piece of equipment; sometimes food and beverage personnel, not realizing the importance of equipment manuals, throw them away or lose them. For these and other reasons, it is a good idea to have the engineering and maintenance department involved in equipment decisions from the beginning.

In the demanding environment of commercial food service, equipment must be readily cleanable and maintainable. These two provisions are addressed in the standards of the National Sanitation Foundation (NSF). NSF develops standards for equipment design, paying special attention to cleanability, durability, and maintainability. It is a good policy to choose equipment constructed to NSF standards. Depending on the type of equipment, other standards are important as well. Gas-fired equipment should meet the American Gas Association's standards, while electrical equipment should have an Underwriters Laboratories (UL) listing.

Equipment Maintenance Needs

There are hundreds of different pieces of food service equipment, and their maintenance needs vary. For this reason, there are two maintenance suggestions everyone should heed: (1) follow the equipment manufacturer's recommended maintenance program, and (2) allow only trained maintenance employees or outside service representatives to work on the equipment.

Maintenance of Preparation and Cooking Equipment. Good maintenance begins with educating the kitchen staff on how to properly use and operate kitchen equipment. Kitchen employees should perform much of the minor maintenance and cleanup of this equipment as part of their daily duties, so they need instruction in these areas. Many operations post a list of daily cleaning and maintenance activities on or near each piece of equipment.

The role of maintenance staff with regard to food preparation and cooking equipment includes installing or helping the manufacturer's service representatives install equipment; stocking repair parts; testing and calibrating controls; replacing filters, heating elements, and other parts which wear out or don't work properly; and inspecting hoses, fittings, connections, and seals. Making sure food service equipment is operating properly may require using such specialized tools as:

- *Air velocity meters*—used to check the air velocity of various ventilating systems.

- *Electrical test meters*—used to measure current flow, voltage levels, and continuity (open or closed circuits).

- *Pyrometers and various types of thermometers*—used to check cooking equipment temperatures to ensure proper calibration and operation of control thermostats.

- *Radio frequency monitor*—used to check for leakage from microwave ovens.

Maintenance employees should follow the equipment manufacturer's maintenance recommendations. A sampling of typical maintenance recommendations for cooking equipment is found in Exhibit 2. Note the indication of shared responsibility for equipment maintenance ("Check that unit is being cleaned properly") with the food and beverage department.

Maintenance of Storage and Service Equipment. Holding or steam tables often have separate thermostats for each of the compartments in which pans of food are placed. These thermostats must be inspected and adjusted periodically. Kitchen personnel help maintain this equipment by keeping it clean.

Exhibit 2   Sample Maintenance Requirements for Cooking Equipment

P.M. PROCEDURES: Gas Stove and Oven
MAINT. ACTION #44
FREQUENCY: Monthly—Semi-Annually

Maint. Action #44M

1. Inspect unit and check operation.
2. Check that unit is being cleaned properly.
3. Advise F&B Director of any cleaning problem.

Maint. Action #44SA

1. Remove top burners. Clean and degrease.
2. Grind in burner gas valves with fine grinding paste.
3. Reassemble and check operation.
4. Check for leaks and adjust burner as required.
5. Remove oven burner. Clean and degrease.
6. Check thermocouple and adjust position in flame.
7. Check gas safety valve operation.
8. Check operation of oven door. Adjust counterweight and chains as required.
9. Replace any missing or damaged controls, knobs, screens.

P.M. PROCEDURES: Flat Top Grill (Gas)
MAINT. ACTION #43
FREQUENCY: Monthly—Semi-Annually

Maint. Action #43M

1. Inspect unit and check operation.
2. Check that unit is being cleaned properly.
3. Advise F&B Director of any cleaning problem.

Maint. Action #43SA

1. Remove grill top. Check for cracks and warping.
2. Remove burner and clean.
3. Clean and degrease base section.
4. Reassemble and check operation.
5. Adjust burner setting as required.
6. Check gas connections for leaks.
7. Replace missing or damaged controls, knobs, screens.

P.M. PROCEDURES: Deep-Fat Fryers
MAINT. ACTION #42
FREQUENCY: Monthly—Semi-Annually

Maint. Action #42M

1. Inspect unit and check operation.

(continued)

Exhibit 2   *(continued)*

---

2. Check that unit is being cleaned properly.

3. Advise F&B Director of any cleaning problem.

4. Check safety cutout if operating.

Maint. Action #42SA

1. Inspect thermostat bulbs for damage.

2. Inspect submersible element for damage.

3. Check all electrical wiring and connections. Tighten or replace as required.

4. Check operation of thermostats. Calibrate as required.

Source: *Maintenance Operating Manual*, Days Inns of America, Inc., Atlanta, Georgia.

Coffee urns and makers must be kept clean in order to produce coffee with the correct flavor and aroma. This maintenance work is performed by kitchen employees. Maintenance employees may be called on to correct thermostat defects that cause brew temperatures to be too high or too low. Older coffee urns powered by gas may have to have their gas-air mixture adjusted; steam units commonly suffer from clogged pipes; the coils of electric units burn out, or wires may break.[24] Leaky faucets must be repaired or replaced.

Maintenance efforts for refrigerators, freezers, and ice machines are generally directed at the refrigeration elements of the equipment. On a semi-annual basis, the refrigerant levels of all refrigeration systems should be checked, evaporator and condenser surfaces cleaned, fans and motors lubricated, and connections inspected to make sure they are tight.

Food service refrigeration equipment can be subject to rather harsh operating conditions, which makes maintenance even more important. For example, the grease in some kitchen areas can build up on a refrigerator's air-cooled condenser. This blocks air flow through the condenser and causes poor heat transfer. The result can be a drop in the cooling ability of the refrigerator, an increase in energy consumption, and a shortened compressor life.

One way to reduce the maintenance needs of refrigeration equipment and improve energy performance is to install equipment that uses either a remote air-cooled condenser or a water-cooled condenser. Remote air-cooled condensers are usually installed outside the building where they use outside air as the cooling source. The results are (1) the air compressor takes in cooler air than that available in the hot kitchen, (2) condenser pressure is lower than it would be if the unit was using kitchen air, (3) conditions are usually cleaner, and (4) there is a drop in energy use and maintenance needs.

Water-cooled condensers are connected to a water loop that uses water from a cooling tower or the operation's chilled-water system. Water-cooled condensers may be located anywhere in the building as long as a source of cool water is available. These condensers are able to reduce energy costs to even lower levels than remote air-cooled units because the water is usually cooler than the outside air,

Exhibit 3   Sample Preventive Maintenance Procedures for a Walk-In Cooler

---

P.M. PROCEDURES: Walk-In Cooler
MAINT. ACTION #55
FREQUENCY: Monthly

Maint. Action #55M

Condensing Unit

1. Blow out condenser coil—use degreaser in kitchen locations.
2. Check operation of unit gas charge and oil level in compressor.
3. Lubricate fan motor with 3 drops of 3-in-1 oil.
4. Check for any loose bolts or screws and tighten.
5. Check electrical connections. Tighten as required.

Walk-In Box

1. Check door seals. Adjust or replace as required.
2. Check hinges for wear and tighten any loose screws.
3. Check latch and strike. Adjust as required, tighten loose screws.
4. Check box temperature. Adjust as required.
5. Ensure product is properly stored and inside is kept clean.
6. Report any problems with storage or cleanliness to F&B Director.

Source: *Maintenance Operating Manual*, Days Inns of America, Inc., Atlanta, Georgia.

resulting in lower condenser temperatures. Some older hotels have water-cooled condensers that use water from the water main as the cooling source and then discharge the water into the sewer. This practice is very wasteful and should not be followed, and may even be illegal in some jurisdictions.

Preventive maintenance needs of walk-in coolers include cleaning various surfaces, checking set points of refrigeration systems against desired storage temperatures, inspecting drain lines and removing blockages, and replacing torn or missing plastic strip curtains or door seals (see Exhibit 3). Doors should close properly; door seals should be inspected to make sure they seal properly. Controls for door heaters (installed to prevent freezing of condensed moisture on freezer doors) should be checked. Defrost operation should be monitored to be sure defrosting is occurring with the proper frequency.

Chapter Appendix B shows how one company presents instructions for ice-maker maintenance to maintenance employees. There is a rather detailed list of instructions regarding what work should be performed. There is also a troubleshooting guide. This is an excellent way to handle maintenance information, given the facts that (1) there can be a high turnover rate among maintenance personnel, (2) some maintenance workers are unfamiliar with food service equipment, and (3) maintenance workers are usually not closely supervised.

Maintenance of Sanitation Equipment. Preventive maintenance activities for dishwashers include checking thermometers and gauges, solenoid valves, seals,

Exhibit 4   Sample Maintenance Checklist for Dishwashers

> **P.M. PROCEDURES: Dishwasher**
> **MAINT. ACTION #37**
> **FREQUENCY: Daily—Monthly**
>
> **Maint. Action #37D**
>
> 1. Inspect machine and check operation.
> 2. Check wash and rinse temperatures. Wash temp. 140°F—Rinse temp. 180°F.
> 3. Check all screens in place.
>
> **Maint. Action #37M**
>
> 1. Carry out Maint. Action #37D.
> 2. Check machine for loose handles, levers, etc.
> 3. Check heating elements, record amperage.
> 4. Check all electrical connections.
> 5. Check pumps, valves, dispensers, etc.
> 6. Check piping to pumps in clear.
> 7. Carry out any repairs to defects found.

Source: *Maintenance Operating Manual*, Days Inns of America, Inc., Atlanta, Georgia.

electrical connections, heating elements, equipment mounting brackets, water temperatures, and pump motors. Maintenance employees should also check for drain leaks and pump obstructions and provide proper water softening for dishwasher water.[25]

If an electric booster heater is used for the dishwasher, it should be inspected. The amp draw of the heater can be checked, and the high-pressure relief valve should be tested to ensure it is functioning properly. Booster heaters should be drained and flushed annually. They may require descaling as well.

Dishwashers require the correct water pressure to operate properly. Water entering dishwashers should be checked under flow conditions to be sure pressure levels are within the range specified by the manufacturer. Exhibit 4 shows a sample maintenance checklist for dishwashers.

The manufacturer's recommendations should be carefully followed for waste disposals. Some manufacturers print instructions for maintenance employees to adjust the disposal's rotors; others recommend that one of their service representatives do this work because the disposal can be destroyed by improper adjustment.[26]

For most disposals the manufacturer outlines a way to fix clogs or jams. Sometimes the rotor can be removed. Some disposals have a reversible motor to relieve jams.

The ground-up food waste must be kept from entering the potable water system. Backflow prevention devices and air gaps on discharge lines are used to ensure this and are often required by health codes. Maintenance personnel should always be on the lookout for unauthorized connections to the water system that may bypass these backflow connections, not only from waste disposals, but from dishwashers and other equipment that discharge wastewater.

Equipment Warranties

New food service equipment generally has a warranty. All too often, the purchaser doesn't know much about the warranty and its limitations nor investigates any optional coverage. The result can be a lack of warranty coverage, ignorance of procedures necessary to keep the warranty in place, or false confidence that problems will be covered by the warranty. In some instances, operations pay repair costs covered by the warranty because they do not know what is in the warranty. Because the maintenance department shares the responsibility of maintaining food service equipment with the food and beverage department, sometimes there is a failure to use warranty cost recovery to its fullest because one department is keeping track of the warranties and the other is calling contractors for maintenance and the two departments are not communicating with each other.

Warranty coverage may begin when the equipment is shipped or from the date of service, with different time periods applying. A standard warranty might state that "Llenroc products are warranted to the original purchaser to be free from defect in materials and workmanship under normal use and service for a period of 90 days from the date equipment is placed in service or 120 days from the date of shipment from the factory, whichever is sooner." The 90-day period may be expanded to one year and the 120-day period to 15 months for some types of equipment. Often the one-year warranty provision covers parts only—you pay all labor and travel costs for service personnel. Some extended warranties have similar provisions in which only a portion of the extended warranty period involves coverage of parts, labor, and transportation, with the balance of the period involving only parts.

Warranties often do not cover minor adjustments or replacement of items such as timers, light bulbs, and indicator lights. Warranty coverage is voided in some instances if the equipment has inadequate utility services, was wired improperly, or mounted poorly. Many manufacturers' authorized service agents will check new installations and make minor corrections if needed, often at no charge. With some manufacturers, equipment warranties are voided if service contracts are not purchased.

Equipment Consultants and Contractors

When they are planning to purchase equipment, hotel and restaurant managers often turn to food service equipment consultants or other professionals such as manufacturer's representatives or equipment distributors. Typically, these professionals help a manager by defining the specifications for the equipment in terms of materials, physical size, utility sources, and production rates (among other things). The equipment is often installed either by a contractor or the equipment's manufacturer. A well-structured and definitive contract with these firms will help ensure that the equipment's design and installation meet the operation's needs. If these needs are met, it is less likely that employees will abuse a piece of equipment by trying to get it to perform a task for which it was not designed. Proper installation means that extra maintenance efforts will not be necessary because of improper installation and start-up.

Equipment maintenance can be performed by outside contractors as well as by maintenance employees. Managers have a number of things to consider when contemplating contract maintenance for equipment. The National Restaurant Association (NRA) suggests these questions should be asked:

- Does the contractor have trained people on staff to meet your maintenance needs?

- Are the contractor's employees trained on a continuing basis?

- Does the contractor have experience with other food service operations?

- How long has the contractor been in business? Is the company fiscally responsible?

- Does the contractor stock adequate spare parts for your equipment, and can it deliver parts you may need that are not in stock?

- Does the contractor possess an adequate library of service manuals?[27]

After screening potential contractors using the criteria above and any other criterion important to the operation, the operation's managers may choose a contractor and sign a contract. The following conditions should be present in the contract, tailored to your specific needs:

- A specific number or frequency of inspections.

- Inclusion of labor and parts, refrigerant, lubricants, filters, and other necessary materials.

- A written report each time your equipment is inspected or serviced.

- A complete listing of the equipment that is covered and its location, instead of general terms such as "all fans."

- Adequate insurance coverage by the service contractor.

- Evidence that the contractor has inspected your equipment thoroughly and knows its condition prior to signing the contract.

- Evidence that the contractor is completely responsible for his or her work, including any damages or breakdowns caused by failure to take appropriate action.

- A clearly spelled-out method of adjustment if the contract calls for annual price adjustments. Terms such as "adjusted at prevailing rates" should not be accepted.

- No limits on the dollar value of parts and materials or the number of labor hours.

- No exclusion of major parts or components.

- A promise that emergency requests will be handled on a 24-hour basis. Breakdown of refrigeration systems in evening hours cannot wait for repair in the morning without loss of food.

- No language that will permit a contractor to cancel the contract without giving advance notice.[28]

Endnotes

1. C. W. Schroeder, "Kitchen Engineering," *The Outfitter,* 1934.

2. Some of the material in this section was adapted from Robert A. Modlin, ed., *Commercial Kitchens,* 7th ed. (Arlington, Virginia: American Gas Association, 1989).

3. Arthur C. Avery, *A Modern Guide to Foodservice Equipment,* rev. ed. (New York: CBI, 1985), pp. 245–246.

4. Some of the material in this section was adapted from Modlin, ed., *Commercial Kitchens.*

5. Avery, p. 48.

6. John B. Knight and Lendal H. Kotschevar, *Quantity Food Production, Planning, and Management* (New York: CBI, 1979), p. 153.

7. Avery, pp. 71–72.

8. Knight and Kotschevar, p. 152.

9. Modlin, ed., *Commercial Kitchens,* p. 62.

10. Knight and Kotschevar, p. 151.

11. Rob Townsend, "Tasty Foods Are Thrilling After Broiler and Griddle Grilling," *Restaurants & Institutions,* June 26, 1991, pp. 131–132.

12. Townsend, pp. 131–132.

13. "Product Knowledge—Storage & Handling Equipment: Reach-In Refrigeration," *Foodservice Equipment & Supplies Specialist,* October 1990, p. 93.

14. "Product Knowledge—Storage & Handling Equipment: Walk-In Refrigeration," *Foodservice Equipment & Supplies Specialist,* October 1990, p. 98.

15. Lendal H. Kotschevar and Margaret E. Terrell, *Foodservice Planning: Layout and Equipment,* 3d ed. (New York: Wiley, 1985), p. 456, and a brochure by Hoshizaki America, Inc.

16. Kotschevar and Terrell, p. 456.

17. "Product Knowledge—Sanitation & Warewashing Equipment: Warewashers," *Foodservice Equipment & Supplies Specialist,* October 1990, p. 125.

18. "Warewashers," *Foodservice Equipment & Supplies Specialist,* p. 126.

19. "Warewashers," *Foodservice Equipment & Supplies Specialist,* p. 122.

20. Karl Scriven and James Stevens, *Food Equipment Facts* (New York: Wiley, 1982), p. 290.

21. "Warewashers," *Foodservice Equipment & Supplies Specialist,* p. 123.

22. Scriven and Stevens, p. 290.

23. Alan T. Stutts and Frank D. Borsenik, *Maintenance Handbook for Hotels, Motels, and Resorts* (New York: VNR, 1990), p. 172.

24. Avery, p. 244.

25. Roland E. Greaves, *The Commercial Food Equipment Repair and Maintenance Manual* (New York: VNR, 1987), p. 126.

26. Avery, p. 268.

27. Adapted from Equipment Maintenance Programs, National Restaurant Association, Chicago, Illinois.

28. Adapted from Equipment Maintenance Programs, National Restaurant Association, Chicago, Illinois.

Key Terms

broiler—A kitchen appliance that cooks food with radiant heat.

deep-fat fryer—An appliance in which foods are cooked by immersing them in heated fat.

dishwashing machine—An appliance that washes and rinses dishes automatically.

food processor—An appliance used for chopping, cutting, grating, pureeing, and combining foods; food processors range from small countertop appliances similar to those used in residential kitchens to large mobile units that discharge food directly into pans. Food processors typically have a number of cutting and blending attachments that slip onto a central shaft as needed for any given task.

freezer—A chilled reach-in or walk-in unit used to maintain the quality of food.

griddle—A cooking appliance with a one-piece polished steel, chrome-plated, or cast-iron plate heated by burners underneath it.

holding table—An appliance that keeps food hot until it is served. Also called a steam table.

ice machine—An appliance that makes cubed, crushed, or flaked ice automatically.

mixer—An appliance used to knead, whip, emulsify, slice, mix, beat, grind, or chop different types of solid food, solid food and liquid(s), or two or more different liquids. Typically, the motor is above the bowl, with the attachments hanging from the motor.

oven—An appliance with a heated cavity in which food is cooked.

range—An appliance that provides a hot, flat surface for cooking food.

refrigerator—A chilled reach-in or walk-in storage unit used to maintain the quality of food.

slicer—An appliance that has a spinning disk with a knife-sharp edge for cutting food; the food is placed in a tray that slides back and forth, pushing the food against the disk's spinning edge.

steam cooker—An appliance that cooks food with a minimum of moisture and nutrient loss by converting water to steam.

tilting braising pan—A versatile kitchen appliance that functions as an oversized skillet. Also called a tilting pan or tilting skillet.

ventilation hood—A piece of kitchen equipment consisting of (1) a metal box or shelf that hangs roughly 3 $1/2$ feet (1.07 meters) above the cooking surface of a piece of cooking equipment, (2) a fan or fans that pull air off the cooking surface, (3) one or more collars to connect the hood to ductwork that removes the air from the kitchen, (4) some form of grease-removal mechanism to prevent air ducts from becoming clogged with grease and creating a fire hazard, and (5) some form of fire suppression equipment. Also called an exhaust hood.

waste disposal—A kitchen appliance, usually part of a sink, that grinds or shreds food waste.

Review Questions

1. What types of mixers, food processors, and slicers are used in commercial kitchens?

2. What are the differences among solid-top, fry-top, and open-top ranges?

3. How is food cooked in a conventional oven? convection oven? microwave oven?

4. What are two types of steam cookers?

5. What is the purpose of holding tables?

6. What are three types of dishwashers?

7. Why should food and beverage department personnel consult with maintenance and engineering department personnel before purchasing equipment?

8. What are the advantages of a remote air-cooled condenser?

9. What are some common problems with equipment warranties?

10. Before hiring a contractor to maintain the operation's equipment, what questions should managers ask?

Internet Sites

For more information, visit the following Internet sites. Remember that Internet addresses can change without notice. If the site is no longer there, you can use a search engine to look for additional sites.

American Gas Association
www.aga.org

Association of Catering Equipment
Manufacturers & Importers
www.cesa.org.uk

Commercial Food Equipment Service
Association
www.cfesa.com

Foodservice Consultants Society
International
www.fcsi.org

Foodservice Equipment Reports
www.fermag.com

Food Warming Equipment, Inc.
www.fweco.com

Groen
www.groen.com

Hardt Equipment
www.hardt.ca

International Foodservice
Manufacturers Association
www.ifmaworld.com

North American Association of Food
Equipment Manufacturers
www.nafem.org

Stephan Machinery Corp.
www.stephan-usa.com

Underwriters Laboratories Inc.
www.ul.com

Univex
www.univexcorp.com

Appendix A

Sample Maintenance Procedures for Kitchen Employees Gas-Powered Equipment

Courtesy of the American Gas Association, Arlington, Virginia.

Appliance	What To Look For	What To Do	How Often	General Pointers
RANGES OPEN TOP CLOSED TOP FRY TOP	Accumulations of grease and dirt that cause corrosion, uneven performance, excessive fuel consumption.	OPEN TOP RANGE: After top grids are entirely cooled, soak in water and a good grease solvent, first removing encrusted matter by scraping off.	Daily.	If it is a closed top range, be sure the cooks understand the arrangement of burners and all the variations of settings to give varying heat on different sections of the top. Then arrange pots and pans to use minimum of heat.
		OPEN TOP: grates and burners should be boiled in a solution of sal soda or other grease solvent. Clean clogged burner parts with stiff wire or ice pick.	Weekly.	* * *
	Proper adjustment of burners. Excessive gas flow to a burner will shorten the life of the range, raise the gas bill and lower operating efficiency. Floating flames and lazy flames with indistinct cones should be corrected.	CLOSED TOP RANGE: After top plates have cooled somewhat, rub vigorously with heavy burlap or steel wool. Remove any grease or dirt lodged under flanges, under lids, rings or plates. Never slop water over range top.	Daily.	Remember, water boils at 212°F (100°C) and can't get hotter by turning the gas higher. Turn down open burners as soon as pots begin to boil. Turn off when not in use. It is seldom necessary to keep the entire area of the closed top at the peak of heat. Often one burner turned low will do the job.
		Have maintenance personnel check all burner adjustments and connections. Tips of flames (when turned on full) should just touch the bottom of the cooking vessel on an "open top" and just touch the undersurface of the plates on a closed top range.	Twice a Year or Oftener.	* * * Turn burner cock handles gently. Keep them greased and adjusted to work easily without sticking. Special high temperature valve grease must be used.

Appliance	*What To Look For*	*What To Do*	*How Often*	*General Pointers*
OVENS CABINET BAKING ROASTING RANGE	Grit and dirt. Encrusted bottoms and linings destroy sheet metal parts. Be sure doors close snugly so no heat escapes. Settling of floors under oven may put appliance out of true, cause uneven heating and unequal strain on metal parts.	Remove boil-overs and spill-overs promptly before material has time to carbonize. Wail until oven is cool and then wipe bottoms and linings with damp (not wet) cloth. Scrape off encrusted material. Never throw water on oven decks to cool them. Guard against broken door hinges and cracks that allow heat to escape by carefully cleaning all crumbs and encrusted matter from around opening. Don't slam or stand on oven doors. Check level of oven. Have maintenance personnel check the oven periodically—burners, thermostats and all working parts.	Daily. Once or Twice a Year.	Learn the exact time required for pre-heating to the temperatures needed. Set thermostat at desired temperature. Higher settings will not shorten pre-heat time but will waste fuel. * * * Schedule roasting and baking to take full advantage of "receding" heat. With large ovens, plan the baking so as not to have to bring oven up to full heat more than once or twice a day. * * * Use low temperature for meat roasting. Saves food and fuel.
DEEP FAT FRYERS COUNTER HEAVY DUTY	Smoking fat means temperature is too high or fat is broken down. Accumulated food crumbs should be removed. Gum in kettle denotes need for thorough cleaning.	Drain fryer and filter fat in commercial filter or through cheese cloth. Wash kettle with hot alkaline solution. Rinse with clear water and $1/2$ cup vinegar. Dry kettle with cloth, not by heat of burner. Replace the fat before lighting the gas burner. Note: When using solid fat with (a) tube type fryers—pack fat around tubes; (b) open pot fryers—set on melt cycle.	Daily. Weekly.	Use different fat for oily foods (mackerel, nutmeg, etc.) than for foods with water soluble flavors (potatoes, onions, etc.). * * * Taste fat for quality. Replace it regularly. Poor fat cannot produce good food.
GRIDDLES RANGE COUNTER	Clean, properly cured frying surface.	Use of spatula or metal scraper to keep surface free of encrusted matter during use. Wipe frequently with heavy grease-absorbent cloth. Polish with griddle stone. Do not scratch! Empty and wash grease receptacle.	Daily.	Don't overheat the griddle. Turn down burners during slack period. * * * A low or medium flame is best for light frying. Only heavy frying requires burner on full. * * * Use thermostat if the griddle is so equipped. It will save money.

Appliance	What To Look For	What To Do	How Often	General Pointers
BROILERS HEAVY DUTY SALAMAN- DER RANGE COUNTER	An accumulation of grease in a broiler will cause excessive smoking, lower production effi- ciency and quality, shorten life of equip- ment.	Empty grease pan and wash with mild sol- vent solution. Wash drip shields and grids. If necessary, scrape grid with three-cor- nered metal scraper. Scrub the whole broil- er chamber and body front.	Daily.	
	Faulty operation of burn- ers. Correct operation of burners makes a world of difference in broiling costs and in uniformity of finished product. A clear flame with a dis- tinct inner cone is best. No floating flames al- lowed. Flames should never strike directly on refractor elements but should just wipe the sur- face.	Clean burners to be sure openings and air shutters are free of lint and grease, using a fine wire to remove obstructions. Handle ceramic refractor units carefully.	Monthly or Oftener.	Turn flame low when broiler is idling. * * * Don't try to broil meat too fast. Longer broiling time at moderate tem- peratures retains juice, flavor and tenderness better than the "burn 'em and serve 'em" tech- nique. Also saves gas.
		Burners should be checked by experienced maintenance personnel for adjustment.	Twice a Year or Oftener.	* * * With a combination broiler-griddle, arrange the menu so both griddle top and broiler chamber are used.
	Watch for cracked or bro- ken ceramics in refractor type broiler.	Replace damaged elements promptly.	Daily.	
HOT FOOD STORAGE TABLE	Don't allow grease and stains to accumulate on stainless steel or nickel and chrome plated parts and surfaces.	Apply a good non-abrasive metal polish to stainless steel and plated parts and surface.	Daily.	If various sections of the storage table are con- trolled by thermostats, learn the proper tem- perature for holding various foods. * * *
		All insets should be thoroughly washed.	Daily.	The hot food storage ta- ble or steam table is not a cooking appliance. It is designed to hold cooked foods at proper serving temperatures.

Appliance	What To Look For	What To Do	How Often	General Pointers
COFFEE URN	A coffee urn must be clean at all times to make good coffee. Residue oils and deposits on the inside of an urn can spoil the best grade of coffee.	Drain leftover coffee from the urn and remove urn bag or metal basket. Wash in clean, cold water (never use soap).	After Each Brew.	Keep urn bags immersed in cold water when not in use. * * * When not in use, keep enough fresh water in the urn to register on the gauge. * * * Use of a thermostat will prevent overheating of coffee during holding periods and preserve coffee quality.
		Clean the liners. Rinse with hot water and drain. Pour 2 gallons of boiling water into each urn. Add reliable urn cleaner material according to instructions. Scrub inside of urn with an urn brush—drain and rinse. Then drain again.	Daily.	
		Clean glass gauges with a gauge brush and rinse. Replace nut and close faucet.	Daily.	
		Drain and refill water jackets twice. Clean urn covers and cups. Clean exterior.	Twice a Week.	
		Clean liners by boiling cleaning solution and water. Turn off the heat; scrub inside wall. Then drain, refill and boil. Drain again.	Weekly.	
		Clean faucet openings—taking faucet apart and scrubbing inside with urn solution. Rinse and return to place. When clean, allow fresh water to run through faucet and other parts.	Weekly.	
GAS TOASTER	Accumulation of crumbs in trays and moving parts.	When the toaster is cool, clean the outside surface. Clean the slanted guide. Remove trays and wash thoroughly in warm water and dry. See that the chain is kept clean and clean frame. Excess crumbs should be removed with a soft brush. Damp cloth and fine abrasive will satisfactorily clean steel surfaces.	Daily.	During idling periods, turn thermostat to lowest setting to save gas and prolong life of appliance.
THERMO-STATS BULB ROD	Failure of a thermostat to control properly does not necessarily mean it is defective. Trouble may be due to improper bypass adjustment.	Call maintenance personnel to locate and remedy trouble. Don't try to adjust or recalibrate thermostat.	Regular Check-Up Periodically.	Don't twist thermostat dials roughly. * * * Learn proper temperature for different foods.
		Remove all grease and dirt from exposed parts.	Daily.	

Appendix B

Sample Instructions for Ice-Maker Maintenance

TASK BREAKDOWN # B b 2

TASK NAME: Clean Ice Machines

POLICY STATEMENT: "The Maintenance Staff services ice machines quarterly to reduce maintenance costs and prolong the life of the equipment. The servicing of ice machines is reported as part of the Preventive Maintenance Program."

EQUIPMENT NEEDED: All-Purpose Cleaner, Rags, Lime-A-Way, Bleach, Preventive Maintenance Cards

WHAT TO DO:	HOW TO DO IT:	ADDITIONAL INFORMATION
1. Remove ice.	1. Remove the front panel. Flip the control switch to the "OFF" position. Turn off the water supply. Remove ice from the bin.	Hot water may be used to melt the ice in the bin or a scoop may be used to scoop out the ice.
2. Remove lime deposits.	2. Mix 3 ounces of Lime-A-Way in one gallon of warm water. See MSDS #12. Use the solution and a sponge to wipe out the storage bin. Put the cleaning solution in the water trough. Turn on the water supply. Flip the control switch to the "WATER PUMP" position. Let the water circulate for about 10 minutes. Drain the water-cleaner solution by removing the drain plug. Let fresh water flush through the water trough for about 30 seconds. Flip the control switch to the "OFF" position. Replace the drain plug.	

WHAT TO DO:	HOW TO DO IT:	ADDITIONAL INFORMATION
3. Sanitize the unit.	3. Mix one teaspoon sodium hypochlorate (chlorine bleach) in one gallon of water. See MSDS #1. Fill the water trough.	
	Flip the control switch to the "WATER PUMP" position. Keep adding solution until the pump is fully primed.	
	Let the solution circulate for one minute.	
	Flip the control switch to the "OFF" position.	
	Drain the solution into the bin to sanitize it.	
	Drain the bin.	
	Flip the control switch to the "WATER PUMP" position.	
	Fill the water trough with fresh water.	
	Flush the system by running the water pump at one minute intervals.	
	Drain the water trough.	
	Flush the bin out several times with clean water.	
4. Turn the unit "ON."	4. Flip the control switch to the "ICE" position.	
	Throw out the first batch of ice. Check for leaks, drainage, and proper water level and flow. If there is a problem, see the *Troubleshooting Guide—Ice Machines*.	
	Replace the front panel.	
5. Record maintenance.	5. Mark completion on the appropriate preventive maintenance card.	

TROUBLESHOOTING GUIDE—ICE MACHINES

PROBLEM:	POSSIBLE CAUSE:	SOLUTION:
1. Compressor won't run; no ice in bin	a. Service switch is in "OFF" position. b. Master switch is in "CLEAN" position. c. Power has been disconnected.	a. Flip switch to "ON" position. b. Flip switch to "ON" position and reposition safety stops. c. Connect power.
2. Compressor runs; no ice in bin	a. Water supply has been shut off. b. Use of ice has been excessive. c. Water inlet tube from valve has not been inserted in return trough.	a. Restore water supply. b. Take machine out of service. c. Insert tube in water return trough.
3. Too much water dripping on ice cubes	a. Water tank is overflowing. b. Overflow hose has not been inserted in the line drain. c. Water return trough is out of place. d. Water inlet tube from water valve has not been inserted in water return trough.	a. Check overflow tube for obstruction. b. Insert overflow hose in line drain. c. Install trough correctly. d. Install tube correctly.
4. Mineral deposits on evaporator plate	a. Mineral content in water is high.	a. Clean ice machine.
5. Ice cube too thin	a. Evaporator thermostat has been set for thin ice cubes. b. Not enough water is being circulated over evaporator.	a. Turn thermostat adjusting screw clockwise to desired cube thickness. b. Check for obstruction in water lines.

PROBLEM:	POSSIBLE CAUSE:	SOLUTION:
6. Ice cubes too thick	a. Evaporator thermostat has been set at or beyond maximum thickness.	a. Turn thermostat adjusting screw counterclockwise to desired cube thickness.
7. Condenser fan won't run during ice cycle	a. Fan blade is binding on shroud.	a. Adjust shroud to clear fan blade.
8. Water tank empty; no ice in bin	a. Shut-off valve is closed. b. Water line is obstructed. c. Water inlet tube from water valve is not directing water to tank.	a. Re-open shut-off valve. b. Clear water line of obstruction. c. Position outlet end of tube into water return trough.
9. "Milky" ice cubes	a. Water supply in tank is insufficient.	a. See #8 above.
10. Water dripping from bottom of machine	a. Drain tube is clogged.	a. Clear drain tube of obstruction.

Courtesy of La Quinta Motor Inns, Inc.

Part III

The Outer Envelope

<table>
<tr><td>

Chapter 13 Outline

The Building
    Roof
    Exterior Walls
    Windows and Doors
    Structural Frame
    Foundation
    Elevators
Exterior Facilities
    Parking Areas
    Storm Water Drainage Systems
    Utilities
    Landscaping and Grounds

</td><td>

Competencies

1. Describe a building's roof, exterior walls, windows and doors, structural frame, foundation, and elevators, including typical problems that each of these building elements have, and preventive maintenance measures that hotel managers can take to keep these building elements in good shape. (pp. 405–413)

2. Describe parking areas, including the materials parking structures are made of (concrete and/or asphalt), structural features, layout considerations, maintenance issues, and ADA requirements. (pp. 414–425)

3. Describe storm water drainage systems, utilities, and landscaping and grounds, including preventive maintenance strategies and inspection tips. (pp. 425–431)

</td></tr>
</table>

13

The Building and Exterior Facilities

The building exterior, grounds, and parking areas of hospitality businesses are the first places seen and experienced by guests. Most hospitality businesses strive for some level of curb appeal and need to maintain it. In addition, the building exterior represents the barrier between the conditioned interior of the facility and the varying and sometimes harsh conditions found in the natural environment.

IN THIS CHAPTER we will discuss the building itself—the shell that protects employees and guests and houses the electrical, HVAC, lighting, telecommunication, and other systems. We will also discuss the facilities exterior to the building— parking areas, storm water drainage systems, utilities, and landscaping and grounds—that provide parking spaces for staff members and guests, protect the building, provide the building with power and other services, and enhance the building's value.

The Building

The building envelope is made up of all the exterior elements of the building: the roof, exterior walls (including doors and windows), structural frame, and foundation. The various parts of a building must work together. If any one part is neglected, it can have an adverse effect on the others.

The functions of a building are to provide usable space and shelter people, equipment, fixtures, and furnishings from the weather. Wind, rain, snow, heat, and cold are excluded or managed by the building envelope.

Roof

The roof is a critically important part of any building. Unfortunately, the roof is often ignored until it leaks. If water gains access to the building through the roof system, great damage can result, first to the roof and later to the structural elements of the building. Interior finishes are also quickly destroyed by roof leaks. For example, a new paint job is ruined by a few minutes of water leakage.

It is not uncommon to find roofs with very few problems over a 20- to 30-year period. On the other hand, some roofs suffer partial or total failure in the first year of a building's operation. A roof's life expectancy depends on the quality of the construction materials, the skill of the builders, and the effectiveness of the preventive maintenance program.

Exhibit 1   Built-Up Roof

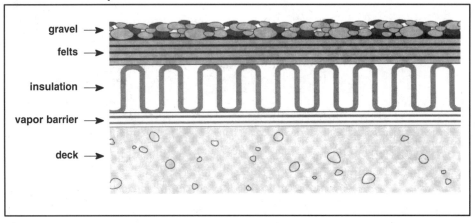

gravel →
felts →
insulation →
vapor barrier →
deck →

A major roof repair can be a very substantial investment that has a profound effect on cash flow as well as day-to-day operations. Therefore, serious efforts should be made to maintain a roof properly and extend its service life.

Basic Structure. A roof is composed of a deck and a covering. The deck is the structural material the covering is placed upon. The deck is usually made of wood, metal, or concrete. A roof system is the combination of all the components of the roof that act together to create a weather and climate barrier for the building.

There are several common types of roofing materials, including asphalt or fiberglass shingles and roll roofing, split wood shakes, sawn wood shingles, clay and concrete tile, steel and aluminum, and various types of built-up and single-ply materials. The roofing material chosen for a building will depend on factors such as economics, the shape of the roof, climate, fire resistance, durability, and aesthetics. Even marketing may play a factor—some operations have distinctive colors or shapes to their roofs that serve to identify the product to prospective guests.

The primary purpose of all of these roofing systems is to keep water from penetrating below the roofing material. For some systems, this is accomplished by having overlapping layers of roofing material oriented on the roof so that water running down the roof will not penetrate under the layers. This is the method used on many homes. For added protection, a layer of asphalt- or tar-impregnated paper called **roofing felt** is installed directly on the roof's deck.

When roofs are relatively flat, multiple layers of felt may be sealed together to form a moisture barrier. These layers are then covered with a surface dressing—often a gravel layer that (1) helps reduce damage due to ultra-violet rays, (2) provides weight to hold down insulation materials, and (3) provides a greater degree of fire protection. This type of roofing system is referred to as a built-up roof (see Exhibit 1).

Many flat roofs are built today with single-ply roofing systems. These systems are a membrane roofing system composed of large pieces of roofing material that are bonded together using heat or chemicals to form a one-piece roof system. The roofing material may adhere to the deck by mechanical means, adhesives, or by the weight of gravel used as a ballast. There are many different materials used for single-ply roofing systems, each of which has particular properties, installation requirements, and maintenance needs.

Most roof structures are pierced by a variety of building mechanical systems, the mounting locations for various equipment, and are subject to foot traffic for periodic inspections, the removal of debris, and the maintenance of equipment. In addition, most flat roofs have integral roof drains for the removal of water. All penetrations of the roof structure must be adequately sealed so that water does not enter below the roofing material at these locations. **Flashing** is installed under the roofing and up the sides of equipment and where roofs contact walls. Flashing is usually formed from sheets of aluminum or copper with edges and joints sealed with elastomeric materials.

In addition, many roofing systems include insulation as part of the roof system. In these instances, the roofing system also plays a key role in controlling energy usage of the building.

Preventive Maintenance. A preventive maintenance program should include regular inspections (before and after the most severe climatic season each year, and after each major storm), removal of all foreign objects (tree limbs, leaves, dirt, and so on), repair of blisters (pockets of air or water between layers of the roof system), exclusion of ponded water, maintenance of all flashing, and maintenance of the ballast. Just because a roof is under warranty docs not mean that it should be neglected. Indeed, failure to routinely inspect the roof may void the warranty.

Inspections. As part of the inspection process, the condition of the roof should be documented. This is especially true if a leak is found. It is then important to locate the spot and write down the conditions under which the leak occurred (such as wind direction and velocity, temperature, and so on). Also note if anyone was on the roof prior to the first time the leak was noticed. A more thorough and detailed inspection by professionals is often called for.

Exterior Walls

Exterior building walls have two basic functions:

1. To enclose the usable parts of the building

2. To provide support for higher floors and the roof system

For walls to function as intended, they must be built to provide protection against the weather and have enough structural strength to support the building.

Exterior walls are constructed of a variety of materials, such as timber, concrete, and steel. A wall may be an integral unit, or be constructed in pre-assembled units and joined together on the job site. A wall's materials and method of construction and assembly have a pronounced effect on maintenance.

Walls can be classified as bearing (supporting) or non-bearing, depending on whether they support other building elements or only themselves.

The useful life of an exterior wall depends on the type of wall and the quality of construction. In general, any exterior wall, properly maintained, should last over 100 years. Without good maintenance, a wall's useful life can be reduced dramatically.

Preventive Maintenance. Preventive maintenance activities for exterior walls include painting, cleaning, and inspecting.

Painting. Painting outside surfaces poses special problems. Wind, sun, rain, and snow can quickly take their toll if these surfaces are not properly protected. The durability of an outdoor paint job depends on many factors, such as the quality of paint selected, the extent of the surface preparation, the skill with which the paint is applied, and local climate and weather conditions.

For the longest-lasting job, top-quality paint should be selected. Surface preparation is also very important. It is a good idea to inspect for difficult areas, such as peeling paint under roof eaves or on gutters and downspouts. If the surface is not correctly prepared, the new paint will not adhere on it properly. Surface preparation should include scraping the outside surfaces clean of peeling paint and rust, and making sure that oil, grease, and dirt are removed.

Graffiti on exterior walls can be a serious problem, especially for masonry walls. The most practical method of minimizing graffiti damage to masonry walls is to apply clear sealers. When masonry pores are sealed, paint and other materials used for graffiti are prevented from penetrating the surface, making cleanup relatively easy. Acrylic sealers are the most promising of all the various sealers applied solely for protection against graffiti.

Cleaning. Cleaning is an important part of the preventive maintenance program for exterior walls. Dirt provides a much greater surface area than clean building materials, and the more surface area that is exposed to atmospheric pollutants, the greater are the possibilities that destructive chemical reactions will start. Dirty areas remain wet longer, resulting in more severe freeze/thaw cycles. And wet, dirty areas can support microorganisms that can cause disintegration, destruction, and staining.

Selecting an appropriate cleaning method can be challenging, because the composition of dirt is so complex. Acidic cleaners can be very damaging, particularly to marble and limestone, and alkaline cleaners can also be harmful. A cleaner should first be tested on a small area to make sure it will not damage the wall.

When cleaning a sealed masonry surface that has been marked with graffiti, the gentlest treatment, such as water mixed with a detergent, should be tried first. A stiff scrub brush, such as a roofing or whitewash brush, is a recommended tool. If this treatment is ineffective, a mild organic solvent, such as mineral spirits, should be tried. If the markings still won't come off, stronger solvents are necessary. These include xylol, lacquer solvents, and paint strippers. These materials may remove some of the acrylic sealer along with the markings. However, as long as the sealer kept the markings from penetrating the wall's pores, it served its purpose.

Inspections. Exterior walls should be inspected at least semi-annually. Things to look for include cracks, loose mortar, mildew, inflow or outflow of water, paint and sealant deterioration, and evidence of wall or building movement. Changes noted since the previous inspection should be investigated to determine why the change occurred. Any evidence or suspicion of wall movement should be thoroughly checked by a structural engineer.

Windows and Doors

Openings are made through a building's exterior walls for windows and doors. These windows and doors need sealants around their edges to keep moisture out, and may be weather-stripped to prevent heat loss or gain. Buildings can lose significant amounts of heat in cold months and cool air in hot months if windows and doors are not properly designed and maintained.

Windows in new, energy-efficient buildings are often fixed (cannot be opened). Casement windows open either outward or inward like a door; vertically hung windows open by sliding the lower half up. The glass in windows is referred to as glazing. Single-glazed windows have one pane of glass; double-glazed windows have two sheets of glass with air or gas in between. They provide better temperature and noise insulation than single-glazed windows. Tinted glass has a coating that reflects heat and keeps a building cooler in summer and warmer in winter.

Doors may be wooden or metallic, solid or hollow. Some doors are mostly glass, such as revolving doors. Revolving doors are used at some hospitality properties because they don't get the wear regular doors receive from constantly being opened and closed, and because they reduce the amount of outside air that gets into the building. Fire safety codes may stipulate that a regular door be installed next to a revolving door as an emergency exit.

Inspections. Windows should be inspected regularly for ease of opening and closing, loose-fitting frames, cracked glazing, damaged hardware, deteriorated caulking, and rust (for windows with metal frames).

Doors also should be inspected periodically. Problems to look for include damage to hinges, locks, and other hardware; damaged frames; surface deterioration; and improper alignment.

Structural Frame

The structural frame of a building is normally thought of as the "skeleton" that provides support for the entire building. If there is failure in the structural frame, the entire building has serious problems. Typical construction materials used in structural framing include steel, concrete (reinforced, pre-stressed), and ordinary or heavy timber.

Preventive Maintenance. Preventive maintenance efforts needed for the structural frame include:

- Inspecting all visible structural members
- Inspecting other building features that might give telltale signs of structural problems (for example, cracks in walls, floors, or ceilings)
- Checking doors and windows for proper alignment and closure

Cracks in walls can indicate underlying structural problems.
(Photo by Jeffrey Lallas)

- Tightening all connections

- Weatherproofing (including painting) structural elements

- Maintaining fireproofing materials

- Checking reinforced concrete members

- Preserving structural steel members

Inspections. The structural frame is usually not exposed to view, but can be inspected fairly easily through access panels and "behind-the-scenes" areas. This inspection should take place at least once a year, and answer at least the following questions:

- Have there been any changes since the previous inspection?
- Are bolts tight and welds intact?
- Is rust at an acceptable level?
- Are structural beams deformed or bent?
- Are fireproofing materials in good condition?
- Are anchors and attachments in good condition?

For multi-story buildings this inspection should be supervised by a structural engineer.

Foundation

Foundations are traditionally constructed of stone or concrete and rest on a solid, underground footing base. If firm foundation material is not available at a reasonable depth, it may be necessary to go deeper by using piles. The decision on footing depth and type is usually left to the architect and structural engineers.

Frost walls commonly surround a building in cold climates and are usually part of the foundation system. Their primary purpose is to exclude entry of frost into the foundation, and their structural uses are normally very limited.

The foundation of a building is structurally designed to carry the various loads of the building: **dead load** (the weight of the building itself), **live load** (the weight of the people, equipment, furnishings, and so on within the building), and loads and stresses imposed by nature (wind, rain, snow, earthquakes). Frequent inspections and a preventive maintenance program are recommended to keep the foundation intact. If maintenance is neglected until it becomes remedial in nature, it is usually too late, and serious problems probably already exist.

Foundation walls commonly also serve as basement walls. In these cases the foundation walls take on the added load caused by lateral pressures from the soil. Normal construction techniques require that foundation walls serving as basement walls be waterproofed. However, many old structures have no waterproofing, and many new structures have inadequate waterproofing systems.

Preventive Maintenance. Preventive maintenance on foundations and footings is difficult to do, since these structural elements are mostly hidden and inaccessible. However, there are some things that can be done:

- If there are footing drains, keep the outlets open, so that no water stands in the drains.
- Keep rodent covers over all drain tiles.
- Relieve excessive water pressure from the outside.
- Maintain the integrity of the exterior waterproofing. If any excavation is done near the foundation, be sure the membrane is not disturbed.

Inspections. Foundations are often difficult to inspect, and generally it is impractical to inspect the underground portion of the foundation system. However, it is essential that the upper portion receive an annual inspection.

The inspector should look for at least the following:

- Any cracks through the foundation wall

- Evidence of water going down adjacent to the foundation

- Spalling or crumbling concrete

- Moisture penetrating the foundation walls into basement areas

Elevators

The building shell must make allowances for the building's "transportation system"—the hallways, stairways, and elevators that are an integral part of the physical facility.[1] Because of the elevator's importance and cost, we will discuss elevators and elevator maintenance in this section.

Components. Elevator systems are made up of several components. A cable elevator system has an elevator shaft, a car or cab, guide rails, cables, counterweights, safety devices, and an elevator motor that supplies the electrical power (see Exhibit 2).

The car is the only component of an elevator system guests see. The car moves passengers and goods up and down within a vertical shaft. Guide rails are positioned in the shaft; the elevator rides on wheels along the guide rails. Cables attach the car to counterweights that move in the opposite direction of the car; counterweights help offset the weight of the car and its passengers, so less energy is needed to move the car. Safety devices keep the car from moving past the lowermost and uppermost floors it serves and properly level the car at each floor. Should the cables holding the car break, rail clamps will slow or stop the descent of the car, and bumpers installed at the bottom of the shaft will absorb the impact, limiting passenger injuries and physical damage to the car.

There are two basic types of elevator systems: **cable** and **hydraulic.** The basic difference between them is that cable elevators move up and down with the help of cables and counterweights; a hydraulic elevator has no cables or counterweights. Instead, the car is mounted on a giant piston inside a cylinder. The cylinder extends into the ground to a depth equal to the height the elevator will rise. An electric pump forces oil into the cylinder, displacing the piston and raising the car. The oil pours out of the cylinder through valves when the car goes down. Hydraulic elevators can only be used in buildings of six stories or less. Cable elevators are used in buildings with more stories.

Maintenance. Many elevator components are covered under a maintenance contract with the elevator's manufacturer. Day-to-day maintenance—cleaning, inspecting, and lubricating—and some minor repair work is typically the responsibility of the property's maintenance department. Because the car is what guests see—and what they use to judge the condition of the entire elevator system—the car should be well maintained at all times. The emergency telephone installed in the car should be checked to make sure it is in working order. Maintenance personnel should ride in the car every day to check ride quality and listen for unusual sounds. Swaying or vibration as the elevator car moves is usually caused by poor

Exhibit 2   Cable Elevator System

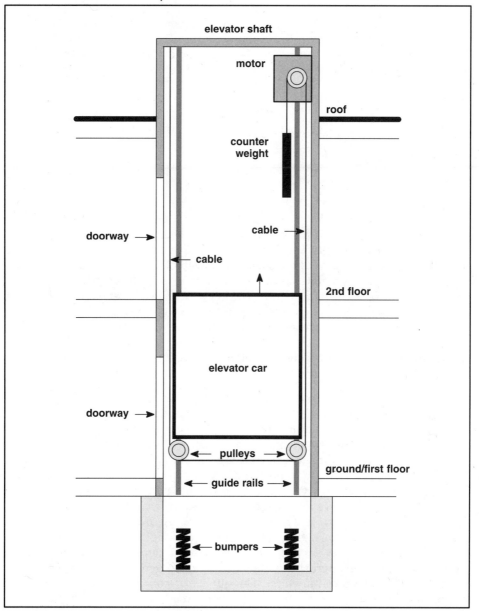

guide-rail alignment, worn car wheels, or incorrect adjustments. The doors should also be checked at this time. Are they opening and closing properly?

The movable parts of the elevator system must be inspected, cleaned, and lubricated periodically. Worn-out cables must be replaced by the elevator's manufacturer.

Exterior Facilities

Some essential facilities are located exterior to the main building. Many of these are underground, and, in a classic illustration of "out of sight, out of mind," are not thought about until there are problems. The function of exterior facilities is to provide essential support services to the building. Common types of exterior facilities are:

- Parking areas
- Storm water drainage systems
- Utilities
- Landscaping and grounds

Parking Areas

Almost every hotel has a parking area of some description for guests and employees. Some center-city hotels may rent space in a municipal parking garage, and the garage is maintained by the city. But most hotels are on their own when it comes to parking area maintenance. In this section we will provide some useful tips on how to properly maintain a parking area. Since most parking lots and garages are built of concrete or asphalt, the section will open with a discussion of these materials and what causes them to deteriorate. Next there are sections on parking lots and garages and the activities necessary to properly maintain them. The section concludes with a discussion of parking lot accessibility requirements mandated by the Americans with Disabilities Act.

Concrete. Concrete is a simple building material formed by a somewhat complex chemical process. Concrete's durability, versatility, and economy have made it the most used construction material in the world.[2] It's no wonder that many developers, builders, and building owners use it to construct their parking lots.

    Fundamentals of concrete. Concrete is basically a mixture of paste and aggregates.[3] The paste is composed of portland cement, water, and entrapped air. Portland cement combines slowly with water to form a hard solid mass. Aggregates are the inert materials in the concrete such as sand, gravel, and crushed stone. Aggregates make up 60 to 75 percent of the volume (70 to 85 percent by weight) of most concrete mixes. Fine aggregates generally consist of natural sand or crushed stone with most particles smaller than .2 inches (.51 centimeters). Coarse aggregates consist of gravel or crushed stone with particles generally between $3/8$ and $1 1/2$ inches (.95 and 3.8 centimeters). The quality of concrete depends to a great extent on the quality of the paste. In properly made concrete, each particle of aggregate is completely coated with paste and all of the spaces between aggregate particles are completely filled with paste.

    Hardening of concrete is a chemical process called "hydration." Hydration is the chemical reaction between cement and water that forms a rocklike material which bonds to aggregate particles, steel, and other materials. Hydration is not the same as drying. In fact, dry cement does not hydrate because with no water the chemical reaction cannot take place. The more cement hydrates, the stronger it becomes.

Hardened concrete becomes a strong, non-combustible, durable, and abrasion-resistant building material that requires little maintenance. However, concrete's relatively low **tensile strength** (the greatest longitudinal stress it can bear without tearing apart) causes it to crack. Exhibit 3 illustrates how cracks can result from shrinkage. Think of a concrete slab as made up of a series of thin vertical segments. Because the top shrinks more than the bottom, each segment becomes slightly narrower at the top than at the bottom, so the segments become slightly wedge-shaped. Because the segments remain in full contact with each other, the slab tends to curl at the edges. This creates enough stress to cause the concrete to crack when loads are applied to its surface.

The existence of a crack usually does not mean the concrete is in danger of collapse or disintegration. Cracks are of serious concern only when they are of a type or frequency that cannot be considered typical for a particular structure. Since a certain amount of cracking is usually unavoidable, builders have developed ways to reduce and control cracking. Joints are the most effective method of controlling unsightly cracking. Joints do not eliminate cracking; they are used to predetermine and control the location of cracks. Cracks along neat, straight joints are much easier to seal and maintain than are random cracks.

Many concrete problems, especially in concrete parking lots, decks, and ramps, can be avoided by applying a high-quality sealant. Sealants fill the pores of the concrete surface and protect it against penetration by waterborne de-icing salts and other contaminants. There are many sealants on the market. Professional advice should be sought as to which is best suited for a particular use and a particular concrete area's exposure conditions.

Concrete deterioration. Concrete deterioration includes crazing, leaching, the deterioration caused by freeze/thaw cycles, and spalling. Most of these problems can be controlled, or at least reduced, by the periodic application of a high-quality protective sealant.

Crazing refers to fine hairline cracks that form a map-like pattern on the surface of concrete. Just as with many other concrete cracks, crazing is caused by shrinkage. These tiny cracks generally do not seriously affect the usability of a concrete floor. However, if the cracks are wider than hairline width the problem may become quite severe and lead to the concrete's disintegration.

Leaching is caused by frequent water migration through a cement floor or through the cracks in the floor. As water migrates through, it takes along part of the cementing constituents and deposits them as a white film, stain, or stalactite on the underside of the concrete. Over a period of years, this process weakens concrete and is accelerated by porous or perpetually moist concrete.

Successive freeze/thaw cycles and the resulting disruption of paste and aggregate eventually will damage concrete. In northern climates, freeze/thaw cycles can cause substantial damage. As the moisture in concrete freezes, the concrete expands. When spring thaws start, the concrete's surface thaws first, and has a tendency to shrink back to its original volume, but the frost continues to hold the expanded concrete below the surface in place. This uneven thawing causes the

Exhibit 3   Concrete Shrinkage and Curling

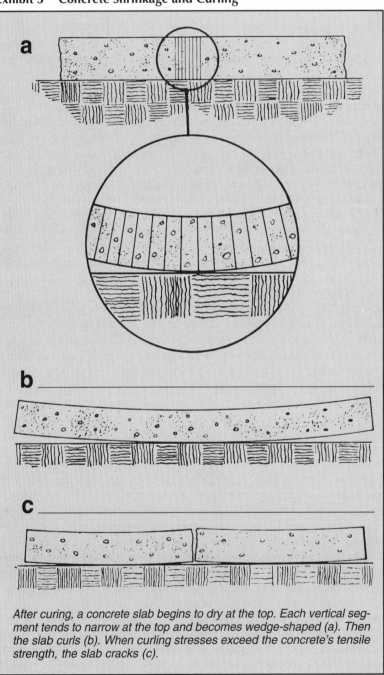

After curing, a concrete slab begins to dry at the top. Each vertical segment tends to narrow at the top and becomes wedge-shaped (a). Then the slab curls (b). When curling stresses exceed the concrete's tensile strength, the slab cracks (c).

Source: American Concrete Institute, *Concrete Craftsman Series—Slabs on Grade* (Detroit, Mich.: American Concrete Institute, 1982), p. 6.

beginning of surface cracks that allow spring rains to penetrate the concrete. When freezing temperatures return, these cracks are widened because the moisture in the cracks freezes and expands. The freeze/thaw cycles are repeated, with cracks continuing to grow wider. Finally, the surface area breaks free of the underlying material and begins to break up during a thaw period. The weakened material breaks loose under the movement of traffic and a pothole is formed.

Reinforced concrete contains embedded bars, wires, or strands made of steel or other materials. Corrosion of the embedded reinforcement can lead to dish-shaped cavities called **spalls.** Metallic corrosion is an electrochemical process that induces progressive deterioration of reinforced concrete. Rust, a byproduct of corrosion, occupies a volume at least 2.5 times that of the parent metal. Therefore, as rust develops on metal surfaces, the metal expands, causing pressure that forms cracks in the concrete surface.

The depth of concrete over and below embedded reinforcement is perhaps the single most important aspect of design and construction that can help prevent spalling. Floor slabs with less than recommended cover over reinforcement, and subject to a lot of de-icing salts, undergo rapid and severe spalling. When preparing maintenance programs for parking facilities, maintenance managers should pay special attention to the areas where reinforcement occurs near the concrete's surface.

Repairing concrete. Repairs to deteriorated concrete range in complexity from simple cleaning and sealing to complete reconstruction. If done properly, patching is generally an effective method of repairing isolated spalls or potholes (see Exhibit 4). A good patch must be durable and must bond well to the concrete surrounding it. Although many patching materials have been tried, the most widely used and effective are generally of portland cement concrete. Other patching materials include epoxy and polymer concretes.

When the area to be patched covers a significant part of the concrete's surface area, an overlay may be more cost-effective than isolated patching. In the case of a concrete floor within an enclosed structure (such as a parking garage), overlays add thickness to the original floor, reduce headroom, and increase the floor's weight. Poorly planned overlays can also cause serious drainage problems. Consulting a qualified engineer can help ensure that the overlay does not cause more problems than it solves.

Asphalt. Asphalt is a dark brown or black thermoplastic material refined from petroleum. Asphalt cement is asphalt that is further refined to make a semi-solid material suitable for paving and other industrial uses. Asphalt is valued because it is strong, durable, waterproof, and resistant to the action of most acids and salts.

Fundamentals of asphalt. Asphalt concrete is asphalt cement combined with aggregate to make a dense paving material. Just as with the aggregate used for cement, there are various types of aggregate, from fine to coarse, used with asphalt. The asphalt cement and aggregate must be heated before they are combined—the asphalt cement to make it fluid, the aggregate to make it dry and hot enough to keep the asphalt cement fluid while it is coating the aggregate particles.

Asphalt paving mixes may be designed and produced from a wide range of aggregate blends, each suited to specific uses or localities. Different types of mixes

Exhibit 4   Concrete Patching

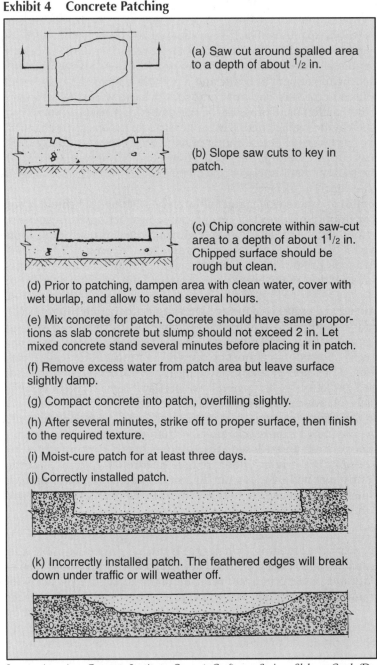

(a) Saw cut around spalled area to a depth of about $1/2$ in.

(b) Slope saw cuts to key in patch.

(c) Chip concrete within saw-cut area to a depth of about $1^1/2$ in. Chipped surface should be rough but clean.

(d) Prior to patching, dampen area with clean water, cover with wet burlap, and allow to stand several hours.

(e) Mix concrete for patch. Concrete should have same proportions as slab concrete but slump should not exceed 2 in. Let mixed concrete stand several minutes before placing it in patch.

(f) Remove excess water from patch area but leave surface slightly damp.

(g) Compact concrete into patch, overfilling slightly.

(h) After several minutes, strike off to proper surface, then finish to the required texture.

(i) Moist-cure patch for at least three days.

(j) Correctly installed patch.

(k) Incorrectly installed patch. The feathered edges will break down under traffic or will weather off.

Source: American Concrete Institute, *Concrete Craftsman Series—Slabs on Grade* (Detroit, Mich.: American Concrete Institute, 1982), p. 65, and Steven H. Kosmatka and William C. Panarese, *Design and Control of Concrete Mixtures,* 13th ed. (Skokie, Ill.: Portland Cement Association, 1990), p. 118.

are preferred, depending on the geographic area. Specifications for asphalt mixes have been created by the American Association of State Highway and Transportation Officials and the American Society for Testing and Materials.

The soil base must be carefully prepared before the asphalt mix is spread. Once spread, the asphalt must be compacted with steamrollers or other heavy equipment. Squeezing out the air in the asphalt mixture and compressing the aggregate and asphalt together strengthens the pavement and makes it more waterproof. In fact, compaction is the single most important factor affecting the quality and life of an asphalt pavement.

Asphalt deterioration. Asphalt problems can result from poorly compacted soil underneath the asphalt or from surface failures caused by weathering or wearing, insufficient asphalt, too much asphalt, unstable mixtures, or poor drainage.

Repairing asphalt. Small asphalt cracks should be cleaned with a broom or a leaf blower to get rid of surface debris. If there are plants growing in the cracks, they should be pulled out (if possible) and weed killer applied to the cracks. It may be necessary to flush the cracks with water to remove coatings of clay or dirt. The cracks must be completely dry before repair work begins, however.

Once clean, small asphalt cracks can be filled with a hot, rubberized crack filler. Squeegeeing the filler into the crack strengthens the repair and makes for a smoother surface. If there are only a few small cracks to repair, they can be repaired manually. If there is a large area of cracking, it may be necessary to apply a slurry seal instead. A slurry seal is a mixture of emulsified asphalt (asphalt cement thinned with water), fine aggregate, mineral filler, and water applied in a uniform, thin coat to an existing pavement.

Repairing large cracks and potholes in asphalt is similar to repairing potholes in concrete. First, the edges of the hole should be squared vertically, and all damaged or loose material removed from the hole. Then a tack coat—a thin, sticky layer of emulsified asphalt—should be applied to the sides and bottom of the hole. The hole can then be filled with an asphalt patching mix and compacted.

The patching mix should be soft and pliable for easy shoveling, raking, and shaping. If possible, the hole should be dry before the tack coat and patching mix is applied. If the hole is wet, the tack coat or patching mix may not stick and the mix will be forced out of the hole by traffic. That is why many potholes repaired in wet winter conditions have to be repaired again in the spring or summer.

Skin patches are generally used to re-level asphalt areas that have settled. Again, the edges of the area to be patched should be squared vertically and the area sprayed with a tack coat to make the asphalt mix stick to the existing pavement.

Parking Lots. In this section we will discuss a parking lot's structural features, layout considerations for parking lots, and parking lot maintenance.

Structural features. The structural features of a ground-level parking lot include the subgrade, subbase, and surface course (see Exhibit 5). The **subgrade** is the soil that has been prepared and compacted to support the surface course. The **subbase** is a layer of sand, gravel, crushed stone, or other granular material that is sometimes placed over the prepared subgrade to enhance uniformity of support, bring the site to the desired grade, and serve as a cushion between the surface

Exhibit 5   Structural Features of a Ground-Level Parking Lot

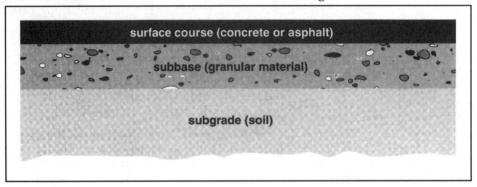

course and the subgrade. The **surface course** usually consists of concrete or asphalt and provides the wearing surface for vehicles to drive on. It also functions as a sealant, preventing moisture from entering the subbase and the subgrade.

The performance of a ground-level parking lot depends in large part on the strength and uniformity of the subgrade. Cracks, slab settlement, and structural failure can often be traced to an inadequately prepared subgrade. The subgrade should be well drained; of uniform bearing capacity; level or properly sloped; and free of sod, organic matter, and frost.

The surface of a parking lot will be subjected to varying, but predictable, vehicle loads throughout its lifetime. To help the parking lot designer determine the optimum thickness of the surface course, the facility's general manager or maintenance manager must supply the designer with estimates of:

- The types of vehicles that will use the parking lot (for example, passenger cars, light trucks, heavy trucks)

- The number of vehicles of each type

- Typical vehicle loads

- The number of vehicles expected in the parking lot each day

These estimates, and traffic studies done for similar types of facilities, can help a designer establish structural design requirements. Exhibit 6 indicates concrete slab thicknesses appropriate under various traffic loads.

Surface parking lots should be designed and constructed to drain well, dry quickly, and be puddle-free. If possible, the grounds surrounding a parking lot should be sloped so that rain water drains away from the lot rather than toward it. In addition, the lot should be designed to provide adequate drainage in all gutters, around all traffic islands and structures, and especially in intersections and pedestrian walkways. Roof drains should not discharge large amounts of water onto a parking lot because maintenance problems can result, such as erosion of surface materials, build-up of algae growth (under certain conditions), and the creation of icy spots in cold weather.

Exhibit 6   Recommended Concrete Thickness for Various Traffic Loads

Allowable Load Applications for Various Slab Thicknesses (20-yr. life)

Type of vehicle	Representative axle loads (lb)		Allowable number of passes per week for indicated slab thickness				
	Front	Rear	4 in.	5 in.	6 in.	7 in.	8 in.
	2,500	2,500	Unlimited				
	2,500	2,500	Unlimited				
	9,000	18,000	*		4	40	Unlimited
	8,000	32,000	*		*	20	Unlimited
	8,000	32,000	*		*	10	Unlimited

*Occasional loads only - consult pavement design manuals.

Source: *Concrete Parking Areas: By Definition—A Classic,* a brochure produced by the Portland Cement Association, Skokie, Illinois.

Layout considerations. Layout considerations for parking lots include determining parking dimensions and establishing parking controls to channel and segregate traffic. Parking lot entrances and exits should be well-defined and located so as to have as little effect as possible on traffic movement on adjacent streets. Local standards usually prescribe lengths of acceleration/deceleration lanes at entrances and minimum distances from intersections. Local zoning regulations usually dictate the minimum number of parking spaces required for various types of buildings. Many local regulations also specify minimum sizes of parking spaces.

A parking lot is not usually expected to serve the broad spectrum of traffic—from very light vehicles to the heaviest trucks—that highways and streets must serve. When parking lots are planned to serve heavy delivery trucks as well as light vehicles, traffic controls are usually imposed to separate and channel the heavy trucks away from areas designed for automobiles and light trucks. If vehicles carry loads beyond those allowed for in a parking lot's structural design, structural failures result. A common cause of structural failures is the garbage truck, which is very heavy and must usually cross the entire parking lot to reach refuse containers at the rear of the property. Some properties install a separate cement pad near the refuse containers for garbage trucks, designed especially for the loading conditions imposed.

Maintenance. A well-designed and well-maintained surface parking lot should have a service life expectancy of 15 to 20 years. The following list indicates typical parking lot maintenance tasks and the frequency with which they should be performed:

Maintenance Task	Frequency
Surface cleaning	Daily
Security inspection	Weekly
Drainage inspection	Monthly
Parking control inspection	Monthly
Waterproofing	Monthly
Minor repair of surface cracks	Monthly
Structural repairs	Monthly
Snow and ice removal	As needed

Each of these tasks should be incorporated into an overall preventive maintenance program.

Parking Garages. Parking garages are commonly constructed of reinforced concrete, prestressed concrete, or concrete surfaces over a steel frame structure. A parking garage is not just a series of concrete floors for parking vehicles. A parking garage also has drainage structures, underground drainage systems, exhaust and ventilating fans, lights, traffic control markings, guardrails, and access ramps.

Maintenance. A well-designed and properly maintained parking garage should have a service life expectancy well in excess of 30 years. The maintenance plan for a parking garage should include regularly scheduled cleaning, inspections, and maintenance activities. In addition, the plan should specify how managers evaluate the effectiveness of the maintenance program.

Parking garage maintenance can vary widely because of features unique to some garages that require special maintenance care. The following items indicate typical maintenance tasks and the frequency with which they should be performed:

Maintenance Task	Frequency
Cleaning	Daily
Parking control equipment inspection	Daily
Safety checks	Daily
Security system inspection	Daily
Painting and striping	Annually
Snow and ice removal	As needed

Each of these tasks should be incorporated into an overall preventive maintenance program.

ADA Accessibility Requirements for Parking Areas. The Americans with Disabilities Act (ADA) requires hospitality businesses to modify their parking areas to make them accessible to people with disabilities.[4] The law requires that modifications must be made that are "readily achievable." However, there are no clear guidelines defining what is meant by readily achievable.

In general, it is recommended that any modifications be completed in accordance with the Justice Department's appendix to the law, called the Americans with Disabilities Act Accessibility Guidelines (ADAAG).

Accessible parking spaces. The ADAAG calls for a sliding scale of **accessible parking spaces** from 4 percent in parking lots with 1 to 100 spaces down to 2 percent when there are more than 1,000 spaces:

Total Parking in Lot	Required Minimum Number of Accessible Spaces
1 to 25	1
26 to 50	2
51 to 75	3
76 to 100	4
101 to 150	5
151 to 200	6
201 to 300	7
301 to 400	8
401 to 500	9
501 to 1,000	2% of total
over 1,000	20, plus 1 for each 100 over 1,000

Accessible parking spaces serving a particular building must be located on the shortest accessible route of travel from adjacent parking to an accessible entrance. Accessible parking spaces are reserved by a sign showing the symbol of accessibility. Signs designating parking spaces for disabled people should be at the front of accessible parking spaces and mounted high enough above the ground so they can readily be seen from a driver's seat. Also, signs must be located so they cannot be obscured by a vehicle parked in the space.

Accessible parking spaces must be wide enough to allow a wheelchair user to open the vehicle door, transfer to a wheelchair, and easily exit to the walkway. These parking spaces should have a minimum width of 13 feet (4 meters)—8 feet (2.4 meters) for the vehicle and 5 feet (1.5 meters) for an access aisle (see Exhibit 7).

Access aisles allow guests to exit and enter vehicles with a device, such as a wheelchair, and travel to the sidewalk or entrance. Access aisles cannot be restricted by planters, curbs, or wheel stops. As shown in Exhibit 7, adjoining accessible parking spaces may share a common access aisle. An essential consideration for any design is having the access aisle level with the parking space. Since a person with a disability must maneuver within the access aisle, the aisle cannot include a ramp or sloped area. The access aisle must either blend with the accessible route or have a curb ramp.

An **accessible route** is an obstruction-free route that connects the parking area to an accessible entrance of the facility. Curb ramps must be provided wherever an accessible route crosses a curb. The minimum width of a curb ramp is 3 feet (91 centimeters), exclusive of flared sides. Transitions from ramps to walks, gutters, or streets must be flush and free of abrupt changes. Also, no obstructions should hang over the accessible route that would present hazards to a person who has a visual impairment. The route should be a minimum of 36 inches (91 centimeters) wide to allow for people who use crutches or wheelchairs and individuals carrying bags. Exhibit 8 shows optional dimensions for accessible walks.

Exhibit 7   Accessible Parking Spaces

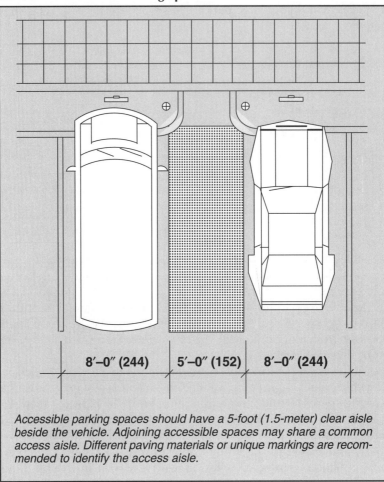

8'–0" (244) | 5'–0" (152) | 8'–0" (244)

Accessible parking spaces should have a 5-foot (1.5-meter) clear aisle beside the vehicle. Adjoining accessible spaces may share a common access aisle. Different paving materials or unique markings are recommended to identify the access aisle.

Source: Thomas D. Davies, Jr., and Kim A. Beasley, *Design for Hospitality: Planning for Accessible Hotels & Motels* (New York: Nichols Publishing, 1988), p. 29.

When accessible parking spaces are designed to meet minimum requirements, at least one (and 12.5 percent of all accessible spaces) must be designated as "van accessible." The access aisle for a van-accessible space must be 8 feet (2.4 meters) wide. A sign is needed to alert van users to the presence of the wider aisle, but the space is not intended to be restricted only to vans. (It should also be remembered that high-top vans, which disabled people or transportation services often use, require higher clearances in parking garages than automobiles.)

An alternative to providing a percentage of van accessible parking spaces is the use of "universal" parking space design. With this design, all accessible spaces are 11 feet (3.4 meters) wide with an access aisle that is 5 feet (1.5 meters) wide. With this design, no "van accessible" signs are needed because all spaces can

Exhibit 8   Optional Dimensions for Accessible Walks

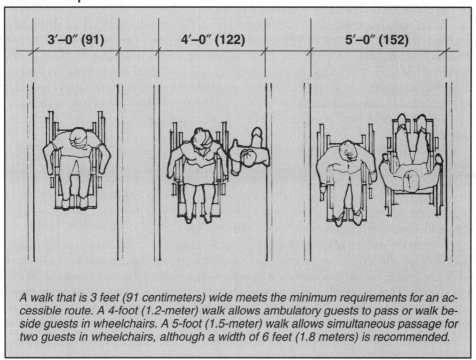

A walk that is 3 feet (91 centimeters) wide meets the minimum requirements for an accessible route. A 4-foot (1.2-meter) walk allows ambulatory guests to pass or walk beside guests in wheelchairs. A 5-foot (1.5-meter) walk allows simultaneous passage for two guests in wheelchairs, although a width of 6 feet (1.8 meters) is recommended.

Source: Thomas D. Davies, Jr., and Kim A. Beasley, *Design for Hospitality: Planning for Accessible Hotels & Motels* (New York: Nichols Publishing, 1988), p. 29.

accommodate a van with a side-mounted lift or ramp. Also, there is no competition between cars and vans for spaces since all spaces can accommodate either.

Valet parking. Not all disabled individuals can use valet parking services. For instance, a disabled individual may use vehicle controls that render the regular controls inoperable, or the driver's seat in a van may be removed. In these situations, another person cannot park the vehicle. It is recommended that some self-parking spaces be provided at valet parking facilities for individuals whose vehicles cannot be parked by another person, and that such spaces be located on an accessible route to the entrance of the facility.

Passenger loading zones. Passenger loading zones are typically located outside the main entrance of a hospitality facility. Accessibility requirements for these zones include an access aisle at least 5 feet (1.5 meters) wide and 20 feet (6.1 meters) long adjacent and parallel to the vehicle pull-up space. If there is a curb between the access aisle and the vehicle pull–up space, then a curb ramp should be provided.

Storm Water Drainage Systems

Storm water drainage systems are designed to carry rain water away from the property. Rain water can also be controlled by allowing it to seep into the soil. If the water is not contained through seepage, it must be transported to a place of storage on the property or discharged from the property.

Sheet flow is a uniform flow of water across the ground until it has ultimately reached its storage point or has been discharged from the property. It is not directed into definite channels of flow. An example of a sheet flow is the flow of water over a surface parking lot. The direction of flow always follows the slope of the ground. Depths of sheet flow seldom exceed $1/2$ inch (1.3 centimeters) and can be controlled by changes in the ground's surface. Sheet flow can cause erosion.

Open-channel flow is water that flows into a defined channel such as a roadside ditch.

An underground drainage system collects surface water through a catch basin or some other type of inlet structure and transports it down through an underground piping system to its ultimate point of discharge from the property.

Usually, the drainage from even a small property is a combination of all these types of flows. The goal of a drainage system is to control the flow of water so that it is not a problem for guests and does not damage the property.

Due to the nature of the type of construction required, no underground drainage facilities should be constructed or installed with a life expectancy of less than 50 years. Extensive earth excavation is necessary to install an underground drainage system. This excavation almost invariably results in conflicts with other existing or planned utilities. Temporary repairs and alterations usually result in so many problems that their value must be questioned. If changes are needed, it is probably best to do all needed work in a permanent manner, and limit the number of times the ground must be opened.

Preventive Maintenance. Preventive maintenance of drainage facilities includes routine inspections after every rain. Were there blockages at any points? Did the water pond or back up during the rain? Did the flow seem sluggish? These are typical questions that should be answered. The answers usually determine the preventive maintenance that is needed. Leaves, twigs, and discarded rubbish and trash that block or clog the drainage system are the causes of most problems. They should be promptly removed.

Manhole and catch basin covers and grates should be kept in place. They are usually set in a frame, but are anchored only by their substantial weight. If the frame is loose, it should be tightened. This usually requires the use of a welding machine. If grates or lids make excessive noise when vehicles cross over them, it may be necessary to anchor or secure them in some way. Do not weld them shut; ease of access is important. Likewise, do not allow manholes to be covered by asphalt or concrete. This may easily happen if a parking lot or driveway is repaved.

Inspections. Inspections of storm water drainage systems should include a thorough visual inspection of the entire system after every hard rain. Problems will usually show up then. Look especially for spots where water is going through a hole into the ground, other than at a catch basin or inlet. These holes are always signs of underground voids. Left uncorrected, these voids will grow larger. Often the water will enter the ground in a swirling motion.

Inspect for blocked or partially functioning inlets. Often they are clogged with debris or leaves. Fast heavy rains closely following grass mowing can carry a significant amount of clippings into the inlet, causing clogs. Look down into the inlets and catch basins while it is raining to see if the water is flowing away smoothly, or if it appears to be impeded by something.

Utilities

Typical utilities used in a hospitality facility include water, sewer, oil, gas, electricity, steam, chilled water, telephone, and cable television.

Externally supplied or purchased utilities are normally brought to a distribution point somewhere on the property. For example, in the case of the water supply, the distribution point is commonly at the property's water meter. Electricity is normally brought to an electric meter's distribution panel.

Ideally, utilities enter the property and are distributed by an underground system to various parts of the property. However, some utilities, such as cable television, telephone, and electric service, are carried above ground at some properties. These above-ground lines are easier to inspect and maintain than underground lines, but they are not as aesthetically appealing.

Normally it is necessary for the facility to maintain the utilities from the facility to their final delivery point. The final delivery point is usually considered to be the meter recording the quantity or volume consumed of the particular utility being provided.

Extreme caution should be used when working around any of the public utilities. Dangers from electrical shock and earth cave-ins are but a few of the problems that can occur. Any time underground digging takes place, the potential for striking an underground utility line is present. Workers should never be allowed to work alone under dangerous conditions.

Preventive Maintenance. Water lines, both potable and non-potable, are normally equipped with valves for control purposes. These valves not only shut off the water, but control the direction and quantity of flow as well. Water control valves should be "exercised" annually. That is, they should be fully opened and closed, to be sure they seat properly and still perform their intended function. If left too long in one position, valves have a tendency to stick in that position, rendering them useless in time of need. A record should be made each time a seldom-used control valve is exercised. Any problems should be noted and taken care of.

Sanitary sewer lines can become clogged by a buildup of solids. This can be caused by the flow being too slow (the sewer grade being too flat), or by the sewer grade being too steep, allowing the liquids to outrun the solids, leaving the solids behind. Sewer slopes should be neither too steep nor too flat.

Sewers that are partially or completely blocked should be rodded or flushed out. Flushing can be done with a high pressure hose, such as a fire hose. A typical garden hose is usually not capable of supplying the quantity of flow or the pressure needed. Rodding is done by mechanical means, usually by inserting a flexible rod into an opening such as a manhole and pushing it through to the next opening. A roto-rooter is a piece of equipment that rotates a cutting bit through the sewer or drain pipe, "rooting" its way through the blockage. The cutting bit is attached to a flexible cable that is rotated by a power source. This equipment is fairly easy to use and is effective in removing blockage. Roto-rooter equipment comes in various diameters and is capable of accepting different turning forces.

Inspections. Inspection of underground utilities is usually limited to observing the surface of the ground above them and looking at the lines themselves through access points such as manholes. Tools are available to do scientific analysis, such as natural gas detectors, moisture and water detectors for water mains, and sewer gas analysis equipment. The necessary equipment ranges from hand-held, reasonably user-friendly equipment to very sophisticated electronic analyzers.

Overhead electric, cable television, and telephone lines can be more easily inspected. If necessary, ladders and lift trucks can be used for detailed inspections.

Landscaping and Grounds

A property's landscaping and grounds set the visual tone for the entire property; they are a large part of the first impression guests receive. Allowing the grounds to decline into mediocrity will severely diminish the property's attractiveness, which may result in lower revenues. To keep the property's "curb appeal" high, the grounds should always be kept at their best.

As landscaping and grounds are planned, consideration should be given to the location and types of driveways, entrances, the first or principal view guests see, drainage conditions, existing trees, the direction of the prevailing wind, underground and overhead utility lines, recreational facilities, the direction of the sun, watering facilities, and—of course—the initial cost of the landscaping and the cost and ease of maintaining it.

Preventive Maintenance. The most common maintenance activities for grounds are mowing, fertilizing, and pruning.

Mowing is necessary to keep a lawn attractive and healthy. The mower's blades should be sharp so that grass blades are cut cleanly, not ripped; ripped, frayed blades invite disease. The grass should be cut when it needs cutting, not according to some arbitrary timetable. Only one third or less of the grass blades should be cut at any one time, otherwise the roots are starved for nutrients and grass health is damaged. Lawns should not be mown too close to the ground because short grass makes it easier for moisture to evaporate and weeds to invade the lawn.

Lawns, plants, and trees usually need fertilization to maintain the healthy appearance guests have come to expect from landscaped grounds. Commercial fertilizers usually contain nitrogen, phosphate, and potash. The amount of each element that is needed depends on the type of soil, the vegetation, and the climate. The manufacturer's instructions should be followed carefully when applying fertilizer.

Trees and shrubs must be pruned with care. Using the wrong technique or pruning at the wrong time of year can ruin or kill a plant. When is the right time to prune? It depends on the plant. For example, deciduous trees should be pruned in

Attractive landscaping adds to a property's appeal. (Courtesy of The Greenbrier, White Sulphur Springs, West Virginia)

winter when they are dormant; evergreens can be pruned in April before new growth begins or in July after new growth has matured. Maintenance employees should consult reference books or call a lawn and garden center if they are unsure of when or how to prune a particular plant.

Regardless of the kind and extent of landscaping work, the maintenance manager is faced with the decision of who should do the maintenance. Many otherwise competent persons in a maintenance department lack the skills to do an acceptable job on landscaping. Extensive training may be necessary. The alternative to training the in-house maintenance staff is to hire a landscaping maintenance service.

The amount of landscaping work varies significantly with the seasons and climate. It is usually best to organize maintenance activities for the grounds into monthly cycles and to subdivide these further into weekly and daily tasks. When rainy days prevent outside work, the landscaping staff must be rescheduled. Following extended rainy periods the landscaping workload may be very heavy.

Inspections. Landscaping and grounds are relatively easy to inspect, since they are readily visible and accessible. The inspector should walk the entire grounds, noting any problems or changes since the last inspection. Problems often develop slowly over a period of time, so detailed notes should be kept. Preferably a scaled drawing should be used. Inspections should be done at least quarterly, and following any significant departure from normal weather.

Irrigation Systems. Many hospitality facilities use irrigation systems to maintain their grounds. The need for irrigation is not universal. It is not necessary in areas where rainfall is equal to the needs of plant life.

In the hospitality industry, the function of irrigation is to artificially provide a reliable source of water for a building's landscape. In some cases the irrigation water is also used as the transport vehicle for soil and plant nutrients. A successful irrigation system not only furnishes water to plants and trees, it supplies the water at the proper time and in the proper quantity.

All irrigation systems must take the following elements into account:

- Rate of water loss through evaporation

- Rate of water infiltration into the soil

- Water-absorption capacity of the soil to which the water is applied

- Depth of infiltration (usually related to depth of the topsoil)

- Depth of plant roots

Lawns and trees usually need large amounts of water. However, it is prudent to stretch the interval between waterings as much as possible, since overwatering wastes water and can have a negative effect on plant life.

The supply or source of water can be one of the following:

- The treated, potable water system of the facility

- A stored supply, such as in a lake or underground tank

- A nearby stream or river

- Gray water

Water that comes from the potable water system must be paid for, and thus carries a significant cost. Potable water used for irrigation should be metered separately. It commonly has had many of the most desirable nutrients removed in the purification process, and often has had chemicals added that are detrimental to plants. It is the most readily available source, but is least desirable. Backflow prevention devices must be used if the irrigation system is connected to the potable water supply.

Water for irrigation can be stored on the surface or underground. Surface storage can either be natural (a lake) or artificial (a tank or a constructed pond). Underground units include cisterns and other underground tanks. These tanks are usually small because of the cost of building a large underground tank.

Gray water is obtained from selected parts of the facility's plumbing system. It originates from the laundry, kitchen, and bathroom sink areas. Its primary pollutants are dirt, food wastes, and laundry detergents. Most of these can be successfully removed by a simple clarification process. The heaviest pollutants settle to the bottom of the clarifier and can be retrieved and dumped into the sanitation sewer. The remaining gray water is rich in nutrients, such as phosphate and nitrogen, and makes excellent irrigation water. Because of the danger of contaminating pathogens, the gray water should be disinfected. Common methods of disinfection include chlorinating and applying ultra-violet light.

A typical irrigation system consists of sprinkler heads or mist applicators. Sprinkler heads are located at the terminals of a piping system. When the water pressure reaches a certain point, the heads begin to spray water. Sprinkler heads are, in general, pressure dependent; the greater the pressure, the greater the flow of water and the greater the area of coverage. Three common types of sprinkler heads are fixed, pop-up, and pulsating.

Mist applicators are similar to the other types of sprinkler heads, except that the nozzle is designed to create a fine mist. Because the discharge nozzles of mist applicators are smaller in diameter, they are easier to clog and thus require more maintenance.

Preventive maintenance. Irrigation systems should be observed daily when in use and inspected in detail monthly. Observers should make note of any sprinkler units that do not seem to deliver the correct quantity of water (either too much or too little). If too little water is delivered it can be a sign of clogged pipes or nozzles, partially closed valves, inadequate water pressure, or other problems.

As part of preventive maintenance, the following should be looked for each day:

- Pump problems

- Leaks in the distribution system

- Sprinkler heads not functioning

All control valves in the irrigation system should be exercised (completely opened and closed) semi-annually. Valves and control devices should be marked with an identifiable code and special paint color. Their location should be documented for easy access.

Irrigation systems located in cold climates must be protected against freezing. As water freezes it expands, bursting pipes and valves. To winterize the system it is usually necessary to remove the water.

Endnotes

1. Some of the information in this section was adapted from Frank D. Borsenik and Alan T. Stutts, *The Management of Maintenance and Engineering Systems in the Hospitality Industry*, 3d ed. (New York: Wiley, 1992), pp. 399–403; and Mel A. Shear, *Handbook of Building Maintenance Management* (Reston, Virginia: Reston Publishing Company, 1983), pp. 508–514.

2. Steven H. Kosmatka and William C. Panarese, *Design and Control of Concrete Mixtures*, 13th ed. (Skokie, Ill.: Portland Cement Association, 1990), p. vii.

3. Much of the material in this section was adapted from Steven H. Kosmatka and William C. Panarese, *Design and Control of Concrete Mixtures*, 13th ed. (Skokie, Ill.: Portland Cement Association, 1990); ACI Committee 330, *Guide for Design and Construction of Concrete Parking Lots* (Detroit, Mich.: American Concrete Institute, 1988); and the

American Concrete Institute, *Concrete Craftsman Series—Slabs on Grade* (Detroit, Mich.: American Concrete Institute, 1982).

4. Although it was published before the Americans with Disabilities Act was passed, and therefore some of its recommendations may not exactly match provisions in the new law, *Design for Hospitality: Planning for Accessible Hotels and Motels* by Thomas D. Davies, Jr., and Kim A. Beasley is a good source of information on how to make properties accessible to disabled people. The book was published in 1988 by the Paralyzed Veterans of America and developed with assistance from the American Hotel & Lodging Association.

🔑 Key Terms

access aisle—An aisle next to an accessible parking space that allows disabled individuals to exit and enter vehicles with a device, such as a wheelchair, and travel to the sidewalk or building entrance.

accessible parking space—A parking space specially designed for disabled persons that meets or exceeds the requirements of the Americans with Disabilities Act.

accessible route—A route that connects the accessible parking area to an accessible entrance of the building the parking lot serves. An accessible route should be a minimum of 36 inches (91 centimeters) wide and have no abrupt surface transitions (from sidewalks to streets, for example) or obstructions that would present hazards to a visually impaired person.

cable elevator system—An elevator system in which an elevator car moves up and down with the help of cables and counterweights.

crazing—Fine hairline cracks that form a map-like pattern on the surface of concrete.

dead load—A structure's own weight.

flashing—Copper, aluminum, or fiber sheeting that joins the roof covering to the building structure where the roof meets a wall, chimney, etc.

hydraulic elevator system—An elevator system with no cables or counterweights. Instead, the elevator car is mounted on a giant piston inside a cylinder that extends underground to a depth equal to the height the elevator will rise.

leaching—The subtraction of cementing constituents from cement due to water migration through the cement.

live load—The weight of the people, equipment, furnishings, and so on within a building.

roofing felt—Fiber-filled paper impregnated with asphalt or tar.

spall—A surface cavity of a cement slab, caused by corrosion of embedded metals.

subbase—In parking lot construction, a layer of sand, gravel, crushed stone, or other granular material that is sometimes placed between a prepared subgrade and the surface course.

subgrade—In parking lot construction, soil that has been prepared and compacted to support a layer of concrete or asphalt.

surface course—A wearing surface for vehicles to drive on, usually made of concrete or asphalt.

tensile strength—The strength to bear longitudinal stress.

Review Questions

1. What is the basic structure of a roof?
2. What are typical preventive maintenance activities for exterior walls?
3. What are some preventive maintenance strategies for a building's structural frame?
4. What should an inspector look for when checking a foundation?
5. Elevator systems are made up of what basic components?
6. What are some of the structural features and layout considerations for parking lots and parking garages (including ADA requirements)?
7. What are some preventive maintenance strategies for storm water drainage systems?
8. What are some preventive maintenance strategies for utility systems?
9. What are some typical maintenance activities for landscaping?
10. Water for irrigation can come from what sources?

Internet Sites

For more information, visit the following Internet sites. Remember that Internet addresses can change without notice. If the site is no longer there, you can use a search engine to look for additional sites.

American Concrete Institute
www.aci–int.org

American Concrete Pavement
Association
www.pavement.com

American Society for Testing and
Materials
www.astm.org

Asphalt Emulsion Manufacturers
Association
www.aema.org

Asphalt Institute
www.asphaltinstitute.org

Asphalt Roofing Manufacturers
Association
www.asphaltroofing.org

Associated Landscape Contractors of
America
www.alca.org

Association of Asphalt Paving
Technologists
www.asphalttechnology.org

Australian Asphalt Pavement
Association
www.aapa.asn.au

British Cement Association
www.bca.org.uk

Canadian Technical Asphalt
Association
www.ctaa.ca

Concrete Reinforcing Steel Institute
www.crsi.org

Concrete Society
www.concrete.org.uk

Construction Specifications Institute
www.csinet.org

Ecological Landscaping Association
www.ela-ecolandscapingassn.org

Elevator Escalator Safety Foundation
www.eesf.org

European Asphalt Pavement
Association
www.eapa.org

European Bitumen Association
www.eurobitume.org

European Cement Association
www.cembureau.be

Indonesia Cement Association
www.inaweb.co.id/asi

Institute for Research in Construction
www.nrc.ca/irc/

International Association for Building
Materials and Structures
www.rilem.ens-cachan.fr/

International Conference of Building
Officials
www.icbo.org

Irrigation & Green Industry Network
www.igin.com

Irrigation Association
www.irrigation.org

Landscape Irrigation Tutorials
www.irrigationtutorials.com

National Asphalt Pavement
Association
www.hotmix.org

National Association of Elevator
Contractors
www.naec.org/naec

National Gardening Association
www.garden.org

National Roofing Contractors
Association
www.nrca.net

Portland Cement Association
www.portcement.org

Roof Consultants Institute
www.rci-online.org

roofinfo.com
www.roofinfo.com

Swedish Asphalt Pavement Association
www.fas.se

Part IV

Facility Design

Chapter 14 Outline

Competencies

1. Describe the hotel development process. (pp. 438–446)

2. Describe site planning. (pp. 447–450)

3. Describe guestroom and suite planning. (pp. 450–456)

4. Describe lobby design. (pp. 456–459)

5. Describe the design of food and beverage outlets. (pp. 459–462)

6. Summarize function space design concerns. (pp. 462–465)

7. Describe the design of recreational facilities and administrative offices. (pp. 465–467)

8. Describe food production area design. (pp. 467–468)

9. Summarize back-of-the-house design concerns. (pp. 468–472)

14

Lodging Planning and Design

This chapter was written and contributed by Richard H. Penner,
Professor, School of Hotel Administration, Cornell University,
Ithaca, New York.

No matter the segment, new hotels must look—and feel—special.

*Location is always a buzzword in hotels. Developers of new hotels
have a new one: design. Whether it's the business-oriented Wingate Inn,
the road warrior's Motel 6, extended-stay Staybridge Suites or exotic
resorts, the goals are distinctiveness and freshness.*

*Cost remains a key concern, prompting chains like HFS, Red Roof
and Accor to use energy- and cost-efficient materials for facilities
that stress consistency. The pricier the segment, however, the more indi-
viduality in design. Resorts, particularly, try to corner the uniqueness
market.*

*For now, the primary medium of new construction is land, and
tried-and-true building techniques rule. To Mike Bruce, corporate architect for Wingate Inns, the key is to tweak the proven. By using concrete
blocks with premanufactured planks and wood frame construction, "We
felt we could hit the whole country," he says.*

*Despite such structural regularity, Wingate Inn is a new concept
designed from the inside out, says Frederick W. Mosser, president and
chief operating officer. "We went to the market first: owners, developers,
operators and consumer groups, and had them tell us what we ought to
include in services, price point and amenities."*

*Since resort developers demand uniqueness, "parachute architec-
ture" is what Mark A. Van Steenlandt wants to avoid. That is architecture in which a firm "plops a generic design into a specific locale without
taking the local flavor into account," says the managing principal of
VOA Associates Inc. of Orlando.*

*"Hospitality projects bring with them a romantic sense," Van
Steenlandt says. "Unlike any other type, as a hospitality project gets
under way, clients can lose it very quickly from the standpoint of staying
focused on the budget."[1]*

Hotel and resort design is an integrative process that brings together the skills
and expertise of owners, managers, architects, builders, and a host of others to con-
ceive and construct a building to meet a variety of business and travel objectives.
Owners see the hotel as a real estate and investment opportunity; managers expect

437

the project to meet certain strategic goals and provide revenue; future guests need accommodations for business or personal travel; and others have myriad reasons for involvement in the development and design process.

Hotels went through an incredible evolution during the nineteenth and twentieth centuries. It wasn't until early in the 1800s that anything comparable to the modern hotel, with its level of comfort and services, was developed. True, there were hundreds of roadside inns and taverns—unsophisticated, even crude places—and a few distinguished spa resorts, primarily in Europe. But hotels as we know them, with private rooms, elegant lobbies, several restaurants and lounges, meeting and banquet rooms, recreational facilities, and back-of-the-house components to serve them, weren't common until the Tremont House in Boston (1829), the Astor House in New York (1836), and numerous copies in North America and Europe marked the first great wave of hotel development.

The latter part of the nineteenth century was marked by technological innovation: central heating; indoor plumbing; gas, then electric, lighting; elevators; telephones; and so forth. Also during this period, as the hotel became the center of much of the social life in cities, owners integrated grand dining rooms and ballrooms. Resorts began to prosper as the industrial revolution created wealthy businessmen who moved their families from the cities to mountain and beach resorts for the summer. Hotel segmentation had begun.

The twentieth century, especially after World War II, saw immense growth in the hotel industry. Developers created roadside motor inns beginning in the 1950s; convention hotels in the 1960s; suburban and airport hotels in the 1970s; economy motels, all-suite hotels, and "fantasy" resorts in the 1980s; and ecotourist retreats and boutique hotels in the 1990s. One wonders what the twenty-first century will bring!

In this chapter, we discuss how an individual hotel is developed and present planning and design guidelines. The development, design, and construction phases often take two years for a relatively small hotel and four or more years for a large urban or resort property. It is important that owners and hotel managers understand the discipline and control needed to organize and manage such a lengthy process, which includes such steps as confirming the hotel's feasibility; selecting the project team; establishing space requirements, operational standards, and construction and engineering criteria; and preparing the budget and schedule. These are only part of the process. The owners and managers also must be familiar with planning and design guidelines for guestrooms, food and beverage outlets, function areas, and back-of-the-house spaces. A hotel's design is instrumental in creating positive guest reactions and enabling management to operate efficiently.

The Development Process

Lodging development can be broken down into several steps but typically begins with the conceptual phase, during which the first idea for a project is envisioned. Often, a cursory analysis suggests that the potential hotel is not practical and the owner or developer moves on to another venture. But where there is proven demand and the resources to develop the project, the development process continues, often for three or four years, until the hotel finally opens.

The development and design process brings together many specialists in an intensive, cooperative effort. The owner and developer require the assistance of legal and financial experts and marketing consultants. They assemble a design team including architects, engineers, interior designers, kitchen specialists, and other design consultants. They establish an agreement with a franchise or hotel management company and involve it in operational decisions. They negotiate both construction and permanent financing agreements. And they contract with a construction firm to build the property.

Hotel development and design is a mammoth organizational effort, one that brings great satisfaction when it is successful and great frustration when problems arise. Critical to the successful project is the organization of the pre-design phase, when criteria are set, the development team is brought together, and preliminary budgets and schedules are established. Some of these tasks are identified in Exhibit 1.

Critical to the whole process is communication. The various members of the development team must understand what the others are doing and, especially, the point-of-view that each person brings to the effort. One effective way of initiating the project is to insist that the full team assemble for a "kick-off" meeting during which they consider different approaches to meet the overall objectives of the owner and operator. This meeting leads to a number of steps—many occurring simultaneously—that will give shape to the future lodging property.

The Feasibility Study

Among the first steps that the developer takes is to study the feasibility of the proposed hotel. The **feasibility study** is usually prepared by a consulting firm and reviewed by the hotel management company. Its purpose is twofold: first, it assesses present and future demand for lodging and such hotel services as meeting rooms, restaurants and lounges, and recreational facilities. Secondly, it estimates the proposed hotel's operating income and expenses for five to ten years after the hotel opens.

A hotel's owner has many reasons for undertaking a feasibility study. Most will use the study to help obtain permanent financing; others may use it to gain a franchise or management agreement, attract equity partners, or support a request for a zoning change. Interestingly, only infrequently do these studies actually assess a project's feasibility, which may largely depend on the owner's investment strategies and tax status. Instead, a feasibility study provides a description of the local area and potential markets, recommends proposed facilities, and projects cash flow. The typical report usually covers the following components:

- *Local area evaluation:* Analyzes the economic vitality of the city or region and describes the suitability of the project site for a hotel.

- *Lodging market analysis:* Assesses the present demand for lodging and other revenue generators and future growth rates for each of several market segments, and identifies the existing supply of competitive properties and their probable growth.

Exhibit 1   Hotel Development Process

PRE-DESIGN PHASE

☐ OWNER/DEVELOPER: Establish project objectives; assemble development team; commission feasibility study; establish preliminary project budget and schedule; obtain option on land; investigate potential financing; negotiate joint venture and hotel management agreements.

☐ FEASIBILITY CONSULTANT: Conduct market study and prepare financial projections.

☐ HOTEL MANAGEMENT COMPANY: Confirm feasibility recommendations; recommend architect and consultants; prepare program; establish design and operation criteria.

☐ ARCHITECT: Analyze site; prepare conceptual design; review program and budget; select consultant team.

DESIGN PHASE

☐ OWNER/DEVELOPER: Schedule kick-off meeting for development team; provide design team with prompt comment and approval; establish design schedule; authorize mock-up guestroom.

☐ ARCHITECT: Prepare schematic designs, outline specification, and preliminary budget; complete design development, including plans, draft of specifications and construction budget; complete construction documents, including all drawings, specifications, and bid documents. Through all phases coordinate with engineers, other design consultants, and management company.

☐ HOTEL MANAGEMENT COMPANY: Review architectural and design submittals; prepare designs for back-of-house areas; prepare budget for operating equipment and supplies; review mock-up room.

☐ INTERIOR DESIGNER: Prepare all interior guestroom, public area, and office designs and specifications; complete specifications for mock-up guestroom.

☐ FOOD-SERVICE CONSULTANT: Prepare all kitchen, bar, and related designs and specifications; coordinate with other back-of-house consultants and management company.

- *Proposed facilities*: Proposes a balance of guestroom and revenue-generating public facilities (restaurants and lounges, function rooms, retail stores, recreational facilities) and assesses the competitive position of the property.

- *Financial analysis:* Estimates income and expenses for the hotel over a five- or ten-year period to show its potential cash flow after fixed charges (before debt service and income tax).

When seeking a feasibility consultant, owners and managers should look for someone with experience and high credibility within the hospitality industry. The consultant must be neutral (lenders are interested in an objective analysis) and should be prepared to provide explanations and documentation to support the underlying assumptions in the report.

New York Marriott, Brooklyn, NY. Developers seek new locations for hotels. In the last decade business-oriented hotels have flourished outside urban centers, at airports, suburbs, and office parks. The new Marriott in Brooklyn is the first major hotel to be built in New York City in 50 years outside of Manhattan and the airports. (Courtesy of William B. Tabler, Architect)

The Space Allocation Program

Following a positive feasibility assessment, the development team establishes the space allocation program for the proposed hotel. The program is a document that lists the design requirements for a project. This is a cooperative effort, with input

Exhibit 2   Guestroom Space per Type of Lodging Property

Lodging type	Number of guestrooms	Service level	% of total space devoted to guestrooms*
Motel	100	Economy to mid-price	85–95
Roadside hotel	100–200	Mid-price	75–85
Commercial hotel	200–400	First-class	75–85
All-suite hotel	150–300	Mid-price to first-class	75–85
Suburban hotel	150–300	Mid-price to first-class	75–85
Convention hotel	400–2,000	First-class	65–75
Resort	varies	Mid-price to luxury	65–75
Mega-resort	>1,000 rooms	First-class	55–65
Conference center	100–300 rooms	Mid-price to first-class	55–65

*Includes guestroom corridors, stairs, elevators, and linen storage.

from the owners, based on the feasibility report and owners' objectives, as well as the objectives of the management company, the architect, and other consultants.

The allocation of space among the principal functions in a hotel varies from property to property. The most obvious difference among properties is the ratio of guestroom space to public and support space. This varies from over 90 percent guestroom space in budget properties and many motels (where there are limited or no food and beverage, meeting, and back-of-the house areas) to less than 65 percent guestroom space in large convention and resort properties, where the public and support functions are essential to the property's ability to gain or keep market share. Exhibit 2 shows the percentage of total hotel space allocated to guestrooms for a range of lodging properties.

For each type of hotel developed at a particular location to meet the needs of a specific target market at a given price range, an experienced developer or management company can provide a tentative list of facilities and an early estimate of space requirements. Until a more detailed space allocation program is established, this gross approximation of the proposed hotel's size is the critical basis for all cost estimates. Exhibit 3 shows fairly typical space allocation requirements for four different types of lodging properties.

The development of the architectural space program does not occur at one time nor does it result in a static document. Usually, at the beginning of **schematic design** (the first design phase), the architect develops a space list and, later, throughout the schematic and design development phases, refines it into a more detailed program. In some cases, where the technical services staff of the hotel operating company has the experience to react quickly and accurately to requests for programmatic information, a new hotel project may proceed without a comprehensive space program. In these situations, the detailed planning and space-use

Exhibit 3   Typical Hotel Space Allocation for Guestrooms

	Roadside	Commercial	Convention	All–Suite
Number of guestrooms	150	300	600	250
Number of bays*	150	315	630	250
Net guestroom area (sf.#)	325	350	350	450
Gross guestroom area@ (sf.)	450	500	500	675
Total guestroom area (sf.)	67,500	157,500	315,000	168,750
Guestroom percentage	80	75	70	80
Total hotel area (sf.)	84,375	210,000	450,000	210,940
Total hotel area per room (sf.)	562	700	750	844

*Guestroom bays indicate additional room modules needed to create suites.
#sf. = square feet
@Gross guestroom area includes an allowance for corridors, stairs, elevators, walls, etc.

information is transmitted through a comprehensive chain-developed design guide or bit-by-bit during the ensuing design phases, as the architect requires more specific technical information. However, with the advent of proprietary computer programs used by many of the companies, detailed space allocation information can be issued early and can be updated easily during the design phases.

Operational Criteria

The complete development program requires a second major element: a thorough description of the future property's operations, including food and beverage concepts, front office procedures, housekeeping systems, typical guest amenities, and so forth. Among the most challenging aspects of hotel design is the need to develop a plan that accommodates several potential guest markets as well as the operational requirements of the hotel. These often conflict and the cost of providing for every need is likely to be prohibitive.

Many operational decisions are changing because of the increased automation and computerization of hotels. The labor-intensive nature of the industry forces hotel management to establish creative new procedures and systems to reduce repetitive tasks while maintaining an appropriate level of service. With the turn of the century, such major management groups as Starwood and Hyatt are increasing the centralization of many services. For example, reservations or purchasing for several hotels in one region might be handled at one location rather than duplicated at each property.

The following list identifies some of the operational decisions affecting the proposed hotel's design and layout that the development team must make:

- *Front desk:* Determine staffing levels, select computer systems, and determine the need for safety deposit and concierge services.

- *Luggage:* Decide how luggage is moved to and from guestrooms; plan a location for luggage storage.

- *Receiving and storage:* Determine responsibilities for purchasing, receiving, and issuing food and other goods.

- *Trash and garbage*: Study waste-holding alternatives (trash cans, compactors), the need for refrigeration, and requirements for recycling.

- *Food and beverage:* Establish concepts for each food and beverage outlet and room service, including hours of operation and production requirements.

The food and beverage program is one of the most complex operational components of the entire hotel. Many operators create a detailed description of each outlet early in the design process, not only establishing its theme and capacity, but specifying service methods, tabletop design, special equipment requirements, interior finishes, and so forth. Later in the chapter, these issues are described in more detail in the discussion of planning food and beverage outlets.

Construction and Engineering Criteria

In addition to estimating and refining space requirements and defining the operational aspects of the proposed hotel, the development team needs to establish preliminary standards for the building materials and engineering systems. While these might not be so prescriptive as to dictate, say, a steel frame versus a reinforced concrete structural system, the team should establish outline specifications that identify such construction details as the primary exterior materials, type of window glass, and quality of interior finishes.

All hotels are subject to a variety of regulations, from zoning codes to health standards to sign ordinances to ADA regulations. Once the proposed hotel meets the zoning requirements regulating use, height, setbacks, and size of the building, the detailed design must comply with local building and fire codes. The intent of these codes is to protect the public against faulty design or construction by assuring that a building will resist fire and other emergencies and protect the occupants until they can exit safely from the premises.

Similarly, the development team needs to establish engineering standards, in part to meet these codes, but further to establish a level of quality in the interior environment. Engineering criteria must be established for heating, air conditioning, ventilation, water, power, lighting, fire protection, and communications systems, all of which can lead to immense detail. The team might dictate exact requirements for each guestroom and guest bathroom, for instance, including lighting levels, water flow, bathroom ventilation, guestroom heating and air conditioning, television cable, telephone systems, smoke detectors, and fire alarms. More detail early in the development process helps the team better define quality levels, establish the project budget, identify which specialists will be needed, and assure that critical elements aren't forgotten or ignored.

Exhibit 4   Preliminary Project Budget

Budget Category	Percent
Land (varies from 2% to 20% or more depending on the location)	not included
General construction	60–65
Building, site work, general conditions	
Furniture, fixtures, & equipment (FF&E)	14–18
Hotel interiors (guestrooms, public areas, administrative offices, signage)	
Equipment (kitchen, bar equipment)	
Expendables (linen, china, glassware, housekeeping equipment, uniforms)	
Special systems (telephones, computers, TV antenna, sound, security, audio-visual systems)	
Development costs	8–12
Architectural/engineering fees	
Design consultant fees (interiors, kitchens, lighting, etc.)	
Purchasing fee	
Financing fee	
Developer fee	
Insurance during construction	
Real estate taxes	
Legal, permits, surveys, etc.	
Interest during construction	4–6
Pre-opening expense and working capital	3–5
Reserve against operation shortfall	2–4

The Project Budget

Among the most important elements of the pre-design phase is establishing a project budget. Too often, grossly inaccurate budgets are established and, only as the design is refined or, later, when prospective contractors submit construction bids, is the inadequacy of the cost estimates apparent. Then, the owner or developer and the management company have to make difficult decisions on which features to eliminate or defer; or, they may decide to seek new equity financing, thereby lowering their share of the ownership.

It is a mistake to rely on an early estimate for the construction cost, before the hotel design is fully established and the building materials, systems, and level of detail are clearly defined. A preliminary budget must include contingency funds, consider inflation, and accurately reflect the final quality standard for the hotel. Too, the developer needs to realize that the construction cost is only about 60 to 65 percent of the total project budget and does not include costs of furnishings, professional fees, financing, and pre-opening expenses, among others (see Exhibit 4).

Because total project costs vary tremendously, from as little as $50,000 per guestroom to well over $250,000, strict budget control throughout the entire process is critical. Budgeting is made more difficult by the common practice in hotel work of using separate architectural and interior design firms. Therefore, the developer must define precisely the design and budget responsibilities of the architect, interior designer, and other consultants; for example, differentiating between the general construction budget and the furniture, fixtures, and equipment (FF&E) budget.

As the project moves through the design phases, the developer modifies the allocation of the contingency funds. Early in the process at least 10 percent should be added to estimates to allow for later changes or refinement. By the time construction begins this may be reduced to 5 percent, but monies still need to be reserved to deal with unforeseen expenses. Some construction managers like to separate the contingency into specific accounts so that FF&E or legal expenses, for example, maintain their own cushion against cost overruns.

The budget also should include a "reserve against operating shortfall" to offset operating loses during the hotel's first one or two years, before revenues are sufficient to meet day-to-day expenses.

The Preliminary Schedule

The owner or developer also must prepare a preliminary schedule for the development and design phases of the project and establish a target date for the hotel's opening. The schedule should identify the myriad pre-design and design tasks, identify the members of the development team to be responsible for each one, and set realistic completion dates.

Many steps during the development phase occur simultaneously. For example, the owner may be negotiating the final management contract or pursuing various financing alternatives at the same time that the developer is selecting the design consultants and the architect is developing the initial building designs. Usually, the owner's legal and financial responsibilities continue through the design and construction phases.

The design phases are relatively orderly and straightforward. The architect typically works through three phases: schematic design, in which alternative plans are studied and a design direction is established for the hotel; design development, in which the plan is firmly set, materials and finishes are selected, interior design and engineering systems are coordinated, and the construction budget is outlined; and construction documents, in which the complete architectural and engineering drawings and specifications are prepared for bidding and construction. The other designers follow the same sequence, although slightly later than the architect, because they must base their designs on the architect's drawings. At the end of each phase, the owner should approve the architect's design and authorize other designers to continue with the next stage.

The Planning and Design Process

Among the first architectural tasks once the design team is assembled is to develop an initial conceptual design for the hotel. In fact, architects often are called upon to prepare a schematic design *before* the developer completes the program or establishes the operational criteria, in part to test the site capacity, generate preliminary construction estimates, and add credibility to a lender's package. While these conceptual studies may occur early in the project schedule, they do make and follow some preliminary assumptions about the number of guestrooms, amount of food and beverage and function space, relative emphasis of such architectural spaces as the lobby, and general massing of the building.

Site Planning

During the one or two months that might be devoted to the initial concept, the architect has to balance preliminary program and operational requirements with a number of site-related and construction issues. The first step is to analyze the site and its constraints and opportunities. The architect is responsible for coordinating the site planning with engineering consultants, who deal with such issues as site drainage and exterior lighting, and the interior designer, who may select paving materials and outdoor furnishings.

The architect should consider how guests arrive at the site, and how they might best approach the building, especially at suburban and resort hotels where the building is not crowded by nearby structures. Even before guests enter the lobby or are greeted by staff, they will have formed an impression of the hotel based on their approach and arrival. Are the grounds landscaped? Does adequate and convenient parking exist? Is there clear signage? Is the building illuminated at night? Does the entrance canopy provide sufficient shelter?

The architect should explore different ways to organize the hotel spaces. Should the hotel be a high-rise structure or a series of low-rise wings? Should the building enclose a public entry plaza or a private garden courtyard? While a flat, treeless site may offer certain advantages—mostly in reduced construction cost—the guest experience may be enhanced when the architect is challenged to creatively design a hotel on a more difficult site.

Thus, the architectural team needs to investigate the site before it can begin to develop the building's form and organization. The following list identifies some of the things the architect must do:

- *Visibility and accessibility*: Consider surrounding street patterns, road access.

- *Surface conditions*: Analyze terrain, vegetation, utilities, existing buildings and roads, environmental constraints.

- *Subsurface conditions*: Investigate water table, bearing capacity of the soil, underground utilities, environmental hazards.

- *Regulatory restrictions*: Research applicable zoning, parking, building, and other codes.

- *Site character*: Study surface conditions (above), adjoining uses, views.

- *Orientation and climate*: Position building and recreational facilities for sun; analyze microclimate (for resorts).

- *Adaptability:* Determine the site's potential for expansion or development for other uses.

Site planning occurs at the same time the building is designed—some of it very early in schematic design when the architect is exploring alternative concepts for the hotel and its siting, other aspects much later when the final construction drawings are produced. For urban hotels and small and mid-size properties, the architect may complete these planning and design tasks with a minimum of consultants, perhaps hiring only a local nursery to help select proper plantings. But for more complex projects, the team may include land planners, who assist the architect with early site analyses and the development of a comprehensive master plan, landscape architects, traffic or transportation specialists, golf course architects, and so forth.

Architects designing a large hotel may develop a number of different entrances to help separate overnight guests from other visitors, reduce the amount of unnecessary traffic through the building, and establish a distinct identity for a restaurant or other facility. Additional entrances, however, may create additional security concerns. Designers should assess the relative need for the following public entrances (in addition to the receiving and trash area and employee entrances):

- Main hotel entrance

- Ballroom/banquet entrance

- Restaurant/bar/nightclub/casino entrance

- Health club/spa entrance

- Tour bus/airport bus drop-off entrance

- Condominium entrance

Among the most prominent entry features is the **porte cochere**, the entry canopy designed to protect guests from inclement weather and to provide visual emphasis to the entrance. The architect's design for the porte cochere should incorporate lighting and signage and be of sufficient height for buses and emergency vehicles. The driveway beneath the porte cochere must be at least two lanes wide, preferably three lanes or more, to facilitate peak numbers of arriving and departing guests. The sidewalk must be wide enough to accommodate groups waiting for taxis or tour buses, and allow for the easy loading and unloading of baggage.

Parking, including the design of the approach, driveways, sidewalks, receiving area, and emergency access, is perhaps the most important entry feature for most lodging properties. The parking requirement usually is specified in the local zoning ordinance and may require more than one parking space per guestroom, especially in small cities and suburban locations. In major urban areas, where a large number of guests will arrive by cab, the final parking agreement may be negotiated between the developer and the city. Providing sufficient parking is critical if a hotel intends to attract banquet and dinner business, so the developer must carefully analyze and balance the need for parking against its cost. Often, nearby garages are used to help accommodate peak parking demand.

The Peninsula Hotel, New York City. The architects for the luxury Peninsula Hotel used lighting to emphasize the scale and grandeur of the historic façade and added an understated porte cochere to shelter arriving guests from rain and snow. (Courtesy of Brennan Beer Gorman Architects)

Hotel Planning

Once the influence of the site on the building program is understood, the architect can begin to plan and design the hotel. Sometimes this is most influenced by the surrounding buildings or natural terrain: a 20-story high-rise tower fits into a downtown location, while a cluster of villas is more appropriate for a remote Caribbean island. Also, mirrored glass and steel may be suitable to the former, while natural materials and elaborate landscaping better suits the latter. The architect must create a building concept and organize the hotel's functions so that they meet the owner's objectives, the operator's functional requirements, and the future guests' expectations. The following sections discuss the variety of planning and design principles that help an architect to meet these demands, beginning with guestrooms and suites, then continuing with public and back-of-the-house areas.

Guestrooms and Suites

Designers and hotel executives—in short, all those involved in the hotel's development and operations—have their own list of which spaces most influence guests. Nearly everyone includes guestrooms, simply because guests are likely to spend the greatest amount of time in them. Therefore, it is natural to try to improve the quality or functionality of guestrooms. But one of the difficulties is that any feature added to a guestroom must be duplicated many times: a decorative valence added to the drapery treatment must be added in every room, a marble vanity counter appears in every bathroom, a more expensive nightstand or bedside lamp appears in every room, and so forth. While each item may add less than $100 to the cost of a single guestroom, this cost soon becomes many thousands of dollars as the item is added to all the guestrooms.

However, instead of studying features to add to the guestroom, more often the owner or architect is analyzing which elements to eliminate. Because guestrooms usually represent between 65 and 85 percent of the total hotel area for most properties, any savings in the construction or furnishings of guestrooms is multiplied many times; a less expensive window treatment, for example, creates a savings in every room. Therefore, the development team—and the interior designer in particular—has to carefully balance the functionality, aesthetic value, and cost of each individual piece of furniture or decorative element to test whether it adds value to the guestroom and to the guest's experience.

To accomplish more in the guestrooms themselves, a major planning goal should be to maximize the amount of saleable guestroom space and keep to a minimum the circulation and supporting areas. Architects initially must resolve such conceptual design issues as building height, massing, exterior materials, location of entrances, and facade details, while at the same time accommodate structural and engineering systems, satisfy the building codes, and work with typically stringent budgets. Given all these issues to resolve, they should be challenged, too, to design as much saleable space into the guestroom floors as possible.

Guestroom Floor Planning. The planning requirements for the guestroom floors are relatively few: there must be a designated number of guestrooms or suites, guest and service elevators should be conveniently located, exit stairways must meet the building code, adequate linen storage and vending areas should be provided, and small electrical and telephone equipment closets are usually necessary. But the way these are arranged can easily affect the total floor area by 10 percent. Therefore, skillful planning makes a substantial impact on the efficiency of the guestroom areas. For example, essentially the same 250-room hotel could vary by 10,000 to 15,000 gross square feet (930 to 1,359 square meters) due entirely to the level of planning efficiency for the guestroom floors; the additional floor area translates into $1 to $2 million in additional project costs, depending on the

Royalton, New York City. This boutique-hotel guestroom is designed with a cool but glamorous style, with great attention to each detail. (Courtesy of Ian Schrager Hotels)

location and quality level of the hotel. For this reason alone, the architect must understand the importance of efficient and economical planning of guestroom areas. The hotel developer and management group should insist that the architect refine and modify the design until it meets a sufficiently high standard.

The more common guestroom floor configurations include the **double-loaded slab**, where rooms are laid out on both sides of a central corridor, the **tower**, in which rooms are grouped around a central vertical core, and the **atrium**, which features rooms off a single-loaded corridor encircling a multi-story lobby space (see Exhibit 5). In general, the double-loaded slab is the most efficient, with about 70

Exhibit 5 Guestroom Floor Configurations

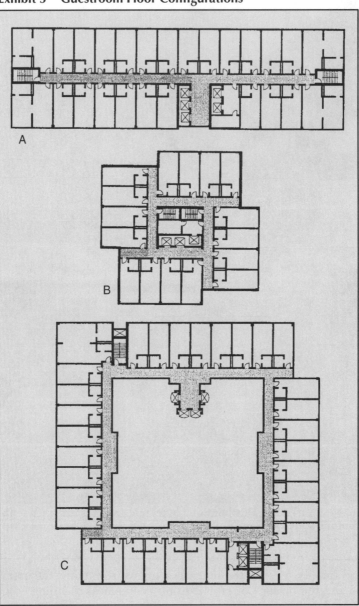

Each guestroom floor configuration has certain characteristics that affect its planning efficiency. (A) Double-loaded slab plans are the most efficient, with a minimum of corridor space per guestroom, back-to-back bathrooms, and many options for elevator and stairway placement. (B) Tower plans are the most compact, with a central core and guestrooms facing the outside. (C) Atrium plans are the least efficient, with single-loaded corridors overlooking the lobby.

percent of the gross floor area devoted to guestrooms; the amount of saleable space drops to 65 and 60 percent, respectively, in the tower and atrium configurations.

The money saved in construction by careful and economical planning of the guestroom floors may be enough to make a marginal project profitable; or those dollars might be diverted to pay for larger guestrooms or better quality furnishings, for such additional public spaces as conference or recreational facilities, or for other types of upgrades or additional guest amenities.

In addition to planning considerations, the architect must recognize a number of programmatic requirements established by the owner or management company. These include, for example, room mix (the number of rooms of each type: **double-double**, king, suite, etc.), the number of rooms for people with disabilities, the number of connecting rooms, and guest bathroom standards. Also, the development team sets exact requirements for each type of guestroom and agrees on model layouts. Similarly, the team establishes requirements for the suites, such as the relative luxury of the living room, the number of adjoining bedrooms, and whether to include a kitchenette or wet bar.

Guestroom Layout. The hotel guestroom is one area where the advances in accommodation over the past century are most obvious. Late in the nineteenth century hotels adopted such modern building systems as central heating, electric lighting, and elevators. But until the Buffalo Statler ("a room and a bath for a dollar and a half") opened in 1908, no major hotel featured private bathrooms. Air conditioning was unheard of and television and in-room movies, direct-dial telephones, electronic door locks, and other technological advances were unknown. In addition, most commercial hotels had small guestrooms, intended for the price-conscious self-employed businessman.

The impressive growth of Holiday Inn (founded in 1952) and other motor inn chains in the 1950s and 1960s was based on providing a consistent product to the traveling public, predominately families who appreciated the two double beds, standard in each guestroom, which easily accommodated parents and children. Today, to better meet the needs of different travelers, designers and operators typically provide a variety of room types: a queen bed for attendees at corporate training centers, a king bed for couples at destination resorts, or two double beds for the convention market. Because many hotels cater to several markets, most properties now have a mix of one- and two-bedded rooms as well as a variety of suites.

The layout of the guestrooms is intertwined with decisions that the architect makes during schematic design when he or she determines the dimensions of the typical guestroom, non-typical room shapes (at corners or behind fire stairs, for instance), and the design of the guest bathrooms. These decisions, along with the target room mix, provide the interior designer with the framework within which to design the various guestrooms and suites. This task includes designing the furniture layouts, selecting interior finishes for the floor and walls, choosing fabrics and colors, specifying lighting, and so forth.

In addition, the designer needs to integrate an understanding of the hotel's typical guests and their needs, establish and respect a furnishings budget, and create a design concept that gives the guestrooms a distinctive character, yet one consistent with the hotel's public areas. One approach is to consider zoning the

Exhibit 6   Guestroom Zoning

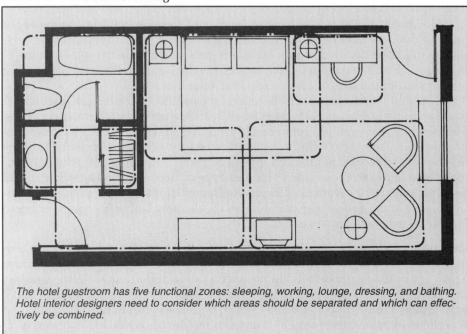

The hotel guestroom has five functional zones: sleeping, working, lounge, dressing, and bathing. Hotel interior designers need to consider which areas should be separated and which can effectively be combined.

guestroom into separate areas, accommodating such overlapping functions as sleeping, working, lounging, dressing, and hygiene (see Exhibit 6). In addition, the interior designer must select individual furnishings that meet a number of basic design criteria:

- *Beds:* Determine the exact room mix for the hotel; provide adequate spacing; include bedside tables and adequate lighting; consider TV viewing angle.

- *Work area:* Provide a desk or worktable, consider chair height and comfort, and provide a phone and adequate lighting.

- *Lounge area:* Provide a soft seating group; consider comfort, lighting, table(s), TV viewing angle, and adequate space for foldout sofa; assess need for mini-bar.

- *Clothes storage/dressing area:* Determine requirements for drawer space, the size of the closet, and luggage storage needs; provide full-length mirror.

- *Bathroom:* Select bathroom fixtures and accessories; consider lighting, counter space, ventilation, and finishes.

- *Décor:* Evaluate furniture, fixtures, and equipment (FF&E)—carpet, wall covering, sheer and blackout drapes, bedspreads, and so forth.

- *Other:* Screen view into guestroom from the corridor; provide a separate dressing area; assess the need for balcony, adjoining rooms, etc.

Sample guestroom layouts are shown in Exhibit 7.

Exhibit 7   Sample Guestroom Layouts

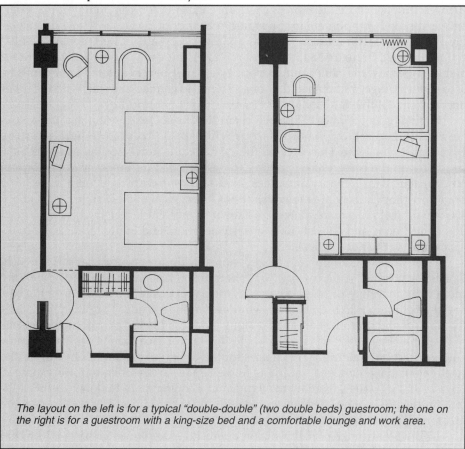

The layout on the left is for a typical "double-double" (two double beds) guestroom; the one on the right is for a guestroom with a king-size bed and a comfortable lounge and work area.

Suite Layout. Through the mid-twentieth century, hotel suites traditionally made up a relatively large part of urban hotels and frequently were occupied by permanent residents. Today, business and convention guests often use suites either for transient upscale accommodations or for hospitality purposes. Large hotels provide a hierarchy of suites, from those with a single-bay living room and a sleeping alcove to others with an oversized living room and as many as four or more adjoining rooms, including a dining or conference room and several bedrooms. (A "**bay**" is the space equivalent of a typical guestroom.) Presidential or other deluxe suites might fill most of a floor; at the 1,550-room Hilton Chicago the magnificent Presidential Suite encompasses the top two floors.

In most commercial hotels the suites are placed on the upper floors. Sometimes suites are stacked vertically in the same location on each floor, especially where they take advantage of an unusual architectural configuration. In the 1980s many operators established "club floors" with upgraded rooms and suites and such additional features as express check-in, concierge services, lounge and conference areas, and complimentary breakfast, tea, and/or cocktails. While in smaller properties these club lounges may be no larger than about 1,000 square feet (93 square meters), in luxury and convention hotels they may be two or three times bigger. Typically, the club lounge requires a small pantry for food preparation, associated storage, and data and phone systems to connect the staff with the other hotel administrative functions.

Beginning in the mid-1970s such chains as Guest Quarters and Granada Royale recognized the opportunity to provide specialized suite hotels for the extended-stay market. They created the first all-suite hotels for the business market. Later, in the early 1980s, Holiday Inn established its Embassy Suites brand; other major management companies soon followed with their own suite hotel brands. Although there are many variations, the typical upscale suite unit is about 450 square feet (42 square meters), or about 40 percent larger than a mid-priced hotel guestroom, and consists of a separate bedroom and living room, guest bathroom, and wet-bar or kitchenette.

There are two common models for suites, with dozens of variations for each. One is the narrow "front-to-back" or "**shotgun**" arrangement in which the living room faces an atrium or outside corridor, the bathroom is in the middle of the bay, and the bedroom is in the rear, with windows to the outside. The other, the "**side-by-side**" configuration, is organized along a double-loaded corridor and consists of two small bays, each with windows to the outside (see Exhibit 8). The operator and architect have a number of choices for the design of the bathroom and for the relative openness between the living and sleeping areas. Sheraton, for example, opts for sliding panels to allow the living and sleeping areas to flow together. Hilton, on the other hand, designs suites with more separation in order to provide greater privacy between the two areas.

In the 1990s, many of the major operating companies created additional budget-suite brands, essentially a reconfigured guestroom to provide a better sitting area, and a small kitchenette. When furnished with one queen or king bed, these "suites" aren't any larger than a standard commercial hotel guestroom, and offer little additional amenity.

The Lobby

In the early nineteenth century hotels did not have lobbies. Then, in 1828, Boston's Tremont House opened and featured, among other innovations, an "office"—today's lobby—and a series of formal lounges, dining, and banquet rooms. By the end of the century a few hotels had fabulous lobbies. For example, the Palace Hotel in San Francisco (1875, destroyed in 1906) featured a seven-story atrium into which horse-drawn carriages delivered guests. The Brown Palace in Denver (1892) is still flourishing. Hotel lobbies for most of the twentieth century—except for those in the grandest urban hotels—were relatively small. Then, in 1967, the Hyatt Regency Atlanta opened, introducing the atrium hotel, with 800 rooms arranged in an open square around a 22-story lobby, marking the shift toward larger lobbies.

Exhibit 8   Sample Suite Layouts

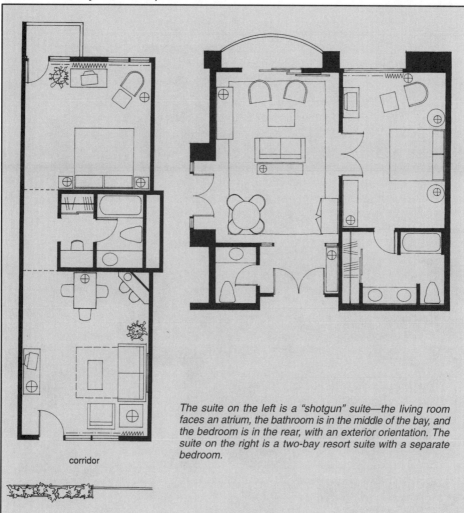

The suite on the left is a "shotgun" suite—the living room faces an atrium, the bathroom is in the middle of the bay, and the bedroom is in the rear, with an exterior orientation. The suite on the right is a two-bay resort suite with a separate bedroom.

corridor

The lobby is the most prominent of a hotel's public spaces. Many hotels serve as the city's gathering spot: for example, for several generations, New Yorkers would arrange to "meet under the clock at the Biltmore." In addition to establishing the image of the hotel, the lobby serves many obvious functional requirements. One of the key planning objectives for hotel architects is to cluster the public facilities—restaurants, lounges, function rooms, front desk, guest elevators, and so forth—around the lobby, ensuring that hotel guests can find the various facilities with a minimum of difficulty. When guests linger in it, the lobby serves as an informal gathering space. It also functions as a control point, with the staff visually overseeing access throughout the building.

Hilton Chicago & Towers, Chicago, IL. Convention hotels often feature large over-scaled suites, to be used for private parties and corporate entertaining. The elegant, two-floor Presidential Suite at the Hilton Chicago was featured in the climax to the film *The Fugitive*. (Courtesy of Hirsch Bedner Associates)

The development team must establish criteria for the planning and design of the lobby, based on the hotel's concept and the guest markets it will attract. These criteria might include the following:

- *Circulation:* Provide clear paths to front desk, elevators, food and beverage (F&B) outlets, function space, etc.

- *Front desk:* Make the front desk visible to entering guests. It should overlook the elevators, have sufficient space for check-in/check-out lines, and have direct access to the front office.

- *Luggage:* Provide areas for bellpersons, luggage storage, and other locked storage.

- *Seating*: Provide seating near the front desk and entrance, with more private seating nearby, and determine need for a lobby lounge.

- *Support functions*: Conveniently locate retail outlets, the concierge desk, public restrooms, house and pay phones, coatrooms, the hotel directory, etc.

- *Décor:* Establish the hotel's image with millwork, furnishings, artwork, lighting, signage, and so forth that are appropriate to the locale.

Food and Beverage Outlets

Hotel food service goes through frequent cycles of changing popularity with the public. Since the mid-1980s, with the increasing need to generate revenue from as much of the hotel as possible, hotel management has striven to create innovative restaurant and lounge alternatives. Operators realize that well-conceived food and beverage outlets increase the demand for guestrooms and meetings, attract guests from the local community, and generate additional profits. The potential F&B outlets, however, can be so diverse that the program and design of each outlet must be developed individually based on a survey of the local market and existing competition.

Occasionally (generally at luxury hotels), it is the hotel restaurant instead of the lobby that creates the overriding image for the property. Many upscale travelers and local businesspeople seek out Lespinasse or Jean Georges in New York, paying scant attention to the exceptional hotels in which they are housed. More commonly, though, the hotel operator provides restaurants and lounges principally as a service to hotel guests.

The design of hotel food and beverage outlets depends on the management company and the quality and price level of the hotel. Franchise and many mid-price chains establish a prototype restaurant concept and then install it in scores of properties nationwide. This may be a corner of the lobby outfitted for breakfast in small economy motels or a three-meal restaurant in mid-price roadside properties. The sameness provides a known quality level and satisfies a particular guest expectation.

On the other hand, upscale hotel management companies attempt to create individual and distinctive outlets in their larger first-class and luxury properties. Some operators carefully script the restaurant or lounge early in the development process, describing the design of the space, the theme, the menu, service style, table decoration—in short, writing full stage directions for the eventual production. Other operators provide relatively generic descriptions of the several outlets, and only when the architectural and interior design directions are established provide the operational detail to bring the outlets to reality. The development and

AT&T Learning Center, Basking Ridge, NJ. Corporate training centers often take on the aura of first-class hotels. Here, the restaurant features many private alcoves and intimate seating groupings, low light levels, and elegant furnishing and fixtures. (Courtesy of Benchmark Hospitality)

design team must determine the most appropriate approach, depending on the need for a distinctive outlet and the talents available.

The initial feasibility study, which investigates the demand and supply characteristics of the market and projects revenues and expenses, is the basis for recommending the number and capacities of food and beverage outlets for the proposed hotel. However, it is necessary for the development team to confirm these recommendations and establish concepts for the F&B areas. As hotels increase in size, developers usually provide additional outlets so that the scale of any one restaurant or lounge doesn't become overbearing.

Restaurants and lounges, because they face such severe outside competition, create the greatest operational and design challenges. Whatever the concept, the food and beverage designer must attempt to meet many generally accepted design criteria:

- *Location:* Position the main three-meal restaurant convenient to the lobby. Consider locating the specialty restaurant with direct exterior access.

- *Service:* Group all food outlets close to the kitchen or a satellite pantry, and provide bars with nearby storage and support areas.

- *Flexibility:* Design large restaurants and bars so that sections can be closed during slow periods.

- *Support areas:* Place public restrooms, coatrooms, and telephones nearby.

- *Layout:* Provide a desk for the host, service stations, and a flexible mix of table sizes. Minimize or eliminate floor-level changes to better accommodate disabled guests.

Hotel Restaurants. Types of hotel restaurants include the three-meal restaurant—frequently named "cafe" or given a signature identity—and a specialty restaurant, often based on a regional theme (Mexican, Italian) or food theme (steak, seafood). If demand merits, a third outlet might be a specialty coffee outlet or a deli. Relatively few hotels now offer a gourmet dining room because of low demand, the exceptions being luxury hotels in major business destinations. Each restaurant has its own image, attracting hotel guests and competing for different groups of diners from the local community.

As hotel operators strive to lower overhead and simplify their operations, many reduce the number of different F&B operations and, instead, develop a single restaurant with several distinct moods that are appropriate to the different meal periods and their general level of formality. For example, one suburban Hyatt Regency features a hotel restaurant with three clearly delineated zones. One is within the atrium, where diners are in a park-like setting among trees and natural light. A second area is at the edge of the atrium, where fabric awnings partially shelter the patrons and provide a semi-private setting not unlike a sidewalk café. The third zone is further back from the atrium, under the upper floors of guestrooms, in a low-ceilinged interior space, giving the diner the effect of having passed from outdoors into a small restaurant. The atrium area is treated most casually, with brick paving and tables with placemats or cloth runners. The intermediate zone is slightly more formal, and the "interior" section includes leather banquettes, table linen, lower lighting levels, and such additional accessories as artwork. The restaurant is highly successful in part because it offers different moods for breakfast or dinner, for family groups or couples, and for informal meals or special-occasion dinners.

Hotel Lounges. Using a process similar to that used for restaurants, the hotel management company establishes the bar and lounge program, the architect prepares preliminary plans to accommodate these requirements, and the interior designer develops the concepts more fully. In a small downtown hotel the primary beverage outlet may be a quiet and luxuriously furnished lobby bar, whereas in a convention or resort property it may be an action-oriented sports bar.

The lobby bar grew in popularity in the 1970s as a method of creating activity and excitement in the open atrium space. After their success as revenue generators was proven, developers began to place lobby bars even in the more traditional hotel lobbies. Open to the lobby space, the lounge provides a small service bar, limited food or tea service, occasional entertainment, and lounge seating that can be used flexibly to expand seating in the lobby.

The choice for a second beverage outlet often is a cocktail bar or entertainment room. This facility is completely enclosed, and features lower light levels and more tightly spaced seating. Depending on the theme, this type of lounge might have distinct sections, including a sit-down bar, an entertainment area with a stage and dance floor, a games area with billiards or backgammon, and quieter seating alcoves.

Function Space

Perhaps the clearest distinguishing feature among the different types of lodging properties is the size and mix of their **function space**: the ballrooms, smaller meeting and banquet rooms, reception and exhibit spaces, and dedicated conference and board rooms. First introduced in the mid-nineteenth century to accommodate important civic and social gatherings, function space now is utilized most often for a variety of corporate and association meetings. The two types of groups have different needs. Corporate groups require relatively small but high-quality spaces for sales and management meetings, new product introductions, and continuing-education programs for executives. The association market primarily needs extensive exhibition space, facilities for large group meetings, and small rooms for seminars and workshops. In addition, local organizations use hotel function space for a variety of meetings, banquets, and receptions; nearby residents use it for wedding receptions and other special occasions.

Generally, the feasibility study for a new hotel suggests a mix of function space based on an analysis of the demand for different types of business and social uses. For example, small mid-price properties generally offer a single multi-purpose ballroom, simply decorated and equipped to accommodate a full range of small meetings, civic lunches, bar and bas mitzvahs, wedding receptions, and local product displays. It only infrequently is used to attract group rooms business.

On the other hand, convention hotels include a major ballroom for 1,000 to 3,000 people, smaller junior ballrooms, and dozens of small multi-purpose meeting and breakout rooms. The ballrooms are designed for major banquets and social functions but include audiovisual and other systems for meetings. The secondary meeting rooms, which have few built-in features or technological systems, often can be combined in numerous configurations.

Conference centers are different still. These hotels are designed for much smaller groups (no larger than 200 to 300 people) and feature dedicated single-purpose banquet, meeting, conference, and boardrooms so that each client has specialized rooms to meet particular needs. Conference centers offer such amenities as extensive foyer and gathering areas, 24-hour use of meeting rooms, additional conference services, and full audiovisual systems.

Because of the differences among the many types of lodging properties and the markets they serve and the highly competitive nature of the meetings business, the design team must review carefully the programming and design criteria for the function areas. In smaller, less-sophisticated hotels the function space may only total 10 to 20 square feet (.93 to 1.86 square meters) per guestroom. However, in convention hotels and dedicated conference centers it commonly reaches 60 and 100 square feet (5.6 and 9.3 square meters) per room, respectively. Considering the additional kitchen and back-of-the-house areas needed to fully support a first-class convention facility, the potential investment in the hotel function space is substantial. Therefore, most successful developers carefully consider the appropriate balance between large and small function rooms, their décor, and equipment.

Just as with the restaurants, where particular consultants deal with specific elements, the planning of the function space may require special consultants, such as acoustic and audiovisual specialists and lighting designers. For large properties the operator may assemble focus groups consisting of meeting planners and others to discuss those features of meeting space that are most critical to them, to help ensure their future business. Such discussions have led to a number of fairly typical planning and design criteria for meeting and banquet space:

- *Location:* Group all function areas in a location easily accessible from the lobby; in major convention hotels consider creating two or more separate function zones.

- *Flexibility:* Include moveable partitions in larger rooms, determine the need for multi-purpose versus dedicated rooms, and create multiple pre-function areas.

- *Access:* Provide a separate entrance to the function area from the street or parking lot, provide public and service access to each function room, and consider the access needs for moving display materials into the ballroom and exhibit areas.

- *Support areas:* Include sufficient restrooms, coatrooms, and telephones for the public and provide banquet pantry, furniture, and audiovisual storage in the back-of-the-house.

- *Structure:* Provide column-free function spaces and locate the ballroom and larger meeting rooms independent of the guestroom tower to simplify the hotel's structure.

- *Ceiling height:* Determine the need for projection booths in the larger function rooms and consider how the high ceilings in these rooms will affect the floor above.

- *Windows:* Determine the need for natural light in function and assembly areas.

For new projects, the architect must address these planning issues early in schematic design because they have a major impact on the hotel's ability to attract group business, obviously essential in the major convention markets. In existing hotels, the owners must assess the scope of any potential renovation to make the meeting and banquet areas more functional both for the public and for the hotel staff. Although it is expensive to modify function space, an older hotel may need to undertake a major renovation to remain competitive.

Once the schematic design is accepted, the architect, interior designer, other consultants, and management staff need to focus on the details of future operations. For example, consider where meeting registration desks or portable bars will be set up in the prefunction area and how guests will move through the space. Or study alternative furniture layouts for each individual meeting or banquet room; that is, test whether the room dimensions accommodate various meeting or banquet configurations efficiently. Such function plans, developed relatively early in design, often show that a minor adjustment to the planning will offer substantial improvement in flexibility or increased capacity (see Exhibit 9).

Experienced designers are familiar with many simple features which result in a better experience for the banquet guest or meeting attendee or which offer operational advantages. Most of these do not cost any more to implement if incorporated into the design at an early stage. For example, some designers typically use a ballroom carpet with an approximately 22-inch (56-centimeter) pattern repeat to help hotel staff quickly arrange chairs in straight rows. Consider the potential problems if banquet guests have unscreened views into the service corridor, or if too few telephones are installed, or if inadequate directional and room signage are provided. The design team must address many of these seemingly insignificant design issues:

- *Floors:* Select a carpet pattern to aid in room setup; use a portable dance floor.

- *Walls:* Apply a chair rail to walls to protect their finish; add fabric panels to improve acoustics and upgrade room appearance.

- *Ceiling:* Organize HVAC, lighting, sound system, fire protection, and other systems into a unified design.

- *Windows:* Add full blackout capability.

- *Furniture:* Select risers, lecterns, stacking chairs, and a balance of rectangular classroom tables and round or oval banquet tables; select high-quality chairs for upgraded conference rooms.

- *Lighting:* Provide a fully dimmable system including, as appropriate, chandeliers, down lights, track lights, fluorescent lighting, and decorative wall fixtures.

- *HVAC/systems:* Provide separate mechanical, electrical, and sound systems for each room division.

- *Communications:* Include TV, telephone, recording, and data lines in each function and control room.

Exhibit 9   Function Area Plan

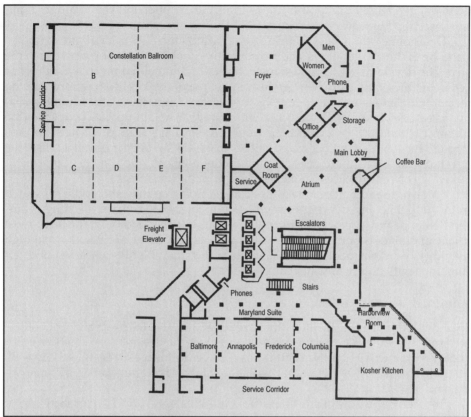

This hotel's function space includes a column-free subdivisible ballroom and several smaller meeting rooms. The Hyatt Regency Baltimore's plan shows how the ballroom is not located under the guestroom structure but in its own wing, whereas pre-function foyers, meeting rooms, and support areas are within the main building. (Courtesy of Hyatt Hotels)

Recreational Facilities

In the 1980s and early 1990s recreational amenities became a larger component in many hotel and resort facilities. The traveling public became more health and fitness conscious and many properties—especially business-oriented urban properties and destination resorts—responded to this trend by adding a health club or spa facilities. A generation ago, the only recreational amenity most lodging properties had was a swimming pool. Over time, developers realized the competitive advantage of more expansive fitness facilities and added exercise equipment and limited health club facilities. Now it is common for first-class or luxury hotels to include a full-size spa to complement other business-oriented facilities; for suburban hotels or small town motels to enclose its pool area to provide a swim and health club for the community; and for conference centers to add extensive out-door jogging, tennis, and golf facilities to its indoor pool and spa to attract high-level executive retreats.

Determining the appropriate mix of recreation facilities is based on an under-standing of the market needs and a competitive analysis of other properties in the area. The development team also may consider the potential revenue that can be generated by selling club memberships to people in the local community. Among the planning issues are considerations for guest access to the facilities and the rela-tive need to isolate them from other building elements. In upscale properties the architect should try to separate the pool area so that guests don't need to pass through the lobby—or other major public areas—in swimwear or robes. Also, the development team should keep in mind that non-guests who use the fitness facili-ties want convenient access to the facilities from parking areas.

Some of the recreational facilities can get noisy, so they should be separated from the public areas and guestrooms if possible. For example, meeting rooms should not be near racquet courts or the swimming pool (although the three-meal restaurant might benefit from views of the pool area). The chlorine odor and high humidity of indoor pools generally require that they be fully enclosed and not combined with non-recreational areas.

Administration Offices

The hotel's design must include office space for the executive staff and front office, accounting, and sales departments. Not only does the design of these offices influ-ence the productivity of the staff, it has a direct influence on the guests as well. Many guests deal with the general manager, sales and catering staff, credit manag-ers, and others.

Typically, the administrative offices are clustered into four groups—front office, accounting, executive, and sales and catering—that, except for the front office, have some flexibility in their location. Even with tremendous advances in technology and communications, it still remains imperative that the front office be located adjacent to the front desk. The front office includes space for the front office manager, reservations, telephone PBX, and a general work area. If possible, the accounting offices should be close by as well, because of the cashier function at the front desk. The accounting area includes offices for the controller and other staff members who take care of payroll, accounts payable, accounts receivable, and management information systems.

In many hotels it is not possible to provide sufficient space near the lobby for the executive and the sales and catering offices. These easily can be located a few floors away, often near function space. An advantage of grouping these together is that executive and sales personnel can share a reception area and conference rooms. If that is not a necessity, these offices can be separate from each other. The executive suite includes offices for the general manager, resident manager, and often the rooms division and food and beverage executive assistant managers, as well as the necessary secretarial support. The sales and catering area includes offices for the marketing and sales directors, several sales and banquet managers, conference services, and general support space.

In the late twentieth century, when hotels were expanding their staffs, operators added offices for such new department heads as director of guest services (in charge of doorpersons, bellpersons, the concierge, etc.) and director of information technology. With the downsizing at the end of the 1990s, many executive suites might have excess space that could be renovated as a business center or another revenue-generating function.

Food Production Areas

Of all the service areas in a hotel, the kitchens and related food production areas require the most design attention, in part because of the extent to which the mechanical, electrical, and plumbing services must be integrated with the functional layout of these spaces. In addition, the design of the kitchen, usually the largest single back-of-the-house area, critically influences labor costs for the life of the building. Distances within the kitchen should be as short as possible, related activities should be located close together, and layouts should be flexible. Therefore, the planning and design aspects of the kitchens require the coordinated attention of a variety of specialized food service and engineering consultants.

Among the many planning requirements that the architect should address during conceptual design, the most important is to locate the receiving and food storage areas, the kitchen(s), and restaurants and banquet rooms on a single floor. When this is not possible (the goal is especially hard to achieve in large hotels), the designer must assess the relative merits of alternate groupings of service and public functions. The following table lists areas that should be linked together if at all possible:

Essential food service connections

- Food storage to main kitchen
- Main kitchen to restaurants
- Room service area to service elevators
- Kitchen or banquet pantry to ballroom

Desirable food service connections

- Receiving to food storage
- Main kitchen to banquet pantry
- Banquet pantry to smaller banquet rooms
- Banquet pantry to pre-function rooms
- Three-meal restaurant pantry to room service area
- Kitchen to cocktail lounges
- Beverage storage to cocktail lounges
- Kitchen to garbage/trash holding
- Kitchen to employee dining

The amount of floor space required in the kitchen and food and beverage storage areas depends on the number of meals served, the complexity of the menu, and the delivery schedule. Because of the high cost of equipment, energy, and labor, one goal should be to design the smallest kitchen that meets the operational objectives. For example, many downtown hotels, where space is at a premium because of high land costs and where most foods are readily available, operate with a minimum food storage area.

After the food production space has been allocated during the early design phases, the food service consultant proposes a preliminary kitchen design. If major planning criteria area met, such as providing a single main kitchen close to the restaurants and function outlets, the overall design can be greatly simplified and the duplication of equipment eliminated. A typical kitchen layout is shown in Exhibit 10. Although the food service consultant prepares the kitchen plan, the architect also needs to understand the flow of food and personnel through the kitchen in order to better plan the surrounding support areas. The food and beverage storage areas usually are located adjacent to either the receiving area or the kitchen, with the latter arranged preferred. The food service layout and operation is improved when designers observe the following objectives:

- Provide a straight-line flow of food from storage to serving.

- Eliminate cross-traffic and backtracking.

- Minimize the distance between the kitchen serving area and restaurant seating.

- Arrange compact work centers.

- Locate secondary storage near each station, as required.

- Place shared facilities centrally (e.g., establish a single ware-washing area convenient to restaurants and banquet facilities).

- Consider sanitation and employee safety.

- Plan for the efficient use of all utilities.

- Provide flexible utility connections to facilitate rearrangement of equipment.

- Group all walk-in refrigerators and freezers together to share common walls and compressors, and save construction and energy costs.

- Incorporate computer technology, such as point of sale computers/printers, into the kitchen layout.

- Provide fire-protection systems throughout, especially over cooking equipment.

- Consider sanitation and employee safety.

Other Back-of-the-House Areas

Although the kitchen may be the most critical of the service functions, it occupies only about three to four percent of the total hotel area; together, the other back-of-the-house functions require approximately twice that amount. Many of these tie

Exhibit 10   Kitchen Equipment Plan

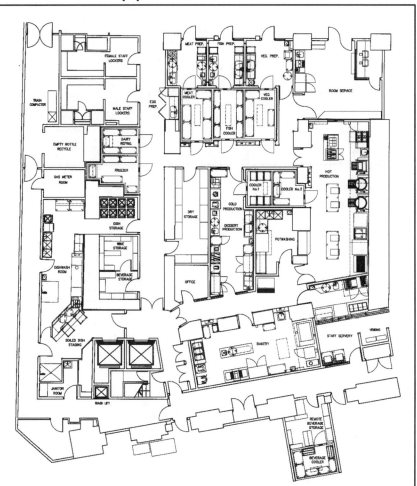

Food-service operations are among the most difficult to coordinate, combining major technical requirements for cooking, refrigeration, and ventilation with functional needs for efficient service flow. This plan shows how a typical kitchen is divided into such discrete work areas as storage, hot production, cold production, room service, and dishwashing. (Courtesy of Four Seasons Hotels)

directly into the kitchen, such as the receiving area and employee dining. Others, such as the laundry and housekeeping areas, are more directly associated with the rooms operation.

Too often the architect and other members of the development and design team defer decisions on the planning of the back-of-the-house until the design development phase, six months or more into the design process. Because these areas are so important to the efficient functioning of the hotel, including its ability

Exhibit 11   Back-of-the-House Plan

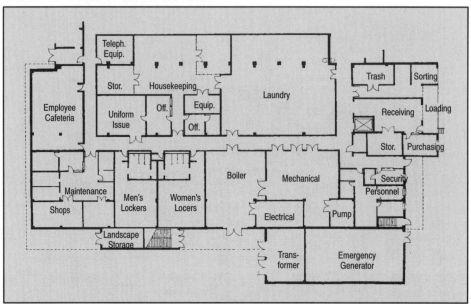

The service areas in this plan are located on a single level (except for the main kitchen, directly above), greatly enhancing back-of-the-house movement among departments. The plan illustrates the successful grouping of related functions: laundry, housekeeping, and uniform issue are in a single block; uniform issue and employee lockers are together; personnel offices are near the employee entrance; maintenance and engineering areas are clustered; and the cafeteria is close to the lockers.

to operate without increased staff levels, the team should establish its back-of-the-house program at the outset, and the architect should consider their planning implications early in schematic design. Throughout the design phase, the management company must carefully review the plans as the architect refines and adds detail to the back-of-the house areas (see Exhibit 11). The following list includes many of the more essential planning objectives:

- Plan the receiving area to accommodate at least two trucks at one time, more for larger operations.

- Enclose the receiving area so that it is secure and protected from the weather.

- Separate the trash/garbage holding area from the receiving dock.

- Position receiving and timekeeper offices so that managers visually control the loading dock and employee entrance.

- Establish employee lockers based on the staffing program for the hotel and the expected male/female ratio.

- Design employee lounge or dining areas with a serving line, dining tables, lounge seating, vending, etc.; if possible provide windows for natural light.

- Provide linen chute from guestroom floor service areas to soiled linen area.

- Establish separate locked linen storage for particular departments (F&B, pool, etc.).

- Group the engineer, assistants' offices, repair shops, etc. around central work area.

- Locate mechanical areas so that noise and vibration don't negatively affect guest areas.

- Design mechanical rooms to allow for eventual equipment replacement.

The following text discusses such back-of-the-house areas as receiving and trash, general storage, employee areas, laundry and housekeeping, and maintenance and engineering.

Receiving and Trash. The receiving and trash areas should be located so that they accommodate the necessary movement of trucks without disrupting guest parking, yet are hidden from the hotel guestrooms and such public areas as restaurants, lounges, and recreational areas. In addition to the major connection to the kitchens for incoming food and liquor and for outgoing trash, sufficient area must be available in the receiving area to inspect goods and move them to storage areas. Often, the purchasing or receiving staff located in an area overlooking the receiving dock provide security at the dock.

General Storage. Hotels require large amounts of storage area. Most storage is associated with specific functions: food storage near the kitchen, furniture storage near the ballroom, and linen storage on the guestroom floors. However, hotels also require space for storing miscellaneous items such as old financial records and extra furnishings and equipment. The general storage area sometimes is located near the receiving area but it can easily be located in a more remote area. It should be secured and perhaps include two or three caged areas, so that different operating departments control separate sections of the room.

Employee Areas. Employee areas form another major part of the back of the house. The usual components—human resources office, staff lockers, and employee dining area—are somewhat independent from each other and relate to other service areas as much as to each other. For example, the human resources function is related closely to the employee entrance, the lockers to the uniform issue area and to the time clock, and the employee cafeteria to the main kitchen. In some destination resorts the operator may have to provide employee housing as well.

Although employee areas may be limited in small properties, it is essential that adequate locker and other space be provided in full-service hotels. During the early stages of design, the architect usually designates large blocks of space to the individual back-of-the-house functions, such as locker rooms. Often, though, these aren't tested to see whether the required functions can be accommodated in the space, which might have columns, an irregular shape, or other constraints. The architect, with additional program information provided by the management company, by the end of schematic design should develop a level of detail to confirm that lockers, restrooms, and so on can be accommodated in the space provided.

Laundry and Housekeeping. The laundry and housekeeping areas are another major back-of-the-house component. Even the smallest motel needs some space for storage and control of guestroom linen; in larger hotels the two functions may total more than 5,000 square feet (465 square meters). Among the key decisions the development team must make is whether to have an in-house laundry. For smaller inns, the high cost to build and equip a laundry may make it more economical to use a commercial laundry service than handle it in-house. On the other hand, virtually all mid-price and above hotels operate their own laundries in order to control quality and ensure availability of linens.

The laundry layout may be designed by the technical services staff of the hotel management company or by the equipment supplier. The laundry preferably should be located on the hotel's lowest floor to prevent noise and vibrations from disturbing guest areas.

The laundry and housekeeping areas are closely related and should be adjacent, even though they are separately managed. But even where the laundry is omitted, extensive areas are required for collecting, loading, receiving, and storing linen. The main function, of course, is to clean and distribute guestroom (bed and bath) and restaurant linen, uniforms, kitchen laundry, and guest clothing. Resort hotels may have additional laundry demand, such as swimming pool towels.

Maintenance and Engineering. A final back-of-the-house component includes the engineering offices, repair and maintenance shops, and mechanical and electrical areas. Too often these activities are given insufficient space—often no more than the areas left over after schematic design. The engineering function operates 24-hours a day and must be centrally located so that the engineering staff can respond readily to both routine and emergency calls. In large hotels the engineering office-and-shops complex may occupy more than 5,000 square feet (465 square meters). Often the area is designed with the maintenance offices, repair shops, and storerooms clustered around a central engineering work area.

The mechanical equipment areas may be scattered throughout the building. They do not need to be immediately adjacent to the engineering offices but, whenever possible, they should be located in proximity to the laundry, kitchen, and other high-energy use areas for most effective operation. For example, it is common to install ballroom air-handlers on a mezzanine or within a separate roof enclosure to put them as close as possible to the function space and to reduce the substantial amount of space required for supply and return ducts. Also, additional mechanical equipment is usually placed on the roof of the guestroom tower.

Endnotes

1. Carlo Wolff, "Fitting In, Looking Fresh," *Lodging and Hospitality,* February 1998, pp. 34–36.

Key Terms

atrium—A guestroom floor configuration in which rooms are laid out off a single-loaded corridor encircling a multistory lobby space.

bay—The space equivalent of a standard guestroom.

double-double room—A guestroom featuring two double beds.

double-loaded slab—A guestroom floor configuration in which rooms are laid out on both sides of a central corridor.

feasibility study—A study, usually conducted by a consulting firm, which assesses present and future demand for a proposed business. Focus of the study is on estimating the business's income and expenses for a period after it opens.

function space—Space such as ballrooms, meeting and banquet rooms, reception and exhibit spaces, and dedicated conference and boardrooms designed to accommodate meetings and a variety of corporate and association conferences.

porte cochere—A canopy designed to protect hotel guests from inclement weather and provide visual emphasis to the main entrance.

schematic design—The first phase of hotel design in which the architect develops a space list and subsequently refines it into a more detailed program.

shotgun suite—A suite in which the living room faces an atrium or outside corridor, the bathroom is in the middle of the bay, and the bedroom is in the rear, with an exterior orientation.

side-by-side suite—A suite that consists of two small bays, each with windows to the outside.

tower—A guestroom floor configuration in which rooms are grouped around a central vertical core.

Review Questions

1. What are the key steps of the development process?

2. What does a feasibility report typically cover?

3. Why is it important for the development team to establish construction and engineering criteria?

4. What are the three design phases the architect typically works through?

5. What are some of the site characteristics an architect must investigate before designing a hotel?

6. What are some of the planning considerations for guestroom floors?

7. What are some of the design criteria for food and beverage outlets?

8. What role do function areas play in a hotel?

9. What food production areas should be linked if possible?

10. What are some back-of-the-house design criteria?

Internet Sites

For more information, visit the following Internet sites. Remember that Internet addresses can change without notice. If the site is no longer there, you can use a search engine to look for additional sites.

American Institute of Architects
www.aia.org

R.S. Means Company (numerous publications and other information)
www.rsmeans.com

U.S. Department of Energy—Center of Excellence for Sustainable Development
www.sustainable.doe.gov/ buildings/gbintro.shtml

U.S. Department of Justice—Americans with Disabilities Act
www.usdojgov/crt/ada/ adahom1.htm

Chapter 15 Outline

Concept Development
    Feasibility
    Regulations
The Project Planning Team
    Planning the Layout
Design of Function Areas
    Receiving Area
    Storage Areas
    The Kitchen
    The Dining Room
    Employee Facilities
    Office Space
Evaluation of Finished Blueprints

Competencies

1. Describe the concept development process for food service facilities, and identify regulations that affect the construction and operation of food service facilities. (pp. 477–481)

2. Explain the makeup and responsibilities of the project planning team, and describe food service facility layout. (pp. 481–486)

3. Summarize design issues in the receiving, storage, and kitchen areas. (pp. 487–503)

4. Summarize design issues in the dining room, employee facilities, and office space areas, and explain how finished blueprints are evaluated. (pp. 503–506)

15

Food Service Planning and Design

This chapter was written and contributed by Carolyn U. Lambert, Ph.D., Associate Professor, School of Hotel, Restaurant & Recreation Management, Pennsylvania State University, University Park, Pennsylvania.

Ron Prescott, a long-time manager for the ABC Restaurant Co., was attending his first design conference on the new restaurant concept the company was planning. As the architects presented the concept, Ron studied the plans. He listened as the architects described how the new building related to the other buildings in the area, how the traffic flow would increase the number of potential guests, and how creative the exterior façade would be. The architects then described the basic layout of the interior, illustrating the locations of the kitchen, dining room, banquet room, and cocktail lounge. Ron noticed that the front of the restaurant had large greenhouse-type windows with no curtains, the dining area included several mezzanines, with no ramps for wheelchairs, and that the cocktail lounge was not easily accessible to the kitchen. He mentioned these concerns to the architects; they replied that the current layout was necessary. Ron realized that the architects did not understand how a restaurant functioned or understand current regulations and decided to talk to his company. He also recognized that he would have to be prepared for each stage of the planning phase to ensure that his company obtained a restaurant concept that would be successful.

SUCCESSFUL FOOD SERVICE DESIGN requires a knowledgeable planning team. The representative of the owners or the restaurant corporation must be aware of the goals and objectives for the restaurant as well as the principles and regulations involved in laying out a restaurant. While this chapter will not qualify the reader to be a food facilities design consultant, it is intended to provide the information necessary for the reader to be a competent member of a planning team—the group of professionals that design a restaurant.

Concept Development

The development of a food service operation usually begins with a concept or idea, suggested by a land developer, a group of investors, or a corporation. After the

Exhibit 1   Preliminary Decisions Needed to Plan Food Service Facilities

Type of Food Service Facility	**Interior Environment**
Coffee Shop	Formal
Cafeteria	Informal
Quick Service	Trendy
Fine Dining	Theme
Menu Description	**Design Objectives**
Number of Menu Items	Number of Turns
Quality of Menu Items	Check Average
Price Range	Quiet Atmosphere
Type of Menu Items	Noisy Atmosphere
Location of Facility	**Operating Characteristics**
Suburban	Days and Hours of Operation
Urban	Number of Seats
Rural	
Service Styles	**Special Characteristics**
Table	Banquet Rooms
Counter	Salad Bars
Tableside	Alcoholic Beverage Service
Take Out	

Source: Adapted from E. A. Kazarian, *Foodservice Facilities Planning*, 3d ed. (New York: VNR, 1989), p. 22.

idea for a restaurant is agreed on, the owners will need to make decisions regarding the specific characteristics of the restaurant, such as the type of facility, the type of menu, and location. A list of these key decisions is shown in Exhibit 1. These initial decisions will direct the entire planning process, so they should be made carefully and the owners must reach a consensus. It simply won't work for one business partner to decide that he or she wants a 24-hour coffee shop, and another to decide that the style of service should be buffet.

While some groups of owners will assume responsibility for making all of these initial decisions, others may delegate the responsibility to an architect or food facilities design consultant. For example, if the owners are entertainers or professional sports figures, they might believe that the architect or consultant would make more informed decisions. Or the owners may not live in the same vicinity or have time to devote to the project. If the responsibility for making preliminary decisions is turned over to the architect or food facilities design consultant, the owners should be represented by a professional food service manager who understands their goals and objectives and who can ensure that their goals are being met (someone like Ron Prescott in the scenario that opened the chapter). A food service manager will be able to understand the terminology used by architects and food facilities design consultants.

There is no absolute order in which the preliminary decisions are made. Sometimes the restaurant's location is decided first, while in other situations the type of service or type of menu may be selected first. These decisions help the owners and the food service manager develop a detailed, descriptive model of the restaurant that includes a market survey, a description of the menu, the restaurant's operating characteristics, and the type of food service facility.

The market survey should include a detailed profile of potential guests. The profile should include information on the occupation, age, sex, geographic location, income, and lifestyle of these guests. The guest profile is the foundation of the other segments of the descriptive model. For example, if the anticipated guests are single adults, the restaurant will need to be open later in the evening than it would be if families were the anticipated guests. The daily and weekly peak periods of dining for these two guest groups or markets are different also.

The menu should reflect the needs and desires of the target market. The description of the menu should include the number of menu items in each category, portion sizes, production techniques, and menu specialty items. This phase of the development process is important, because the majority of decisions made during planning are dictated by the menu. For example, as the complexity of menu items increases, the kitchen must be larger to allow for more equipment and work space.

Defining the market and the menu will help determine the restaurant's operating characteristics. Operating characteristics include the annual operating days, daily business hours, forecasted volume, and forecasted peak periods. The restaurant's organizational structure also needs to be identified, including such aspects as personnel policies and procedures and control measures for purchasing, receiving, issuing, production, and cash.

The specific type of food service facility, such as coffee shop, fine dining, or quick service, may be identified as a result of decisions about the menu and style of service, if it wasn't decided prior to planning the menu. Each type of food service facility requires a different type of layout.

Feasibility

After the descriptive model for a restaurant is developed, the proposed restaurant will need to be analyzed to determine its profitability. Usually a profitability, or feasibility, study is conducted by a professional hospitality business consultant. However, in some cases the owners may decide to complete it. The feasibility study should take into account the specific site of the restaurant. Each feasibility study should be unique, as each restaurant will have distinct characteristics. The number of seats in the dining room and the forecasted check average are used to predict the number of guests each day and total sales. These data are then used in a projected income statement. The consultant will also forecast food and beverage costs using menu and market information. Estimates of labor, overhead, and other operating costs such as china, glassware, and uniforms are determined. Finally, costs for the land, building, furniture, fixtures, and equipment must be calculated. The consultant will compare projected income with estimated costs to determine if the restaurant will be profitable. With these figures, the owners should monitor the designers to ensure that design costs don't exceed the original budget.

Regulations

While the feasibility study is being performed, regulations governing construction and operation of the restaurant should be studied. Numerous regulations exist on local, state, and federal levels that influence restaurant design, including:

- Zoning codes

- Department of Agriculture (1999 Food Code)[1] regulations

- The Americans with Disabilities Act of 1990

Zoning Codes. Zoning codes are the regulations that dictate the types of businesses and buildings allowed in specific geographic areas. Zoning codes may include regulations for **setback** (a building's distance from the street), parking (the number and size of parking spaces and the design of parking lots), easements (allowances for utility lines), height (the maximum height of buildings), and construction standards (quality and safety requirements for buildings). Construction standards include the National Electrical Code, the Building Officials and Code Administrators code, and the Life Safety Code from the National Fire Protection Association.

Some zoning codes include a section on compatibility. This section allows city officials to decide if the proposed building fits in with the surrounding buildings and environment, regardless of whether it meets all of the other restrictions. A compatibility section allows communities to protect the local character. For example, all buildings in Alexandria, Virginia, must conform to the local architectural style. One of the restrictions in Alexandria is that restaurants cannot display large neon signs on the exterior of their buildings.

Each community has a distinct set of zoning codes, so restaurant owners should check with City Hall to obtain a copy of the specific codes in force for the area in which they want to build. A municipal zoning officer can stop construction at any time he or she determines that the zoning codes are not being followed. When construction is completed, a building inspector must tour the building to determine if the zoning codes have been met. If zoning codes are not complied with, the owners of the newly built restaurant may not be granted an occupancy permit to open the business.

Department of Agriculture (1999 Food Code) Regulations. The 1999 Food Code is a reference document for regulatory agencies responsible for monitoring food safety in restaurants and other food service operations. While it isn't a federal law, it was developed jointly by the Food and Drug Administration, the Department of Agriculture's Food Safety and Inspection Service, and the Centers for Disease Control and Prevention to provide a uniform system of regulation. The Food Code includes information on the plan review process that is required for all new restaurants. The Food Code also includes Hazard Analysis and Critical Control Points (HACCP) guidelines to help food service operators and employees produce safe food. While HACCP implementation is voluntary, managers should strive to design food services that decrease the risk of food hazards. The 1999 Food Code states "the likelihood of the occurrence of a hazard in a finished product is definitely influenced by facility and equipment design, construction, and installation, which play a key role in any preventive strategy."[2]

Many states require that properly prepared blueprints of a new restaurant and detailed descriptions of equipment be submitted to appropriate authorities to ensure that all regulations are followed. The plans must include a description of the restaurant's building, physical surroundings, water supply, type of equipment, refuse disposal system, and sewage disposal system. The 1999 Food Code contains a food establishment plan review document to assist regulatory personnel achieve uniformity in the plan review process. Although the 1999 Food Code has not been adopted by all states, the plan review document can help regulators ensure that plans for new restaurants comply with nationally recognized food safety standards. The National Sanitation Foundation (NSF) governs the installation of food equipment, which is an integral part of the plans. For specific information about NSF regulations, food service managers should contact their state's department of health.

ADA Regulations. The Americans with Disabilities Act of 1990[3] provides civil rights protection for individuals with disabilities. The ADA states that disabled individuals cannot be discriminated against if they can, with reasonable accommodation, perform the job and are not a threat to the health and safety of other employees. What is "reasonable accommodation"? According to the law, possible accommodations include providing work areas that are wheelchair accessible and acquiring special equipment such as Braille devices and telephone handset amplifiers. The law does not compel employers to make accommodations that would result in undue hardships for them.

Title III of the ADA states that all public accommodations operated by private entities must provide barrier-free facilities. Modifications to make existing structures barrier-free must be made if they are "readily achievable" and do not create "undue hardship" for the facility. Restaurant managers need to be aware of these regulations as they plan a new facility or renovate an existing one. The U.S. Department of Justice maintains an Internet site that has information managers can use to learn about accessibility issues.

The Project Planning Team

Once the owners have defined the concept and approved the feasibility study, the project planning team can be assembled. The project planning team for a restaurant is responsible for implementing the ideas developed by the owners. The makeup of the team will depend on the owners' expertise, the time available, and the amount of available capital. A typical team includes one of the owners or a representative of the owner (such as the food service manager), an architect, a food facilities consultant, an interior designer, and a graphics designer. Additional team members may include a lighting consultant, an acoustical engineer, and a landscape architect.

Each team member should be selected carefully, since one weak or incompetent member can ruin a project. For example, the food facilities consultant must be able to communicate effectively with the architect and designers and defend his or her ideas in team meetings. If the consultant is inexperienced or unprepared, the architect may assert his or her own ideas and design a restaurant different from the intended one. The owners should request credentials and evidence of past projects from all team members and evaluate each candidate's ability to work on the team before hiring.

The owners should discuss the restaurant's concept and business objectives with the planning team to avoid costly misunderstandings. For example, if the owners' business objective is to operate a formal restaurant with an extensive menu, a high guest-check average, and a 90-minute average length of stay, the interior designer will need to coordinate the dining room's color scheme, type of furniture, and lighting to provide the type of upscale atmosphere that will match this objective.

The owners or their representative, such as the food service manager, approve the blueprints created by the project planning team. The owners sign all legal documents and are responsible for securing financial support for the restaurant. One of the owners, or the food service manager representing the owners, may act as chairperson of the team. However, the owners may delegate this responsibility to the architect or food facilities design consultant if they (or the food service manager) aren't knowledgeable about architecture and construction. If the project is part of a larger property, the architect may have responsibility for the restaurant design. However, in cases where the restaurant is the entire project, the food facilities consultant may assume the lead role in implementing the design planned by the team.

The architect is responsible for designing the physical structure to support the restaurant's concept as defined by the owners. The architect may coordinate the work of the interior designer, graphics designer, and landscape architect.

Frequent communication between team members is essential during the planning stage. The plans for the restaurant's physical structure will undergo many changes before the design is finalized, so all team members must be accessible to provide their expertise when needed. The architect or owner's representative will need to develop a time schedule for completion of the construction planning documents and the construction process. Indecision on design issues can cause the restaurant opening to be delayed, which will impact the profitability of the restaurant.

Once the planning team has agreed on the restaurant's concept, and business objectives have been clearly defined, the project planning team can begin working on the layout.

Planning the Layout

Initial total space estimates were made in the feasibility phase in order to forecast the restaurant's construction costs and annual sales volume. The next step in planning the layout, the arrangement of workstations and equipment, is to divide the total space by estimating the amount of space needed for the dining room, kitchen, storage rooms, and other sections of the restaurant. An exact declaration of space requirements is difficult, since many factors must be considered. For preliminary estimates, charts and graphs have been developed (see Exhibit 2). The planning team should realize that these guidelines are "rules of thumb" only. They should

Exhibit 2   Sample Industry Guidelines

Work Center Allocation by Approximate Percentage of Total Space (Includes Aisles Prorated to Work Centers)

Area	Hospital	Restaurant	Cafeteria
Receiving	3	3	3
Refrigeration (shelf)	11	12	12
Freezer	5	7	6
Unrefrigerated Storerooms	9	14	12
Meat Preparation	2	3	4
Vegetable and Salad Preparation	7	8	8
Production Cooking	12	14	14
Pot Washing	4	5	4
Bakery	5	6	5
Offices	5	5	5
Tray Service	11		
Serving Line (Area)	11	12	14
Dishwashing	12	11	13
Tray Cart Storage	3		

Kitchen Area Requirements

Type of Service	Sq. Ft. of Kitchen Area per Dining Area Seat	Total Back of House Area per Dining Area Seat
Cafeterias, Commercial	6–8	10–12
Lunch Rooms and Coffee Shops	4–6	8–10
Table Service Dining Rooms	5–7	10–12

Dining Room Square Feet Per Person and Turnover Characteristics of Various Service Methods

Type of Service		Dining Room Sq. Ft. per Seat to be Allotted	Turnover in Patrons per Seat per Hour
Cafeterias Not Including Serving Counter	Commercial	13–18	$1^{1}/_{2}$–$2^{1}/_{2}$
	Industrial	12–16	2–3
	School	10–15	2–3
Lunch Rooms and	Counter service only Area includes counter and serving aisle.	18–26	2–$3^{1}/_{2}$
Coffee Shops	Counter and Table service	15–17	2–3
Waiter Service Restaurants	Deluxe	13–18[1]	$^{1}/_{2}$–$1^{1}/_{4}$
	Popular priced	11–15	1–$2^{1}/_{2}$
Banquet Service	Churches	9–12	
Community Meals	Churches Lodges Social Centers	9–15	

[1]Not usually satisfactory for design. Much depends on room dimensions and luxuriousness of service.

Source: Robert A. Modlin, ed., *Commercial Kitchens*, 7th ed. (Arlington, Virginia: American Gas Association, 1989), pp. 104–111.

only be used as rough estimates, as they do not consider menu items, production methods, or peak periods of service. For example, the "Kitchen Area Requirements" table in Exhibit 2 states that table-service restaurants should allocate 5 to 7 square feet (.5 to .7 square meters) to the kitchen for each seat. However, if the restaurant will use ready-made entrées, frozen vegetables, and frozen desserts, that might be too much kitchen space. The restaurant will pay overhead costs for space that isn't used.

The menu provides the foundation for planning space requirements and equipment layouts in the restaurant. The menu was planned in the concept stage; now it needs to be reviewed and any changes made before layout work begins. For example, if the owner or owner's representative decides to buy ready-made desserts, a bakeshop is not required. But if he or she decides to offer a signature breads, the restaurant will need a bakeshop. These menu decisions should be carefully weighed before the food facilities design consultant begins laying out the kitchen and its equipment.

A menu analysis (see Exhibit 3) can be helpful at this time. The menu analysis identifies the restaurant's menu items, their major ingredients, the equipment required for production, and the quantities of food required. When the menu is not

Exhibit 3 Sample Menu Analysis

Menu Item/ Portion Size	Approximate Quantities (Volume or Portions)	Ingredient(s)	Purchase State	Equipment to Store	Equipment to Pre-Prepare	Equipment to Cook	Production Schedule of (Time: Number of Batches)	Equipment to Hold/Serve
Steamed Shrimp (8)	10 serv/peak hour	Shrimp	Fresh	Refrig.	—	Compt. Steamer	Cooked to Order	—
Steamed Clams (8)	15 serv/peak hour	Clams	Fresh	Refrig.	—	Compt. Steamer	Cooked to Order	—
French Onion Soup (6 oz)	40 serv/night	Onions Beef Broth Cheese	Fresh Canned	Refrig. Dry	Steam Kettle	Steam Kettle	Batch - 1/Day	Soup Well
Cream of Crab (6 oz)	50 serv/night	Cream Crab	Fresh Fresh	Refrig.	—	Steam Kettle	Batch - 1/Day	Soup Well
Crab Cake (2–4 oz)	20 serv/peak hour	Crab Bread Crumbs	Fresh Dry	Refrig. Dry	Food Chopper	Grill	Cooked to Order	—
King Crab (16 oz)	25 serv/peak hour	Crab	Fresh	Refrig.	—	Combo-Oven	Cooked to Order	—
Chicken Delmarva (6 oz)	10 serv/ 30-min peak	Chicken Breast Ham Crab	Frozen Canned Fresh	Freezer	—	Convection Oven	Cooked to Order	Heat Lamp
Broiled Sirloin (8 oz)	20 serv/night	Sirloin Cut Roast	Fresh	Refrig.	Knife	Broiler	Cooked to Order	—
Broiled Flounder (6 oz)	30 serv/night	Flounder	Fresh	Refrig.	—	Broiler	Cooked to Order	—
Beef Teriyaki (8 oz)	30 serv/night	Beef Cubes Onions Tomatoes	Fresh Fresh Fresh	Refrig. Refrig.	Knife Marinade Slicer	Convection Oven	Batch - 50/Batch	Steam Table
Baked Potato (1)	300 serv/night	Potato	Fresh	Dry	Sink	Convection Oven	Batch - 50/Batch	Heat Lamp
French Fries	30 serv/peak hour	—	Frozen	Freezer	—	Deep Fat Fryer	Cooked to Order	Heat Lamp
Tossed Salad (6 oz)	280 serv/ evening	Lettuce Tomato Carrots	Fresh	Refrig.	Sink Slicer	—	Batch - 1/Day	Refrig.

Exhibit 4   Sample Bubble Diagram

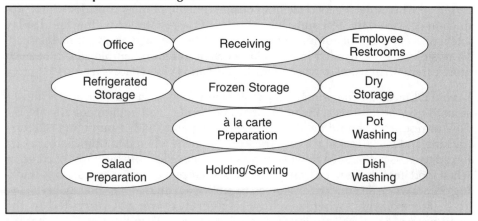

known, the food facilities design consultant may provide more equipment than necessary to protect against an inadequately equipped kitchen. Using the menu analysis, the consultant can assign similar activities to the same section of the restaurant and create work or function areas, such as salad preparation, dessert preparation, and entrée production areas. With these function areas identified, the consultant can draw a relationship or bubble diagram to show the relationships between them and how food will flow through the restaurant. The bubble diagram shown in Exhibit 4 is based on the menu analysis in Exhibit 3. As indicated by the type of menu items listed in the menu analysis, a bakeshop area is not required in this limited-menu restaurant. Therefore, there is no bakeshop area on the bubble diagram. A bubble diagram is also helpful for developing HACCP flow charts. For HACCP compliance, critical control points (points in a food's production when a potential hazard can be controlled or eliminated) must be identified. For example, if storage for a potentially hazardous food is located at a distance from the cooking area, the risk of contamination increases.[4]

When determining initial space allocations, the consultant should first consider all factors that relate to the menu. These factors include the market form of food (the amount of processing the food item has received before it is delivered); the number and variety of menu items; menu specialty items (such as flaming desserts, Caesar salad, and boiled lobster); the volume of meals served; the style of service (sit-down, buffet, or cafeteria); production techniques (sous-vide, cooking to order, or batch cooking); and holding methods (holding tables or heat lamps). Each of these factors affects the amount of space required in specific kitchen areas. For example, if the owners want to offer an all-you-can-eat fish night, they will need to increase the number of fryers, which increases the space requirements in the à la carte preparation area. If the owners want to offer a 100-item menu, a large amount of space will be needed in the storage and preparation areas.

If the owners decide they would like to have a display, or exhibition, kitchen, this will greatly affect the kitchen's layout. A display kitchen provides great advertising for specialty items, such as fresh pasta, fresh fish, or stir-fry. However, most patrons don't want to hear the sound of dishwashers or smell the odors of frying oil. Therefore, the food facilities design consultant must consider which production activities are best suited for display. In a restaurant with a full display kitchen, every piece of equipment must be neatly arranged and well-maintained. More sinks may be needed in a display kitchen to remind employees to be even more careful than usual to wash utensils and hands when necessary.[5]

Layout Objectives. The primary objective of any food service design is to achieve a smooth flow of resources, including food, personnel, and equipment. Ideally, the flow of resources should be along straight-line paths, with a minimum of cross-tracking and back-tracking. **Cross-tracking** happens when two traffic streams are forced to cross paths, such as when food servers have to cross the paths of cooks or when food items have to be transported across employee traffic aisles. **Back-tracking** occurs when an employee is forced to retrace a path that has already been covered. For example, when reach-in refrigerators are not provided in the salad-preparation area, employees have to go to a walk-in refrigerator to get the salad ingredients, then take the prepared salads back to the walk-in refrigerator for temporary storage.

In some cases, the ideal flow of food, personnel, and equipment must be compromised to arrive at a workable layout. For example, providing dishwashing machines at various locations throughout the kitchen would prevent cross-tracking; however, this would require a lot of space and be costly. Therefore, even though some cross-tracking will result, it is better to have kitchen employees carry dirty dishes to one dishwashing area. When making such layout decisions, the food facilities design consultant has to consider the most costly resource. In this example, clearly the cost of providing numerous dishwashing machines throughout the kitchen exceeds the cost of employees walking to one dishwashing machine in one location. Food safety will also need to be considered. For example, the designer should be sure that raw food does not cross paths with ready-to-eat items or food waste.

In addition to the smooth flow of resources, other layout objectives include efficiently using equipment, utilities, space, and personnel; meeting safety and sanitation regulations; and providing optimum working conditions. Food facilities design consultants should be aware of these objectives as they complete the layout. In the area of sanitation, the consultants should try to arrange work areas so they are easily cleaned, place hand sinks where employees will use them, and avoid specifying hard-to-clean shelves.

With these layout objectives in mind, the food facilities design consultant can begin planning specific function areas in the restaurant. The menu analysis can guide the planning of each function area.

Design of Function Areas

Function areas are sections of the restaurant where similar activities occur. Each function area should be designed as a work station or group of work stations. A **work station** is a space planned for a specific set of tasks. After the work stations have been designed, they can be arranged within each function area to meet the overall design objectives for the restaurant.

The following sections describe specific aspects of planning each function area. Restaurant function areas include receiving, storage, kitchen, dining room, employee, and office areas.

Receiving Area

The receiving area is the area designated for the delivery and inspection of inventory items. It is the first control point for food and supplies. It sets the foundation for the quality of the menu items served, as the basic quality of the food brought in cannot be improved on. Therefore, food has to be carefully checked to make sure suppliers do not deliver products that are below the restaurant's desired quality standard or have been stored or shipped outside of acceptable temperature ranges.

The receiving area consists of an area outside the restaurant, called the back dock, and an area inside the restaurant, sometimes called the inspection area.

Back Dock. The back dock (also called the delivery or receiving dock) should be easily accessible from the restaurant's delivery driveway (see Exhibit 5). The dock should be hidden from street traffic and any dining room windows. These objectives may be accomplished with landscaping or by building a wall around the area. When possible, the dock should be visible from a back window to allow management to monitor activities. Ideally, the back dock should be covered.

The driveway to the back dock should be large enough for trucks to back up and turn around. The exact size of the dock will depend on the frequency and size of deliveries. Generally, a dock that measures 10 feet (3.1 meters) from front to back provides enough space so that employees can unload items and still have enough room to walk around them. The length of the dock depends on the restaurant's size and the number of deliveries it will handle. If it will not be uncommon for more than one truck to arrive at the same time to unload cargo, the dock may be made long enough to handle two or more trucks at a time. The door into the facility should be at least 4 feet (1.2 meters) wide.

The back dock should be elevated when possible to increase the convenience of deliveries; drivers can simply wheel the cases off the truck directly onto the back dock. Suggested equipment for unloading deliveries includes hand trucks (two-wheeled vehicles for moving a few cases of inventory items) and platform carts for transporting 10 to 20 cases. For restaurants that use standard case goods, a conveyor roller system will facilitate moving cases to the storeroom quickly.

Inspection Area. The area used for inspecting items should be located inside the restaurant, adjacent to the delivery door. This location helps to ensure that the delivered items are actually checked in. Floors should be smooth to allow easy handling of hand trucks. The area should be well-lighted to allow visual inspection of items.

The amount of space required for the inspection area depends on the volume and type of food received. If the restaurant receives a wide variety of fresh produce, adequate space will be needed to open cases, inspect and weigh the product, and repackage the product for storage. Normal activities include counting,

Exhibit 5   Elevated Back Dock

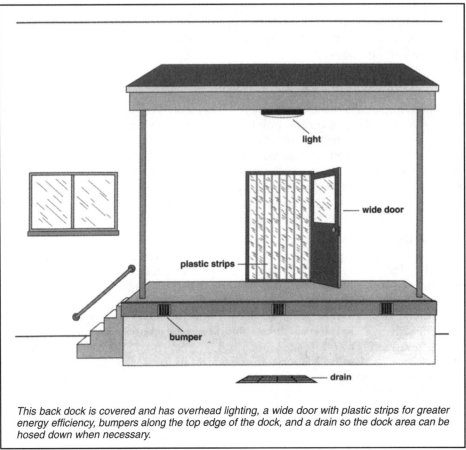

This back dock is covered and has overhead lighting, a wide door with plastic strips for greater energy efficiency, bumpers along the top edge of the dock, and a drain so the dock area can be hosed down when necessary.

inspecting, weighing, and repackaging food. Some facilities may allocate space for a small office in this area for maintaining records of items ordered and invoices for items received. If space is not allotted in this area, these records may be kept in the restaurant manager's office.

Scales are a necessity, and more than one type of scale is needed. For items purchased in units smaller than cases, a table scale is appropriate. For food items like meat, built-in floor scales are suitable. Other recommended equipment items include tables for breaking down cases, tools for opening cases, and hand trucks and platform carts for moving cases. Ideally, a computer is used to record items received.

Storage Areas

Once food items are received, they are transported to either dry, refrigerated, or frozen food storage areas. Storage areas should be positioned between the

Exhibit 6   Sample Inventory Spreadsheet

ITEM	PACKAGE	WEIGHT (LBS/GAL/OZ)	CUBIC FEET	QUANTITY/DAY (No. of Pkgs)	STORAGE PERIOD (No. of days)	TOTAL DELIVERY (LBS/GAL/OZ)	STORAGE (Cu. ft)
CHICKEN BASE	CAN-LB.	6	1.02	1.00	7.00	42.00	7.14
CHIPS, TORTILLA	7.25OZBX-LB.	0.453	0.49	2.00	7.00	6.34	6.93
COFFEE	128BG/CS.-LB.	20	1.63	0.50	7.00	70.00	5.69
COOKING OIL	CAN-LB.	5	0.68	3.00	0.00	0.00	0.00
CORNSTARCH	BAG-LB.	25	0.80	0.25	7.00	43.75	1.40
CROUTONS	BAG-OZ.	5	0.09	1.00	7.00	35.00	0.63
FLOUR	BAG, LB.	50	1.22	0.50	7.00	175.00	4.28
GELATIN, UNFLAV.	BOX-LB.	1	0.03	1.00	7.00	7.00	0.22
GELATIN, FLAV.	BOX-OZ.	6	0.01	4.00	7.00	168.00	0.30
JELLY	JAR-OZ.	10	0.01	1.00	7.00	70.00	0.09
MAYONNAISE	JAR-GAL.	1	0.19	0.50	7.00	3.50	0.67
MOUSSE MIX	10PKG/CS.-LB.	5	0.22	1.00	7.00	35.00	1.56
N.E. CHOWDER	CAN-LB.	6	1.02	1.00	7.00	42.00	7.14
OIL, PEANUT	JUG-LB.	35	0.70	0.00	0.00	0.00	0.00
ONIONS	SACK-LB.	100	3.78	0.10	7.00	70.00	2.65
PASTA	BOX-LB.	5	0.10	1.00	7.00	35.00	0.70
POTATOES	SACK-LB.	100	3.78	0.10	7.00	70.00	2.65
	TOTAL						42.03

receiving area and the kitchen. Generally, they should be closer to the kitchen, as the number of trips made from the kitchen to the storage areas exceeds the number of trips from the receiving area to storage.

The amount of storage space required is ideally determined by considering the number of meals prepared, the frequency of deliveries, the variety of menu items, and inventory policies. Some managers like to maintain a high level of inventory, while others store only enough inventory to last till the next delivery. Realistically, the cost of space will influence the amount of space devoted to storage. As the cost per square foot of space increases, the owners usually look for areas to decrease. Since storage is not a revenue-producing area, its size may be reduced. This reduction is acceptable if the frequency of deliveries can be increased. In some U. S. cities, restaurants may receive deliveries twice a day to decrease storage space and cost.

Many references exist that have formulas for calculating the amount of storage space needed. However, these are general figures, and not always pertinent to a particular facility. If managers need a rough estimate for initial space planning and haven't completed a menu analysis, there is a formula in the 1999 Food Code that can help them estimate their storage space needs.

If a menu analysis has been completed, the amount of dry, refrigerated, and frozen storage space required can be determined using a spreadsheet package such as Excel. The food facilities design consultant can estimate the number of cartons, bags, or boxes needed per inventory item on a daily basis (see Exhibit 6, column 5, "Quantity/Day"). For example, this consultant has estimated that the planned restaurant will need one 6-pound (2.7-kilogram) can of chicken base each day. The number of packages needed per day can be multiplied by the number of days between deliveries—in other words, the storage period (column 6)—to determine the amount of goods requiring storage space. The storage period for the chicken base is 7 days, therefore the delivery will total 7 packages. This total number of packages (7) is multiplied by the cubic feet per package (column 4) to yield the total cubic feet necessary for storage. For the chicken base, 7 packages multiplied by its cubic feet per package—1.02 (.029 cubic meter)—equals 7.14 cubic feet (.2 cubic meter) of storage space.

To determine the amount of linear shelf space required to store the inventory items, the cubic feet must be converted to linear feet of shelving. This is done by dividing the total cubic feet by the height and width of the shelving. To allow for some extra room above the products on each shelf to facilitate stocking and allow for air circulation, subtract at least 2 inches from the shelving's height before dividing it into the total cubic feet figure. Using the chicken base example, suppose the shelving is 2 feet (61 centimeters) deep and 14 inches (36 centimeters) high. Subtract 2 inches from the height and then divide 7.14 cubic feet by the shelving's depth (2 feet) and height (1 foot). This calculation indicates that approximately 3.57 linear feet (1.1 meter) of shelving is necessary to store the chicken base. Now suppose that your calculations for all inventory items indicate that 100 linear feet of shelving is needed to store the items. This does not mean you need a single shelf 100 feet long. Rather, any combination of shelves that totals 100 linear feet will meet your needs (for example, five 20-foot-long shelves, ten 10-foot-long shelves, twelve 5-foot-long shelves and four 10-foot-long shelves), as long as the height and width of these shelves matches the height and width figures you used in your calculations. The shelves can be configured in a variety of patterns to fit into the designed storage space.

Not all items come in standard-size cartons or cans, therefore the consultant may want to add a cushion of space to allow for irregularly sized items. The percentage of this cushion may vary from 0 to 100 percent, depending on the number of irregularly sized items. In Exhibit 6, the croutons, flour, onions, and potatoes come in bags or sacks, so an additional 20 to 30 percent of storage space may be added to their calculated total.

Design Factors for Food Storage. In dry storage facilities, ventilation should be sufficient to minimize odors and prohibit condensation on walls and equipment. All surfaces should be easy to clean. Floors are usually concrete or tile; walls are usually masonry or gypsum board with a washable finish. The room temperature should be between 50°F and 70°F (10°C and 21°C). The room should not have non-insulated steam and water pipes, refrigerator condensing units, or other heat-generating units. Windows should not be included, unless they are dictated by local regulations. If windows are required, they should be secured to prevent theft. Lighting levels should be at least 15 footcandles. For the optimal distribution of light, the lamps should be located over the center of each aisle.

Walk-in refrigerators and freezers are used for long-term storage of ingredients and products and short-term storage of prepared foods. Walk-ins may be either pre-fabricated or built-in. Pre-fabricated walk-ins are made from urethane-insulated panels. The surface materials available include stainless steel, galvanized steel, and aluminum. The panels are attached to form walls, ceilings, and floors (although some planners prefer to use quarry tile for floors). These pre-fabricated walk-ins may be dismantled if they need to be moved or changed. Built-in walk-ins typically have glazed tile walls, quarry tile floors, and aluminum or stainless steel ceilings with styrofoam insulation. Lighting levels in the walk-ins should be at least 15 footcandles.

Recommended shelving materials include corrosion-resistant metals, such as steel with a galvanized or chrome coating, or polymer composite material, which is less costly than stainless steel, corrosion-resistant, and NSF approved for food contact surfaces. Recent alternatives to standard shelving units include track shelving, cantilevered shelving, and vertical shelving. These shelving systems may increase the capacity of the storage area.

The compressor and condenser units of walk-in refrigerators and freezers may be either remote or self-contained. Remote compressor and condenser systems are placed in a distant location to decrease noise and heat levels in kitchens. Self-contained refrigeration systems may be hidden behind panels on top of walk-ins. In these cases, the space above the walk-ins needs to be sufficiently ventilated to minimize heat buildup.

Design Factors for Non-Food Storage. Alcoholic beverages should be stored in a lockable area. In large operations, closed-circuit television may also be used to increase security. The storage area needs to be big enough to maintain stock in an organized manner, so physical inventory can be completed easily.

Since some alcoholic beverages will deteriorate when stored improperly, temperature and humidity requirements must be considered when planning the beverage storage area. Unpasteurized beers should be stored at 36°F to 38°F (2°C to 3°C). Generally, red wines should be stored around 55°F (13°C); white wines and sparkling wines should be stored around 50°F (10°C).[6] The humidity of the wine storage area can be crucial to the quality of the wine. When the humidity is low, corks will dry out, permitting air to enter the bottle and damage the wine. Wines should be stored in a wine cellar or in a room with cool temperatures and controlled humidity. Bottled wines and beers should be stored in dark areas, as light will cause the product to deteriorate.

The amount of storage space required for paper and cleaning supplies depends on the number of items, the volume used, and the frequency of deliveries. A restaurant that uses straws, paper or plastic cups, paper napkins, and plasticware will need to forecast the number of guests per day and the desired duration of storage to determine the amount of space required.

Cleaning supplies must be stored separately from food to avoid accidental food contamination. The storage area for cleaning supplies must be large enough to contain cases of detergents and cleaning agents and 55-gallon (208-liter) drums. The manager should determine the amount of cleaning supplies required daily and the frequency of deliveries.

The Kitchen

The kitchen should be located between long-term storage areas and the dining room. While specific work areas in the kitchen will differ based on the menu, most restaurants will have a pre-preparation area, a cold-food (or salad) preparation area, and a hot-food preparation area (see Exhibit 7). Restaurants that offer "homemade" desserts may have a separate bakery area.

Exhibit 7   Sample Kitchen Layout

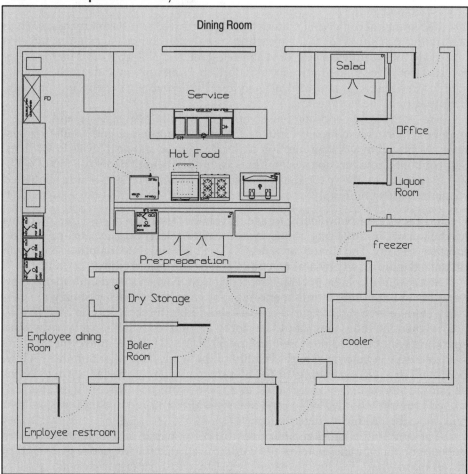

Pre-Preparation. A pre-preparation area is necessary if lettuce, tomatoes, and other produce items are purchased in a raw, unprocessed state. Specific activities in this area might include cleaning lettuce, slicing carrots, and mixing salad dressings. Typical equipment items needed for these tasks include sinks, work tables, mixers, vertical cutter/mixers, and food processors. Equipment should be arranged to minimize the number of steps employees must take to do their jobs. In a small restaurant, the pre-preparation area may be combined with the cold-food preparation area.

Cold-Food Preparation Area. The cold-food preparation area, or pantry, is designed for making salads, appetizers, and sandwiches. In large-volume restaurants and for banquet service, these items may be prepared in advance of the meal period and stored for serving later. Work tables and refrigerators are the major

This kitchen features face-to-face cooking lines divided by large work tables. Mobile equipment and stainless steel wall panels aid in clean-up. (Courtesy of Hammer Design Associates, Inc., Pittsburgh, Pennsylvania)

equipment items required for the cold-food preparation area. A two-compartment sink is needed if the vegetables haven't been pre-prepared. Slicers and a food processor may also be included in this area. If the menu has a special section for cold appetizers and entrées, a large cold-food preparation area will be needed.

Hot-Food Preparation Area. The hot-food preparation area is where chefs or cooks prepare entrées, soups, sauces, and vegetables. Work stations within a hot-food preparation area may include broiler, fryer, griddle, soup and sauce, steaming, and sauté stations. Short-term, or quick, cooking stations—the broiler, fryer, griddle, and sauté stations—are generally located on the front or "hot" line, close to holding and service. In the soup and sauce, and bakery areas, menu items are prepared in larger quantities and do not need to be located adjacent to the service line. To increase the flexibility of these work stations, some of the equipment items can be purchased with quick-disconnect hoses and casters so they can be moved when necessary.

   Broiler. The broiler station may be used for preparing steaks, fillets, and pork chops. This station should be located on the "hot line," as broiling is a quick cooking method. If necessary, gas or electric broilers may be stacked to save floor space. This area will be warm due to the heat given off by the broiler. Therefore, the broiler station is usually placed at the end of an equipment line in the hot-food preparation area.

Fry station. Deep-fat fryers are standard equipment in most restaurants. They are used to prepare French fries and deep-fried fish, chicken, and vegetable items. The fry station should have space for loading and unloading products, and refrigerator or freezer space to store uncooked products. The number and size of fryers will depend on the number of fried menu items.

Griddle. A griddle station is used for cooking such menu items as eggs, hamburgers, and pancakes. Space for storing ingredients and condiments and holding cooked products should be allocated for this work station.

Soup and sauce. Inclusion of a distinct soup and sauce work station depends on the number of sauces required and whether soups are made from scratch. Equipment for this station may include ranges, steam-jacketed kettles, and tilting braising pans. The soup and sauce station will need counter space, and space for ingredients and utensils. If possible, a water source should be located nearby so it will be convenient to add water to soups and clean the steam-jacketed kettles. These kettles should be located in a section with a depressed floor or with a curb to prevent liquids from spilling on the floor. Prepared soups or sauces may be held on the range top or in the kettles.

Steaming. Steamers are used for cooking vegetables, fish, pasta, and rice. Based on the menu, either a high-pressure or pressureless steamer may be needed.

Sauté. In restaurants that offer many sautéed items, a separate work station may be needed. Since sautéed items should be cooked and served quickly, the sauté station needs to be designed for efficiency. The major piece of equipment required is a range top. Space for uncooked items, condiments, sauté pans, and finished items is required in this station.

Bakery. If restaurant owners decide to offer extensive pastry and dessert items, the project planning team needs to design a production area for baking. If space is not available, bakery production will have to be arranged around the hot-food production schedule so the same equipment can be used. The baking production area may include mixing, dough-proofing, dough-rolling, cooking, cooling, and decorating areas. Equipment includes mixers, ovens, dough dividers/shapers, dough-rolling equipment, and refrigerators. Table space and space for storing ingredients and utensils are necessary in all of these areas.

Because kitchen design is so important to the success of a restaurant, the following sections will cover designing work stations in the kitchen in more detail.

Designing Kitchen Work Stations. The first phase in planning a kitchen work station (or any work station) is to identify the task or tasks. Exhibit 8 lists the menu items and preparation procedures that might be found in a short-order work station. Next, the food facilities design consultant decides who will be doing the tasks, as the skill level of the employee or employees may affect the layout of the work station. The preparation procedures can be used to identify the equipment, tools, and storage space needed in this station. Using the preparation procedures in Exhibit 8, the planner should recognize that a waffle iron, grill, warming drawer, toaster, microwave oven, refrigerator, and plate lowerator are needed in this work station. (A plate lowerator is a piece of equipment for storing and dispensing plates.) Tools required include spatulas, spoons, knives, and a butter spreader.

Exhibit 8   Menu Items and Preparation Procedures for a Short-Order Work Station

MENU ITEMS

Bacon, Ham, Eggs, Pancakes, Toast

PREPARATION PROCEDURES

A.   Bacon

1.   Remove raw bacon from counter refrigerator, count portions, and return rest to refrigerator.
2.   Place bacon on preheated grill and weight to ensure flat, even cooking.
3.   Turn with spatula.
4.   Take plate from cart, garnish with two slices of toast, and move to grill to add finished bacon and other items.
5.   Place completed order on shelf for pick up.
6.   Scrape excess bacon grease into grease well on grill.

B.   Ham

1.   Remove pre-cut ham portion from refrigerator and place on grill.
2.   Remove spatula from counter or grill location and turn ham.
3.   Return spatula to counter or grill location.
4.   Remove plate from rack and prepare with toast.
5.   Place cooked ham on plate with spatula.
6.   Place completed order on shelf for pick up.
7.   Return spatula to counter or grill location.

C.   Eggs

1.   Brush grill with cooking oil.
2.   Remove eggs from refrigerator.
3.   Crack eggs and place on grill.
4.   Cook eggs for either sunny-side up or over easy.
5.   Remove finished eggs with spatula and add to order.

D.   Pancakes

1.   Remove pitcher containing pancake batter from refrigerator.
2.   Place correct number of portions on grill.
3.   Return pitcher to refrigerator.
4.   Use spatula to turn pancakes.
5.   Take plate from cart and prepare with garnish.
6.   Place completed order on shelf.

E.   Toast

1.   Take bread slices from loaf of bread on shelf next to toaster.
2.   Load toaster.
3.   When finished, butter toast with brush in butter pan.

Storage space is needed for the tools and ingredients. Exhibit 9 is a possible layout for this work station

The physical environment. The physical environment—the working conditions—in the kitchen should be addressed at the same time the work stations are laid out. Employees need a comfortable environment to work most productively. Factors that should be considered include temperature and humidity, lighting type and level, noise levels, aisle widths, and equipment design. One authority states

Exhibit 9   Sample Work Station Layout

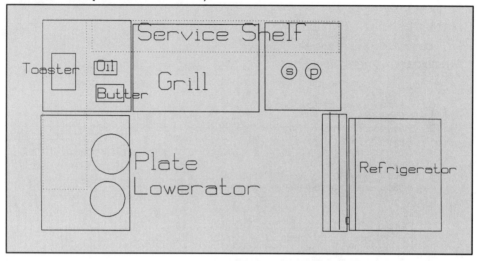

that the ideal temperature range in a kitchen is between 68°F and 72°F (20°C and 22°C) in winter and 74°F and 78°F (23°C and 26°C) in summer, with a relative humidity of 40 to 45 percent.[7] These conditions may be attained if the kitchen is air conditioned. When the kitchen is not air conditioned, the food facilities design consultant should consider placing fans in appropriate areas.

Lighting will also affect employee productivity. The type and level of lighting should be specified by the planner, and should depend on the particular tasks being performed. Direct lighting may cause enough glare on a shiny surface (such as stainless steel) to hamper employees. The 1999 Food Code recommends a light level of at least 50 footcandles at a surface where employees are performing food preparation activities such as chopping, slicing, or mixing.

The color of surfaces in a kitchen contribute to the lighting levels. Light-colored surfaces reflect light, so the kitchen will be brighter when ceilings and walls are painted white. White is typically used to meet the sanitary standards. The consultant should check with the owners to determine their color preferences.

Noise levels in kitchens are typically high, in part because of the types of kitchen surfaces required for the safe preparation of food. All food-preparation surfaces must be non-porous, non-toxic, and resistant to moisture and microbial contamination. To meet these requirements, the best surface is stainless steel. Floors must be non-slippery, grease-resistant, and non-porous. Preferred materials are quarry tile and sealed concrete. Walls must be non-porous, grease resistant, heat resistant, and able to withstand cleaning, so materials of choice include ceramic tile, filled concrete block painted with epoxy paint, and drywall of an appropriate fire-resistance rating that is taped, filled, and covered with an epoxy-type coating. Ceilings must be grease-resistant and washable, which limits the choice of materials to such coverings as metal-clad or plastic-coated fiber board, and plastic-laminated panels. All of these surfaces are hard, which makes sound reverberate.

The food facilities design consultant should make a special effort to decrease noise levels in the kitchen. Possible techniques include designing the kitchen so that refrigerator compressors are in remote locations, locating dishwashers in separate areas, specifying sound-absorbing materials on the underside of stainless steel counters, and using rubber mats on tables under counter-type machines.

The width of kitchen aisles should differ depending on whether they are work aisles or traffic aisles. Traffic aisles should be planned according to the number of people and carts expected in the area. Aisle widths should take into account the aisle requirements of the Americans with Disabilities Act, so that if an employee in a wheelchair is hired, modifications do not have to be made.

Selecting equipment. Food service equipment for the work stations should not be selected hastily. Each piece should be researched to ensure it is the most appropriate for the food service operation. The food facilities design consultant should be knowledgeable about the different types of equipment so that he or she can recommend the most appropriate pieces of equipment for the restaurant. If the owners hired a food service manager to represent them, he or she should also have expertise in equipment selection and coordinate this activity with the food facilities design consultant.

There are many sources of information on food service equipment, including equipment and supply dealers, independent manufacturers' sales representatives, broadline distributors, manufacturers, and food facility design consultants. Food service equipment and supply dealers stock all types and brands of equipment. Dealers typically provide delivery, installation, and demonstration services; some dealers offer free design services as well. Independent manufacturers' sales representatives serve to educate consultants, distributors, and dealers about equipment features. These representatives work for a commission or a percentage of the equipment's price. They do not offer competing lines of products. Broadline distributors are large food distributors that have expanded to offer supplies and equipment. These distributors have changed the market place due to their buying power beyond the traditional equipment dealer. A manufacturer may employ a direct sales team. Although this is a fixed cost, the manufacturer gains a dedicated, full-time salesperson. Food service consultants are independent contractors with expertise in food service design and equipment specifications, hired by the food service operator or owner.

Equipment should be selected with care, because not all brands of equipment are equal. For example, deep-fat fryers vary by the amount of fat used, the energy required for operation, the ease of cleaning, and the location of controls. Equipment selection criteria include:

- Need and function
- Flexibility
- Training requirements
- Safety and sanitation
- Employee use (and abuse)
- Construction methods and materials

- Service requirements

- Maintenance requirements

- Energy requirements

- Capacity

- Costs

The food facilities design consultant should be sure that the equipment is necessary and that it will perform the desired function. Equipment flexible enough to do a variety of jobs should be considered. A tilting braising pan that can be used as a griddle and a steam kettle may be a better purchase than either a griddle or a steam kettle.

The amount of training required to operate the equipment should be identified. For example, employees will need more training to operate combination oven/steamers than microwave ovens.

Equipment should have the appropriate safety features. Equipment with hot surfaces or exposed blades should be carefully considered in view of employee skills. Unskilled employees may not be as careful around equipment as more experienced employees. Additionally, the potential abuses of equipment should be anticipated. If employees might place heavy pans on open oven doors, heavy-duty hinges should be specified.

Equipment should be selected and placed so employees don't have to bend or reach excessively. Although deck ovens may be stacked three high and steamers can be stacked four high to save floor space, they could cause employees to get burned. Employees who are shorter than average will be unable to place pans in the top compartment, while tall employees will have trouble bending down to check products in the bottom compartment.

The equipment's construction materials and methods should be evaluated to be sure they will withstand the amount of expected use. If equipment will receive heavy use, it should be stainless steel rather than aluminum. The type of maintenance the equipment will need and the availability of service are factors that cannot be ignored. If routine maintenance is too complex for employees to perform, it won't be performed. If the manufacturer's service personnel are an hour away, service calls will be expensive.

The energy requirements of the equipment should be identified. The question of whether to use gas or electric equipment may depend on the preference of the chef or cook. The food facilities design consultant or food service manager will make the ultimate decision and should be aware of the differences in cost of these two utility sources.

Equipment capacity should be checked to be sure it is correct for the restaurant. Managers need to be aware that the stated capacities in equipment catalogs are not always the actual capacities. For example, a 30-gallon (113-liter) steam-jacketed kettle realistically only holds 66 to 75 percent of 30 gallons because the 30-gallon capacity is based on filling the kettle to the rim. Manufacturers' data on oven capacities may be based on full loads rather than realistic operating loads. Food facilities design consultants should check the menu analysis to determine if

Exhibit 10   Straight-Line Equipment Configuration

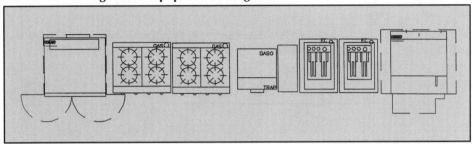

food items will be cooked in large batches or on an as-needed basis. When a restaurant makes one 50-gallon (189-liter) batch of soup each week, it will need a larger kettle than if a daily batch of 8 gallons (30 liters) is made.

Cost is an important criterion, but it should not be the primary one. Also, it should be remembered that the equipment cost includes not only the purchase price, but the installation price, the maintenance cost, and the service cost.

Equipment configuration. Within each work area of the kitchen (pre-preparation, cold-food, hot-food, and bakery), equipment is usually laid out in one of five configurations: straight-line, L-shaped, U-shaped, parallel back-to-back, or parallel face-to-face. The use of a particular layout will depend on the specific situation, as each layout has inherent advantages and disadvantages.

A straight-line configuration (Exhibit 10) is good for low-volume restaurants with limited menus. All of the necessary equipment is in one line, which allows a single employee to watch all the pieces of equipment in the line at the same time. If there is more work than one employee can handle, the line may be divided into more than one work station. This configuration is easily placed against a wall.

The L-shaped configuration (Exhibit 11) is suitable when space is limited. This configuration decreases travel distances between the equipment on the ends of the line.

The U-shaped configuration (Exhibit 12) is most appropriate when specific tasks need to be isolated, like baking or dishwashing. Depending on the equipment in the configuration, the area may be difficult to supervise. Therefore, this arrangement is suitable for areas that do not require close supervision. In many older kitchens, the different types of preparation areas are located in separate alcoves with U-shaped configurations. This complicates the supervision process, as the manager has to travel excessive distances to determine the progress of employees.

The parallel, back-to-back configuration (Exhibit 13) is suitable when the linear space available in the kitchen is insufficient for a straight-line arrangement. A parallel, back-to-back arrangement may need only one ventilation hood, which will lower equipment costs. Additionally, all utility connections may be placed between the lines of equipment. If a half-wall is placed between equipment, communication is possible between these areas. A full-height wall will deter communication and make supervision more difficult.

Exhibit 11   L-Shaped Equipment Configuration

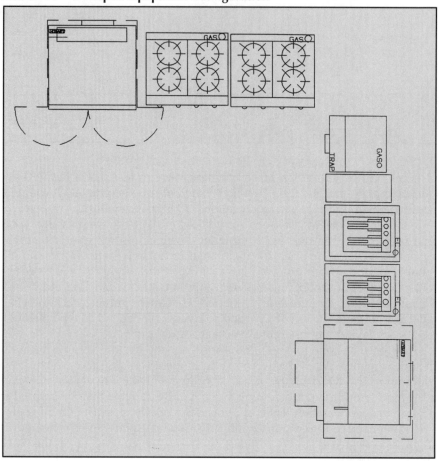

The parallel face-to-face configuration (Exhibit 14) is usually used in large facilities. This arrangement is easier to supervise, as employees are all visible from one location. A disadvantage of this configuration is that two ventilation hoods are required, and more than one set of utility lines is needed.

Other Kitchen Areas. Other areas within the kitchen that need to be designed include holding and service, pantry, warewashing, and potwashing areas.

Holding and service. This area should be located between the kitchen's food production areas and the dining room (see Exhibit 7). Following production, food must be held until it is served. The holding and service area is the servers' pick-up site. Hot items are kept on holding tables or under heat lamps until servers arrive to pick them up. Holding tables can hold casseroles, vegetables, and sliced meats; heat lamps are best for sandwiches, French fries, and pizza-type items. Holding (also called steam) tables are available in standard sizes that hold from one to eight 12- by 20-inch (30- by 51-centimeter) serving pans. In addition to holding tables,

Exhibit 12   U-Shaped Equipment Configuration

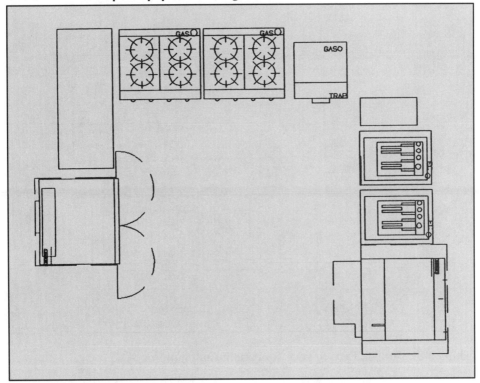

this area may include plate holders, refrigerated drawers, roll warmers, soup warmers, and a microwave oven.

In many restaurants, a service bar is located adjacent to the holding and service area. Service bar layout depends on many variables, including the volume of business, the variety of beverages offered, the type of beverage dispensing system used, and the level of security desired.

Pantry. The cold-food holding area, or pantry, may be located adjacent to the holding and service area. The pantry holds desserts, ice creams, salads, and beverages. In small restaurants a pantry may be used for preparation of salads and desserts, while in large facilities it is usually separated from the salad preparation area. When **service stations** are located in dining rooms, some of the holding equipment for cold foods will be located in the service stations.

Warewashing. Activities in the warewashing area include removing flatware, food, and non-food items from plates; sorting cups and glasses; scraping, sorting, and stacking dishes; placing items in dishwashers; removing items from dishwashers; and sorting flatware.

Ideally, the warewashing area should be located close to the dining room. This placement allows servers to drop off dirty dishes as they enter the kitchen to obtain another order. It also keeps servers and buspersons out of food production areas.

Exhibit 13 Parallel, Back-to-Back Equipment Configuration

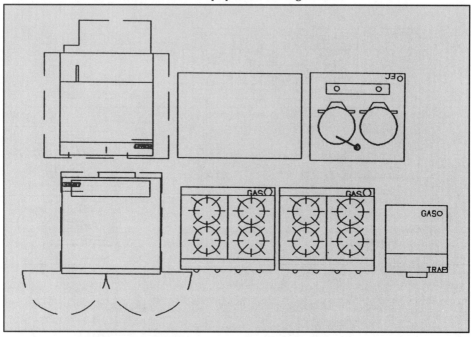

Exhibit 14 Parallel, Face-to-Face Equipment Configuration

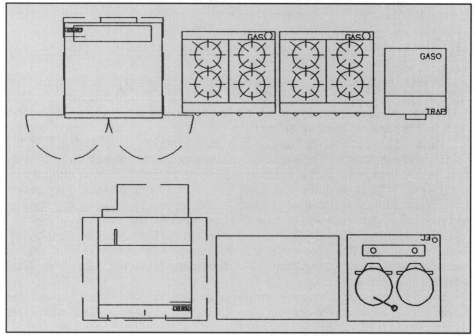

The major piece of equipment in the warewashing area is the dishwashing machine. Dishwashing machines may vary from a single-tank door-type dishwasher to a three-tank conveyor machine or even a flight-type dishwasher. The food facilities design consultant will need to determine the number of dishes that will require washing and how fast they will need to be processed. The cycle time of each type of dishwashing machine varies. The larger machines allow more dishes to be processed in a shorter time; however, they require more space and a larger monetary investment. The larger machines may decrease the number of employee hours required.

Potwashing. The potwashing area may be located adjacent to the warewashing area or close to the hot-food production area; employees in the hot-food production area use pots the most. The 1999 Food Code requires a three-compartment sink for manual potwashing. The first compartment is for soaking and washing, the second for rinsing, and the third for sanitizing. If the facility uses sheet pans that are 18 by 26 inches (46 by 66 centimeters), the first compartment should be at least 20 by 30 inches (51 by 76 centimeters) to allow the pans to soak. The second and third compartments may be 24 by 24 inches (61 by 61 centimeters). Drain boards for dishes should be at least 3 feet (.92 meters) long, with a slight pitch toward the sink.

Potwashing machines are becoming more common. These machines are similar to dishwashing machines, except they have larger motors to increase the water's velocity. The machine's compartment size depends on the size of pots to be washed.

The Dining Room

The dining room should be located adjacent to the holding and service area so food temperatures can be maintained to the point of guest service. When dining rooms are located in distant locations from the holding and service area, heated carts or mobile holding tables can be used to keep hot food hot, and refrigerated carts can keep cold food cold.

The number of seats within a dining room and the number and sizes of tables should be based on the restaurant's forecasted market share. For example, if the feasibility study indicated that the restaurant should serve 500 dinners during the dinner period, the manager will need to decide on the number of table turns and the number of 2-tops (tables designed to accommodate two diners), 4-tops, 6-tops, etc. that are needed. Since not all groups are even-numbered, 100 percent occupancy is rarely achieved. To increase flexibility, tables that can be moved together to handle large groups are recommended. The size and type of tables and chairs, the arrangement of the tables, and the space requirement for service stations will all influence the size of the dining room.

Dining room furniture should be carefully considered, as the choice of chair and table designs will influence the length of time guests stay. Guests tend to stay longer if the chairs have arms, or if the booths have high backs. Chairs used in fine dining restaurants are generally large with well-padded arm rests. The width of tables will influence the amount and noise level of conversation; wider tables tend to make people either talk less or talk louder. Unfortunately, most research studies concerning the impact of the physical environment on guests are conducted by private companies and are not available to the industry at large.

The arrangement of tables on diagonal rather than straight lines will increase the number of seats per square foot. Booths can also be used to increase the number of seats per square foot, because booths are arranged back-to-back, while tables are separated with aisles. For fire safety, the National Fire Protection Association's Life Safety Code dictates that 15 square feet (1.4 square meters) of space, per seat, be provided for assembly areas of less concentrated use, without fixed seating, such as dining rooms.[8] The design of the dining room will affect the efficiency of service and therefore should not be left entirely to the architect or interior designer. A food facilities design consultant, with the food service manager, should be involved in the design decisions as they affect the restaurant's overall operation.

Service Stations. Service stations are small work islands located in the dining room. Placement and design of service stations can save trips to the kitchen, allowing service personnel to be more attentive to guests. Items that may be stocked at a service station include bread, butter, coffee, tea, soft drinks, cups and saucers, glasses, milk, cream, silverware, crackers, napkins, and condiments.

Employee Facilities

Facilities should be provided for employees that promote good employee morale and ensure sanitary and safe practices. These facilities should include lockers, restrooms, and a break room for employees. Providing employee lockers will minimize the number of personal belongings piled on shelves or in the manager's office. If uniforms are required, changing space is recommended. Employee restrooms encourage frequent hand-washing and decrease the time employees spend away from work. When employees have to share restrooms with guests, their efficiency is affected. An employee break room eliminates the practice of employees spending breaks in the dining room or on the back dock, and managers will have an easier time locating employees when needed. The size of the break room will depend on the number of employees per shift and employee break policies.

A separate employee entrance is recommended whenever possible, so employees can go directly to their locker room or break room without walking through the kitchen or dining room. Having employees enter the restaurant through the back dock is not ideal, since there are more opportunities for them to pilfer food and other products in the back dock area.

Office Space

Office space is necessary for the restaurant manager, assistant managers, the chef, and secretarial personnel. Office space provides an area for managers to perform job duties such as hiring, disciplining, and firing employees; completing financial reports; and talking to salespeople or guests. The number of offices required will depend on the complexity of the restaurant. If the manager is responsible for planning banquets or catering, a second office may be beneficial. This office should be large enough for the number of visitors expected.

Exhibit 15   Sample Elevation

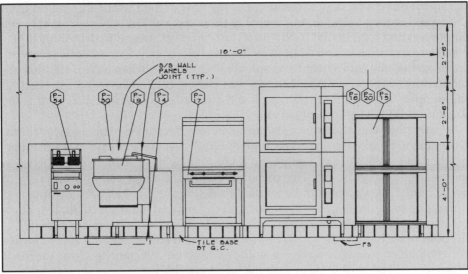

Source: Hammer Design Associates, Inc., Pittsburgh, Pennsylvania.

If there is only one office, it should be easily accessible to guests and the kitchen employees. Space is limited in small restaurants, so the office may be located close to the receiving area. This arrangement allows the manager to watch the activities of employees in the receiving and storage areas, but may limit guest access.

An office should be a minimum of 60 square feet (5.6 square meters). This allows sufficient space for a desk, file cabinet, computer, and one or two chairs for visitors. An office should present a professional image, especially if the manager meets with salespeople and guests there. When managers are forced to use storage areas, private dining areas, or a corner of the dining room as office space, it reflects poorly on their image and the restaurant.

Evaluation of Finished Blueprints

When the layout for the restaurant is complete, the owners, the design consultant, and the food service manager need to decide whether the design goals have been met. The design consultant will prepare a set of drawings, called blueprints, which include plan, elevation, and section views of the restaurant. A **plan view** is a horizontal cut through the restaurant at approximately three feet (.92 meters) above the finished floor that shows the placement of all equipment. An **elevation** is a vertical view of any wall or row of equipment in the restaurant, and shows, for example, equipment heights, distances between equipment, and placement of shelves and drawers (see Exhibit 15). A **section** is a vertical cut showing a side view of a piece of equipment, counter area, or table.

As mentioned earlier, the major goal of restaurant layout is to establish a smooth flow of resources, with a minimum of back-tracking or cross-tracking.

Using this criterion, the food service manager and owners can first evaluate how the layout directs the flow of resources. Is the flow of food relatively straight from the receiving area to the dining room? Is there too much cross-tracking between employees and food items? Next, the layout can be evaluated to determine if personnel, space, utilities, and equipment are used effectively. Is there sufficient work space around the equipment for employees? Does the kitchen have aisles that are too narrow or too wide? Are there gas and electric connections where needed? Is the equipment correct for the menu? Is the capacity of equipment sufficient? Is the working height of equipment suitable for employees?

Safety and sanitation concerns can be reviewed from the plans and elevations. Questions to be asked include: Is equipment placed so that it is easy to clean underneath? Does each piece of equipment adjoin the next, or is there room between pieces for dirt to build up? Are the equipment controls placed appropriately to avoid burns? Plan views can be studied to determine if fryers have loading and unloading space, and see the location of trash cans and hand sinks. Section views will show whether it will be easy to clean under-counter shelving. For example, if the bottom shelf is 6 inches (15 centimeters) above the finished floor and 30 inches (76 centimeters) deep, employees will probably be reluctant to clean the shelf because it will be hard to clean it all the way to the back.

Endnotes

1. U.S. Department of Health and Human Services, Public Health Service, and Food and Drug Administration 1999 Food Code.

2. U.S. Department of Health and Human Services, Public Health Service, and Food and Drug Administration 1999 Food Code.

3. Department of Justice, The Americans with Disabilities Act of 1990.

4. Food and Drug Administration, "Managing Food Safety: A HACCP Principles Guide for Operators of Food Establishments at the Retail Level."

5. Steven Starr, "See-Through Kitchens," Contractmagazine.com, December 1998.

6. Lendal H. Kotschevar and Mary L. Tanke, *Managing Bar and Beverage Operations* (Lansing, Mich.: Educational Institute of the American Hotel & Lodging Association, 1991), pp. 144, 238–239.

7. Arthur C. Avery, *A Modern Guide to Foodservice Equipment*, rev. ed. (New York: CBI, 1985), p. 17.

8. Ron Coté, *Life Safety Code Handbook*, Eighth Edition (National Fire Protection Association, 2000), p. 184.

Key Terms

back-tracking—Occurs when an employee is forced to retrace a path that has already been covered.

cross-tracking—Two traffic streams forced to cross paths.

elevation—A vertical view of any wall or row of equipment in a restaurant that shows equipment heights, distances between equipment, and placement of shelves and drawers.

plan view—A horizontal cut (on a drawing or blueprint) through a restaurant or other building that shows the placement of all equipment.

section—A vertical cut (on a drawing or blueprint) showing a side view of a piece of equipment, counter area, or table.

service station—A small work island located in a dining room.

setback—A zoning term referring to a building's distance from the street.

work station—A space planned for a specific set of tasks.

zoning codes—The local regulations that define the types of businesses and buildings allowed in specific geographic areas.

Review Questions

1. How does the menu affect a restaurant's layout?
2. What are some regulations that influence restaurant design?
3. Who are typical members of a project planning team?
4. What are typical layout objectives?
5. What are some design factors for food and non-food storage?
6. What are some factors to keep in mind when designing kitchen work stations?
7. What criteria can help guide equipment selection?
8. What are some typical equipment configurations?
9. What should a designer keep in mind when planning a dining room?
10. What kinds of drawings are included in a set of blueprints?

Internet Sites

For more information, visit the following Internet sites. Remember that Internet addresses can change without notice. If the site is no longer there, you can use a search engine to look for additional sites.

American Institute of Architects
www.aiaonline.com

Foodservice Consultants Society
International
www.fcsi.org

National Fire Protection Association
www.nfpa.org

USDA Food Safety and Inspection
Service
www.fsis.usda.gov/index.htm

U.S. Department of Justice
www.usdoj.gov

Competencies

1. List typical reasons for renovating a hotel, summarize the life cycle of a hotel, and describe types of renovation. (pp. 510–514)

2. Describe how a renovation plan is created. (pp. 514–524)

3. Explain how a renovation plan is implemented, including the design phase and construction phase. (pp. 525–538)

4. Describe issues that must be addressed after a renovation project is completed (if not before). (pp. 538–539)

16

Renovation and Capital Projects

This chapter was written and contributed by Jan deRoos, Ph.D.,
Associate Professor, School of Hotel Administration, Cornell University,
Ithaca, New York.

*[B]y the early 1970s, a stingy maintenance budget had once again let
[New York City's Plaza Hotel] decline to a frightful state of disrepair.
Cracks opened up in ceilings, wallpaper peeled off walls, faucets leaked,
hot water was in short supply.*

*As the physical plant decayed, so did staff morale. Guests found
themselves greeted by sullen, insolent employees who could take no pride
in their hotel. Many regulars deserted the place and shifted their alle-
giance to the Pierre or the Waldorf. The hotel started losing money.*

*When Westin bought the hotel, another extensive renovation began,
in staggered fashion, portions of floors at a time. Between 1975 and early
1988, at a cost of $100 million, Westin managed to redo every room.
Attention was given to the most minute details. Sixteen layers of paint
were peeled from window frames to reveal the original copper. Not surprisingly, the mood of employees simultaneously began to pick up.*[1]

RENOVATION OF LODGING FACILITIES is an enormous undertaking. It is estimated
that the annual volume of renovation work in the United States exceeds $6 billion
per year.[2] Virtually every hotel undertakes an annual renovation plan; using typical renovation cycles, approximately 750,000 guestrooms are renovated each year.
Given the competitive nature of the industry, renovation is necessary to maintain
and enhance business volume and hence the financial health of individual hotels.

There are many terms used in the industry to describe where the money
comes from to pay for renovation, including "reserve for replacement," "capital
expenditures," "Cap-X," "CapEx," and "FF&E reserve." In fact, there is a debate
within the industry over accounting and valuation rules related to the classification of renovation expenditures. In this chapter, we distinguish renovations from
other expenditures by categorizing renovations as work on the property for which
the benefits extend over a multi-year period. This includes not only work that simply replaces furniture, fixtures, and equipment that are worn out, but also work
performed on major building systems such as plumbing systems and roofs, work
performed to reposition a property or space within a property, work performed to

meet new government regulations, work performed to meet new market demands, and work performed to keep the property current with improvements in the technology arena.[3]

In this chapter we examine why hotels should renovate and discuss the life cycle of a hotel. We also discuss different types of renovation and the planning, design, and construction phases of the renovation process. The chapter concludes with a section on after-renovation activities. Although the chapter will focus on hotels, much of the material applies to restaurants as well.

Hotel Renovation

Generally speaking, **renovation** is the process of renewing and updating a hospitality property, usually to offset the ravages of use or modify spaces to meet the needs of changing markets. Renovation freshens the look and feel of interior spaces; it provides a means to update and modernize the engineering systems that provide a safe, comfortable, and convenient interior environment; and it allows managers to change the mix and type of services and facilities offered to the public.

Several trends have emerged over the past decade that impact the manner in which renovations are approached:

- First, a clear trend is to construct smaller lodging properties and place them closer to individual demand generators. This gives customers more choices and allows individual properties to capture specific segments of demand that were served by traditional full-service hotels. A result is that, proportionally speaking, the number of properties a given hotel competes with is increasing much faster than the number of rooms in a market.

- Second, increased segmentation within the hotel industry gives consumers many more choices when deciding which property to select. For example, many locales have several traditional full-service hotels of varying quality levels, economy and limited-service properties, extended-stay hotels, and suite hotels—all serving the same market.

- Third, technology has changed significantly in the past decade; customers have very different expectations about in-room technology and in-hotel business-center capabilities today than they did even five years ago.

These factors combine to produce a much more competitive environment for hotels. Existing hotels must renovate or become the physically and functionally obsolete properties within their markets. A hotel can no longer plan to use its systems and interior finishes without change for 15 to 20 years. Technological, functional, and stylistic obsolescence forces most hotel managers to introduce changes within five years of opening a new facility, with extensive changes taking place over a typical 12- to 15-year cycle.

Reasons to Renovate

There are many reasons to renovate a hotel. Some of the most common are:

- Equipment reaches the end of its lifetime.

- Building elements reach the end of their lives and must be replaced; if the roof, for example, is not replaced at the proper time, the hotel risks significant business interruption, due to serious leaks in revenue-generating areas that force those areas to shut down for repairs.

- The furnishings and finishes within the facility are worn out.

- The interior design is out-of-date and a source of embarrassment or is directly linked to declining revenues.

- The market for the mix of facilities offered by the hotel has changed, and new opportunities are available only through renovating and redeploying under-utilized facilities to meet changing guest demands. Examples include converting a restaurant to a catering or meeting venue, or adding retail space.

- Present or previous ownership has not spent the funds necessary to keep the hotel in a fully updated condition, and the physical plant has deteriorated. As a direct result, business volume has declined to a point where revenues do not support the hotel's level of debt. In this case, a decision must be made to hold and renovate versus sell the property.

- Acquiring and renovating an existing hotel presents an opportunity that is superior to constructing a new hotel in terms of location, timing, and costs.

- New technology must be installed to meet customer needs.

- The property has physical or environmental issues that must be dealt with. For example, a hotel might need to renovate to meet the needs of physically challenged customers, or to cure indoor-air-quality problems.

As a property ages, the renovation strategy needs to change. Maintaining the original design is important in the early years; making extensive changes to meet changing guest needs and expectations becomes important in later years. It is tempting to accelerate the process of changing the original design, but few facilities can justify speeding up major changes on a return-on-investment basis.

Most owners of lodging facilities want funds spent on renovations to provide a return on their investment. The question for an owner is, Which makes the most sense financially—should I put money into the hotel (renovate it) and keep it, or should I sell it? For this and other reasons, most owners require a detailed financial analysis of each major renovation project. This change has occurred slowly, but conducting a financial analysis for a proposed renovation is now the norm, not the exception, for most renovation projects. Major responsibilities of the owner's asset manager are to (1) ensure that renovation projects indeed add value to the property, and (2) assist property managers in setting a strategic direction for the renovation plan.

Additionally, someone at the property must take responsibility for creating and maintaining a long-term renovation plan. Such a plan provides for continuity over time, provides a linkage between a property's business plan and the physical condition the property must maintain to achieve the business plan, and becomes a repository of wisdom regarding project economics.

The Life Cycle of a Hotel

All commercial businesses have an identifiable life cycle, and hotels are no exception. In many cases, the cycle is typified by the following scenario:

> A hotel is constructed to meet the needs of a growing community and becomes a dominant force in the market for a number of years, enjoying higher occupancies and rates than its competitors. During this robust first phase, the property may be the preferred site for local social and business functions. Other hoteliers, seeing this hotel's success, enter the market with equal or superior products, especially in communities that are growing in population and business activity.
>
> In the second phase, the hotel's occupancy and average daily rate decline over time as new competitors enter the market and "steal" market share from existing properties. This process is hastened if ownership and management do not invest in the renovation of the hotel.
>
> In the third phase, the market changes as well, demanding new services different from those the hotel is capable of offering in its current state. If the hotel is part of a chain, in many cases the franchise is lost or changed during this phase. Over time it becomes apparent that revenues will not support the property's required returns. The hotel's decline has two possible outcomes: disposal of the hotel (by selling it, for example) or a change in its focus, meaning repositioning or rehabilitation. The critical factor at this point is whether investments in the facility will bring higher returns than the returns associated with selling the hotel and reinvesting the money elsewhere.

This process of dominance, decline, and rehabilitation or reuse is illustrated in Exhibit 1. Renovation work should be used to extend the phase-one period of strong performance and minimize any periods of decline. Renovating early in a hotel's life preserves and extends its healthy phase-one period. Renovations in the second phase incorporate changes in response to market forces. Third-phase renovations involve significant changes to the building to reposition it within the market and upgrade support systems (such as mechanical, life-safety, or technology systems) that are outdated.

Types of Renovation

Renovations typically fall into four categories, depending on the scope of work performed: special projects, minor renovation, major renovation, and restoration.

Special Projects. The scope of a **special project** is to perform work related to a specific system upgrade that can be handled without changing the hotel's interior design in any substantial way. As such, special projects have typically been related to technology or engineering systems. Examples include: installation of electronic locking systems, installation of equipment for high-speed Internet access, and fire sprinkler system retrofits.

Minor Renovation (6-Year Cycle). The scope of a **minor renovation** is to replace or renew the non-durable furnishings and finishes within a hotel space without changing the space's use or physical layout. For example, minor renovation of a meeting room would include replacing carpets and wall coverings, repainting

Exhibit 1   The Life Cycle of a Hotel

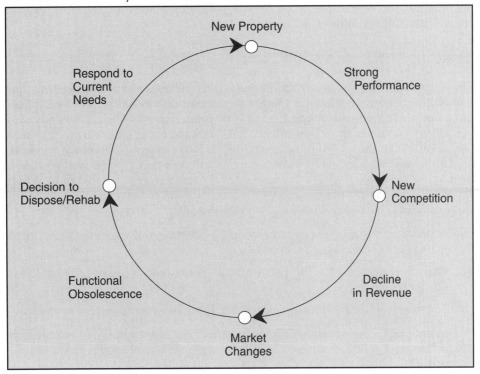

doors and frames, and other minor work. Minor renovation of a guestroom would include replacing carpets, wall coverings, drapery, and bedspreads; minor painting; and touching up the furniture.

Major Renovation (12- to 15-Year Cycle). The scope of a **major renovation** is to replace or renew all furnishings and finishes within a space, and may include extensive modifications to the use and physical layout of the space itself. For example, major renovation of a restaurant can include changing the concept; changing the location of the entrance(s); replacing all seating and tables; replacing all floor, wall, and ceiling treatments; changing mechanical, electrical, and lighting systems; and installing an up-to-date point-of-sale (POS) transaction-management system. Major renovation to a guestroom would include everything involved in a minor renovation plus replacement of all furniture, bedding, lighting, and artwork. In many cases, the bathroom also is upgraded, which might include replacing ceramic tile with marble or granite and replacing the vanity and lavatory.

Restoration (25- to 50-Year Cycle). The scope of a **restoration** is to completely gut a space and replace systems that are technically and functionally obsolete, while restoring furnishings and systems that can still be used, given the current needs of the facility. Examples include wholesale replacement of kitchen and laundry facilities; interior demolition of entire guestroom floors to reconfigure the mix of rooms and placement of bathrooms; replacement of all mechanical, electrical, and plumbing systems; and restoration of a ballroom, including plaster filigree work, crystal chandeliers, and ornamental woodwork.

Creating the Renovation Plan

The planning process for renovation work is often called the capital budgeting process. Traditionally, the planning process for renovation projects starts by establishing a budget that is some percentage of total property revenues. Historically, this percentage was set at three percent, but has moved to four percent during the past two decades. This does not mean that three or four percent of property revenues actually provided adequate funding for all capital projects, but it was seen as a benchmark measure. It is now recognized that these percentages are below actual experience. Two important studies by the International Society of Hospitality Consultants (ISHC) have demonstrated several indisputable facts:

1. A property's capital needs vary widely over time and can only be approximated by a percentage of revenues.

2. Capital needs tend to "lump" in certain years and increase significantly as properties age.

3. There are significant differences in capital spending across property types.[4]

In answer to the question "Should CapEx" (that is, capital expenditures or expenditures for renovation) "be analyzed as a percentage of total revenue or on a per-available-room basis?" the *CapEx 2000* report states the following:

> Despite the simplistic nature of estimating future CapEx as a percentage of total revenues, it is our opinion that it is the most reliable measure which can be *consistently* utilized within our industry. This does not lessen the need for a proper micro analysis of a particular hotel asset based on the property's age, market position, physical condition, history of maintenance and capital expenditures, and professional design and engineering reviews.[5]

The report also states that the percentage should be applied within a type of property, and presents data on full-service hotels, limited-service hotels, and all-suite hotels. Exhibit 2 provides summary data from the *CapEx 2000* report; Exhibits 3 through 6 give some detailed information from the report.

One industry writer makes the case that the capital expenditure reserve should be 7 to 11 percent of total revenue.[6] The author makes his argument by pointing out that replacement of furniture, fixtures, and equipment will need between 4 and 5 percent of total revenues, the structure and other "permanent" parts of the property will require 1 to 3 percent, and technology systems will require 2 to 3 percent. While his figures are in excess of the experience recorded in the ISHC study, there is some validity to his argument.

Increasingly, the industry is recognizing that the most correct way to forecast capital expenditures is to establish a space-by-space schedule of renovation needs over a very long time horizon, such as 20 to 30 years. Such a schedule is based on the expected life of various components within each space and the cost to replace

Exhibit 2   Capital Expenditure Spending from 1988–1998

	Percent of Total Revenues	Dollars per Available Room per Year
All Hotels	5.6%	$ 1,502
Full-Service Hotels	6.1%	$ 2,219
Limited-Service Hotels	5.5%	$ 1,111
All-Suite Hotels	4.9%	$ 1,402

Source: S. Mellen, K. Nylen, and R. Pastorino, *CapEx 2000: A Study of Capital Expenditures in the U.S. Hotel Industry* (Alexandria, Virginia: International Society of Hospitality Consultants, 2000).

Exhibit 3   Composition of Capital Expenditures

Component	Full-Service Hotels	Limited-Service Hotels
Rooms & Corridors	33%	29%
Food and Beverage	11%	10%
Other Public Space	16%	13%
Building	14%	24%
Technology	8%	8%
ADA/Life Safety	3%	5%
Other	15%	11%

Source: S. Mellen, K. Nylen, and R. Pastorino, *CapEx 2000: A Study of Capital Expenditures in the U.S. Hotel Industry* (Alexandria, Virginia: International Society of Hospitality Consultants, 2000).

Exhibit 4   Capital Expenditures by Hotel Location

Location	Full-Service Hotels			Limited-Service Hotels			All-Suite Hotels		
	Avg. Age	CapEx Percent	CapEx /Rm	Avg. Age	CapEx Percent	CapEx /Rm	Avg. Age	CapEx Percent	CapEx /Rm
All Properties	20.5	6.1%	$2,219	12.0	5.2%	$ 1,111	10.1	4.9%	$1,402
Airport	17.5	6.7%	$2,693	9.8	5.4%	$1,268	9.5	9.2%	$3,091
Urban	23.6	6.6%	$2,527	15.2	4.3%	$ 820	12.1	6.2%	$1,807
Resort	17.7	6.0%	$2,475	N/A	N/A	N/A	N/A	N/A	N/A
Highway / Small City	24.7	4.9%	$1,365	9.2	5.1%	$ 773	11.1	4.4%	$1,087
Suburban	15.6	5.4%	$1,826	10.5	5.7%	$1,172	8.4	4.2%	$1,188

Source: S. Mellen, K. Nylen, and R. Pastorino, *CapEx 2000: A Study of Capital Expenditures in the U.S. Hotel Industry* (Alexandria, Virginia: International Society of Hospitality Consultants, 2000).

Exhibit 5   Capital Expenditures by Hotel Age

Location	Full-Service Hotels		Limited-Service Hotels		All-Suite Hotels	
	CapEx Percent	CapEx /Rm	CapEx Percent	CapEx /Rm	CapEx Percent	CapEx /Rm
All Properties	6.1%	$ 2,219	5.5%	$1,111	4.9%	$1,402
Before 1983 (> 15 years old)	6.4%	$ 2,009	6.5%	$1,372	6.1%	$1,677
1983–1993 (5–15 years old)	6.5%	$ 3,335	4.8%	$ 897	5.3%	$1,662
After 1993 (< 5 years old)	0.9%	$ 479	3.0%	$ 547	1.6%	$ 421

Source: S. Mellen, K. Nylen, and R. Pastorino, *CapEx 2000: A Study of Capital Expenditures in the U.S. Hotel Industry* (Alexandria, Virginia: International Society of Hospitality Consultants, 2000).

Exhibit 6   Capital Expenditures, Dollars per Room/Year

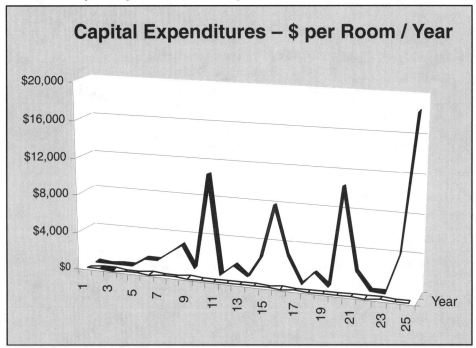

Source: S. Mellen, K. Nylen, and R. Pastorino, *CapEx 2000: A Study of Capital Expenditures in the U.S. Hotel Industry* (Alexandria, Virginia: International Society of Hospitality Consultants, 2000).

them at the end of their expected life. By proceeding in this manner, management obtains a very accurate picture of the property's capital needs over a long time. Not only is a budget established that accounts for the physical needs of the building, management obtains a very thorough understanding of the required phasing of the building's needs. Known generically as **facility life-cycle cost studies**, these studies are increasingly seen as part of the asset manager's role to preserve and enhance the value of the property.[7]

Note that facility life-cycle cost studies do not need to use the physical life of building components as the basis for the replacement cycle; indeed, in many cases they should not. As an example, it is widely recognized that the economic life of a cocktail lounge is considerably less than its physical life. Scheduling the replacement of furnishings and finishes on a three-year cycle but the replacement of equipment on a six-year cycle recognizes that some items must be replaced to maintain income, others because they are worn out.

By producing a well thought out facility life-cycle cost study, management will come to understand that the property will require, for renovation purposes, perhaps 4 percent of revenues during the first decade of business, 5.5 percent during the second decade, and 6.5 percent during the third. Such a study provides managers with a benchmark that is based on the business and physical needs of the property. Facility life-cycle cost studies cannot anticipate everything, however; there will always be expenditures for unforeseen needs, such as the need to renovate certain spaces to comply with new laws or new brand standards imposed by corporate headquarters (if the property is part of a hotel chain).

The Planning Phase

The planning phase for property renovation consists of several steps:

- Conduct a strategic review

- Survey the property and create a preliminary project list

- Estimate project costs and benefits

- Set priorities and choose projects

We'll take a look at each of these steps in the following sections.

Conduct a Strategic Review. The annual renovation process should begin with an understanding of the hotel's long-term needs, ideally arrived at through a facility life-cycle cost study. However, this plan is normally based on the typical life of building components, without regard to current competitive pressures. Therefore, in addition to this long-term plan, management must have a strategy to contend with the property's immediate competitive environment.

Owners and managers need to take a step-by-step approach to the assessment of the property's current and desired operational mission; there should be a rigorous periodic evaluation of the property, a **strategic review**. In most organizations, this step is usually handled as a joint effort between management and ownership, typically conducted by the property's general manager and the owner's representative or asset manager. In large hotel chains, regional or divisional managers are also involved. Steps in this strategic review are as follows:

1. Conduct an honest evaluation of the hotel's current market position. Using historical performance data and information from competing properties, evaluate the existing reputation of the property and its strengths, weaknesses, opportunities, and threats.

2. Identify the key trends in the local area that will drive the lodging market as a whole for the foreseeable future.

3. Combine the above analyses to formulate the best market position for the property, consistent with constraints such as location. In many cases it will become obvious that the property should change its positioning within the market, while in others, maintenance of the current market position is optimal.

By subjecting the property to a rigorous strategic review and seeking to understand both the current and desired market position, management will then be prepared to craft the renovation plan in a manner that brings the most value to the property. This step should establish consensus about the property's main renovation concerns and create a preliminary phasing plan. It is wise to remember that renovation is not the objective, only the means, to greater objectives: to increase a property's competitive position and maximize its value. Every renovation, large or small, must also be appropriate to the property's rate structure, target markets, franchise affiliation, sales strategy, and level of service. The next job is to identify the renovation projects that will best support the findings of the strategic review. This is done through a property survey.

Survey the Property and Create a Preliminary Project List. The need to properly survey the property cannot be overemphasized. A thorough survey of the property helps management determine what areas and facilities need to be renovated. A proper survey includes input from all department heads. The survey is meant to identify needs and stimulate ideas. Another reason to survey is to force managers responsible for the renovation to inspect the spaces to be renovated. Exhibit 7 contains a checklist of areas that should be surveyed on a regular basis. In many cases, two surveys are appropriate. The first survey is typically performed by the hotel's management to identify needs. Once renovation projects have been determined, a follow-up survey is done by the manager in charge of the renovation along with the designer(s) and/or engineer(s) to determine the exact scope of the renovation work.

When surveying the property for the first time, managers should keep in mind the relationship between the economic life of building systems and the physical life of these systems. In most cases the physical life exceeds the economic. Most owners can easily see the wisdom of replacing a still functioning but obsolete manual front office system with a computerized front office system, even though the old equipment is still working. The same analysis can be applied to laundry equipment, kitchen equipment, and engineered systems, to achieve both labor savings and energy savings. Thus, when identifying opportunities for renovation, one has to do more than just identify those items that are worn out.

Identifying renovation opportunities requires sensitivity to the available range of options for the property. It is here that the previous work of evaluating market position becomes valuable, because managers can eliminate renovation options that are clearly inconsistent with the goals of the property, and can focus attention on those choices that are most promising.

Exhibit 7   Hotel Survey Checklist

FRONT-OF-THE-HOUSE SPACES

Rooms Division
- ☐ Guestrooms, guestroom baths, suites, and corridors
- ☐ Guestroom amenities and accessories—safe, mini-bar
- ☐ Guestroom technology—Internet access, in-room movies, VCR/DVD, radio, bedside controls
- ☐ Bathroom accessories—pulsating shower heads, lighted mirrors, towel warmers, shoe polishers, whirlpools, and steam baths
- ☐ Support areas—front desk, reservations, guest services areas

Food and Beverage Outlets
- ☐ Restaurants and lounges—concepts, condition, consistency, competition
- ☐ Support areas—coat check room, entrances, restrooms

Public Areas
- ☐ Ballrooms, meeting rooms, banquet rooms, lobbies
- ☐ Pools, health and recreation facilities
- ☐ Elevator interiors

ENGINEERED SYSTEMS

Heating, Ventilating, and Air Conditioning Systems
- ☐ Temperature, humidity, fresh air, and odor control
- ☐ Mechanical noise and vibration control

Life–Safety Systems
- ☐ Sprinklers, standpipes, hose racks, fire extinguishers
- ☐ Smoke detectors, fire alarms, voice communication system, command post
- ☐ Emergency power generator, lighting, fire pumps, elevators
- ☐ Kitchen hood protection, computer protection

Energy Conservation Systems
- ☐ Computerized energy management systems
- ☐ Heat recovery systems (kitchen and laundry hot water and exhaust)
- ☐ Exhaust recirculation (air purifying systems)
- ☐ Insulating windows (double and solar glazing)

Telephone and Communications Systems
- ☐ Computerized least-cost routing, accounting, wake-up call

MANAGEMENT SYSTEMS

Computerized Property Management Systems
- ☐ Reservations, room status, guest histories
- ☐ Accounting, auditing, inventories
- ☐ Point-of-sale billing

SECURITY SYSTEMS

- ☐ Card-locking systems, peepholes, secondary locks
- ☐ TV surveillance of entrances, service dock, elevators, escalators
- ☐ Alarms for exit stairs, cashier
- ☐ Cashier's vault, safe deposit boxes

Source: Adapted from Walter A. Rutes, Richard H. Penner, and Lawrence Adams, *Hotel Design, Planning, and Development* (New York: W.W. Norton, 2001).

At the end of the property survey, the hotel's management has generated a list of potential renovation projects. Senior management should take a close look at the list to determine which projects are consistent with the strategic review. Those that aren't should be discarded or tabled. This leaves management with a list of appropriate renovation projects that must be evaluated further. This step is important to communicate to the hotel staff, so that there is a clear understanding of which projects will proceed, the priority of those projects, and the reasons for discarding certain projects.

Estimate Project Costs and Benefits. Concurrent with generating the project list, management should estimate the costs and benefits of each project. This process will identify projects that should be dropped from the list because their costs exceed their benefits.

Estimating costs. In new construction, managers have the advantage of being able to completely plan and analyze projects before construction begins. There are relatively few unknowns on the cost side. Because renovations involve work that will be performed (in most cases) in a property that will remain open for business, they pose a different set of problems, such as maintaining public circulation while the renovation work goes on, and finding ways to reuse existing mechanical and electrical systems. Without proper estimating and analysis, management can make poor decisions, leading to delays and cost overruns.

In many renovation projects the choice is not whether to proceed but how to choose among alternative ways to proceed. For instance, when renovating a lounge, at what point does it make sense to move the bar to improve guest traffic circulation? Only an objective analysis of the benefits and costs associated with this move can answer the question. If revenue can be greatly enhanced by moving the bar (an expensive option due to the plumbing work involved), the idea merits consideration.

All cost-estimating methods are based on breaking projects into various components and estimating the cost of each component. For managers, the question is: What estimating technique should I use, given my current decision needs? There is a direct relationship between the amount of time and information needed to prepare an estimate and the accuracy of the estimate. Four commonly used estimating methods are:

1. *Order of magnitude.* Order-of-magnitude estimates are commonly called "ballpark" estimates. This is the quickest and least accurate (plus or minus 30 percent) method of estimating. The purpose is to create only an approximate estimate of costs. It is common to estimate by a percentage of revenues—for example, a lounge renovation will cost 50 percent of annual revenues; or by a percentage of physical value—for example, a restoration of a guestroom costs approximately 75 percent of the per-room cost of new construction. Order-of-magnitude estimates require very little information and are based on information from previous projects or from general industry sources.

2. *Occupancy-based estimates.* Occupancy-based estimates produce more refined estimates (plus or minus 20 percent) of project costs. These estimates are prepared by using standard units, such as cost per room for guestrooms, cost per

seat in food and beverage outlets, or cost per square foot in meeting rooms (adjusted for known complicating factors). Thus, occupancy-based estimates can be used only when the scope of renovations is known—for example, the number or guestrooms or the amount of meeting-room space to be renovated.

3. *Systems estimates.* Systems estimates are created by estimating the cost of the different construction systems used in a renovation. This estimating method gives a more detailed cost estimate than occupancy-based estimates (plus or minus 10 percent) but requires more information, including detailed information about new construction and work to be reused. For example, a systems estimate for a guestroom includes the installed cost of a new vanity top, the installed cost of a new air conditioning unit, the removal of old wall vinyl, the installation of new wall vinyl, and so on, with a complete estimate being the total cost of all the items that will be involved in the renovation. This estimating method is very appropriate during the design phase of a project.

4. *Unit-price estimates.* This is the most detailed and accurate (plus or minus 5 percent) method of estimating. With unit-price estimates, the estimator prices materials, shipping costs, taxes, and labor separately for each item, and then adds up the totals for the items. For example, a drapery system would be estimated by pricing the cover material, liner material, the cost of flame-proofing, the cost of new drapery rods, shipping costs, taxes, and the cost of installation. A unit-price estimate for a new vanity would break the work into the demolition and removal of the old vanity top and sink; trash removal; wall repair; installation of the new vanity top and sink; installation of the plumbing; and clean up. This method takes considerably longer than the other methods and requires complete information about the project. This method is suited for the preparation of construction bids and for securing furnishings bids.

Order-of-magnitude estimates are useful for preparing a renovation wish list or quickly comparing the costs of different projects. Occupancy-based estimates are appropriate when you only need to select among alternatives. Once a project is approved and is moved to the design phase, it should be estimated using a more accurate method, which requires higher levels of estimating expertise.

Information for making occupancy-based estimates for the major spaces in economy, mid-price, first-class, and luxury properties is presented in the chapter appendix. This information is based on national average costs in 2000 and represents "turn-key" costs, including sales tax (8 percent), freight, warehousing, and installation costs. The price differences among property types are due to differences in the quality of the materials used, size of rooms, amount of furniture, and level of customization of the furnishings. The appendix guidelines can provide a reasonable basis for preliminary decision-making at most properties, especially if they are modified by the particular circumstances at a specific property. For example, the appendix shows that a major guestroom renovation will cost $7,000 per room at a mid-range property. If, however, you know that the rooms need new televisions but not bedding, simply adjust the per-room price for these two items and then multiply by the number of rooms. Remember to include sales tax, freight, warehousing, and installation costs when making these adjustments.

Many times the indirect costs of a renovation project are not included in the estimate. Examples of indirect costs include:

- Extra cleaning of all areas due to construction dust and dirt
- Complimentary goods and services or billing adjustments to soothe unhappy guests (typically, managers comp drinks or meals, but may even comp guest-rooms if that is necessary to keep goodwill)
- Loss of revenue due to out-of-service facilities
- Loss of valued employees and the hiring and training costs to replace them.

In many cases, simple changes to the renovation plan can significantly reduce these indirect costs. These and other operational issues are discussed later in the chapter.

Estimating benefits. There are two types of benefit analysis: one for projects directly affecting revenues, and the other for projects that support revenues. An example of a project directly affecting revenues is the renovation of a lounge; an example of a project that supports revenues would be replacing the roof.

The key to analyzing projects directly affecting revenues is to compare the net benefits (i.e., increase in revenues due to renovation) with the renovation costs, using the appropriate present value techniques for revenues that are projected to occur in the future.[8]

To evaluate the potential benefits of a renovation project, managers must prepare an estimate (over some reasonable time period) of the operational revenues the hotel will earn without the renovation. This "base" revenue estimate is compared with an estimate of the revenues the hotel may earn if the renovation is undertaken, over the same time period. The difference between these estimates is the estimate of the net revenues that will be gained by renovating. The net revenues are then compared with the cost of performing the renovation, to determine if the renovation produces the desired returns. It is very typical to use a net present value analysis as an aid to make decisions. Projects for which the present value of the benefits is greater than the present value of the costs are typically considered for funding.

For example, let's say a hotel is considering changing the concept of its lounge, estimated to have a five-year life cycle. Sample projections of revenues are shown in Exhibit 8. As you can see from the exhibit, this analysis shows that the renovation should be undertaken, because the property will earn more revenues over time if it renovates than if it does not ($95,000 more by the end of 2006).

This type of analysis should be performed on all proposed renovation projects affecting revenues. Projects can then be ranked according to their net present value or net present value to cost ratio, from most beneficial to least beneficial. Ranking is especially important when the projected costs of the renovation projects exceed the available funds.

The purpose of analyzing support projects is to identify those projects that will produce the greatest savings for the property. The methodology is very similar to that for projects affecting revenues, but the orientation shifts from estimating potential revenues to estimating the total cost of each alternative under consideration.[9]

Exhibit 8   Sample Projections of Revenues and Costs

	2002	2003	2004	2005	2006
With Renovation					
Revenues	750,000	800,000	875,000	975,000	1,100,000
Costs	650,000	680,000	740,000	825,000	935,000
Net Income	100,000	120,000	135,000	150,000	165,000
No Renovation					
Revenues	700,000	725,000	750,000	775,000	800,000
Costs	625,000	650,000	675,000	700,000	725,000
Net Income	75,000	75,000	75,000	75,000	75,000

Estimated Revenue with Renovation	$ 670,000
Estimated Revenue with No Renovation	$ 375,000
Estimated Additional Revenue with Renovation	$ 295,000
Estimated Cost of Renovation	$ 200,000
Estimated Additional Revenue after Deducting Renovation Costs	$ 95,000

As shown in Exhibit 9, life-cycle costing involves comparing the total cost of ownership for each alternative under consideration. The example in Exhibit 9 is generic, but illustrates the point that the life of each alternative need not be the same. In the example, Alternative A has a higher initial cost than Alternative B, but has the lowest annual total cost of ownership. In essence, the longer life and lower operating costs of Alternative A outweigh its higher initial cost. The lodging industry has many opportunities to use this analysis; common examples include:

- Equipment replacement—laundry, kitchen, engineering

- Lighting replacements—especially replacement of incandescent lamps with fluorescent

- Repair versus replacement decisions—hotel van, kitchen equipment, roof

- Replacement/retrofit of chillers and refrigeration equipment with machinery that uses environmentally acceptable refrigerants.

- Replacement of through-wall HVAC units using electric heat with heat pump units

- Installation of a micro turbine to generate electricity

In many cases, higher initial costs of a given alternative are more than offset by much lower operating costs, including both energy and labor savings.

Exhibit 9   Total Cost of Ownership Example

Alternative A

| | | Inflation Rate | | 3% |
| | | Opportunity Cost of Capital | | 10% |

Year	Initial Cost	Op. Cost	Salvage	Total
0	$ (12,000.00)			$ (12,000.00)
1		$ (2,000.00)		$ (2,000.00)
2		$ (2,060.00)		$ (2,060.00)
3		$ (2,121.80)		$ (2,121.80)
4		$ (2,185.45)		$ (2,185.45)
5		$ (2,251.02)		$ (2,251.02)
6		$ (2,318.55)		$ (2,318.55)
7		$ (2,388.10)		$ (2,388.10)
8		$ (2,459.75)	$1,500.00	$ (959.75)
			NPV =	$ (22,987.16)
		Annual Total Cost of Ownership =		$ (4,308.81)

Alternative B

| | | Inflation Rate | | 3% |
| | | Opportunity Cost of Capital | | 10% |

Year	Initial Cost	Op. Cost	Salvage	Total
0	$ (7,000.00)			$ (7,000.00)
1		$ (2,500.00)		$ (2,500.00)
2		$ (2,575.00)		$ (2,575.00)
3		$ (2,652.25)		$ (2,652.25)
4		$ (2,731.82)		$ (2,731.82)
5		$ (2,813.77)	$1,000.00	$ (1,813.77)
			NPV =	$ (16,385.58)
		Annual Total Cost of Ownership =		$ (4,322.47)

Set Priorities and Choose Projects. At the completion of the estimating process, management has a list of projects ranked from most beneficial to least beneficial to the property. Senior management and the property's owner(s) must choose which projects to undertake, keeping in mind the funds available for renovation.

Decision-makers usually pick those projects that offer the greatest economic returns or fulfill the most pressing needs. Good judgment is required to make this final list, because, from this point on, most approved projects are constructed. If poor projects are included, or good projects excluded, management has wasted opportunities.

Implementing the Renovation Plan ——————————

Once the planning process is complete and projects have been approved, the hotel's managers can move on to the implementation of the renovation plans—the design and construction phases.

The Design Phase

The first implementation step is to prepare, for each approved project, a design—or more precisely, a set of design documents—that serves as:

- The visual embodiment of the desires of ownership and management
- A tool to secure building permits and licenses
- A means to communicate to contractors the scope and detail of the work to be completed
- A set of specifications that can be used to purchase furnishings

While it may seem unlikely that one set of design documents can serve all these functions, in the end it must, for failure in any of these areas renders the documents virtually useless. For example, if the design is complete but does not meet local building codes, the renovation project cannot proceed, for lack of a building permit. In this instance, the plans must be modified until the code requirements are met.

The extent and level of detail required in the design vary widely from project to project. Some projects may require only a simple sketch and some performance specifications, while complex renovations involve a complete set of construction plans, specifications, and schedules.

The Design Team. Whether the renovation is large or small, the design work for the renovation is usually the product of a team. The number of team members will vary widely from property to property and project to project, but all renovation projects should have a team composed of:

- Property managers
- Design professionals
- Contractors
- Purchasers

To achieve success, these team members must integrate their respective needs and responsibilities while keeping in mind the maxim, "Good design costs no more than bad design." Exhibit 10 lists the responsibilities of team members and shows where those responsibilities overlap.

Because of the nature of renovation work, many renovation designers are specialists. Some specialize in the restoration of historic properties, others in southwest mission-style design, life-safety system retrofits, or seismic retrofits. Managers should interview designers to probe for their strengths and weaknesses before hiring them. If a design firm has experience with your type of facility or the specific nature of your project, it should be better able to understand your needs and those of your guests.

Exhibit 10 Responsibilities of the Design Team

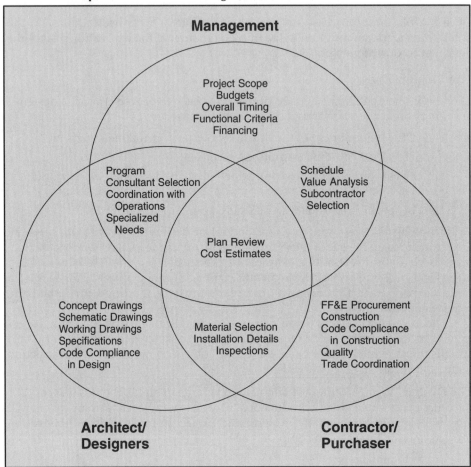

Bringing in professional designers is justified for all but the very smallest projects. Designers bring a breadth of experience to the project and have access to the most current materials, furnishings, and construction technology. They see to it that the designs meet building code requirements, and provide the documents needed by local building officials. A design firm's services are usually paid for through a fixed-price contract based on a specific amount of work called "Basic Services," with payments made according to a schedule of completion. The client (in most cases, the hotel owner) usually reimburses the design firm for the costs of travel, drawing reproduction, and other reimbursables. Fees are usually based on a percentage of the work to be performed. A typical fee schedule for renovation work is:

- Architectural design—3 to 6 percent of construction costs
- Structural design—2 to 5 percent of construction costs

- Mechanical-electrical-plumbing design—1 to 4 percent of construction costs

- Interior design—4 to 10 percent of furniture, fixtures, and equipment costs

- Specialty design (i.e., elevator, telephone, kitchen, signs)—5 to 10 percent of specialty work costs

In many renovations, the choice of one particular designer—the interior designer—is a key decision. The interior designer sets the boundaries of the project in a physical, aesthetic, and economic sense. The interior designer's decisions will affect the renovation budget, the renovation schedule, and the appearance of the facility for many years. It is important to select an interior designer with utmost care, since a poor designer will adversely affect all of the other design professionals as well as the property.

The Design Process. Design work has many phases, and in each phase the design firm will ask the client to approve the work before the firm goes on to the next phase. If the client has a change of heart after an approval and decides to do something different, the design firm will comply, but typically will request a fee for the additional work. By using this approach, the design firm and the client (in this case, the hotel's owner and managers) balance the need for the designer to make decisions on the client's behalf with the client's right to have ultimate control over those decisions. Done properly, the process results in completed projects that reflect the client's desires. Failure of this process results not only in bad design, but also in the creation of spaces that do not work as desired or intended, thus compromising revenue and property value.

Phase 1—conceptual design. Conceptual design sets the bounds and scope of a renovation project. It begins with the hotel's written renovation program being delivered to the design firm, and ends with the hotel's approval of concept documents prepared by the designers. The renovation program comes from the property survey process. The designers' work includes drawings; models; presentations of interior fabrics, colors, and materials; and sets of outline specifications. Through these documents, designers at the design firm demonstrate their understanding of the owner's needs and desires. In many cases, the design team will also produce a set of measured drawings that document existing as-built conditions. Especially in older buildings, this work can significantly reduce project uncertainty and lead to much better results.

Phase 2—schematic design. This phase fleshes out the conceptual design, fixing the location of design elements—a bar, front desk, or entry door, for example—establishing rigid boundaries, and showing the limits of demolition. This phase ends when the schematic design drawings are approved. The approved drawings show final colors and the final choices of the materials the major design elements are made of—stone rather than tile, vinyl rather than paint, wood rather than laminate, for example. Schematic design also shows how the work will be scheduled.

Phase 3—design development. Design development drawings are highly detailed, allowing the reader to determine accurate counts on numbers of seats, number of square feet, and quantities of materials. Construction materials and methods are specified, and design details between surfaces (for example, door moldings and jambs) and materials (for example, carpet to stone) are worked out.

During this phase, design professionals coordinate and resolve any difficulties between each other's work, so that the completed design achieves the owner's objectives. Examples include coordinating gas and electrical service to kitchen equipment, reconfiguring duct work to accommodate ceiling changes, planning an aesthetically pleasing sprinkler-head layout in a ballroom, and incorporating all code-required changes. Approval of this set of drawings signals the client's desire to proceed with the work as designed. Changes after this point will affect construction of the work.

Phase 4—construction documents. Construction documents (also known as working drawings) constitute the final design phase. They are necessary primarily for two purposes: (1) to provide construction guidelines and guidelines for procuring materials, and (2) to secure the necessary building permits required to perform the work. This set of documents requires the highest level of detail and the longest time to prepare. It is also the most straightforward work, assuming no changes are made. Changes in the scope or nature of the renovation at this time will cause long delays in the production of the documents and will increase design costs.

Good construction documents eliminate uncertainty and result in lower costs, higher quality, and faster work. They allow the contractor to focus on the work exactly as shown on the documents and allow the purchaser to know precisely what and how much of each item to obtain.

The Construction Phase

Once construction documents are completed, contractors can be hired to begin construction.

Construction Contracts. The standard construction contract is a lump-sum contract that includes the following:

- A complete description of the work to be done (construction documents are used for this purpose)

- A description of the duties and responsibilities of hotel management, the contractor, and the design firm

- The cost of the work and the method of payment

- The date of commencement and the date of completion (for renovation work, this is particularly important and may include several interim dates as deadlines for phased work)

- The conditions that define final completion and acceptance of the contractor's work

The American Institute of Architects (AIA) has developed sample contracts that do a good job of protecting the interests of all parties. One contract in particular is well done—AIA Document A101, Standard Form of Agreement Between Owner and Contractor. Although AIA's sample contracts are good places to start, you should always modify them (with the help of an attorney) for the particular work at hand. AIA Document A101 is used for large jobs with complex scopes or complex relationships between the parties. For smaller jobs, AIA Document

Eight Steps to a Successful Renovation Project

1. *Define project goals* Take the time to clearly establish the project's mission and objectives.

2. *Establish the scope of work.* This should be in the form of a written program prepared by the hotel's renovation team. This step sets both the quantity and quality of the work.

3. *Set a definite budget.* A realistic yet aggressive budget will save time and prevent misunderstandings throughout the project. Everyone should understand what is included (and not included) in each line item.

4. *Survey existing conditions.* Careful examination of existing conditions prevents budget-busting surprises.

5. *Establish a realistic schedule.* Every hotel closes some of its operations for a renovation; the questions are, How much is closed at a time and for how long? Anticipate the impact on guests and plan accordingly. A missed deadline significantly affects the hotel's operations and reputation.

6. *Communicate.* The renovation's progress must be communicated continually to the hotel's staff members, so they can answer guest questions knowledgeably and honestly. The members of the renovation team also must do a good job of communicating with each other, in order to properly manage the project troika of time, budget, and quality.

7. *Pay attention to security.* A renovation should not create an environment that endangers guests and staff or encourages theft. It is vital to establish clear renovation policies for staff members and set appropriate limits for staff members and guests regarding access to areas undergoing renovation.

8. *Inspect work in process.* It is much better to correct flawed work while it is still in progress than to have the attitude that unsatisfactory work can be identified during the walk-through at the project's end and corrected later. Not only is quality higher with ongoing inspections, the hotel's owner and managers are assured that they are paying for work actually completed.

A107—Abbreviated Form of Agreement Between Owner and Contractor—is used. It is a shorter version of AIA Document A101.

There are several variations to the standard owner-contractor agreement that have been used with success, such as:

*   *Design/build contracts.* In this arrangement, the contractor serves as the designer as well as the builder. This arrangement is particularly well-suited for work requiring significant engineering design, such as life-safety, mechanical, or electrical work. It is also well-suited for dealing with specialty contractors, such as kitchen equipment suppliers, electronic equipment suppliers, and sign companies. There is a risk with this arrangement, however, in the sense that there is no separation of the design and construction disciplines, but the risk can be minimized or eliminated by selecting a good contractor.

- *Guaranteed Maximum Price ("GMP").* This type of agreement is used when the scope of the renovation or the conditions that might be encountered during the renovation are uncertain. The owner describes the work to be accomplished; the contractor, because of the uncertainties of the project, sets a somewhat high maximum price, guaranteeing that the owner will not pay more for the work; however, if the contractor can manage to perform the work for less, the contractor shares in the savings (the contractor might ask for 20 percent of the savings as an incentive to get the project completed for less than the guaranteed price). This approach is particularly suited for work with a very short time frame, in which design details will be settled after construction begins. If used with incomplete documents, this construction contract leaves the owner exposed to the possibility of many change orders and extras.

- *Owner as contractor.* For many small jobs or for renovations in large properties, management needs design expertise, but the work can be performed by in-house staff. The risk with this approach is that the ongoing, day-to-day maintenance needs of the property tend to get pushed aside, because the property's staff is concentrating on the renovation work. If the renovation is properly managed, this problem can be minimized.

Before signing a contract, management will typically obtain bids from several contractors. In private work, one can choose the contractors allowed to bid. It is wise to prequalify contractors and create a bidder's list of firms able to perform the work. This is done via interviews and a review of each firm's technical and financial capabilities.

Each prequalified bidder receives a bid package consisting of the construction documents, a copy of the proposed construction contract, and a bid form. The bid form requests the contractor to provide a cost and a time to complete the work detailed in the construction documents. By submitting a signed form, the contractor certifies that he or she is able and willing to do the work for the price quoted in the time specified, and to abide by the terms of the contract.

Managers often neglect to use penalty and/or bonus clauses to encourage the contractor to finish on time. These clauses, coupled with good design documents, can help ensure timely completion and avoid hard feelings or litigation.

Purchasing. Purchasing furnishings, supplies, and equipment for renovation projects is a function with no uniformly defined status across hospitality firms. For some hotels, purchasing is performed by a corporate-level purchasing department, for others it is performed by a purchasing manager at the hotel, for still others it is performed by a third-party purchasing agent.

Even though much purchasing today can be done via the Internet through on-line business-to-business exchanges, someone or some team still must take responsibility for renovation purchases. It is essential to manage renovation purchasing as a project distinct from operational purchasing. There are four key elements to success that the purchasing agent for the renovation project should keep in mind:

- Purchase materials of proper quality
- Purchase materials in the proper quantities

- Make sure materials are on hand when needed

- Stay within budget guidelines

In many cases, the purchasing agent buys materials for the contractor to use during construction. Examples are kitchen and bar equipment, wall coverings, accessories (bath or closet, for example), lighting fixtures, and attached seating. In these cases, close coordination between the purchasing agent and the contractor concerning lead times, delivery dates, and handling of the material before installation are vital to maintaining the construction schedule. Failures by the purchasing agent can become excuses for the contractor to delay progress.

When purchasing material, the purchasing agent relies heavily on specifications and documents produced by the design firm. The furniture, fixtures, and equipment selection process is illustrated in Exhibit 11.

Purchasing agents need to know whether they can vary from the specifications in order to stay within the budget. While the adage "You get what you pay for" is usually true, part of a good purchasing agent's expertise is knowing manufacturers that have the ability to meet the design specifications at a lower cost than the manufacturer named in the specifications. The process of securing quotes on other manufacturers' goods is known as obtaining "knock-offs." **Knock-offs** are equipment or materials that are functionally, operationally, and aesthetically equivalent to the items specified, but are produced by a different manufacturer at a lower cost. Buying knock-offs is a well-established practice in the purchasing field, and has significant potential for savings, especially when buying furniture, seating, lighting, wall coverings, fabrics, and carpeting. Knock-off goods should be approved by the designer to ensure that the design intent is not violated. When knock-offs are used, it is important to proceed in a manner that respects the copyrighted designs of the original manufacturer or suppliers.

One of the most difficult responsibilities of the purchaser is the expediting process. Expediting is the formal follow-up process used to ensure that goods are produced and shipped on schedule while maintaining the quality specified. A good expediting effort is often the key to meeting a renovation project's completion date. In many cases, however, expediting is performed haphazardly, leading to missed deadlines or the need to use expensive express-delivery services. The manager in overall charge of the hotel's renovation project(s) should insist on being familiar with the purchasing agent's expediting procedures.

One final issue in purchasing is the question of what to do with the old furnishings. In some cases, selected pieces can be incorporated into the renovation, subject to cleaning, re-upholstering, or restoration. These pieces should be set aside for a restoration specialist to work on. In other cases, managers want the entire lot of existing furnishings to just go away.

There are two ways to get rid of existing goods. One is to contract with a furnishings handler to remove them for a fixed price. The agreement is usually very specific and lists material to be removed, when it is to be removed, and payment terms. The other way to get rid of goods is to have a liquidation sale at the hotel. While in-house staff can handle the liquidation, it is better to use the services of a professional liquidator, who in most cases will get higher prices for the goods. The advantage of contracting with a furniture handler is the speed with which the

Exhibit 11 The Furniture, Fixtures, and Equipment Selection Process

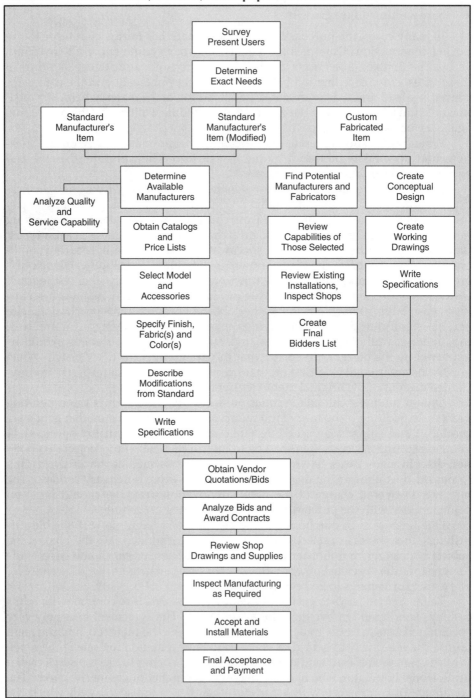

furnishings disappear; the advantage of a liquidator is that the hotel will receive higher prices for the furnishings. Only management can determine which objective, minimum bother or maximum revenue, is best under the circumstances.

Managing Construction. In new construction, the essence of project management is to simultaneously maximize quality, minimize time, and meet the budget. In renovation work, the further objective of minimizing disruptions in operating sections of the facility is added. Achieving all four objectives is a tall order, but not impossible. It requires dedication, attention to detail, and a willingness to confront minor problems before they become major ones.

Two key issues in project management are documenting work and changes to the work, and managing conflict. Documenting work consists of preparing a record of decisions that affect the project. Examples of documentation are:

- Approvals of sample materials, workmanship, or shop drawings

- Written requests for interpretation of the drawings and a written reply

- Minutes of job meetings

- Written telephone conference records

- Change proposals and change orders, signed and accepted by the contractor, design professionals, and renovation manager

In short, the most important thing to remember in managing construction is to "get it in writing." Changes to the construction drawings invariably occur, and all changes should be written down and signed off on by everyone involved. Such documentation keeps conflict to a minimum.

A certain amount of conflict is inevitable in construction. It is not humanly possible for designers to foresee all possible contingencies and indicate every bit of work to be done. The owner, renovation manager, and contractor must understand that the construction drawings convey the designer's intentions, but may not show every minute detail. It is up to the individuals in charge of the project to equitably and properly work out any omissions or errors in the drawings and specifications.

Much conflict can be avoided if all parties to the renovation understand their roles and completely understand the scope of work to be completed. Hotel managers must know that they cannot tell the contractor and subcontractors what to do, except through the chain of command. Construction personnel must understand that the renovation is taking place in an operating business, and that construction workers do not have free run of the premises, nor can they make arbitrary changes to the design to reduce costs or help the schedule. If all parties to the project work as a team, with trust and understanding, the result can be a high-quality renovation completed on time within the budget.

Issues that come up during construction that deserve special attention include coordinating the renovation with ongoing operations, the effect of building codes and new legislation on renovations, and cost and quality control.

Coordination with operations. One of the most important decisions in any hotel renovation is the decision about what spaces will be closed and how long they will be closed. The general industry consensus is that a hotel should stay open unless the work cannot be completed without closing. In some cases, it becomes apparent that the necessary closings are so extensive that the entire hotel should be shut down. The benefits and liabilities of closing are:

Benefits of Closing the Hotel

- Faster construction schedule, because all spaces are available

- Lower construction cost—no temporary facilities, shorter schedule, more efficient work

- Possibility of higher quality—no start/stop transitions; the ability to attract the best subcontractors

- No guests disgruntled by construction work

Liabilities of Closing the Hotel

- Loss of income during closing

- Loss of goodwill and market presence during closing

- Loss of good employees during closing (they move on to other jobs)

There are ways to manage a renovation so that construction problems are minimized and the hotel can remain open. For example, a kitchen may be relocated to an on-site trailer if conditions require it. Spaces under renovation can be temporarily put in working order to accommodate a sell-out or high occupancy period. Employees can be informed of renovation plans and progress via an in-house newsletter, an attachment to their paycheck, and frequent postings of pertinent information. Guests can be accommodated by moving a restaurant or lounge to a meeting room on a temporary basis. When a property remains open, it is important to convey to guests that the level of service hasn't changed, even though the number of services offered may be temporarily reduced. One way to retain valued employees is to have them work on the project or on a temporary assignment in another department, rather than institute layoffs. This sends a clear message to employees that they are valued.

If the hotel remains open (albeit with some of its spaces temporarily closed), the renovation manager must communicate often and clearly with the sales staff, so the staff can properly manage the inventory of rooms and meeting space. Sales employees should treat the renovation manager like a client and block space to be renovated in the same manner they do with other clients; the renovation manager then has the responsibility to vacate the space on the agreed-upon date, like any other client. Following this type of procedure is vital in guestroom renovations, which typically take place in blocks of rooms. The renovation manager gets a new block upon completion of the old block. In many cases it is possible to set up a system whereby the contractor takes a given number of rooms per day or per week and returns a given number after a certain interval. By rotating the rooms in this manner, renovation work can be done more efficiently because construction workers have a constant workload.

Another management concern during a renovation is temporary facilities. Temporary facilities take the form of physically moved or relocated facilities and

"Lots of Noise, Dust, and No Discounts"

So reads the headline from a *Wall Street Journal* article about hotel renovations.[10] The article's author, Jonathan B. Weinbach, goes on to suggest how hotels undertaking renovation work should treat travel agents and guests:

- *Give travel agents fair warning.* You may lose some business in the short run, but will gain loyal agents in the long run.

- *Give guests fair warning when they arrive.* Pet peeves among guests include drilling or hammering at early hours, lack of response to complaints, and lack of attention to special requests. The particular example of a professional hockey team that was unable to take afternoon naps during the playoffs due to noisy construction was cited in the article as an illustration of what not to do.

- *Take the safety concerns of guests seriously.* One guest was upset to be "stepping off the elevator to find a corridor with uncarpeted floors, exposed wires, and walls scarred by drill marks—including one hole so large that the guest feared her daughter could fall through."

The article sums up by saying that guests expect four things from hotels undergoing renovation: notification, security, a quiet environment, and a discount if they are seriously inconvenienced. Hotel managers should keep these expectations in mind as they plan and oversee the renovation work at their hotels.

constructed physical barriers. When considering temporary facilities, you should take the attitude that something worth doing is worth doing right. When relocating facilities, guests will tolerate some inconvenience, but you run the risk of asking so much of guests that they are alienated. It is here that friendly, competent service will greatly assist the renovation effort, for if guests perceive that the staff is not in control of the situation, they will become irritated and may not return. It is important to finish temporary barriers properly. A wall of unpainted plywood or drywall is ugly and intimidating. Usually, temporary walls can be used to display plans and colored drawings of the work being performed. In addition to separating construction from guests, barriers should control noise and dust. If these are not controlled, they can increase housekeeping costs and annoy guests.

A further factor in coordinating renovation work with ongoing operations, as alluded to earlier, is accommodating construction crews. The attitude of most hotel managers is that construction trades people are a necessary evil of renovation, and, from their perspective, it is an accurate assessment. Most trades people are not used to working on jobs that involve an operating business, and bring with them habits developed from years of work on new construction. It is important that the hotel's renovation manager establish clear and precise rules for the workers to follow. Most construction workers will comply with reasonable rules. Rules should address parking, entrances and exits, restroom facilities, lunch facilities, smoking, use of radios, hours of work, and identification of employees. To maintain discipline and order on the job, violations should be quickly dealt with. It should be made clear to construction workers that these rules are not designed to infringe on their ability to do their jobs; rather, they are designed to facilitate the delivery of services to the hotel's guests and address the safety concerns of guests and construction workers.

Building codes and new legislation. A critical factor to consider for any renovation project is the impact that building codes and new legislation will have on the work. Most buildings were built to meet the codes in effect at the time they were first constructed and are typically not required to be upgraded to meet code changes as they are adopted and applied to new construction over the years. However, upon renovation, many of the new codes could come into play, requiring changes to:

- Entrances and exits (configuration, location, and number)

- Life-safety systems

- Parking areas

- Construction materials (an upgrade in fire-resistance levels, for example)

Due to federal legislation, one area of particular interest continues to be building codes designed to accommodate disabled individuals. These codes have moved well beyond simply requiring businesses to provide ramps for people who use wheelchairs. The Americans with Disabilities Act of 1990 broadens the definition of "disabled" to include people with vision or hearing impairments, arthritis, heart conditions, emphysema, shortness of stature, amputated limbs, and AIDs. The ADA requires all commercial buildings to provide a much broader range of facilities for disabled individuals than have been traditionally installed. These regulations are triggered by renovations.

Design considerations for disabled persons include:

- *Security.* Disabled people are especially vulnerable to crime and violence. Good lighting throughout the property, controlled access to the property, and good locking systems are important.

- *Temperature regulation.* Some people with disabilities are especially sensitive to temperature extremes and find it desirable to control the temperature in their guestrooms based on their own subjective feeling of comfort. Designs also should minimize drafts in guestrooms and other areas.

- *Independence.* Designs should allow disabled individuals to do as many things as possible without special assistance. It is important to install devices that assist individuals but do not limit their independence.

- *Safety.* Persons with impaired mobility should be able to find refuge within buildings during emergencies (rather than being forced to exit), if at all possible.[11]

In summary, hotel owners should consider the needs of people with disabilities during renovations. Often, making changes to accommodate disabled guests will allow better service to non-impaired guests by providing a safer, more "user-friendly" environment for all.

Cost and quality control. Achieving the proper balance between cost and quality requires skill, attention to detail, and vision. There never seems to be enough funds for renovation. Good renovation managers spend endless hours revising budgets, seeking alternatives, and surgically adjusting the renovation's scope to achieve the most renovation for the funds expended. But cost-cutting should not be overdone. After the renovation is complete, the brief satisfaction of saving a few dollars fades quickly if it turns out that quality was sacrificed to achieve budget objectives, for the facility must live with the renovated space until the next renovation cycle. Mistakes to avoid include:

- *Not hiring design professionals.* It is difficult for many people to see the value of design professionals. Competent designers save their fees many times over by specifying the correct materials for the job, fixing problems on the plans rather than working them out in the field, knowing where to find competent manufacturers and contractors, achieving a consistent look to a space, and—most importantly—creating spaces that work aesthetically and functionally.

- *Allowing unqualified contractors to bid or work on a project in an attempt to lower construction costs.* This is perhaps the most destructive form of penny-wise, pound-foolish judgment. It is the renovation manager's responsibility to select competent contractors and trades people and pay them a fair price for the work. Some facilities have been ruined by contractors who did not have the ability to do the work properly. While the manager received a low price for the work, the end result was not worth the savings.

- *Reducing the renovation's scope to the point that the renovation becomes meaningless.* One does not renovate a lobby by replacing the drapes and reupholstering the furniture. If this work is all that needs to be done, it should be performed in harmony with the existing interior design, and not be called a renovation. This does not mean that this type of work should be avoided, but one should make decisions based on the needs of the space, not simply apply a few dollars to a space and call it "renovated."

When considering renovation, look for ways to save money without sacrificing quality. Some examples are:

- Asking food and beverage purveyors to supply equipment at no cost or reduced cost, if you use their products. Examples include coffee makers, juice dispensers, and soda equipment.

- Purchasing used equipment that has been refurbished. This is an especially appropriate idea for kitchens, laundries, and engineered systems.

- Buying equipment that may be show samples, last-year's models, or discounted because of superficial damage during shipping.

- Allowing renovation funds to build in a bank account; the funds will grow as interest is added. This may require delaying renovation projects for several months or even a year, a trade-off that should be considered if funds are especially scarce.

- Using textured wall coverings that will hide a poor subsurface and avoid costly wall preparation.

- Refinishing or re-upholstering existing furniture if the quality and style are appropriate for the renovation.

- Using synthetic stone on walls and ceilings rather than the solid stone used for floors.

While these ideas may make some people cringe, they should be considered, along with other money-saving ideas, if the renovation budget is tight.

Final Completion and Acceptance. Final completion and acceptance is an important phase of all renovation projects. It signifies both physical acceptance of the work, as completed, and compliance with the legal requirements of the construction contract—meaning that the contractor is entitled to full payment of money owed.

It is common to formalize acceptance of the contractor's work by using a document called the Certificate of Substantial Completion. The essence of this document is that the renovation manager, design professional(s), and contractor agree that the work is fit for its intended purpose, that it meets the requirements of the construction contract, and that it is ready for occupancy. The renovation manager usually does not sign this document unless he or she has secured a Certificate of Occupancy from the appropriate local authorities and (if necessary) has attached a list, called a **punch list**, of work that does not conform to contract specifications. Once the renovation manager signs the Certificate of Substantial Completion, the contractor is paid in full (usually within 30 days) except for the value of the work on the punch list.

While the standard AIA contracts call for the contractor to prepare the punch list, this is not common in practice. Usually the design firm, in conjunction with the renovation manager, prepares the punch list for review by the contractor. The contractor may object to certain punch-list items on the grounds that they were not part of the original agreement; in this case, they are crossed out, if the renovation manager and designers agree. If they do not agree, the items must be negotiated.

Another issue during the final-completion-and-acceptance phase is clean-up. In many cases, the hotel's housekeeping staff will assist the contractor in the clean-up effort, in order to help meet the schedule and ensure proper housekeeping standards. The amount of cleanup the housekeeping staff will do should be worked out before signing the Certificate of Substantial Completion.

After the Renovation

Even after the renovated areas of the hotel are finished and open for business, the renovation is not yet complete. Several items should be addressed at this point (if not before), including:

- Employee training
- Grand re-openings
- Impact of the renovation on operating budgets

Employee Training. Employee training is often neglected or ignored until a renovation is complete and management suddenly realizes that the employees who work in the renovated space need re-orientation and training to maximize the benefit of the renovation. The interior designer should take part in the training to ensure that employees work within and maintain the space as envisioned by the renovation manager and designer. Training should address:

- New or changed service standards

- New or changed methods of production, holding, and presentation of food and beverage items

- How to operate new equipment, especially electronic systems (training requirements should be written into purchasing contracts with suppliers of this equipment)

One often hears the refrain, "Oh, I didn't know we could do that!" months after a renovation is complete. Managers and employees discover by accident or from suppliers how systems or equipment work or should be maintained. Examples include discovering capabilities in the new sound systems or lighting systems that managers and employees knew nothing about, or continuing to maintain a floor in the same old way when the new floor requires much simpler maintenance procedures. In these cases, management has lost opportunities and the employees have been done a disservice by a lack of proper training.

Grand Re-Openings. Often it is appropriate to involve the hotel's marketing department or even the corporate office (if the hotel is part of a chain) in a public celebration of the renovation. The objective of the celebration should be to build awareness among potential guests, travel agents, and meeting planners that the new and improved facilities are available for use. The re-opening is often a grand occasion, with dignitaries and the media invited. These events should be planned and budgeted as part of the original scope of renovation work.[12]

Impact of the Renovation on Operating Budgets. As mentioned earlier in the chapter, the feasibility of renovation projects is based in part on projections of future revenue or future cost reductions. Once projects are completed, there should be a formal tracking procedure to determine whether each renovation project has the financial impact management projected. This tracking will be valuable for future renovations, providing managers with solid information with which to base future decisions.

Endnotes

1. Sonny Kleinfield, *The Hotel—A Week in the Life of the Plaza* (New York: Simon & Schuster, 1989), pp. 25–26.

2. Two good estimates are available for calendar 2000. One is to multiply the national room inventory of 3.9 million rooms by the average renovation expenditure of approximately $1,550 per room; the other uses the average capital expenditure ratio to total revenues of 5.6 percent, multiplied by total lodging industry revenues of $110 billion.

3. In particular, see Raymond S. Schmidgall, James W. Damitio, and A. J. Singh, "What Is a Capital Expenditure? How Lodging Industry Financial Executives Decide," *Cornell Hotel and Restaurant Administration Quarterly,* August, 1997; and S. Mellen, K. Nylen, and R. Pastorino, *CapEx 2000: A Study of Capital Expenditures in the U.S. Hotel Industry* (Alexandria, Virginia: International Society of Hospitality Consultants, 2000).

4. *CapEx 2000* and *CapEx 1995: A Study of Capital Expenditures in the U.S. Hotel Industry* (Memphis, Tennessee: International Society of Hospitality Consultants, 1995).

5. *CapEx 2000.*

6. S. Rushmore, "Maybe the Reserve for Replacement Should be 7% to 11% of Revenue," *Hotels,* August 1999.

7. See, for example, G. Denton, "Managing Capital Expenditures: Using Value Engineering," *Cornell Hotel and Restaurant Administration Quarterly,* April 1998. Whitestone Research of Seattle, Washington, specializes in publishing databases that estimate the life of various building components (www.whitestoneresearch.com).

8. No attempt will be made to detail present value techniques in this chapter. Two excellent sources for this information are Raymond S. Schmidgall, *Hospitality Industry Managerial Accounting,* Fourth Edition (Lansing, Mich.: Educational Institute of the American Hotel & Lodging Association, 1997), and William P. Andrew and Raymond S. Schmidgall, *Financial Management for the Hospitality Industry* (Lansing, Mich.: Educational Institute of the American Hotel & Lodging Association, 1993). Each book has a chapter on the financial analysis of capital expenses.

9. For a detailed discussion, see Rosalie T. Ruegg and Harold E. Marshall, *Building Economics: Theory and Practice* (New York: Van Nostrand Reinhold, 1990).

10. J. Weinbach, "Lots of Noise, Dust, and No Discounts," *Wall Street Journal,* June 20, 2000.

11. Adapted from Thomas D. Davies and Kim A. Beasley, *Accessible Design for Hospitality: ADA Guidelines for Planning Accessible Hotels, Motels, and Other Recreational Facilities,* Second Edition (New York: McGraw-Hill, 1994).

12. See Frederick Knapp, *Hotel Renovation: Planning and Design* (New York: McGraw-Hill, 1995) for an excellent illustrated book that visually demonstrates what is possible through renovation.

⚷ Key Terms

facility life-cycle cost study—A space-by-space schedule of the projected renovation needs for a given building over a very long time horizon (such as 20 to 30 years), based on the expected life of various components within each space and the cost to replace them at the end of their expected life.

knock-off—Material, furniture, or equipment that is functionally, operationally, and aesthetically equivalent to a more expensive item produced by another manufacturer.

major renovation—Replacement or renewal of all furnishings and finishes within a space, and, in some instances, extensive modifications to the use and physical layout of the space.

minor renovation—Replacement or renewal of non-durable furnishings and finishes within a space, without changing the space's use or physical layout.

punch list—A list of non-conforming construction work, attached to the Certificate of Substantial Completion, that a contractor must correct before receiving payment for the work.

renovation—The process of renewing and updating a hospitality property, usually to offset the ravages of use or modify spaces to meet the needs of changing markets.

restoration—A complete gutting of a space that involves replacing systems that are technically and functionally obsolete, while restoring furnishings and systems that can still be used.

special project—A renovation task related to a specific upgrade, service, or system that can be handled distinctly from renovation work that is tied to changing an interior design. As such, special projects in hospitality businesses have usually been related to technology or engineering systems.

strategic review—A periodic, rigorous evaluation of a property, usually by the property's general manager and the owner's representative or asset manager (in large organizations, regional or divisional managers may also be involved); in this evaluation, managers and ownership representatives conduct an honest evaluation of the hotel's current market position, identify key trends in the local hospitality market, and combine the above analyses to formulate the best market position for the property and plan for future renovations.

Review Questions

1. Why should a hotel renovate?

2. What are the differences among the four types of renovation?

3. What is a facility life-cycle cost study?

4. The planning phase for property renovation can be broken down into what four steps?

5. How are renovation costs and benefits estimated?

6. What are the four phases of design work?

7. What is included in a standard construction contract? What are some variations to a standard owner-contractor agreement?

8. What are some issues hotel managers should keep in mind while managing construction work?

9. What are some of the benefits and liabilities of closing a hotel while it is being renovated?

10. What are some areas that managers should address after a renovation is complete (if not before)?

Internet Sites

For more information, visit the following Internet sites. Remember that Internet addresses can change without notice. If the site is no longer there, you can use a search engine to look for additional sites.

American Institute of Architects
www.aiaonline.com

Associated Builders and Contractors Inc.
www.abc.org

Association of Restorers
www.assoc-restorers.com

Association of Specialists in Cleaning and Restoration
www.ascr.org

Construction Management Association of America
www.cmaanet.org

Construction-Net Online
www.construction-net.com

Hotel Renovators
www.hotelrenovators.com

International Society of Hospitality Consultants
www.ishc.com

Appendix

Renovation Cost Guidelines

	Economy Property (2-Star)	Mid-Range Property (3-Star)	First-Class Property (4-Star)	Luxury Property (5-Star)
ROOMS				
A. GUESTROOMS—*Major Renovation* All casegoods, softgoods, wall vinyl, bath tile, flooring, and lighting. Does not include TV, vanity, major electrical or mechanical changes. ADD $2,000 PER MODULE FOR MAJOR BATH WORK.	$5,000	$7,000	$10,000	$13,000 Per Module
GUESTROOMS—*Minor Renovation* Primarily softgoods replacement (carpet, spreads, drapes, vinyl minor accessories, upholstered goods, lamp shades, and artwork).	$3,000	$5,000	$7,500	$9,000 Per Module
B. SUITES—*Major Renovation* All casegoods, softgoods, vinyl bathroom tile(s) and stone, some construction, redesign of space, lighting, related elec. and mech. work, and artwork.	N/A	$25,000	$32,000	$40,000 Per Module
SUITES—*Minor Renovation* Softgoods replacement (carpet, drapes, spreads, upholstery), furniture replacement, and minor lighting. Does not include millwork or changes to bar/bathroom.	N/A	$10,000	$15,000	$20,000 Per Module
C. CORRIDORS—*Major Renovation* Carpet, vinyl, all graphics, ceiling work, paint trim, lighting. Add $250–$300/door for door replacement. Add $250/door for electronic locks. Add $50/door to replace closers.	$750	$900	$1,000	$1,200 Per Door
CORRIDORS—*Minor Renovation* Carpet, vinyl, graphics, and lighting.	$500	$600	$750	$900 Per Door
D. "CONCIERGE" LOUNGE Create a new two-module lounge from existing guestrooms.	N/A	$60,000	$80,000	$100,000
Renovate existing two-module lounge	N/A	$30,000	$40,000	$50,000
E. MODEL ROOM (Complete)	◄——— $20,000	to	$60,000 ———►	
FOOD AND BEVERAGE				
A. COFFEE SHOP—*Major Renovation* Total renovation of space: carpet, vinyl, furniture, counters, lighting, elec./mech., minor construction, ceiling work, uniforms, menus, graphics, concept change. Does not include kitchen equipment upgrades or changes to the cooking lines.	$2,000	$3,500	$5,000	$7,000 Per Seat

	Economy Property (2-Star)	Mid-Range Property (3-Star)	First-Class Property (4-Star)	Luxury Property (5-Star)
COFFEE SHOP—*Minor Renovation* Replacement of carpet, chairs, tables: reupholster, banquettes; minor millwork changes and decorative lighting.	$1,400	$2,200	$3,000	$3,800 Per Seat
B. BAR/LOUNGE—*Major Renovation* Same criteria as coffee shop including concept change. Does not include changing bar location.	$2,000	$3,500	$4,500	$6,000 Per Seat
BAR/LOUNGE—*Minor Renovation* Same criteria as coffee shop. Does not include changing bar location.	$1,400	$2,200	$3,000	$3,800 Per Seat
C. SPECIALTY REST—*Major Renovation* Same criteria as coffee shop including concept change.	$3,500	$5,000	$6,500	$8,000 Per Seat
SPECIALTY REST—*Minor Renovation* Same criteria as coffee shop.	$2,000	$2,800	$3,600	$4,500 Per Sq. Ft

PUBLIC AREAS

	Economy Property (2-Star)	Mid-Range Property (3-Star)	First-Class Property (4-Star)	Luxury Property (5-Star)
A. BALLROOM—*Major Renovation* Total renovation of space including carpet, vinyl, millwork, lighting, ceiling, doors/hardware, graphics, elec./mech. work, repair/relevel/recover movable walls. Does not include any FF&E, major chandelier work, sound system, or major HVAC work.	$50	$65	$80	$90 Per Sq. Ft.
BALLROOM—*Minor Renovation* Replace carpet, vinyl, paint and trim work, recover/repair movable walls.	$25	$40	$50	$60 Per Sq. Ft.
B. PREFUNCTION AREA—*Major Renovation* Same criteria as ballroom, except no ceiling work. Includes furnishings replacement.	$30	$40	$50	$60 Per Sq. Ft.
PREFUNCTION AREA—*Minor Renovation* Replace carpet, vinyl, paint and trim work, reupholster/replace furnishings.	$18	$25	$34	$45 Per Sq. Ft.
C. MEETING ROOMS—*Major Renovation* Same criteria as ballroom.	$50	$65	$80	$90 Per Sq. Ft.
MEETING ROOMS—*Minor Renovation* Same criteria as ballroom. (If a guestroom is converted to a meeting room, the cost will be $50–$100/sq. ft.)	$25	$40	$50	$60 Per Sq. Ft.
D. LOBBY Cost determined by individual components.	$15–$40	$20–$50	$25–$60	$30–$100 Per Sq. Ft.

GENERAL ITEMS

	Economy Property (2-Star)	Mid-Range Property (3-Star)	First-Class Property (4-Star)	Luxury Property (5-Star)
A. CARPET Delivered and installed, including padding.				
Guestrooms	$12	$15	$20	$20
Suites	$14	$20	$25	$30
Corridors	$25	$40	$40	$50 Per Sq. Yd.

Hand-Woven Wool Area Rugs—$30–$50 per sq. ft.

	Economy Property (2-Star)	Mid-Range Property (3-Star)	First-Class Property (4-Star)	Luxury Property (5-Star)
B. WALLCOVERING				
Delivered and installed.				
Guestrooms/Bathrooms	$2.00	$4.00	$5.50	$6.00
Suites	$4.50	$6.00	$10.00	$12.00
Restaurants	$6.00	$11.00	$15.00	$15.00+
Public Areas	$6.00	$11.00	$15.00	$15.00+
Wall Carpet	$8.00	$8.00	$12.00	$12.00
(Ballroom movable walls, service areas, elevators, etc.)				Per Linear Yd.

Adapted from a format used by Hyatt Hotels Corporation.

Appendix 1
Engineering Principles

This Appendix discusses some of the key principles of physics and chemistry and their application to commonly encountered situations in the design and operation of buildings. Many of these principles are presented in courses which hospitality students may take in food chemistry or physical sciences courses at colleges and universities. A substantial background in mathematics and the physical sciences is used in the design of building systems. An understanding of the basic principles governing engineering systems will provide a worthwhile dimension to the reader's understanding of the technical aspects of building operations.

Basic Principles

Mass, Force, Power, and Energy

Mass, force, power, and energy are key engineering concepts. Mass refers to the quantity of matter. In the English system of measurement, the unit of mass is the pound (lb). The pound is also the unit used for force in the English system, a rather unfortunate circumstance. An object with a mass of one pound will exert a force of one pound when subjected to the gravity of the earth (at certain standard conditions). In the metric system, the unit of mass is the gram (gm), a rather small unit defined as the quantity of water occupying one cubic centimeter of space. Since this unit is rather small, we often use the kilogram (kg) when speaking of mass in the metric system. One kilogram is equal to 2.205 pounds (mass).

Force is the product of mass and acceleration (or change of velocity). For example, weight, the action of the acceleration of gravity on a mass, is a force. The units of force in the English system are lb (mass)-ft/second-second or, as we have mentioned, the pound (force). In the metric system, the unit of force is the newton which is defined to be one kg-meter/sec-sec. One pound (force) is equal to 4.448 newton.

Power is defined as the rate of doing work or the work per unit time. Work can be thought of as a force acting through a distance. If a force of 1 lb acts through a distance of 1 ft, we say that 1 ft-lb of work has been performed, a basic unit of work in the English system. A power term commonly used is the horsepower, which is defined as 550 ft-lb/sec. In the metric system, the unit of work is the newton-meter (n-m) and the common unit of power the kilowatt, a term equal to 102 n-m/sec. One horsepower is equal to 0.746 kilowatt.

Energy is the capability of doing work. This capability can be present by virtue of either the condition or the position of a body. An additional form of energy is that which is due to energy chemically stored in an object such as a fuel. Energy by virtue of position means an object will do work if it is released. An example would be an object tied to a rope and suspended in the air from a pulley and connected to another weight. If the object is released, work could be performed. This type of energy is also known as potential energy. Energy by virtue of condition has as its most common form energy contained by virtue of motion or kinetic energy. In the English system, the units of energy are the British thermal unit (Btu) and the ft-lb (force). In the metric system, the units of energy are the joule and the kilowatt-hour. Since the joule is a very small unit of energy, the kilowatt-hour is more commonly used when dealing with building systems. The Btu is equal to 778 ft-lb (force) and the kilowatt-hour is equal to 3,413 Btu.

Laws of Conservation

Laws of conservation define relationships in engineering systems. Just as a proper accounting system is able to track the flow of all money entering and leaving a business, the laws of conservation account for all mass and energy in engineering systems.

The law of conservation of mass states that the mass of a body remains unchanged by any ordinary physical or chemical change to which it may be subject. Simply speaking, this law means when we start with a pound (mass) of something and process it, we are left with a pound at the end. For many normal processes, we extend this to entire systems. For example, the water which enters a building water system at the water meter should be accountable in terms of water which is used for various purposes in the building.

The law of conservation of energy states that energy can be neither created nor destroyed, but only converted from one form to another.

Application of the two laws of conservation to building systems and equipment will often provide the answers to problems relating to their operation and provide clues which will assist in optimizing their performance.

General Engineering Data and Metric Conversions

General engineering data concerning such things as the various properties of water and air and the meaning of certain terms is frequently needed by or useful to those performing the engineering function at a lodging property. Exhibit 1 contains a variety of potentially important data. For properties adhering primarily or solely to the metric system, Exhibit 2 presents a number of approximate metric conversion factors.

Water, Air, and Steam Flow ——————————————

Water, air, and steam are all fluids which are commonly used in building engineering systems. Water is a non-compressible fluid under the conditions in which we normally encounter it, while air and steam are both compressible. The term compressible means that when the material is subjected to changes in pressure, its volume changes. Each of these fluids obeys basic laws of energy and mass conservation as it is used in the building. Because of the uses made of these fluids, there are some other parameters of interest which become important to the property designer and the operating engineer. These parameters include pressure, friction, and the means of providing energy to the fluid steam (pumping, compressing, or by means of fans).

Exhibit 1   Engineering Data

Water
    volume
        1 gallon = 8.33 lb = 0.134 cu. ft.
        1 cu. ft. = 7.48 gal. = 62.3 lb
    pressure
        1 lb/sq. in. = 2.31 ft. of water
        1 foot column of water = 0.4331 lb/sq. in.
    specific heat
        liquid = 1.0 Btu/lb-F°
        ice at 32°F = .487 Btu/lb-F°
        steam at 212°F; 14.7 psia = .482 Btu/lb-F°
    latent heat of fusion = 144 Btu/lb
    latent heat of vaporization = 970 Btu/lb
        (at 212°F; 14.7 psia)

Air (at 75°F; 14.7 psia)
    volume
        1 cu. ft. = .075 lb
        1 lb = 13.5 cu. ft.
    specific heat = .24 Btu/lb-F°

Power
    ton of refrigeration = 12,000 Btu/hr
    horsepower = .746 kw
    horsepower = 550 ft.-lb/sec
    boiler horsepower = 33,475 Btu/hr
    watt = 3.413 Btu/hr
    kw = 1,000 watts
    lumen = .0015 watt

Energy
    kwh = 3,413 Btu
    therm = 100,000 Btu
    MBtu = 1,000 Btu
    MMBtu = 1,000,000 Btu

Volume
    ccf = 100 cu. ft.
    mcf = 1,000 cu. ft.

Pressure

The pressure of a fluid is measured in force per unit area, with the most commonly encountered units being pounds per square inch or psi. The force which creates pressure can be developed as the result of a large mass of fluid, the storage of energy in the fluid, or fluid flow. The pressure readings which are talked about on the evening news weather report are due to the force of the mass of the column of air which extends to the end of the earth's atmosphere. The pressure which occurs inside a pressure cooker is caused by the transfer of energy into the water inside causing it to change to steam. The ability of an airplane to achieve lift is due to a difference between the forces on the top and the bottom of the wings generated by different rates of air flow over each wing surface.

The pressure caused by the atmosphere of the earth is continuously present. Rather than have this pressure show up on our measuring devices, we have calibrated most of them not to include the atmospheric pressure. If this were not true, a

Exhibit 2   Approximate Metric Conversion Factors

Symbol	When You Know Number of	Multiply by	To Find Number of	Symbol
	Length			
in	inches	2.54	centimeters	cm
ft	feet	.305	meters	m
yd	yards	0.9	meters	m
mi	miles	1.61	kilometers	km
	Area			
sq in	square inches	6.5	square centimeters	sq cm
sq ft	square feet	0.093	square meters	sq m
sq yd	square yards	0.836	square meters	sq m
sq mi	square miles	2.6	square kilometers	sq km
	acres	0.4	hectares	ha
	Weight (mass)			
oz	ounces	28	grams	g
lb	pounds	0.45	kilograms	kg
	short tons (2,000 pounds)	0.91	metric tons	Mg
	Volume			
tsp	teaspoons	5	milliliters	mL
Tbsp	tablespoons	15	milliliters	mL
cu in	cubic inches	16	milliliters	mL
fl oz	fluid ounces	30	milliliters	mL
c	cups	0.24	liters	L
pt	pints	0.47	liters	L
qt	quarts	0.95	liters	L
gal	gallons	3.78	liters	L
cu ft	cubic feet	0.028	cubic meters	cu m
cu yd	cubic yards	0.76	cubic meters	cu m
	Pressure			
inHg	inches of mercury	3.4	kilopascals	kPa
psi	pounds per square inch	6.89	kilopascals	kPa
	Temperature (exact)			
Btu	British thermal unit	.252	kilocalories	kcal
°F	degrees Fahrenheit	5/9 (after subtracting 32)	degrees Celsius	°C
	Other			
	Btu/sq ft	2.71	kilocalories/square meter	kcal/sq m
mpg	miles per gallon	.43	kilometers/liter	km/L
	Btu/lb	.556	kilocalories/kilogram	kcal/kg
cfh	cubic feet/hour	.028	cubic meters/hour	cmh
cfm	cubic feet/minute	.028	cubic meters/minute	cmm

Adapted from U.S. Department of Commerce, *Metric Style Guide for the News Media* (Washington, D.C.: National Bureau of Standards, 1976).

bathroom scale which was 1 ft square (144 square inches) would show a weight of 2,117 lbs (14.7 psi due to the atmosphere times 144 square inches). Pressure measurements which use the atmospheric pressure as a datum (zero value) are called gauge pressures and would commonly be represented by the units psig. Measurements which include the atmospheric pressure are noted by the units psia. If the units are given as psi, the assumption is generally made that gauge pressure is being used.

Exhibit 3   Pressure and Temperature for Saturated Steam

Gauge Pressure (psi)	Temperature (°F)
0	212
5	227
10	240
20	260
50	298
75	320
100	337
125	353

In water systems, we are concerned about the pressure produced by and required for tall columns of water in the piping systems in high-rise buildings. A column of water one foot high with a density of 62.3 pounds per cubic foot exerts a pressure of .433 psi. Therefore, a building which is 20 stories tall with an average floor-to-ceiling height of 12 feet has a pressure at the base of a water pipe of 104 psi due to the weight of the water. If we are to move water in this pipe to the top of the building, we must inject the water into the base of the pipe at 104 psi or greater, a pressure which is higher than that usually available from the local water utility.

In air systems, we are rarely concerned about the pressure created by tall columns of air since even for a 100-story building the resulting air pressure would be less than 1 psi. Building air-handling systems are concerned with friction and pumping (fan) requirements to move air about the building. Compressed air may be used in the building for operation of the building control system, but this is a specialized application.

Steam systems create pressure by confining water within a boiler and steam piping and by heating the water until it evaporates. The eventual steam/water temperature depends on how high the pressure is allowed to go (assuming heat is continually added). Exhibit 3 illustrates the relationship between the pressure of steam and the temperature. This relationship is true only for what is known as saturated steam—steam that has just left the surface of a pool of boiling water.

Friction

Friction represents the resistance of an object to the flow or movement of another object along its surface. The presence of friction in fluid flow results in a drop in the pressure of the fluid. Charts are available for flow systems (both pipes and ducts) which correlate the pressure drop (in psi per unit of length) with the flow rate of the fluid and the diameter of the pipe or duct. Valves and other devices installed in these systems will also create pressure losses. There are tables which list the losses in pressure associated with these devices as well.

The amount of friction in a flow system is dependent upon the characteristics of the pipe or duct, the material flowing through the pipe or duct, and the velocity of flow. Of particular concern is the velocity of flow, since the amount of friction is proportional to the square of the velocity. The Darcy-Weisbach equation illustrates these factors for liquid flow in a circular pipe where

$$\text{Loss of pressure due to friction} \quad = \quad \frac{f \times L \times V^2}{d \times 2g}$$

where *f* is a dimensionless friction factor derived from test data for the pipe; *L* is the length of the pipe; *d* is the pipe diameter; *V* is the velocity; and *g* is the acceleration of gravity. This equation allows us to determine the amount of energy which must be input to the fluid in order to overcome friction.

Pumping

In order to overcome friction, energy is added to a fluid. This energy addition is accomplished by pumps for water systems, fans for air-handling systems, and a combination of pumps and the addition of heat for steam systems. In each instance, the pressure of the fluid is increased in order to compensate for the losses in pressure which will occur because of friction.

For water systems, the pumps will also compensate for differences in water pressure required because of the height of water in the building piping.

Exhibit 4 illustrates the relationships between various parameters which define pump or fan performance. Capacity refers to the quantity of fluid moving through the pipe, usually expressed in gallons per minute (pumps) or cubic feet per minute (fans). Pressure refers to the discharge pressure from the pump or fan. For a pump, this term is often referred to as head in units of feet of water. For a fan, the units are psi or inches of water. Efficiency refers to the percentage of the input energy to the pump or fan which is transferred to the fluid and power is the rate of input of energy to the pump or fan. System pressure losses represents the pressure drop which is expected for the system on which the pump or fan is operating at the flow rate given on the horizontal axis.

Exhibit 4 illustrates several important factors in pump/fan selection and operation. Since a pump/fan is normally chosen for some peak level of flow (the load), a knowledge of the pressure needed to supply this load is important. For water systems, the head is a combination of the amount of lift we must give the fluid above the pump position, the friction in the pipe from the pump to the load, and the desired pressure at the load itself. Air systems will generally have systems curves which incorporate the friction in the duct work and the desired delivery pressure at the load. An increase in the overall pressure of the system which must be matched by the pump/fan will reduce the quantity of fluid delivered by the pump. In addition, there is a certain range at which the pump/fan operates with a high efficiency. When selecting equipment for a given application, consideration of its operating efficiency in the application is important. Applications with highly varying flow requirements may warrant the use of variable speed equipment capable of operating close to its maximum efficiency over a range of applications or the installation or multiple pieces of equipment with a staging capability.

Electricity

Electricity is a form of energy consisting of a quantity of electrons (measured in amperes or amps) flowing between two points of different electrical potential

Exhibit 4   Relationships Between Capacity and Maximum Values of Head, Efficiency, Power, and Pressure Losses for Flow Systems

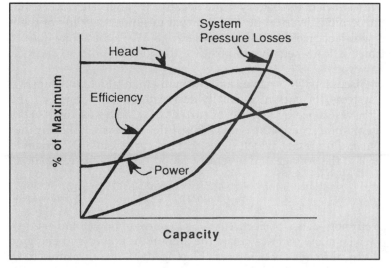

(measured in volts). One ampere represents 6.251×10^{18} electrons per second passing through a cross section of the conductor. The voltage between two points represents a net difference between the number of negative charges (electrons) at the two points. A point or object with more negative charges than another point or object is said to have a negative voltage. Note that voltage is a relative measurement. A voltage measurement is either made relative to ground—usually the earth at a given location—or relative to some other point, such as the voltage between two terminals of a battery.

In electrical systems, the flow of electricity does not proceed unhindered. The characteristic which measures the difficulty that electricity has in flowing through a material is called resistance. The lower the resistance of a material, the better a conductor of electricity the material is. Good conductors such as copper and aluminum are used to make building wiring. Poor conductors, such as glass, porcelain, rubber, and some plastics, are used to make insulating materials which protect us from electricity. The equipment being powered (called the load) also has resistance.

As an aid to understanding electrical systems, analogies are sometimes made between electrical and water systems. The flow of water is similar to the flow of electricity; the pressure in a water system is similar to the voltage in an electrical system; and the resistance of a wire to the flow of electricity is similar to the friction which occurs when water flows through a pipe. The analogies can further extend to pieces of equipment found in the systems as well—for example, the similarity between a pump and a battery and between a valve and a switch.

Current, Resistance, and Power—DC Systems

The discussion of the mathematical relationships which govern electricity will begin with the form of electricity known as direct current or DC. This is the type of electricity produced by a battery. It is characterized by current flow in a single direction, with the normal convention of electrical terminology showing flow from the positive (+) cell of the battery to the negative (−) cell. This rather strange convention concerning electrical flow is due to a misunderstanding of the nature of electricity which occurred hundreds of years ago. While the actual flow of electricity (electrons) is from negative to positive, the convention is to show flow from positive to negative.

When discussing DC systems and the mathematical relationships which govern these systems, the current is usually designated in equations by I, the voltage by V, and the resistance by R. Units of current flow are amps, units of voltage are volts, and units of resistance are ohms. These three terms are linked by the relationship known as Ohm's law, which states that the current in a DC circuit is directly proportional to the voltage and inversely proportional to the resistance. In equation form, Ohm's law is

$$I = V/R$$

Since our normal use of electricity is as a source of power and energy, the relationships which allow us to calculate the amount of power and energy available from an electrical source are of interest. Electrical power is measured in watts (W), where watts are the product of current (I) and voltage (V). When we couple this with the relationship for Ohm's law, we can define electrical power by the following formulas:

$$W = VI = I^2R = V^2/R$$

These formulas reveal some interesting characteristics of electrical power. If we increase the voltage (V) supplied to a constant load, denoted in the equation by the R value, the power required will increase by the square of the voltage. Therefore, if the voltage is increased by a factor of two, the power will be increased by a factor of four. A similar increase occurs if the current is doubled.

The item which we control in electrical systems is the voltage. The resistance is a physical characteristic of the load and the current results from Ohm's law given the voltage and resistance. If we think of the R value in the power equation as representing the resistance of the wires carrying the electricity, we can see why higher voltages are used to deliver higher power requirements. If we wish to provide 100 watts of power using a 20 volt source, we will need 5 amps of current. If this current flows through a wire with a resistance of 2 ohms, the resulting power loss in the line will be 50 watts. In order to deliver 100 watts, we will have to provide 150 watts due to the losses in the line. On the other hand, if we provide electricity at 40 volts, the required current will be 2.5 amps and the power loss in the line only 12.5 watts, only one-fourth of that calculated previously. Providing electrical energy at higher voltages greatly reduces line losses. It also reduces the need for large wires to carry high levels of current flow.

Energy measurements in electrical systems are made by simply multiplying the power by the length of time that level of power is used. If 1,000 watts of power are used for one hour, the amount of energy consumed is 1,000 watt hours or one kilowatt-hour.

Exhibit 5   Wave Representation of AC Current or Voltage

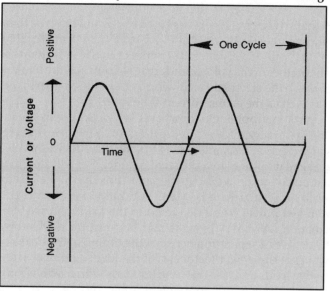

Current, Impedance, and Power—AC Systems

While the relationships and physics associated with DC power systems are relatively straightforward, the realm of AC systems is more complex and less easily grasped. Since the vast majority of our uses of electricity are in the form of AC power, an understanding of this common form of electricity is particularly helpful. Fortunately, several of the characteristics of DC electricity are also true of AC.

While the flow of electricity in a DC system is always in one direction, the direction of flow in an AC system oscillates following a generally symmetrical pattern known as a sinusoidal (or sine) wave. Exhibit 5 illustrates several waves of AC current. When the curve begins to repeat itself, we say one cycle of AC current has passed. The distance along the horizontal axis which is associated with the curve beginning to repeat itself is called a cycle. The standard North American power system operates at 60 cycles per second, also known as 60 hertz. Therefore, the time required for one cycle is 1/60th of a second. The number of cycles per second is also known as the frequency.

The voltage and the current in AC systems are sine waves with the same frequency. Because of the wave nature of AC voltage and current, it is not possible to actually assign a constant value to either of these parameters. Also, because their average value is zero, the use of an average value is useless. The value we use to measure the current and voltage is actually the peak value of each divided by 1.414 (the square root of 2). All electrical instruments commonly used to measure AC current and voltage are set up to divide the peak value of the AC sine wave by 1.414 and show this on the display of the instrument.

In AC systems, the unit of current is still the amp and the unit of voltage the volt with the symbols I and V used to denote each. The unit of resistance is somewhat more complex than in DC circuits. It is denoted by a Z and referred to as impedance, a term which incorporates both resistance as it is thought of in DC circuits and reactance, an additional type of resistance. Reactance occurs in AC circuits because of the changing (cyclic) nature of the voltage and current flows and the tendency of the material through which the electricity is flowing to resist the change in the voltage and current flows as well as the actual current flow itself.

If an AC circuit is supplying only what is known as a resistive load, the same power relationships are used for AC as are used for DC. However, if the load being supplied has any reactive resistance, as is true of such devices as electric motors, then we must calculate power in a different manner. We will find that the voltage and the current do not occur at exactly the same time due to the reactive resistance that is present. As a result, there is a time separation between their peak values which results in less power being delivered to the load than we would calculate from the calculation ($W = V \times I$) we would perform for a DC power source. A measure of the degree of separation between the timing of the peaks of the voltage and current waves is the power factor (pf) of the load, a number with a value of 1 for purely resistive loads and less than one for loads with reactive components. For such circumstances, the equation for power is given by

$$W = V \times I \times pf$$

This equation is actually valid for both single-phase AC and DC calculations, since the power factor for DC is 1. Energy calculations are still performed by multiplying the power by the time (in hours) over which the power is used.

The world of AC power is further complicated by the presence of three-phase power systems. In three-phase systems, there are three wires, each of which functions like a single AC line. Exhibit 6 illustrates wave forms for a three-phase power supply. Within any single cycle of the power system, a load connected to a three-phase power supply will receive three impulses of current and voltage. Such a load, such as a three-phase motor, will have a wire for each of the three phases connected to separate connections on the motor and is only capable of operating properly when provided with three-phase electricity. For applications which need a single phase, such as a wall outlet, one of the three phases is used.

With three-phase power, it should be obvious that standard power relationships will not work properly since we are dealing with three lines providing power. Power calculations in three-phase circuits are governed by the relationship

$$W = V \times I \times pf \times \sqrt{3}$$

The relationships discussed and developed between current, voltage, power, and energy for AC and DC circuits are useful for property engineers when dealing with electrical systems at lodging facilities. Exhibit 7 presents sample calculations which use the relationships developed in this Appendix in the context of problems which might face a property engineer. The problems are simplified for the purpose of these examples.

Exhibit 6   Wave Representations of Three-Phase AC Current or Voltage

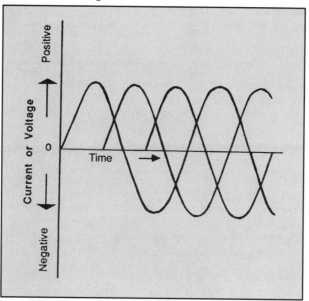

Thermodynamics

Temperature

Temperature must be defined in an indirect manner using the concept of equality of temperature. When two bodies, one hot and the other cold, are placed in contact with each other, the hot body will over time become cooler and the cold body will become warmer. Eventually, all changes in the properties of the bodies will cease and the bodies will be at thermal equilibrium (that is, they will have the same temperature). Therefore, two bodies or systems have equal temperature when no changes occur in their properties when they are brought in contact with each other.

A practical temperature scale has been developed by assigning specific, yet arbitrary, values of temperature to two easily reproducible temperatures: the freezing and boiling points of water at standard atmospheric pressure. In the English system of units, the Fahrenheit scale assigns a temperature of 32°F to the freezing point and 212°F to the boiling point.

So far, this definition of temperature only applies between the freezing and boiling point of water. But the temperature scale can be extrapolated beyond these boundaries in both directions. Therefore, the temperature in a blast freezer and a boiler can be measured as −10°F and 250°F, respectively.

Heat

Heat is a form of energy defined by temperature. When two bodies of different temperatures are brought in contact with each other, they eventually reach thermal

Exhibit 7   Sample Electrical Calculations

Problem 1: Evaluate the cost of lighting a guestwing corridor.

A corridor in the guestwing of a property is lighted by 50 lighting fixtures, each of which contains a 100-watt lamp. The lamps operate 24 hours a day, 365 days a year. The local cost of electrical energy is $.08 per kwh. What is the annual operating cost of the lamps?

The starting point for this problem is to determine the total lighting power (P) and from this to determine the energy (E) consumed by multiplying the power by the number of hours the lamps operate. The cost is then calculated by multiplying the amount of energy by the cost per unit of energy.

P = 100 watt/lamp × 50 lamps = 5,000 watts or 5 kw
E = P × time = 5 kw × 24 hrs/day × 365 days/year = 43,800 kwh/year
Cost = E × rate per kwh = 43,800 kwh/year × $.08/kwh = $3,504/year

Problem 2: Determine the current draw of a resistive load.

Determine the current draw (how many amps) of the lighting system in Problem 1. (Such a calculation may be required if additional equipment is to be connected to the lighting circuit to determine whether adequate capacity is available in the system.)

Each lamp is rated at 100 watts. Using the definition of power (P = V × I), we can calculate the current draw of each lamp. P is 100 and V is the voltage of the lamps, 120 volts being common. Solving for the current, we have

I = P/V = 100 watts per lamp/120 volts = .833 amps per lamp

The total current flow is 41.7 amps (.833 × 50).

Problem 3: Determine the efficiency of an electric motor.

An electric motor producing 5 HP (horsepower) is operated at 208 volts, single phase. The nameplate of the motor indicates the motor has a power factor of 85% and draws a full load current of 27 amps at rated horse-power. What is the motor efficiency? (A calculation of this type is necessary if a comparison is to be made between the existing motor and a new motor.)

Efficiency = Output/Input
Output = 5 HP × .746 kw/HP = 3.73 kw
Input = V × I × pf = 208 volts × 27 amps × .85 = 4.774 kw
Efficiency = 3.73 kw/4.774 kw = .78 or 78%

Problem 4: Determine the heating capacity of an electric heating element operated at other than its rated voltage.

An electric water heater installed as a booster heater for a dishwasher is rated at 4.5 kw when installed on a single phase 240 volt line. The electric service in the kitchen is 208 volts. What is the heating capability of the heater?

In this problem, the resistance of the heater is a constant value. Using a combination of a power relationship and Ohm's law, we can calculate the resistance of the heater from the following equation

P = V^2/R = 240 volts × 240 volts/R = 4.5 kw

Solving for R:

R = 240 volts × 240 volts/4.5 kw = 12.80 ohm

When operated at 208 volts, the resulting power delivered by the heating element (heating capability) is

P = V^2/R = 208 volts × 208 volts/12.80 ohm = 3.38 kw

equilibrium and a common temperature. The energy that was transferred between the two bodies because of their temperature difference is defined as heat. The direction of the heat flow will always be from the body with the higher temperature to the body with the lower temperature, with the convention that the flow of heat out of a body is considered negative and the flow of heat into a body is considered positive.

The amount of heat can be measured by raising the temperature of the mass of a specific material by a specific temperature difference. The Btu (British thermal unit) is defined as the amount of heat required to raise one pound of water by one Fahrenheit degree. Materials other than water require more or less heat to increase their temperatures by one Fahrenheit degree. This amount of heat is defined as the specific heat, C_P, for that material. Air, for example, has a specific heat of .24 at typical atmospheric conditions.

States of Matter

At the environmental temperatures normally associated with buildings, all matter exists in three states: solid, liquid, or gaseous. These states can be distinguished by observation of certain characteristics of the material. A solid is rigid and maintains its shape without the help of a container. Its volume changes only slightly as the environmental conditions change. A liquid takes the shape of the lower portion of its container, but maintains a horizontal upper surface. Its volume also changes only slightly as the environmental conditions change. A gas fills the entire container without maintaining shape or volume.

The same substance can exist in any of the three different states, depending on its temperature and pressure. At standard atmospheric pressure, water exists as ice (a solid) when its temperature is below 32°F, as steam (a gas) when its temperature is above 212°F, and as a liquid when the temperature is between these two values. As the pressure changes, the temperatures that identify the boundaries between the states change. At a pressure of 15 psig, water will remain in the liquid state up to a temperature of 249.7°F. At a pressure of 50 psig, the boiling point of water increases to 297.7°F.

These specific conditions of water can be observed readily in a lodging facility. The temperature of the ice in the bin of an ice maker must be lower than 32°F, while the temperature of a drink made with shaved ice is exactly 32°F. Water boiling in a stock pot is approximately 212°F. The temperature of the cooking environment or the steam in a high-pressure steam cooker is approximately 250°F because the pressure in such a unit is 15 psig. The steam being produced from a boiler set at 50 psig must be at a temperature greater than approximately 298°F.

Many of the important thermal processes that occur in a lodging property operate on the basis of a change of state for the working substance. During these changes of state, energy is either added to or extracted from the substance. Ice is produced in an ice maker by extracting heat energy from water, thus changing its temperature and state from liquid to solid. Steam is produced in a boiler by adding heat to water, thus increasing its temperature and changing its state from liquid to gaseous. A phase change in the reverse direction is used to cook food in a steamer. Water changing from the gaseous state to the liquid state as the steam is condensed in the steamer gives off heat that is used to cook the vegetables. The Freon in a guestroom air conditioner cools the room by undergoing a change from the liquid state into the gaseous state, taking the necessary heat from the room.

The two changes of state that are common are the change between the solid and liquid states and the change between the liquid and gaseous states. The first change is usually called melting or freezing, depending on the direction of the change. The latter is commonly called boiling or evaporation when the change is from the liquid to the gaseous state and condensation when the change occurs in the opposite direction. Although uncommon in a property, the third possible change of state—from a solid to a gas—is called sublimation. When dry ice (solid CO_2) is used to create "smoke" for a display, the carbon dioxide is changing directly from the solid state to the gaseous state.

An exchange of energy is always associated with any change of state. This addition or subtraction of energy does not affect the temperature of the substance, but rather only affects the form of the substance. At standard atmospheric pressure, both ice and liquid water exist at 32°F and both liquid water and steam exist at 212°F. When water at either of these two conditions changes from one state to the other, it does not change its temperature even though energy has been added or subtracted from it. The energy connected with these changes is designated latent energy, because no temperature change occurs in the process. The energy associated with the change from a solid to a liquid is called the latent heat of fusion, while the energy involved in the change of state from liquid to gaseous is called the latent heat of vaporization. For water at standard atmospheric pressure, the values are 144 Btu/lb and 970 Btu/lb, respectively.

Heat Transfer

Heat energy is transferred between two bodies that have different temperatures by three modes: conduction, convection, and radiation. In the conduction mode, energy is transferred by the direct interaction of molecules. The vibrational energy of one molecule is passed on to its neighbors by direct contact or collision, but the molecules themselves do not move a significant distance through the substance. Conduction occurs in all three states of matter, but is usually associated with solids. The heat that is transferred from the burner of a range into the stock in a stock pot is conducted through the metal container.

Heat transfer in the convection mode is accomplished through the large-scale motion of molecules in currents. Using the example of the heating of a stock in a stock pot, the molecules of the stock that touch the inside surface of the container are heated by conduction. When they are warmed, the density of the liquid decreases and the warmed molecules begin to rise through the stock. As these molecules rise, they are cooled by the surrounding cooler stock. The cooled molecules then return to the bottom of the container. This cyclical heating and cooling of the molecules sets up convection currents in the liquid. The heating of the entire liquid is accomplished by the continuous mixing caused by these currents. Convection is only associated with liquids or gases and does not occur in solids.

Radiation heat transfer occurs when energy from a hot body is converted into electromagnetic energy and is transmitted to another body with a lower temperature. This transmission of energy occurs even through a vacuum without any intermediate medium and is essentially the same as the transmission of radio or television signals. This mode of transfer usually occurs between two solids, with the color of the surfaces of the solids greatly affecting the amount of radiation transfer. Black surfaces emit and absorb energy very readily, while white surfaces inhibit the emission and absorption of radiation energy. In a radiation broiler, the heating element is heated to an extremely high temperature, and the cooking of a steak is accomplished by the radiation of heat from the element to the surface of the steak.

In most actual situations, the heat transfer between two bodies or systems is accomplished by a combination of the three modes. In the stock pot example, the heat is convected and radiated from the gas flame in the burner to the bottom surface of the container, conducted through the metal to the stock that is touching the inside surface of the container, and convected to the remaining stock through currents. For the steak, the heat is initially transferred to the surface of the meat primarily by radiation, although some convection heating also occurs. The heat is then conducted into the center of the steak. In the heating season, heat is lost through the walls of a guestroom because of the difference between the inside air temperature and the outside air temperature. The heat is convected to the inside surface of the wall, conducted through the inside surface material, convected and radiated through any air spaces in the wall, conducted through the outside surface material, and finally convected to the outside air.

In these practical situations where more than one mode of heat transfer occur, the effects of the individual modes are combined into an overall heat transfer coefficient. The total heat transfer can be determined based on the geometric configuration, material properties, and terminal temperatures. The theory for combining modes of heat transfer is based on the concept of thermal circuits or thermal resistance, a direct analogy with electrical circuits and electrical resistance.

Combining the separate effects, however, requires an understanding of the equations and terminology for each of the three modes. For the conduction of heat through a solid, three thermal properties of the material are defined: conductivity (k), conductance (C), and thermal resistance (R). The definition of conductivity is best shown by performing an experiment with a specific material in the following way.

A one-inch thick slab of the material with a surface area of one square foot is subjected to a one Fahrenheit degree temperature difference between the two flat surfaces of the slab. Heat will flow through the one-inch dimension of the material because of the temperature difference. The conductivity (k) of the material is defined as the rate of heat in Btu/hr that flows in this specific configuration, and is expressed in units of Btu/hr-ft^2-F°-in. Therefore, this thermal property only applies to a one-inch thick sample of the material.

Since the materials in most practical situations have a thickness different than one inch, the property of conductivity is generalized to the property of conductance (C) for a specific thickness of the material other than one inch. Conductance is defined by the following equation, where x is the specific thickness in inches, and is expressed in units of Btu/hr-ft^2-F°:

$$C = k/x$$

When x is one inch, then C = k as it should by definition. When x is greater than one inch, the conductance is less than the conductivity because a thicker sample of the material conducts less heat. Conversely, the conductance is greater than the conductivity when the thickness is less than one inch because a thinner sample of

Exhibit 8   Thermal Properties for Some Typical Building Materials

Building Material	k (Btu/hr-ft²-F°-in)	C (Btu/hr-ft²-F°)	R (hr-ft²-F°/Btu)
Gypsum plasterboard (.5 in)	1.11	2.22	0.45
Fiberglass insulation (4 in)	0.25	0.0625	16.0
Brick, common (4 in)	5.0	1.25	0.80
Concrete block, 3 oval cores (8 in)	----	.90	1.11
Plywood (.5 in)	0.806	1.61	0.62
Plate glass (.25 in)	2.77	11.1	0.09

Reprinted by permission from *1985 ASHRAE Handbook—Fundamentals.*

Exhibit 9   Typical Convection Heat Transfer Coefficients

Situation	h_c (Btu/hr-ft²-F°)
Still air; vertical surface	1.46
7.5 mph wind; vertical surface	4.00
15 mph wind; vertical surface	6.00
Still water; vertical surface	1.00

Reprinted by permission from *1985 ASHRAE Handbook—Fundamentals.*

the material conducts more heat. Finally, a thermal resistance (R) for the material is defined as the reciprocal of the conductance, in units of hr-ft²-F°/Btu:

$$R = 1/C$$

While the conductance is a measure of the amount of heat that flows through a layer of material, the resistance is a measure of the material's ability to resist the flow of heat. Hence, the two properties are reciprocal in nature. Values of these thermal properties for some typical building materials are shown in Exhibit 8.

For the convection heat transfer in a liquid or gas, the entire effect is expressed in a convection coefficient, h_c, in units of Btu/hr-ft²-F°. The coefficient includes the effects of the type of convection (natural or forced), the geometry of the situation, and the type of fluid (for example, water or air). Values for some common situations are given in Exhibit 9. A larger value for h_c indicates a higher rate of heat flow. The interpretation of the coefficient is analogous to that for the conductance of a solid. The resistance to convective heat flow is the reciprocal of the convection coefficient.

Similarly, the overall effect of radiation heat transfer is expressed by a radiation coefficient, h_r, with the same units. This coefficient also includes all of the effects due to the properties of material (for example, surface color) and geometry of the situation. Again, the analogy with the conductance of a solid holds, and the resistance to radiation heat flow is the reciprocal of the radiation coefficient.

Exhibit 10   Thermal Effects of Combining Building Materials

	k	h or c	R
Outside air film	---	4.00	.25
Layer 1	5.0	1.25	.80
Layer 2	---	.90	1.11
Inside air film	---	1.46	.68
Total resistance			2.84

U factor $= 1/R_T = 1/2.84 = .352$

With the heat transfer characteristics of individual layers of materials defined, they may be combined into composite assemblies that represent actual configurations that are common in hospitality properties. Refer to Exhibit 10 for this discussion. The exterior wall of a guestroom could be built of several layers of building materials (for example, wall board, concrete block, face brick), but in this example only two layers are used. The conductivities or conductances of the solid layers are obtained from tables of design values for such materials. Two additional layers of air (inside air film and outside air film) contribute to the thermal properties of the wall. The heat transfer coefficients for these layers are obtained from tables similar to Exhibit 9. In addition, the value of any radiation heat transfer coefficient should be obtained if it is appropriate. The resistances for each of these layers can then be calculated by taking the appropriate reciprocals.

The overall heat transfer capability of the entire wall may now be determined by combining the effects of the individual layers using the concept of thermal resistance. When the layers of the wall are in series (that is, all of the heat flows through each layer), the total resistance of the composite wall is the sum of the individual resistances for each layer. A common sense analysis of the situation

Exhibit 11   Spectrum of Electromagnetic Radiation

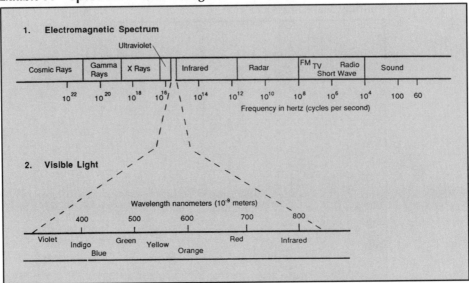

supports this method for combining separate layers. As more layers are added to a wall, the amount of heat that flows through it is reduced, thus increasing the wall's resistance to heat flow. Note that it is not the conductances (the ability to transfer heat) but rather the resistances (the ability to resist heat transfer) of the individual layers that are added together to determine the overall thermal effect of the composite wall. If the conductances were added as the number of layers were increased, then the heat flow through the wall would increase, and this effect is contrary to actual experience.

The overall thermal effect of the wall could remain expressed in terms of its resistance, but most applications require the effect expressed in terms of its ability to transfer heat. Therefore, an overall coefficient, the *U factor*, expressed in units of Btu/hr-ft^2-F°, is calculated by taking the reciprocal of the total resistance:

$$U = 1/R_T$$

This U factor represents the aggregate effect of all the layers, including the air films, on the ability of the wall or any other configuration (for example, the stock pot when heating water) to transfer heat from the higher temperature region on one side of the barrier to the lower temperature region on the other side.

Light

Light is defined most simply as radiated energy that can be seen by the human eye. Light exhibits wave properties similar to other phenomena such as radio, microwave, and X rays, and is part of the electromagnetic spectrum as shown in Exhibit 11.

As such, light has both wave length and frequency as do all these types of radiation. These two properties are inversely related through the constant for the speed of light as follows. With frequency in cycles per second (Hz or cps), wave length in meters (m), and the speed of light as 3×10^8 m/sec, the relationship is expressed as

$$l = c/f$$

where l represents the wave length, f the frequency, and c the speed of light. Note that metric units have been used here because most of the literature on lighting uses them.

Color

Different wave lengths or frequencies of light are interpreted by the human eye as different colors of light. The wave lengths of visible light extend from 380 nanometers (a nanometer is 10^{-9} meters) to 760 nanometers, with the former frequency corresponding to violet light and the latter corresponding to red light. Light of wave lengths in between these two values is associated with the common colors as shown in the second section of Exhibit 11. The acronym ROY G BIV identifies these colors as red, orange, yellow, green, blue, indigo, and violet. White light contains energy in equal amounts at all the wave lengths in this range.

Light Sources. Light that is produced by practical sources has different color characteristics because the light is emitted at various frequencies rather than just one. The frequencies that dominate in the spectrum cause the human eye to interpret the light as the colors associated with the dominant frequencies. Exhibit 12 shows the spectral distributions of the following common light sources: noon sunlight, a typical light bulb with a tungsten filament, and a typical fluorescent lamp that has not been corrected for color rendition.

The human eye interprets daylight as having a near-white quality, but with a slight tone of yellow, while it sees the color of the light from the artificial sources as substantially different from that of daylight. The light from the incandescent (tungsten filament) bulb is seen as yellow-orange and the light from the fluorescent lamp appears stronger in the blue range and very weak in the orange-red range. Therefore, the lamps that are used to light the interiors of buildings may not give the building's interiors the same color characteristics exhibited during the daylight hours.

Effect of Surfaces. When the light from a source strikes a surface, the light is absorbed, reflected, or transmitted in various proportions, depending on the material characteristics of the surface. Some of the light always is absorbed and converted into energy that increases the temperature of the surface. The remaining light is predominantly either reflected or transmitted, thus categorizing the material as either opaque or transparent, respectively.

The color of the light that is either transmitted or reflected by the surface depends on the interaction of the color of the incident light and the absorption characteristics of the surface material. Since the color of the transmitted or reflected light is interpreted by the eye as the color of the object, this interaction is extremely important in determining the color of objects as perceived by people in actual settings.

Exhibit 12 Spectral Characteristics of Light Sources

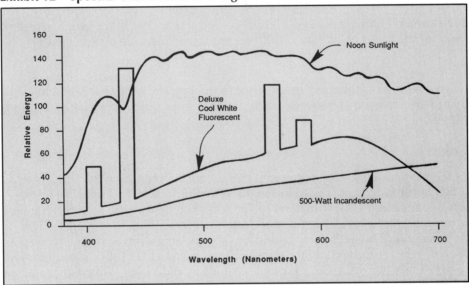

Different frequencies of light are absorbed by materials in different amounts by a process of selective absorption in which most of the light is absorbed and the remaining light is reflected or transmitted in a very narrow band of frequency. This reflected or transmitted light exhibits a distinct color or hue. For example, a red napkin absorbs almost all of the light from the visible spectrum except for those frequencies associated with the color red; yellow flowers in the atrium absorb all of the frequencies except those for yellow.

The color spectrum of the incident light is modified by the selective absorption characteristics of the surface material to determine the color of the object. When white light is incident on the surface, all colors in the spectrum are present in the incident light and the perceived color of the object is dependent on which light frequencies are absorbed by the material. For example, white light on a "red" surface appears red. When light of a specific color is incident on a surface, only light of the frequencies associated with that color is present and the perceived color of the object is dependent on which light frequencies remain after the existing light frequencies are absorbed selectively by the surface. There are two possible situations. One, when (for example) violet light strikes an object in which the material absorbs all the frequencies except those associated with the color violet, the object looks violet to the observer. Two, when the same violet light strikes an object in which the material absorbs all the frequencies except those associated with the color red, the object appears black because little or no light is reflected from the object.

Knowledge of this interaction between the color of the light source and the color absorption characteristics of an object influences many of the lighting decisions that affect the appearance of lodging facilities to their guests and employees. Foods such as beef or tomatoes that are rich in red and orange colors must be lighted by artificial sources that contain a sufficient amount of light in the red and orange frequencies or they appear dull, dark, and unappetizing to the dining room guest. Human skin must also be lighted by a source with desirable color character-istics so that it shows its natural beauty to guests as they view themselves in any of a property's mirrors.

Intensity

Power of Light Source. A standardized light source that emits radiation equally in all directions from one point is used to define the power of practical light sources. The output of the standardized light source is quantified by measuring the amount of light which strikes a spherical surface that is centered on the light source and has a radius of one foot. The unit of measurement for the total quantity of visible radi-ation emitted by the source is the lumen. The amount of light in a lumen is based on the light output of a wax candle, which emits approximately 12.57 lumens.

The efficacy, or the efficiency of the production of light, of a light source is ex-pressed by an input-output ratio. For an electrically powered light source, the effi-cacy is measured in lumens per watt, where lumens measure the output of the light and watts measure the electrical input. While the theoretical maximum efficiency of light production is approximately 220 lumens per watt, the efficacies of actual light sources are substantially less than this value (usually 15 to 150 lumens/watt) because a large proportion (typically 75–95%) of the input energy is converted into heat which is dissipated by the light bulb.

Inverse Square Law. The light output of a light source is measured using a spheri-cal surface centered on the light source with a radius of one foot. The extension of the measurement of light intensity to distances other than one foot requires the de-velopment of the relationship between the amount of light (lumens) and the inten-sity or density of light (lumens/ft^2). A *footcandle (fc)* is defined as the intensity of light of one lumen per square foot.

For a standardized light source emitting 12.57 lumens, the intensity of light measured at the surface of the unit sphere is one footcandle because the output of 12.57 lumens shines equally on 12.57ft^2 of surface area. The intensity of light on a spherical surface centered on the same light source with a radius of two feet, how-ever, is only .25 fc because the surface area of the sphere is 50.28 ft^2, while the out-put of the light source is 12.57 lumens.

This reduction in the intensity of light as the distance from the light source in-creases is governed by the inverse square law. The relationship can be expressed mathematically by

$$fc = lm/(12.57 \times d^2)$$

where the distance *(d)* from the light source is measured in feet. For a light source of a given power, the intensity of the light decreases in proportion to the square of the distance from the source, hence the name "inverse square law."

Effect of Surfaces. When the light from a source shines on a surface, some of the light is absorbed and the remainder is transmitted or reflected, depending on whether the surface is primarily transparent or opaque. In either case, the intensity of the light that leaves the surface is dependent on two factors: (1) the intensity of the light striking the surface and (2) the material properties and geometry of the surface. The relationship among these variables can be expressed as

$$fc = fc_I \times factor$$

where fc_I is the intensity of the light incident on the surface, *factor* represents the aggregate effect of the surface on the intensity of the light, and fc is the intensity of the light leaving the surface.

The actual factors are expressed as values in percentages ranging from 0% for a surface that absorbs all the incident light to 100% for a surface that returns all the incident light, and are described in the literature as either the reflectance or transmittance of the surface, depending on whether the surface primarily reflects or transmits the incident light.

Appendix 2
Psychrometrics and
Human Comfort

Psychrometry

Psychrometry is the study of the thermodynamic properties of a combination of dry air and water vapor. A manager should be aware of this subject because the comfort of guests and the comfort and productivity of the employees is highly dependent on the conditions of the air inside a hospitality building. In order to maximize guest satisfaction and employee productivity with minimal cost, the conditions of the environment within the facility must be controlled properly and carefully. Knowledge of the appropriate conditions and of the best methods for control is based on the scientific properties of moist air, the mixture of dry air, and water vapor.

The properties of moist air that are important to the understanding of psychrometrics are dry-bulb temperature (°F db), wet-bulb temperature (°F wb), moisture content (pounds of water vapor per pound of dry air), relative humidity (percent rh), dew point (dp), specific enthalpy (h in Btu/lb of dry air) specific volume (ft3/lb of dry air). The definitions for each property are developed in the following sections.

Temperature

Dry-bulb and wet-bulb temperatures are best defined by a simple experiment in which two identical common thermometers are used to measure the temperature of a sample of moist air. One of the thermometers measures the dry-bulb temperature and the other the wet-bulb temperature. A wick or piece of fabric that is soaked with water is attached around the mercury reservoir of the wet-bulb thermometer, while nothing is attached to the reservoir of the dry-bulb thermometer. When the mercury reservoir of the dry-bulb thermometer is exposed to the air sample, the reading obtained from the scale is called the dry-bulb temperature—the temperature of the air as reported in weather reports. The wet-bulb temperature is read from the scale on the wet-bulb thermometer in exactly the same manner.

The two temperature readings are usually different because of the effect of the soaked wick on the reservoir of the wet-bulb thermometer. If the air sample is able to absorb some of the water in the wick, then the water in the wick evaporates into the air sample. When this evaporation occurs, the necessary heat of vaporization is extracted from the wick and the mercury reservoir, thus cooling the reservoir. Therefore, the reading from the wet-bulb thermometer is lower than the reading from the dry-bulb thermometer. This difference between the dry-bulb and wet-bulb temperatures is inversely related to the amount of water vapor that is in the air sample. If the air sample contains a substantial amount of water vapor, then the

Exhibit 1   The Saturation Line

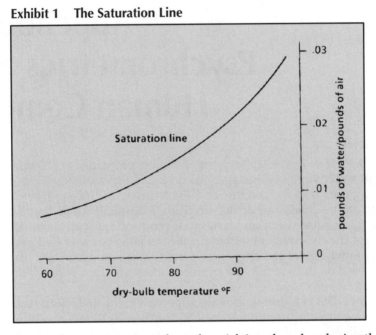

amount of water that can evaporate from the wick is reduced, reducing the cooling effect and the temperature difference between the two temperature readings. Conversely, if the air sample contains little or no water, then the amount of water that evaporates is increased, increasing the cooling effect and the temperature difference.

Thus, the two temperature readings together indicate both the actual temperature of the air and the amount of water vapor in a sample of moist air. These two temperatures are the bases for defining the other important properties of moist air.

Moisture Content

The following experiment assists in the development of the definition of moisture (or water) content. A one-pound sample of dry air at standard atmospheric pressure and a specific temperature is exposed to a source of water at the same temperature. The water is allowed to evaporate into the sample of air and heat is added to maintain the specified temperature. After some time, the air sample cannot absorb any more water from the water source. The moist air in the sample at this condition is defined as *saturated* because no more water can be evaporated into it. The amount of water that was evaporated in the process is recorded. The same experiment is run several times at various specific temperatures. The data from such an experiment is plotted in Exhibit 1. Note that the amount of water that can be evaporated into a sample of dry air increases as the temperature of the dry air increases. Since this curve represents the maximum amount of water that can be evaporated into dry air, it is called the saturation line. On this line, the air is 100 percent saturated or is in a state of 100 percent relative humidity.

Exhibit 2   Relative Humidity

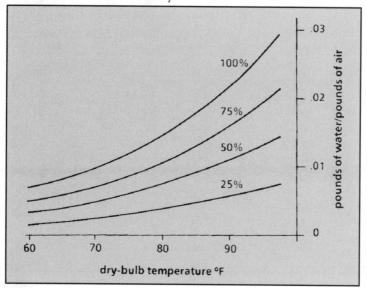

At a given dry-bulb temperature, the relative humidity of the moist air is determined by the amount of water vapor that is actually evaporated into the air compared to the maximum that could be evaporated. If the actual amount is one half the maximum, then the relative humidity of the moist air is 50 percent. For each dry-bulb temperature, the necessary amount of water for 50 percent relative humidity can be determined by comparison with the saturation amount of water at that given temperature. These amounts of water can be plotted on a graph as shown in Exhibit 2. This line is labeled as the 50 percent relative humidity line. Likewise, the lines for all other possible relative humidity levels can be plotted and labeled.

The moisture content of a sample of moist air is defined as the amount of water vapor actually held in the sample measured in pounds of water per pound of dry air. Since this parameter represents only the numerator of the ratio that determines the relative humidity of the moist air, the distinction between the moisture content and the relative humidity is very important. The moisture content measures the actual amount of water vapor in the air in an absolute sense, while the relative humidity measures this amount in a relative sense in comparison to the maximum that could be present. Notice in Exhibit 2 that the moisture content of air at a condition of 95°F db and 50 percent relative humidity actually is greater than the moisture content of air at a condition of complete saturation at 70°F db, even though the relative humidity of the former is lower.

Psychrometric Chart

The graphs plotted in the previous section are the basis for the development of the psychrometric chart, a graphical presentation of the important parameters of moist

Exhibit 3   Wet-Bulb Scale

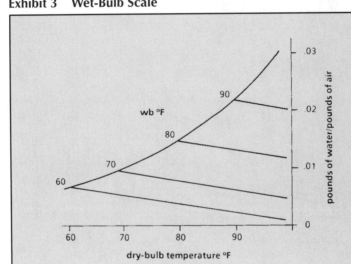

air. The three parameters—dry-bulb temperature, moisture content, and relative humidity—have already been included on the chart as shown. The four remaining important parameters—wet-bulb temperature, dew point, specific enthalpy, and specific volume—can be added through their relationship to the present parameters in the following ways.

The wet-bulb temperature and the dry-bulb temperature of saturated air are the same as explained in the definition of the wet-bulb temperature. Therefore, the saturation line on the graph can be labeled with wet-bulb temperatures for every dry-bulb temperature, as shown in Exhibit 3.

With this new temperature scale, the definition of wet-bulb temperature can be extended to all conditions of moist air shown on the graph. When the moist air is at a condition of less than saturation, the wet-bulb temperature is always lower than the dry-bulb temperature and the reading depends on the amount of water vapor in the air. Therefore, the relative humidity and the wet-bulb temperature of a sample of air are interrelated and lines of constant wet-bulb temperature can be added to the graph to show this interconnection. These straight parallel lines slope from the upper left region to the lower right region of the graph. For example, moist air at the condition of 80°F db and 50 percent relative humidity has a wet-bulb temperature of approximately 67°F wb.

Another of the parameters, dew point, can be added to the graph by referring to a common occurrence in everyone's experience. When warm moist air is brought in contact with a cold surface such as a cold glass of water or a cold windowpane in the winter, some of the water vapor in the moist air condenses on the cold surface, forming water droplets. This occurs because the moist air is cooled below saturation by the cold surface and the water is forced to condense because the air is no longer able to hold it. This process can be traced on the graph as

Exhibit 4   Dew Point Scale

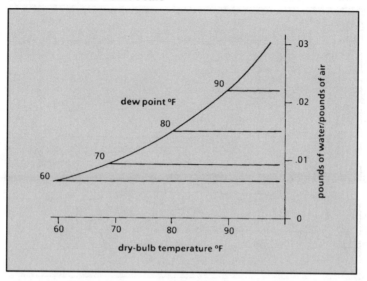

follows. Warm moist air at 75°F db and 50 percent rh is cooled as it contacts the cold surface through convection of heat from the air to the surface. As the air cools, the condition of the air changes initially by a lowering in the dry-bulb temperature without any reduction of the moisture content. Therefore, the initial trace of the process on the graph is a horizontal line moving to the left from the beginning condition of the air. As the air continues to cool, this horizontal line intersects the saturation line. At this point, the air holds the maximum amount of water that it can contain at this temperature. This temperature is designated as the dew point for the condition of the original air because if the air is cooled below this temperature, water droplets or dew will form.

Lines of constant dew point and a dew point scale that has exactly the same values as the wet-bulb temperature can be added to the graph as shown in Exhibit 4. These straight parallel lines are horizontal on the graph and each is related to a moisture content. Therefore, the dew point of air at a specific condition is determined by the moisture content and not the relative humidity.

The final two parameters—specific enthalpy and specific volume—can be added by the measurement of two properties of the moist air. The total energy that is contained in the moist air, from both dry air and water vapor, is determined in Btu/lb of dry air and is called specific enthalpy (h). The values of specific enthalpy are based on a reference of zero specific enthalpy at 0°F. The scale for this quantity of energy is added above the saturation line and the wet–bulb temperature scale. Lines of constant specific enthalpy are essentially parallel to the lines of constant wet-bulb temperature and for common usage they are considered the same lines. Specific volume (v) is the volume of one pound of dry air at a given condition. Although the value for this parameter varies over the range of conditions normally associated with air mixtures on hospitality properties, an approximate value of 13.5 ft3/lb is used. This value corresponds with a specific density of dry air of .075

Exhibit 5   Specific Volume Scale

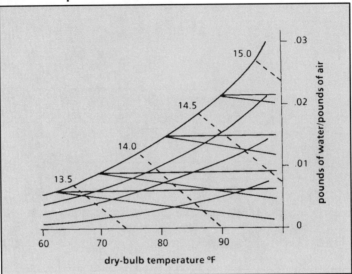

lb/ft3. Lines of constant specific volume are overlaid on the graph as shown in Exhibit 5.

The completed graph as shown in Exhibit 5 contains all of the important information about the parameters of the mixture of dry air and water vapor and is called the psychrometric chart. A similar chart that is published by the Carrier Corporation is shown in Exhibit 6. This chart or similar charts are the basis from which all calculations regarding heating, ventilation, and air conditioning systems and determinations about human comfort are made.

Applications

Changing the conditions of moist air is accomplished through four distinct processes which are differentiated by their direction of movement on the psychrometric chart. The process that moves the condition of the air horizontally while increasing its dry-bulb temperature is designated *sensible heating*, because the air is being heated without changing its moisture content. Likewise, the process that moves the condition of the air horizontally while decreasing its temperature is called *sensible cooling*. A process that increases the moisture without changing the air temperature is designated *humidification*, while one that decreases the moisture without changing the air temperature is called *dehumidification*.

In practice, the conditioning of the air in hospitality facilities is usually a combination of these four basic processes. In the summer, warm and moist air is both dehumidified and cooled in order to maintain the guests' and employees' comfort. In a northern location in the winter, the cold and dry outdoor air is heated and sometimes humidified to maintain desirable inside comfort conditions. In

Exhibit 6 Psychrometric Chart

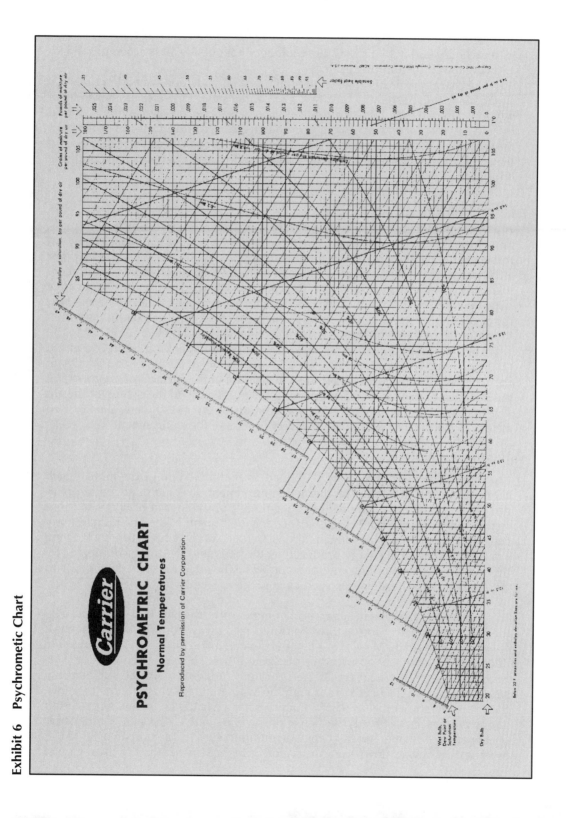

PSYCHROMETRIC CHART
Normal Temperatures

Reproduced by permission of Carrier Corporation.

extremely dry and hot locations, the cooling of hot outside air is accomplished by allowing the air to humidify itself.

The characteristic of the dew point of moist air is demonstrated in numerous situations within hospitality facilities. The condensation of water on the inside of window panes in the winter, the condensation of water on a glass containing a cold beverage, the formation of an ice coating on cooling coils of a freezer, the formation of water droplets on the inside surfaces of a walk-in refrigerator, and the condensation of water on the outside of cold water pipes are all examples of this phenomenon.

Human Comfort

A guest's opinion of a hospitality property is extremely dependent on the condition of the thermal environment. When the thermal environment makes the guest feel comfortable, then he or she completely forgets about it and enjoys the other attractions and amenities of the facility. However, when the thermal environment makes the guest feel uncomfortable, then he or she usually focuses on the negative sensations and does not notice the positive attributes of the facility. Consequently, the operator of a facility should strive to maintain environmental conditions within the range of comfort while minimizing the costs of providing them.

There are several factors that influence the environmental comfort of a guest: (1) the dry-bulb temperature of the air, (2) the humidity of the air, (3) the velocity of the air moving over the guest, (4) the temperature of the surfaces of the room, (5) the volume of fresh air that is supplied to the guest, and (6) the quality of the air. The first four factors affect the thermal comfort of the guest, while the last two factors are considered primarily life-safety aspects of the environment.

Thermal Comfort

The thermal comfort of a guest is defined as that condition of the mind which expresses satisfaction with the thermal environment. It is the mind's interpretation—a very subjective judgment—of the body's physiological reactions to those factors that influence the energy balance for the human body. The human body automatically attempts to maintain a constant deep body temperature by keeping a balance between the energy produced by the body and the energy dissipated by the body to the surrounding environment, while the mind registers the reaction to the environment in categories such as cold, cool, slightly cool, neutral, slightly warm, warm, and hot.

For the body to remain at a constant temperature, the heat that is produced by the body's metabolic process must be transferred away from the body. This heat balance, expressed by $M + C + R + E = 0$, is dependent on the metabolic production of energy (m), the heat absorbed or dissipated through convection with the surrounding air (c), the heat transferred through radiation with the surrounding structures (r), and the heat lost through the evaporation of perspiration (e). When the air temperature is below 98.6°F, C always has a negative sign, and when the air temperature is above 98.6°F, the sign is positive. As with C, the sign of R depends on the surface temperatures of the surrounding structures compared to 98.6°F, because heat always flows from the region of higher temperature to the region of lower temperature. E always has a negative sign because the body can only lose energy through evaporation.

The body's metabolic production of heat energy is extremely dependent on the activity level of the individual. The relationship is shown in Exhibit 7 where the amount of heat production is expressed in *met units*. A met unit is the energy produced by a seated person at rest. For an average individual, a value of 1.0 met is equivalent to an energy production of 360 Btu/hr. For hospitality employees, the metabolic heat production ranges from a low of 1.0 met for seated work up to 3.4 met for heavy housecleaning tasks; for guests, the range is from .7 met for sleeping up to 7.2 met for playing squash.

The body's thermal control systems regulate the amount of energy dissipated through convection, radiation, and evaporation in order to balance the amount of heat production so that the body has no net heat gain. Within the normal comfort region, this control is accomplished by changing the surface temperature of the body through the control of blood flow near the surface of the skin and by changing the amount of sweat secreted from the skin. The body's surface temperature affects the transfer of heat through convection and radiation because these mechanisms are dependent upon a temperature differential between the heat source and the region that absorbs the heat; the amount of sweat secretion affects the quantity of water and corresponding heat of vaporization that is removed from the body

Environmental factors also affect these three mechanisms. The air temperature of the room has an effect on the amount of heat that is convected from the body; a lower air temperature increases the heat flow, while higher air temperature decreases the flow. The temperatures of the surfaces in a room (that is, ceilings, walls, floors) influence the amount of radiation heat transfer; a higher average surface temperature allows less heat transfer, while a lower surface temperature requires more heat flow. The humidity of the air affects the amount of evaporated heat loss; air with a lower relative humidity permits a faster rate of evaporation than does air with a higher relative humidity

When the body's thermal control systems respond to changes in metabolic rate or environmental factors, the body first relies on the convective and radiative mechanisms before it uses the evaporative mechanism. In the case of a seated person at rest who produces 1.0 met or 360 Btu/hr in a room at 60°F and 45 percent rh, the body is dissipating almost all of the 360 Btu/hr of heat through convection and radiation. As the air temperature in a room increases, the amount of heat transferred through these two mechanisms decreases because there is a lower temperature difference between the body and its surroundings. Therefore, the body must dissipate an increasing amount of heat through evaporation in order to maintain the total dissipation rate of 360 Btu/hr. This trend continues until the room temperature is 98.6°F, at which point the entire 360 Btu/hr is being lost through evaporation. Exhibit 8 summarizes this effect.

In the case of a similar person in a room in which the temperature is lowered, the body takes action to maintain the total heat loss at 360 Btu/hr even though the temperature difference is increased. First, it shuts down the evaporative mechanism. If that does not have enough of an effect, the body begins to lower its surface temperature in order to reduce the temperature difference. If that is not sufficient,

Exhibit 7   Metabolic Rate at Different Typical Activities

Activity	Metabolic Rate in Met units
Resting	
Sleeping	0.7
Reclining	0.8
Seated, quiet	1.0
Standing, relaxed	1.2
Walking	
On the level mph	
2	2.0
3	2.6
4	3.8
Miscellaneous Occupations	
Bakery (e.g., cleaning tins, packing boxes)	1.4 to 2.0
Brewery (e.g., filling bottles, loading beer boxes onto belt)	1.2 to 2.4
Carpentry	
Machine sawing, table	1.8 to 2.2
Sawing by hand	4.0 to 4.8
Planing by hand	5.6 to 6.4
General Laboratory Work	1.4 to 1.8
Machine Work	
Light (e.g., electrical industry)	2.0 to 2.4
Heavy (e.g., steel work)	3.5 to 4.5
Shop Assistant	2.0
Teacher	1.6
Watch Repairer, Seated	1.1
Domestic Work, Women	
House cleaning	2.0 to 3.4
Cooking	1.6 to 2.0
Washing by hand and ironing	2.0 to 3.6
Shopping	1.4 to 1.8
Office Work	
Typing	1.2 to 1.4
Miscellaneous office work	1.1 to 1.3
Drafting	1.1 to 1.3
Leisure Activities	
Stream fishing	1.2 to 2.0
Calisthenics exercise	3.0 to 4.0
Dancing, social	2.4 to 4.4
Tennis, singles	3.6 to 4.6
Squash, singles	5.0 to 7.2
Golf, swinging and golf cart	1.4 to 1.8

Reprinted by permission from 1985 ASHRAE Handbook—Fundamentals

Exhibit 8   Distribution of Heat Loss for a Human

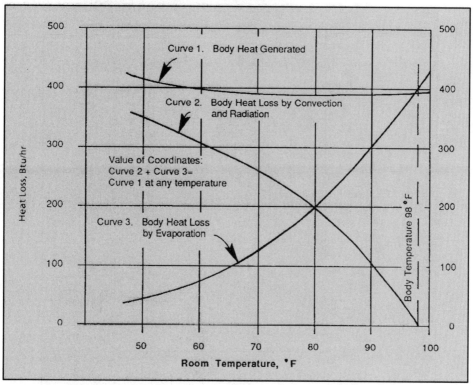

the body attempts to produce more metabolic energy to offset the increased rate of heat loss by inducing involuntary muscle action or shivering.

The Comfort Zone

From this discussion, it is obvious that the thermal comfort of the guest is connected to several factors that have an interrelated effect on the guest's perception of the thermal environment. The aggregate effect of these factors has been combined into a concept called *comfort zone*. This zone is defined as containing all the combinations of air temperature and relative humidity that satisfy at least 80 percent of the population with regard to their thermal comfort.

In Exhibit 9, the comfort zones for typical winter and summer clothing are plotted separately on a portion of a psychrometric chart. The almost vertical boundaries (that is, the left and right sides) of the zones were determined by extensive testing of samples of people exposed to different air conditions. Each boundary represents those combinations of temperature and relative humidity that are perceived by the guest to be equivalent to one another and that are comfortable to exactly 80 percent of the people.

The steep downward slope of the boundaries shows an inverse tradeoff between the temperature of the air and its relative humidity in determining the

Exhibit 9 The Comfort Zone

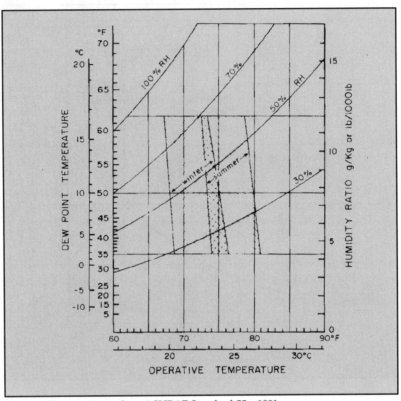

Reprinted by permission from ASHRAE Standard 55—1981

comfort of a guest. For example, air at 68.5°F and 30 percent rh offers the same level of comfort as air at 67.0°F and 70 percent rh. This tradeoff is a result of the interaction of the heat transfer mechanisms that depend on a temperature difference (convection and radiation) with the mechanism that depends on the humidity in the air (evaporation). The loss in evaporative heat transfer due to the increase in relative humidity must be offset by an increase in the convective and radiative losses accomplished by a lower air temperature.

The horizontal boundaries of the comfort zones (that is, the top and bottom) are set for considerations that partially relate to thermal comfort as well as to other practical considerations. Air that contains less moisture than is in the air at the lower boundary (a dew point temperature of 35°F) causes people to exhibit symptoms of very dry skin, dry throats, and respitory problems. The same air also contributes to the excessive drying and deterioration of wood furniture, some building materials, and painted surfaces. Air that is wetter than the air at the upper boundary (a dew point temperature of 62°F) causes mold growth and condensation of water droplets on cool building parts such as cold water lines which are not insulated or the inside surfaces of windows in the winter. Consequently, air that is either too dry or too wet is undesirable for the successful operation of a facility.

The primary difference between the comfort zones for the winter and the summer is the amount of clothing worn by the test subjects. For the winter, the typical description of the clothing is heavy slacks, long sleeve shirt, and sweater; for the summer, the description is light slacks, and a short sleeve shirt. Therefore, the apparent distinction between two different seasons is not due to intrinsic aspects of the seasons such as acclimatization, but rather to the differences in the amount of clothing that is normally worn during these seasons.

The comfort zones shown in Exhibit 9 are based on several assumptions regarding the factors that affect the thermal comfort of guests. The activity level is light, mainly sedentary with a met value of 1.2. The average temperature of the room's surfaces (mean radiant temperature, abbreviated as MRT) is assumed to be the same as the air temperature. The velocity of air movement is less than 30 feet per minute (fpm) for the winter zone and less than 50 fpm for the summer zone.

The two comfort zones can be extended to include situations that have characteristics different from the assumptions listed above. An increase in activity level for each 0.1 met moves the winter comfort zone by approximately 1.0°F and the summer comfort zone by approximately 0.8°F toward cooler temperatures. A change in the MRT of the room surfaces for each 1.0°F moves the comfort zones approximately 0.5°F; the comfort zones move toward warmer temperatures when the MRT decreases and toward cooler temperatures when the MRT increases. Air movement in excess of the stated limit of 30 fpm for the winter comfort zone is not acceptable, while an increase in air movement is acceptable for the summer comfort zone, when the comfort zone is moved 1.0°F toward warmer temperatures for each 30 fpm increase in air movement up to a maximum air movement of 160 fpm. Air movement beyond this level causes visible movement of loose paper, hair, and other light objects.

Maintaining Acceptable Indoor Air Quality

Both the physiological and psychological needs of humans require that an adequate supply of outside air of acceptable quality be circulated through a building. For physiological reasons, the air circulation system must supply the necessary amount of oxygen for metabolism and remove the by-products of metabolism that are present in the exhaled air, as well as control the amount of carbon dioxide in the air so that minimum standards are met. The system also must control the level of various contaminants that enter the air from either outside sources (such as general industrial pollution) or inside sources of pollutants (such as formaldehyde from insulation or carbon monoxide from faulty heating systems). For psychological reasons, the body odor of occupants and the moisture contributed to the air either by humans or other sources (for example, cooking, taking showers) must be removed from the occupied space.

Except in the locations where the quality of the outdoor air is unacceptable, the ventilation system of a building could in theory maintain acceptable indoor air quality just by circulating massive amounts of outdoor air. However, this is not a viable practical solution because the circulated outdoor air must be conditioned when it is brought into the building. When the outside air is cold, the heating system must heat the air to an acceptable temperature; when the outside air is hot and

Exhibit 10   Outdoor Air Requirements for Ventilation—Commercial Facilities

	Estimated Occupancy, persons per 1000 ft.³ or 100 m² floor area. Use only when design occupancy is not known.	Outdoor Air Requirements		Comments
		Smoking	Non-Smoking	
Food & Beverage Services		cfm/person		
Dining rooms	70	35	7	
Kitchens	20	--	10	
Cafeterias, fast food facilities	100	35	7	
Bars and cocktail lounges	100	50	10	
Hotels, Motels, Resorts, Dormitories, & Correctional Facilities		cfm/room		
Bedrooms (single, double)	5	30	15	} Independent of room size
Living rooms (suites)	20	50	25	}
Baths, toilets (attached to bedrooms)		50	50	Independent of room size installed capacity for intermittent use.
		cfm/person		
Lobbies	30	15	5	
Conference rooms (small)	50	35	7	
Assembly rooms (large)	120	35	7	
Gambling Casinos	120	35	7	
Offices				
Office Space	7	20	5	
Meeting & waiting spaces	60	35	7	
Public spaces		cfm/ft² floor		
Corridors & utility rooms		0.02	0.02	
		cfm/stall or urinal		
Public restrooms	100	75	--	
		cfm/locker		
Locker & dressing rooms	50	35	15	
Sports & Amusement Facilities		cfm/person		
Ballrooms & Discos	100	35	7	
Bowling alleys (seating area)	70	35	7	
Playing floors (e.g., gymnasiums, ice arenas)	30	--	20	{ When internal combustion engines are operated for maintenance of playing surfaces, increased ventilation rates will be required.
Spectator areas	150	35	7	
Game rooms (e.g., cards & billiards rooms)	70	35	7	
Swimming pools		cfm/ft² area		
Pool & deck areas	--	--	0.5	{ Higher values may be required for humidity control.
		cfm/person		
Spectators area	70	35	7	

humid, the air conditioning system must cool and dehumidify the air to an acceptable temperature. Both of these processes consume substantial amounts of energy. In addition, large circulation fans powered by electric motors consume energy just to circulate the air. Therefore, the designers of building ventilation systems specify the minimum ventilation rate, which will provide desirable indoor air quality in order to minimize the construction and operating costs of the building. There are two methods—the *ventilation rate procedure* and the *indoor air quality procedure*—

that indicate how to achieve acceptable air quality. The first procedure is prescriptive in nature in that specified minimum ventilation rates of acceptable outside air are provided. This method assumes that this "clean" outside air should dilute and remove the contaminants from interior sources so that their levels in the interior air are acceptable. The second procedure is performance-oriented in that the maximum allowable levels of contaminants are provided for acceptable indoor air quality. No specified ventilation rates are provided, however; their actual choice is at the discretion of the designer of the ventilation system as long the allowable levels of contaminants are not exceeded.

Ventilation Rate Procedure. The acceptable level of pollutants for outdoor air can be obtained from several sources.[1] If the outdoor air in a specific location satisfies these levels, then the air may be used directly to ventilate a building. However, if the outdoor air contains contaminants that exceed these levels, then the air must be treated before it may be used in a building's ventilation system.

Exhibit 10 shows the outdoor air requirements for ventilation for various types of businesses or buildings. The requirements are stated in cfm/person, cfm/ft^2 of floor area, or cfm/functional unit (for example, a room in a hotel or a bed in a hospital). By the application of this method, indoor air quality is considered acceptable if the required rates of acceptable outdoor air are provided for the occupied space and no unusual contaminants are present.

Higher ventilation rates are specified for the spaces in which smoking is permitted, because tobacco smoke is one of the most difficult contaminants to control at the source. When smoking is not permitted in designated spaces, the lower values of ventilation rates may be applied. In numerous applications, this reduction in ventilation rates can substantially affect the operating cost of the heating, ventilating, and air conditioning (HVAC) system. Therefore, use of no smoking areas in lodging properties should be strongly encouraged because of its desirable effect on the operating costs of the building.

Indoor Air Quality Procedure. Under this method, acceptable indoor air quality is provided by the ventilation system if the level of contaminants in the *indoor* air does not exceed the levels as specified for *outdoor* air. In addition, acceptable levels of contaminants from indoor sources must also be met.

There are, however, numerous substances for which no regulations have yet been developed (for example, mercury), substances that have not yet been identified as harmful to humans (for example, unknown environmental carcinogens), and substances for which no regulations are likely to be developed because they are such complex mixtures (tobacco smoke). In order to respond to these substances, this method allows a subjective evaluation of the indoor air quality.

The following steps should be used to ensure the validity of the subjective evaluation. A panel of at least 20 untrained observers should enter a space in the manner of a normal visitor and should render a judgment of acceptability within 15 seconds. Each observer should make the evaluation independently of the other observers and without influence from a panel leader. The air can be considered acceptably free of annoying contaminants if at least 80 percent of the observers deem the air to be not objectionable.

Endnote

1. See, for example, ASHRAE Standard 62–1981—*Ventilation for Acceptable Indoor Air Quality* (Atlanta, GA.: American Society of Heating, Refrigerating, and Air–conditioning Engineers, 1981), and *1985 ASHRAE Handbook—Fundamentals* (Atlanta: American Society of Heating, Refrigerating, and Air–conditioning Engineers, 1985), Chapter 11.

Index